TURKISH:
A COMPREHENSIVE GRAM

Routledge Comprehensive Grammars

Comprehensive Grammars are available for the following languages:

Modern Written Arabic
Cantonese
Catalan
Chinese
Danish
Dutch
Greek
Indonesian
Japanese
Slovene
Swedish
Turkish
Ukrainian
Modern Welsh

Titles of related interest

Colloquial Turkish: A Complete Course for Beginners
Jeroen Aarssen and Ad Backus

Dictionary of the Turkic Languages
*Kurtuluş Öztopçu, Zhoumagaly Abuov, Nasir Kambarov
and Youssef Azemoun*

TURKISH:
A COMPREHENSIVE
GRAMMAR

Aslı Göksel and
Celia Kerslake

 Routledge
Taylor & Francis Group

LONDON AND NEW YORK

First published 2005
by Routledge
2 Park Square, Milton Park, Abingdon, Oxon OX14 4RN

Simultaneously published in the USA and Canada
by Routledge
270 Madison Ave, New York, NY 10016

Routledge is an imprint of the Taylor & Francis Group

Typeset in Times by Florence Production Ltd, Stoodleigh, Devon
Printed and bound in Great Britain by MPG Books Ltd, Bodmin, Cornwall

British Library Cataloguing in Publication Data
A catalogue record for this book is available from the British Library

Library of Congress Cataloging in Publication Data
has been applied for

ISBN 0–415–11494–2 (pbk)
ISBN 0–415–21761–X (hbk)

CONTENTS

ACKNOWLEDGEMENTS

The present book would not have been in the form it is had it not been for the generous feedback of the following colleagues, friends and students, linguists and teachers and users of Turkish, who read and commented on parts of the manuscript: Didar Akar, Öznur Ayman, Ercan Balcı, Cem Çakır, Georgia Catsimali, Monik Charette, Ruth Christie, Ann Denwood, Dilek Elçin, Eser Erguvanlı-Taylan, Kate Fleet, Jorge Hankamer, Katerina Hardiman, Atakan İnce, Meltem Kelepir, Elisabeth Kendall, Wilfried Meyer-Viol, Mine Nakipoğlu-Demiralp and A. Sumru Özsoy. We are grateful to all these people for sparing the time to help us in this way.

We owe special thanks to Ceyda Arslan for reading the whole manuscript meticulously. Her detailed and insightful corrections helped us avoid many errors.

Dimitris Antoniou and Andras Riedlmayer provided valuable help in pointing us to some of the statistics about Turkish speakers outside Turkey, and Mehmet Ölmez, Şükriye Ruhi and Güneş Müftüoğlu kindly responded to our questions about reference grammars in current use for teaching purposes in Turkey. We are indebted to Meltem Kelepir, Zeynep Kulelioğlu, Mine Nakipoğlu-Demiralp, Gülen Ergin and Müfide Pekin for their readiness to give us their acceptability judgements on problematic constructions, and to Onat Işık for his technical help in transferring several files from one computer system to another. We are also grateful to our students at Boğaziçi and Oxford Universities, who (whether they were aware of it or not) constantly brought to our attention aspects of Turkish that we might not otherwise have thought about.

Gratitude is due to our successive editors at Routledge, Simon Bell, Sophie Oliver, Sarah Butler, Liz O'Donnell and Ruth Jeavons for their feedback and patience throughout the years, and to several anonymous reviewers for their comments.

During the preparation of this book we have drawn heavily on the work of others, some of it unpublished. Unfortunately the format of this book does not allow us to acknowledge our sources at the appropriate points in the text. We hope that this will not give the impression that all the observations and descriptions presented in the book belong originally to us, and that we will be forgiven for having to content ourselves with simply including our sources in the bibliography. Needless to say, responsibility for any shortcomings that this book may have rests entirely with ourselves.

Finally, we should like to thank our closest friends and our families for their unfailing support in what has been a prolonged and often too absorbing task.

Aslı Göksel
Celia Kerslake
July 2004

INTRODUCTION

TURKISH AND ITS SPEAKERS

Turkish belongs to the Turkic family of languages, which have been spoken for many centuries across a vast territory from the Balkans to China. Within this family, which includes such languages as Uighur, Uzbek, Tatar and Kazakh, Turkish forms part of the southwestern or Oghuz branch. Its closest relatives are Gagauz (spoken by less than 200,000 people of Orthodox Christian religion, mostly in southern Moldova), Azerbaijanian (spoken by up to 20 million people in Iran and Azerbaijan) and Turkmen (spoken by some 3 million people in Turkmenistan and by about 400,000 in Iraq).

Turkish itself is spoken predominantly in the Republic of Turkey, of which it is the official language. No statistics are available as to how many of Turkey's population of 70 million have Turkish as their first language. Most of the ethnic minorities have undergone considerable (in some cases, total) linguistic assimilation. In the largest ethnic minority, that of the Kurds (which is variously estimated to make up between 8 per cent and 20 per cent of the country's population), a large number of people are bilingual. A reasonable estimate would probably be that Turkish is now the first language of 55–60 million of Turkey's citizens, with another few million people speaking it with equal fluency to their native language.

Turkish speakers outside Turkey fall into two groups. The first consists of communities located in various lands that were formerly, for several centuries, part of the Ottoman Empire. There are populations of this kind in Bulgaria (760,000), Greece (115,000), Macedonia (80,000) and Romania (23,000). Cyprus, also former Ottoman territory, has seen its Turkish-speaking population considerably enlarged by migration from Turkey since 1974. There may be as many as 150,000–200,000 Turkish speakers living in the Turkish Republic of Northern Cyprus at the time of writing.

The second group of Turkish speakers outside Turkey comprises those who, since the 1960s, have taken up residence in various western European countries, Australia and North America. The number in western Europe is nearly 4 million, of whom half live in Germany. The Australian Turkish community numbers some 40,000, and the number of Turkish speakers in North America is 50,000–60,000. Although in all these migrant communities there is a tendency for the use of Turkish to decline with each succeeding generation, it can probably be stated with reasonable certainty that Turkish is spoken as a first language or with native fluency by about 65 million people worldwide.

BREAK WITH THE OTTOMAN PAST

The Turkish language underwent two kinds of radical change as part of the revolutionary reform programme launched by Mustafa Kemal (Atatürk) after the establishment of the Republic in 1923. The first was a sudden and comprehensive change in the medium in which it was written, with the introduction of a specially adapted form of the Latin alphabet in 1928, accompanied by a total prohibition on any further use of the Arabic script for teaching or publication in Turkish. The second affected the substance of the language itself, particularly its lexicon, and comprised a systematic campaign, launched by the official Turkish Language Foundation in 1932, to 'liberate' Turkish from its 'subjugation' to other languages, i.e. to Arabic and Persian. In order to give some indication of the significance of this change it will be necessary to say something about the Ottoman form of Turkish, the precursor of the modern language.

As a linguistic term, 'Ottoman' denotes the form of Turkic which became the official and literary language of the Ottoman Empire (1300–1922). This was, essentially, the variety of Oghuz Turkic which developed in Anatolia after that region was settled by Oghuz Turks in the eleventh to thirteenth centuries. It was written in the Arabic script, the form of writing adopted not only by the Oghuz but by all the Turkic-speaking peoples who, from about the tenth century onwards, had accepted the Islamic faith. The primacy accorded in Islam to the Arabic language itself, the language of the Qur'an, had a profound impact on the intellectual life of Ottoman society. The language of scholarship and of Islamic law, and the medium of instruction in the only schools available to the Muslim population before the nineteenth century, the *medrese*s, was Arabic. In literature, on the other hand, the influence that was more directly felt was that of Persian, since it was the aesthetics of Persian poetry and ornate prose that provided inspiration for the Ottoman literati. A truly cultured Ottoman was expected to have a fluent command of 'the three languages', and many Turkish-speaking Ottomans did indeed write treatises in Arabic and/or poetry in Persian.

As far as Ottoman itself was concerned, the degree to which written texts reflected the spoken idiom varied greatly according to the level of education of the writer and the purpose and intended readership of the document. In any kind of sophisticated writing the Turkish structural base became all but submerged, surfacing mainly in the inflectional morphology and in other non-lexical items such as pronouns, determiners, and auxiliary verbs. Arabic and Persian borrowings were not confined to the lexicon, but included grammatical elements also. Arabic words were often used in their distinctive plural forms, and adjectives were made to agree with them in terms of gender, as they would in Arabic itself. A host of Arabic prepositional phrases, completely alien to Turkish syntax, were imported more or less as lexical units. A number of Persian constructions became particularly prevalent. One was the ubiquitous *izafet*, by which the head of a noun phrase was linked to the modifying noun or adjective that *followed* it (as in *asakir-i İslam* 'armies of Islam' or *memalik-i Osmaniye* 'Ottoman dominions'). Another was the compound adjective, used mainly for ornamental or rhetorical reasons, and often designed to rhyme with its head noun (as in *padişah-ı alem-penah*, 'world-sheltering monarch' or *vezir-i Asaf-tedbir* 'vizier wise as Asaf'). It should be noted that the majority of these imported elements were totally absent from the language of the unschooled Turkish-speaking masses. On the other hand, some common words of Arabic or Persian origin, such as *perde* 'curtain', *kitap* 'book', *namaz* 'ritual prayer', *cami* 'mosque', had become fully integrated into the general lexicon. The only significant foreign *grammatical* influence to be seen in the popular language was the Indo-European type of subordinate clause (introduced by a subordinating conjunction, and having a finite verb. (See the clauses with *ki* discussed in Chapters 24–6 of this book.)

The term 'Ottoman' was not applied to the language of the Ottoman state until the mid-nineteenth century, when, as part of the reform movement known as the Tanzimat, attempts were made by the government to foster a sense of Ottoman identity that might save the ailing empire. Before then, when it was necessary to distinguish Turkish from any other language, it had been called precisely that (*Türki* or *Türkçe*), however impregnated it might have been with Arabic and Persian elements. It was in the Tanzimat period that Turkish (under the politicized name 'Ottoman') first began to be taught in schools, the new state schools designed to train soldiers, bureaucrats and technical experts for the service of a modernized state. There was now a clear need for the language to be defined and streamlined, through the production of grammars and dictionaries, in order to maximize its effectiveness as a means of public communication. A newly emerging class of Turkish intellectuals, who had access to Western writings and were full of new ideas that they wanted to convey to a wide public, shared the state's interest in regularizing and simplifying the language, although their standpoint – liberal and patriotic – was largely opposed to the government. The new genres of writing in which they were involved, principally journalism, drama and the novel, all played their part in the evolution of a modern form of Ottoman, shorn of much of its rhetorical opacity, and with a regularized, transparent sentence structure much closer to that of modern Turkish.

The closing decades of the life of the Ottoman Empire witnessed the emergence of a new sense of ethnic identity among the Turkish educated elite, which had hitherto defined itself only as Ottoman and Muslim. The discoveries of European Turcologists drew attention to the long-forgotten linguistic and cultural links existing between the Turks of the Ottoman Empire and other peoples spread out far across Asia. The first scholarly dictionary of Ottoman Turkish to be written by a Turk, the *Lehçe-i Osmani*

(Ottoman Dialect) of Ahmet Vefik (1877), clearly identified Ottoman as just one branch of a much wider, 'Turkish' language.[1] This revolutionary idea was at the heart of an incipient Turkish national consciousness that gathered strength as the empire increasingly fell victim to internal disintegration and the predations of the European powers.

After the constitutional revolution of 1908 the politically dominant Committee of Union and Progress gave all but overt encouragement to the formation of a number of societies and publications devoted to the promotion of this new sense of Turkish nationhood, which was incompatible with the official ideology of Ottomanism. As the Ottoman state teetered on the brink of final collapse, the Turkish language became for many intellectuals and writers the key to unlocking the spirit of unity and common purpose that alone, they believed, would enable the nation (in some as yet unknown form) to survive.

This message was first clearly enunciated in 1911 in the journal *Genç Kalemler* (Young Pens), which called on young writers to put themselves in the service of the nation by creating a 'national literature' in a 'new language'. The rules of this 'new language' (*yeni lisan*) were defined quite precisely: no Arabic and Persian grammatical constructions were to be used, except in lexicalized phrases for which there was no available alternative; Arabic and Persian plural forms were to be avoided; Arabic and Persian words that were not current in the spoken language, and for which a Turkish equivalent was in common use, should similarly be rejected (e.g. for 'water' Arabic *ma* and Persian *ab* should both be abjured in favour of Turkish *su*). Already at this period there were extremists who wanted to see *all* Arabic and Persian loan words, even those long integrated into the popular language, replaced by Turkish synonyms, if necessary retrieved from old texts or imported from eastern 'dialects'. But at this stage the moderate view prevailed, and the 'new language' campaign was remarkably successful in its aims. By the period of the First World War the use of a natural, unadorned Turkish, close to the language of speech, had become the unquestioned stylistic imperative of literary writing. However, bureaucratic, legal and scholarly discourse remained more resistant to change, as evidenced even in the diction of Atatürk's famous six-day speech of 1927, the *Nutuk*.

The Kemalist language reform (*dil devrimi*) begun in the 1930s differed from all previous efforts in two important ways.[2] First, despite the nominally autonomous status of the Turkish Language Foundation (Türk Dil Kurumu, TDK), this was an openly state-sponsored campaign, funded by annual grants from the state budget and having at its disposal all the implementational apparatus of the bureaucracy, the education system, and the

---

[1] The Turkic/Turkish distinction is a recent terminological innovation of western origin.

[2] For a recent study in English of the language reform movement see Lewis (1999).

state radio monopoly. Second, the aims and scope of this project were far more radical and ambitious than anything that had gone before. There was now an overt commitment to complete purification of the language, and any word that was deemed worthy of acceptance was designated *öztürkçe* 'pure Turkish'. This new lexicon included, in addition to native words already in general use, the following new categories: (1) words used in Anatolian dialects but not part of the current standard language of the urban elite; (2) obsolete Turkish words discovered by searching through relatively unpretentious texts from the early and middle Ottoman periods; (3) neologisms derived from Turkish roots and suffixes; (4) other more dubious coinages, often similar in form to European words, which were justified by pseudo-etymologies. It should be noted that there was very little antagonism to the quite conspicuous European borrowings (such as *otobüs*, *gazete*, *elektrik*, *demokrasi*) which had entered the language as part of the general process of modernization from the late eighteenth century onwards, predominantly from French.

The remarkable fact about the project of socio-linguistic engineering comprising the language reform is the enthusiasm with which it was embraced by a large majority of the Turkish educated class. This applies not only to first-generation Kemalists but also to their children, some of whom, in the 1960s and 1970s, were inspired as much by socialism as by nationalism. In the middle decades of the twentieth century the 'language question' was a subject of fierce controversy, with the Kemalists and left-ists equally committed to the purist ideal, regarding it as representing all that was modern, secular and progressive, while conservatives fought a rearguard action in defence of the nation's cultural heritage, and the moral, emotional and aesthetic values attached to many of the words that had been consigned to disuse. Since the 1980s the heat has gone out of this debate, but this is due as much as anything to the fact that in large measure the aims of the reformers have been achieved, and that, for better or for worse, the lexicon of Turkish in the early twenty-first century is radically different from that of the early twentieth century.

PREVIOUS GRAMMARS OF TURKISH

The first comprehensive modern treatment of Turkish grammar was Jean Deny's monumental *Grammaire de la langue turque, dialecte osmanli* (Paris, 1921). This was a significant first step towards the creation of a terminology that would accurately reflect the features of the language without trying to assimilate them to Indo-European preconceptions. While Deny's main focus was on the standard spoken and written language of Istanbul at the time of writing (pre-1914), his work also encompasses current popular and dialectal forms and older Ottoman usages. A Turkish translation by Ali Ulvi Elöve, with useful additional notes, was published twenty years later by the Turkish Ministry of Education (*Türk Dili Grameri (Osmanlı Lehçesi)*, 1941).

Within Turkey itself, the change of alphabet and the language reform movement generated both a surge of interest in the structure of the language and a great pedagogical need for a new conceptualization and a new terminology. Tahsin Banguoğlu's *Ana Hatlariyle Türk Grameri* (Outlines of Turkish Grammar) (1940), was produced in response to a ministerial request for a work that might serve as a basis for school text-books. Modern in its approach, and drawing on contemporary French linguistics, Banguoğlu's book identified itself as a descriptive, not a histor-ical grammar, and was rich in examples reflecting the spoken language. It was reprinted in 1974 with updated terminology, under the title *Türkçenin Grameri* (The Grammar of Turkish), and is still highly regarded. Ahmet Cevat Emre's *Türk Dilbilgisi* (Turkish Grammar) (1945) was the earliest comprehensive grammar to be published by the Turkish Language Founda-tion (TDK). It was less systematic than Banguoğlu's work, and was not reprinted, but it remains of considerable historical interest.

Muharrem Ergin's *Türk Dil Bilgisi* (Turkish Grammar) (1952), a histor-ical grammar of Oghuz Turkic, is a very different kind of work, and was written from a standpoint opposed to the radicalism of the TDK. It is highly traditional in its approach, and concentrates almost entirely on phonolog-ical and morphological phenomena.

The next milestone in the description of Turkish was the grammar published in Russian by the Soviet Turcologist A. N. Kononov in 1956. This work, unfortunately not linguistically accessible to the present authors, is recognized as having provided a highly valuable and original synthesis of research on Turkish down to that date.[3] Four years later appeared the *Osmanisch-Türkische Grammatik* of H. J. Kissling (Wiesbaden, 1960). Despite its title (which was intended to emphasize the essential continuity between Ottoman and modern Turkish), this book was designed as a prac-tical reference tool for German-speaking learners of Turkish.

The first Turkish grammar to be written from a theoretical-linguistic standpoint was Lloyd B. Swift's *A Reference Grammar of Modern Turkish* (Bloomington, Ind., 1963). This was a pioneering attempt to describe the grammatical phenomena of Turkish in structural terms, i.e. as a complete system, and it marked an important new beginning in conceptual terms. At about the same time, two further grammars of a broadly pedagogical nature appeared in Turkey. Haydar Ediskun's *Yeni Türk Dilbilgisi* (New Turkish Grammar) (1963), reissued as *Türk Dilbilgisi* in 1985 and regularly reprinted down to today, was designed as a university textbook for non-specialist students. It includes an introductory section on language in general, and on the Turkish language reform movement in particular. Tahir

[3] See Hazai (1978), 77; Johanson (1990), 152.

Nejat Gencan's clearly arranged and readable *Dilbilgisi* (Grammar), published by the TDK in 1964 and reprinted many times since, had the avowed objective of deriving the rules of Turkish from a wide-ranging assemblage of examples from admired writers (old and new), and from time-honoured usages such as proverbs.

The two grammars that are best known to English-speaking learners of, and researchers on, Turkish are those of Lewis (1967) and Underhill (1976). Geoffrey Lewis's philologically based *Turkish Grammar* (2nd edition 2000) is insightful and highly readable. The author uses examples drawn from mid-twentieth-century Turkish literary and journalistic texts, and devotes particular attention to the structures that are most alien to an English-speaking learner of Turkish. Robert Underhill's *Turkish Grammar* (Cambridge, Mass., 1976) is arranged as a coursebook. This means that pedagogical concerns determine the way in which the material is organized, and some space is allocated to vocabulary, exercises and matters of usage. Nevertheless, this work by a linguist from the generative tradition brought increased clarity to a number of topics, and continues to be much in demand both as a teaching tool (particularly in the USA) and as a resource for linguists.

The influence of generative linguistics had already been seen in the concise survey of Turkish grammar published by Yüksel Göknel in 1974 under the title *Modern Türkçe Dilbilgisi* (Modern Turkish Grammar). This includes, as well as a description of Turkish phonology, morphology and syntax, a section in which linguistic theories, predominantly generative, are applied to the structures discussed. A more recent comprehensive grammar in Turkish, Mehmet Hengirmen's *Türkçe Dilbilgisi* (Turkish Grammar) (1995), which describes itself as a textbook for students and teachers, is also inspired by this approach. In addition to the sections on Turkish grammar, it has a chapter on the application of generative theories of syntax to Turkish, as well as a chapter on the Turkic languages.

Jaklin Kornfilt's volume *Turkish* (London, 1997), is the most recent comprehensive grammar to appear in English. It forms part of Routledge's Descriptive Grammars series, addressed mainly to linguists who seek data on specific points across languages. The structure of the book is determined by a research questionnaire that has been applied uniformly to all the languages covered in the series. Kornfilt's analyses are well supported by examples, some illustrating little discussed or hitherto unnoticed aspects of Turkish.

The last few years have also seen the appearance of pedagogical presentations of Turkish grammar in both French and German. Bernard Golstein's *Grammaire du Turc: ouvrage pratique à l'usage des francophones* (1997; second edition 1999) and Brigitte Moser-Weithmann's *Türkische Grammatik* (2001) are addressed respectively to French-speaking and German-speaking learners of Turkish. Despite their limitations of scope and analysis, the French-Turkish and German-Turkish comparative dimensions of these works furnish some interesting insights.

Scientific linguistic research on the structure and use of contemporary Turkish was a rare phenomenon before 1970.[4] The situation has, however, changed radically in the last three decades, as modern linguistic methodologies have increasingly made their impact. Already by the beginning of the 1980s there was sufficient research activity, both in and outside Turkey, for a series of biennial international conferences on Turkish linguistics to be launched, and the twelfth of these was about to take place as this book went to press. Attempting a scholarly description of Turkish grammar is no longer an isolated struggle. On the contrary, it requires an engagement with the collective achievement of an international body of scholars in a field that is increasingly well connected to the linguistic mainstream.

AIMS AND ORGANIZATION OF THIS GRAMMAR

What we have aimed to do in this book is to provide a description of the structure of contemporary standard Turkish that is both systematic and comprehensive. We have divided the book into three main parts, dealing respectively with phonology (the sound system), morphology (the structure of words) and syntax (the structure of sentences). We have paid particular attention to the distinction between morphology and syntax, in order to bring out as clearly as possible the systems in place at each level.

The chapters in Part 2 are concerned exclusively with the forms that words can take. In Turkish, because of its highly agglutinative structure, the description of word structure is largely a matter of identifying the different categories of suffixes, and the rules determining what kinds of stem they may attach to and in what order. All discussion of how words combine into phrases, clauses and sentences is confined to Part 3. This is also where semantic issues, i.e. the effects of structure on meaning, are discussed.

There is a hierarchy among the structures discussed in Part 3. For example, adjectival structures (Chapter 15) usually form part of noun phrases (Chapter 14). Noun phrases, for their part, can occur as complements within the verb phrase (Chapter 13), and/or combine with verb phrases to form clauses or sentences (Chapter 12). Furthermore, there is a parallelism between the phrasal structures described in Chapters 14–16 (having respectively a nominal, adjectival and adverbial function) and the clausal structures described in Chapters 24–6 (which follow the same sequence). The ample use that we have made of cross-references throughout the text serves in part to draw attention to the systematic links between different levels of the language. It also makes it possible to draw the reader's attention from one use of a particular form (e.g. a suffix or clitic)

---

[4] See Underhill (1986).

to others described in another part of the book, and in so doing to help readers both to connect and to distinguish between different functions of the one form.

The book is intended to be useful to a wide range of people interested in Turkish, first and foremost university students and other advanced learners of the language, but also teachers and translators of Turkish, and academic linguists. Our methodology has been informed by questions of concern to general linguistic scholarship, but we have taken care to make all our explanations accessible to those without a formal linguistic training. We have strictly avoided any involvement with theoretical issues, and have kept our terminology as simple and neutral as possible. Every point has been clearly illustrated with examples. All the examples are translated, and selective use has also been made of linguistic glosses, which indicate the grammatical functions of individual suffixes. It should be noted that in the examples which are thus glossed, the segmentation is morphological, not phonological, i.e. the hyphens show the boundaries between roots and suffixes, and between the suffixes in a sequence; they do not mark syllable boundaries (as required by the conventions of Turkish orthography). A glossary of grammatical terms has been provided at the end of the book, and terms that can be found in the glossary are shown in bold on their first occurrence in a chapter.

Limitations of space make any claim to totally comprehensive coverage unrealistic, and we have had to exercise a degree of selectivity with regard to forms or usages that have marginal currency. Where we regard an item as in fairly common but declining use we have placed a triangle (∇) in front of it. This happens mainly in the case of words of Arabic origin which are adverbials or form part of postpositional or converbial structures, and are increasingly being replaced in actual usage by native or coined equivalents. Arabic and Persian inflectional forms are no longer a productive part of the Turkish language, and we have therefore excluded them entirely.

It is very important to note that this is a descriptive, not in any sense a prescriptive, grammar. In other words we have tried to record how the language is actually used at the present time, without offering any judgements as to what is 'right' or 'wrong'. We have sought to reflect *variety* of usage as well as regularity, and in this connection we have had to indicate in some places that a particular construction is used only by some speakers and not favoured by others. Another kind of variation is that relating to register, i.e. to the formality or otherwise of the speech situation or text type. In our discussion of particular forms and constructions we have been careful to mention if there is any stylistic restriction on their use. A downwards arrow (↓) has been placed in front of any form that is confined to very informal contexts. Otherwise, unless we have mentioned in the text that a particular form or construction is formal, informal, colloquial, etc., it can be assumed that it is in unrestricted use.

Most suffixes in Turkish are variable in form according to the rules of vowel harmony and consonant alternation, which are explained in Chapters 3 and 6 respectively. In this book any parts of a suffix that are subject to such variation are shown in capital letters, e.g. *-lAr, -sIn, -DI*. Similarly, many suffixes have an initial vowel or consonant that is dropped in certain contexts. Such deletable elements are shown in brackets when a suffix is cited, e.g. *-(y)mIş*.

The English translations of the example sentences have been made as idiomatic as possible. Where the structure of the idiomatic translation is so different from that of the Turkish as to make it possibly difficult to see how it was arrived at, we have added in brackets a literal translation of all or part of the sentence. Where translations are provided for individual words (e.g. in Parts 1 and 2) it should not be assumed that these represent the only meanings that these words can have.

ABBREVIATIONS

ABL	ablative case
ACC	accusative case
ADJ	adjective/adjectival/adjectivizer
ADV	adverb/adverbializer
AOR	aorist
AT	attributive
AUX	auxiliary verb
C	consonant
CL	clitic
COM	comitative
COND	conditional
COND.COP	conditional copula
CONJ	conjunction/connective
COP	copula
CV	converb marker
DAT	dative case
DEF	definite
DER	derivational suffix
DET	determiner
EMPH	emphatic
ENUM	enumerator
EV.COP	evidential copula
EV/PF	evidential/perfective
FUT	future
GEN	genitive case
GM	generalizing modality
IMP	imperative
IMPF	imperfective
INDEF	indefinite
INF	infinitival
INFL	inflectional suffix
INS	instrumental
INT	interrogative
INTR	intransitive
lit.	literally
LOC	locative case
N	noun

NC	noun compound
N.DER	noun/nominal-deriving suffix
NEG	negative
NEG.AOR	negative aorist
OBL	oblique case
OBLG	obligative
obs.	obsolete
OPT	optative
PART	participle
PASS	passive
P.COP	past copula
PF	perfective
PL	plural
POSS	possessive
POT	potentiality
PROG	progressive
PRON	pronominalizer
PSB	possibility
REC	reciprocal
REF	reflexive
RP	relative pronoun
SG	singular
s/he	she, he (also 'it', depending on the context)
s.o.	someone
s.t.	something
s.w.	somewhere
SUB	subordinator
TAM	tense/aspect/modality
TR	transitive
V	vowel
V.DER	verb deriving suffix
VN	verbal noun marker
1	first person
2	second person
3	third person
Ø	zero

LIST OF CONVENTIONS
OBSERVED IN THIS BOOK

italics in the text or in lists are used for Turkish examples

italics in the text are used for highlighting a point in the text

italics in the English translations correspond to the highlighted parts in the Turkish examples

bold in the Turkish examples highlights the point which is being discussed

bold italics in the Turkish examples emphasize a particular part in a highlighted section

bold in the text (apart from headings) is used to highlight the key concepts under discussion in a chapter, and/or to indicate a term that is explained in the glossary

. (full stop) between two English words in the glosses indicates that the corresponding item in Turkish is either one word, or two (or more) words which do not have a word-for-word translation into English

' ' indicates a letter in the alphabet

' ' in the text indicates a mention of a part of a suffix, or one of the forms of a suffix

' ' indicates English translations of Turkish words, phrases and sentences

/ shows that either form is grammatical

/ / indicates the phonemic representation of a phonological unit

| indicates the boundary between two intonational phrases

[ ] indicates the phonetic realization of a phonological unit (i.e. the sound of a particular segment)

[ ] in the Turkish examples indicates a subordinate clause

[ ] in the translations indicates either (i) a word or phrase which is required for the grammaticality of the English translation or for stylistic reasons, but which does not occur in the Turkish example or (ii) in cases where a subordinate clause is marked in the Turkish example, a subordinate clause

( ) in a suffix indicates that the enclosed item is present only under certain morpho-phonological conditions

( ) in an example indicates that the item enclosed is optional

(. . .) indicates the omission or dislocation of a particular item

{ } used selectively to mark the boundaries of a noun phrase

∇ indicates that a form is dated or in decreasing use in standard Turkish

∇ indicates a verbal inflectional suffix which is in use but is limited in productivity

↓ indicates that the form is very informal

- (hyphen) in front of a form indicates that it is a suffix

- (hyphen) after a form indicates either that it is a verb (e.g. *gül-* 'laugh')
or that it cannot occur without a suffix (e.g. *bura-* 'here')
- (hyphen) in the Turkish glosses indicates suffix boundaries
~ indicates syllable boundaries
'A.' and 'B.' at the beginning of examples indicate different speakers
capital letters in the suffixes indicate variability
capital letters in the Turkish examples and English translations indicate
stressed words or syllables
small capital letters in the Turkish examples indicate secondary stress
´ (acute accent) indicates stress within individual words

THE TURKISH ALPHABET AND WRITING CONVENTIONS

The list below provides a rough guide to the pronunciation of the 22 consonants and 8 vowels in Turkish. Only the most prominent aspects of pronunciation are highlighted. The explanations are based on the speech habits of native speakers of British English and should be read in conjunction with Section 1.1.

Letter   *Pronunciation*

A, a   pronounced as *u* in 'c*u*p'

B, b   *b* as in '*b*it'

C, c   *j* as in '*j*am'

Ç, ç   *ch* as in '*ch*ip'

D, d   *d* as in '*d*eep'

E, e   *e* as in 't*e*n'

F, f   *f* as in '*f*it' or '*f*ull'

G, g   *g* as in '*g*et' or '*g*ull'

ğ   either lengthens the sound of the vowel preceding it or is silent between two vowels

H, h   *h* as in '*h*ope'; pronounced also in word medial and final positions and sometimes silent between two vowels

I, ı   pronounced as *a* in '*a*mong', '*a*lone'

İ, i   a shorter form of *ee* as in 'b*ee*t' or *i* as in 'b*i*t'

J, j   *s* as in 'lei*s*ure'

K, k   *k* as in '*k*ept', '*c*ure' and '*c*alf'

L, l   *l* as in '*l*amp', 'bu*ll*' or '*l*urid'

M, m   *m* as in '*m*ilk'

N, n   *n* as in '*n*o'

O, o   *o* as in '*o*ff'

Ö, ö   resembles the sound which is produced when *e* as in 'b*e*t' is pronounced with the lips rounded, as in the German sound 'ö'

P, p   *p* as in '*p*in'

R, r   produced with the tip of the tongue touching the alveolar ridge

S, s   *s* as in 'hi*ss*'

Ş, ş   *sh* as in '*sh*eep'

T, t   *t* as in '*t*ime'

U, u   *u* as in 'c*u*te' or p*u*t'

Ü, ü   resembles the sound which is produced when *i* as in 'b*i*t' is pronounced with the lips rounded, as in the German sound 'ü'

V, v   *v* as in '*v*ery'
Y, y   *y* as in '*y*ou'
Z, z   *z* as in '*z*igzag'

CIRCUMFLEX

In the writing system, a circumflex '^' is sometimes placed over a vowel to indicate that it is long, e.g. *kâtil* [kʰa:tʰil] 'murderer', but this is neither regular nor a reliable means of identifying a long vowel (see 1.1.2.2).

Again, in some words of Persian or Arabic origin, a circumflex may be placed on a vowel to palatalize the previous consonant:

kâr   'profit'
gâvur   'foreigner' (derogatory)

In words such as *hâlâ* 'still', the circumflex fulfils both functions by showing as long the vowels (in both syllables) and palatalizing 'l'.

In view of the functional ambiguity of the circumflex, and the fact that its use is declining, it has been avoided altogether in this book except in the cases of *hâlâ* 'still', *kâr* 'profit', *kâh . . . kâh* 'now . . . now', where its omission could lead to ambiguity.

APOSTROPHE

The apostrophe is used for separating a proper noun from its inflectional suffixes, as in:

Semra'dan   'from Semra'
Hürriyet'te   'in *Hürriyet*' (a newspaper)

When a derivational suffix (Chapter 7) is attached to a proper name, the apostrophe can be placed before or after it:

Ankaralı'lar/Ankara'lılar   'the people of Ankara'

If the proper name is a -*(s)I* compound (10.2) the apostrophe is placed after -*(s)I* or -*lArI*:

İçişleri Bakanlığı'ndan   'from the Home Office'
İçişleri'ne   'to the Home Office' (shortened form)
Ticaret Odaları'nın   'of the Chamber of Commerce'

(Note that the 'n' of the suffixes -*(s)I(n)* and -*lArI(n)* is placed *after* the apostrophe.)

Proper names are spelt as in their bare form, even in cases where the addition of a suffix changes the pronunciation (2.1):

| *Ahmet'in* | [axmedín] | 'Ahmet's' |
| *Tarık'ın* | [tʰa:rí:n] | 'Tarık's' |

SYLLABIFICATION AND DIVIDING A WORD AT THE END OF A LINE

All syllables contain one vowel in Turkish. A vowel cannot be the first item in a syllable unless it is at the beginning of a word, i.e. it always belongs to the same syllable as a preceding consonant if there is one:

a~ta~ma~dım   'I could not throw'

A syllable cannot begin with two consonants, except at the beginning of loan words:

| *at~tım* | 'I threw' |
| *park~tan* | 'from the park' |

Note that the silent consonant 'ğ' conforms to the conditions on consonants:

ba~ğı~ra~ma~ya~ca~ğım   'I will not be able to shout'

At the end of a line, a word can be divided at any syllable boundary, *irrespective of whether the division breaks up a single semantic unit* (such as a stem or a suffix):

| *park* | 'park' | *par~ka* 'to the park' |
| *git-* | 'go' | *gi~di~le~me~ye~ce~ği~ne* 'instead of [one] not being able to go [there]' |

(Note that in the second example the verb root 'git', the passive suffix 'il' and the converbial suffix 'yeceğ' are broken up.)

PART 1
PHONOLOGY: THE SOUND SYSTEM

1 PHONOLOGICAL UNITS

Words are made up of sequences of distinct **phonological units** called **consonants** and **vowels**. Some consonants and vowels sound the same wherever they occur within a word, and have a single pronunciation. Others have more than one way of being pronounced, depending on the surrounding sounds. The various pronunciations of a phonological unit conditioned by its position are called its **allophones**.

Phonological units are indicated by double slashes (/ /), and their allophones by square brackets ([ ]). The corresponding Turkish alphabetical symbols are indicated by inverted commas (' '). Long vowels and doubled consonants are indicated by a following colon (:).

1.1 CONSONANTS AND VOWELS

1.1.1 CONSONANTS

The consonants in Turkish differ from each other in terms of whether they are **voiced** or **voiceless**, their **point of articulation** and their **manner of articulation**. The voiced/voiceless contrast is the most prevalent one in processes involving phonology and word structure (2.1, 6.1.2).

Voiceless consonants	*Voiced consonants*
/p/	/b/
/t/	/d/
/k/	/g/
/c/('k')	/ɟ/('g')
/tʃ/('ç')	/dʒ/('c')
/f/	/v/
/s/	/z/
/ʃ/('ş')	/ʒ/('j')
/h/	
	/ɣ/('ğ')
	/m/
	/n/
	/ɫ/('l')
	/l/
	/r/
	/j/('y')

1.1.1.1 Consonants and their allophones

The following factors affect the pronunciation of particular consonants in certain environments:

(i)   **palatalization** (producing a consonant with the tongue against the hard palate) affects the velar consonants /k/, /g/ and /ł/, and the glottal consonant /h/ in front vowel environments

(ii) **aspiration** (producing a consonant with force) affects the voiceless plosives /p/, /t/, /k/, /c/, and the voiceless affricate /ʧ/

(iii) **bilabialization** (producing a consonant by bringing the lips together) affects the voiced labio-dental consonant /v/ and to a lesser extent, its voiceless counterpart /f/

The descriptions below regarding the pronunciation of consonants in 'word-final position' apply only to those cases where a word is followed by a pause or uttered in isolation. Otherwise, the pronunciation of a word-final consonant is, in most cases, conditioned by the initial sound in the following word. For example, /p/ which is described below as aspirated at the end of a word or before a vowel sounds so only if it is followed by a pause or a word beginning with a vowel. If it is followed by a word starting with a consonant it is an unaspirated /p/. In other words, the 'p' of *tıpa* 'stopper', *Tıp Ansiklopedisi* 'Encyclopaedia of Medicine' and *tıp* 'medicine' (pronounced in isolation) are all aspirated, whereas the 'p' in *tıpkı* 'just like' or in *Tıp Dergisi* 'Journal of Medicine' is unaspirated.

Another point about pronunciation concerns two identical consonants that occur next to each other. Such clusters are pronounced with a delayed release as in *attım* [atʰ:ım] 'I threw [it]' (as opposed to *atım* [atʰım] 'my horse') and *kaç çocuk* [kʰaʧ:oʤukʰ] 'how many children' (as opposed to *kaç okul* [kʰaʧokʰuł] 'how many schools').

The consonants of Turkish and their allophones are given below. Where the phonetic symbol is different from the orthography, the latter is indicated in brackets (e.g. /ʧ/ ('ç')).

/p/   [p]   *şapka* 'hat', *aptal* 'stupid', *kitapçı* 'bookshop', *iplik* 'thread'
      [pʰ] *para* 'money', *pirinç* 'rice', *pırasa* 'leek', *top* 'ball', *ip* rope',
            kapak 'cover', *ipek* 'silk'

[p] is an unaspirated voiceless **bilabial plosive** which occurs before a consonant. [pʰ] is an aspirated voiceless bilabial plosive which occurs before vowels or in word-final position.

/b/   [b]   *bebek* 'baby, doll', *bora* 'gale', *biz* 'we', *ebe* 'midwife', *öbek* 'group', *abla* 'elder sister'

[b] is a voiced bilabial plosive. It does not occur in word-final position except in a few loan words such as *rab* '(the) Lord', *rob* 'robe' and *ab* 'water', and is rare in syllable-final position.

/t/ [t] *katla-* 'fold', *saatçi* 'clockmaker', *etnik* 'ethnic', *atkı* 'scarf'
 [tʰ] *tarak* 'comb', *tirşe* 'aquamarine', *türev* 'derivative', *etek* 'skirt', *otuz* 'thirty', *ütü* 'iron', *inat* 'insistence', *it-* 'push'

[t] is a voiceless unaspirated **denti-alveolar** plosive which occurs before a consonant. [tʰ] is an aspirated dental plosive which occurs before a vowel or in word-final position.

/d/ [d] *dere* 'stream', *dam* 'roof', *doğru* 'correct', *diz* 'knee', *dümen* 'wheel', *kadın* 'woman', *badem* 'almond', *ödün* 'compromise', *adlı* 'named'

[d] is a voiced denti-alveolar plosive. It does not occur in word-final position except in a few words such as *ud* 'lute', *had* 'limit', *ad* 'name', most of which are borrowed, and is rare in syllable-final position.

/k/ [k] *bakla* 'broad beans', *sıkma* 'squeezed', *okşa-* 'caress', *parkta* 'in the park'
 [kʰ] *kafa* 'head', *sıkı* 'tight', *doruk* 'zenith', *sok-* 'push in', *kazak* 'sweater'
 [c] *ikna (et-)* 'convince', *ekle-* 'add', *eksi* 'minus'
 [cʰ] *keçi* 'goat', *kömür* 'coal', *iki* 'two', *sök-* 'dismantle', *bölük* 'squadron', *erk* 'power'

[k] is a voiceless unaspirated **velar** plosive which occurs at the end of a syllable containing a **back vowel** (one of /ı/, /a/, /o/ or /u/) and before a consonant. Its aspirated counterpart [kʰ] occurs before a back vowel and in word-final position following a back vowel. [c] and [cʰ] are voiceless **palatal** plosives which occur with **front vowels** (one of /e/, /i/, /ö/ or /ü/). [c] occurs at the end of a syllable containing a front vowel and before a consonant, and its aspirated counterpart [cʰ] occurs before a front vowel and in word-final position following a front vowel. The palatalization of [cʰ] is more pronounced when it follows /i/ or /ü/ and occurs at the end of a word, as in *yörük* 'nomad' or the final 'k' in *küçük* 'small'.

An even more palatalized version of [cʰ] occurs before palatalized back vowels in some loan words, as in *kağıt* 'paper', *kufi* 'Cufic', *katip*, 'clerk, secretary', *mahkum* 'prisoner'. Note that [cʰ] in these instances constitutes a separate phonological unit (/c/), as it contrasts with [kʰ]: *kar* [kʰaɾ̥] 'snow' and *kâr* [cʰaɾ̥] 'profit'.

/g/   [g]   *gaz* 'gas', *gıdıkla-* 'tickle', *gocuk* 'duffle coat', 'anorak', *gaga* 'beak'

       [ɟ]   *gez-* 'stroll', *giy-* 'wear', *göç* 'migration', *Ege* 'Aegean'

[g] is a voiced velar plosive which occurs in syllables with the back vowels /ı/, /a/, /o/, and /u/. Its palatal counterpart [ɟ] occurs in syllables with the front vowels /i/, /e/, /ö/ and /ü/. /g/ does not occur in syllable-final or in word-final position except in loan words such as *program* 'programme', *psikolog* 'psychologist', *lig* 'league' and *katalog* 'catalogue'.

A slightly more palatalized version of the sound [ɟ] can also occur before a palatalized back vowel in loan words, as in *yegane* 'only', *gavur* 'infidel' (derogatory), *dergah* 'dervish convent'. Here [ɟ] belongs to the separate phonological unit /ɟ/, which is a voiced palatal plosive.

/tʃ/ ('ç')   [tʃ]   *biçki* 'cutting out', *saçma* 'nonsense', *içmeler* 'springs'

           [tʃʰ]   *çene* 'chin', *çabuk* 'quickly', *çöp* 'rubbish', *uçuk* 'pale', *ölçü* 'measurement', *kılıç* 'sword', *ilgeç* 'postposition'

[tʃ] is a voiceless **post-alveolar affricate** which occurs before a consonant. Its aspirated counterpart [tʃʰ] precedes vowels and also occurs in word-final position.

/dʒ/ ('c')   [dʒ]   *caz* 'jazz', *cebir* 'algebra', *cuma* 'Friday', *cins* 'type', *acı* 'pain', *böcek* 'insect'

[dʒ] is a voiced post-alveolar affricate. It does not occur in syllable-final position and rarely occurs in word-final position (e.g. *hac* 'pilgrimage' and *sac* 'sheet iron', mostly for purposes of distinguishing these words from words containing its voiceless counterpart /tʃ/, i.e. *haç* 'cross' and *saç* 'hair').

/f/   [Φ]   *ufuk* 'horizon', *küfür* 'curse', *kof* 'rotten', *örf* 'common usage', 'custom'

       [f]   *fakat* 'but', *nefes* 'breath', *defter* 'notebook', *lif* 'fibre'

[Φ] is a voiceless bilabial **fricative** which occurs in the pronunciation of some speakers before the rounded vowels /u/, /ü/, /o/ and /ö/ and to a lesser extent in word-final position following a rounded vowel. [f] is a voiceless **labio-dental** fricative which occurs elsewhere.

/v/   [ω]   *tavuk* 'chicken', *kavun* 'melon', *havuç* 'carrot'

       [β]   *vücut* 'body', *vur-* 'hit', *ov-* 'massage', *döv-* 'beat'

       [v]   *virgül* 'comma', *vatan* 'motherland', *ev* 'house', *tava* 'frying pan'

[ω] is a bilabial **glide** which occurs between two vowels where at least one of the vowels, usually the one following it, is rounded. [β] is a voiced bilabial fricative which also occurs with rounded vowels but only when it is not intervocalic (i.e. when it is in word-initial or syllable-final position). The difference between [ω] and [β] is very slight and is not audible in the speech of some speakers. [v], the voiced labio-dental fricative, occurs elsewhere.

/s/   [s]   *sarı* 'yellow', *somurt-* 'sulk', *su* 'water', *süt* 'milk', *ısı* 'heat', *askı* 'hanger', *pas* 'rust'

[s] is a voiceless denti-alveolar fricative.

/z/   [z]   *zar* 'dice', 'membrane', *zehir* 'poison', *otuz* 'thirty', *doz* 'dosage', *uzun* 'long, tall', *azınlık* 'minority'

[z] is a voiced denti-alveolar fricative.

/ʃ/ ('ş')   [ʃ]   *işlek* 'busy', *şiir* 'poem', 'poetry', *şarkı* 'song', *aşık* 'lover', *meşin* 'leather', *kaş* 'eyebrow', *güneş* 'sun'

[ʃ] is a voiceless post-alveolar fricative.

/ʒ/ ('j')   [ʒ]   *jüpon* 'underskirt', *jet* 'jet', *jilet* 'razor blade', *garaj* 'garage', *bej* 'beige', *Jülide* (a name), *ajan* 'agent', *ejderha* 'dragon'

[ʒ] is a voiced post-alveolar fricative. It occurs in words borrowed from Indo-European languages, in particular from Persian and French.

/ɣ/ ('ğ')   *soğuk* 'cold', *bağır-* 'shout', *eğik* 'bent', *dağ* 'mountain', *gittiğim* 'that I went'

The so-called 'soft g' lacks a corresponding 'consonantal' sound in standard Turkish, although it is pronounced as a voiced velar fricative in some dialects. It behaves like a consonant when a suffix follows it (see 6.1.3), and is either inaudible as a consonant or may be pronounced as a palatal glide in the environment of front vowels and as a bilabial glide in the environment of rounded vowels. In particular:

(i)   When it is in word-final or syllable-final position, it lengthens a preceding back vowel (*dağdan* [daːdan] 'from the mountain' and *sığ* [sɯː] 'shallow'), but may be pronounced as a palatal glide when following a front vowel (*eğlen-* [ejlæn] 'have fun').

(ii)   Between identical back vowels it is inaudible (*sığınak* [sɯːnakʰ] 'shelter', *uğur* [uːɾ̥] 'good luck').

(iii) Between identical front vowels it is either inaudible (*sevdiğim* [sevdi:m] 'that I love') or sounds like a palatal glide (*düğün* [düjün] 'wedding').

(iv) Between rounded vowels it is mostly inaudible but can also be pronounced as a bilabial glide *soğuk* ([souk^h] or [soɯuk^h] 'cold').

(v) Between a rounded vowel and an unrounded vowel it is mostly inaudible but can also be pronounced as a bilabial glide (*soğan* [soan] or [soɯan] 'onion').

(vi) 'a + ğ + ı' sequences may either sound like a sequence of /a/ followed by /ı/ or like a sequence of two /a/ vowels (*ağır* [aıɾ] or [a:ɾ] 'heavy').

(vii) 'ı + ğ + a' sequences, on the other hand, are pronounced as sequences of /a/ followed by /ı/ (*sığan* [sıan] '[one] which fits').

(viii) When 'ğ' occurs between an 'e' and an 'i' it is either inaudible or pronounced as a palatal glide [j], hence words with the sequences 'e + ğ + i' and 'i + ğ + e' can sound like words written with a 'y', as in *değil* [dejil] 'not' and *diğer* [dijæɾ̥] 'other' (the former being similar to words *written* with a palatal glide, e.g. *meyil* 'slope'). 'e + ğ + i' sequences may also sound like a sequence of two /i/ vowels, hence *değil* is often pronounced [di:l] in colloquial speech.

For the pronunciation of 'ğ' in forms containing the future/participle suffix *-(y)AcAK*, see 8.2.3.3.

Note that vowel sequences formed as a result of an intervening 'ğ' are made up of two distinct syllables and are not diphthongs or long vowels. In these vowel sequences stress falls on the second syllable, provided that other conditions on word stress are met (see Chapter 4).

/h/   [ç]   *hile* 'trick', *ihtimal* 'possibility', *Salih* (a name)

       [x]   *ıhlamur* 'linden', *ahşap* 'wooden', *kahve* 'coffee', *sabah* 'morning'

       [h]   *hala* 'paternal aunt', *horla-* 'snore', *ahır* 'barn'

[ç] is a voiceless palatal fricative that occurs with front vowels in the following environments: before a front vowel, between a front vowel and a consonant, and after a front vowel in word-final position. When the vowel is /i/, the palatalization is more pronounced. [x], the voiceless velar fricative, follows a back vowel and precedes a consonant, or follows a back vowel in word-final position. [h], the voiceless glottal fricative, occurs before a back vowel. /h/ may be silent between two identical vowels, as in *pastahane* [pʰastʰa:nɛ] 'bakery shop' and *daha* [da:] 'more', or between a vowel (usually /a/) and a consonant, causing the preceding vowel to lengthen as in *kahve* [kʰa:vɛ] 'coffee' and *Ahmet* [a:metʰ].

/m/ [m] *masal* 'fairytale', *mine* 'enamel', *müzik* 'music', *emin* 'sure', *kumar* 'gambling', *kambur* 'hunchback', *tarım* 'agriculture', *ekim* 'October'

[m] is a bilabial **nasal**.

/n/ [n] *nasıl* 'how', *nine* 'grandmother', *on* 'ten', *ünlü* 'famous', *inek* 'cow', *sorun* 'problem'

[ŋ] *yangın* 'fire', *banka* 'bank', *mangal* 'brazier'

[ɲ] *engin* 'boundless', *dingin* 'calm'

[n] is a dental nasal which occurs in all positions except when it is followed by /k/ or /g/. /n/ is realized as a velar nasal [ŋ] following a back vowel and preceding a velar plosive, and as a palatal nasal [ɲ] following a front vowel and preceding a palatal plosive.

There is no audible difference between 'n' and 'm' when either of these occurs before a labio-dental fricative ('f' or 'v'). In such cases, the vowel preceding 'n' or 'm' becomes slightly nasalized: *Enver* [ẽvæɾ̩] (a name), *amfi* [ãfi] 'lecture room'.

/l/ [l] *leylek* 'stork', *lira* 'lira', *elli* 'fifty', *gül* 'rose', *ölüm* 'death'

[ɫ] *oluk* 'gutter', *kalın* 'thick', *bal* 'honey', *pul* 'stamp'

[l] is a palatalized post-alveolar **lateral** which occurs adjacent to front vowels, and [ɫ] is a velarized dental lateral which occurs adjacent to back vowels. /l/ generally gets assimilated with a preceding /n/ in fast speech, e.g. *kadınlar* 'women' may be pronounced [kʰadınnaɾ] and *anla-* 'understand' as [anna].

The palatal sound [l] can also occur adjacent to back vowels in loan words such as *lale* [la:le] 'tulip', *laf* 'word(s)', *ilah* 'god', *rol* 'role'. Here it belongs to the phonological unit /l/.

/r/ [r] *rahat* 'comfort', *renk* 'colour', *iri* 'big', *artık* 'waste', *oruç* 'fasting'

[ɾ̥] *tür* 'type', *ger-* 'stretch', *iksir* 'elixir', *kar* 'snow', *mor* 'violet'

[r] is a voiced alveolar **tap** produced with the tip of the tongue touching the alveolar ridge. It occurs in initial and medial positions. Its devoiced counterpart [ɾ̥] occurs in word-final position. /r/ is sometimes deleted in colloquial speech, in particular in the imperfective suffix -*Iyor* (see 8.2.3.3 for details) and in *bir* 'a', 'one'. In the case of *bir*, this usually occurs when it is not stressed (*bir ev* [bi év] 'a house') but also sometimes when it is stressed (*bir daha* [bída:] 'again', *sadece bir ev* [sa:deʤɛ bí ev] 'only one house').

/j/ ('y')   [j]   *yer* 'place', *yoğurt* 'yogurt', *yağ* 'oil', *ayak* 'foot', *oyun* 'game', *ayna* 'mirror', *kay-* 'slide', *huy* 'disposition'

[j] is a palatal glide. The sequence 'i + y' can be realized as a long vowel, as in *iyi* [i:] 'good' and *diyeceğim* [di:ʤæm] 'I will say'.

The **glottal stop** survives mainly in the speech of some elderly speakers, and is going out of usage. It is confined to words of Arabic origin, and mostly to those in which it is intervocalic (*saat* [sa'aṭʰ] 'clock', 'watch', *fiil* [fi'il] 'verb', *teessüf* [tʰe'es:üɸ] 'sorrow', *taarruz* [tʰa'ar:uz] 'assault'). Note that an intervocalic glottal stop can also be pronounced as a long vowel (1.1.2.2).

1.1.2 VOWELS

Turkish has a very symmetrical vocalic system, consisting of the eight vowels /a/, /e/, /ɯ/ ('ı'), /i/, /o/, /œ/ ('ö'), /u/, /y/ ('ü'). The symbols /ɯ/, /œ/ and /y/ will henceforth be replaced by their counterparts in the Turkish orthography, /ı/, /ö/ and /ü/ respectively. These vowels differ from each other in terms of the height of the tongue, the **rounded**ness of the lips and the **front**ness of the tongue.

	High		*Non-high (mid and low)*	
	Rounded	*Unrounded*	*Rounded*	*Unrounded*
Front	ü	i	ö	e
Back	u	ı	o	a

In addition, Turkish has the long vowels /a:/, /u:/, /i:/ and /e:/ in loan words of Arabic and Persian origin.

1.1.2.1 Vowels and their allophones

Vowels can occur at the beginning and end of words, and between two consonants. In words of native origin, /o/ and /ö/ occur only in the first syllable (except for words which contain the imperfective suffix *-Iyor*, see 3.4 (vi) and 8.2.3.3).

Some general factors which affect the pronunciation of vowels are the following: the back vowels /a/, /o/ and /u/ are palatalized when following or preceding the palatal consonants /c/, /ɟ/ and /l/, which occur only in loan words. All vowels except /a/ and /o/ get lowered in word-final position.

/a/   [a]   *kara* 'black', *aşı* 'vaccination', *kurak* 'arid', *algı* 'perception', *banka* 'bank'

[a]   *laf* 'word(s)', 'banter', *lapa* 'mush', *alfabe* 'alphabet', *kağıt* 'paper'

[a] is a low, back and unrounded vowel. Its **fronted** allophone [a̧] occurs with the palatal consonants /c/, /ɟ/ and /l/ in loan words.

/e/   [e]   *sevgi* 'love', *ekim* 'October', *bez* 'cloth', *senin* 'your'
       [ɛ]   *ile* 'with', *küfe* 'large basket', *bale* 'ballet', *dene-* 'try'
       [æ]   *gel-* 'come', *ver-* 'give', *ben* 'I', *sen* 'you', *gizem* 'mystery'

The non-high, front and unrounded vowel /e/ has three allophones. Going from the highest, i.e. mid, to the lowest, these are: the mid, front, closed vowel [e], its lowered counterpart [ɛ], an open-mid, front vowel, and [æ], a low front vowel. [e] sounds like a shorter form of the vowel sound in the English word *late*, [æ] resembles a shorter form of the vowel sound in *bat*, and [ɛ] is between the two, with a sound similar to the vowel in *air* in English.

[æ] occurs before /l/, /m/, /n/, /r/ in instances where the sequences '*er*', '*em*', '*en*' and '*el*' are not followed by a vowel, as in *her* 'each, all', *gerdi* 's/he stretched', *kent* 'town', *pergel* 'pair of compasses'. [ɛ] occurs in word-final position. [e] occurs elsewhere. All three occur in words such as *gezegende* [gezegændɛ] 'on the planet', *perende* [perændɛ] 'somersault' (see also 2.5). Note that /e/ may be pronounced either as [e] or [æ] in a limited number of words before /l/, /m/ and /n/. Hence, some speakers pronounce *elbise* 'dress', *kendi* 'self' or *hem* 'both' with [e], others with [æ].

/i/   [i]   *erik* 'plum', *iletişim* 'communication'
       [ɪ]   *ilgi* 'interest', *deri* 'skin', *kedi* 'cat'

[ɪ] is a higher-than-mid, front, unrounded vowel which occurs in word-final position. Its pronunciation resembles the vowel sound in *bit* in English. [i], which occurs elsewhere, is a front, high, unrounded vowel, a shorter version of the vowel sound in *beat* in English.

/ı/   [ɯ]   *asıl* 'real', *kışla* 'barracks', *ılık* 'lukewarm', *kırmızı* 'red'

[ɯ] is an unrounded, high, back vowel.

/o/   [o]   **o** 'he/she/it/that', *bol* 'abundant', *otur-* 'sit', *kop-* 'snap',
           protokol 'protocol'
       [o̧]   *lokum* 'Turkish delight', *rol* 'role'

[o] is a mid, back, rounded vowel. Its palatalized counterpart [o̧] occurs adjacent to /l/ in loan words. /o/ occurs only in the initial syllable in words of Turkic origin, but may appear in any syllable in loan words.

/ö/   [ö]   *göl* 'lake', *ölçü* 'measurement', *dökül-* 'be spilt', *sözlük*
           'dictionary', *kuvöz* 'incubator', *şoför* 'chauffeur'

[ö] is a mid, front, rounded vowel. In loan words /ö/ can occur in any syllable, but like /o/ it appears only in the first syllable in native words.

/u/ [u] *buluş* 'finding', *ufak* 'small', *koşul* 'condition'
     [ʉ] *lut* 'lute', *blucin* 'denims', *lugat* 'dictionary', *kufi* 'Cufic'
     [ʊ] *bu* 'this', *kutu* 'box', *ordu* 'army'

[u] is a rounded, high, back vowel which sounds like the vowel in the English word *truth*. [ʉ] is its palatalized allophone, which occurs adjacent to the palatal consonants /c/, /ɟ/ and /l/ in loan words. [ʊ] is more lowered than [u] and occurs in word-final position. It is pronounced in a similar way to the vowel in *put* in English.

/ü/ [ü] *üzüntü* 'sadness', *püre* 'mash', *süprüntü* 'rubbish', *ömür* 'life'
     [ʏ] *üzüntü* 'sadness', *örgü* 'knitted', *sövgü* 'curse'

[ü] is a rounded, high, front vowel. [ʏ] is more lowered than [ü] and occurs only in word-final position.

1.1.2.2   Long vowels

Long vowels occur in words borrowed from Persian and Arabic. These have two separate sources. They are either long vowels in the original language or they originally contained a glottal stop (1.1.1.1), which, together with the vowel that precedes it, has become a long vowel in Turkish. Sometimes long vowels are indicated by a circumflex (^) in the orthography. Those long vowels which derive from an intervocalic glottal stop are usually written as two vowels. The list below provides a few examples without distinguishing between these distinct sources:

/a:/ *matbaa* 'press', *kira* 'rent', *mavi* 'blue', *arif* 'wise person'
/u:/ *mevzu* 'topic', *suret* 'copy', *buse* 'kiss', *Numan* (a name)
/i:/ *fiil* 'verb', *ilan* 'advertisement', *sine* 'bosom', *Didem* (a name)
/e:/ *teessüf* 'sorrow', *temin* 'acquisition', *tesir* 'effect'

See 1.1.1.1 for the effect of 'ğ' and 'h' on preceding vowels, and 2.4 for vowel length under other circumstances.

1.2   THE DISTRIBUTION OF CONSONANTS AND VOWELS

In Turkish roots are predominantly monosyllabic, i.e. they contain a single vowel. There are no vowel sequences in Turkish, except in loan words (see 1.1.2.2).

The most common combinations of consonants (C) and vowels (V) are VC (*at* 'horse', *ol-* 'be', *in-* 'descend', *iş* 'work', *üç* 'three') and CVC sequences (*gel-* 'come', *bak-* 'look', *güz* 'autumn', *göl* 'lake'). There are also CV sequences such as *bu* 'this', *şu* 'that', *su* 'water', *ne* 'what', *de-*, 'say', but these are fewer in number and those which are nominals usually require an additional consonant ('n' or 'y') when they combine with suffixes (6.1.3). Other types are VCV sequences such as *ara-* 'look for', *ile* 'with', *öte* 'far side', and VCC and CVCC sequences such as *ört-* 'cover', *sert* 'hard', *genç* 'young'. There is a single occurrence of a root which consists only of a single vowel, the word *o* 'he, she, it, that'. This word requires a consonant when it combines with a suffix (6.2 (ii)).

In this book we treat the following words also as roots, although they have more than one syllable:

(i) Loan words such as *hazır* 'ready', *kitap* 'book', *köşe* 'corner' and *otomatik* 'automatic'. Some such words are derived forms in their original language but cannot be broken up into smaller units in Turkish.

(ii) Words of Turkic origin which do not have a recognizable monosyllabic root in modern Turkish, such as *damar* 'vein', *ördek* 'duck', *eski* 'old', *ana* 'mother', *bekle-* 'wait', *oku-* 'read' and *çalış-* 'work'.

In the overwhelming majority of cases, a word which contains more than one syllable in Turkish is a derived word (see 7.2). For the rules of syllabification in Turkish see p. xl.

1.2.1 CONSONANT CLUSTERS

Consonant clusters, i.e. sequences of two different consonants, occur word-initially only in loan words. Some speakers insert one of the vowels /i/ or /ɪ/ in or before the cluster:

	Alternative pronunciation
spor 'sport'	[ispʰoɾ, sipʰoɾ]
stil 'style'	[istʰil, sitʰil]
stres 'stress'	[sitres]
tren 'train'	[tʰiræn]
psikoloji 'psychology'	[pʰiscʰoloʒi, pʰisicʰoloʒi]
kral 'king'	[kʰɪraɫ]
grev 'strike'	[gɪrev]
plan 'plan'	[pʰilan]

Consonant clusters are frequently found in word-final position, as in *ilk* 'first', *alt* 'lower', *sark-* 'hang', *kork-* 'fear', *zamk* 'adhesive', *renk* 'colour', *kart* 'tough', *üst* 'top', *aşk* 'love', *baht* 'luck', *teyp* 'tape recorder', *genç* 'young', *felç* 'paralysis', *bronz* 'bronze', *şans* 'luck', *alarm* 'alarm'.

2 SOUND CHANGES PRODUCED IN THE STEM BY SUFFIXATION

There are a number of contexts where the addition of a suffix causes a change in the quality of the last consonant or vowel of a stem. Certain of these changes are confined to specific lexical items, whereas others occur as part of a general phonological process in the language. Those which occur only in certain words are:

(i) A voiceless consonant alternating with its voiced counterpart, e.g. *kitap* 'book' but *kitabım* 'my book' (2.1)

(ii) A single consonant alternating with its doubled counterpart, e.g. *sır* 'secret' but *sırrım* 'my secret' (2.2)

(iii) A high vowel alternating with zero (i.e. absence of that vowel), e.g. *burun* 'nose' but *burnum* 'my nose' (2.3)

(iv) A short vowel alternating with a long vowel, e.g. *zaman* 'time' but *zamanım* [zama:nım] 'my time' (2.4)

The changes which are part of a general phonological process are:

(v) Final 'k' alternating with 'ğ' in nominals, e.g. *çocuk* 'child' but *çocuğum* 'my child' (2.1)

(vi) [æ] alternating with [e], e.g. *ben* [bæn] 'I' but *benim* [benim] 'mine' (2.5)

(vii) Final 'a', 'e', 'u' and 'ü' alternating with 'ı' or 'i', e.g. *de-* 'say' but *diyecek* 's/he will say' (2.6)

2.1 ALTERNATIONS OF VOICELESS/VOICED CONSONANTS: 'p'/'b', 't'/'d', 'k'/'g', 'k'/'ğ', 'ç'/'c'

In some stems ending in one of the voiceless consonants 'p', 't', 'k' and 'ç', this final consonant changes to its voiced counterpart before a suffix beginning with a vowel.

'p'	is replaced by	'b'
't'	is replaced by	'd'
'(n)k'	is replaced by	'(n)g'
'ç'	is replaced by	'c'
'k'	is replaced by	'ğ'

Some of these alternations take place in words borrowed from Arabic or Persian, where the word originally ends in a voiced consonant ('b', 'd', 'g' or 'c', as in *kitab* 'book'). As Turkish does not have any of these consonants in final position (1.1.1) the final segment is devoiced in the bare form (hence *kitap*) or in syllable-final position (i.e. when followed by a suffix beginning with a consonant, e.g. *kitaptan* 'from the book'). The original voiced consonant is retained when it is followed by a suffix beginning with a vowel (e.g. *kitabım* 'my book'). Alternations in voiceless/voiced consonants also occur in many words of Turkish origin. Note that only some of the words which in their bare form end in a voiceless consonant are subject to change.

(i)   final 'p'   →   'b'

     dolap 'cupboard'   *dolaba* 'to the cupboard'
     cep 'pocket'   *cebim* 'my pocket'

(ii)   final 't'   →   'd'

     kilit 'lock'   *kilidim* 'my lock'
     kanat 'wing'   *kanadı* 'its wing'

There are relatively few nominal roots that undergo 't'/'d' alternation. The class of nouns ending in a non-changing 't' includes the large number of Arabic borrowings which end in the Arabic feminine suffix *-et/at*, such as *cumhuriyet* 'republic' → *cumhuriyetin* 'of the republic', and French loan words ending in 't', e.g. *bilet* 'ticket' → *biletim* 'my ticket', *ceket* 'jacket' → *ceketim* 'my jacket'.

(iii)   final 'n' + 'k'   →   'n' + 'g'

     renk 'colour'   *renge* 'to the colour'
     denk 'equal'   *dengi* 'his/her/its equal'

'k' alternates with 'g' only when it is preceded by 'n' (otherwise it alternates with 'ğ'; see (v) below). Nouns of this form which have been borrowed in recent times from European languages do not normally undergo 'k'/'g' alternation:

     tank 'tank'   *tankı* 'his/her/its tank'
     bank 'bench'   *bankı* 'his/her/its bench'

(iv) final 'ç'   →   'c'

ağaç 'tree'	*ağacı* 'his/her/its tree'
güç 'power'	*gücün* 'your power'
taç 'crown'	*taca* 'to the crown'

(v)   While the scope of the aforementioned alternations is limited to particular words and is a lexical matter, the next alternation is a general rule which applies to nominals ending with 'k' when they are combined with a vowel-initial suffix. In such cases 'k' alternates with 'ğ'. Due to the pronunciation properties of 'ğ' (1.1.1.1) this process is also referred to as 'k'/Ø alternation.

final 'k'   →   'ğ'

yaprak 'leaf'	*yaprağı* 'its leaf'
gök 'sky'	*göğe* 'to the sky'
otomatik 'automatic'	*otomatiğe* '(in)to automatic'

Note that only a final 'k' which is preceded by a vowel undergoes 'k'/'ğ' alternation. Final 'k' alternates with 'g' when preceded by 'n' (see (iii) above), otherwise it remains as 'k' (eg. *zamk* 'adhesive' and *zamkı* 'the adhesive' (ACC)). 'k'/'ğ' alternation also affects suffixes ending in 'k', such as *-DIK* (8.5.1.1), *-(y)AcAK* (8.2.3.3, 8.5.1.1) and *-mAK* (8.5.1.2):

gelecek 's/he's going to come'	*geleceğim*	'I'm going to come'
aldık 'we bought'	*aldığımız*	'the one/that we bought'

In the case of *-mAK*, 'k' also alternates with 'y':

almak 'to buy'	*almaya/almağa* '(in order) to buy' (also pronounced [aɫmıja] or [aɫma:])

'k'/'ğ' alternation does not affect words with long vowels (2.4). For example, *tebrik* 'congratulation(s)', where 'i' is originally long, does not undergo 'k'/'ğ' alternation, hence, *tebriki* [tʰebri:cʰɪ] 'his/her congratulation(s)'.

There are certain categories to which alternations of voiceless/voiced consonants do not generally apply:

(a) Most monovocalic nominal roots are not subject to these changes:

saç	'hair'	*saçım*	'my hair'
yük	'load'	*yüküm*	'my load'
top	'ball'	*topum*	'my ball'
at	'horse'	*atım*	'my horse'

(**b**) The vast majority of verbal roots are not subject to these changes. A verbal root such as *kap-* 'snatch' retains its final consonant in suffixation, hence *kapın* 'snatch!', although the identical-sounding nominal root *kap* 'container' reverts to its original voiced consonant when a suffix beginning with a vowel is added: *kabın* 'your container'. Similarly the verb *ak-* 'flow' retains its final consonant under suffixation (e.g. *akan* 'flowing') but the adjective *ak* 'white' may not (cf. *ağar-* 'become white', but *akı* 'its white (part)'). There are only a few verbs that have a change in their final consonant when followed by a vowel-initial suffix:

et-	(auxiliary verb/'do')	*eder*	's/he does'
git-	'go'	*gidiyor*	's/he is going'
güt-	'cherish'	*güdecek*	's/he will cherish'
tat-	'taste'	*tadınca*	'upon tasting'

The only way to be sure whether a noun ending in 'p', 't', 'k', or 'ç' is subject to alternation with 'b', 'd', 'g'/'ğ' or 'c' is to look in a dictionary. Despite the fact that the nominals which do not undergo change outnumber those that do, the standard practice adopted in dictionaries is to take the pattern of change shown above as the norm, and to mark only those nouns which retain a final 'p', 't', 'k', or 'ç'. Thus *ağaç*, *çocuk*, *kitap* and *kağıt* (all of which undergo change) will be found without annotation, whereas *saç*, *top* and *millet* are presented in the form *saç* (*-çı*), *top* (*-pu*), *millet* (*-ti*).

2.2 ALTERNATIONS OF SINGLE CONSONANTS WITH DOUBLE CONSONANTS

In a small number of nouns ending in 'b', 't', 'd', 'k', 'l', 's', 'z', 'm' and 'n' the final consonant is duplicated when a vowel is attached to it. These are words borrowed from Arabic, which, in their original roots, have geminates, i.e. doubled consonants. In Turkish such words appear with a single consonant in their bare form or when followed by a suffix beginning with a consonant.

hak 'right'	*haklar* 'rights'	*hakkın* 'your right'
his 'emotion'	*histen* 'of the emotion'	*hissi* 'emotional'
sır 'secret'	*sırlar* 'secrets'	*sırrımız* 'our secret'
hat 'line'	*hatlar* 'lines'	*demiryolu hattı* 'railway line'
zıt 'opposite'	*zıtsa* 'if [it's] the opposite'	*zıddı* 'the opposite of it'

Some of these words keep their original double consonants when they combine with the auxiliaries *et-* 'do' and *ol-* 'be' (13.3.2): *hallet-* 'solve', *hallol-* 'be solved', *hisset-* 'feel'. Others appear in nominal-verb compounds with a single consonant: *hak et-* 'deserve'.

It should be noted that since bare stems do not give any indication that they end in geminates, such words have to be learned individually. Nouns belonging to this class are indicated in dictionary entries in the form *sır* (*-rrı*), *hat* (*-ttı*), *zıt* (*-ddı*). The form of any nominal-verb compounds derived from these words also has to be checked in a dictionary.

2.3   VOWEL/Ø ALTERNATION

There are a number of nouns in which the high vowel ('ı', 'i', 'u' or 'ü') of the final syllable in the bare form does not appear when a suffix beginning with a vowel is attached to the root (e.g. *isim* 'name' but *ismi* 'his/her name'). Many of these are words of Arabic origin which do not have a vowel in this position. For example, the Arabic word *ism* 'name' does not contain a vowel between 's' and 'm'. In Turkish when such a word appears in its bare form an **epenthetic vowel** is inserted, hence the second 'i' in *isim*.

It is important to remember that this is not a general phonological process. It occurs in some words of Arabic origin and in a very few roots of Turkish origin. When such roots combine with a stressable suffix (4.3.1) containing a high vowel, such as the accusative case marker *-(y)I*, there is invariably no epenthetic vowel in the inflected form. However, there may be variation among speakers regarding the inclusion of epenthetic vowels in words with a suffix containing a non-high vowel (such as the dative case marker *-(y)A*).

Root	Root + I (e.g. -(y)I (ACC))	Root + A (e.g. -(y)A (DAT))
karın 'belly'	*karnı*	*karna* or *karına*
şehir 'town'	*şehri*	*şehre* or *şehire*
izin 'permission'	*izni*	*izne* or *izine*

It is not possible to know without looking in a dictionary whether the final high vowel in the bare form of a root is epenthetic or not. Stems which look identical may differ in this respect:

koyun 'bosom'	→	*koynu* 'his/her bosom'
koyun 'sheep'	→	*koyunu* 'his/her sheep'
nehir 'river'	→	*nehri* 'the river' (ACC)
Nehir 'Nehir' (a name)	→	*Nehir'i* 'Nehir' (ACC)

If a root containing an epenthetic vowel is followed by an auxiliary verb beginning with a vowel (*et-* 'do' or *ol-* 'be' (13.3.2)), the epenthetic vowel does not appear, and the noun and verb coalesce into a single word:

sabır 'patience'	*sabrı* 'his/her patience'	*sabret-* 'be patient'
kahır 'distress'	*kahrı* 'his/her distress'	*kahrol-* 'be damned'

In the rare cases where a root with an epenthetic vowel is followed by an unstressable suffix (4.3.2) beginning with a vowel, e.g. the group 2 person marker -(y)Im (8.4), the epenthetic vowel is retained for purposes of stress; thus *nehrím* 'my river' but *nehírim* 'I am a river' (poetic).

2.4 SHORT/LONG VOWEL ALTERNATIONS

In a number of stems which have 'a', 'u' or 'i' in the final syllable, these vowels are replaced with their long counterparts /a:/, /u:/ and /i:/ when a suffix beginning with a vowel is attached:

meram 'plight'	*mera:mını* 'your/his/her plight' (ACC)
hukuk 'law'	*huku:ken* 'legally'
zaman 'time'	*zama:nım* 'my time'
zemin 'ground'	*zemi:ni* 'the ground' (ACC)

As in gemination (2.2) and in most cases of epenthesis (2.3), the alternation of short vowels with their long counterparts occurs in words of Arabic origin, in this case those which originally contain a long vowel. These words have to be learned individually, as there is no indication in the roots that they contain a long vowel. This process can also take place across word boundaries when such words are followed by an auxiliary verb beginning with a vowel (*et-* 'do' or *ol-* 'be' (13.3.2)):

merak 'curiosity'	*mera:k et-* 'be curious'
emin 'sure'	*emi:n ol-* 'be sure'

Short/long vowel alternation does not affect proper nouns that are derived from common nouns with long vowels:

murat 'wish'	→	*mura:dı* 'his/her wish'
Murat 'Murat' (a name)	→	*Murat'ı* ([muratʰɪ] or [muradɪ]) 'Murat' (ACC)

2.5 æ/e ALTERNATION

[æ], which is a lowered allophone of /e/, does not occur in environments where it is followed by a consonant + vowel sequence (1.1.2.1). In cases where a stem or suffix has [æ] but is followed by a consonant + vowel sequence as a result of (further) suffixation, this [æ] is replaced by [e]:

gel- 'come' [ɟæl]	[ɟældim] 'I came'	[ɟeliɾ] 's/he comes'
evler 'houses' [evlæɾ]	[evlærdɛ] 'in (the) houses'	[evlerim] 'my houses'
sen 'you' [sæn]	[sændɛ] 'on you'	[senin] 'your'

2.6 ALTERNATION OF 'a', 'e', 'u' AND 'ü' WITH 'ı' AND 'i'

In the spoken language, some suffixes which conjoin to a stem by means of the consonant 'y' (6.1.3) may affect the pronunciation of a preceding 'a', 'e', 'u' or 'ü'. The presence of 'y' often causes these vowels to be pronounced as 'i'. Alternatively, 'a' and 'u' can be pronounced as 'ı'. The suffixes that most commonly cause such a change are the suffix *-(y)AcAK* (8.2.3.3, 8.5.1.1), the participle suffix *-(y)An* (8.5.2.1), the adverbial suffix *-(y)IncA* (8.5.2.2) and the combination of the optative suffix with the 1st person optative marker: *-(y)AyIm* (8.2.3.1, 8.4). In the case of the verb roots *de-* 'say' and *ye-* 'eat', the change is reflected in the orthography:

de- 'say'	*di-yen* (say-PART) '(the one) who says'
ye- 'eat'	*yi-yecek* (eat-FUT) 's/he will eat'

In most cases, however, only the pronunciation is affected:

atla- 'jump'	*atlayan* (jump-PART) '(the one) who jumps', pronounced [atɫayan], [atɫıjan] or [atlijan]
özle- 'miss'	*özleyince* (miss-CV) 'upon missing', pronounced [özɫejindʒɛ] or [özɫiːndʒɛ]
oku- 'read'	*okuyacak* 's/he is going to read', pronounced [okʰ uʤakʰ] or [okʰ iʤakʰ]
üşü- 'be cold'	*üşüyeyim* 'let me be cold', pronounced [üʃiːm] [üʃijejim]

Note that the effect of 'y' on a previous vowel can result in the violation of vowel harmony (e.g. [atliyan] above).

Inflectional suffixes which end in 'a' or 'e' also tend to be affected by a following 'y'. For example, the vowel of the negative suffix *-mA* is usually replaced (in pronunciation) with a high vowel when followed by a suffix beginning with 'y':

atlama- 'not jump'	*atlamayabiliyorum* (jump-NEG-PSB-IMPF-1SG) 'I [may or] may not jump', pronounced [atɫamajabilijorum]/[atɫamıjabilijorum]/ [atɫamijabilijorum]

The imperfective suffix *-(I)yor* has a similar effect on the final 'a' or 'e' of the stem it attaches to; see 8.2.3.3.

3 VOWEL HARMONY

Vowel harmony is a phonological process which determines what vowel will appear in all but the first syllable of a word. In roots with more than one syllable, the second vowel harmonizes with the first one:

kabak 'marrow'   *etek* 'skirt'
uzak 'far'   *ipek* 'silk'

Similarly, when a suffix is attached to a stem, it harmonizes with the properties of the vowel in the preceding syllable, irrespective of whether the stem is of native or foreign origin:

kuş-lar 'birds'   *ev-ler* 'houses'
puma-lar 'pumas'   *otobüs-ler* 'buses'

After describing the types of vowel harmony in 3.1, we discuss how vowel harmony operates in suffixes (3.2) and in roots (3.3). In 3.4 exceptions to vowel harmony are given.

3.1   TYPES OF VOWEL HARMONY

As a result of vowel harmony, only the following sequences are permissible in native Turkish words:

	'a'	can only be followed by	'a' or 'ı'
Back	'ı'	can only be followed by	'a' or 'ı'
vowels	'o'	can only be followed by	'a' or 'u'
	'u'	can only be followed by	'a' or 'u'
	'e'	can only be followed by	'e' or 'i'
Front	'i'	can only be followed by	'e' or 'i'
vowels	'ö'	can only be followed by	'e' or 'ü'
	'ü'	can only be followed by	'e' or 'ü'

Vowel harmony in Turkish is a combination of two kinds of harmonization process. One of these is **fronting harmony**, which is the assimilation of a vowel with the vowel in the preceding syllable in terms of frontness. A front vowel can only be followed by a front vowel and a back vowel can only be followed by a back vowel, as in *aç-ıl-dı* '[it] was opened', *güç-tü* '[it] was difficult, *böl-üm* 'part', *düş-en* 'falling'.

The other type of harmony process is **rounding harmony**, which is the assimilation of a vowel with the vowel in the preceding syllable in terms of roundedness. Unless it is in the first syllable of a word, a rounded vowel occurs only when it is preceded by another rounded vowel. (For exceptions see 3.3.) Roundedness is thus a property which is copied from the rounded vowel of the previous syllable. This process only affects suffixes and clitics with high vowels. Some examples are *üz-ül-dü-nüz* 'you became sad', *sor-ul-ur* 'it is asked', *öv-ün-dük* 'we boasted'.

The vowels 'o' and 'ö' only occur in the initial syllable of a word, except in loan words such as *lodos* 'south-westerly gale', *otobüs* 'bus' and *protokol* 'protocol'.

3.2 VOWEL HARMONY IN SUFFIXES AND CLITICS

A handful of exceptions aside (see 3.4), vowel harmony operates in all suffixes and clitics, irrespective of whether these are attached to words of native or foreign origin. In terms of vowel harmony, there are two types of suffix in Turkish, I-type and A-type. In this chapter, we use the term 'suffix' as a cover term for suffixes proper and clitics (Chapter 11).

3.2.1 VOWEL HARMONY IN I-TYPE SUFFIXES

The vowels of I-type suffixes are high, but they get their other features (i.e. frontness and roundedness) from the preceding vowel. Fronting and rounding harmonies determine whether the vowel in this type of suffix will be 'i', 'ı', 'ü', or 'u' when affixed to a particular word. For example, a stem with a front unrounded vowel combines with the form which contains the front unrounded vowel 'i', and a stem with a back rounded vowel combines with the form with the back rounded vowel 'u'. When an I-type suffix is attached to a root or stem:

'**ı**' is selected if the preceding vowel is 'ı' or 'a'	'**i**' is selected if the preceding vowel is 'i' or 'e'
kız-ın 'your daughter' *baş-ın* 'your head'	*diz-in* 'your knee' *el-in* 'your hand'
'**u**' is selected if the preceding vowel is 'u' or 'o'	'**ü**' is selected if the preceding vowel is 'ü' or 'ö'
burn-un 'your nose' *kol-un* 'your arm'	*yüz-ün* 'your face' *göz-ün* 'your eye'

Examples of I-type suffixes are the genitive suffix -(n)ın, -(n)in, -(n)un, -(n)ün, the accusative suffix -(y)ı, -(y)i, -(y)u, -y(ü) and the evidential/perfective suffix -mış, -miş, -muş, -müş. The consonants and vowels in brackets are deletable (6.1.3). Capital letters indicate alternating sounds (6.1.2).

Stem	I-type suffix	Forms	Stem + I-type suffix
çay 'tea'	-(I)m (1SG.POSS)	-m, -ım, -im, -um, -üm	çay-ım 'my tea'
su 'water'	-lI (ADJ)	-lı, -li, -lu, -lü	su-lu 'watery'
güzel 'nice'	mI (INT)	-mı, -mi, -mu, -mü	güzel mi 'is it nice'
sor- 'ask'	-DI (PF)	-dı, -di, -du, -dü -tı, -ti, -tu, -tü	sor-du 's/he asked'

3.2.2 VOWEL HARMONY IN A-TYPE SUFFIXES

The vowels of A-type suffixes are unrounded and non-high, but are variable in terms of whether they are back or front. The choice of the appropriate vowel in an A-type suffix depends on whether the vowel in the syllable preceding it is front or back. A stem with a front vowel combines with the 'e' form of the suffix; a stem with a back vowel combines with the 'a' form. A-type suffixes are only affected by fronting harmony. The roundedness or unroundedness of the preceding vowel does not affect them. When an A-type suffix attaches to a root or stem:

'a' is selected if the preceding vowel is 'a', 'ı', 'o' or 'u'	'e' is selected if the preceding vowel is 'e', 'i', 'ö' or 'ü'
hava-dan 'from the air'	ev-den 'from the house'
kız-dan 'from the girl'	biz-den 'from us'
yol-dan 'by the road'	göl-den 'from the lake'
şun-dan 'of this'	tür-den 'of the type'

Examples of A-type suffixes are the plural suffix -lar, -ler, the dative suffix -(y)a, -(y)e, the conditional suffix -sa, -se and the future marker -(y)acak, -(y)ecek.

Stem	A-type suffix	Forms	Stem + A-type suffix
tür 'type'	-lAr (PL)	-lar, -ler	tür-ler 'types'
yık- 'destroy'	-mA (NEG)	-ma, -me	yık-ma 'don't destroy'
gelenek 'tradition'	-sAl (ADJ)	-sal, -sel	gelenek-sel 'traditional'

3.3 VOWEL HARMONY IN ROOTS

Vowel harmony operates in native roots, e.g. *kabak* 'marrow', *oda* 'room', *uzak* 'far', *erik* 'plum' and *inek* 'cow'. With only a few exceptions (3.4 (i)), fronting harmony occurs in all native roots.

As for rounding harmony, again the majority of native words display this, but there are a few cases where the vowel in the second syllable is rounded despite the fact that the preceding vowel is not. This is usually the result of an intervening labial consonant ('p', 'b', 'f', 'v' or 'm'): *savun-* 'defend', *tavuk* 'chicken', *kabuk* 'shell', 'skin'.

3.4 EXCEPTIONS TO VOWEL HARMONY

(**i**)   A few native roots, such as *anne* 'mother' and *elma* 'apple', and stems which contain invariable suffixes, such as *kardeş* 'sibling' are non-harmonic.

(**ii**)   Compounds (some of which are written as a single word, see Chapter 10) are non-harmonic: *bugün* 'today', *keçiboynuzu* 'carob', *Karagöz* (a shadow theatre character).

(**iii**) Loan words often violate the rules of vowel harmony, e.g. *kitap* 'book', *kalem* 'pencil', *lale* 'tulip', *penaltı* 'penalty', *fasulye* 'bean(s)', *marul* 'lettuce', *masum* 'innocent', *jaluzi* 'Venetian blind' and *lobi* 'lobby'.

(**iv**)   The vowel of a suffix may get harmonized as a front vowel even where a loan word does not have a front vowel in the last syllable:

hakikat-siz	(truth-ADJ)	'disloyal'
bahs-i	(topic-ACC)	'the topic (ACC)'
harb-in	(war-GEN)	'of the war'
kalp-ler	(heart-PL)	'hearts'

This happens regularly in loan words that end in a palatal 'l':

gol-ü	(goal-3SG.POSS)	'his/her goal'
etol-den	(scarf-ABL)	'from the scarf'
hal-im	(condition-1SG.POSS)	'my condition'

Loan words that behave in this way appear in the dictionary as *hakikat(-ti)*, *gol(-lü)*, etc.

(v)   Suffixes and prefixes of foreign origin are invariable:

-*izm*: *Şamanizm* 'Shamanism'
-*en*: *tamamen* 'completely'
anti-: *antidemokratik* 'antidemocratic'
bi-: *bihaber* 'unaware', 'ignorant'

(vi) A few native suffixes, or parts of suffixes, are invariable:

(a)   The second vowel in the bound auxiliaries *-(y)Abil*, *-(y)Iver*,
      ▽*-(y)Agel*, ▽*-(y)Adur*, ▽*-(y)Akal*, and ▽*-(y)Ayaz* (8.2.3.2): *kalkabildi*
      's/he managed to stand up'; the non-deletable vowel of the imperfec-
      tive suffix *-(I)yor* (8.2.3.3): *görüyorum* 'I see'; the converbial marker
      -(y)ken (8.5.2.2): *bakmışken* 'having looked'

(b)   The vowels in the following derivational suffixes (7.2.2.2):

      -gen: *altıgen* 'hexagon'
      -gil: *halamgil* 'my aunt and her family'
      -(I)mtrak: *pembemtrak* 'pinkish'
      -leyin: *sabahleyin* 'in the morning'

(c)   The suffix *-ki* (8.1.4) optionally undergoes vowel harmony after *gün*
      'day' and *dün* 'yesterday': *dünki/dünkü* 'yesterday's'.

(vii) The following clitics are invariable (11.1): *bile*, *ki*, *ya*, *ile* and *ise*:
baktım ki 'upon seeing', *söyledim ya* 'but I have said [it]', *Korhan ile*
'Korhan and . . .', *bunlar ise* 'as for these'.

See also 2.6.

4 WORD STRESS

The term **stress** refers to the high pitch and loudness with which a syllable is pronounced relative to others in the same word or sequence of words. This chapter discusses the position of stress in isolated words. The syllable which is stressed in an isolated word is the same one which is stressed when that particular word is the most prominent one within a sequence of words (see Chapters 5 and 23). In this chapter an acute accent will be used to indicate a stressed syllable. The conditions determining **sentence stress**, i.e. which particular word within a sentence is to be stressed, are discussed in Chapter 23.

4.1 STRESS IN ROOTS

4.1.1 REGULAR ROOTS

Most roots in Turkish (including all polysyllabic verbal roots and some loan words) are stressable on the final syllable:

kadín	'woman'
kalabalík	'crowd'
cumhuriyét	'republic'
hastá	'ill'
kutú	'box'
beklé-	'wait'
öğrén-	'learn'

Where a particular root is stressable on a syllable other than the last, this is indicated in dictionary entries.

In vocative forms, i.e. forms of address, stress is placed on the penultimate syllable:

Kádın!	'Hey woman!'
Çocúklar!	'Hey kids!'
Hüséyin!	'Hüseyin!'

If a diminutive suffix (*-CIK*, 7.2.2.2, or its inflected form *-CIğIm*) is added to a form of address, the stress remains in its original position:

Semrá'cığım	'Semra darling!'

4.1.2   IRREGULAR ROOTS AND STEMS

The following groups of words have irregular root stress:

(i)   Adverbs are mostly stressable on the first syllable:

şímdi	'now'
bélki	'perhaps'
yárın	'tomorrow'
áncak	'only', 'only just'

Note that this rule does not apply to words which function primarily as adjectives (16.1.2), but to those that are adverbs in their primary function (16.1.1). Thus in *Bunu koláy yaptım* 'I did this easily', the adjectival *koláy* 'easy' retains its regular stress position even though it functions as an adverb in this sentence.

(ii)   Many nouns of foreign origin (in particular, those which are borrowed from a language other than Arabic or Persian) do not conform to the stress pattern of native words, and are stressed on a syllable other than the final one:

lokánta (Italian)	'restaurant'
bánka (Italian)	'bank'
iskémle (French)	'chair'
táksi (French)	'taxi'
lóbi (English)	'lobby'
fútbol (English)	'soccer'
péncere (Persian)	'window'
politíka (Greek)	'politics'
iskéle (Greek)	'quay'
satsúma (Japanese)	'satsuma'

(iii)   Place names have a non-final stress position:

Tűrkiye, Ánkara, İstánbul, Táksim, Adána, İngiltére, Fránsa, Afríka

Exceptions are place names ending in the suffix *-istan*, which are stressed on the last syllable:

Hindistán	'India'
Gürcistán	'Georgia'

Some speakers place the stress in place names ending in *-istan* on the penultimate syllable (e.g. *Gürcístan*).

Note that the difference in stress is the only distinguishing factor between some place names and otherwise identical common nouns:

mısír 'maize'   *Mísır* 'Egypt'
ordú 'army'   *Órdu* (a city on the Black Sea coast of Turkey)
bebék 'baby'   *Bébek* (a district in Istanbul)

(**iv**) The following question words and those that contain the suffix -*rA* (see 4.3.2 (iii)) are stressed on the first syllable:

hángi   'which'
háni   'where' (informal)
násıl   'how'
níçin   'why'

(**v**) Stems which have reduplicative prefixes (Chapter 9) and most of the stems containing loan prefixes (7.4) are stressed on the prefix:

kápkara   'pitch black'
ásosyal   'antisocial'

(**vi**) Stems that contain unstressable suffixes, see 4.3.1.

(**vii**) Stems which are compounds (4.2).

4.2 STRESS IN COMPOUNDS

Most noun compounds are stressed on (the stressable syllable of) the first element:

búgün (*bu* 'this' + *gün* 'day')   'today'
báşbakan (*baş* 'head' + *bakan* 'minister')   'prime minister'

This is also true of -*(s)I* compounds (10.2), irrespective of whether the two roots are written together or separately:

sokák lambası   'street light'
telefón rehberi   'telephone directory'
çáy bardağı   'tea glass'
dérs kitapları   'textbooks'
búzdolabı   'refrigerator' (lit. 'ice cupboard')
kasímpatı   'chrysanthemum' (lit. 'November aster')
deréotu   'dill' (lit. 'stream weed')

However, there are exceptions, and some compounds are stressed on the final syllable, like regular stems:

alışveríş (*alíş* 'taking' + *veríş* 'giving') 'shopping'
bilgisayár (*bilgí* 'knowledge' + *sayár* '[something] that counts')
  'computer'
kabakulák (*kaba* 'coarse', 'puffy' + *kulak* 'ear') 'mumps'

In compounds consisting of two verbs (13.3.1.2) or a nominal and a verb (13.3.2), stress falls on (the stressable syllable of) the first word:

anlamíş ol-	'have understood'
bitiríyor gözük-	'seem [to] be finishing'
yardím et-	'help'
hastá ol-	'become ill'

For stress in compound verb forms containing bound auxiliaries, see 4.3.1 (iii).

4.3   STRESS IN SUFFIXES

In terms of stress, the suffixes of Turkish are divided into two classes: stressable and unstressable.

4.3.1   STRESSABLE SUFFIXES

The great majority of Turkish suffixes belong to this class. The effect of stressable suffixes on the position of potential word stress is as follows:

(i)   When a stressable suffix is added to a root in which the final syllable (whether part of the root, or itself a suffix) is also stressable, the position of word stress moves to the new final syllable.

kitáp	'book'
kitap-lár	'books'
kitaplar-ím	'my books'
kitaplarım-dá	'in my books'
kitaplarımda-kí	'the one in my books'
kitaplarımdaki-lér	'the ones in my books'
kitaplarımdakiler-é	'to the ones in my books'
kír-	'break'
kır-íl	'be broken'

kırıl-acák	'it will be broken'
krılacak-lár	'they will be broken'

(ii) When a stressable suffix is added to a root in which the final syllable is not stressable (4.1.2), i.e. is irregular, the position of word stress remains on the stressed syllable of the root:

iskémle	'chair'
iskémle-ler	'chairs'
iskémleler-imiz	'our chairs'
iskémlelerimiz-de	'on our chairs'
iskémlelerimizde-ki	'the one on our chairs'
iskémlelerimizdeki-ler	'the ones on our chairs'

Afríka	'Africa'
Afríka-lı	'African'
Afríkalı-lar	'Africans'
Afríkalılar-ın	'of Africans'

As a result, inflected common nouns and inflected place names have different stress patterns:

mısırdakilér 'the ones in the maize'
Mísır'dakiler 'the ones in Egypt'

(iii) Some suffixes which are polysyllabic, e.g. -(y)ArAk (8.5.2.2), -mAksIzIn (8.5.1.2), -sAna, -sAnIzA (8.4), -(I)yor (8.2.3.3) and -(y)Iver, ▽-(y)Agel, ▽-(y)Akal, ▽-(y)Adur and ▽-(y)Ayaz (8.2.3.2), are stressed on their first syllable. The other syllables in these suffixes are unstressable:

kaz-	'dig'	kaz-árak	'by digging'
bak-	'look'	bak-máksızın	'without looking'
gel-	'come'	gel-íyor	's/he is coming'
tut-	'hold'	tut-úver	'hold'
şaş-	'be astounded'	şaş-ákal-dı-m	'I was astounded'

The first syllable of these polysyllabic suffixes bears the word stress even when other stressable suffixes follow:

gel-íyor-lar	'they are coming'
tut-úver-miş	'apparently s/he suddenly took hold of [it]'

When they attach to irregular roots they either retain their stress, or they lose it and the original stress of the root reemerges:

Afrikalılaşárak or *Afríkalılaşarak* 'by becoming Africanized'
Afrikalılaşíyor or *Afríkalılaşıyor* 's/he is becoming Africanized'

If two suffixes of this group of stressable suffixes occur on the same word, the first one is stressed:

tut-úver-iyor 's/he suddenly takes hold of [it]'

4.3.2   UNSTRESSABLE SUFFIXES AND CLITICS

There are a number of suffixes and **clitics** in Turkish which do not take stress and are pre-stressing except in certain cases where two of them occur within the same intonational phrase (see 11.2). These are:

(i)   The copular markers *-(y)DI*, *-(y)mIş*, *-(y)sA* (8.3.2), the converbial marker *-(y)ken* (8.5.2.2) and the generalizing modality marker *-DIr* (8.3.3):

gel-sé-ymiş 'if s/he had arrived'
gid-ér-se 'if s/he goes'
otur-úr-ken 'while sitting'
oku-yacák-tır 's/he will most certainly read'

(ii)   The marker *-(y)lA/ile* 'with', 'by', 'and' (8.1.4):

elíyle 'with his/her hand', 'his/her hand and . . .'
Alí'yle 'with Ali', 'Ali and . . .'

(iii)   The derivational suffixes *-(A/I)cIK, -CA, -CAsInA, -en, -(y)In, -lA* (7.2.2.2), *-leyin, -rA*:

úfacık 'tiny'	*kadínca* 'womanly'
uçárcasına 'as if flying'	*tamámen* 'completely'
kíşın 'in winter'	*yáyla* 'plateau'
néreye '[to] where'	*órada* 'there'

(iv)   The following person markers (8.4):

(a)   the 1st and 2nd person markers belonging to group 2, i.e. *-(y)Im, -sIn, -(y)Iz, -sInIz*:

uyúrum 'I sleep', 'I will sleep'
anlamíşsın 'you have understood'

(b) The 2nd person markers of group 4, i.e. *-yIn*, *-yInIz*, and those belonging to group 3, i.e. *-sIn*, *-sInIz*. (Note that the other *-sIn*, i.e. the 3rd person optative and imperative suffix (groups 3 and 4) is stressable):

> *anlayásınız (diye)* '(so that) you understand'

(c) The 3rd person plural suffix *-lAr* of group 2 when it is attached to a non-case-marked subject complement:

> *Tutsáklar* 'They are prisoners' (see also 8.4, 22.3 (34)).

(v) The particle *bile* 'even' (11.1.1.1):

> *Ahmét bile* 'even Ahmet'

(vi) The clitic *mI* (11.1.1.5):

> *gittiníz mi?* 'did you go?'

(vii) The clitic *-(y)sA/ise* (11.1.1.3):

> *bénse* 'as for me'

(viii) The negative marker *-mA* (8.2.2) and composite suffixes containing it (e.g. *-mAdAn* (8.5.2.2)):

> *gít-me-dik* 'we didn't go'
> *bák-madan* 'without looking'

Note that one exception is the occurrence of *-mA* in the negative aorist form *-mA(z)* (8.2.3.3), which is stressable, e.g. *bak-máz-dık* 'we were not in the habit of looking', *yaz-má-yız* 'we will not write'.

(ix) The clitics *dA* (11.1.1.2 (ii–iii)), *ki* (11.1.1.4) and *ya* (11.1.1.6):

> *anlıyorúm da* 'I understand, but . . .'
> *bakmıyordúm ki* 'but I WASN'T looking'
> *gördǘm ki* 'I realized that . . .'
> *gördǘm ya* 'I HAVE seen (it)'

4.3.2.1 The effect of unstressable suffixes and clitics on word stress

The addition of unstressable suffixes and clitics to a word may or may not change the existing position of stress within that word. (Note that clitics attach to phrases which may be made up of one or more words (Chapter 11)).

Regular roots
The addition of any one of the unstressable suffixes and clitics except the negative suffix and the clitics in (ix) above (i.e. *dA, ki* and *ya*) to a regular root does not change the existing position of stress in that word:

geldilér 'they have arrived'	*geldilér-se* 'if they have arrived'
	geldilér bile 'they have already arrived'
yorgún 'tired	*yorgún-um* 'I'm tired'
	yorgún mu 'is s/he tired?'
bisiklét 'bicycle'	*bisiklét-le* 'by bicycle'
	bisiklét-se 'as for the bicycle'
çocúk 'child'	*çocúk-ça* 'childish(ly)'

Irregular roots
The addition of (i)–(iv) in 4.3.2 (i.e. the copular markers, the generalizing modality marker, the marker *-(y)lA/ile*, and the adverbial and person markers specified there) to an irregular root tends not to change the existing position of stress within that word:

İstánbul	*İstánbulda-ydım* 'I was in Istanbul'
	İstánbul-la 'with Istanbul'

The addition of *bile* 'even', *mI* (interrogative), *-(y)sA/ise* 'as for' (i.e. (v)–(vii) in 4.3.2) and *dA* (in its additive function described in 11.1.1.2 (ii)) to an irregular root may or may not change the existing position of potential stress within that word. The stress may either remain in its original position, or it may be attracted to the position just before the clitic:

İstánbul	*İstánbul bile/İstanbúl bile*	'even Istanbul'
	İstánbul mu?/İstanbúl mu?	'Istanbul?'
	İstánbulsa/İstanbúlsa	'as for Istanbul'
	İstánbul da/İstanbúl da	'Istanbul too'

Co-occurrence of unstressable suffixes and clitics
When two or more of the above-mentioned suffixes or clitics (i)–(ix) co-occur in a word, stress falls on the syllable immediately before the unstressable suffixes or clitics or immediately before their unstressable segments:

otur-úyor-muş-sun bile 'apparently you were already sitting'
otur-acák-sa da mı 'even if s/he's going to sit?'
iste-míş mi-ydi-n ki 'had you asked for [it], then?'

An unstressable suffix followed by a stressable suffix

The addition of a stressable suffix to one of the unstressable suffixes or clitics does not alter the position of stress. In the examples below, *-DI* and *-lAr* are stressable suffixes following an unstressable suffix:

otúrma 'don't sit down'	*otúr-ma-dı* 's/he hasn't sat down'
okuldá 'at school'	*okuldá-ymış-lar* 'apparently they are/were at school'

Stress and the negative suffix

The addition of the negative suffix changes the existing position of potential stress within a word, attracting it to the syllable before itself:

sevíyor	's/he likes [it]'
sévmiyor	's/he doesn't like [it]'
İstánbullulaş	'become like a native of Istanbul'
İstanbullulás-ma	'don't become like a native of Istanbul'

Stress and the clitics *dA*, *ki* and *ya*

The addition of these clitics ((ix) in 4.3.2) has the effect of placing stress on the immediately preceding syllable, even if this syllable is otherwise unstressable:

istemíştim 'I had wanted [it]'	*istemiştím ki* [*otursun*] 'I had wanted [him/her to sit down]'
anlayámıyorum 'I can't understand [it]'	*anlayamıyorúm ki* 'but I can't understand [it]'
söylémemiş 's/he hasn't said [it]'	*söylememíş ya* 'but s/he HASN'T said [it]'
yürüyorum 'I (can) walk'	*yürüyorúm da koşamıyorum* 'I can walk, *but* I can't run'

Note that 'continuative' *dA* (11.1.1.2 (i)) does *not* place stress on the preceding constituent. See 11.2 for the stress pattern in sentences with more than one clitic.

5 INTONATION AND SENTENCE STRESS

Intonation refers to the rising and falling of the voice in terms of pitch. The continuous flow of speech may be seen as divided into consecutive sections known as **intonational phrases**. An intonational phrase, which may be as short as a single word, but usually consists of several, is the unit of speech within which a single primary **stress** and a single **intonation contour** occur. There may be pauses between intonational phrases. If a sentence contains more than one intonational phrase the stress which is the most prominent is called sentence stress.

In this chapter we describe the main intonation contours of Turkish and the position of primary and secondary stress in unmarked sentences. The syllable which is acoustically the most prominent one in an intonational phrase is said to have primary stress, indicated by capital letters below. A syllable which is less acoustically prominent than the one which has primary stress but which still stands out among the others is said to have secondary stress, indicated below by small capital letters. Where an example consists of more than one intonational phrase, the boundary between them is shown by a vertical stroke. The effect of shifting the position of stress, and the interaction of this with the order of constituents in a sentence, are discussed in Chapter 23. The effect of clitics on sentence stress is discussed in 11.2.

5.1 THE INTONATION CONTOURS OF TURKISH

There are three types of intonation contour in Turkish:

(i) Slight rise followed by fall:
This is the standard contour for statements (including negative statements) regarded by the speaker as complete, and also for the last intonational phrase in more complex statements.

(1) O HER zaman yemek-ler-in-i loKANta-da yer.
s/he every time meal-PL-3SG.POSS-ACC restaurant-LOC eats
'S/he always eats in a restaurant.'

(ii) High rise followed by fall:
This is the standard contour for yes/no questions (expressed with *mI* (19.1)).

(2) Dün çocuk-LAR okul-a git-Tİ mi?
yesterday child-PL school-DAT go-PF INT
'Did the children go to school yesterday?'

(iii) Slight rise, followed by fall-rise:
This occurs:

(a) in questions involving a wh-phrase (e.g. *ne* 'what', *nereye* 'where', *kim* 'who' (19.2)).

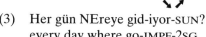

(3) Her gün NEreye gid-iyor-SUN?
every day where go-IMPF-2SG
'Where do you go everyday?'

(b) in all intonational phrases whose content is not complete in itself and needs continuation. Important examples are conditional clauses, other adverbial clauses and all but the last of any co-ordinated series of items and of lists:

(4) Eğer sokağ-a çık-mak isTİ-yor-SAN . . .   (Conditional clause)
if street-DAT go.out-VN want-IMPF-COND.COP-2SG
'If you want to go out . . .'

(5) Bugün Ziya-yla buluş-tuĞ-UN zaMAN . . .   (Adverbial clause
today Ziya-COM meet-CV-2SG.POSS time   of time)
'When you meet Ziya today . . .'

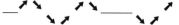

(6) EVE gitTİM, ÇANtamı alDIM . . .   (Co-ordinated items)
'I went home, took my bag . . .'

5.2 POSITION OF STRESS IN THE INTONATIONAL PHRASE

5.2.1 PRIMARY STRESS

In a simple sentence which is uttered as a single intonational phrase the unmarked position of primary stress is the stressable syllable of the word which is situated just before the predicate:

(7) Aydın bana çiÇEK getir-di.
Aydın I(DAT) flower bring-PF
'Aydın brought me flowers.'

(8) Şu anahtarı HANginize vereyim?
'Which of you shall I give this key to?'

(9) Dışarda bir köPEK var.
'There's a dog outside.'

Two factors may cause a change in the position of stress:

(i) Clitics and the negative suffix:
When a clitic occurs in a sentence, primary stress is placed on the stressable syllable of the phrase before it (see also 4.3.2.1, 11.2):

(10) LONdra-ya **mı** gid-ecek-siniz?
London-DAT INT go-FUT-2PL
'Are you going to go to London?' (i.e. 'Is it London you're going to go to?')

(11) Londra'ya gideCEK **mi**siniz?
'Are you going to go to London?'

(12) Ahmet'TE **de** bunlardan bir tane var.
'There's one of these in Ahmet's office too.'

(13) Turgut nasıl bilSİN **ki**?
'How on earth should Turgut know?'

The negative marker causes primary stress to occur on the syllable before it (4.3.2(viii), 8.2.2):

(14) [Herkesin burada olduğun]-u BİLmiyordum.
'I didn't know [everyone was here].'

(ii) Focusing a constituent:
Focusing a constituent may cause primary stress to appear on a constituent other than the one which immediately precedes the predicate:

> (15) Zeki babasıNI onbeş yıldır görmüyormuş, annesini deĞİL.
> 'Zeki hasn't seen his FATHER for 15 years, not his mother.'

For a detailed discussion of the interaction of focusing and primary stress, see 23.3.1.

5.2.2 SECONDARY STRESS

Secondary stress occurs mainly on the following types of constituent (where it is indicated in small capital letters):

(i) The stressable syllable of subject and topic (23.3.3) noun phrases:

> (16) Dün **Zeki-nin aBla-sı** iş-TEN ayrıl-mış.   (Subject)
> yesterday Zeki-GEN sister-3SG.POSS work-ABL leave-EV/PF
> 'Zeki's sister left her job yesterday.'

> (17) **Arkadaş-lar-ımIZ-la** BUrada buluş-acağ-ız.   (Topic)
> friend-PL-1PL.POSS-COM here meet-FUT-1PL
> 'We're going to meet our friends here.'

(ii) Adverbs which are not in the immediately preverbal position (in which case they have primary stress), in particular *daha* 'more' and *en* 'most':

> (18) Çamaşır-lar-ı GEne makina-nın iç-in-DE bırak-mış-ım.
> laundry-PL-ACC again machine-GEN inside-3SG.POSS-LOC leave-EV/PF-1SG
> 'I seem to have left the laundry in the washing machine *again*.'

> (19) Kitapları HEP yerDE bırakıyorsun.
> 'You *always* leave the books on the floor.'

> (20) Bundan **daHA** uygun bir sözcük düşüNEmiyorum.
> 'I can't think of a *more* appropriate word.'

> (21) Bu hayvanların arasında EN vahşisi kapLANmış.
> 'Apparently the *most* savage these animals is the tiger.'

(iii) Most quantificational constituents, i.e. determiners (15.6) such as *her* 'every', numerals (15.7), pronominalized determiners (18.4 (iv)) such as *bazısı* 'some [people]', *kimi* 'some [people]' and pronominal quantifiers (18.6.1) such as *herkes* 'everyone', *her şey* 'everything':

(22) Halk politikacıların **çoğuna** güVENmiyor.
      'The people don't trust *most* politicians.'

5.3 SENTENCES WITH MORE THAN ONE INTONATION CONTOUR

Complex sentences containing an adverbial clause or a conditional clause have more than one intonation contour:

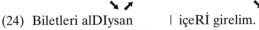

(23) Bugün Ziya-yla buluştuğuNUZ zaMAN | bana teleFON ed-in.
      today Ziya-COM meet-CV-2PL.POSS time I(DAT) telephone
                                                    make-2PL.IMP
      'When you meet up with Ziya today give me a ring.'

(24) Biletleri alDIysan | içeRİ girelim.
      'If you've got the tickets, let's go in.'

PART 2
MORPHOLOGY: THE STRUCTURE OF WORDS

6 PRINCIPLES OF SUFFIXATION

In Turkish the vast majority of words which contain more than one syllable are complex. Processes of word formation create words that can be very long and sometimes correspond to whole sentences in English. The main word formation process in Turkish is **suffixation**, the formation of a new word by attaching an affix to the right of a **root**. Any linguistic item to which suffixes can be added, whether this is a simple root or a combination of a root plus suffix(es), is referred to as a **stem**.

The principles that apply to the attachment of a suffix to a stem also apply to some of the **clitics** that can be placed after the final suffix of a phrase (Chapter 11).

In 6.1 we describe the conditions which determine the vowels and the consonants in suffixes and clitics and the changes that take place at the boundaries between stems and suffixes. In 6.2 irregular alternations to the stem are discussed, and 6.3 explains the order of suffixation in a word.

6.1 THE FORM OF SUFFIXES

Almost all suffixes in Turkish have more than one form. The initial consonant in some suffixes and the vowels in almost all suffixes depend on the consonants or vowels that precede them. For example, the plural suffix has two forms, -*lar* (as in *kuş*-**lar** 'birds') and -*ler* (as in *kedi-***ler** 'cats'), with only the vowel alternating between 'a' and 'e', whereas the perfective suffix has eight forms, -*dı*, -*di*, -*du*, -*dü*, -*tı*, -*ti*, -*tu*, -*tü* (as in *kal-***dı** 'remained' but *düş-***tü** 'fell'), where both the consonant and the vowel are subject to alternation. The alterable sounds in a suffix are indicated in this book by capital letters, hence the plural suffix is written as -*lAr*, and the perfective suffix as -*DI*.

6.1.1 VOWEL ALTERNATION IN SUFFIXES

The vowel of a particular suffix is selected on the basis of the rules of vowel harmony, which are explained in 3.2. Some suffixes and clitics do not undergo vowel harmony (see 3.4).

6.1.2 CONSONANT ALTERNATION IN SUFFIXES: 'ç'/'c', 't'/'d' AND 'k'/'g'

Some suffixes in Turkish begin with the voiceless/voiced pairs 'ç'/'c' (e.g. the occupational suffix -*CI* (7.2.2.2), 't'/'d' (e.g. the locative suffix -*DA*

(8.1.3) or 'k'/'g' (e.g. the adjective-forming suffix -*GAn* (7.2.1.1)). The choice between using the voiced or voiceless variant depends on the last phonological unit in the stem. When a suffix beginning with one of these pairs is attached to a stem ending in any one of the voiceless consonants, the voiceless variant in the pair is used as the initial consonant of the suffix. Otherwise (i.e. when the stem ends in a vowel or a voiced consonant) its voiced counterpart is used. To summarize:

'p', 't', 'k', 'f,' 'h', 'ç', 'ş', 's'   are followed by 'ç', 't', 'k'
'b', 'd', 'c', 'v', 'l', 'm', 'n', 'j', 'r', 'z', 'y', 'ğ'   and vowels are followed
                                            by 'c', 'd', 'g'

These alternations are shown by the use of capital letters. Thus 'C' represents 'ç'/'c', 'D' represents 't'/'d', and 'G' represents 'k'/'g':

C:	*posta-cı*	'postman'	*süt-çü*	'milkman'
D:	*oda-da*	'in the room'	*sokak-ta*	'in the street'
G:	*diz-gi*	'print'	*as-kı*	'hanger'

6.1.3 THE ATTACHMENT OF A SUFFIX TO A ROOT OR STEM: DELETABLE VOWELS AND CONSONANTS

In Turkish, vowels do not occur next to each other. Therefore if a suffix beginning with a vowel is attached to a stem ending in a vowel, either the initial vowel of the suffix is deleted, or the consonant 'y' is added. As a result, suffixes are divided into two groups: those which can lose their initial vowel and those which can acquire the buffer consonant 'y'. All such vowels and consonants are shown in brackets in the citation forms of suffixes.

Examples of the first type are the 1st person possessive suffix -*(I)m*, the aorist suffix -*(A/I)r* and the adjectival suffix -*(I)mtrak*. Most **derivational suffixes** (Chapter 7) are of this type.

*pul-**um*** 'my stamp'	but	*kafa-**m*** 'my head'
*gör-**ür*** 's/he sees'	but	*ara-**r*** 's/he searches'
*yeşil-**imtrak*** 'greenish'	but	*sarı-**mtrak*** 'yellowish'

Some examples of suffixes which take the consonant 'y' are the converbial suffix -*(y)IncA*, the dative suffix -*(y)A* and the future marker -*(y)AcAk*. Most **inflectional suffixes** (Chapter 8) are of this type.

*gel-**ince*** 'upon coming'	but	*dene-**yince*** 'upon testing'
*Yusuf-**a*** 'to Yusuf'	but	*Emine-**ye*** 'to Emine'
*sor-**acak*** 's/he will ask'	but	*atla-**yacak*** 's/he will jump'

A suffix beginning with a consonant is directly attached to a root or stem ending in a consonant, as is the case with the ablative suffix *-DAn*, the perfective suffix *-DI* and many others:

*ev-**den*** 'from the house'
*git-**ti*** 's/he left'

However, there are three exceptions. One of these is the genitive suffix (8.1.3), which has a deletable initial 'n'. Another is the 3rd person possessive suffix, which has a deletable initial 's'. Finally, the distributive suffix contains a deletable 'ş'. These consonants appear in order to avoid vowel sequences; otherwise they are deleted. In the citation forms of suffixes these are shown in brackets:

Genitive *-(n)In* (8.1.3):

*Yusuf-**un***	(Yusuf's)	but	*Suna-**nın***	(Suna's)
*Betül-**ün***	(Betül's)	but	*Emine-**nin***	(Emine's)

3rd person possessive marker *-(s)I(n)* (8.1.2):

*ev-**i***	(his/her house)	but	*elbise-**si***	(her/his dress)
*kitab-**ı***	(his/her book)	but	*kafa-**sı***	(his/her head)

(For the (*n*) in *-(s)I(n)* see 6.2 (iib).)

Forms which contain suffixes with deletable initial sounds can be ambiguous, as it may not always be clear which segment a particular vowel or consonant belongs to:

diz-im 'my knee' (*diz* 'knee'-1SG.POSS)
dizi-m 'my serial' (*dizi* 'serial'-1SG.POSS)

Note that a stem ending in 'ğ' (1.1.1.1) combines with the vowel-initial variant of a suffix:

dağ-ın 'of the mountain/your mountain'
bağ-ımız 'our vineyard'
iç-tiğ-im 'that I have drunk'

6.2 IRREGULAR CHANGES IN ROOTS AND SUFFIXES UNDER (FURTHER) SUFFIXATION

Apart from the sound changes described in Chapter 2, some roots and suffixes undergo additional changes when a suffix is added. These changes are as follows:

(i)   The pronouns *ben* 'I' and *sen* 'you' become *bana* 'to me' and *sana* 'to you' when the dative suffix -*(y)A* is added.

(ii)   At the end of certain types of stem 'n' appears when particular suffixes are added:

(a)   In the case of the 3rd person pronoun *o* (18.1.1) and the demonstrative pronouns (18.2), 'n' appears when the following are attached:

>   the plural suffix -*lAr* (8.1.1)
>   case suffixes (8.1.3)
>   the adverbial suffix -*CA* (7.2.2.2)
>   the adjectival suffix -*sIz* 'without' (7.2.2.2)

Some examples are: *ona* 'to him/her/it', *onlar* 'they', *onca* 'according to him/her', *onsuz* 'without him/her/it', *bunu* 'this (one) (ACC)', *şunlar* 'those', *bunsuz* 'without this', *bunca* 'this much'.
   The same applies in the case of the colloquial usage in which the comitative/instrumental and conjunctive suffix -*(y)lA* 'with' (8.1.4) is affixed to the non-case-marked, rather than to the genitive-marked, form of these pronouns: ↓*onla* 'with him/her' (cf. *onunla*), ↓*bunla* 'with this' (cf. *bununla*).

(b)   There are a number of other pronominal stems and two suffixes in which an 'n' appears when either case suffixes (8.1.3) or the adverbial suffix -*CA* (7.2.2.2) are attached. These are the following:

– the personal pronoun *kendi*- (in its 3rd person reflexive, simple pronominal and emphatic usages (18.1.3)): *kendinde* 'at/on him/her(self) (colloquial)', *kendince* 'according to him/her(self)'. *Kendi* behaves differently from the other two groups listed below in that in informal speech -*(y)lA* can also attach to it by means of an intermediary 'n': ↓*kendinle* 'with him/her(self)'.
– the 3rd person possessive suffixes -*(s)I* (singular) and -*lArI* (plural) (8.1.2) and pronouns containing them: *kendisi* 'self', 's/he' (18.1.2), *kendi kendisi* 'self' (18.1.3), *birbiri/birbirleri*- 'each other' (18.1.4), and all of the pronominalized determiners listed in 18.4 (iv):

kendisine 'to himself/herself', *birbirlerini* 'each other (ACC)', *bazılarından* 'from some of them', *hepsinde* 'in all of them', *birine* 'to one of them'.

- the suffix *-ki* in its pronominal usage 'the one . . .' (18.5): *evdekinde* 'in/on/at the one in the house', *buradakinden* 'from the one which is here'.

(iii) In the case of just two stems, *su* 'water' and *ne* 'what', 'y' appears at the junction with any of the following suffixes:

(a)   the possessive suffixes, except the 3rd person plural
(b)   the genitive suffix

e.g. *suyum* 'my water', *suyun* 'your water', 'of the water', *neyimiz* 'what (of ours)', *neyi* 'what (of his/hers)' (also *nesi*, but *neleri* 'what (of theirs)', *sular* 'waters'). Note that the forms ↓*nem* and ↓*nen* for *ne*+possessive can be used in informal contexts.

(iv)   Certain adjectives, some of which are themselves derived forms, lose their final consonant ('k') when combining with derivational suffixes:

alçak 'low'	+ *-(A)l*	_	*alçal-* 'decline'
ufak 'small'	+ *-(A/I)cIK*	_	*ufacık* 'tiny'
küçük 'small'	+ *-mAn*	_	*küçümen* 'rather small'

Others lose their final vowel in such circumstances:

kuru 'dry'	+ *-(A)K*	_	*kurak* 'arid'
sarı 'yellow'	+ *-(A)r*	_	*sarar-* 'fade'

In speech, the locative pronouns *bura-* 'here', *şura-* 'here', 'over there' and *ora-* 'there' (18.3.1) and the wh-phrase *nere-* 'where' (19.2.1.3) may lose their final vowel when a locative or ablative case marker is added:

bura- 'here'	+ *-DA*	_	*burda/burada* '(in) here'
nere- 'where'	+ *-Dan*	_	*nerden/nereden* 'from where'

(v)   Surnames ending in *-oğlu*: Note that *-oğlu* 'son of' contains the 3rd person singular possessive suffix *-(s)I* (8.1.2), hence conforms to the pattern mentioned in (iib) above, as in *Senemoğlu'nu*, *Senemoğlu'ndan*. However, case suffixes (but not *-CA*) can also combine directly with such names, without an intermediary 'n', as in *Senemoğlu'yu*, *Senemoğlu'dan*, etc. (but *Senemoğlu'nca*).

6.3 THE ORDER OF SUFFIXATION

In Turkish a large number of suffixes and clitics can be added to a single root. In the overwhelming majority of cases, derivational suffixes (Chapter 7) precede inflectional suffixes (Chapter 8). Clitics (Chapter 11) occur after inflectional suffixes.

(1) suç-lu-luk-la mı
crime-N.DER-N.DER-INS INT
DER-DER-INFL CL
'in a guilty manner?'

(2) diz-ge-ler-im-de
arrange-N.DER-PL-1SG.POSS-LOC
DER-INFL-INFL-INFL
'on my lists'

(3) yap-ı-laş-tır-ıl-ma-mış
build-N.DER-V.DER-CAUS-PASS-NEG-EV/PF
DER-DER-INFL-INFL-INFL-INFL
'has not been built up'

Note that the clitic *dA* 'also', 'and', which regularly occurs after all the inflectional suffixes in a word, in colloquial usage may appear between the two segments of *-(y)Abil* (8.2.3.2):

(4) Gid-ebil-ir-im **de**.
go-PSB-AOR-1SG also
INFL-INFL-INFL CL
'*And* I can [indeed] go.'

(5) Gör-üş-tür-ül-e-me-ye **de** bil-iyor mu-ydu-nuz?
see-REC-CAUS-PASS-PSB-NEG-PSB also PSB-IMPF INT-P.COP-2PL
'Did it *also* sometimes happen that you were not allowed to see each other?'

The attachment properties of each suffix and clitic are described in the relevant sections of Chapters 7, 8 and 11. See also 7.3 for the internal ordering of derivational suffixes.

7 WORD CLASSES, DERIVATION AND DERIVATIONAL SUFFIXES

This chapter discusses the word classes of Turkish and the means by which new words are formed by using **derivational suffix**es. Section 7.1 introduces the word classes of Turkish, such as noun, adverb, verb, etc. 7.2 is on **derivation**, the formation of a new word by means of attaching a suffix to a **root**. In 7.2.1 and 7.2.2, we list the derivational suffixes that attach to verbs and nominals respectively, and in 7.3 we discuss the ordering of derivational suffixes. 7.4 is on prefixation, a process which has a very limited range of application in Turkish.

7.1 WORD CLASSES

A word in Turkish can belong to one of the following classes: nominal (noun, pronoun, adjective or adverb), verb, postposition, conjunction or discourse connective, interjection.

7.1.1 NOMINALS

The group **nominal** contains four word classes: **noun, pronoun, adjective** and **adverb**. In Turkish the boundaries between noun, adjective and adverb are somewhat blurred. Many lexical items are able to occur with the typical functions of more than one of these classes, although in almost all such cases one function or another is dominant in the actual usage of that item. We call this its primary function. For example, the word *güzel* can occur as a noun in *güzelim* 'my beauty' (affectionate mode of address), or as an adverb, as in *Güzel konuştu* 'S/he spoke well'. But in by far the majority of its occurrences the function of the word *güzel* is adjectival, as in *güzel bir köpek* 'a beautiful dog'. Below we describe the criteria for identifying the primary function of any specific word belonging to the nominal group.

(i) Nouns:
A noun is a word used for a thing (e.g. *ağaç* 'tree'), a person (e.g. *kadın* 'woman'), an abstract concept (e.g. *mutluluk* 'happiness'), or the proper name of a person (e.g. *Suzan*) or place (e.g. *Londra*). Nouns in Turkish can be inflected for **number** (8.1.1, 14.3.1), **person** (8.1.2, 14.3.2), and **case** (8.1.3, 14.3.3).

(ii) Pronouns:
A pronoun (Chapter 18) is a word which is substituted for a noun phrase in contexts where it is either not necessary to name the referent explicitly or where it is impossible to do so. Examples are *sen* 'you', *bu* 'this (one)', *başkası* 'another (one)', *ne* 'what', *kimse* 'anyone', 'no one'. Pronouns are inflected for number, person and case: *bunlar* 'these', *hepimiz* 'all of us', *şurada* 'here', 'over there'. There is no gender distinction in Turkish pronouns.

(iii) Adjectives:
An adjective (15.2) ascribes some property, quality or status to the entity denoted by a noun. Examples are *sarı* 'yellow', *yumuşak* 'soft', and *dürüst* 'honest'. Adjectives in Turkish can be modified by adverbials such as *çok* 'very', *son derece* 'extremely' and *oldukça* 'rather', as in *çok önemli* 'very important', *oldukça yumuşak* 'rather soft' (15.4.1.1). They can be expressed in comparative or superlative forms by the addition of the modifiers *daha* 'more' or *en* 'most', as in *daha dürüst* 'more honest', and *en yumuşak* 'soft-est' (15.4.2 and 15.4.3). **Determiners**, such as *bir* 'a/an', *her* 'each', *bütün* 'all' and *bu* 'this', 'these' (15.6), and **numerals**, such as *iki bin* 'two thousand', *üçüncü* '(the) third' (15.7) are functionally related to the adjective class.

Most lexical items which occur primarily as adjectives can also occur as nouns, taking plural, possessive and case suffixes as required, or they can function as adverbs, in particular as circumstantial adverbs of manner (16.4.3). An example of the first type is the word *küçük* 'small', which is primarily used as an adjective, as in *küçük kızlar* 'little girls', but which can also be used as a noun, as in *küçükler* '(the) little ones'. An example of the second type is the word *kötü* 'bad', as in *kötü araba* '(a) bad car', which when placed immediately before the verb in a sentence functions as an adverb meaning 'badly', as in *kötü yüzmek* 'to swim badly'.

(iv) Adverbs:
An adverb modifies, that is to say provides further specification of the meaning of, a verb, an adjective, another adverb, or a whole sentence (Chapter 16). Adverbs that modify verbs typically provide information about the manner, time or degree of the occurrence of an event: *yavaşça* 'slowly', *hep* 'always', *çok* 'a lot'. Adverbs that modify adjectives or other adverbs specify the degree to which the concepts they denote apply, such as *biraz* 'somewhat' and *çok* 'very' in *biraz büyük* 'somewhat large', *çok sık* 'very often'. Examples of adverbs that modify a whole sentence are *belki* 'perhaps' and *maalesef* 'unfortunately'. Occasionally, words that occur primarily as adverbs can be inflected as nouns. Thus *şimdi* 'now' can appear in the form *şimdilerde* 'nowadays', which includes number and case markers.

7.1.2 VERBS

A **verb** is a word which expresses an action, event, process or state, such as *koş-* 'run', *bit-* 'end', *ol-* 'be', 'become', *kal-* 'remain', 'stay'. Verbs in Turkish are inflected for **voice** (8.2.1, 13.2), **negation** (8.2.2, 20.1), **tense, aspect** and **modality** (8.2.3, Chapter 21) and person (8.4, 12.2.1). Verb stems, derived or non-derived, are indicated in this book by a following hyphen.

7.1.3 POSTPOSITIONS

Postpositions (Chapter 17) are words which take noun phrase complements. Examples are *karşı* 'against' (e.g. *bana karşı* 'against me'), *sonra* 'after' (e.g. *toplantıdan sonra* 'after the meeting', and *için* 'for', e.g. *kimin için* 'for whom'). Lexical items that occur primarily as postpositions (17.2) are not inflected when functioning as such. However, an important sub-class of postpositions (17.3) is formed from nouns by the addition of possessive and case markers (e.g. *ön-ün-de* 'in front of' from *ön* 'front'). Some lexical items which function primarily as postpositions may also occur as nouns. For example, *karşı* can also be used meaning 'the other side', and in this case it can be inflected like a noun, as in *karşıdan* 'from the other side'.

7.1.4 CONJUNCTIONS AND DISCOURSE CONNECTIVES

Conjunctions join two or more items which have the same syntactic function. Examples are *ve* 'and', *fakat* 'but', and *de . . . de* 'both . . . and', as in *Hasan ve Hüseyin* 'Hasan and Hüseyin', *Git ama kalma* 'Go but don't stay [there]', and *Can da sen de* 'both Can and you'. **Discourse connectives** are used between, or sometimes inside, sentences for purposes of cohesion in discourse. Among other functions, they can introduce statements which are a further development of a previous statement, e.g. *hatta* 'moreover', *üstelik* 'and on top of that', or they can be used for expanding on a previous statement e.g. *yani* 'in other words', or for presenting a fact that appears to contradict what has just been said, e.g. *halbuki* 'whereas'. Conjunctions and discourse connectives constitute the only word class that cannot be inflected. They are discussed in detail in Chapter 28.

7.1.5 INTERJECTIONS

These are words which express feelings, such as *ay* 'ouch!', 'wow!', *hay allah* 'oh dear!', *vah vah* 'what a shame!', *allah allah* 'good heavens!', or which are used to initiate conversation or to express the speaker's attitude towards the hearer, such as *yahu* 'hey'. A few interjections in Turkish can be used as nouns and can combine with inflectional suffixes (e.g. *ahlarımdan* 'from my sighs') or derivational suffixes (e.g. *ahla-* 'sigh').

7.2 DERIVATION

Derivation is the creation of a new **lexical item** (i.e. a word form which would be found in a dictionary). The vast majority of derivation in Turkish is achieved through suffixation. Prefixation is used, to a very limited extent, for **reduplication** (Chapter 9), and in a few loan words (7.4). **Compounding**, which is another type of word formation process, is discussed in Chapter 10. In very rare cases, word formation does not involve any of the above derivational processes, as in the case of *kuru* 'dry' and *kuru-* '(to) dry'.

When a derivational suffix attaches to a stem it produces a new word connected in meaning to that stem. Some derivational suffixes change the class of the word they attach to. For example, the nominal-deriving suffix *-I* combines with verbal stems such as *kaz-* 'dig' and *güldür-* 'cause to laugh' to form the nouns *kazı* 'excavation' and *güldürü* 'comedy'. Other derivational suffixes create words of the same class as the stem to which they are attached. For example, the suffix *-lIk* can derive nouns from nouns, as in the case of *krallık* 'kingship', 'kingdom' from *kral* 'king'.

In most cases, the meaning of a word which contains a derivational suffix is not predictable by segmenting it into parts. For example, the words *kayık* 'boat', *kayak* 'ski' and *kaydırak* 'slide' are all derived from the verb *kay-* 'slide', and although the suffixes themselves indicate that these words are nominals, they do not give an indication as to the exact meaning of the new words they form. Similarly, the particular suffix that a word can take is not predictable. For example, the suffixes *-lA*, *-lAş*, *-(A)l* and *-(A)r* can all change adjectives into verbs that express the process of changing state (i.e. become what the adjective denotes), but the adjectives they attach to are not chosen on the basis of a particular grammatical condition, as witnessed by the words *genişle-* 'widen', *kalınlaş-* 'broaden', *incel-* 'become thin' and *kabar-* 'swell'.

The roots that derivational suffixes attach to may not always be identifiable words in modern Turkish. Some derivational processes took place a long time ago, and while the derived word is still in use the root may have become obsolete (e.g. **yayla** 'plateau'). It may also be the case that the root of the word is still in use in some parts of Turkey but is no longer used in modern standard Turkish (e.g. **dilim** 'slice').

Productive derivational suffixes are those which regularly have particular meanings and can be used freely with a particular type of stem. For example, the suffix *-lI*, in one of its meanings, can be used freely with almost all place names, to indicate that a person comes from, or is a native of, the place specified, as in *Londra'lı* 'Londoner', *Kuzey İrlanda'lı* 'native of Northern Ireland', *oralı* '(person) from there'. The majority of derivational suffixes, however, are unproductive. This means that although they may be present in a number of words that are still in use, they are no longer perceived by speakers as items usable in the production of new words (e.g. *utangaç* 'shy').

Derivational suffixes were widely used as a means of coining new words to replace their non-native counterparts during the language reform movement that was launched in the early 1930s. Words of mostly Arabic and Persian origin, but also some other loan words, were replaced by new words made up by adding derivational suffixes to Turkish or Turkic roots. While most of the derivational suffixes employed were Turkish, a few were borrowed from other Turkic languages (e.g. -tay in kurultay 'conference'). Many of the new words thus formed have replaced their loan counterparts, or are in the process of doing so; others proved short-lived, and yet others co-exist with their synonyms or near-synonyms of foreign origin, e.g. teklif (Ar.) and öneri 'proposal', mesela (Ar.) and örneğin 'for example', teorik (Fr.) and kuramsal 'theoretical'.

7.2.1   SUFFIXES THAT ATTACH TO VERBS

Suffixes that attach to verbs create new words which are either nominals (noun, adjective or adverb) or verbs.

7.2.1.1   Suffixes that attach to verbs to form nominals

Nominal-forming suffixes that combine with verbs mostly create words that function primarily as nouns. They may also create adjectives, and in rare instances adverbs. Most suffixes of this type are unproductive.

-A	Forms nouns: süre 'time span', yara 'wound'. Less commonly it forms adverbs: geçe 'past' as in ikiyi çeyrek geçe 'quarter past two'.
-(A)C	Forms nouns: süreç 'process', kaldıraç 'pulley', bağlaç 'conjunction'.
-(A)cAn	Forms adjectives: sevecen 'loving'.
-AğAn/-AgAn	Forms adjectives. The more frequently used form is the one containing 'ğ': olağan 'usual', durağan 'still', gezegen 'planet' (see also -GAn below).
-(A)K	Forms (i) nouns, usually denoting concrete objects: elek 'sieve', adak 'sacrifice', kayak 'ski'; (ii) adjectives: ürkek 'timid', korkak 'cowardly'.
-(A)l	Forms (i) nouns: okul 'school', kural 'rule'; (ii) adjectives: sanal 'virtual'.
-(A)m	Forms nouns: kuram 'theory', dönem 'period', anlam 'meaning'.
-(A)mAK	Forms nouns: basamak 'step', kaçamak 'evasion'.
-(A)nAK	Forms nouns: tutanak 'minutes', ödenek 'subsidy', görenek 'custom'.

-(A/I)r	Forms: **(i)** nouns: *keser* 'adze', *yarar* 'benefit', 'use', *gelir* 'income' **(ii)** adjectives: *çalar saat* 'alarm clock', *okuryazar* 'literate' **(iii)** adjectival clauses: *uzaktan farkedilebilir bir renk* 'a colour (which is) noticeable from far away'.
-(A)v	Forms nouns: *sınav* 'examination', *görev* 'duty', *türev* 'derived form'.
-(A)y	Forms (i) nouns: *olay* 'event', *deney* 'experiment'; (ii) adjectives: *yapay* 'artificial', *düşey* 'vertical'.
-C/-InC	This pair of suffixes (*-ç* is added to verbs ending in *-n*, otherwise *-Inç* is used) forms (i) nouns: *direnç* 'resistance', *basınç* 'pressure'; (ii) adjectives: *iğrenç* 'disgusting', *gülünç* 'ridiculous'.
-DI	Forms nouns: *uydu* 'satellite', *alındı* 'receipt', *çıktı* 'print-out'.
-DIK	Forms (i) nouns: *tanıdık* 'acquaintance'; (ii) adjectives: *bildik* 'familiar', *tanıdık* 'familiar'. See 25.1.1.2 (v) for a special adjectival usage.
-GA/-(A)lgA	Forms nouns: *dizge* 'system', *süpürge* 'broom', *çizelge* 'table' (i.e. tabulated information).
-GAC	Forms (i) nouns: *süzgeç* 'sieve', *kıskaç* 'pincers', *yüzgeç* 'fin'; (ii) adjectives: *utangaç* 'shy'.
-GAn	Forms (i) nouns: *etken* 'factor', *sürüngen* 'reptile'; (ii) adjectives: *konuşkan* 'talkative', *kaygan* 'slippery'.
-GI	Forms nouns, mostly denoting concrete objects: *silgi* 'eraser', *sürgü* 'bolt', but also abstract nouns such as *bilgi* 'knowledge', *sevgi* 'love'.
-GIC	Forms nouns: *dalgıç* 'diver', *başlangıç* 'beginning'.
-GIn	Forms (i) nouns: *baskın* 'raid', *sürgün* 'exile'; (ii) adjectives: *etkin* 'active', *durgun* 'calm'.
-I	Forms (i) nouns: *yazı* 'writing', *güldürü* 'comedy', *batı* 'west'; (ii) adjectives: *dolu* 'full', *duru* 'clear'.
-(I)K	Forms (i) nouns: *konuk* 'guest', *kayık* 'boat'; (ii) adjectives: *soluk* 'faded', *kırık* 'broken'.
-(I)lI	A compound of *-I* (above) and *-lI* (7.2.2.2). Forms adjectives and adjectival phrases: *yazılı* 'written', (*kağıda*) *sarılı* 'wrapped (in paper)'.
-(I)m/-(y)Im	Forms nouns from underived verb roots: *bölüm* 'department', 'chapter', 'part', *seçim* 'choice', 'election', *deneyim* 'experience', or from derived intransitives with *-(I)l/-n*: *gerilim* 'tension', *devinim* 'movement'.

-(I)n	Forms nouns: *basın* '(the) press', *yayın* 'publication', 'broadcast', *yığın* 'heap'.
-(I)ntI	Forms nouns: *söylenti* 'rumour', *girinti* 'indentation', *alıntı* 'quotation'.
-(I)t	Forms nouns: *geçit* 'crossing', 'pass', *yazıt* 'inscription', *umut* 'hope'.
-mA	Forms (i) nouns: *basma* 'printed cloth', *kıyma* 'minced meat', *inme* 'paralysis', 'stroke'; (ii) adjectives: *dökme* '(of metal) cast'.
-mAC	Forms nouns: *bulamaç* 'thick soup', *yırtmaç* 'slit'.
-mAcA	Forms nouns: *bulmaca* 'puzzle', *koşmaca* 'tag (game)', *çekmece* 'drawer'. This is a complex suffix made up of *-mA* and *-CA* (7.2.2.2).
-mAdIK	Forms adjectives. The form *-mAdIK*, which contains the negative suffix, is a productive suffix, unlike its affirmative counterpart *-DIK* (see above). It can attach directly to verb stems or to their passive form: *kırmadık* 'unbroken', *görmedik* 'unseen', *görülmedik* 'unseen', 'unprecedented'.
-mAK	Forms nouns: *ekmek* 'bread', *çakmak* 'lighter', *yemek* 'food', 'meal'.
-mAn	Forms (i) nouns indicating a person's occupation: *öğretmen* 'teacher', *danışman* 'adviser', *eleştirmen* 'critic'; (ii) adjectives: *şişman* 'fat' (see also *-mAn*, 7.2.2.2).
-mAz	Forms: (i) nouns: *açmaz* 'impasse', *tükenmez* 'ball-point pen' (ii) adjectives: *bitmez* 'endless', *anlaşılmaz* 'incomprehensible' (iii) adjectival clauses: *gözle görülemez* (*bir ayrıntı*) '(a detail) which is invisible to the [naked] eye'.
-mIK	Forms nouns: *kıymık* 'splinter', *kusmuk* 'vomit'.
-mIş	Forms nouns from intransitive verb stems: *geçmiş* '(the) past', *dolmuş* 'car operating like a bus', *ermiş* 'saint'.
-sAK	Forms nouns: *tutsak* 'prisoner' (see also *-sAK*, 7.2.2.2).
-sAl	Forms adjectives: *görsel* 'visual', *işitsel* 'aural' (see also *-sAl*, 7.2.2.2).
-sI	Forms nouns: *tütsü* 'incense', *yatsı* 'ritual worship performed by Muslims two hours after sunset', *giysi* 'garment'.
-tay	Forms nouns denoting an institution or organized meeting: *Danıştay* 'Council of State', *çalıştay* '(academic) workshop' (see also *-tay*, 7.2.2.2).

-tI	Forms nouns from two-syllable stems ending in *-l* or *-r*: *doğrultu* 'direction', *bağırtı* 'shout', *morartı* 'bruise'.
-(y)AcAK	Forms nouns: *yiyecek* 'food', *içecek* 'drink', *gelecek* 'future'. See 25.1.1.2 (v) for a special adjectival usage.
-(y)An	Forms nouns: *sıçan* 'rat', *bakan* 'minister'.
-(y)AsI, *-(y)AsIcA,* *-(y)AsIyA*	*-(y)AsI* forms adjectives which mean 'worthy of . . .', but these forms are going out of usage: ∇*görülesi* 'worth seeing'. Both *-(y)AsI* and *-(y)AsIcA* form adjectives used in expressing ill-wishes: *kahrolası(ca)* 'damned', *lanet olası(ca)* 'cursed'. *-(y)AsIyA* forms adverbs indicating the degree to which an action is performed, in terms of the imagined endpoint: *ölesiye* 'to the point of dying', *doyasıya* 'to the point of fulfilment/satisfaction'.

-(y)IcI/-cI   Probably the most productive suffix in this category, this forms:

(i) nouns expressing:

  (a) a person practising a certain profession, or having a certain occupation: *koruyucu* 'guardian', *öğrenci* 'student', *dilenci* 'beggar'.

  (b) a tool, machine or substance performing a particular function: *yazıcı* 'printer', *yatıştırıcı* 'sedative', *uyuşturucu* 'narcotic'.

(ii) adjectives denoting that the action of a verb is an inherent quality of the person or thing to which the adjective is applied: *yapıcı* 'constructive', *üzücü* 'distressing', *yorucu* 'tiring'.

(iii) adjectival clauses that mark an attribute which is regarded as an inherent property of the entity denoted by the noun that the adjectival construction qualifies. The noun which is qualified is always inanimate and is the subject of the root verb: *nezleyi önleyici (ilaçlar)* '(medicines) that prevent the common cold', *endişelerimizi giderici (sözler)* '(words) that ease our worries'.

Note that the *-cI* form of this suffix occurs only after '-n'. See also *-CI* in 7.2.2.2, the counterpart of this suffix which is added to nominals.

-(y)Iş   Forms nouns: *direniş* 'resistance', *giriş* 'entrance', *yürüyüş* 'walk', 'march'.

7.2.1.2 Suffixes that attach to verbs to form verbs

-(A/I)klA   Indicates repetitive or intermittent action: *uyukla-* 'doze', *dürtükle-* 'prod continually'.

-AlA	Indicates the suddenness of the onset of an action: *şaşala-* 'be bewildered', *durala-* 'suddenly stop (to reflect)'.
-(I)n	In the vast majority of cases this suffix, which is identical in form to the reflexive suffix (8.2.1.3), forms intransitive verbs: *sevin-* 'be happy', *görün-* 'appear', 'seem', *kaçın-* 'avoid', but it can also form transitive verbs: *edin-* 'acquire'.
-(I)ş	This suffix, which is identical in form to the reciprocal suffix (8.2.1.4), indicates one or other of the following:

    (i) that the action denoted by the root verb is performed in an unorganized manner: *koşuş-* 'run back and forth', *uçuş-* 'fly about'

    (ii) a shared act: *bölüş-* 'share', ↓*kırış-* 'share', *fısıldaş* 'whisper among themselves'

    (iii) the intensity of a property of the root verb: *kokuş-* 'give off a putrid smell', 'become rotten' (from *kok-* 'smell').

-(I)ştır	(*-(I)ş* + *-DIr* (reciprocal + causative, 8.2.1.4, 8.2.1.1)) Indicates intensive or repetitive action: *araştır-* 'investigate', *itiştir-* 'push back and forth'.

7.2.2 SUFFIXES THAT ATTACH TO NOMINALS

Suffixes that attach to nominals create both verbs and other nominals (nouns, adjectives and adverbs).

7.2.2.1 Suffixes that attach to nominals to form verbs

-A	Added to nouns: *kana-* 'bleed', *türe-* 'spring up', 'derive' and adjectives: *boşa-* 'divorce'.
-(A)l	Added to adjectives of quality, to form intransitive verbs: *kısal-* 'become short(er)', *daral-* 'become narrow(er)', *incel-* 'become thin(ner)'.
-(A)r	Added to adjectives, particularly those denoting colour, to create verbs that indicate the process of acquiring that colour or state: *karar-* 'turn black', *ağar-* 'turn white', *delir-* 'go mad'.
-(A)ş	Added to nouns: *yanaş-* 'approach'.
-(A)t	Added to nouns: *gözet-* 'safeguard'.
-DA(n)	Added mostly to onomatopoeic stems: *kıpırda(n)-* 'move', 'fidget', *çatırda-* 'crack', *şakırda-* 'jingle', *vızılda(n)-* 'hum', 'buzz', 'whinge'. The '*-n*' is added only where the subject is human.
-GIr	Occurs in words with onomatopoeic stems that do not stand independently: *fışkır-* 'spurt out', *püskür-* 'spray'.

-(I)K	Makes intransitive verbs from (i) adjectives: *acık-* 'become hungry', *gecik-* 'be delayed'; (ii) nouns: *gözük-* 'seem', 'appear'.
-(I)msA	Added to adjectives to form transitive verbs: *azımsa-* 'underestimate', *özümse-* 'assimilate', 'make one's own'. Also used with the pronoun *ben* 'I': *benimse-* 'consider [s.t.] one's own'.
-lA	Added to:

(i) nouns: *tuzla-* 'put salt on', *avla-* 'hunt'

(ii) adjectives: *akla-* 'acquit', *kurula-* 'dry (transitive)'

(iii) onomatopoeic stems indicating the sound produced by animals: *gıdakla-* 'crow', *miyavla-* 'miaow', *havla-* 'bark'

(iv) interjections: *ahla-* '(to) sigh', *ofla-* '(to) huff'.

The result of (i) and (ii) is most often a transitive verb, but there are cases where *-lA* can also create intransitive verbs: *çabala-* 'try hard', *şişmanla-* 'become fat', *zayıfla-* 'grow thin'.

-lAn	(*-lA* + *-n* (passive/reflexive, 8.2.1.2, 8.2.1.3)) Added to (i) adjectives: *kurulan-* 'dry oneself', 'be dried', *hazırlan-* 'get ready', (ii) nouns: *avlan-* 'hunt', *güneşlen-* 'sunbathe', *hırslan-* 'get angry'. All of these verbs are intransitive. Most of those which are derived from adjectives also have a transitive form (see *-lA* above), but the vast majority of those that are derived from nouns do not have a transitive counterpart. *-lAn* combines with the causative suffix *-DIr-* (e.g. *evlendir-* 'to marry (two people to each other)', *hırslandır-* 'make [s.o.] angry') only in cases where the corresponding *-lAt* suffix (see below), for idiosyncratic reasons, does not combine with a particular root.
-lAş	(*-lA* + *-(I)ş* (reciprocal, 8.2.1.4)) Added (i) to adjectives of quality to form intransitive verbs that indicate the process of attaining that particular quality: *güzelleş-* 'become beautiful', *koyulaş-* 'darken', 'thicken', *kırlaş-* 'turn white (of hair)'; (ii) to nouns to indicate mutual activity: *haberleş-* 'communicate with one another', *mektuplaş-* 'communicate with each other by letter', *e-mailleş-* 'e-mail (each other)'.
-lAt	(*-lA* + *-t* (causative 8.2.1.1)) Added to adjectives to form transitive/causative verbs: *kirlet-* 'make [s.t.] dirty', *serinlet-* 'make [s.o.] cool down', *genişlet-* 'expand [s.t.]'. Some of these verbs do not have a corresponding *-lA* form.

-sA	Added (i) to nouns to form transitive or intransitive verbs: *önemse-* 'consider important', *susa-* 'become thirsty'; (ii) to adjectives to form transitive verbs: *garipse-* 'consider strange', *hafifse-* 'consider trivial'.

7.2.2.2   Suffixes that attach to nominals to form nominals

A few of these suffixes are of Arabic or Persian origin. Words containing Arabic and Persian suffixes are increasingly giving way to their synonyms of Turkish origin.

-(A)C	Attaches to nouns to form adjectives: *anaç* 'motherly', *kıraç* 'infertile'.
-(A/I)cIK	See -CAK
-(A)K	Attaches to adjectives to form adjectives: *solak* 'left-handed', *kurak* 'arid'.
-(A)l	Attaches to nouns to form adjectives: *yerel* 'local', *ulusal* 'national', *yasal* 'legal'. This suffix was introduced as part of the language reform movement alongside *-sAl*, and has the same function.
-(A)n	Attaches to nouns or adjectives to form nouns: *köken* 'origin', *düzen* 'system'.
-ane	A suffix of Persian origin (pronounced [a:nέ]) which attaches to nouns borrowed from Arabic and Persian to form adjectives: *şairane* 'poetic', *dostane* 'friendly'.
-(A)rI	The spatial nominals *iç* 'inside' and *dış* 'outside' can be used in their bare form only as adjectives (e.g. *iç taraf* 'inner part', *dış kapı* 'outer door'). Otherwise they always have to have possessive marking (e.g. *evin içi* 'the inside of the house'). The addition of the derivational suffix *-(A)rI* allows these words to appear on their own and to be case-marked: *dışarı (çık-)* '(go) outside'.
-(A)t	Attaches to nouns or adjectives to form nouns or adjectives: *özet* 'summary', *başat* 'dominant'.
-(A)y	Attaches to nouns to form adjectives: *güney* 'south'.
-baz	A suffix of Persian origin which is added to nouns to form nouns: *cambaz* 'acrobat', *düzenbaz* 'cheat'.
-CA	(unstressable) This is a productive suffix which:
	(**i**) creates adjectives
	(**a**) from nouns, meaning 'characteristic of a . . .', describing actions or attitudes: *çocukça* 'childish', *aptalca* 'idiotic'
	(**b**) from the pluralized form of a 'round' numeral, expressing a large number in an

imprecise fashion: *binlerce* 'thousands of' *yüzlerce* 'hundreds of', or of a measure expression, again suggesting a large amount: *kilolarca* 'kilograms of', *hektarlarca* 'acres of'

(ii) creates nouns, adjectives or adverbs denoting a language from nouns of nationality: *Japonca* '(in) Japanese', *İsveççe* '(in) Swedish'

(iii) creates adverbs (see 16.1.6 for details).

Also combines with the verbal noun suffix *-mA* (see *-mAcA* (7.2.1.1)).

-CA   (stressable) Reduces the intensity of adjectives: *güzelcé* 'prettyish', *hızlıcá* 'quite fast', *küçükçé* 'rather small'. The same function is more often performed by a modifying adverbial of degree such as *oldukça* 'quite' (16.5).

-CAK, -CAğIz, -CIK, -(A/I)cIk are all diminutive suffixes which are used for expressing endearment and/or pity. The choice of the appropriate suffix is not predictable: *çocukcağız* 'the poor/dear child', *kedicik* 'the poor/dear little cat', *kuşcağız* 'the little birdie', *yavrucak* 'the poor child'. *-CIK* also (i) indicates smallness: *sözcük* 'word', *adacık* 'little island', (ii) unproductively combines with adjectives which contain (unstressable) *-CA*, as in *yakíncacık* 'close by', *hémencecik* 'immediately', usually with the effect of emphasizing the quality expressed by the adjective. In the same way, *-(A/I)cIK*, both of which are unstressable, are added to adjectives, intensifying the degree of diminutiveness they express: *dáracık* 'very narrow', *ázıcık* 'very little', *küçücük* 'tiny'.

-CAK   Apart from its diminutive usage mentioned above, this suffix derives:

(i) adjectives from adjectives (synonymous with adjectival (stressable) *-CA*): *büyücek* 'rather large' from *büyük* 'large'

(ii) nouns from nouns: *oyuncak* 'toy', or from verbs: *salıncak* 'swing'

(iii) (in colloquial registers) adverbs from nouns: *evcek* 'the whole household together', *mahallecek* 'as a neighbourhood' (in contexts such as 'We objected as a neighbourhood')

(iv) occasionally adverbs from adverbs indicating haste: *çabucak* 'very quickly' (from *çabuk* 'quickly').

-CAnA   Colloquial form of unstressable (adverbial) *-CA*: *güzelcene* 'nicely', *yavaşçana* 'slowly', *kolaycana* 'easily'.

-CAsI	(*-CA* + 3rd person possessive) Unproductive composite suffix which forms modal adverbs (16.3): *hakçası* 'in truth', 'frankly', *erkekçesi* 'honestly'.
-CAsInA	Derives manner adverbs from adjectives with a negative connotation: *aptalcasına* 'stupidly', *salakçasına* 'like a twit', see also 8.5.2.2.
-CI	A productive suffix which, when added to nouns, forms:

    (i) nouns indicating a person associated with a profession: *güreşçi* 'wrestler', *lokantacı* 'restaurant owner', *Almancacı* 'German teacher'. Also occurs in the question word *neci* used to inquire about someone's occupation.

    (ii) nouns or adjectives indicating ideological adherence to a person, cause or idea: *devrimci* 'revolutionary', *gerici* 'reactionary'

    (iii) nouns indicating a person engaged in a particular activity: *yolcu* 'traveller', *kapkaççı* 'snatch-and-run thief'

    (iv) nouns indicating one who likes or is in the habit of consuming a particular type of food or drink: *içkici* 'boozer', *tatlıcı* 'someone with a sweet tooth'

    (v) adjectives indicating the habitual involvement of a person with the entity denoted by the root: *palavracı* 'liar', 'lying (person)', *şüpheci* 'sceptical (person)'.

    See also *-(y)IcI*, the counterpart of *-CI* which is added to verbs, 7.2.1.1.

-CIl	Added to nouns to form adjectives and nouns, this suffix indicates love or affinity towards what is denoted by the stem: *insancıl* 'humane', 'philanthropic', *evcil* 'domesticated', *öncül* 'premise'. It is also added to the pronoun *ben* 'I': *bencil* 'selfish'.
-DA	Added to nouns to form nouns and adjectives: *gözde* 'favourite'.
-DAm	Added to nouns to form nouns: *gündem* 'agenda', *yöntem* 'method'.
-DAn	Added to nouns or adjectives to form adjectives and nouns: *sıradan* 'ordinary', *neden* 'reason', *içten* 'sincere', *toptan* 'wholesale'.
-dan	A suffix of Persian origin which is attached to nouns to form nouns: *şamdan* 'candlestick', *cüzdan* 'wallet'.
-dar	A suffix of Persian origin which is attached to nouns to form (i) nouns: *kasadar* 'cashier'; (ii) adjectives: *dindar* 'religious'.

-Daş/-Deş	Added to nouns to form nouns denoting possessors of a shared attribute: *yandaş* 'supporter', *kardeş* 'sibling' (from *karın* 'abdomen'), *meslektaş* 'colleague (i.e. person of the same profession)'.
-en	An unstressable Arabic suffix which is attached to nouns to form adverbs: *şahsen* 'personally', *hakikaten* 'really'.
-engiz	A suffix of Persian origin which is added to nouns to form adjectives: *esrarengiz* 'mysterious', *dehşetengiz* 'awesome'.
-gen	Added to numerals to form names given to geometric figures: *dörtgen* 'quadrilateral', *altıgen* 'hexagon'.
-gil	This suffix indicates group membership, especially when referring to species of animals or plants, and is used with the plural suffix: *baklagiller* 'legumes', *turunçgiller* 'citrus fruits'. In non-standard usage it may also refer to human groups, being attached to (i) proper names: *Ahmetgil* 'Ahmet and his family/group', and (ii) nouns indicating family members (in which case *-gil* is preceded by a possessive suffix: *amcasıgil* 'his/her uncle (and his family)'.
-(h)ane	The word *hane* 'house', borrowed from Persian, appears as a suffix in words denoting places (pronounced [a:nɛ́]): *hastahane* 'hospital', *pastane* 'cake shop', *kayıkhane* 'boat house'.
-I	This suffix forms adverbs of time from the pluralized form of nominals denoting time: *sabahları* 'in the morning(s)', *önceleri* 'formerly' (see 16.4.1.1 (63)).
-(I)msAr	Attaches to adjectives to form adjectives: *iyimser* 'optimistic', *karamsar* 'pessimistic'.
-(I)msI	Attaches to nouns or adjectives to form adjectives expressing similarity to the entity denoted by the root noun: *barakamsı* 'shed-like', *meyvamsı* 'fruity' (see also *-sI* below).
-(I)mtraK	Attaches to adjectives which express colour and taste, to express approximation to what that adjective denotes: *mavimtrak* 'bluish', *ekşimtrak* 'sourish'.
-(I)ncI	Added to cardinal numbers to derive ordinal numbers: *ikinci* 'second', *yüzüncü* 'hundredth' (15.7.2). Also used with the question word *kaç* 'how many' to inquire about the number of a particular item in an ordered list: *kaçıncı (gün)* 'which (day)', and optionally with *son* 'last': *sonuncu* 'last'.
-istan	A Persian suffix which forms names of countries or regions: *Macaristan* 'Hungary', *Arabistan* 'Arabia'.

-(I)t	Forms adjectives and nouns: *eşit* 'equal', *karşıt* 'opposite'.
-iye	An Arabic suffix which forms nouns: *maliye* 'public finance', *Harbiye* 'Military Academy'.
-iyet	An Arabic suffix which forms nouns: *maliyet* 'cost', *medeniyet* 'civilization'.
-(I)z	Attaches to numerals to indicate (a member of) a group of siblings born in a single birth: *dördüz* 'quadruplet(s)', *ikiz* 'twin(s)'.
-kar	A suffix of Persian origin (pronounced [cʰaɾ]) which is added to nouns to form nouns indicating a person associated with a profession or occupation: *sanatkar* 'artist', *hizmetkar* 'servant'.
-lA	Attaches to nouns to designate a place associated with the concept in the root: *yayla* 'plateau' (from *yay* (obs.) 'summer'), *tuzla* 'salt mine'. This suffix is unstressable, and stress remains on the root.
-lAm	Attaches to nouns to derive nouns: *denklem* 'equation', *önlem* 'precaution'.
-lAmA	Attaches to nouns to derive nouns or adverbs: *gözleme* 'pancake', *şekerleme* 'crystallized fruit', 'nap', *balıklama (atla-)* '(dive) head-first'.
-leyin	Unstressable suffix attaching to terms denoting times of the day to derive adverbials: *sabahleyin* 'in the morning', *geceleyin* 'at night' (see also *-(y)In* below).
-lI	This a productive suffix which derives:

(i) nouns and adjectives where the entity described possesses, is characterized by, or is provided with the object or quality expressed by the stem:

(a) from nouns and adjectives: *atlı* 'horseman', 'horsedrawn', *sevgili* 'lover', 'dear', *akıllı* 'clever', *mavili* 'in blue', *hızlı* 'rapid'. Also occurs in the question word *neli,* used to inquire about the attribute of something (e.g. *neli dondurma* 'what kind of ice cream').

(b) from nouns of place and locative pronouns (18.3.1) to indicate a person belonging to or coming from that place: *üniversiteli* 'university student', *Londralı* 'Londoner', *köylü* 'villager', *buralı* 'from here'. Also occurs in the question word *nereli* 'from where', used to ask about a person's country (or town, etc.) of origin.

(c) from numerals to indicate groups made of items containing that number of objects: *üçlü* 'threesome', 'trio', *altılı* 'sextet'.

(ii) adjectival phrases from noun phrases, which express that the entity described possesses, is characterized by, or is provided with the object or quality expressed by the noun phrase: *kısa saçlı* 'short-haired', *dört çocuklu* 'with four children', *mavi elbiseli* 'in a blue dress', *bindokuzyüzlü yıllar* 'the nineteen hundreds'. If the adjectival phrase thus formed is derived from a *-(s)I* compound (10.2), the compound marker *-(s)I* is deleted before *-lI* is added: *deniz manzaralı* 'with a sea view' (cf. *deniz manzarası* 'sea view'), *üç yatak odalı* 'three-bedroomed' (cf. *yatak odası* 'bedroom').

The double usage of this suffix, *-lI ... -lI*, produces adjectives: *kızlı oğlanlı (bir grup)* '(a group) of girls and boys', or adverbs: *geceli gündüzlü (çalış-)* '(work) day and night'.

-lIK This productive suffix derives:

(i) nouns from nouns, adjectives or adverbs to indicate:

(a) the state relating to a particular concept: *krallık* 'kingship', *sağırlık* 'deafness', *iyilik* 'goodness', *çabukluk* 'speed'

(b) an application, embodiment or institutionalization of the concept in question: *krallık* 'kingdom', *iyilik* 'good deed', *askerlik* 'military service'

(c) an object or garment associated with a body part: *gözlük* 'spectacles', *başlık* 'headgear'

(d) a storage place or container for a particular type of object: *odunluk* 'woodshed', *kitaplık* 'bookcase', *pabuçluk* 'shoe rack'

(e) a place where the entity denoted by the root noun is found collectively: *zeytinlik* 'olive grove', *mezarlık* 'cemetery'

(f) a person whose relationship is analogous to the blood relationship indicated by the root noun: *analık* 'stepmother', *evlatlık* 'child servant'

(g) a banknote: *onluk* 'tenner'.

(ii) adjectives which indicate:

(a) when added to nouns, suitability for the type of entity denoted by the root: *dolmalık* 'for stuffing', *elbiselik* 'for a dress', *karakolluk* 'requiring police intervention'

(b) when added to nouns denoting periods of time, recurrent production or occurrence: *günlük* 'daily', *aylık* 'monthly'

(c) when added to numerals, the approximate age of a person: *ellilik* 'in (his/her) fifties', or the value or price of something: *yüz milyonluk* 'worth a hundred million'.

(iii) adjectival phrases from quantitative expressions of the form numeral + noun, which according to the meaning of this noun can express weight, length, capacity, duration, value, price, etc.: *beş kiloluk* 'weighing five kilos', *üç saatlik* 'three-hour', *iki kişilik* 'suitable for two people', *beş yüz milyon liralık* 'worth five hundred million lira'.

-mAn Forms adjectives and nouns with idiosyncratic meanings: *sarman* 'ginger' (used of cats), *toraman* 'sturdy', *katman* 'layer' (see also *-mAn* in 7.2.1.1).

-rA Unstressable suffix which attaches to demonstrative pronouns and *ne* 'what', to form locative pronouns (18.3.1) *bura-* 'here', *ora-* 'there', *nere-* 'where'. In some dialects these can appear on their own, but in standard Turkish they must combine with one of the nominal inflectional suffixes (the plural suffix, case and person suffixes).

-sAK Forms nouns: *tümsek* 'mound', *bağırsak* 'intestine' (see also *-sAk* in 7.2.1.1).

-sAl A suffix introduced as part of the language reform to replace the Arabic suffix *-(v)i*, it attaches to nouns to form adjectives that express the notion of relationship to the concept denoted by the root noun: *tarihsel* 'historic(al)', *yapısal* 'structural', *küresel* 'global'. In rare cases it also forms nouns: *kumsal* 'sandy beach'. See also *-sAl* in 7.1.1.1.

-sI Like *-(I)msI* and *-(I)mtrak*, this suffix expresses approximation to a particular quality. Added only to nouns to form adjectives: *kadınsı* 'feminine', *çocuksu* 'naïve'.

-sIl Forms adjectives: *yoksul* 'poor', *varsıl* 'wealthy'.

-sIz This productive suffix is added to

(i) nouns to form adjectives denoting that the entity described lacks whatever is expressed by the root: *parasız* 'penniless', 'free (of charge)', *eşsiz* 'unequalled', *sınırsız* 'unlimited'

(ii) nouns and pronouns to form adverbs denoting the non-involvement in an event of whatever is expressed by the root: *arabasız* 'without a/the car', *parasız* 'free of charge', 'without paying', *sensiz* 'without you'

(iii) nouns to form nouns (a rare usage): ↓*aynasız* (slang) 'police officer', *telsiz* 'wireless', 'walkie-talkie', *Hamursuz* 'Passover'.

-*(ş)Ar*   This distributive suffix is added productively to numerals (15.7.3): *üçer (kişi)* 'three (people) each', *onaltışar (kitap)* 'sixteen (books) each', and to the question word *kaç* 'how many': *kaçar* 'how many each'. When combining with *yarım* 'half', the initial consonant remains: *yarımşar* 'half each'.

-*tay*   Added to nouns to form nouns denoting an institution: *Yargıtay* 'Supreme Court' (see also -*tay* in 7.2.1.1).

-*tI*   Added to onomatopoeic stems to form nouns: *gıcırtı* 'squeak', *takırtı* 'rattle', *gürültü* 'noise'.

-*vari*   A suffix of Persian origin (pronounced [va:rí:]) but going out of usage: *gangstervari* 'gangsterlike', *Amerikanvari* 'American-style'. Both vowels in this suffix are long.

-*(v)i*   An Arabic suffix (pronounced [vi:]) which forms adjectives: *milli* 'national', *resmi* 'official', *hukuki* 'legal', *ananevi* 'traditional'.

-*(y)A*   An Arabic suffix which indicates feminine gender: *müdire* 'female director'. Also appears on names given to women: *Aliye*, *Fazıla*.

-*(y)at*   An Arabic suffix which forms nouns: *tahkikat* 'investigation', *ihracat* 'exports', *maddiyat* 'material things'.

-*(y)In*   Unstressable suffix which attaches to terms denoting seasons, deriving adverbials: *yazın* 'in (the) summer', *kışın* 'in (the) winter' (see also -*leyin* above).

-*zede*   A suffix of Persian origin, which when added to nouns forms nouns indicating the victim of some catastrophic event: *depremzede* 'earthquake victim', *felaketzede* 'victim of a (certain) disaster'.

7.3 THE INTERNAL ORDERING OF DERIVATIONAL SUFFIXES

There are no clear-cut rules governing all combinations of derivational suffixes. However, there are a few points which apply to the majority of cases:

(i) Unproductive derivational suffixes tend not to co-occur.

(ii) Suffixes which are unproductive tend to precede productive ones (although it may be very difficult in many cases to decide which category a suffix belongs to). For example, the productive noun-forming suffix *-lIk* follows the unproductive *-(y)An*:

bak- 'look' + *-(y)An* → *bakan* 'minister' + *-lIk* → *bakanlık* 'ministry'

But the same suffix *-lIk* can occur before or after an equally productive one, e.g. the noun-deriving suffix *-CI*:

göz 'eye' + *-lIK* → *gözlük* 'spectacles' + *-CI* → *gözlükçü* 'optician'
göz 'eye' + *-CI* → *gözcü* 'guard' + *-lIK*   → *gözcülük* 'being a guard'

It can also recur in the same word:

göz-lük-çü-lük 'the profession/business of an optician'

7.4 PREFIXATION

Apart from the reduplicative prefixes discussed in Chapter 9, the only prefixes Turkish has are of foreign origin:

antidemokratik 'antidemocratic'
postmodern 'postmodern'
gayrimüslim 'non-Muslim'
bihaber 'unaware', 'ignorant'
namütenahi 'infinite'

With the exception of *anti-*, which has some degree of productivity, these prefixes occur only with loan words. Most of the words thus formed are stressed on the (first syllable of the) prefix.

8 INFLECTIONAL SUFFIXES

Inflectional suffixes indicate how the constituents of a sentence relate to each other, and express functional relations such as **case**, **person** and **tense**. In this chapter a description of the forms and attachment properties of these suffixes is provided; for the meaning and usage of each suffix, the reader is referred to the relevant chapters in Part 3.

In section 8.1 we discuss the inflectional suffixes that attach to nominals, and in section 8.2 those that attach to verbs. Sections 8.3 and 8.4 focus on the **copular markers** and **person markers**, both of which can attach to nominals and to verbs. Section 8.5 explains the attachment properties of suffixes that form subordinate clauses.

8.1 NOMINAL INFLECTIONAL SUFFIXES

The suffixes that attach to nominals are those marking **number, possession** and case. The only number suffix is the plural suffix -lAr. The possessive suffixes indicate the person of the possessor. The order in which nominal inflectional suffixes appear on the stem is number-possession-case (see 14.3.1.2 (38) for an exception):

(1) çocuk   -lar   -ın   -a
     child   -PL   -2SG.POSS   -DAT
               NUMBER   POSSESSION   CASE
     'to your children'

These forms can further be combined with the copular markers (8.3.2), -DIr (8.3.3) and person markers (8.4) to form **predicates** (12.1.1.2):

(2) Ev   -ler   -imiz   -de   -ymiş   -ler.
     home   -PL   -1PL.POSS   -LOC   -EV.COP   -3PL
     'Apparently they are/were at our homes.'

8.1.1 THE PLURAL SUFFIX -lAr

The suffix -lAr (14.3.1.1) is used primarily to indicate plurality: köpek**ler** 'dogs', su**lar** '[glasses, etc. of] water', şun**lar** 'these', sarı**lar** 'the yellow [ones]'; see 14.3.1.2 for other functions. This suffix should not be confused with the 3rd person plural marker -lAr which appears, as at the end of example (2) above, on predicates to indicate subject agreement (8.4 and 12.2.2).

8.1.2 POSSESSIVE SUFFIXES

The forms of the possessive suffix are:

1st person singular		*-(I)m*	'my'
2nd person singular	(familiar)	*-(I)n*	'your'
	(formal)	*-(I)nIz*	'your'
3rd person singular		*-(s)I(n)*	'his', 'her', 'its', 'their'
1st person plural		*-(I)mIz*	'our'
2nd person plural		*-(I)nIz*	'your'
3rd person plural		*-lArI(n)*	'their'

Examples:

*ev-**im***	'my house'	*araba-**m***	'my car'
*ev-**in***	'your house' (familiar)	*araba-**n***	'your car' (familiar)
*ev-**iniz***	'your house' (formal)	*araba-**nız***	'your car' (formal)
*ev-**i***	'his/her/their house'	*araba-**sı***	'his/her/their car'
*ev-**imiz***	'our house'	*araba-**mız***	'our car'
*ev-**iniz***	'your house'	*araba-**nız***	'your car'
*ev-**leri***	'their house(s)'	*araba-**ları***	'their car(s)'

For the number ambiguity in the 3rd person forms, see 14.3.2 and 14.4.

Apart from indicating the possessor in a noun phrase (14.3.2, 14.4), possessive suffixes are also added to the subordinating suffixes *-DIK*, *-(y)AcAK*, *-mA* and *-(y)Iş* (8.5.1) to mark the subject of the subordinate clause: *ilgilendiğimiz* (*konular*) '(the topics) that we are interested in', *gidecekleri* (*ülke*) '(the country) that they will go to', *anlamanız* (*için*) 'so that you understand', (*kitabı*) *okuyuşu* 'his/her reading the book'. For a full discussion see Chapters 24–6.

Possessive suffixes can be followed by case markers: *odamda* 'in my room', the marker *-(y)lA/ile* 'with', 'by', 'and' (8.1.4): *annemle* 'with my mother', 'my mother and . . .' and to a limited extent by the adverbial suffix *-CA* (7.2.2.2): *kanımca* 'in my opinion'.

The 3rd person singular form *-(s)I(n)* appears as *-(s)I* when no other suffix follows it: *tepesi* 'its top', *yüzü* 'his/her face'. When it is followed by a case suffix or by the adverbial suffix *-CA*, it appears as *-(s)In*: *tepesinde* 'at its summit/top', *yüzüne* 'to his/her face', *fikrince* 'in his/her opinion'. Similarly, the 3rd person plural form *-lArI(n)* appears as *-lArI* when no other suffix follows. However, when there is a case suffix or *-CA* following it, it appears as *-lArIn*: *elbiselerine* 'to their dress(es)'. (See 14.4 for the ambiguity of forms containing the 3rd person plural possessive form, e.g. *ev-**lerin**-e* 'to their house(s)' and forms containing the plural suffix + 3rd person singular possessive marker, e.g. *ev-**ler-in**-e* 'to his/her houses', 'to their houses'. See 6.2 for other forms containing 'n'.) In this book, for reasons of simplicity, we use the forms *-(s)I* and *-lArI* when referring to these suffixes.

The suffix *-(s)I* has a number of functions in addition to those that it shares with the other possessive suffixes:

(**i**)   it marks the head of a noun compound: *düğün pastası* 'wedding cake' (10.2)

(**ii**)   it marks the head of a partitive construction: *kitaplardan üç tanesi* 'three of the books' (14.5.2–3)

(**iii**) it forms pronominals from a variety of word classes: *burası* 'here', *içerisi* 'inside', *eskisi* 'the old one', *hiçbiri(si)* 'none of them' (18.3–4)

(**iv**)   it appears on (impersonal) verbal nouns which contain *-mA*: *okuması zor* '[it] is difficult to read' (8.5.1.2, 24.4.2.2)

(**v**)   it occurs in some composite suffixes: *anlamazmışçasına* 'as if uncomprehending' (8.5.2.2, 26.3.6).

8.1.3   CASE SUFFIXES

Turkish has five case suffixes:

-(y)I   marker of the **accusative** case: *sarayı* 'the palace (ACC)', *suyu* 'the water (ACC)', *küçüğü* 'the small one (ACC)'.

-(y)A   marker of the **dative** case: *Kars'a* 'to Kars', *dereye* '(in)to the river', *masaya* 'on (to) the table', *size* 'to you'.

-DA   marker of the **locative** case: *radyoda* 'on the radio', *evde* 'at home', *sepette* 'in the basket'.

-DAn   marker of the **ablative** case: *okuldan* 'from/of/out of (the) school', *sonuçtan* 'from/of the result', *sisten* 'from/of the fog'.

-(n)In/-Im   marker of the **genitive** case: *çocuğun* 'the child's', *Fatma'nın* 'Fatma's', *bahçenin* 'of the garden'. *-Im* attaches to 1st person pronouns: *benim* 'my', *bizim* 'our'.

The function of these suffixes is discussed in 14.3.3.

8.1.4   OTHER NOMINAL INFLECTIONAL MARKERS

-(y)lA/ile   This marker can have comitative, instrumental or conjunctive meaning. In all of these functions it appears predominantly in the suffixal form *-(y)lA*, and only rarely as the separate form *ile*. The comitative/instrumental marker forms postpositional phrases (17.3). Like the dative, locative and ablative case markers it attaches to noun phrases, enabling them to function as oblique objects (13.1.2.2) or adverbials (13.1.3). However, unlike the case suffixes it is unstressable (4.3.2):

Ahmét'le 'with Ahmet' (comitative), *kalémle* 'with a pen/ pencil' (instrumental), *baltáyla* 'with an axe' (instrumental). This marker also functions as a noun phrase conjunction: *Ahmet'le Mehmet* 'Ahmet and Mehmet', *kedimle köpeğim* 'my cat and my dog' (see 28.3.1.1 (ii)).

In the standard language, *-(y)lA* attaches to the genitive-marked forms of the following pronouns (i.e. **genitive-attracting pronouns**), except where the plural suffix *-lAr* is also present (see 17.2.1):

(i)   simple personal pronouns (18.1.1): *benimle* 'with me'
(ii)   demonstrative pronouns (18.2): *şununla* 'with this/that one'
(iii) *kim* 'who' (19.2.1.1): *kiminle* 'with whom'.

The free-standing form *ile* is not used with genitive-attracting pronouns. In everyday speech, *-(y)lA* may be attached directly to pronouns without an intervening genitive case marker: ↓*benle* 'with me', ↓*şunla* 'with this/that one', ↓*kimle* 'who with'. In very informal speech contexts 'l' may be pronounced as [n] and the marker itself may be followed by [n]: ↓*Fatma'ynan*, ↓*şunnan*, ↓*kimnen*.

-ki(n)   This is a stressable suffix whose vowel is invariable except that, in some cases, it harmonizes with a preceding 'ü': *evdeki* '(the one) in the house', *oradaki* '(the one) over there', *sizinki* 'yours', *kızınki* 'the one belonging to the girl', *suyunki* 'the one belonging to (the) water'. When it follows *dün* 'yesterday' and *gün* 'day' (and words containing *gün*) it is generally pronounced (and spelt with) 'ü': *bugünkü/bugünki* 'today's', *dünkü/dünki* 'yesterday's'. In all other cases where it follows 'ü' it is more likely to be pronounced as 'i': *gülünki* 'that of the rose'. The consonant 'n' appears only when *-ki* is followed by a case suffix or *-CA*: *evdekinde* 'in/on/at the one in the house' (see 6.2). In this book, for reasons of simplicity. we refer to this suffix as *-ki*. (The suffix *-ki* should not be confused with the clitic *ki*, for which see 11.1.1.4)

-ki has two main functions: to form attributive adjectival phrases (15.3.6–7) and to form pronominal expressions (18.5). These are formed in the following ways:

(i)   By attaching *-ki* directly to adverbials which express a location in time: *yarınki (gazete)* 'tomorrow's (newspaper)', *bu seneki (portakallar)* 'this year's oranges', *her zamanki* 'the usual (one)'.

Note that where the temporal adverbial takes the form of a *-(s)I* compound, the compound marker is deleted before the affixation of -ki: *Salı günkü (programlar)* 'Tuesday's (programmes)'.

(ii) By attaching -ki to noun phrases and postpositions which contain the locative suffix: *sokaktaki araba* 'the car on the street', *önünüzdeki* 'the one in front of you'.

(iii) By attaching -ki to noun phrases which contain the genitive suffix: *seninki* 'yours', *adamınki* 'the man's [one]', *odanınki* 'the one belonging to the room'. (Expressions formed in this way are pronominal only.)

Any *pronominal* form containing -ki can be further inflected by adding:

(i) the plural suffix -lAr: *masadakiler* 'the ones on the table', *masanınkiler* 'the ones which belong to the table'. As a result, words which contain -ki can sometimes have more than one plural suffix: *masalardakiler* 'the ones on the tables'.

(ii) a case suffix, which can be added to a singular or plural form: *bendekine* 'to the one that I have', *evinkileri* 'the ones belonging to the house (ACC)', *bahçedekinden* 'of/from the one in the garden'. As a result, words which contain -ki can sometimes have more than one locative or genitive marker: *anneminkinin (rengi)* '(the colour) of my mother's one', *evdekilerde* 'at/on/in the ones in the house'.

(iii) one of the markers -(y)lA/ile (see above), -CA 'according to', 'by' (16.1.6), or -sIz 'without' (7.2.2.2). The combination with -(y)lA/ile is regular: *sokaktakiyle* 'with the one on the street', *mutfaktakilerle* 'with the ones in the kitchen', *arabanınkiyle* 'with the one belonging to the car', *perdeninkilerle* 'with the ones belonging to the curtain'. On the rare occasions when -ki combines with -CA or -sIz, these attach to the plural form: *Amerika'dakilerce* 'by the ones in America', *bahçedekilersiz* 'without the ones in the garden'.

-ki can combine with a genitive or locative form that already contains -ki:

ev-de-ki-ler-in-ki	'the one belonging to those at home'
anne-m-in-kin-de-ki	'the one **on** my mother's'

8.2 VERBAL INFLECTIONAL SUFFIXES

There are two distinct types of verb form in Turkish: **finite** and **non-finite**.

(i) Finite verb forms:
The inflectional suffixes that can appear in finite verb forms are the following:

> voice suffixes (8.2.1)
> the negative marker (8.2.2)
> tense/aspect/modality markers (8.2.3)
> copular markers (8.3)
> person markers (8.4)

A finite verb form in Turkish obligatorily contains a **person marker** from groups 1–4 (8.4), which indicates the subject:

(3) Otur-acağ-**ım**.
sit.down-FUT-1SG
'I'm going to sit down.'

Note that a 3rd person singular subject is indicated by the *absence* of any person marker from groups 1, 2 and 4:

(4) Şu anda evden çık-tı.
leave-PF
'S/he has just left the house.'

In all forms except the 2nd person imperative and the 3rd person optative, a verb contains one of the **tense/aspect/modality** suffixes from position 3 (8.2.3):

(5) Yüz-**üyor**-uz.
swim-IMPF-1PL
'We're swimming.'

Voice suffixes, the negative marker and **copular markers** may also occur in finite verb forms:

(6) Yık-**ıl**-**ma**-mış-**tı**.
demolish-PASS-NEG-PF-P.COP
'It had not been demolished.'

The order in which the suffixes appear in a finite verb form is:

ROOT-VOICE-NEGATION-TENSE/ASPECT/MODALITY-COPULAR
MARKER-PERSON MARKER-*DIr*

(7)	Döğ	-üş -tür -t -ül	-me	-yebil-iyor	-muş	-sunuz	-dur.
	beat	-REC-CAUS-CAUS-PASS	-NEG	-PSB-IMPF	-EV.COP	-2PL	-GM
		VOICE	NEGATIVE	TAM	COPULAR	PERSON	MODALITY
		SUFFIXES	MARKER	SUFFIXES	MARKER	MARKER	MARKER

'It is presumably the case that you sometimes were not made to fight.'

Irregular combinations are explained in the description of individual suffixes.

(ii) Non-finite verb forms:
The inflectional suffixes that can appear in non-finite verb forms are the following:

voice suffixes (8.2.1)
the negative marker (8.2.2)
tense/aspect/modality markers from positions 1 and/or 2 (8.2.3.1–2)
subordinating suffixes (8.5)
nominal inflectional suffixes (8.1)

Non-finite verb forms obligatorily contain a **subordinating suffix** (also called a **subordinator**). Because these are **nominalized forms**, most of them can be followed by some or all of the nominal suffixes described in 8.1 (see 8.5 for details).

(8) sev-***mek***-le
     like-SUB-INS
     'by loving [him/her/it]'

The order of the suffixes in a non-finite verb form is the following:

ROOT-VOICE-NEGATION-SUBORDINATING SUFFIX-NOMINAL
INFLECTIONAL MARKERS

(9)	bak	-tır	-ma	-dığ	-ın	-dan
	check	-CAUS	-NEG	-SUB	-2SG.POSS	-ABL
		VOICE	NEGATIVE	SUBORDINATOR	PERSON	CASE
		SUFFIX	MARKER		MARKER	MARKER

'because you haven't had [it] checked', 'from the one you didn't have checked'

8.2.1 VOICE SUFFIXES

These are the **causative**, **passive**, **reflexive** and **reciprocal** suffixes. Voice suffixes come immediately after the verb root preceding all other suffixes. The only exception to this is the combination of the passive suffix with *-(y)Iver* (see 8.2.3.2). For the effect a voice suffix has on the structure of a clause see 13.2, and for the ordering of voice suffixes see 13.2.4.

8.2.1.1 Causative

The causative suffix attaches to **transitive** and **intransitive verb** stems. It has the following forms:

-DIr	*yaptır-* 'make/let [s.o.] do/make/build [s.t.]', *koydur-* 'have/make [s.o.] put [s.t.] [s.w.]', *öldür-* 'kill', *doldur-* 'fill [s.t.]'
-t	*kapat-* 'close [s.t.]', *daralt-* 'reduce', *uyut-* 'make/let [s.o.] sleep'
-It	*sarkıt-* 'dangle [s.t.]', *ürküt-* 'scare', *korkut-* 'scare'
-Ir	*düşür-* 'drop', *bitir-* 'finish [s.t.]', *duyur-* 'announce', *pişir-* 'cook [s.t.]'
-Ar	*çıkar-* 'extract', *gider-* 'remove'
-Art	*çökert-* 'crush'

Which form of the causative suffix occurs with any particular verb stem is predictable, at least in part, from the form of the stem. Around thirty monosyllabic stems, most of which are intransitive, combine with one of the forms *-It*, *-Ir*, *Ar* or *-Art*. Polysyllabic stems ending in a vowel, 'l' or 'r' combine with *-t*. In all other circumstances *-DIr* is used.

It is possible for more than one causative suffix to appear simultaneously on a single verb stem. Such combinations conform to the rules given above. Thus *-t* follows *-DIr*, *-Ir* or *-Ar* (as these suffixes end in 'r') and *-DIr* follows *-t* or *-Art*: *bit-**ir**-**t**-**tir**-di* 's/he arranged for it to be finished'. For the syntactic properties of multiple causativization see 13.2.1.1.

Some intransitive verbs do not combine with the causative suffix, and instead have unrelated transitive counterparts. For example, the transitive counterpart of *gir-* 'enter' is *sok-* 'insert' (also 'allow to enter'). These can be further causativized (as in *sok**tur**-*). Another irregular verb is *em-* 'suck', for which the transitive form is *em**zir**-* 'breastfeed'. Some verbs which contain a form that looks like a causative suffix are not derived directly from an existing non-causative root, e.g. *getir-* 'bring', *götür-* 'take', *kaldır-* 'raise' (derived from *kalk-* 'rise'), none of which contain separable roots.

8.2.1.2 Passive

The passive suffix *-Il/(I)n* (can be attached to transitive and intransitive stems. It turns a transitive verb into an intransitive one, as in *sev-* 'love' → *sevil-* 'be loved', or an intransitive verb into a subjectless predicate (see 13.2.2.3–4).

The passive suffix has the following forms:

-n	*aran-* 'be searched (for)', 'be rung up', *tıkan-* 'be blocked', *yıkan-* 'be washed'
-In	*bilin-* 'be known', *delin-* 'be punctured/perforated'
-Il	*yapıl-* 'be done/made/built', *görül-* 'be seen'

-n is attached to stems ending in a vowel, *-In* is attached to stems ending with the consonant 'l', and *-Il* is attached to stems ending with all other consonants.

8.2.1.3 Reflexive

The reflexive suffix *-(I)n* is an unproductive suffix, which combines only with a few roots. It attaches to transitive verbs, to form an intransitive verb denoting an action that one can perform on or for oneself.

yıka- 'wash [s.t.]'	→	*yıkan-* 'have a bath/shower'
kurula- 'dry [s.t.]'	→	*kurulan-* 'dry oneself'
tara- 'comb'	→	*taran-* 'comb one's hair'
ört- 'cover'	→	*örtün-* 'cover oneself'
sar- 'wrap' (tr.)	→	*sarın-* 'wrap oneself (in)'
giy- 'put on [a garment]'	→	*giyin-* 'get dressed' (intr.)

For the syntactic effects of reflexivization see 13.2.3.1. For the non-reflexive usage of the suffix *-(I)n* see 7.2.1.2.

Note that the reflexive suffix shares a form with the passive suffix. As a result, the reflexive and passive forms of some verbs are identical, e.g. *yıkan-* can mean 'be washed (by someone)' or 'have a bath/shower', depending on the context.

8.2.1.4 Reciprocal

The reciprocal suffix *-(I)ş* combines with only a few transitive and intransitive stems, and indicates mutual involvement in an action. When it combines with a transitive stem it usually indicates the reciprocity of an action (i.e. A does x to B and B does x to A):

araş- 'ring each other', *öpüş-* 'kiss each other', *seviş-* 'make love', 'love each other', *görüş-* 'see/meet up with each other'

Stems containing the reciprocal suffix tend not to combine with the similar-sounding verbal noun suffix *-(y)Iş* (8.5.2.1). Instead they combine with *-mA* (8.5.1.2). Some verbs that seem to have a segment identical to a reciprocal suffix are not transparently related to a non-reciprocal stem, e.g. *konuş-* 'speak'. (See also *-(I)ş*, 7.2.1.2 and *-lAş* 7.2.2.1.)

8.2.2 THE NEGATIVE MARKER

The negative marker *-mA* is situated between voice suffixes and tense/ aspect/modality markers. It is unstressable and causes the syllable before it to receive stress, except in most combinations with the aorist suffix (see 8.2.3.3 for details): *anlámadık* 'we did not understand', *anlaşílmasın* 'let it not be understood', *anlamáz* 's/he does not understand'. (See 4.3.2 (viii), 4.3.2.1 and 11.2.2 for the combination of *-mA* with other unstressable suffixes and clitics.) There are irregularities in the combination of the negative marker with:

(i)   the aorist *-(A/I)r* (producing the combination *-mA-z*) (8.2.3.3)
(ii) the possibility suffix *-(y)A* (8.2.3.1)
(iii) the non-premeditative suffix *-(y)Iver* (8.2.3.2).

The vowel of the negative suffix becomes a high vowel ('ı' or 'i') when it is followed by *-(I)yor* (8.2.3.3), *-(y)AcAk* (8.2.3.3) and a few other suffixes beginning with 'y' (see 2.6). In the case of the *-mA* + *-(I)yor* combination the vowel also undergoes vowel harmony like an I-type suffix (3.2.1), which is reflected in the orthography: *anlamıyor* 's/he does not understand', *görmüyor* 's/he does not see' (see 2.6 for other examples).
The negative marker occurs in composite suffixes such as *-mAdAn* and *-mAzdAn* (8.5.2.2). For its occurrence in compound verb forms see 20.1.2.

8.2.3 TENSE/ASPECT/MODALITY MARKERS

Most of the suffixes falling into this group have more than one function, and may simultaneously mark tense, aspect and/or modality. The syntactic and semantic properties of these suffixes are discussed in detail in Chapters 21 and 27, and are summarized in Appendix 2.
When tense/aspect/modality markers co-occur, they appear in the order given below:

1	2	3	4 Copular markers	5
-(y)A (possibility)	*-(y)Abil* (possibility)	*-DI* (perfective)	*-(y)DI* (past copula)	*-DIr*
	-(y)Iver (non-premeditative)	*-mIş* (perfective/ evidential)	*-(y)mIş* (evidential copula)	(generaliz-ing
	▽-*(y)Agel*	*-sA* (conditional)	*-(y)sA* (conditional copula)	modality)
	▽-*(y)Ayaz*	*-(A/I)r/-z* (aorist)		
	▽-*(y)Akal*	*-(y)AcAK* (future)		
	▽-*(y)Adur*	*-(I)yor* (imperfective)		
		-mAlI (obligative)		
		-mAktA (imperfective)		
		-(y)A optative		

The following points should be noted:

(i) Suffixes which are in the same column cannot co-occur on a single stem.

(ii) Finite verbs (except for imperative forms and 3rd person optative forms) obligatorily contain a suffix from position 3:

> (10) Geç-**ti**-n.
> pass-PF-2SG
> **3**
> 'You've pass*ed*.'

> (11) Bitir-e-me-**miş**-tir.
> finish-PSB-NEG-PF-GM
> 1   **3** 5
> 'S/he *has* probably not be*en* able to finish [it]'.

> (12) Oku-yabil-**ecek**-miş.
> read-PSB-FUT-EV.COP
> 2 **3** 4
> Apparently s/he *will* be able to read [it].'

(iii) The markers in positions 4–5 can also attach directly to a subject complement, to *değil* or to the existential expressions *var/yok* in nominal sentences (8.3, 12.1.1.2).

> (13) Yazın Paris-te-**ydi**-k.
> Paris-LOC-P.COP-1PL
> **4**
> 'We *were* in Paris during the summer.'

> (14) Mutlaka zamanı var-**dır**.
> existent-GM
> **5**
> 'I'm sure s/he has the time.'

(iv) Non-finite verb forms obligatorily contain a subordinating suffix (8.5), but they can also contain suffixes from positions 1–2.

> (15) otur-**abil**-mek
> sit-PSB-VN
> **2**
> 'to *be able to* sit [down]'

8.2.3.1   Position 1

-*(y)A*   The possibility suffix -*(y)A* (21.4.2.1) appears only in negative verb forms. It is the only tense/aspect/modality suffix that precedes the negative suffix: *bakamayız* 'we cannot look', *göremiyordur* 's/he probably can't see'. It can co-occur with the possibility suffix -*(y)Abil* from position 2: *bakamayabiliriz* 'we may/might not be able to look'.

8.2.3.2   Position 2

The suffixes in this group consist of one of the verb roots *bil-* 'know', *ver-* 'give', *yaz-* 'make a mistake (obs.)', *dur-* 'stay' and *kal-* 'remain'. All of these suffixes except for -*(y)Abil* are stressed on the first syllable (4.3.1 (iii)). They occur with one of the suffixes in position 3.

-*(y)Abil*   The possibility suffix -*(y)Abil* (21.4.2.1) can occur with any of the suffixes in position 3: *gidebileceğim* 'I shall be able to go', *görebildiğim* '(the one) that I can see'. See also -*(y)A* above.

-*(y)Iver*   This suffix can occur with all the suffixes in position 3 except for -*mAktA*: *bitirivermiş* 'apparently s/he finished [it] without effort', *pişiriverirdim* 'I would just have cooked it'. It can either follow or, less commonly, precede the negative suffix: *yapmayıverdi* 's/he simply didn't do [it]', *yapıvermedi* 's/he refrained from simply doing [it]'. Although it follows voice suffixes in general, it may precede the passive suffix: *yapılıverdi/yapıverildi* 'it was suddenly done'.

▽-*(y)Agel*, ▽-*(y)Adur*, ▽-*(y)Ayaz* ▽-*(y)Akal*
    These markers mostly occur in (semi-)lexicalized forms, or are obsolescent: *yapagelmişizdir* 'we have gone on doing [it]', *düşeyazdım* 'I almost fell'. The least lexicalized one is -*(y)Adur*: *okuyadur* 'go on reading' (13.3.1.1).

8.2.3.3   Position 3

-*DI*   The **perfective** suffix can be followed by a person marker from group 1, one of the copular markers -*(y)DI* or -*(y)sA*, but not by -*(y)mIş* or -*DIr*: *olduk* 'we became', *gittiydin* 'you had left' (see -*(y)DI* below), *beklediysen* 'if you have waited'.

-*mIş*   The **evidential/perfective** suffix can be followed by a person marker from group 2, any one of the copular markers, and by -*DIr*. When it is *not* followed by another tense/aspect/

modality marker, *-mIş* indicates both evidentiality and perfectivity: *koşmuş* 'apparently s/he ran/has run', *unutmuşum* 'I seem to have forgotten'. When it is followed by a copular marker or *-DIr*, it indicates only perfectivity: *başlamıştık* 'we had started', *anlamamışsa* 'if s/he has not understood', *görmüşlerdir* 'they must have seen [it]'. Similarly, when *-mIş* is followed by an auxiliary verb in compound verb forms (13.3.1.2) it indicates only perfectivity: *yapmış olduk* 'we have done [it]', *görmüş bulunuyorum* 'I have seen [it]'.

-sA   The **conditional** suffix can be followed by a person marker from group 1, or by *-(y)DI* or *-(y)mIş*, but not by *-(y)sA* or *-DIr*: *düşünsen* 'if you thought/were to think', *hazırlamasaydın* 'if you had not prepared [it]'. In colloquial contexts *-sA* can be replaced by the optative suffix *-(y)A* (see below) when followed by a copular marker: *arasaydın/arayaydın* 'if (only) you had rung', 'you should have rung'.

-(A/I)r/-z   The **aorist** suffix is phonologically irregular, as it displays a variation between six vowels, 'ı', 'i', 'ü', 'u', 'a' and 'e'. It is also the only suffix that has a different form (*-z*) when used with the negative marker. The aorist suffix may be followed by a person marker from group 2, or any one of the copular markers, but not by *-DIr*: *okurum* 'I read', *gülerdin* 'you used to/would laugh'.

The distribution of the different forms is as follows:

(i)   *-(I)r* attaches to polysyllabic stems: *konuşur* 's/he speaks', *koparır* 's/he breaks [it]', and to monosyllabic stems which already contain a suffix: *ye-n-ir* 'it is eaten' (but *yen-er* 's/he beats [s.o]').

(ii)   Monosyllabic verbs ending in 'l' or 'r' are unpredictable in terms of which form they combine with. Of the forty-odd monosyllabic stems that end in 'l' or 'r', the following combine with *-Ir*: *al-* 'take', *bil-* 'know', *bul-* 'find', *dur-* 'stop', *gel-* 'come', *gör-* 'see', *kal-* 'stay', 'remain', *ol-* 'be', *öl-* 'die', *var-* 'reach', *ver-* 'give', *vur-* 'hit': *bilir* 's/he knows', *kalır* 's/he stays', *görür* 's/he sees', *bulur* 's/he finds'. Other stems ending in 'l' or 'r' combine with *-Ar*: *örer* 's/he knits', *kurar* 's/he establishes'.

(iii)   Monosyllabic verbs ending in any other consonant combine with *-Ar*, with the exception of *san-* 'imagine': *sanırım* 'I think'.

(iv)   The way in which the aorist suffix combines with the negative suffix *-mA* is highly irregular:

(a) The suffix itself takes a completely different form, -z, when it follows -mA: gitmez 's/he doesn't/won't/ wouldn't go', anlamazsın 'you wouldn't understand'.

(b) Where a negative aorist verb form does not contain a copular marker, the -z is deleted in the 1st person singular and plural: yemem 'I won't/wouldn't eat', kalmayız 'we won't/wouldn't stay'. This means that, in these particular forms, the aorist is expressed by the *absence* of a distinct suffix.

(c) Unlike the negative suffix in other contexts (8.2.2), the negative-aorist combination -mAz is *stressed*, except where (i) it is preceded by the possibility suffix -(y)A, or (ii) it is followed by the 3rd person plural marker -lAr.

The table below shows the negative-aorist forms of the verb bak- 'look', both with and without the presence of a copular marker. In the second column the past copula -(y)DI is used as an example of a copular marker.

	Negative + aorist	*Negative + aorist + copular marker*
1st person sg.	bak-**má**-m	bak-**má**-z-dı-m
2nd person sg.	bak-**má**-z-sın	bak-**má**-z-dı-n
3rd person sg.	bak-**má**-z	bak-**má**-z-dı
1st person pl.	bak-**má**-yız	bak-**má**-z-dı-k
2nd person pl.	bak-**má**-z-sınız	bak-**má**-z-dı-nız
3rd person pl.	bak-**ma**-z-lár	bak-**ma**-z-lár-dı

-(y)AcAK The future suffix may be followed by a person marker from group 2, any one of the copular markers or by -DIr: geleceğim 'I shall come', silecektiniz 'you were going to erase [it]', bulacaktır 'I'm sure s/he'll find [it]'.

Despite being written with 'a' or 'e', the initial syllable of the future suffix is often pronounced like an I-type suffix (3.2.1): kalacak 's/he will stay' [kʰałɯdʒakʰ], dönecek 's/he will return' [dönüdʒecʰ]. When this suffix is followed by a person marker starting with a vowel, the final 'k' is replaced by 'ğ' (1.1.1.1). In formal speech, the inflectional sections of forms such as seveceğim 'I will love' and alacağım 'I am going to take [it]' are pronounced as two consecutive vowels with stress on 'ce' or 'ca': [sevedʒéim] or [sevidʒéim], [aładʒáım] or [ałɯdʒáım]. But in everyday speech the combination of the future marker with person markers has a contracted version, as shown for the verb *in-* 'go/come down' in the table below. See also 2.6 for a general discussion of the effect of the initial *-(y)* of a suffix on a preceding vowel.

Future marker *-(y)AcAk* + person marking:

		Formal	Familiar
1st p. sg. *ineceğim*		[ineʤéim]/[iniʤéim]	↓[iniʤǽm]
2nd p. sg. *ineceksin*		[ineʤécsin]/[iniʤécsin]	↓[iniʤǽn]
3rd p.sg. *inecek*		[ineʤéchʰ]/[iniʤéchʰ]	[iniʤéchʰ]
1st p. pl. *ineceğiz*		[ineʤéiz]/[iniʤéiz]	↓[iniʤǽz]
2nd p. pl. *ineceksiniz*	[ineʤécsiniz]/[iniʤécsiniz]	↓[iniʤæ:níz]
3rd p.pl. *inecekler*		[ineʤeclǽɾ]/[iniʤeclǽɾ]	[iniʤeclǽɾ]

In the case of forms with back vowels, the [æ] in the future suffix is replaced by [a]: [jazıʤán] 'you are going to write', etc.

-(I)yor The **imperfective** suffix *-(I)yor* contains the obsolete verb stem *yor-*, which is invariable. Except where the negative marker is present, *yor-* assigns stress to the preceding vowel, whether this vowel is *-(I)* or the final vowel of the stem that *-(I)yor* attaches to: *koşúyor* 's/he runs', *korúyor* 's/he protects'. (For the effect of the negative suffix on word stress see 4.3.2.1.)

-(I)yor combines regularly with stems ending in a consonant: *satıyor* 's/he sells/is selling', *görüyor* 's/he sees'. Stems ending in a vowel combine with the component 'yor'. In the case of stems ending in a high vowel ('i', 'ı', 'ü' or 'u') 'yor' is added directly to the stem: *eriyor* 'it melts/is melting', *kuruyor* 'it dries/is drying'. However, where a stem ends in 'a' or 'e', the combination with 'yor' causes this vowel to become high (see 2.6). This high vowel is then subject to vowel harmony (3.2.1):

anla- 'understand' → *anlıyor* 's/he understands'
okşa- 'caress' → *okşuyor* 's/he caresses/is caressing'
bekle- 'wait' → *bekliyor* 's/he waits/is waiting'
özle- 'miss' → *özlüyor* 's/he misses'

The same situation occurs when *-(I)yor* is attached to the negative marker:

saklama- 'not hide' → *saklamıyor* 's/he doesn't hide/ is not hiding'
söyleme- 'not tell' → *söylemiyor* 's/he doesn't tell/ isn't telling'

-(I)yor may be followed by a person marker from group 2, any one of the copular markers or by *-DIr*: *çalışıyorum* 'I work/am working', *arıyordu* 's/he was looking for [it]', *anlıyorsa* 'if s/he understands [it]', *gidiyordur* 's/he's probably going'. In colloquial speech the 'r' at the end of the suffix is often not pronounced when it is followed by a suffix beginning with a consonant: *gidiyorsun* 's/he goes/is going' [ɟidíjosun]/[ɟidíjorsun], *ödüyorduk* 'we were paying' [ödǘjodukʰ]/[ödǘjordukʰ], or when it is at the end of a word: *sarıyor* 's/he wraps' [saríjo]/[saríjoɾ]. 'r' is retained when it is followed by a suffix beginning with a vowel: *seviyorum* 'I love/like' [sevíjorum].

-mAlI   The obligative suffix (21.4.2.2) may be followed by a person marker from group 2 or by any one of the copular markers: *oturmamalısın* 'you must not sit', *anlattırmalıydılar* 'they should have made [him/her] tell [the story]'. In formal texts it can also be followed by *-DIr* when the verb is in the 3rd person singular or plural form: *gitmelidir(ler)* 's/he/(they) should go', *yapılmamalıdır* 'it should not be done'.

-mAktA   This is an **imperfective** suffix which is mostly used in formal contexts. It may be followed by a person marker from group 2 or any one of the copular markers: *okumaktasın* 'you are (in the process of) reading', *bitirmekteydim* 'I was (in the process of) finishing'. It can also be followed by *-DIr* when the verb is in the 3rd person singular or plural form: *dönmektedirler* 'they are (in the process of) returning', *görülmemektedir* 'it is not seen/observed'.

-(y)A   The **optative** suffix occurs mostly in the 1st person singular and plural forms: *gideyim* 'let me go', 'I'll go', *oturalım* 'let's sit (down)'. It may also occur in the 2nd person singular and plural forms, usually in adverbial clauses of purpose with the subordinator *diye* or *ki* (26.1.1.2, 26.1.2.2): *gösteresin (diye)* '(so that) you [can] indicate'. Apart from the person markers in group 3, *-(y)A* may be followed by *-(y)DI* or *-(y)mIş*: *gideydim* 'if I had gone'. In these combinations with copular markers *-(y)A* is an informal alternative to the conditional suffix *-sA* (see above).

8.3 THE COPULA 'BE', COPULAR MARKERS AND -DIr

The copular markers in position 4 are composite. They are made up of the copula *-(y)-* and the suffixes *-DI*, *-mIş* and *-sA*.

8.3.1 THE COPULA 'be'

The copula, which in most cases corresponds to the verb 'be', has different forms. These are:

(i) *-(y)-*: This appears in *-(y)DI*, *-(y)mIş*, *-(y)sA* and in the converbial form *-(y)ken* (8.5.2.2 and 26.3.16). The segment 'y' in these markers should not be confused with the consonant which occurs at the beginning of many suffixes for purposes of attachment (6.1.3). The markers containing the copula *-(y)-* are unstressable (4.3.2 (i)). *-(y)-* is the contracted form of *i-*, see below.

(ii) The bound stem *i-*: This is an obsolescent stem which appears in the now seldom used forms ∇*idi*, ∇*imiş* ∇*ise* and ∇*iken*, e.g. *seviyor* **idiysen** 'if (as you imply) you loved [him/her]'. In the limited cases in which they are used, they are most often the stressed word within the whole sentence and they are stressed on their second syllable. This is because they are used primarily for purposes of emphasizing the tense or modality that a particular copular marker expresses, especially by contrast to another tense or modality expressed in the preceding utterance. For example, in a context where someone makes a statement to the effect that Ahmet likes horror films, whereas the hearer believes that Ahmet used to like horror films but no longer does, s/he could respond by saying:

Sever idí.
'He *used* to.'

(iii) *ol-* (see 12.1.1.2–3).

8.3.2 THE COPULAR MARKERS -(y)DI, -(y)mIş AND -(y)sA

These markers are the contracted forms of ∇*idi*, ∇*imiş* and ∇*ise* (8.3.1 (ii)). They attach to:

(i) Verbs containing one of the suffixes in position 3 (see the description of individual suffixes for exceptions): *bırakmıştı* 's/he had left', *yürümekteymişler* 'apparently they are/were walking', *koşuyorsak* 'if we are running', *bitirmiş olacaklardı* 'they were supposed to have finished [it]'.

(ii) To nominals (7.1.1) to form nominal predicates (12.1.1.2): *hastaydı* 's/he was ill', *evdeymişler* 'apparently they are/were at home', *hevesliysek* 'if we are enthusiastic'.

Note that the component *-(y)-* is omitted following a consonant: *satıyorduk* 'we were selling [it]', *yemişti* 's/he had eaten', *oynarsan* 'if you play'. *-(y)DI* and *-(y)sA* are followed by person markers belonging to group 1, and *-(y)mIş* by person markers belonging to group 2 (see 8.4 for details and exceptions). The copular markers are unstressable, and place stress on the (stressable) syllable before them (see 4.3.2 (i) and 4.3.2.1).

-(y)DI   The **past copula** can attach to:
  (i) All suffixes in position 3 on a verb stem: *koşuyordu* 's/he was running', *kalkmalıydı* 's/he should have got up'. The forms *-DIydI* and *-mIştI* are identical in meaning, but the former is restricted to informal registers: *gelmişti* 's/he had arrived', ↓*geldiydi* 's/he had arrived'.
  (ii) Nominals: *öğretmenimdiniz* 'you were my teacher', *buradaydım* 'I was here', *hastaydık* 'we were ill'.
  Note that *-(y)DI* can also occur *after* a person marker which is attached to the perfective marker *-DI* (8.2.3.3): *gittimdi* 'I have been [there]', as well as before it: *gittiydim*.
  For the combination of the past copula with the conditional copula see *-(y)sA* below.

-(y)mIş   The **evidential copula** can attach to:
  (i) all suffixes in position 3 on a verb stem except for *-DI*: *anlıyormuşsun* 'apparently you understand/understood', *otursaymışlar/otursalarmış* 'apparently, if they had sat ...'
  (ii) nominals: *öğretmenmiş* 'apparently s/he is/was a teacher', *evimmiş* 'it is/was apparently my house'.
  See *-(y)sA* below for the combination of the evidential copula with the conditional copula.

-(y)sA   The **conditional copula** can attach to:
  (i) all suffixes in position 3 on a verb stem except for *-sA*: *görmüşse* 'if s/he has (apparently) seen', *seviyorsan* 'if you love [him/her]'.
  Note that *-(y)sA* can also occur *after* a person marker which is attached to the perfective marker *-DI* (8.2.3.3): *gittimse* 'if I have gone [there]', as well as before it: *gittiysem*.
  (ii) nominals: *şoförse* 'if s/he is a driver', *yaşlıysa* 'if s/he is old', *evdeysem* 'if I am at home'

(iii) the copular markers *-(y)DI* and *-(y)mIş*. When it combines with these other copular markers, *-(y)sA* usually follows them: *gidiyorduysan* 'if (as you imply) you were going', *bakıyormuşsan* 'if (as seems to be the case) you were said to be looking'. However, some speakers use the reverse order with *-(y)DI*: *gidiyorsaydın*.

In nominal predicates the free-standing forms *idiyse* and *imişse* are generally preferred to the suffixed combinations *-(y)DIysA* and *-(y)mIşsA*: *masada idiyse* 'if it was on the table'.

8.3.3 *-DIr*

The **generalizing modality marker** *-DIr* follows person markers (8.4), except in the case of the 3rd person plural suffix *-lAr*, which it may precede or follow:

1st person singular		*gid-iyor-um-dur* 'I'm presumably going'
2nd person singular (familiar)		*gid-iyor-sun-dur* 'you're presumably going'
	(formal)	*gid-iyor-sunuz-dur* 'you're presumably going'
3rd person singular		*gid-iyor-dur* 's/he's presumably going'
1st person plural		*gid-iyor-uz-dur* 'we're presumably going'
2nd person plural		*gid-iyor-sunuz-dur* 'you're presumably going'
3rd person plural		*gid-iyor-lar-dır/gid-iyor-dur-lar* 'they're presumably going'

-DIr occurs in:

(i) verbal forms which already contain one of the position 3 suffixes *-mIş*, *-(y)AcAK*, *-(I)yor*, *-mAlI*, *-mAktA*: *anlamışlardır* 'they've probably understood', *unutacağızdır* 'we will almost certainly forget', *sanıyordur* 's/he's probably assuming', *bilmelidir* 's/he must know', *gitmektedir* 's/he is going'. *-DIr* co-occurs with *-mAlI* and *-mAktA* only in the 3rd person singular and plural forms.

(ii) verbal forms which have the combination *-(I)yormuş* (the imperfective suffix followed by the evidential copula). This occurs only in colloquial registers: ↓*bitiriyormuştur* 's/he must have been finishing [it]'.

(iii) nominal predicates: *yırtıcı bir kuştur*, 'it's a bird of prey', *güzelsindir* 'you are definitely pretty', *burdadır* 's/he's probably here', *vardır* 'there is/must be'.

(iv) expressions denoting a period of time: *bunca zamandır* 'for all this time' (see 16.4.1.2 (iii)).

When -*DIr* is attached to an indefinite noun phrase which is the subject or object in a sentence, it emphasizes the scale of the event described: *Bir curcunadır gidiyordu* 'There was pandemonium', *Bir inattır tutturdu* 'S/he is being totally unreasonable'.

8.4 PERSON MARKERS

Person markers are attached to both verbal and nominal predicates, to indicate the (grammatical person of the) subject. They follow all other suffixes: *kaçsan* 'if you ran away', *çalışıyoruz* 'we're working', *bakayım* 'let me see', *gidin* 'go!', *odamdayım* 'I'm in my room', except in the following cases, where they optionally or obligatorily precede another suffix:

(i) 1st and 2nd person forms which contain -*DIr* (see 8.3.3)

(ii) verb forms with -*DI* followed by -*(y)DI* or -*(y)sA* (see group 1 below)

(iii) the 3rd person plural suffix -*lAr*: When this suffix occurs in a form which contains a position 3 suffix and a copular marker, its preferred position is between these two, but it may also come at the end:

    kat-sa-lar-dı/kat-sa-ydı-lar 'if they had added [it]'
    bak-acak-lar-mış/bak-acak-mış-lar 'apparently they are/were going to look'

In nominal predicates the 3rd person plural suffix normally follows a copular marker:

    öğrenci-ydi-ler 'they were students'
    hasta-ymış-lar 'apparently they are/were ill'

However, there are two exceptions:

(a) When suffixed to a locative-marked noun phrase -*lAr* may precede a copular marker, although this is less common:

    orada-ydı-lar (or *orada-lar-dı*) 'they were there'
    evde-yse-ler (or *evde-ler-se*) 'if they are at home'

(b) When suffixed to one of the negation markers *değil* or *yok* (20.2–3), -*lAr* normally precedes a copular marker, although the reverse order is also possible:

    öğrenci değil-ler-di (or *değil-di-ler*) 'they were not students'
    evde yok-lar-mış (or *yok-muş-lar*) 'apparently they are/were not at home'

A non-case-marked subject complement to which the 3rd person plural predicate marker *-lAr* has been added should not be confused with a noun phrase containing the number suffix, i.e. the plural marker *-lAr*. In the former case *-lAr* is unstressable, whereas in the latter case it is stressable (see also 4.3.2 (ivc) and 22.3 (34)):

Öğretménler. 'They are teachers.' (3rd person plural predicate marker)
öğretmenlér '(the) teachers' (number suffix)

For the circumstances under which the 3rd person plural predicate marker can be used or omitted see 12.2.1–2. The conditions that apply to the usage of the familiar and formal 2nd person singular forms in the groups below are the same as those described for the selection of the 2nd person singular pronouns *sen* 'you' (familiar) or *siz* 'you' (formal) in 18.1.1.

There are four groups of person markers that occur in predicates.

Group 1

1st person singular		*-m*
2nd person singular	(familiar)	*-n*
	(formal)	*-nIz*
3rd person singular		-
1st person plural		*-k*
2nd person plural		*-nIz*
3rd person plural		*(-lAr)*

The 3rd person singular is expressed by the absence of any suffix: *geldi* 's/he has arrived', *kalsa* 'if s/he were to stay', *yazmıştı* 's/he had written'.

The markers in this group are used after:

(i)   The position 3 verbal suffixes *-DI* and *-sA*: *çekildiniz* 'you retreated', *baktılar* 'they looked', *bıraksak* 'if we were to leave [it]', *uyusan* 'if you slept', *kaldılar* 'they stayed'.

(ii) The copular markers *-(y)DI* and *-(y)sA*: *çekilirdiniz* 'you used to retreat', *bırakıyorsak* 'if we are leaving [it]', *evdeydik* 'we were at home', *hastaysalar* 'if they are ill'.

When a verb form contains *-DI* followed by *-(y)DI* or *-(y)sA*, the person markers can occur either after *-DI* or after the copular marker: *geldinizse/geldiyseniz* 'if you have arrived', *baktıydık/baktıktı* 'we had looked'.

Group 2

1st person singular		*-(y)Im*
2nd person singular	(familiar)	*-sIn*
	(formal)	*-sInIz*
3rd person singular		-
1st person plural		*-(y)Iz*
2nd person plural		*-sInIz*
3rd person plural		*(-lAr)*

The 3rd person singular is indicated by the absence of any suffix: *okuyormuş* 'apparently s/he's reading', *bakacak* 's/he's going to look', *orada* 's/he's there'.

The markers in this group are used after:

(i) The position 3 verbal suffixes *-mIş*, *-(A/I)r*, *-(y)AcAK*, *-(I)yor*, *-mAlI*, *-mAktA*: *unutmuşsun* 'you seem to have forgotten', *biliriz* 'we know', *hatırlamalıyım* 'I must remember', *gideceğim* 'I shall go', *ilgilenmemişler* 'apparently they did not take any notice'.

(ii) The copular marker *-(y)mIş*: *çalışmalıymışız* 'apparently we have to work', *söylüyormuşsunuz* 'apparently you've been saying'.

(iii) Nominals which are part of nominal predicates: *okuldayım* 'I'm at school', *hastasınız* 'you're ill', *buradalar* 'they're here'.

In colloquial speech, the 's' in the forms *-mIşsIn(Iz)* (evidential/perfective suffix + 2nd person singular/plural) and *-(y)mIşsIn(Iz)* (evidential copula + 2nd person singular/plural) can be deleted, reducing these forms to *-mIşIn(Iz)* and *-(y)mIşIn(Iz)*: *satmışın* 'I hear you've sold [it]', *bitiriyormuşunuz* 'I gather you're finishing [it]'. The combination of group 2 person markers with the future suffix also has a colloquial version (see *-(y)AcAk*, 8.2.3.3).

Group 3

1st person singular		*-yIm*
2nd person singular	(familiar)	*-sIn*
	(formal)	*-sInIz*
3rd person singular		*-sIn*
1st person plural		*-lIm*
2nd person plural		*-sInIz*
3rd person plural		*-sIn(lAr)*

All of the person markers above except the 3rd person forms attach to the optative suffix -(y)A (8.3.3.1, 21.4.4.3): *bakayım* 'let me see', *oynaya-bilesiniz* '[so that] you would be able to play', *kaçalım* 'let us escape'. The 3rd person forms -sIn and -sInlar do not attach to the optative suffix (or to any other position 3 suffix) but conjoin directly with the verb (which may contain a suffix from position 2): *git-**sin*** 'let him/her go', *oynasınlar* 'let them play', *kalkmayıver**sin*** 'let him/her just not get up', *bitirebil**sinler*** '[so that] they are able to finish [it]'.

Group 4

2nd person singular	(familiar)	-, -sAnA
	(formal)	-(y)In, -(y)InIz, -sAnIzA
3rd person singular		-sIn
2nd person plural		-(y)In, -(y)InIz, -sAnIzA
3rd person plural		-sIn(lAr)

These are person markers used in imperative forms. They attach directly to the verb stem: *okut**un*** 'make [him/her/them] read', *gel* 'come here!'. The 2nd person persuasive imperative forms ↓-sAnA and ↓-sAnIzA are composite forms containing the conditional suffix, the 2nd person markers from group 1 and the harmonized interjection A. These two person markers are mostly used for expressing suggestions rather than orders: ↓*otursanıza* 'why don't you sit down', *oturun* 'sit down!' (see 21.4.4.2).

8.5 SUBORDINATING SUFFIXES

Suffixation is the primary means of forming subordinate clauses in Turkish. Subordinating suffixes are nominalizing suffixes. They combine with verb stems to form nominals, some of which can be inflected with the plural suffix (8.1.1), the possessive marker indicating the subject of the subordinate clause (8.1.2), a case suffix (8.1.3), -(y)lA or -ki (8.1.4). Any verb form which contains a subordinating suffix is non-finite. Non-finite verb forms are of the three following types:

(i) **verbal nouns**: these are non-finite verbs of **noun clauses** (Chapter 24)
(ii) **participles**: these are non-finite verbs of **relative clauses** (Chapter 25)
(iii) **converbs**: these are non-finite verbs of **adverbial clauses** (Chapter 26).

Some examples are:

(16) [Sorun **yarat-*acağ*-ı**] belli.   (Verbal noun)
        problem create-VN-3SG.POSS clear
        'It is clear [*that s/he will create* problems].'

(17) [Sorun **yarat-*an***] kuruluş-lar uyar-ıl-dı.   (Participle)
problem create-PART organization-PL admonish-PASS-PF
'The organizations [*that were creating* problems] were admonished.'

(18) [Sorun **yarat-*maktansa***] sonuç-lar-ı kabullen-di.   (Converb)
problem create-CV consequence-PL-ACC accept-PF
'[*Instead of creating* problems] s/he accepted the consequences.'

The majority of subordinating suffixes in Turkish form only one of the three types of non-finite verb. However, certain subordinators, namely *-DIK*, *-(y)AcAK*, *-mA* and *-mAK* can form more than one type of subordinate clause. In some cases they do this by combining with other suffixes or words. In this section we describe the attachment properties and morphological characteristics of each subordinating suffix. For a full discussion of their functions see Chapters 24–7. Note that where person marking is obligatory in a particular non-finite form, this is indicated below by the 3rd person singular form.

8.5.1 MULTI-FUNCTIONAL SUBORDINATING SUFFIXES: *-DIK*, *-(y)AcAK*, *-mA*, *-mAK*

8.5.1.1 *-DIK* and *-(y)AcAK*

-DIK and *-(y)AcAK* form all three types of subordinate clause. They can be followed by possessive suffixes and case suffixes. Where they function as participles in headless relative clauses (25.3), they can be followed by all of the nominal inflectional suffixes described in 8.1, including the plural marker, *-(y)lA* and *-ki*: *sattıklarımınki* 'the one belonging to those that I sell/sold'.

-DIK This suffix usually expresses present or past time. It forms:

(**i**) Verbal nouns: *gittiğini* (*bil-*) '(know) that s/he has left', *kıskandırdığınızı* (*anla-*) '(understand) that you are making/have made [s.o.] envious' (24.4.3).

(**ii**) Participles: *göremediğim* (*film*) '(the film) that I was not able to see', *öpüştüğü* (*kız*) '(the girl) whom s/he has kissed/is kissing' (25.1.1.2).

(**iii**) Converbs: *baktığımızda* 'when we look/looked', *anladığımdan* 'because I understand/(have) understood'.

-DIK has a converbial function when it occurs in one of the following combinations (26.2–3), some of which involve postpositions (Chapter 17):

> -*DIğIndA*: *yürüdüğümde* 'when I walk'
> -*DIkçA*: *koştukça* 'the more [s.o.] runs'
> -*DIğIndAn* (*beri/dolayı/ötürü*): *geldiğimizden beri* 'since we arrived'
> -*DIğI* (*için/zaman/sırada/anda/halde/kadarıyla/takdirde/gibi/sürece/nispette*): *bakmadığım için* 'because I haven't looked/am/was not looking', *gördüğüm anda* 'the moment I saw [it]'
> -*DIğInA* (*göre*): *istemediğinize göre* 'since you don't/didn't want [it]'
> -*DIktAn* (*sonra/başka*): *aldıktan sonra* 'after taking [it]', *anladıktan başka* 'in addition to understanding'

-*(y)AcAK* This subordinator indicates (relative) future time, and forms:

(**i**) Verbal nouns: *anlayacağımı* (*san-*) '(imagine) that I would understand', *iteceğini* (*düşün-*) '(think) that s/he would push' (24.4.3).

(**ii**) Participles: *okuyacağım* (*kitap*) '(the book) that I am/was going to read', *sevemeyeceğim* (*bir kişi*) '(a person) that I shall/would not be able to like', *görüşeceği* (*doktor*) '(the doctor) whom s/he is/was going to see' (25.1.1.2).

(**iii**) Converbs: *öğreneceğine* 'instead of learning', *isteyeceğimden* 'because I am going to want'.

-*(y)AcAK* has a converbial function when it occurs in one of the following combinations (26.2.3), some of which involve postpositions (Chapter 17).

> -*(y)AcAğI* (*için/zaman/sırada/anda/halde/gibi*): *kalkacağın zaman* 'when you are going to get up', *oturmayacağı için* 'because s/he isn't/wasn't going to stay', *gideceği gibi* 'in addition to the fact that s/he is/was going to go'
> -*(y)AcAğIndAn* (*dolayı/ötürü*): *satmayacağından ötürü* 'on account of the fact that s/he is/was not going to sell [it]'
> -*(y)AcAğInA* (*göre*): *içmeyeceğime göre* 'since I'm/I was not going to drink [it]'
> -*(y)AcAk* (*kadar/derecede*): *saklayacak kadar* 'to the point of hiding [it]'

Note that words containing the subordinating suffix -*(y)AcAK* have a different stress pattern and pronunciation from words containing the future marker -*(y)AcAK* (8.2.3.3). The finite forms which contain the future marker -*(y)AcAK* combine with the unstressable (group 2) person markers (4.3.2 (iv)) and have short vowels, whereas the non-finite forms which contain the subordinator -*(y)AcAK* are followed by stressable possessive markers (8.1.2). However, in the informal contracted forms that occur in non-finite as well as finite future verbs, this distinction in stress is neutralized in the 1st and 2nd person singular and the 2nd person plural. (Compare the table below with that given for the same verb *in-* 'go/come down' in 8.2.3.3.)

Subordinator *-(y)AcAk* + possessive marking:

		Formal	Familiar
1st p. sg. *ineceğim*	[inedʒeím]/[inidʒeím]	↓[inidʒǽ:m]
2nd p. sg. *ineceğin*	[inedʒeín]/[inidʒeín]	↓[inidʒǽ:n]
3rd p.sg. *ineceği*	[inedʒeí]/[inidʒeí]	↓[inidʒǽ:]
1st p. pl. *ineceğimiz*	[inedʒeimíz]/[inidʒeimíz]	↓[inidʒæ:míz]
2nd p. pl. *ineceğiniz*	[inedʒeiníz]/[inidʒeiníz]	↓[inidʒæ:níz]
3rd p.pl. *inecekleri*	[inedʒeclerí]/[inidʒeclerí]	[inidʒeclerí]

8.5.1.2 *-mA* and *-mAK*

Both *-mA* and *-mAK* form verbal nouns and converbs. These two suffixes differ in respect of which nominal inflectional markers they can combine with. The plural suffix attaches to *-mA* only: (*evden*) *kaçmalar* 'incidents of running away (from home)'. Combinability with possessive suffixes is the most significant difference between the two subordinators. While *-mA* is often followed by one of the possessive markers, *-mAK* cannot combine with them:

-mA	*-mAK*
koşmam (için)	*koşmak (için)*
'(in order for) me to run'	'(in order) to run'

These forms can be inflected for case:

gitmenizi (bekliyor)	*gitmeyi (bekliyor)*
's/he expects you to leave'	's/he expects to leave'
şarkı söylemene (bayılıyor)	*şarkı söylemeye (bayılıyor)*
's/he loves [the way] you sing'	's/he loves singing'
koşmamda (ısrar etti)	*koşmakta (ısrar etti)*
's/he insisted that I run/ran'	's/he insisted on running'
konuşmamdan (korkuyor)	*konuşmaktan (korkuyor)*
's/he is scared that I might talk'	's/he is scared of talking'

-mA can also combine directly with the genitive case-marker, whereas *-mAK* cannot: *üniversiteye gitmenin (anlamı)* '(the significance) of going to university'. Some speakers attach the locative case marker directly to *-mA*:

cevap vermede (geciktim) 'I am/was late in responding', but forms where the locative suffix is attached to *-mAK* are more widespread: *cevap vermekte (geciktim)* 'I am/was late in responding'.

Note that when *-mAK* combines with a suffix beginning with a vowel, as in the case of the accusative and dative suffixes, the resulting form is spelt and pronounced more commonly nowadays as *-mayı, -meyi* (ACC) and *-maya, -meye* (DAT), rather than *-mağı, -meği* (ACC) and *-mağa, -meğe* (DAT). Since a case marker can also attach to *-mA* directly without an intervening possessive marker (as seen above in the case of the genitive and locative case markers), it may not always be clear whether the accusative or dative case marker has attached to *-mA* or to *-mAK*. In this book we adhere to the new spelling of these forms (with 'y' rather than 'ğ') and consider these forms as a combination of *-mAK* + ACC/DAT.

-mAK This subordinator forms:

(i) Verbal nouns: *almak (iste-)* '(want) to buy', *sevmeyi (öğren-)* '(learn) to love', *ağlamaya (başla-)* '(start) crying' (24.4.1)

(ii) Converbs: *içmeksizin* 'without drinking'.

-mAK has a converbial function when it occurs in one of the following combinations (26.2–3), some of which involve postpositions (Chapter 17):

> *-mAk (üzere/için/yerine/suretiyle/şartıyla)*: *vermek için* 'in order to give'
> *-mAklA (birlikte)*: *okuyabilmekle birlikte* 'although able to read'
> *-mAksIzIn (formal)*: *dönmeksizin* 'without returning'
> *-mAktAn (öte/başka/gayrı)*: *satmaktan öte* 'apart from selling [it]'
> *-mAktAnsA: bitirmektense* 'rather than finishing [it]'.

-mA This subordinator forms:

(i) Verbal nouns: *anlamamamı (iste-)* '(want) me not to understand' (24.4.2)

(ii) Converbs: *yürümekten başka* 'apart from walking'.

-mA has a converbial function when it occurs in one of the following combinations (26.2–3), some of which involve postpositions (Chapter 17):

> *-mAsI (için/halinde/durumunda/yüzünden)*: *öksürmesi halinde* 'in the event of his/her coughing'
> *-mAsIndAn (itibaren/önce/sonra/ötürü/başka/dolayı)*: *seçilmesinden önce* 'before s/he was elected', *istemememizden ötürü* 'because we don't/didn't want [it]'

-mAsInA (*rağmen/karşın*): *anlaşmanıza rağmen* 'in spite of your getting along well together'.

8.5.2 SUBORDINATING SUFFIXES WHICH HAVE A SINGLE FUNCTION

8.5.2.1 *-(y)An* and *-(y)Iş*

-(y)An This suffix forms participles: *okuyan (çocuk)* '(the child) who studies/is studying' (25.1.1.1). When it occurs in headless relative clauses (25.3) and pronominalized complex adjectivals (18.4 (vi)), it can be followed by all of the nominal inflectional suffixes described in 8.1: *okuyanlarımıza* 'to the ones among us who study/are studying'.

Much less productively than in its usage as a participle, *-(y)An* can be used idiomatically in informal contexts to express the unexpectedly large number of people involved in a particular activity. In these cases it is reiterated on identical and adjacent verb stems, and the second verb has dative case marking: *Konsere giden gidene* 'Masses of people went to the concert'. *Şu saçma dergiyi de alan alana!* 'Everyone's buying this ridiculous magazine!'

-(y)Iş This suffix can combine with the plural marker, possessive suffixes and case suffixes. It forms verbal nouns: *oturuşumu (beğen-)* '(like) my way of sitting', *konuşuşunuz* 'the way you talk' (24.4.4).

8.5.2.2 Subordinating suffixes which only form converbs

The following suffixes form converbs (26.2–3). With the exception of *-mIşÇAsInA*, none of these suffixes combine with person markers:

(i) Converbial suffixes containing the negative marker *-mA* or *-mAz*

-mAdAn (*önce/∇evvel*): The forms containing *-mA* are stressed on the syllable preceding the negative marker (cf. 4.3.2 (viii)), e.g. *yıkílmadan* 'before being demolished'.

-mAzdAn (*önce/∇evvel*) (*-mA* combined with the negative aorist form *-z*): The forms containing *-mAz* occur with *önce* or *∇evvel*. They are stressed on the case suffix following the negative marker, e.g. *yıkılmazdán önce* 'before being demolished'. The form *-mAzdAn önce* is slightly more formal than *-mAdAn önce*.

(ii) Other converbial suffixes:

-(y)IncA   *yüzünce* 'when [s.o.] swims/swam', *kalkmayınca* 'when [s.o.] doesn't/didn't get up'.

-(y)ArAk   *koşarak* 'running', *büyüyerek* 'growing up', *çalışarak* 'by working'. Also ↓*-(y)ArAktAn*: *bakaraktan* 'looking'.

↓*-(y)AlI (beri)*   *düşüneli* (*beri*) 'since thinking about [s.t.]', *geleli beri* 'since arriving', 'since [s.o.] arrived'. Colloquial form of *-DIğIndAn beri*.

-(y)IncAyA (kadar/değin/dek)/↓-(y)AnA (kadar)
                    gidinceye kadar 'by the time [s.o.] went'. *-(y)AnA* is a colloquial version: ↓*oturana kadar* 'by the time [s.o.] sat down'.

-(A/I)r/-(y)AcAk/-mIş/-(y)mIş/-(I)yor gibi
                    kalkacak gibi 'as if about to get up', *anlar gibi* 'as if understanding', *içki içmiş gibi* 'as if having drunk alcohol'.

-(A/I)rcAsInA/-mIşçAsInA
                    hissedercesine 'as if feeling'. With the form *-mIşçAsInA*, there is the possibility of adding person marking: *konuşuyormuşumcasına* 'as if I was talking'.

-(y)Ip   *koşup al-* 'run and get', *girip otur-* 'enter and sit down'. Because of its conjunctive function, this suffix is discussed in 28.2.

-(y)ken   The segment *-(y)-* is the copula (8.3.1). Because of this, *-(y)ken* attaches not directly to the verb stem, but instead to a position 3 verbal suffix or to a nominal (cf. 8.3.2, 26.2.3 (ii)): *bakarken* 'when/while ([s.o.] is/was) watching', *çocukken* 'when/as a child', 'when [s.o.] was a child', *sokaktayken* 'while in the street', *bizimken* 'when [s.t.] is/was ours'. Unlike the other copular markers, it cannot combine with person markers, except optionally with the 3rd person plural suffix *-lAr*: *gider(ler)ken* 'as they go/went'. It is invariable (i.e. its vowel does not undergo vowel harmony, see 3.4).

A few converbial subordinators are added to pairs of verbs that follow immediately after each other:

-(y)A . . . -(y)A   Added to identical or similar verb stems or to semantically contrasting ones: *baka baka* 'staring', *yedire yedire* 'continuously making [s.o.] eat', *bağıra çağıra* 'at the top of his/her voice', *gide gele* 'going back and forth', *bata çıka* 'sinking and rising'.

↓*-DI . . . -(y)AlI*   Added to identical verb stems. The first stem has person marking: *duydum duyalı* 'ever since I heard [it]', *baktırdın baktıralı* 'ever since you had [it] checked', *alındı alınalı* ' ever since it was bought'.

-(A/I)r . . . -mAz   This pair of suffixes consists of the aorist and negative-aorist position 3 verbal suffixes (8.2.3.3). These produce a converbial form when added to consecutive identical verb stems without any person marking: *yer yemez* 'as soon as [s.o.] eats/ate', *gider gitmez* 'as soon as [s.o.] leaves/left'.

9 REDUPLICATION

Reduplication is the repetition of a word or part of a word. There are three types of reduplicative process in Turkish:

(i) emphatic reduplication: *kıpkırmızı* 'stark red' (9.1)
(ii) *m*-reduplication: *çirkin mirkin* 'ugly, or anything like that' (9.2)
(iii) doubling: *yavaş yavaş* 'slowly' (9.3).

9.1 EMPHATIC REDUPLICATION

Emphatic reduplication is used for accentuating the quality of an adjective:

uzun 'long'   →   *upuzun* 'very long'
güzel 'pretty'   →   *güpgüzel* 'very pretty'

It occurs mainly with underived adjectives, and occasionally with adverbs.
  In emphatic reduplication, a prefix is attached to the stem. If the stem begins with a vowel the prefix consists of this vowel and the reduplicative consonant 'p':

ince 'thin'   →   *i* + **p** + *ince*   →   *ipince* 'very thin'
eski 'old'   →   *e* + **p** + *eski*   →   *epeski* 'very old'

If the stem begins with a consonant, the prefix consists of this consonant, the vowel following it and one of the reduplicative consonants 'p', 's', 'r' or 'm':

sarı 'yellow'   →   *sa* + **p** + *sarı*   →   *sapsarı* 'bright yellow'
katı 'hard'   →   *ka* + **s** + *katı*   →   *kaskatı* 'hard as a rock'
temiz 'clean'   →   *te* + **r** + *temiz*   →   *tertemiz* 'clean as a pin'
siyah 'black'   →   *si* + **m** + *siyah*   →   *simsiyah* 'pitch black'

In some cases the reduplicated segment contains an additional segment:

(i)   *-A*:

gündüz 'daytime', 'by day' *gü* + **p** + **e** + *gündüz* 'in broad daylight'
sağlam 'in good condition' *sa* + **p** + **a** + *sağlam* 'in very good condition'
yalnız 'alone'   *ya* + **p** + **a** + *yalnız* 'all alone'
                                               (also *yapyalnız*)

(ii)   *-Il* or *-Am*, in some cases where the reduplicative consonant is 'r':

çıplak 'naked'   *çı* + **r** + **ıl** + *çıplak* 'stark naked' (also *çırçıplak*)
parça 'piece'   *pa* + **r** + **am** + *parça* 'torn to shreds', 'smashed to pieces'

The occurrence of a particular reduplicative consonant is, to a degree, based on the consonants in a stem. For example, the reduplicative consonant cannot be the same as the first or second consonant of the stem. The number of stems which can undergo emphatic reduplication is limited. A list of such stems with their reduplicated forms is given in Appendix 1.

Words which undergo emphatic reduplication are stressed on the initial syllable (e.g. *kápkara, sápasağlam, ápaçık*) except when the reduplicated form contains *-Il* or *-Am*, in which case this latter syllable bears stress (e.g. *çırílçıplak*). Emphatically reduplicated words cannot occur with the modifiers in 15.4 (such as *çok* 'many' or *en* 'most').

9.2   *m*-REDUPLICATION

The function of *m*-reduplication is to generalize the concept denoted by a particular word or phrase to include other similar objects, events or states of affairs. This is a colloquial usage.

(1)   Doktor önce hastanın **gözüné** *mözüné* baktı, sonra sorunu anlamadığını söyledi.
'The doctor first checked the patient's *eyes, etc.*, then said that s/he didn't understand the problem.'

(2)   Eve çat kapı bir alıcı geldi, **odalarí** *modalarí* dolaştı.
'Today a prospective buyer came unannounced, [and] looked around the *rooms, etc.*'

(3)   **Soner'í** *monerí* görmedim.
'I didn't see *Soner or anyone.*'

m-reduplication involves the repetition of a word or phrase in a modified form. If this word or phrase begins with a vowel, the modifying consonant 'm' is prefixed to its second occurrence:

etek metek 'skirt(s) and the like'
içecek miçecek 'drinks and the like'

If the word or phrase begins with a consonant, this consonant is *replaced* by 'm' in its second occurrence:

kapı mapı 'door(s) and the like'
çay may 'tea and the like'

In most cases the reduplicative form immediately follows the word which it reduplicates. One exception is noun compounds, where the entire compound is repeated, with only its first word undergoing *m*-reduplication:

(4) Ben adam **tarih hocasıymış *m*arih hocasıymış** anlamam. Fransız tarihini ondan daha iyi biliyorum.
'I don't care if he is *a history teacher or whatever*. I know more about French history than he does.'

9.3 DOUBLING

Doubling is the simple repetition of a word. It occurs with nouns, adverbs, adjectives and measure terms.

(**i**) Doubled adverbs, doubled nouns, doubled adjectives and doubled distributive numerals (15.7.3) all occur with an adverbial function (see 16.1.3):

yavaş yavaş	'slowly'
çabuk çabuk	'quickly'
kapı kapı	'from door to door'
damla damla	'in drops'
sabah sabah	'early in the morning'
usul usul	'slowly and softly'
rahat rahat	'comfortably', 'easily'
birer/ birer	'one by one'

(**ii**) Doubled adjectives are also used as modifiers with plural nouns, both to draw attention to the quality denoted by the adjective and to indicate a large quantity of the item in question:

koca koca (ağaçlar)	'many huge (trees)'
sarı sarı (evler)	'many yellow (houses)'

(**iii**) When doubled nouns are used adjectivally they are usually used without plural marking on the noun that is modified. These forms indicate a large quantity or a great variety of the item in question:

çeşit çeşit yiyecek(ler)	'all kinds of (dishes)'
boy boy kutu(lar)	'boxes of all sizes'
kutu kutu kitap	'many boxes of books'

(**iv**) The particle *mI* (11.1.1.5) inserted between two occurrences of an adjective intensifies its meaning. These forms are colloquial, and are usually used either as predicative adjectives or in indefinite noun phrases:

Adam kurnaz mı kurnaz   'The man is extremely sly'
güzel mi güzel bir kız   'a remarkably pretty girl'

Forms doubled with the aid of *mI* can occasionally be used as adverbs:

yavaş mı yavaş (okuyor)   '(s/he reads) very slowly'

9.3.1   DOUBLING IN LEXICAL FORMATIONS

There are a number of idiomatic expressions that are created by doubling. Some of these contain similar sounding words which may or may not exist independently, or they may be formed by two words that denote similar concepts:

konu komşu   'neighbours'
ufak tefek   'tiny'
paldır küldür   'with an enormous noise'
çoluk çocuk   'wife and children'
süklüm püklüm   'in a crestfallen manner'

10 NOUN COMPOUNDS

In this chapter we discuss noun compounds, word-like units which are made up of two nouns or an adjective and a noun. There are two types of noun compound:

(i)   bare compounds: *kız kardeş* 'sister', *naylon torba* 'plastic bag', *Yeşilbahar Sokak* 'Yeşilbahar Street', *büyükbaba* 'grandfather'

(ii)   *-(s)I* compounds: *at arabası* 'horse-drawn carriage', *gaz sobası* 'gas stove', *Atatürk Bulvarı* 'Atatürk Boulevard', *buzdolabı* 'refrigerator'.

In both types the first noun or adjective modifies the second noun, which is called the **head**. As seen in the above examples, some compounds are written as one word.

Noun compounds whose modifiers are clauses (e.g. s*avaşın uzun bir süre devam edeceği korkusu* 'the fear that the war would go on for a long time') are discussed in 24.6. See 4.2 for stress in compounds.

10.1   BARE COMPOUNDS

These are of two types: bare noun compounds and adjective-noun compounds.

10.1.1   BARE NOUN COMPOUNDS

These consist simply of two juxtaposed nouns, with no suffixation to mark the relation between them. This type of compounding is of restricted occurrence. Its main areas of usage are listed below.

(i)   Compounds in which the first noun specifies the sex or the profession of the person denoted by the second noun:

erkek kardeş	'brother'
kız arkadaş	'girlfriend'
kadın doktor	'woman doctor'
avukat kadın	'woman who is a lawyer'

(ii)   Compounds in which the first noun specifies the nationality of the person denoted by the second noun (also expressed by *-(s)I* compounds (10.2)):

Alman mimar	'German architect'
Türk çocuklar	'Turkish children'

(**iii**) Compounds in which the first noun specifies the material from which the item denoted by the second noun is made:

çelik kapı	'steel door'
taş duvar	'stone wall'
yün çorap	'wool sock(s)'

(**iv**) The names of various cooked dishes:

şiş kebap	'shish kebab'
kuzu fırın	'oven-cooked lamb'

(**v**) Street names in which the second noun is *sokak* 'street':

Akgül Sokak	'Akgül Street'

The use of bare noun compounds for street names is a fairly recent development, and forms such as *Akgül Sokak* are used interchangeably with the corresponding *-(s)I* compound form (with *Sokağı* instead of *Sokak*; see 10.2). Even official usage is not consistent, and the abbreviation '*Sok.*', commonly used in postal addresses and on street signs, obscures this variation.

10.1.2 ADJECTIVE-NOUN COMPOUNDS

These compounds are made up of an adjective and a noun. As in bare-noun compounds, there is no suffixation to mark the relation between the two components. The majority of these compounds are written as single words:

karabiber	'pepper'
karafatma	'cockroach'
darboğaz	'(economic) bottle-neck'
kabakulak	'mumps'
akciğer	'lung(s)'
sarı humma	'yellow fever'

10.2   *-(s)I* COMPOUNDS

This is by far the more common type of compounding in Turkish. *-(s)I* compounds consist minimally of two juxtaposed nouns, the first of which has no suffixes while the second is marked with the 3rd person possessive suffix -*(s)I* (8.1.2). Some examples are:

*otobüs bilet-**i***	'bus ticket'
*el çanta-**sı***	'handbag'
*masa örtü-**sü***	'tablecloth'
*çay bardağ-**ı***	'tea glass'
*çocuk bahçe-**si***	'children's playground'

The plural of a -*(s)I* compound is formed by attaching the 3rd person possessive suffix (in this case always -*I*) to the plural form of the second noun:

*otobüs biletler-**i***	'bus tickets'
*el çantalar-**ı***	'handbags'
*çay bardaklar-**ı***	'tea glasses'

In the case of -*(s)I* compounds that are written as one word, there is some variation in how the plural is formed. In most such words the plural suffix precedes the possessive suffix, just as in the separately written compounds:

*buzdolap-**lar**-ı*	'refrigerators'
*yayınev-**ler**-i*	'publishing houses'

There are a few cases, however, where the possessive suffix is treated as an integral part of the word, and the plural suffix follows it:

*ayakkabı-**lar***	'shoes'
*yüzbaşı-**lar***	'(army) captains'
*binbaşı-**lar***	'(army) majors'

In a very small number of cases the plural can be formed either way:

*kasımpatı-**lar**/kasımpat-**lar**-ı* 'chrysanthemums'

The function of the 3rd person possessive suffix (8.1.2) in -*(s)I* compounds is not to signify possession of one thing by another. It simply serves as a grammatical indicator of the compounding of the noun to which it is affixed with the immediately preceding noun.

A particular function of -*(s)I* compounds is to unite the particular names of topographical features, institutions and geopolitical entities with the noun denoting the category of item in question:

Ağrı Dağ-ı	'Mount Ararat'
Van Göl-ü	'Lake Van'

Efes Lokanta-sı	'Ephesus Restaurant'
Türkiye Cumhuriyet-i	'Republic of Turkey'

A similar usage is seen in time expressions in which a date or the name of a day or month is compounded with the noun denoting the unit of time in question (see 16.4.1.1):

1912 yıl-ı	'the year 1912'
cuma gün-ü	'Friday'
ocak ay-ı	'the month of January'

-(s)I compounding is obligatory in cases where something non-human is specified as peculiar to, or characteristic of, a specified nation. Turkish words expressing nationality (e.g. *Türk, İngiliz, Alman*) are nouns, not adjectives:

Türk kahve-si	'Turkish coffee'
Türk Lira-sı	'Turkish Lira'
Alman ekmeğ-i	'German bread'
Fransız edebiyat-ı	'French literature'

Note that for some nationalities, the noun used as a modifier in *-(s)I* compounds is not necessarily identical with the word used to designate a person of that nationality:

Yunan müziğ-i	'Greek music'
Hint diller-i	'Indian languages'

When the head noun is one that denotes human beings, adjectival forms with *-lI* (7.2.2.2) are preferred:

Yunanlı doktor	'Greek doctor'
Hintli müzisyen	'Indian musician'

Note that in the case of *Yunan(-lı)* and *Hint(-li)*, noun phrases on the pattern of *Hint-li doktor* (adjective + noun) replace the bare noun compound forms such as *Alman mimar* shown in 10.1.1.

In the case of countries for which Turkish does not have a separate noun of nationality, the name of the country is used in place of it in *-(s)I* compounds:

Çin fener-i	'Chinese lantern'
Brezilya takım-ı	'the Brazilian team'

Names of other geographical or geopolitical entities (e.g. continents, regions, cities) are also used in *-(s)I* compounds in the same way:

bir Afrika ülke-si   'an African country'
Ortadoğu siyaset-i   'Middle East(ern) politics'
Akdeniz iklim-i   'Mediterranean climate'
Uşak halı-sı   'Uşak carpet' (carpet made in Uşak, or in that style)

As we saw in 10.1.1 (ii) above, when nouns of nationality (*Türk, Alman,* etc.) occur in compounds denoting human beings, the second noun can be left unsuffixed, forming a bare noun compound. However, in these cases a *-(s)I* compound is also possible:

İngiliz çocuklar-ı   'English/British children'
Türk işçiler-i   'Turkish workers'
Japon askerler-i   'Japanese soldiers'
bir Rus sporcu-su   'a Russian athlete'
Yunan başbakan-ı   'the Greek prime minister'

There is a subtle difference between the meanings of the bare compound and the *-(s)I* compound in such cases. While the bare compound identifies one or more individuals who just happen to have a certain nationality, the *-(s)I* compound either (i) expresses a whole class or group generically (such as British children, or the Turkish workers in a particular factory, town, or country), or (ii) presents a person not primarily as an individual human being but as someone functioning in some capacity on behalf of his/her nation or country.

10.3   EMBEDDING COMPOUNDS WITHIN OTHER COMPOUNDS

Compounds can often be embedded within other compounds. For example, compounds such as *İngiliz edebiyatı* 'English literature' or *göz hastalıkları* 'diseases of the eye' can act as modifiers in other compounds:

İngiliz Edebiyat-ı Bölüm-ü   'Department of English Literature'
göz hastalıklar-ı hastane-si   'hospital for diseases of the eye'

Note that in these cases the marker *-(s)I* occurs on the head of each compound. Hence longer forms can contain several markers, one for each head:

Türkiye Cumhuriyeti Milli Eğitim Bakanlığı Kadıköy Kız Yüksek Meslek Okulu Müdürlüğü 'The Directorate of the Kadıköy Technical College for Girls under the Ministry of National Education of the Republic of Turkey'

The head of this multi-layered compound is *müdürlük* 'directorate', which is modified by the following construction, itself a *-(s)I* compound:

Türkiye Cumhuriyet-i Milli Eğitim Bakanlığ-ı Kadıköy Kız Yüksek Meslek Okul-u 'Kadıköy Technical College for Girls under the Ministry of National Education of the Republic of Turkey'

The head of this compound is *okul* 'school', which has two simple modifiers, *meslek*, here meaning 'technical' and the adjective *yüksek* 'high', which when combined with *okul* means 'college'. *Kız* 'girl' modifies *yüksek meslek okulu* 'technical college', and *Kadıköy* modifies *kız yüksek meslek okul-u* 'technical college for girls'. *Kadıköy Kız Yüksek Meslek Okulu* is modified by *Türkiye Cumhuriyeti Milli Eğitim Bakanlığı*, which is also a construction with embedded compounds. The head of this compound is *bakanlık* 'ministry', modified by the noun phrase *milli eğitim* 'national education'. The compound *Milli Eğitim Bakanlığı* 'Ministry of National Education' is modified by *Türkiye Cumhuriyeti* 'Republic of Turkey', itself a compound.

Note that when a compound acts as the head of another compound, only one occurrence of *-(s)I* on the head is possible:

Kadıköy Kız **Yüksek Meslek Okul-u** 'Kadıköy Technical College for Girls'
Polonya **gölge tiyatro-su** 'Polish shadow theatre'

10.4 SEPARABILITY OF THE CONSTITUENTS OF COMPOUNDS

The constituents of bare noun compounds and *-(s)I* compounds usually form a single unit and are inseparable. However, there are two exceptions:

(i) Conjoined compounds:
When two compounds have the same head, they can be conjoined by *ve* (28.3.1.1), and the first occurrence of the head can be deleted. The head in such cases may or may not have plural marking:

kız ve erkek çocuklar	'female and male children', 'girls and boys'
İngiliz ve Alman sineması/sinemaları	'(the) British and German cinema(s)'

(ii) Adjectives modifying the head:
Adjectives, determiners and numerals modifying the head noun are placed before the whole compound in the same order as they are placed before the head of a noun phrase (see 15.9):

güzel bir masa örtüsü   'a beautiful tablecloth'
birtakım ilginç çocuk kitapları 'some interesting children's books'

However, in compounds which refer to official bodies, an adjective (but not determiners or numerals) may be placed before the head noun:

eski *Dışişleri Bakanı/Dışişleri* **eski** *Bakanı*
'the former Foreign Secretary'

11 CLITICS

Clitics are particles that are attached to phrases. The clitics in Turkish follow the suffixes that occur on the final word of a phrase. Most clitics can attach to any type of phrase, and thus have freedom of movement inside a clause, unlike suffixes, which are fully integrated with the word to which they are attached. Some clitics undergo vowel harmony (Chapter 3) like suffixes, but others are non-harmonic. They are all unstressable, and in the majority of cases cause stress to occur on the phrase they are attached to (see 11.1.1.2–3) for some exceptions concerning *dA* and *-(y)sA/ise*, and 19.1.5 for an exception concerning *mI*). For details of the position of stress within a word followed by clitics, see 4.3.2.1. For the stress effects of combinations of clitics see 11.2.

11.1 THE CLITICS OF TURKISH

The clitics of Turkish are the following:

(**i**)   the particle *mI* (the most typical function of which is to form yes/no questions)
(**ii**) the discourse connectives *dA*, *-(y)sA/ise*, and *ya*, and the discourse connective and subordinator *ki*
(**iii**) the additive connective *bile* 'even'
(**iv**) the copular markers *-(y)DI*, *-(y)mIş*, *-(y)sA* (8.3.2), the adverbial marker *-(y)ken* (8.5.2.2) and the generalizing modality marker *-DIr* (8.3.3)
(**v**)   the person markers belonging to group 2 (8.4)
(**vi**) the comitative/instrumental and conjunctive marker *-(y)lA/ile* (8.1.4).

Of these, the last three groups are discussed elsewhere in this book. The clitics discussed in this chapter, with the exception of *-(y)sA*, are written separately from the preceding word.

11.1.1 THE PROPERTIES OF PARTICULAR CLITICS

11.1.1.1 *bile*

This is an additive connective which is non-harmonic (see also 28.3.1.1 (iv)):

yolladım **bile** 'I have *already* sent it'
ev **bile** '*even* a/the house'

11.1.1.2 *dA*

The first consonant of this marker is invariable and is pronounced [d], but its vowel harmonizes with the vowel in the preceding syllable:

*annem **de*** 'my mother *too*'
*yaparım **da*** 'I will do [it], *too*'

When it combines with a form containing the possibility suffix *-(y)Abil*, it can be inserted after *-(y)A* in colloquial speech:

*bakabilirim **de*** 'I can *also* look'
*baka **da** bilirim* 'I can *also* look' (colloquial)

The clitic *dA* is a conjunction and discourse connective with additive, adversative, continuative/topic-shifting and enumerating functions. It occurs after stressed constituents, except when it functions as a continuative/topic-shifting connective. Its functions are as follows:

(i)   Continuative/topic-shifting connective (23.3.3.1 (i), 28.3.1.1 (iiia)):

*Bu hediyeyi **de** Envér aldı.*
'*As for* this present, Envér bought it.'

(ii)   Additive (28.3.1.1 (iiib)):

*seyrétmedim **de***
'*and moreover* I didn't watch [it]'

When *dA* functions as an additive connective the stressable syllable of the word preceding it bears stress.

(iii)   Adversative 28.3.4.5 (i):

*seyretmedím **de** (anlattılar).*
'I didn't watch [it] *but* ([people] told [me about it])'.

When *dA* functions as an adversative connective the *syllable* preceding it bears stress.

(iv)   Enumerating (28.3.2):

*Ayşe **de** Semra **da***
'*both* Ayşe *and* Semra'

In these constructions *dA* attaches to each item that is enumerated.

See also its usage in combination with *-sA* (27.4.2.1) and *-(y)sA* (27.4.2.2)

11.1.1.3 -(y)sA/ise

This is a discourse connective with topic-shifting and contrastive functions (23.3.3.1 (ii), 28.3.4.5 (iii)). Although it assigns stress to the syllable preceding it, the stressed constituent never carries primary stress within a sentence. This clitic either occurs as -(y)sA, or less commonly as the separate form *ise*. It is mostly added to 1st and 2nd person pronouns or proper nouns, and can follow case markers:

bense 'as for me'
*Ahmet'se/Ahmet **ise*** 'as for Ahmet'
Zehra'yıysa 'as for Zehra (ACC)'
onlarınsa (hiç parası yok) 'as for them (they don't have any money)'

It can also attach to any adverbial expressing location in time:

Öğleden sonraysa yürüyüşe çıktık.
'And in the afternoon, we went for a walk.'

When this clitic attaches to the 3rd person singular pronoun *o* 'he/she/it', only its free form can be used:

o ise 'as for him/her/it'

Note that the form *oysa* (28.3.4.4) is a discourse connective with the quite different meaning of 'whereas'.

11.1.1.4 ki

ki is of Persian origin and, unlike the adjectival/pronominal -*ki(n)* (8.1.4), cannot be stressed. In the first four of its functions listed below, it assigns stress to the syllable preceding it, even if this syllable is otherwise unstressable (4.3.2.1). It has the following functions:

(i) Subordinator connecting a noun clause to a superordinate clause (24.3.2):

*İnanıyorum [**ki** herşey düzelecek].*
'I believe [*that* everything will come right].'

(ii) Subordinator connecting an adverbial clause to a superordinate clause (26.1.2):

*Sana bunu söylüyorum [**ki** sonradan şaşırmayasın].*
'I'm telling you this [so that you won't be surprised later].'

(iii) Repudiative discourse connective (28.3.4.6):

Anlayamıyorum ki! 'I just can't understand.'

(iv) Exclamation (12.4):
In exclamations, *ki* comes at the end and is used with *o kadar* or *öyle(sine)* 'so':

Londra sonbaharda o kadar güzel olur ki!
'London is so beautiful in autumn!'

(v) Relative clause marker (25.6):

(a) Comment (25.6.3):
In this function, *ki* introduces a clause that supplies a comment or additional information about the phrase that has just been uttered:

Bugün hava açarsa, [ki açacağını pek sanmıyorum,] bahçede mangal yakacaklarmış.
'If the weather brightens up today, *which* I don't really think it will, apparently they're going to have a barbecue in the garden.'

(b) In non-restrictive relative clauses (25.6.1):

Semra [ki partileri sevmez], o bile eğlendi.
'Even Semra, [who doesn't like parties,] had fun.'

(c) In restrictive relative clauses (25.6.2):

Bir şöför [ki park etmeyi bilmesin], ona güvenip arabasına binilmez.
'A driver [who doesn't know how to park a car] isn't to be trusted to drive one around.'

(d) *ki* can also be used following the demonstrative pronoun *şu* (18.2) to present the content of a fact, belief, desire, etc., referred to by a headless relative clause (25.3):

[Bildiğim] şu [ki, herkesin tatile ihtiyacı var].
'All [I know] is [*that* everyone needs a holiday].'

11.1.1.5 *mI*

The clitic *mI* has the following functions:

(i) Question particle in yes/no questions (19.1.1), and alternative questions (both direct (19.1.2) and indirect (24.4.3.2)).

When *mI* is added to a main clause predicate, its position depends on what kind of suffixes or clitics (if any) appear at the end of the predicate. *mI* immediately *precedes* any of the items listed below:

(a)   the copular markers *-(y)DI* and *-(y)mIş* (8.3.2):

      *Gitse **miydik?*** 'Should we have gone?'
      *Başlamış **mıydınız?*** 'Had you started?'
      *Burada **mıymış?*** 'Was it here?'

(b)   the person markers in group 2, except for the 3rd person plural marker (8.4) and the colloquial combinations with *-(y)AcAK* mentioned in (e) below):

      *Gidiyor **musun?*** 'Are you going?'
      *İster **miyiz?*** 'Would we want [to]?'
      *Hazır **mısınız?*** 'Are you ready?'

(c)   the generalizing modality marker *-DIr* (8.3.3) in 3rd person forms:

      *Unutmuş **mudurlar?*** '[Do you think] they have forgotten?'
      *Evde **midir?*** '[Do you think] s/he/it's at home?'/'Is s/he at home?'

Otherwise, i.e. in forms with *-DIr* containing markers of the other persons, it immediately precedes the person marker:

      *(Acaba) geçmiş **miyimdir?*** 'I wonder if I have passed.'

On the other hand, *mI* immediately *follows* any of the items listed below:

(a)   the person markers in group 1:

      *Gördün **mü?*** 'Did you see?'
      *Gitsek **mi?*** 'Should we go?'
      *Yürüdünüz **mü?*** 'Did you walk?'

(b)   the person markers in group 3 (except for the 2nd person forms, which do not combine with the question particle for semantic reasons):

      *Kalayım **mı?*** 'Shall/should I stay?'
      *Başlasın **mı?*** 'Should s/he start?'

(c)   the 3rd person plural form *-lAr*:

>   *Gittiler mı?* 'Have they left?'
>   *Uyanırlar mı?* 'Will they wake up?'
>   *Okuldalar mı?* 'Are they at school?'

(d)   a subject complement (12.1.1.2) that is not followed by any predicate markers:

>   *Akıllı mı?* 'Is s/he intelligent?'
>   *Benimki mi?* 'Is it mine?

(e)   the colloquial forms of the combination of future marker with 1st or 2nd person markers (8.4):

>   [arıjʤan **mı**] 'Are you going to look [at it]?'
>   [jürijʤæz **mi**] 'Are we going to walk?'

mI places stress on the stressable syllable in the preceding word (4.3.2.1; for an exception, see 19.1.5).

(ii)   Adverbial clause marker (26.1.6 and 27.6.2):
When *mI* functions as an adverbial clause marker it follows verb forms which have the perfective suffix *-DI*:

>   *gittin **mi*** 'as soon as you go'
>   *evini sattın **mı*** 'once you've sold your house'

Clauses with *mI* functioning as an adverbial have a slight rise of intonation at the end, unlike questions, where the intonation falls at the end (see 5.1).

(iii)   Intensifier in doubled forms (9.3):

>   *ilginç **mi** ilginç* 'very interesting'
>   *hızlı **mı** hızlı* 'very fast'

11.1.1.6   *ya*

The clitic *ya* is non-harmonic and typically places stress on the syllable that precedes it, even if this syllable is otherwise unstressable (4.3.2.1). It has the following functions:

(i)   Contrastive adversative conjunction ('but') (28.3.4.5 (ii)):

>   *Gittim **ya** onu göremedim.* 'I went there but couldn't see her/him.'

This usage is colloquial, and occurs only where an affirmative sentence is followed by a negative one.

(ii) Repudiative discourse connective that occurs in sentence-final position (28.3.4.7):

Görmedim dedim ya! 'I told you I didn't see him/her!'

(iii) Reminding discourse connective that occurs in sentence-final position (28.3.12):

Hani sana göstermiştim ya, işte o elbise. 'Remember the dress I showed you? That one.'

(iv) For the stressable discourse connective *ya* that precedes a phrase and introduces alternatives or a speculative question, see 28.3.3.1 and 28.3.1.1 (vii):

Ya parası yoksa? 'What if s/he doesn't have any money?'

The clitic *ya*, which has a short vowel, should not be confused with the interjection *ya*, the contracted form of *yahu*, which has a long vowel.

11.2 CLASSIFICATION OF CLITICS BY RELATIVE POWER

Clitics vary in the degree of prominence, particularly height of pitch, which they produce in the affected syllable. From this aspect clitics fall into two classes, the first having a stronger effect:

I   *ki, mI* and *ya*
II   *bile, dA* (in its additive function, see 28.3.1.1 (iiia)) and *-(y)sA/ise*

11.2.1 COMBINATIONS OF CLITICS WITHIN THE INTONATIONAL PHRASE

If two clitics are present within the same intonational phrase (Chapter 5), only one of them retains its stress-generating force (for clitics which occur adjacently see 4.3.2.1):

(i) If both clitics are from the same class, the one which occurs earlier in the intonational phrase predominates. For semantic reasons, the only possible combination of this type involves *mI* and *ki*:

(1)   Tohumları soğukTA **mı** bırakmıştın **ki**?
       'Had you left the seeds in the cold, then?'

(ii) If the two clitics are from different classes, the one which belongs to class I predominates:

(2) Kağıtları **da** okuMUŞ **mu**?
'Has s/he read the papers too (i.e. in addition to doing other things)?'

(3) Çerçeveleri **bile** temizlemişSİN **ya**!
'But you have even cleaned the frames!'

11.2.2 THE COMBINATION OF CLITICS WITH THE NEGATIVE MARKER -mA

-*mA* usually generates stress, causing it to fall on the syllable preceding it (4.3.2.1). However, when it occurs in combination with one of the clitics *mI* (interrogative), *dA* (in its additive function, see 28.3.1.1 (iiia)) or *bile*, stress falls before whichever one occurs first in the sentence:

(4) Bu gözlükle sahneYİ **mi** göre**mi**yormuş?
'Can't s/he see the STAGE with these glasses?'

(5) Yeni öğrencilerini daha GÖRme**din mi**?
'Haven't you seen your new students yet?'

(6) BEN **de** iç**me**yeceğim.
'I'm not going to have [any] either.'

(7) Semra ücretini aLA**mamış bile**.
'Semra couldn't even [succeed in] getting her wages.'

The pre-stressing effect of *ki*, *ya* or adversative *dA* (28.3.4 (i)) in sentence-final position is strong enough to neutralize the pre-stressing effect of a preceding -*mA*. When -*mA* occurs with *ki* or *ya* stress falls on the syllable preceding *ki* or *ya*:

(8) Kimseyi görme**DİM ki**!
'But I didn't see anyone!'

This happens even if the syllable in question is otherwise unstressable (see 4.3.2):

(9) (Hani) eski gazeteleri at**mamış**TIM **ya** . . .
'Remember I hadn't thrown away the old newspapers? . . .'

PART 3
SYNTAX: THE STRUCTURE
OF SENTENCES

12 SIMPLE AND COMPLEX SENTENCES

From the structural point of view, sentences are either **simple** (i.e. contain only a main clause, as in (1)) or **complex** (i.e. contain a main clause and one or more subordinate clauses, as in (2)):

(1) Dün okullar açıldı.
    'The schools opened yesterday.'

(2) Dün [yolda giderken] [yıllardır görmediğim] bir arkadaşıma rastladım.
    'Yesterday, [as I was walking along the street], I ran into a friend [whom I hadn't seen for years].'

In this book we indicate **subordinate clauses** using '[ ]' (square brackets).

In 12.1 we discuss the main constituents of simple sentences, and in 12.2 we focus on the agreement between the subject and the predicate. The structure of complex sentences is summarized in 12.3, and different types of subordinate clauses are discussed in detail in Chapters 24–7. Sentences can also be classified functionally, as **statements**, **questions**, **volitional utterances** and **exclamations**. These are discussed in 12.4.

12.1 CONSTITUENTS OF A SENTENCE: SUBJECT AND PREDICATE

12.1.1 PREDICATE

The **predicate** expresses an event, a process or a state in which the **subject** is involved:

(3) Necla bir hafta içinde projeyi **bitirecek**.
    'Necla *will complete* the project within a week.'

(4) Bu çocuk **hasta**.
    'This child *is ill*.'

The predicate of a simple sentence, or of the main clause in a complex sentence, is described as **finite**. According to the type of predicate they have, sentences in Turkish are divided into two main groups, verbal sentences and nominal sentences.

12.1.1.1 Verbal sentences

These are sentences whose predicates are **finite verbs** (8.2 (i)):

(5) Bu gün evde **kal-a-ma-m**.
            stay-PSB-NEG.AOR-1SG
    'I *can't stay* at home today.'

For a detailed discussion of the properties of such sentences, see Chapter 13.

12.1.1.2 Nominal sentences

These are sentences whose predicate either does not contain an overt verb at all or whose verb is one of the forms of the **copula** (*ol-* 'be', 'become', 'exist' or *-(y)-* 'be'; see 8.3.1). This type of predicate is called a nominal predicate.

(6) Necla **öğretmen**.
    'Necla *is a teacher*.'

Non-modalized utterances with non-recurrent present time reference, such as (6), do not have an overt copula. Past tense (21.2.1) or evidential modality (21.4.3) can be indicated by **copular markers** (8.3.2):

(7) (**a**) Necla **öğretmen-*di***.
            teacher-P.COP
    'Necla *was a teacher*.'

    (**b**) Necla **ev-de-y*miş***.
            home-LOC-EV.COP
    '*Apparently* Necla *is/was at home*.'

For the expression of other types of tense, aspect and modality it is necessary to use the suppletive form *ol-* of the copula (12.1.1.3):

(8) Necla **öğretmen** *ol-acak-tı*.
            teacher be-FUT-P.COP
    'Necla *was going to be a teacher*.'

Turkish nominal sentences are of two kinds: **linking** and **existential**.

Linking sentences
These correspond to the pattern *x is y*, and contain the following:

(i)   a subject (if overtly expressed; see 12.1.2, 18.1.5)
(ii) a subject complement as (part of) the predicate
(iii) a copular marker (suffixed to, or immediately following, the subject complement). In present-tense sentences which are not aspectually or modally marked the copula has no overt expression. Person/number marking of the predicate is attached to the copular marker, if there is one, otherwise to the subject complement
(iv) (optionally) one or more adverbials.

(9) Ben   o sırada   öğretmen-di-m.
     SUBJECT   ADVERBIAL   SUBJECT.COMPLEMENT-COPULAR.
                               MARKER-PERSON. MARKER
                               (PREDICATE)
     I   at.that.time teacher-P.COP-1SG
     'I was a teacher at the time.'

The function of the **subject complement** is to provide some kind of description of the subject, such as identification, characterization, location, state of belonging, etc. The subject complement may be an adjectival, a noun phrase or a postpositional phrase. If a noun phrase, it may be marked for any grammatical case except the accusative case:

(10) **Biraz yorgun**dum.   (Adjectival)
     'I was *rather tired*.'

(11) Siz **çok iyi bir doktor**sunuz.   (Non-case-marked noun phrase)
     'You're *a very good doctor*.'

(12) Sözüm **sana**ydı.   (Dative-marked noun phrase)
     'My words were *for you*.'

(13) Herkes **ona karşı**ymış.   (Postpositional phrase)
     'Apparently, everyone is/was *against him/her*.'

Linking sentences are negativized by means of the expression *değil* 'not', which is placed between the subject complement and the copular marker:

(14) Dün ev-de **değil**-di-k.
         home-LOC not-P.COP-1PL
     'We were*n't* at home yesterday.'

For the various functions of *değil* see 20.2.

Existential sentences
Whereas linking sentences present, or assume knowledge of, a subject and relate some attribute or identification to it, existential sentences merely assert the existence or presence of a subject. The statement is usually made in relation to either (i) a location in time or space, or (ii) a possessor. There are thus two kinds of **existential sentence**: **locative** and **possessive**.

Locative existential sentences
These are of the type *there is an x (in y)* or *x has y*. The basic constituents of a locative existential sentence (listed in the order in which they occur) are:

(i) at least one adverbial of place or time
(ii) the subject (shown in bold below)
(iii) one of the two expressions *var* 'present/existent' and *yok* 'absent/non-existent'. (These can only be used in predicative function. For the usage of the copula *ol-* instead of *var/yok* see 12.1.1.3.)
(iv) a copular marker (as in linking sentences, not present in the case of present-tense sentences which are not marked for aspect or modality).
(v) 1st or 2nd person marking if required. (*Yok* but not *var* may also take a 3rd person plural marker.)

   (15) Buzdolabın-da **iki şişe bira** var.
        fridge-LOC two bottle beer existent
        'There are *two bottles of beer* in the fridge.'

   (16) O gün **ben** yok-tu-m.
        that day I non.existent-P.COP-1SG
        '*I* wasn't [there] on that day.'

When the expression indicating 'location' denotes persons or institutions, locative existential sentences express the concept *x has y*:

   (17) Ben-de **bir kitap** var.
        I-LOC
        'I have *a book*.'

If the subject of such a sentence is **definite/specific**, it may be topicalized (see 23.3.3) and thus placed at the beginning of the sentence:

   (18) **Bu kitap** bende var.
        'I have *this book*.'

Although close in meaning, locative existential sentences of the type *there is an x (in y)* cannot be used interchangeably with linking sentences (i.e. *x is y*) where the subject complement is a locative noun phrase:

(19) Banyoda MuRAT vardı.   (Locative existential sentence)
      'MURAT was in the bathroom.'

(20) Murat BANyodaydı.   (Linking sentence)
      'Murat was in the BATHROOM.'

The difference between these two is that (19) would be used in a situation where one wanted to indicate who the person in the bathroom was (hence 'Murat' is focused) whereas (20) would be used in a situation if one wanted to indicate Murat's whereabouts (hence 'bathroom' is focused). Note that the negative form of (20) can be expressed by either *değil* or *yok*; see 20.3 (36) for an example.

Possessive existential sentences
These express the concept *x has y*. Their basic constituents are:

(i)   a genitive-possessive construction (14.4) or a possessive-marked noun phrase, which is the subject (shown in bold in the examples below)
(ii) (optionally) one or more adverbials
(iii) *var* 'present/existent' or *yok* 'absent/non-existent'
(iv) a copular marker (not overtly expressed in the case of present-tense sentences which are not marked for aspect or modality).

The adverbials, if there are any, are generally placed before the possessive-marked noun phrase. They may either precede or follow the genitive-marked possessor constituent (if there is one):

(21) **Ayten-in** İstanbul'da **iki arkadaş-ı** var./İstanbul'da **Ayten-in iki arkadaş-ı** var.

      Ayten-GEN   two friend-3SG.POSS   Ayten-GEN two friend-3SG.POSS

      'Ayten has two friends in Istanbul.'

(22) O gün **paramız** yoktu.
      'We had no money that day.'

Note that the concept *x has y* can be expressed by both possessive existential sentences, as in (23), and locative existential sentences, as in (17):

(23) Benim bir kitabım var.
      'I have a book.'

Possessive existential sentences are used for expressing possession or relations between people and things which are either of a permanent nature or are considered as such. The possessed constituent in these constructions cannot be definite or specific. Possessive existential sentences are mainly used for expressing the following:

(i)   Familial and other personal relations, as in (21).

(ii)   Part-whole relations:

    (24) Masanın üç ayağı var.
           'The table has three legs.'

(iii) Authorship:

    (25) Shakespeare'in birçok oyunu var.
           'Shakespeare has [written] many plays.'

(iv)   Ownership:

    (26) Murat'ın yatı var.
           'Murat has a yacht.'

Locative existential sentences, on the other hand, denote contiguity between persons or things at a particular time:

    (27) Nejat'ta sadece 10 dolar varmış.
           'It seems Nejat only has 10 dollars [on him].'

The subject in these constructions can be definite or **non-definite**:

    (28) Murat'ta bu resim/bir resim var.
           'Murat has this/a picture.'

12.1.1.3   The complementarity of -(y)- and *var/yok* with *ol-*

The complementarity of -(y)- and *ol-*
When the concept *be* is expressed by the copula -(y)- (8.3.1, 8.3.2) this takes one of the following forms, with the meanings shown:

(i)   past tense, in which case the copular form -(y)DI is used (21.2.1 and 21.3.4.1)
(ii)   evidential modality, in which case -(y)mIş is used (21.4.3)
(iii) conditional modality, in which case -(y)sA is used (Chapter 27)

(It is also present in the non-finite form -(y)ken, see 26.2.3 (ii).)

(29) Buranın adı Koyundere-**ymiş**.
Koyundere-EV.COP
'*I am told* that this place *is* called Koyundere.'

In finite verbal predicates *-(y)-* appears after verbs inflected with position
3 suffixes (8.2.3) and does not always correspond to 'be' in English:

(30) Ahmet eve git-ti-**yse** . . .
go-PF-COND.COP
'If Ahmet has gone home . . .'

Note that *-(y)-* is omitted after a stem ending in a consonant:

(31) Bu bina eskiden okul**muş**.
'This building used to *be* a school.'

ol-, which is another form of the copula (8.3.1), is used in all other instances,
e.g. when a nominal predicate expresses:

(i)   Future tense (21.2.3):

(32) Bugün iş-te **ol-*acağ*-**ım.
today work-LOC be-FUT-1SG
'I *shall be* at work today.'

(ii)   Habitual aspect (21.3.2):

(33) Her gün iş-te **ol-*uyor*-**um.
every day work-LOC be-IMPF-1SG
'I *am* at work every day.'

(iii) Necessitative modality (21.4.2.2):

(34) Bugün iş-te **ol-*malı*-**ydı-m.
work-LOC be-OBLG-P.COP-1SG
'I *should* have *been* at work today.'

(iv)   Possibility (21.4.2.1):

(35) Bugün iş-te **ol-*abil*-**ir-di-m.
work-LOC be-PSB-AOR-P.COP-1SG
'I *could* have *been* at work today.'

(v)   Commitment (21.4.4.6)

(36)   Bugün iş-te **ol-*ur*-um**.
       work-LOC be-AOR-1SG
       'I *will be* at work today.'

It is also used to express the nominal predicates of subordinate clauses:

(37)   [bugün iş-te **ol-*an***] kadın
         work-LOC be-PART woman
       'the woman who *is/was* at work today.'

The complementarity of *var/yok* and *ol-*
In a way closely parallel to its function as a suppletive form of the copula
-(y)-, *ol-* is used (instead of *var/yok*) to produce future-tense and aspectually or modally marked existential predicates, as in:

(38)   Eskiden bütün otobüslerde biletçi **ol-*ur*-du**.   (Habitual aspect)
                               be-AOR-P.COP
       'There *used to be* a conductor on all the buses.'

(39)   Daha büyük bir arabamız **ol-*sa*** keşke.   (Volitional modality)
                         be-COND
       '*If only* we *had* a larger car.'

ol- is used instead of *var/yok* also in non-finite existential predicates:

(40)   [ev-de su **ol**-ma-dığ-ı zaman] (cf. Evde su **yok**.)
       house-LOC water exist-NEG-CV-3SG.POSS time
       'when there *is*n't any water in the house'

(41)   [bahçe-si **ol**-an] ev (cf. Evin bahçesi **var**.)
       garden-3SG.POSS exist-PART house
       'the house that *has* a garden'

For further discussion of aspectual distinctions in nominal sentences,
including the use of *ol-* to express *become*, see 21.3.4. *Ol-* is also used as an
auxiliary verb in compound verb forms (13.3.1.2).

12.1.2   EXPRESSION OF THE SUBJECT

In Turkish the subject is not always overtly expressed within the sentence.
Sentences without an overtly expressed subject, and the conditions under
which these occur, are discussed in 18.1.5.

If the subject is expressed, this is always by some kind of **noun phrase** (Chapter 14), which can be simple, such as a single pronoun as in (42), or a noun modified by determiners, numerals and/or adjectives as in (43):

(42) **Ben** o adamı sevmiyorum.
'*I* don't like that man.'

(43) Her yıl bu kentte **iki bin beş yüz yeni bina** yapılıyor.
'Every year *two thousand five hundred new buildings* are constructed in this town.'

It can also be complex, i.e. a noun clause (Chapter 24):

(44) [**Jale'nin işten çıkartıldığı**] doğru değilmiş.
'Apparently it's not true [*that Jale has been dismissed from her job*].'

The subject of a simple sentence or main clause is always in the non-case-marked form. Subjects of certain kinds of relative clauses and of most noun clauses, on the other hand, receive genitive case marking (see Chapters 24–25).

For the factors determining the position of the subject in the sentence, see 23.2–3.

12.2   AGREEMENT OF SUBJECT AND PREDICATE

The predicate shows agreement with the subject in terms of person and number.

12.2.1   PERSON AND NUMBER MARKING ON THE PREDICATE

First and second persons
In all sentences which have a 1st or 2nd person subject, the addition of the appropriate person suffix (see 8.4) to the predicate is obligatory whether or not the subject is separately represented in the sentence by a pronoun. (The only exception to this is sentences which have pronominalized determiners as subjects; see 12.2.2.3 (72), (75)–(76).)

(45) (Ben) yorgun-**um**.
(I)   tired-1SG
'I'm tired.'

(46) (Siz) yeni komşularımızla tanıştı**nız** mı?
'Have you met our new neighbours?'

(See also 12.2.3 (88) for 1st and 2nd person marking on the predicate with sentences which have pronouns as subject complements.)

Third person singular

Turkish does not have overt marking of the 3rd person singular on predicates:

(47) Annem yorgun.
'My mother's tired.'

(48) Ahmet hiçbir şey yapmadı.
'Ahmet hasn't done anything at all.'

The only exception is the imperative/optative, where the 3rd person singular is marked by -*sIn*:

(49) Öğleden sonra bize gel**sin**.
'Let him/her come round to us this afternoon.'

Where a 3rd person singular subject is a person or thing that the speaker assumes can be unambiguously identified by the hearer (either through previous mention or because of the shared experience of the speech situation), it is the *absence* of any person markers on the predicate that indicates the 3rd person singular identity of this subject:

(50) A.– Annen nasıl?
'How's your mother?'

B.– Yorgun.
'(She's) tired.'

Where the subject is overtly expressed by a noun phrase denoting a collectivity of human beings, such as *aile* 'family' or *halk* 'people', this predicate does not have plural person marking.

(51) **Anadolu halkı** denizden çok dağları bilir.
'*The people of Anatolia* are more familiar with mountains than with the sea.'

A sentence which has an explicitly singular 3rd person human subject may be given a plural-marked predicate if the speaker wishes to express deference towards that individual.

(52) Selim Bey evde**ler** mi acaba?
'Is Selim Bey at home, I wonder?'

Third person plural
Where a 3rd person plural subject is not expressed by an overt noun phrase, and the referents are animate, plural marking of the predicate is *obligatory*:

(53) Bodrum'a gitti**ler**.
'They've gone to Bodrum.'

(54) Dün çok yorgundu**lar**.
'Yesterday they were very tired.'

In most cases where the subject is overtly expressed by a noun phrase containing a numeral modifier, the predicate does *not* take plural marking:

(55) Bu sınıfta **elli iki öğrenci** var.
'There are *fifty-two pupils* in this class.'

(56) Dün **otuz üç mektup** geldi.
'Yesterday *thirty-three letters* came.'

However, where the subject noun phrase is the head of a partitive construction (14.5), refers to human beings, and is situated at some distance from the verb, plural marking of the verb may occur:

(57) {Yarışmacılar arasından **iki üç kişi**}, jürinin ısrarına rağmen yaşlarını söylememiş(ler).
'{**Two or three** of the competitors}, despite insistent requests from the judges, have apparently not stated their ages.'

In other contexts, the use of a non-case-marked noun phrase containing a numeral modifier in a sentence with a plural-marked verb is usually adverbial (equivalent to a phrase with *olarak* see 16.1.9 (iib)), indicating that the action denoted by the verb is/was performed as a group:

(58) **İki kızkardeş** seyahate gittiler.
'They went on holiday, *[just] two sisters [together]*.'

12.2.2 AGREEMENT OF THE PREDICATE WITH DIFFERENT TYPES OF PLURAL SUBJECT

12.2.2.1 Subject marked with the plural suffix

In a sentence where the subject is overtly expressed by a plural-marked noun phrase, the 3rd person plural marker is often omitted from the predicate. The regularity with which this happens differs according to whether the entities referred to by the subject are human or non-human, and whether they are specific or non-specific.

(i) Specific human subjects:
In the case of specific human subjects, plural marking of the predicate is optional but common. It draws attention to the distinctness of the individuals constituting the set which is referred to, and may imply that the participation of each one in the action or state described by the predicate is not identical but in some way individuated. If the predicate in such a sentence is not given plural marking, the implication is that the speaker is more interested in the event or state as a whole than in the internal make-up of the group of individuals involved. (59) and (60) illustrate the optionality of plural marking of the predicate in sentences with an overtly expressed, specific and plural-marked human subject.

(59) **Bazı arkadaşlarımız** bu fikre katılmadı(**lar**).
'*Some of our colleagues* didn't agree with this idea.'

(60) **Senin çocuklar** burada değil(**ler**).
'*Your children* are not here.'

Where the idea of individuated action by the participants is inherent in the meaning of the predicate, plural marking of the predicate is more or less obligatory:

(61) **Öğrenciler** sürekli aralarında konuşuyorlardı.
'*The students* were talking among themselves all the time.'

(ii) Specific animal subjects:
In the case of specific animal subjects, use or non-use of plural marking on the predicate depends on the speaker's attitude to animals. If s/he views them as broadly comparable to human beings in terms of having individual identity, then plural marking of the predicate is possible:

(62) **Köpekler** geceleri hep havlar(**lar**)dı.
'At night *the dogs* would always bark.'

(iii) Specific inanimate subjects:
As for sentences with specific inanimate subjects, plural marking of the predicate is usual here in the case of entities seen as moving or acting through a force that is in some way inherent to them:

(63) **Ağaçlar** artık yapraklarını döküyordu/döküyorlardı.
'By now *the trees* were shedding their leaves.'

(64) **Arabalar** çok hızlı geçiyordu/geçiyor**lardı**.
'*The cars* were speeding past.'

Otherwise, where the sentence expresses a situation in which the role of the inanimate plural-marked subject is not an *active* one, plural marking, although not usual, is sometimes encountered:

(65) **Buradaki odalar** banyoluymuş.
'Apparently *the rooms here* have ensuite facilities.'

(66) **Anahtarlar** buraya bırakılıyor.
'*The keys* are left here.'

(iv) Indefinite subjects:
Even if human, animate or quasi-animate, a plural-marked subject which is indefinite, as in (67a), does not trigger plural marking on the predicate:

(67) Bu resimleri **çocuklar** yapmış.
(**a**) '*Children* painted these pictures.'
(**b**) '*The children* painted these pictures.'

Sentences with plural-marked subjects and no plural marking on the predicate can be ambiguous, as (67) illustrates. The addition of plural marking to the predicate, however, indicates unambiguously the *definite* status of the subject:

(68) Bu resimleri **çocuklar** yapmış**lar**.
'*The children* painted these pictures.'

12.2.2.2 Subjects containing determiners

Where the subject noun phrase contains one of the determiners that occur with non-plural-marked noun phrases, such as *birkaç* 'a few', 'several', *birçok* 'many', *kaç* 'how many' and *her* 'every' (15.6.1 (ii)), the predicate is not plural marked:

(69) **Birçok kişi** çocukluğunu pek düşünmez.
'*Many people* don't think much about their childhood.'

12.2.2.3 Pronominalized determiners as subjects

When the subject is a pronominalized determiner (18.4 (iv)), such as *hiçbirimiz* 'none of us', *bazılarınız* 'some of you', *hangileri* 'which of them', 'which (ones)' or one of the pronominalized forms derived from the adverb *hep*

(18.4 (v)) such as *hepimiz* 'all of us', marking of the predicate with the appropriate person suffix may or may not be obligatory, depending on the quantified pronoun.

(i) *Hepimiz/hepiniz/hepsi* ('all of us/you/them'):
With the 1st and 2nd person forms of these quantified pronouns referring to all-inclusive groups, person marking is obligatory in both nominal and verbal predicates:

> (70) **Hepimiz** tatilde deniz kıyısına gidiyor**uz**.
> '*All of us* go to the seaside in the vacation.'

The 3rd person form is most commonly used without a person marker, but it may also be used with a 3rd person plural marker:

> (71) Oyuncuların **hepsi** yeni kostümler istiyor(**lar**).
> '*All the actors* want new costumes.'

(ii) *Hiçbirimiz/hiçbiriniz/hiçbiri* ('none of us/you/them'):
Where the 1st or 2nd person form of this pronoun occurs as subject, 1st or 2nd person marking of a verbal predicate is optional:

> (72) **Hiçbirimiz** bugün sokağa çıkmadı(**k**).
> '*None of us* went out today.'

Most speakers, however, regularly add person marking to nominal predicates:

> (73) Neden **hiçbiriniz** evde değil**siniz**?
> 'Why are *none of you* at home today?'

With the 3rd person form *hiçbiri* 'none of them', the predicate is never plural marked:

> (74) **Hiçbiri** gelmeyecek.
> 'None of them is going to come.'

(iii) *Bazı(ları)mız/bazı(ları)nız/bazısı/bazıları/kimimiz/kiminiz/kimisi/kimileri* ('some of us/you/them'):
With the 1st or 2nd person forms of these pronouns, person marking is optional on both verbal and nominal predicates:

> (75) **Bazılarımız** bu konudan hoşlanmıyor(**uz**).
> '*Some of us* don't like this topic.'

(76) **Kiminiz** burada değildi(**niz**).
'*Some of you* weren't here.'

With the 3rd person forms *bazısı, bazıları/kimisi/kimileri* 'some of them', the preferred form is for the predicate not to have plural marking:

(77) **Bazıları** evde yoktu.
'Some of them weren't at home.'

12.2.2.4   Conjoined subjects

Where a pair or series of conjoined subjects includes *ben* 'I' or *biz* 'we', the predicate is marked for 1st person plural:

(78) **Arkadaşlarımla ben** bu akşam dışarı çıkmıyor**uz**.
'*My friends and I* aren't going out tonight.'

Where a pair or series of conjoined subjects includes *sen/siz* 'you' and excludes *ben* 'I' or *biz* 'we', the predicate is marked for 2nd person plural:

(79) **Sen ve arkadaşların** Almanya'ya hangi yıl gitti**niz**?
'What year did *you and your friends* go to Germany?'

Where a group of conjoined subjects includes both a 1st person pronoun and a 2nd person pronoun, the tendency is for the 1st person pronoun to be the last in the series of conjoined subjects:

(80) **Ya Ahmet ya siz ya da ben** hazırlıklara gönüllü katılmalıyız.
'*Either Ahmet or you or I* must volunteer for the preparations.'

When both or all in a series of conjoined subjects are 3rd person, the predicate may or may not have plural marking, according to the principles explained in 12.2.2.1.

(**i**)   Subjects conjoined by the conjunctions *ve* 'and' (28.3.1.1 (i)), *veya* 'or', *ya da* 'or', *ya . . . ya* 'either . . . or' (28.3.3.1), *hem . . . hem, gerek . . . gerek* 'both . . . and', *dA . . . dA* 'both . . . and' (28.3.2), *ne . . . ne* 'neither . . . nor' (20.4)

These subjects can be in any order among themselves:

(81) **Ne Ayşe ne ben** yalandan hoşlanmıyoruz.
'*Neither Ayşe nor I* like lying.'

(82) **Sen *ya da* Ahmet,** bugün oraya gidip bu işi bitirin.
'*You or Ahmet* should go there and finish it off today.'

(ii)   Subjects conjoined with *-(y)lA/ile* 'and':
-(y)lA/ile is a common means of joining two noun phrases (8.1.4, 28.3.1.1 (ii)):

(83) **Annemle babam** üniversitede tanışmış(**lar**).
'*My mother and father* met at university.'

(84) **Bulaşıkla çamaşır** mutlaka birer makine ister.
'*Dish washing and laundry* definitely each require a machine.'

If one of the items conjoined by *-(y)lA/ile* is a personal pronoun, it usually occurs as the second item. Since the person marker on the predicate indicates this person, this pronoun may be omitted (see also 18.1.5):

(85) **Ahmet'le (ben)** dün deniz kenarında yürüyüş yaptık.
'Yesterday *Ahmet and I* went for a walk on the seashore.'

Note, however, that sentences where the pronoun of a conjoined subject is deleted may be ambiguous. Since the predicate of such a sentence has plural marking (in the case of the 1st and 2nd persons and in the case of the 3rd person, when it has plural marking) it may be unclear whether the 'hidden' pronoun is singular or plural:

(86) **Ahmet'le** dün deniz kenarında yürüyüş yaptı**k**.
   (**a**) 'Yesterday *Ahmet and I* went for a walk on the seashore.'
   (**b**) Yesterday *we and Ahmet* went for a walk on the seashore.'

Note also that *-(y)lA/ile* functions as a conjunction only when it is between the two items it conjoins. Otherwise it functions as a postposition:

(87) **Ben Ahmet'le** dün deniz kenarında yürüyüş yaptı**m**.
'Yesterday I went *with Ahmet* for a walk on the seashore.'

In such a case the constituent bearing *-(y)lA/ile* is not part of the subject, but forms with the comitative marker an adverbial of manner (16.4.3 (iv)); hence the predicate in (87) has 1st person singular marking because of its agreement with *ben* 'I'. For the postpositional function of *-(y)lA/ile* see 17.3.1.3 (v) and 13.2.3.2. For the inclusive nature of *-(y)lA/ile*, see 28.3.1.1 (ii).

12.2.3   PERSONAL PRONOUNS AS SUBJECT COMPLEMENTS

When the subject complement of a linking sentence is a personal pronoun, the person marker agrees with this pronoun rather than with the subject:

(88) Ayşe **ben-im**.
Ayşe I-1SG
'*I am* Ayşe.'

Note that (88) is a sentence where the subject complement and the subject of a regular linking sentence such as (89) are swapped:

(89) Ben Ayşe-yim.
I Ayşe-1SG
'I am Ayşe.'

This kind of reversal can occur only where the subject complement (*Ayşe* in (89)) is a non-case-marked noun phrase.

There is an important difference in the meaning of these sentences (rendered by the position of sentence stress in English) in that (88) corresponds to '*I* am Ayşe' (i.e. a response to the question *Who is Ayşe?*) whereas (89) corresponds to 'I am *Ayşe*' (i.e. a response to the question *Who are you?*).

12.3 COMPLEX SENTENCES AND SUBORDINATION

Complex sentences contain at least one subordinate clause in addition to a main clause. Structurally, the predicate of a subordinate clause can be **finite** (i.e. identical in form to a main clause):

(90) [Maç birazdan **başla-yacak**] de-n-iyor.
match soon start-FUT say-PASS-1MPF
'It is said [that the match *will be starting* soon].'

(91) [Çocuğun babası **kim**] bilinmiyor.
'It's not known [*who* the father of the child *is*].'
(lit. '[Who is the father of the child] is not known.')

But the majority of subordinate clauses are **non-finite** (i.e. contain a verbal predicate with one of the subordinating suffixes in 8.5):

(92) [Maç-ın birazdan **başla-*yacağ*-ı**] söyleniyor.
match-GEN soon start-SUB-3SG.POSS
'It is said [*that* the match *will be starting* soon].'

(93) [Maç **başla-*yınca***] herkes ayağa fırladı.
match start-SUB
'[*When* the match *started*] everyone jumped to their feet.'

(94) [Maç-ı **izle-*yen***] kişiler yağmurdan sırılsıklam olmuşlar.
match-ACC watch-SUB
'The people [*who watched* the match] got soaked.'

A finite subordinate clause can be directly connected to the superordinate clause (as in (90) and (91)), or it can be linked to the superordinate clause by means of a subordinator (e.g. *diye*):

(95) [Maç birazdan **başlayacak**] *diye* biliyorduk.
'We thought [(*that*) the match *would be starting* soon].'

The subordinators that link finite clauses to superordinate clauses are the following: *diye* (24.3.1 and 26.1.1), *ki* (24.3.2 and 26.1.2), *madem (ki)* (26.1.3), *nasıl (ki)* (26.1.4), *mI* (26.1.6 and 27.6.2), the clitic *dA* (26.1.7) and some other obsolescent subordinators containing *ki*, such as ∇*ola ki*, ∇*meğer ki*, ∇*kim ki*, ∇*ne zaman ki*. The Persian-derived subordinator *ki* stands at the beginning of its clause, in the manner of Indo-European subordinators such as its French and Italian cognates *que*, *che*.

Subordinate clauses have three different functions:

(i) **noun clauses** function as subjects or objects
(ii) **relative clauses** function as adjectival phrases
(iii) **adverbial clauses** function as adverbials

These clauses are discussed in detail in Chapters 24–7.

The clause within which a subordinate clause occurs is called the **superordinate clause**. The superordinate clause may either be the main clause of the sentence or another subordinate clause. In the examples below the superordinate clauses are shown in bold italics. The superordinate clause is a main clause in (96) (where the subordinate clause is an adverbial clause), a relative clause in (97) (where the subordinate clause is a noun clause) and a noun clause in (98) (where the subordinate clause is an adverbial clause):

(96) *Füsun bu kitap-lar-ı* [öğretmenlik yap-ar-**ken**] *kullan-mış-tı*.
Füsun this book-PL-ACC teaching do-AOR-SUB use-PF-P.COP
'*Füsun used these books* [*when* she was work*ing* as a teacher].'

(97) [*Füsun-un bu kitap-lar-ı kullan-dığ-ın*]*-ı duy-an* kişiler
Füsun-GEN this book-PL-ACC use-SUB-3SG.POSS-ACC hear-SUB people
'the people *who heard [that Füsun was using these books]*'

(98) *Füsun'un* [kullan-ıl-mı-yor **diye**] *kitap-lar-ı sat-ma-sı*
Füsun-GEN use-PASS-NEG-IMPF SUB book-PL-ACC sell-SUB-3SG.POSS
'*Füsun's selling the books* [on the grounds that they were not being used]'

Note that a clause which contains *ki* can only be subordinate to a main clause.

12.4   FUNCTIONAL SENTENCE TYPES

Sentences can be classified functionally, that is according to the type of utterance that they express. The four major types of utterance are statements, questions, volitional utterances and exclamations, all of which can be expressed by both verbal and nominal sentences.

(i)   Statements:

> (99)   Köyde Bayram'ın ailesi zengin sayılıyormuş.
> 'In the village Bayram's family is apparently considered rich.'

> (100)   Bayram'ın ailesinin diğer köylülerden daha çok toprağı var.
> 'Bayram's family has more land than the other villagers.'

(ii)   Questions:
What marks a sentence as a question is the presence either of the interrogative clitic *mI* or of a **wh-phrase** such as *ne zaman* 'when' or *kaç* 'how many'. For a full discussion of how questions are expressed in Turkish see Chapter 19.

(iii)   Volitional utterances:
These are utterances which express the speaker's attitude towards the possible performance of an action or the occurrence of an event. The most common types include commands, suggestions and wishes (21.4.4).

> (101)   Saat ikiden sonra beni telefonla ara.   (Imperative)
> 'Ring me after two o'clock.'

> (102)   Bu akşam dışarda yiyelim.   (Optative)
> 'Let's eat out this evening.'

> (103)   Çabuk bitirseler bari.   (Conditional with optative meaning)
> 'I hope at least they finish quickly.'

(iv)   Exclamations:
Exclamations often contain a wh-phrase, such as (19.2): *ne* 'what', *ne kadar* 'how (much)', *nasıl* 'how', or *ne biçim* 'what kind (of)'. Exclamations of this kind have the intonation pattern of statements, and are thus distinguishable from questions (5.1).

(104) Burası **ne _güzel_** bir yer!
'*What* a *beautiful* place this is!'

(105) Ay **nasıl** güldük!
'Oh, *how* we laughed!'

Exclamations can also be expressed with *o kadar/öyle(sine)* ... *ki* 'so' (26.1.2.3) or *pek* (*de*):

(106) Su **o kadar** soğuktu **ki!**
'The water was *so* cold!'

(107) Çocuğu **öylesine** seviyor **ki** ...
'S/he loves the child *so much* ...'

(108) **Pek de** tatlı bir oğlunuz varmış!
'*What a* sweet son you have!'

13   THE VERB PHRASE

A verb phrase consists of a **verb**, its **complements**, and **adverbials** that modify the verb. At its simplest, a verb phrase consists of an (inflected) verb alone:

(1)   **Otur**uyorum.
      'I am *sitting down*.'

(2) shows a verb phrase consisting of a verb and an adverbial:

(2)   **Yavaş yürü**.
      '*Walk slowly*.'

(3) shows a phrase consisting of a verb, its complement (the direct object *suyu* 'water') and three adverbials (*yavaşça* 'slowly', *sürahiden* 'from the jug', *masadaki bardağa* 'into the glass on the table'):

(3)   **Suyu yavaşça sürahiden masadaki bardağa dök**tü.
      'S/he *slowly poured the water from the jug into the glass*.'

Both main clauses (4) and subordinate clauses (bracketed section in (5)) contain verb phrases. Most examples in this chapter are sentences consisting of only one (main) clause.

(4)   Ahmet **çay-ı bardak-tan iç**-ecek.
      Ahmet tea-ACC glass-ABL drink-FUT
      'Ahmet will *drink the tea* from a glass.'

(5)   [Ahmet-in **çay-ı bardak-tan iç**-me]-si gerek-iyor-du.
      Ahmet-GEN tea-ACC glass-ABL drink-VN-3SG.POSS be.necessary-
      IMPF-P.COP
      'Ahmet was supposed to *drink the tea from a glass*.'

Types of verb and the constituents of the verb phrase are discussed in 13.1. In 13.2 we describe the structure of verb phrases which have causative, passive, reflexive and reciprocal verbs, and in 13.3 we discuss auxiliary verbs.

Other elements that are associated with verb phrases are discussed elsewhere, namely negation in Chapter 20 and tense, aspect and modality in Chapter 21. The ordering of verbal inflectional suffixes is discussed in 8.2 (see also 6.3). The majority of sentences in this chapter have the unmarked word order *subject-object-verb*; see Chapter 23 for variations in word order.

13.1 CONSTITUENTS OF THE VERB PHRASE

13.1.1 THE VERB

The internal structure of a verb phrase depends primarily on the transitivity or intransitivity of the verb. This distinction relates to the ability of a verb to take a direct object. Verbs which cannot take direct objects (see 13.1.2.1) such as *git-* 'go', *düş-* 'fall', *otur-* 'sit', *kork-* 'be afraid (of)', *sevin-* 'be happy (about)' are **intransitive**:

(6) Londra'ya gidelim.
     'Let's go to London.'

(7) Ayşe çok hızlı koşuyordu.
     'Ayşe was running very fast.'

Verbs such as as *ye-* 'eat', *gör-* 'see', *yaz-* 'write', *boya-* 'paint', on the other hand, have direct objects (bold in the examples below), and are thus **transitive**:

(8) Erol **duvar-lar-ı** yanlışlıkla boyamış.
         wall-PL-ACC
     'Apparently Erol painted *the walls* by mistake.'

(9) Bugün sınıfta **çok önemli konular** işledik.
     'Today in class we covered [some] *very important topics*.'

However, there is a group of intransitive verbs that can also be used transitively. These are verbs of motion such as *yüz-* 'swim', *koş-* 'run' and *yürü-* 'walk', and they may take direct objects expressing distances:

(10) Normal bir koşucu **100 metre-lik bir mesafe-yi** 20 saniyenin
                             100 metre-ADJ a distance-ACC
     altında koşabilir.
     'An ordinary athlete can run *a distance of 100 metres* in under twenty seconds.'

In the majority of cases, the direct object and the adverbials in a verb phrase can be omitted if they are recoverable from the context. For example, the verb *işle-* 'cover (a topic)' can appear without its direct object in a context such as the one below (see also 28.4.3):

(11) A.– Bugün sınıfta **önemli konular** işlediniz mi?
'Did you cover *important topics* in class today?'

B.– İşledik.
'[Yes,] we did.'

13.1.2 COMPLEMENTS OF THE VERB

In a verb phrase, a **complement** is a constituent that 'completes' the meaning of the verb, and that stands in a particular structural relationship to it. The complement of a verb is always a noun phrase, which can be simple or complex (Chapters 14 and 24). It represents the person(s) or thing(s) – other than the subject – affected by the action of the verb. Some verbs (e.g. *gül-* 'laugh' or *yüz-* 'swim') have meanings which are complete in themselves and do not have any kind of complement. Other verbs, such as *yık-* 'destroy', *anla-* 'understand', *kork-* 'fear', denote actions or states which require complements. There are two types of complement, **direct objects** and **oblique objects**.

13.1.2.1 Direct object

A direct object denotes a person or thing which is brought into being, or to which something is done, by the action of the subject. In Turkish the noun phrase which constitutes the direct object is usually non-case-marked if non-definite (i.e. indefinite or categorial, see 22.2 and 22.3), but if definite it has the accusative case marker *-(y)I*.

Indefinite direct object:

(12) **Bir mektup** yaz-dı-m.
a letter write-PF-1SG
'I wrote *a letter*.'

Categorial direct object:

(13) Yaz-lar-ı açık hava sinema-sın-da **film** seyr-ed-er-ler-di.
summer-PL-NC open air cinema-NC-LOC film watch-AUX-AOR-
3PL-P.COP
'They used to watch *films* in outdoor cinemas in the summer.'

Definite direct object:

(14) **Bu parça-yı** ancak çok iyi bir piyanist çal-abil-ir.
this piece-ACC only very good a pianist play-PSB-AOR
'Only a very good pianist can play *this piece*.'

13.1.2.2 Oblique object

Oblique objects denote persons or things which are not directly affected by the action of the verb but which are an integral part of its meaning. They have one of the dative, locative, ablative or comitative/instrumental markers. They occur with intransitive verbs especially with those which express emotion, such as *hoşlan-* 'like', 'fancy', *kork-* 'fear', *sevin-* 'be happy (about)', *üzül-* 'be sad (about)' and *kız-* 'be angry (about/with)'. Which particular case marker appears on the complement noun phrase is determined by the verb.

Dative-marked oblique object
Verbs such as *inan-* 'believe', *güven-* 'trust', *acı-* 'feel sorry (for)', *sevin-* 'be pleased (about)', *üzül-* 'be sad (about)', *kız-* 'be angry (about/with)', *kıy-* 'be merciless (towards)', *bayıl-* 'adore', *tap-* 'worship', and compound verbs such as *razı ol-* 'agree (to)', ↓*gıcık ol-/*↓*kıl ol-* 'be irritated (by)' (slang), *boyun eğ-* 'submit (to)', *sıkıl-* 'be upset (by)' and *uy-* 'match', 'comply (with)' take complements with dative case marking:

(15) Herkes **piyanist-*e*** bayıl-dı.
pianist-DAT adore-PF
'Everyone adored *the pianist*.'

(16) Bazı insanlar [**tatsızlık çıkar-may**]-*a* bayıl-ıyor.
conflict create-VN-DAT love-IMPF
'Some people love [*creating conflicts*].'

Locative-marked oblique object
Verbs such as *karar kıl-* 'decide (on)', *kusur et-* 'fail (in)', *diret-* 'insist (on)', *ısrar et-* 'insist (on)' take complements in the locative case:

(17) Kocası **evin rengin*de*** ısrar ediyor.
'Her husband is being insistent *about the colour of the house*.'

(18) Çocuk [**okul-a git-me-mek**]-*te* diret-iyor.
school-DAT go-NEG-VN-LOC insist-IMPF
'The child insists *on [not going to school]*.'

Ablative-marked oblique object

Verbs such as *hoşlan-* 'like', 'fancy', *iğren-* 'be disgusted (by)', *soğu-* 'lose one's love (for)', *bık-* 'get fed up (with)', *sıkıl-* 'get bored (with)', *faydalan-* 'take advantage (of)', 'benefit (from)', *kork-* 'be afraid (of)', *şüphelen-* 'suspect', *vazgeç-* 'give up' and some compound verbs such as *nefret et-* 'hate', *memnun kal-* 'be happy (with)' take complements in the ablative case:

(19) Nermin kazadan sonra **evinden** soğudu.
'After the accident, Nermin became apprehensive *about* [living in] *her house.*'

(20) Nermin bir gün geldi ki [**yemek yap-mak**]-*tan* bık-tı.
food-make-VN-ABL be.fed.up.-PF
'The day came when Nermin got fed up *with* [*cooking*].'

Comitative/instrumental-marked oblique object

Verbs such as ↓*dalga geç-* 'make fun (of)', *ilgilen-* 'show an interest (in)', *alay et-* 'make fun (of)' take complements which have the comitative/instrumental marker:

(21) Serap **kızkardeşiyle** hep dalga geçiyor.
'Serap always makes fun *of her sister.*'

(22) Erol **sinema-yla** çok ilgilen-iyor-du.
cinema-COM/INS very be.interested-IMPF-P.COP
'Erol was very interested in films.'

The oblique objects of some verbs are not uniquely associated with a single case suffix. For example, if the complement of the verb *utan-* 'be ashamed/embarrassed' is simple, it has ablative case marking, but if it is a clause (24.4.1.3), it can have either ablative or dative marking:

(23) Erol o kadar utangaç ki **doktordan** bile utanıyor.
'Erol is so shy that he is even embarrassed [to be seen] *by the doctor.*'

(24) . . . [**konuş-mak**]-*tan*/. . . [**konuş-may**]-*a* bile utanıyor.
speak-VN-ABL   speak-VN-DAT
'. . . that he is even embarrassed *to speak.*'

Some verbs which take oblique objects also have direct objects, such as *mahkum et-* 'sentence (to)', 'condemn (to)', *it-* 'lead (into)', *sürükle-* 'drag (into)', *zorla-* 'force (to/into)'. The oblique objects of these verbs are either abstract nouns or clauses formed with *-mAK* (24.4.1.3).

> (25) Allahtan **kimse-yi ölüm-e** mahkum etmediler.
>   no.one-ACC death-DAT
>   'Luckily they didn't condemn anyone to death.'

(See (35) in Chapter 23 for another example.)

13.1.3 ADVERBIALS

The adverbials in a verb phrase modify the verb by describing:

(i)   Its destination or target (indicated by the dative case marker):

araba-ya (*git-*)	'(go) to the car'
ayna-ya (*bak-*)	'(look) in the mirror'
oğlan-a (*paket-i ver-*)	'(give the package) to the boy'

(ii)   Its location (indicated by the locative case marker):

kanape-de (*uyu-*)	'(sleep) on the sofa'
biz-de (*kal-*)	'(stay) at our place'
durak-ta (*otobüs bekle-*)	'(wait for a bus) at the bus stop'

(iii) The source of the action or the space through which an action takes place (indicated by the ablative case marker):

büro-dan (*kağıtlar-ı al-*)	'(take the papers) from the office'
mutfak-tan (*yemeğ-i getir-*)	'(bring the food) from the kitchen'
evlerin üstün-den (*geç-*)	'(pass) over the houses'

(iv)   The manner in which the action takes place indicated by:

the comitative/instrumental marker

bıçak-la (*ekmek kes-*)	'(cut bread) with a knife'

a simple adverb

yavaş (*yürü-*)	'(walk) slowly'

a derived adverb

korkak-ça (*kaç-*)	'(run away) in a cowardly fashion'

an adjective used adverbially

güzel (*oku-*)   '(study) well'

For a full discussion of adverbials see Chapter 16.

13.2 TRANSITIVITY AND VOICE

In many instances where English has unrelated stems for transitive and intransitive pairs (e.g. *drop* and *fall*), or identical verbs with transitive and intransitive meaning (e.g. *change* (something) and *change* (in the sense of *go through a change*)), Turkish uses **voice suffix**es to alter the transitivity of a verb. There are four voice suffixes in Turkish (8.2.1): the **causative**, the **passive**, the **reflexive** and the **reciprocal**. In the overwhelming majority of cases the final suffix of a verb derived in this fashion automatically indicates the transitivity or intransitivity of a stem. Almost all verb stems ending in the passive, reflexive or reciprocal suffixes *-Il*, *-(I)n*, *-(I)ş*, or the composite suffixes *-lAn* or *-lAş*, are intransitive (see 7.2.1.2 for exceptions), and verb stems ending in the causative suffix (*-DIr*, *-t*, *-It*, *-Ir*, *-Ar*, *-Art*) or the composite suffix *-lAt* are transitive.

Transitivizing an intransitive verb by attaching the causative suffix (8.2.1.1):

değiş- 'change'	*değiş-tir-* 'change (s.t.)'
uğraş- 'be busy (with)'	*uğraş-tır-* 'preoccupy'
yürü- 'walk'	*yürü-t-* 'make (s.o.) walk'
ürk- 'be scared (of)'	*ürk-üt-* 'scare'
düş- 'fall'	*düş-ür-* 'drop'
çık- 'go/come out'	*çık-ar-* 'remove, get (s.t.) out'

Intransitivizing a transitive verb by attaching the passive (8.2.1.2) or reflexive suffix (8.2.1.3):

yık- 'destroy'	*yık-ıl-* 'fall apart', 'be destroyed'
eğ- 'bend (s.t.)'	*eğ-il-* 'bend over'
sakla- 'hide (s.t.)'	*sakla-n-* 'hide'
yıka- 'wash'	*yıka-n-* 'be washed', 'get washed', 'have a bath/shower'
ört- 'cover'	*ört-ün-* 'cover oneself'

Voice suffixes alter the function of the major constituents in a sentence, as explained below.

13.2.1   CAUSATIVE CONSTRUCTIONS

The causative suffix (i.e. one of the forms *-DIr*, *-t*, *-It*, *-Ir*, *-Ar*, *-Art*, see 8.2.1.1) can attach to transitive and intransitive verbs.

(i)   When it attaches to a transitive verb, it expresses the concepts 'cause', 'make', 'have', and, in negative environments or with reference to involuntary acts, 'let', 'allow' or 'be unable to prevent':

(26)   Her gün camlar-ı sil-**dir**-iyor-lar.
       every day windows-ACC wipe-CAUS-IMPF-3PL
       'They *have* the windows cleaned every day.'

(27)   Ev-i çoktandır boya-**t**-ma-dı-k.
       house-ACC for.a.long.time paint-CAUS-NEG-PF-1PL
       'We haven't *had* the house painted for a long time.'

In a causative construction based on a transitive verb (e.g. *aç-* 'open'), the performer of the action denoted by this verb (the **causee**) can be expressed by a dative-marked noun phrase. The causee is usually human, but can also be an inanimate entity to which inherent power is attributed, such as a car or other machine.

(28)   Nuran **Deniz-*e*** kapı-yı aç-**tır**-dı.
             Deniz-DAT door-ACC open-CAUS-PF
       'Nuran *made Deniz* open the door.'

(29)   **Annesine** bulaşık yıkatmıyor.
       'S/he doesn't *let his/her mother* wash the dishes.'

(30)   Şule elini **makina*ya*** kaptırdı.
       'Şule *got* her hand caught *in the machine.*'

Causative constructions with dative-marked noun phrases can sometimes be ambiguous, because a dative-marked noun phrase could have an adverbial function (see 13.1.3):

(31)   Bu ev-i **Ahmet-e** yap-tır-dı-m.
       this house-ACC Ahmet-DAT make-CAUS-PF-1SG

This sentence can mean 'I got *Ahmet* to build this house', where the dative-marked noun phrase *Ahmet'e* denotes the person who has built the house, or it may mean 'I had this house built *for Ahmet*', where this same noun phrase marks the beneficiary. To resolve such ambiguities beneficiaries can be expressed by postpositional phrases:

(32) Bu evi **Ahmet için** yaptırdım.
      Ahmet for
      'I had this house built *for Ahmet.*'

It should be noted that sentences in which the beneficiary is indicated by other means (e.g. a postpositional phrase) are preferred to sentences where both the causee and the beneficiary are indicated by a dative-marked noun phrase.

(**ii**) In the case of intransitive verbs, the person or thing that is made to perform or undergo the action denoted by the root verb is in the accusative case:

(33) Bütün atık su-lar-ı deniz-e **ak-*ıt*-tı-lar**.
      all waste water-PL-ACC sea-DAT flow-CAUS-PF-3PL
      'They *release*d all the waste water into the sea.'

(34) Adamı üç bıçak darbesiyle **öl-*dür*-düler**.
      'They *kill*ed the man by stabbing him three times.'

Causation can also be expressed by means of a complex sentence containing verbs like *zorla-* 'force' (24.4.1.3 (58)), *sağla-* 'ensure' or *yol aç-* 'cause' (24.4.2.2 (84)).

13.2.1.1 Multiple occurrences of the causative suffix

The causative suffix can also attach to a stem already containing a causative suffix:

(35) Su-lar-ı durmadan **temizlikçi-ye** balkon-dan aşağı **ak-*ıt-tır*-ıyor**.
      water-PL-ACC continuously cleaner-DAT balcony-ABL down flow-
      CAUS-CAUS-IMPF
      'S/he is always *getting/making* the cleaner (to) *run* the water down off the balcony.'

Whether the root verb is intransitive or transitive, causative sentences without a dative-marked noun phrase (indicated in brackets above) are more common than those that have one. In the event of the dative noun phrase being omitted from (35), the sentence would mean 'S/he is always getting the water run down off the balcony'.

If the root verb is transitive (e.g. *kes-* 'cut'), an additional causative suffix is often used simply as a means of emphasizing causation, but it may also imply the addition of another intermediary. In most cases, a transitive stem with two causative suffixes is identical in meaning to its single causative counterpart:

(36) (**a**) Saç-ım-ı kes-**tir**-di-m.
hair-1SG.POSS-ACC cut-CAUS-PF-1SG
'I *had* my hair cut.'

(**b**) Saçımı kes-**tir-t**-ti-m.
cut-CAUS-CAUS-PF-1SG
'I *had* my hair cut.'

If the causee is expressed, the addition of a second causative is generally preferred:

(37) Saçımı **berber-e** kes-**tir-t**-ti-m.
hairdresser-DAT cut-CAUS-CAUS-PF-1SG
'I *got the hairdresser* to cut my hair.'

The double occurrence of the causative is even more clearly preferred when the causee and the beneficiary are both expressed in the sentence:

(38) **Karı-sın-a/karısı için** bir ev yap-**tır-t**-mış **bir İngiliz mimar-ın-a**.
BENEFICIARY   CAUSEE
wife-3SG.POSS-DAT/wife-3SG.POSS for a house make-CAUS-CAUS-EV/PF a British architect-NC-DAT
'He got *a British architect* to build a house *for his wife*.'

In informal speech, a third occurrence of the causative suffix only highlights the fact that the event was caused, rather than adding one more intermediary to the clause.

13.2.1.2 Causatives of verbs of emotion

Causative constructions based on certain verbs of emotion such as *kork-* 'fear', *ürk-* 'be scared/intimidated', *kız-* 'be angry (with)' and *sevin-* 'be happy (about)' have a special structure. Their oblique objects function as the subject in their causativized counterparts (39b):

(39) (**a**) Hayvan-lar **güneş tutulmasın-dan** ürk-üyor.
animal-PL solar eclipse-ABL be.frightened-IMPF
'Animals are frightened *by solar eclipses*.'

(**b**) **Güneş tutulması** hayvan-lar-ı ürk-*üt*-üyor.
solar eclipse animal-PL-ACC be.frightened-CAUS-IMPF
'*Solar eclipses* scare animals.'

Note that there are some verbs of emotion which do not follow this pattern, and causativize just like intransitive verbs which do not have oblique objects (such as *soğu-* 'lose one's love (for)', *nefret et-* 'hate'). On the other hand, there are also a number of verbs which involve an action rather than an emotion, and which display the pattern illustrated in (39) (e.g. *uğraş-* 'be busy with').

13.2.2 PASSIVE CONSTRUCTIONS

In Turkish both transitive and intransitive verbs can combine with the passive suffix (8.2.1.2).

13.2.2.1 Passivizing a transitive verb

This is usually done for purposes of topicalizing (23.3.3) the direct object and suppressing the agent or perpetrator of the action denoted by the verb. The process of passivization has the effect of making the direct object of a transitive verb the subject of a passive one. In the examples below the corresponding active sentence is shown in brackets:

(40) **Ev** bu yıl artık sat-**ıl**-acak. (cf. Biz **evi** bu yıl artık satacağız.)
house this year finally sell-PASS-FUT
'*The house* will finally *be* sold this year.'

(41) **Televizyon** şu anda tamir ed-**il**-iyor. (cf. Tamirci **televizyonu** tamir ediyor.)
TV at.the.moment repair AUX-PASS-IMPF
'The television set is *being* repaired at the moment.'

13.2.2.2 Expressing the agent in a passive sentence

Although one of the reasons for passivizing a direct object is to suppress the agent of an action, it is still possible to express the agent in a passive clause. The agent is expressed either by using the postposition *tarafından* (17.3.2), a locative or ablative noun phrase or the adverbial suffix *-CA* (16.1.6).

In a *tarafından* phrase the agent acts as the complement of the postposition (*tarafından* 'by'). These phrases are equivalent to 'by' phrases in English, but used less frequently. Agentless passive sentences are much more common in Turkish than those containing a *tarafından* phrase.

(42) En iyi oyun **birinci sınıf öğrencileri tarafından** hazırlanmış.
'The best play was performed *by the first year students*.'

A *tarafından* phrase usually comes immediately before the verb in a passive sentence. Phrases with *tarafından* can normally only refer to animate entities, usually to human beings. Occasionally they can be used (with personifying effect) to refer to machines (e.g. *makina tarafından* 'by the machine'). An inanimate agent can usually only be expressed by means of some other type of adverbial, particularly by an ablative- or locative-marked noun phrase. (For the causal meaning of the ablative case marker see 14.3.3.5 (i))

(43) (a) **Ayışığ-ı** keten-i parçala-r-mış.
           moonlight-NC linen-ACC destroy-AOR-EV.COP
           'Apparently *moonlight* fragments linen.'

      (b) Keten **ayışığ-ın-*dan*/*da*** parçala-n-ır-mış.
           linen moonlight-NC-ABL/LOC destroy-PASS-AOR-EV.COP
           'Apparently linen gets fragmented *by moonlight*/[as a result of being] *in the moonlight*.'

(44) (a) **Fırtına** bütün evleri yıktı.
           '*The storm* destroyed all the houses.'

      (b) **Fırtına-*da*** bütün evler yıkıldı.
           storm-LOC
           'All the houses were destroyed *in the storm*.'

Another way of expressing the agent in a passive construction is by attaching the suffix -*CA* (7.2.2.2, 16.1.6 (iii)) to the agentive noun phrase. This can be done only when the agent of an action is an official body, such as a ministry, or an organization or group of people. This usage is typical of formal discourse, and is mostly confined to official speeches and broadcasts.

(45) Bugün **Başbakanlık-*ça*** vergi-ler konusunda önemli
      today government-ADV tax-PL regarding important
      bir açıklama yap-**ıl**-acak-mış.
      an announcement make-PASS-FUT-EV.COP
      'Apparently, an important announcement regarding taxes is expected to be made today *by the government*.'

(46) Bu toplantı **okulumuzca** düzenlendi.
      'This meeting was organized *by our school*.'

The verb phrase 151

13.2.2.3 Impersonal passives

The addition of a passive suffix to an intransitive verb produces an impersonal passive construction:

(47) Adalara artık deniz otobüsüyle mi gid-**il**-ecek?
　　　　　　　　　　　　　　　　　　　　 go-PASS-FUT
'Will hovercraft be the way that [people] go to the islands now?'

In such constructions there is no particular person or group of persons that is understood as performing the action denoted by the verb, hence such sentences cannot have agent phrases. The closest English equivalents are active sentences with 'people', 'one' or the impersonal 'you' as subject.

Impersonal passives occur most often with aorist marking, to express a general property of a particular entity (see 21.4.1.1). (48) below indicates a property of cobblestone streets:

(48) Arnavut kaldırım-ı üst-ün-de topuklu pabuç-la yürü-**n**-mez.
cobblestone.street-NC top-3SG.POSS-LOC high.heeled
shoe-COM walk-PASS-NEG.AOR
'[You] can't walk on cobblestone streets wearing high-heeled shoes.'

In impersonal passive constructions the action denoted by the verb is understood to be attributed to human beings; hence sentences such as the following cannot refer to actions by inanimate entities.

(49) Parmaklık o kadar alçak ki balkondan aşağı düş-**ül**-ebil-ir.
　　　　　　　　　　　　　　　　　　　　　　　　fall-PASS-PSB-AOR
'The railing is so low that [one] could fall off the balcony.'

13.2.2.4 Double passive constructions

When a transitive verb combines with two passive suffixes, the result is again an impersonal passive which refers to a property of a particular entity. These constructions are quite marginal, and are almost always used with the aorist suffix. In double passive constructions the first occurrence of the passive suffix has an intransitivizing function.

(50) Böyle laf-a **kır-ıl-ın**-ır.
such word-DAT hurt-PASS-PASS-AOR
'[One] can *be hurt* by such words.'

(51) Bu duruma tabii ki **üz-*ül-ün*-ebil-ir.**
                        sadden-PASS-PASS-PSB-AOR
    '[One] can of course *be upset* by this situation.'

In colloquial Turkish some speakers tend to use a second passive suffix after the suffix *-(y)Abil* as in *yap-ıl-abil-in-ir* '[it] can be done'. This duplication does not serve any syntactic function.

For the obligatory occurrence of passive morphology in the main clause of a sentence whose subject is a *-mAK* noun clause that is itself passive, see 24.4.1.4.

Some irregular cases

(i) Some forms which have two passive suffixes (such as *söyle-n-il-* 'be told', *de-n-il-* 'be said' and *ye-n-il-* 'be eaten') are not 'double passive' constructions in the sense described above, but are identical in meaning to their counterparts with a single passive suffix (i.e. *söyle-n-* 'be told', etc.).

(ii) In the spoken language, the form *ko-n-ul-* 'be placed' is the more frequently used passive form of *koy-* 'place', 'put', rather than *koy-ul-* 'be placed'.

(iii) The passive form of *kapa-* and *kapat-* 'close' is *kapat-ıl-*:

(52) Okul meğer belediye başkanı tarafından kapat-**ıl**-mış.
                                    close-PASS-EV/PF
    'The school was apparently closed down by the mayor.'

The stem *kapan-*, unless used in a reflexive sense (13.2.3.1), denotes the action of closing in an intransitive sense:

(53) Köşedeki dükkan yedide kapa-**n**-ıyor.
                          close-PASS-IMPF
    'The shop on the corner closes at seven.'

(iv) Anlaşıl- 'be understood', 'be clear' is an irregular passive form whose root is *anla-* 'understand'.

13.2.3   CONSTRUCTIONS WITH NON-PRODUCTIVE VOICE SUFFIXES

The reflexive and reciprocal suffixes are intransitive. These combine with only a limited number of verbs.

13.2.3.1 Reflexive constructions

Reflexive constructions contain the reflexive suffix -*(I)n* (8.2.1.3), which combines only with transitive verbs. In the most common type of reflexive construction, the agent of an action performs the action on himself/herself:

(54) Bu kız daha sabahleyin yıka-**n**-mış-tı.
                        wash-REF-PF-P.COP
     'This girl had taken a bath/shower only that morning.'

(55) Sarman durmadan yala-**n**-ıyor-du.
                    lick-REF-IMPF-P.COP
     'Sarman was licking himself incessantly.'

(56) O sıralarda bütün kadınlar eve kapa-**n**-mış-tı.
                              close-REF-PF-P.COP
     'In those days all women used to stay indoors/kept themselves at home.'

In another type of reflexive construction, the way in which the agent is affected by the action is somewhat indirect, as in *giyin-* 'get dressed', *sürtün-* 'rub (oneself) against [s.t.]':

(57) Aferin! Çabucak giy-**in**-di-n.
                 wear-REF-PF-2SG
     'Good for you! You got dressed very quickly.'

The vast majority of reflexive verbs are intransitive. However, there are a few transitive ones:

(58) Hergün **kokular** sür**ün**üyor.
     'S/he puts on *perfume* every day.'

Although the reflexive suffix and the pronoun *kendi* 'self' are mutually exclusive when *kendi* functions as a reflexive pronoun, there are some instances when the reflexive suffix can co-occur with *kendi* in its other functions. This happens when *kendi* is:

(**i**) Used emphatically (18.1.2.2 (i)):

(59) Çocuklar **kendi**-leri yıka-**n**-abil-ir-ler.
                  self-3PL.POSS wash-PASS-PSB-AOR-3PL
     'The children can have a shower *themselves.*'

(**ii**) Used in its doubled form *kendi kendi-* (18.1.3) with dative case marking:

(60) Çocuklar **kendi kendi**-lerin-e yıka-**n**-abil-ir-ler.
self self-3PL.POSS-DAT wash-REF-PSB-AOR-3PL
'The children can have a shower *by themselves.*'

See also 7.2.1.2 for the derivational usage of -*(I)n*.

13.2.3.2 Reciprocal constructions

Reciprocal constructions are intransitive constructions which describe an event in which at least two agents perform the same action upon each other. The verb is marked with the reciprocal suffix -*(I)ş* (8.2.1.4), as in *dövüş*- 'fight each other':

(61) Kemal-le Zeki döv-**üş**-tü(-ler).
Kemal-CONJ Zeki beat.up-REC-PF(-3PL)
'Kemal and Zeki had a fight.'

In reciprocal constructions there is more than one way of expressing the two (or more) agents of the action. One of these is by using a conjunction such as *ve* or -*(y)lA/ile* 'and' (28.3.1.1 (i–ii)), which forms a composite subject as in (61) above. In such cases the verb can have plural person marking.

Alternatively, one of the agents can be expressed as an adverbial of manner (16.4.3 (iv)), by means of the comitative suffix -*(y)lA/ile* 'with' used as a postposition (17.2.1 (iii)):

(62) Kemal Zeki-**yle** dövüştü.
Zeki-COM
'Kemal fought *with* Zeki.'

In these constructions there is only one subject (here *Kemal*) and the verb therefore has singular person marking (see also 12.2.2.4 (ii)). There is a slight difference between the meanings of the two constructions. While in (61) the two agents of the action, Kemal and Zeki, have equal standing as agents of the verb, (62) is a statement about an action performed by Kemal, in which Zeki is also involved.

The reciprocal pronoun *birbir*- 'each other' (18.1.4) can be used in reciprocal constructions with -*(y)lA* as an adverbial of manner:

(63) Kemal-le Zeki **birbir-leri-yle** döv-üş-tü-ler.
Kemal-CONJ Zeki each.other-3PL.POSS-COM beat.up-REC-PF-3PL
'Kemal and Zeki fought *(with) each other.*'

For other examples of verbs to which the reciprocal suffix can be added see 8.2.1.4. The reciprocal suffix also appears in the verb-forming suffix -*lAş* (7.2.2.1).

13.2.4 COMBINATIONS OF VOICE SUFFIXES

More than one voice suffix can attach to a verb. Since these suffixes affect the transitivity of a clause, the order in which they are attached is very important. The last suffix to appear determines the (in)transitivity of the stem.

Apart from the double occurrences of the passive and the causative which are explained above, other combinations are also possible. When the passive suffix attaches to a verb, the only other voice suffix that can attach to it is a second passive, as discussed in 13.2.2.3–4.

Causative (+ causative) + passive
This is the most productive of combinations. In such constructions the verbal complex as a whole (e.g. *dik-tir-il-* below) is passive, and therefore the sentence does not contain a direct object:

(64) **Herkes-e** birer ağaç dik-**tir-il**-di.
    everyone-DAT a tree plant-CAUS-PASS-PF
    (**i**) 'It *was arranged* that a tree be planted *for everyone*.'
    (**ii**) '*Everyone was made* to plant a tree.'

Where, as in (64), there is just one causative suffix on the verb, a dative-marked noun phrase (such as *herkese*) is more often used to express a beneficiary (as in (64 (i)), than to express the causee (as in (64 (ii)). By contrast, when a passive suffix is attached to a double causative, the more likely interpretation is the one where the dative-marked noun phrase expresses the causee, as in (65 (i)):

(65) **Bütün öğrenci-ler-e** resim-ler yap-**tır-t-ıl**-dı.
    all student-PL-DAT picture-PL paint-CAUS-CAUS-PASS-PF
    (**i**) '*All the students* were made to paint (pictures).'
    (**ii**) 'It was arranged for pictures to be painted *for every student*.'

The addition of a causative suffix followed by a passive suffix produces a stem different in meaning and structure from the corresponding root. For example, both the root *piş-* 'cook (intransitive)' and the stem *piş-ir-il-* (*piş-*CAUS-PASS) 'be cooked' are intransitive, but a sentence with *piş-ir-il-* can contain an agent, whereas this is not a possibility with simple verbs.

(66) Fasulye [kart ol-duğ-un-dan] üç saat-te **piş**-ti.
    bean stringy be-CV-3SG.POSS-ABL three hour-LOC cook-PF
    '[Because the beans were stringy] they took three hours to *cook*.'

(67) Keşke şu fasulye-ler **doğru dürüst bir ahçı tarafından piş-*ir-il*-se-
ydi!
if.only this bean-PL proper a cook by cook-CAUS-PASS-COND-
P.COP
'If only these beans *had been cooked by a proper cook*!'

Reciprocal + causative
In these sequences the last voice suffix is causative; the stem is therefore
transitive and the sentence contains a direct object:

(68) Baba-ları **kardeş-ler-i** öp-*üş-tür*-dü.
father-3PL.POSS sibling-PL-ACC kiss-REC-CAUS-PF
'The(ir) father *made* the sisters/brothers kiss *each other*.'

(Note that -*(I)ştır* may also function as a derivational suffix, see 7.2.1.2.)

Reciprocal + passive
Reciprocal + passive sequences produce impersonal constructions (cf.
13.2.2.4):

(69) Bu arena-da her zaman döv-**üş-ül**-müş-tür.
This arena-LOC always beat.up-REC-PASS-PF-GM
'People have always fought in this arena.'

Reciprocal + causative + passive
This sequence produces intransitive stems with a passive sense:

(70) Onlar bura-da döv-**üş-tür-ül**-dü.
They here-LOC beat-REC-CAUS-PASS-PF
'They *were made* to fight *each other* here.'

Reflexive + passive
These are impersonal passive constructions (13.2.2) because the stem to
which the passive is added is intransitive:

(71) Bu hamam-da iyi yıka-**n-ıl**-ır.
this bath-LOC well wash-REF-PASS-AOR
'[*One*] can *get washed* pretty well in this bath house.'

13.3 AUXILIARY VERBS

An auxiliary verb cannot stand on its own and occurs with another verb or
nominal. There are three types of auxiliary verb in Turkish:

(i) Bound auxiliaries:
These are the suffixes *-(y)Abil, -(y)Iver,* ∇*-(y)Ayaz,* ∇*-(y)Adur,* ∇*-(y)Akal.*

(ii) Free auxiliaries:
These are verbs such as *ol-* (which is also one of the forms of the copula), *et-, gel-, dur-, kal-, düş- bulun-,* ∇*eyle-* and ∇*buyur-.*

(iii) *i-/-(y)-:*
These are also forms of the copula, see 8.3.1–2.

13.3.1 COMPOUND VERB FORMS

These are formed by using bound and free auxiliaries.

13.3.1.1 Compound verb forms containing bound auxiliaries

The verb roots *bil-* 'know', *ver-* 'give', *gel-* 'come', *yaz-* 'make a mistake' (obs.), *dur-* 'stay', *kal-* 'remain' can also function as bound (i.e. suffixed) auxiliaries appearing as part of the composite suffixes *-(y)Abil, -(y)Iver,* ∇*-(y)Agel,* ∇*-(y)Adur,* ∇*-(y)Ayaz* and ∇*-(y)Akal* (8.2.3.2), which appear in position 2 on the verb stem.

The most common of these suffixes is the possibility suffix *-(y)Abil* (21.4.2.1).

(72) Her gün çikolata yi-**yebil**-ir-im.
every day chocolate eat-PSB-AOR-1SG
'I could eat chocolate every day.'

-(y)Iver mostly indicates swiftness and suddenness of an action, as in (75), or the ease with which an action is performed, as in (76):

(73) O anda odaya bir adam gir-**iver**-di.
enter-AUX-PF
'*Suddenly* a man entered the room.'

(74) Şu pencereyi kapa-**yıver**-sene.
'[*Why don't* you] just close that window?'

The remaining bound auxiliaries are either (semi-)lexicalized or obsolescent. ∇*-(y)Agel* indicates that the action denoted by the verb is habitual and customary:

(75) Onlar [Hristiyan olmamalarına rağmen] yıllardır Noel'i
kutla-yagel-miş-ler-dir.
'They have been celebrating Christmas for years, [even though they aren't Christians].'

The compounds containing ⱱ-*(y)Adur* and ⱱ-*(y)Akal* are semi-lexicalized. ⱱ-*(y)Adur* is mostly used with motion verbs such as *git-* 'go', *yürü-* 'walk', *koş-* 'run', to indicate the continuous nature of the action. Verbs with ⱱ-*(y)Adur* are usually imperative:

(76) Sen yürü**yedur**, ben sana yetişirim.
'You *keep on* walking, [and] I'll catch you up.'

ⱱ-*(y)Akal* is almost exclusively used with the verbs *bak-* 'look', *don-* 'freeze' and *şaş-* 'be surprised', producing the forms *bakakal-* 'be amazed', *donakal-* 'be stunned' and *şaşakal-* 'be dumbfounded':

(77) [Söylediklerini duyunca] don**akal**dık.
'We were stunned [when we heard what you said].'

The verb roots *dur-* 'stay' and *kal-* 'remain' can also be used as free forms. These separate verb forms are more productive than their suffixed counterparts ⱱ-*(y)Adur* and ⱱ-*(y)Akal*, and are used following the conjunctive suffix *-(y)Ip* (28.2):

(78) Şan derslerine **gid-ip** *dur-***uyor** ama şarkı söylediği yok.
                 go-CONJ AUX-IMPF
'S/he *keeps going* to singing lessons, but s/he doesn't sing.'

(79) Burada böylece **otur-up** *kal-***dı-k**.
                sit-CONJ AUX-PF-1PL
'We were just *left sitting* here.'

13.3.1.2 Compound verb forms containing free auxiliaries

The free auxiliaries *ol-* and *bulun-* can form compounds with verbs. *Ol-* is fully productive, while *bulun-* is limited in usage. These auxiliaries function as buffer stems which, acting as carriers for tense/aspect/modality suffixes, supplement the tense/aspect marking that is already present on the lexical verb in a finite clause (e.g. *bitir-* in (80)):

(80) Bu arada da ders-imiz-i **bitir-miş** *ol-***acağ-ız**.
     meanwhile and lesson-1PL.POSS-ACC finish-PF AUX-FUT-1PL
'And in the meantime *we will have finished* our homework.'

For a survey of the wide range of compound verb forms in common use in finite clauses see 21.5. For those occurring in conditional clauses see 27.2.1.3 and 27.2.6.

In non-finite compound verb forms the free auxiliaries act as bearers of
the subordinating suffix, freeing the lexical stem to carry a tense/aspect
marker (see 24.4.7, 25.4.1, 26.2.3 (i)):

(81) [Semra'yla **konuş-uyor** *ol*-**duğ-un** sırada] bütün sırlarını
anlatmıştın.
speak-IMPF AUX-CV-2SG.POSS
'[At the time when you *were on speaking terms* with Semra], you
told [her] all your secrets.'

The auxiliary verb *bulun-* is generally confined to formal or pedantic
discourse:

(82) Kayıtları bugün saat 17 itibariyle **kapat-mış** *bulun*-**uyor-uz**.
finish-PF AUX-IMPF-1PL
'*We* [officially] *finished* registration at 5 p.m. today.'

However, it can have the different function of attributing an element of
involuntariness to the action denoted by the verb, suggesting that it was
carried out either by mistake or as an unintended result of some other
action. In compound verbs with *bulun-*, the lexical verb has to be inflected
with *-mIş*:

(83) [Ankara'ya bir kere **gel-miş** *bulun*-**duğ-umuz-a** göre] bari Kale'yi
come-PF AUX-CV-1PL.POSS-DAT seeing.that
gezelim.
'[Since we *have landed up* in Ankara *anyway*], why not let's visit
the castle?'

In compound verbs with free auxiliaries, only the lexical verb can carry
voice suffixes; *-(y)Abil* (and to a lesser extent *-(y)Iver*) can occur on the
auxiliary verb or the main verb:

(84) Gör-ül-müş **ol-*abil*-ir** mi-yiz?
see-PASS-PF AUX-PSB-AOR INT-1PL
'*Could* we have been seen?'

(85) Anne-sin-i **gör-*ebil*-miş** ol-du.
mother-3SG.POSS-ACC see-PSB-PF AUX-PF
'S/he *has managed to see* his/her mother.'

For the combination of compound verb forms with the negative suffix, see
20.1.2.
A rather less productive compound verb form contains *-mAzlIktAn gel-*.
This construction is restricted to verbs of perception and cognition, such as

duy- 'hear', *anla-* understand', etc., and is identical in meaning to its negative counterpart *-mAmAzlIktAn gel-*. Sometimes it occurs as *-mAzdAn gel-*:

(86) Beni *duymazlıktan/duymamazlıktan/duymazdan geldi.*
      'S/he pretended not to hear me.'

13.3.2 NOMINAL-VERB COMPOUNDS

Nominal-verb compounds are made up of a bare nominal (noun or adjective) followed by a verb used as a free auxiliary. *Ol-, et-, yap- gel-, dur-, kal-, çık-, düş-, Vbuyur-, Veyle-* form nominal-verb compounds such as *sebep ol-* 'cause', *yardım et-* 'help', *inat et-* 'be obstinate', *takdir et-* 'appreciate', *karşı gel-* 'oppose', *karşı dur-* 'resist', *mecbur kal-* 'be obliged', *karşı çık-* 'oppose', *zayıf düş-* 'become weak', *Vaf buyur-* 'forgive' (only used in requests), *Vistirham eyle-* 'ask for mercy', *işbaşı yap-* 'start work'. In some cases, the nominal and the auxiliary verb are joined up: *affet-* 'forgive', *hallet-* 'solve', *hallol-* 'be solved' (for the phonological properties of words combining with *et-* see 2.2). These compounds are inflected like ordinary verbs:

(87) Ahmet arkadaş-lar-ın-a hep **yardım ed**-er.
      Ahmet friend-PL-3SG.POSS-DAT always help AUX-AOR
      'Ahmet always *helps* his friends.'

(88) [Beni anlamamak]-ta **inat ed**-iyor.
      'S/he *obstinately refuses* to understand me.'

14 THE NOUN PHRASE

A noun phrase is any sequence of words that can function as the subject of a sentence:

(1) Bunu **sen** al.
    '*You* take this one.'

(2) [**Her gün oraya gidip gelmek**] zor.
    'It's difficult [*to go there and back every day*].'

A noun phrase can also function as some kind of complement, such as:

An object:

(3) **Yeni komşuları** tanımıyordum.
    'I didn't know *the new neighbours*.'

A subject complement:

(4) O sırada **lise öğrencisi**ydik.
    'We were *high school students* at the time.'

The complement of a postposition:

(5) Bunları [**Amerika'nın dış politikasını daha iyi anlamak isteyenler**] *için* yazıyorum.
    'I'm writing all this *for people who want to understand American foreign policy better*.'

The most complex kinds of noun phrases are subordinate clauses, which are discussed elsewhere in this book: noun clauses (exemplified in (2) above) form the subject of Chapter 24, and headless relative clauses (as in (5) above) are explained in 25.3.

In this chapter we look first at the structure of the noun phrase (14.1), then consider the extent to which distinctions of countability are grammaticalized (14.2). The next sections explain how noun phrases are inflected for number (14.3.1), possession (person) (14.3.2) and case (14.3.3). The last two sections examine composite structures involving a combination of two

noun phrases: the genitive-possessive construction (14.4) and partitive
constructions (14.5).

14.1 STRUCTURE OF THE NOUN PHRASE

The Turkish noun phrase consists of an obligatory constituent, called the
head, and one or more optional constituents, known as **modifiers**. (6)–(8)
are noun phrases of varying degrees of complexity. In each case the head
is shown in bold:

(6) **oda**
     'the *room*'

(7) büyük bir **oda**
     'a large *room*'

(8) [Mustafa'nın çalışma odası olarak kullandığı] **oda**
     'the *room* that Mustafa uses as a study'

All modifiers in the Turkish noun phrase, however complex, precede the
head. The head is the location for any inflectional suffixes that pertain to
the noun phrase as a whole:

(9) {Bu kattaki en güzel oda-**lar-ımız**}-ı size ayırdık.
                          room-PL-1PL.POSS-ACC
     'We've given you {our best rooms on this floor}.'

14.1.1 ITEMS WHICH CAN FUNCTION AS THE HEAD OF A
NOUN PHRASE

There are three word classes that can function as the head of a noun phrase:
nouns, noun compounds, and pronouns. Some examples of each are given
below:

(**i**) Nouns:

(**a**) common nouns
        adam 'man', *para* 'money', *tarih* 'history'

(**b**) proper nouns
        Mustafa, İstanbul, Avrupa

(**ii**) Noun compounds (Chapter 10):

(**a**) bare compounds
        kız öğrenci 'female student', *taş duvar* 'stone wall'

(b)   *-(s)I* compounds
    otobüs bileti 'bus ticket', *Türk kahvesi* 'Turkish coffee'

(iii)   Pronouns (Chapter 18):
sen 'you', *bu* 'this', *orası* 'that (place)', *hangisi* 'which (one)', *öteki* 'the other'

Of these three classes, pronouns differ from the other two in that they very rarely occur with any modifiers.

14.1.2   MODIFIERS IN THE NOUN PHRASE

Modifiers that may be present in a noun phrase fall into two classes: **determiners** and **adjectivals**.

   Determiners (15.6) constitute a small class of items whose function is to specify the limitation (or lack of limitation) of the potential referent of a noun phrase, such as *bu* 'this', *aynı* 'the same', *her* 'every', etc.

   Adjectivals (15.1–5) attribute some kind of quality to the head of a noun phrase. Turkish adjectivals range from simple adjectives, such as *iyi* 'good', *yeni* 'new', *zengin* 'rich', *yüksek* 'high', through various kinds of more complex forms and phrases to relative clauses (Chapter 25), which have a sentence-like internal structure.

(10)   **küçük**   **bir**   kız
       little   a   girl
       ADJ   DET   N
       'a little girl'

(11)   **şu**   **raf-ta-ki**   **bütün**   **eski**   kitap-lar
       that   shelf-LOC-ADJ   all   old   book-PL
       DET   ADJ   DET   ADJ   N
       'all the old books on that shelf'

(12)   **[Deniz-in**   **sev-diğ-i]**   **bazı**   Türk yemek-ler-i
       Deniz-GEN   like-PART-3SG.POSS   some   Turk dish-PL-NC
       ADJ   DET   NC
       'some Turkish dishes that Deniz likes'

14.2   COUNTABILITY

There is no clear grammatical distinction in Turkish between countable and uncountable nouns. As shown in 14.2.1 and 14.3.1.2, both the indefinite article and the plural suffix can be used with almost any noun. However, nouns denoting non-discrete, continuous entities such as *su* 'water', *toprak* 'earth', *müzik* 'music' are not normally combinable with numerals or with the quantifying determiners *kaç* 'how many', *birkaç* 'a few,' 'several', or *birçok* 'many', unless the context makes clear that the counting is based upon either a conventional *measure* of the substance in question, as in (13), or distinct *types* of the substance, as in (14):

(13) Bakkaldan **birkaç bira** al.
              a. few beer
    'Get *a few* [*bottles of*] *beer* from the corner shop.'

(14) Bu memleketin en az **beş altı müziğ**-i var
                   five six music-3SG.POSS
    'There are at least *five or six* [*kinds of*] *music* in this country.'

Conversely, the quantifier *biraz* 'a little', 'some' cannot normally be used as a determiner with nouns that denote discrete, countable entities, such as *çocuk* 'child', *şehir* 'city', *resim* 'picture'. However, in very informal registers this combination can occur where a speaker envisages a group of items in a vague, undefined way, without giving any importance to their individuality:

(15) Masada **biraz kalem, kitap** falan vardı galiba.
    'I think there were *some pens, books* and suchlike on the table.'

All words denoting fruits and vegetables are used interchangeably to refer either to an individual item (16) or to the type (17):

(16) Dün **üç şeftali** yedim.
    'I ate *three peaches* yesterday.'

(17) Şuradan **biraz şeftali** alalım.
    'Let's get *some peaches* from here.'

14.2.1 USES OF THE INDEFINITE ARTICLE *bir* WITH NOUN PHRASES THAT DO NOT DENOTE DISCRETE ENTITIES

(i)   As in the case of numerals in general, *bir* 'one', 'a(n)' can designate a conventional measure of the substance in question:

(18) Bana **bir su** ver.
    'Give me *a* [*glass of*] *water*.'

(ii)   It can also refer to one instance of a quality or state:

(19) İçime **bir rahatlık** girdi.
    '*A* [*sense of*] *relief* came over me.'

(iii) In combination with an adjectival, it attributes a quality to a particular instance of the class denoted by the noun:

(20) **Güzel bir pirinç** buldum.
'I've found *a nice [kind of] rice*.'

14.3   NOMINAL INFLECTION

The inflectional suffixes that can be added to the head of a noun phrase are those set out in 8.1. In this section we look at how three of these sets of suffixes, namely the plural suffix (8.1.1), possessive suffixes (8.1.2) and case suffixes (8.1.3), affect the meaning of a noun phrase.

14.3.1   NUMBER

14.3.1.1   Plural marking with *-lAr*

The only suffix marking number in Turkish nominals is the plural suffix *-lAr*. The basic meaning of this suffix is to denote more than one item from the class indicated:

boş oda-lar	'vacant rooms'
kim-ler	'who' (referring to more than one person)

Noun phrases that have to be plural-marked:
A noun phrase containing one of the quantifying determiners *bazı/kimi/bir kısım* 'some', 'certain', *birtakım* 'some', 'a number of', normally has to be plural marked:

(21) **Bazı insan-*lar*** çocuklarına tuhaf adlar koyarlar.
some person-PL
'*Some people* give their children strange names.'

However, there are some fixed expressions in which singular nouns do occur with these determiners, e.g. *kimi/bazı zaman* 'sometimes', *bazı kimse* 'some people'. In the case of the quantifiers *bütün/tüm* 'all', 'the whole', the meaning of the noun phrase is crucially affected by whether the head is plural marked or not:

(22) **Bütün sınıf** ayağa kalktı.
'*The whole class* rose to its feet.'

(23) Bu yıl **bütün sınıflar** daha kalabalık olacak.
'This year *all the classes* are going to be larger.'

Restrictions on the use of plural marking:

(**i**)   *-lAr* is not used where plurality is already indicated by the presence of a numeral as a modifier in the noun phrase:

üç çocuk	'three children'
yirmi beş dakika	'twenty-five minutes'

The only exceptions to this rule are the proper names of well-known groups:

Üç Silahşörler	'the Three Musketeers'
Yedi Cüceler	'the Seven Dwarfs'

(**ii**)   Where certain quantifying determiners (15.6.1), i.e. *çok* 'a lot of', 'many', *fazla* 'too much', 'too many', *az* 'not much', 'not many', *biraz* 'a little', *birkaç* 'a few', 'several', *bir miktar* 'some', *bu kadar/şu kadar/o kadar* 'this much/that much', 'so much', *kaç* 'how many', and *her* 'every', are used in a noun phrase, the head noun is always left in the singular form:

her Türk vatandaşı	'every Turkish citizen'
kaç kişi	'how many people'
birkaç boş oda	'a few empty rooms'
çok kitap	'a lot of books'

The determiner *birçok* 'many' sometimes occurs with a plural-marked head noun, although the non-marked form is generally preferred, and is obligatory in the case of *kişi* 'person':

birçok kadın(lar)	'many women'
birçok kişi	'many people'

(**iii**)   The combination of *bir* and *-lAr*:
The head of a noun phrase which includes the indefinite determiner *bir* 'a(n)' (15.6.1) normally has to be in the singular form. However, in the case of the pluralized forms of the pronouns *bir şey* 'something' (18.6.1) and *bir yer* 'somewhere', the sequence *bir . . . lAr* regularly occurs in informal contexts:

(24)   Harun o gün bana **bir şeyler** söyledi.
        'Harun told me *some things* that day.'

(25)   Bu yaz **bir yer(ler)e** gidiyor musunuz?
        'Are you going *anywhere* this summer?'

The combination *bir . . . lAr* is occasionally encountered (again in informal usage) with other nouns. It conveys that the referent is conceived as being plural, but that its identity is unknown or unknowable.

(26) **Bir sesler** duydum galiba.
'I think I heard *something*' (lit. 'some sounds').

14.3.1.2 Further uses of the plural suffix *-lAr*

There are several other uses of *-lAr* which are observed particularly (although not exclusively) in nouns whose primary denotation is an uncountable substance.

(i) A plurality of conventional measures or portions of the thing concerned:

(27) **Çay-lar**-ı koyayım mı?
tea-PL-ACC
'Shall I pour out *the tea*?'

This particular use of *-lAr* can occur even with nouns whose primary denotation is a countable entity:

(28) **Balıklar** yendikten sonra **tavuklar** geldi.
'After *the fish* had been eaten *chicken* arrived.'

(ii) A plurality of separate quantities of the thing concerned:

(29) **Kir(ler)** bir türlü çıkmıyordu.
'*The dirt* just wouldn't come out.'

(30) Bu işte **büyük para(lar)** var.
'There's *big money* involved in this business.'

(iii) In the case of substances with a granular composition, the addition of the plural suffix shifts attention from the substance en masse to its constituent elements:

(31) **Kum-lar**-ı parmaklarının arasından geçiriyordu.
sand-PL-ACC
'She was sifting *the (grains of) sand* through her fingers.'

(iv) The plural suffix can be used to designate a plurality of types of a substance:

(32) Bizim Migros'ta güzel **şaraplar** var.
'There are nice *wines* at our Migros.'

(v) Certain expressions can be intensified by the addition of *-lAr* to the noun, for example:

(33) **Kan(lar)a** bulanmıştı.
'He was covered *(all over) in blood.*'

(vi) The addition of *-lAr* can also highlight the spatial extent of the substance referred to, whether in area or volume terms:

(34) **Kum(lar)a** uzandım.
'I lay down on *the sand.*'

(vii) In the case of nouns expressing abstract states, the addition of the plural suffix usually expresses a plurality of occurrences of this state:

(35) Böyle **tembellikler**im çok oluyor.
'I'm often lazy like this.' ('Such *acts of laziness* on my part occur often.')

(viii) *-lAr* can be added to certain expressions of time and place, giving a sense of approximation, or giving the expression a wider meaning. The list below gives some common examples. Although the locative case-marked form is shown for several items, other case markings also occur according to context.

buralarda	'around here'
bir yerler	'anywhere', 'somewhere'
oralar (güzel)	'(It's nice) round there.'
Erzurum taraflarında	'around Erzurum', 'in the Erzurum area'
uzaklarda	'in the distance'
1995 ortalarında	'about the middle of 1995'
mayıs başlarında	'at about the beginning of May'
bu haftanın sonlarına doğru	'towards the end of this week'
o sıralarda	'at about that time'
o tarihlerde	'around that date', 'at that period'
şimdilerde	'these days'
sonraları	'later on'
bir zamanlar	'once' (= at some time in the past)

Approximations about people's age fit into the same pattern:

kırkbeş yaşlarında bir adam   'a man of about forty-five'
o yaşlarda   'at about that age'

(**ix**) For the use of *-lArI* to express recurrent time (*sabahları* 'in the morning(s)', *cumartesileri* 'on Saturdays', etc.) see 16.4.1.1 (63).

(**x**)
(**a**)   When attached to the name of a famous person, *-lAr* means 'and people like that':

> (36) Dünya'dan **Atatürk'ler, Nehru'lar** geçmeseydi şimdiye kadar
>   ne hale gelirdik?
>   'If *people like Atatürk and Nehru* had not passed through
>   the world, what state would we be in by now?'

(**b**)   Another function of *-lAr* attached to the name of a person is to produce an expression referring to the group normally associated with that person. This group could consist just of the named person and his/her spouse/partner, or it could be their family, group of friends, etc. The precise meaning varies with the context, and this usage is confined to informal situations.

> (37) **Ahmet'ler** gelmedi.
>   '*Ahmet and his wife/girlfriend/family/gang* didn't come.'

The same usage can occur with expressions of relationship. Note that in such expressions the possessive suffix *precedes* the plural suffix.

> (38) **Abla-m-lar** nerede?
>   elder.sister-1SG.POSS-PL
>   'Where are *my elder sister and her boyfriend/husband (etc)*?'
>   (cf. abla-lar-ım (elder.sister-PL-1SG.POSS) 'my elder sisters')

14.3.1.3   Transnumeral uses of the unmarked form

A noun phrase that is unmarked for number, i.e. whose head does not carry the plural suffix and which does not have a numeral or other quantifying determiner among its modifiers, may be either singular or **transnumeral** (number-neutral) in meaning. If it has definite status it will have singular meaning, but if it has generic or categorial status it will have transnumeral meaning. These various referential statuses are discussed in detail in Chapter 22.

(39) **İlaç** bana çok iyi geldi.
'*The medicine* did me a lot of good.'

(40) **İlaç** hastaya göre seçilmelidir.
'*The medicine/Medicines* must be chosen according to the patient.'

(41) Doktor bana **ilaç** yazmadı.
'The doctor didn't prescribe me *any medicine(s)*.'

The noun phrase *ilaç* 'medicine' is definite and therefore singular in (39), generic and therefore transnumeral in (40), and categorial, therefore again transnumeral, in (41).

14.3.2 POSSESSION

The possessive suffixes (8.1.2) correspond to the six grammatical persons. A noun phrase marked with a possessive suffix (except where this is a 3rd person suffix functioning as a compound marker (10.2) or pronominalizer (18.4)) is understood as denoting a person or thing that is possessed. The possessive suffix indicates only whether the possessor is 1st, 2nd or 3rd person, singular or plural.

(42) Arkadaş-lar-**ınız** ne kadar kalacaklar?
friend-PL-**2PL.POSS**
'How long are *your* friends going to stay?'

(43) Ahmet oda-**sın**-ı arıyordu. Numara-**sı** akl-**ın**-da kalmamıştı.
room-**3SG.POSS** -ACC number-**3SG.POSS** mind-**3SG.POSS**-
LOC
'Ahmet was looking for *his* room. *Its* number was no longer in *his* head.'

If there is a need to be more explicit about, or to emphasize, the identity of the possessor, this can be done by a genitive-possessive construction, that is, by modifying the possessed constituent with a genitive-marked noun phrase (see 14.4 below).

Certain combinations of the possessive suffixes with plural and/or case suffixes give rise to potential ambiguity:

(**i**)   Following a consonant-final stem, the sequences [2SG.POSS + case] and [3SG.POSS + case] are indistinguishable, because of the 'n' that is included in the 3rd person possessive suffix before a case suffix or -*CA* (6.2, 8.1.2). (44) can therefore be read in two ways:

(44)   Ev-**in**-i daha gör-me-di-m.
  (**a**) house-**2SG.POSS**-ACC
        'I haven't seen *your* house yet.'

  (**b**) house-**3SG.POSS**-ACC
        'I haven't seen *his/her* house yet.'

(**ii**)   A single -*lAr* can sometimes express two different notions of plurality simultaneously: plurality of the thing possessed, and plurality of the (3rd person) possessor. The form -*lArI* on a subject noun phrase is capable of three interpretations:

(**a**)   plural + 3rd person singular possessive
(**b**)   3rd person plural possessive
(**c**)   plural + 3rd person plural possessive

This ambiguity is illustrated in (45):

(45) (**a**) Bilet-**ler-i** burada.
           ticket-PL-3SG.POSS
           '*His/her* tickets are here.'

     (**b**) Bilet-**leri** burada.
           ticket-3PL.POSS
           '*Their* ticket is here.'

     (**c**) Bilet-**leri** burada.
           ticket-PL.3PL.POSS
           '*Their* tickets are here.'

In (a) -*lAr* indicates the plurality of the tickets. In (b) it is part of the suffix -*lArI*, indicating a 3rd person plural possessor ('their'). In (c) it is performing both functions simultaneously.

(**iii**) The 2nd/3rd person ambiguity identified in (i) is sometimes compounded with the 3rd person singular/plural ambiguity identified in (ii):

(46) (**a**) Arkadaş-**lar-ın**-a soralım.
           friend-**PL-2SG.POSS**-DAT
           'Let's ask *your* friends.'

     (**b**) Arkadaş-**lar-ın**-a soralım.
           friend-**PL-3SG.POSS**-DAT
           'Let's ask *his/her* friends.'

(c) Arkadaş-**ların**-a soralım.
friend-**3PL.POSS**-DAT
'Let's ask *their* friend.'

(d) Arkadaş-**ların**-a soralım.
friend-**PL.3PL.POSS**-DAT
'Let's ask *their* friend*s*.'

In (d) the element -*lAr* is again expressing plurality both of the possessor and of what is possessed (here 'friends'). Such potential ambiguities are resolved by using modifiers and forming genitive-possessive constructions, as explained in 14.4 below.

14.3.2.1 Marking possession in -*(s)I* compounds

Because only one possessive suffix can be attached to a noun at any one time, if a suffix indicating possession is added to a -*(s)I* compound (10.2) the compound marker -*(s)I(n)* has to be dropped. As a result, the non-possessed forms and the 3rd person possessed forms of any particular -*(s)I* compound are indistinguishable:

> *yatak oda-sı*
(i) bed room-NC   'bedroom'
(ii) bed room-3SG.POSS   'his/her bedroom'

> *yatak oda-m*
bed room-1SG.POSS   'my bedroom'

In the case of noun compounds that end in a consonant, where case marking is present the 2nd/3rd person ambiguity discussed in 14.3.2 (i) also arises:

(47)   Ders kitab-**ın**-ı beğenmedim.
    (a) lesson book-**NC**-ACC
      'I didn't like *the* textbook.'

    (b) lesson book-**2SG.POSS**-ACC
      'I didn't like *your* textbook.'

    (c) lesson book-**3SG.POSS**-ACC
      'I didn't like *his/her* textbook.'

Where a plural suffix is present the kinds of ambiguity discussed in 14.3.2 (ii) and (iii), regarding whether the plurality affects the possessed item, the possessor, or both, also arise:

(48) (a) Telefon numara-**lar-ın-ı** yazdım.
    (i) telephone number-**PL-NC**-ACC
        'I've written down *the* telephone number*s*.'

    (ii) telephone number-**PL-2SG.POSS**-ACC
        'I've written down *your* telephone number*s*.'

    (iii) telephone number-**PL-3SG.POSS**-ACC
        'I've written down *his/her* telephone number*s*.'

    (**b**) Telefon numara-**ların-ı** yazdım.
    (i) telephone number-**3PL.POSS**-ACC
        'I've written down *their* telephone number.'

    (ii) telephone number-**PL.3PL.POSS**-ACC
        'I've written down *their* telephone number*s*.'

In all of these cases, except for the non-possessive (47a) and (48a (i)), the use of a genitive-marked noun phrase or pronoun can eliminate the ambiguity (see 14.4).

14.3.3 CASE

Turkish has five case suffixes (8.1.3), which mark respectively the **accusative**, **dative**, **locative**, **ablative** and **genitive** cases. (The comitative/instrumental marker *-(y)lA/ile*, which shares some properties with case suffixes, is discussed in 8.1.4 and 17.2.1.) The function of case marking (or its absence) is to indicate the relationship between the noun phrase to which it is attached and other sentence constituents.

14.3.3.1 The non-case-marked noun phrase

A noun phrase is left without case marking when it functions as one of the items listed below:

(i) The **subject** of one of the following types of clause:

A main clause:

(49) Bunu belki **siz** bilebilirsiniz.
      'Perhaps *you* may know this.'

A finite subordinate clause:

(50) [**Herkes** görsün diye] kartı masanın üstünde bırakıyorum.
      'I'm leaving the card on the table [so that *everyone* will see it].'

An adverbial clause (for exceptions see 26.2.1):

> (51) [**Ahmet** gelince] ona sorabiliriz.
> '[When *Ahmet* comes] we can ask him.'

A conditional clause:

> (52) [**Ahmet** gelirse] ona sorabiliriz.
> '[If *Ahmet* comes] we can ask him.'

A relative clause of the type where the verb in the relative clause is marked with -*(y)An* and contains a subject (25.1.1.1 (ii-a)):

> (53) [**kapısı** açık dur*an*] bir oda
> 'a room, *the door of which* is/was open'

(ii)   A subject complement:

(a)   in nominal sentences (12.1.1.2):

> (54) Hakan'ın karısı **mimar**mış.
> 'Apparently Hakan's wife is *an architect.*'

(b)   in small clauses (24.5):

> (55) Bence [bu resim **sanat eseri**] sayılmaz.
> 'In my opinion this picture can't be considered *a work of art.*'
>
> (56) [Tanju'yu **arkadaş**] sayıyorduk o zamanlar.
> 'In those days we regarded Tanju as *a friend.*'

(iii) A non-definite (i.e. indefinite (22.2) or categorial (22.3)) **direct object:**

> (57) Bu konuda **kitap(lar)** okumuş.
> 'It seems he has read *books* on this subject.'
>
> (58) Bana da ver **bir çay**.
> 'Give me too *a (glass of) tea.*'

Note that indefinite direct objects sometimes have to, or may, take accusative case marking (see 14.3.3.2).

(iv) The **complement** of certain postpositions:

(a) The bare postpositions *gibi* 'like', *için* 'for', *ile/-(y)lA* 'with', *kadar* 'as
  ... as' (17.2.1):

> (59) O adam **para *için*** her şeyi yapar.
>   'That man would do anything *for money*.'

(b) Possessive-marked postpositions denoting spatial relations, such as
  iç-in-de 'in(side)', *alt-ın-da* 'under', *arka-sın-da* 'behind'. The non-
  case-marked form (as opposed to the genitive-marked form) occurs
  where the complement is non-specific or the postposition is used in a
  metaphorical or non-spatial sense (see 17.3.1.2):

> (60) Ellerim **çamur *içinde*** kalmıştı.
>   'My hands were *covered in mud*.'

(c) Other possessive-marked postpositions, such as *boyunca* 'all along',
  'throughout', *yüzünden* 'on account of' (for list see 17.3.2):

> (61) **Yol *boyunca*** konuştu.
>   'He talked *all the way*.'

(v) An adverbial, especially of time or distance (see also 16.1.4):

> (62) **O gün** siz yoktunuz.
>   'You were not there *that day*.'

14.3.3.2 The accusative case marker

The sole function of the accusative case marker is to indicate the direct
object of a transitive verb. However, as seen in the previous section, some
direct objects are left in the non-case-marked form. The rules for the use
and omission of accusative case marking are as follows:

(i) The use of the accusative suffix is obligatory where the direct object
is **definite**:

> (63) **Bütün arkadaşlarımızı** çağıralım.
>   'Let's invite *all our friends*.'

(ii)   Accusative case marking is also necessary where a **non-definite** direct object precedes the verb but does not occupy the immediately pre-verbal position:

> (64) **Birçok şey***i* şu raflara koyabiliriz.   (Indefinite)
>   '*A lot of things* we can put on these shelves.'

> (65) **Patlıcan***ı* her gün yiyebilirim.   (Categorial)
>   'I could eat *aubergines* every day.'

(iii)   An **indefinite** direct object which is in the immediately pre-verbal position must still take the accusative suffix in the following crcumstances:

(a)   If the direct object is marked with a possessive suffix:

> (66) **Bir arkadaş-***ım-ı* getireceğim.
>   a friend-1SG.POSS-ACC
>   'I'm going to bring *a friend of mine*.'

The only exception to this rule is where a 3rd person possessive suffix is functioning as the marker of a *-(s)I* compound. Thus the indefinite direct object in (67) is non-case-marked:

> (67) Her yemekten sonra **bir Türk kahve-***si* içer.
>   a Turk coffee-NC
>   'After every meal s/he has *a (cup of) Turkish coffee*.'

(b)   If the direct object is an indefinite or plural **generic** (see 22.4.3).

(c)   If the direct object refers to a member or members of a previously mentioned or implied group:

> (68) Paketin içindekiler eksik çıktı. **İki kitab***ı* göndermemişler galiba.
>   'The contents of the parcel are incomplete. I think they've failed to send *two [of the] books*.'

> (69) Salon kalabalıktı. **Kapıya yakın duran bir adam***ı* tanıdım.
>   'The room was crowded. I recognized *a man standing near the door*.'

For an explanation of other factors that can trigger accusative marking of indefinite direct objects see 22.2.1.

14.3.3.3 The dative case marker

The functions that may be performed by a noun phrase marked with the dative case suffix are listed below.

(i) An **adverbial** indicating one of the following:

(a) The recipient or beneficiary of an action:

(70) **Çocuğa** doğru dürüst bakamıyor.
'S/he can't look after *the child* properly.'

(71) **Aysel'e** anahtar verdim.
'I've given *Aysel* a key/keys.'

(b) The destination or target of an action:

(72) Beni **Paris'e** gönderdiler.
'They sent me *to Paris.*'

(73) Bu koltuk **oturma odasına** konacak.
'This armchair is to be put *in the sitting-room.*'

(c) The price at which something is sold or offered for sale:

(74) Bu bisikleti **iki yüz milyona** almıştım.
'I bought this bicycle *for 200 million* [*lira*].'

(d) Purpose:
This kind of dative-marked noun phrase is almost always a *-mAK* clause (26.3.12):

(75) [**Seni gör***mey*]*-e* geldim.
'I've come *to see you.*'

(ii) The **oblique object** (13.1.2.2) of many verbs of emotion, e.g. *sevin-* 'be pleased (about)', *üzül-* 'be sorry (about)', *kız-* 'be angry (with/about)', *can-ı sıkıl-* 'be annoyed (about)', and certain other verbs, e.g. *benze-* 'resemble', *uy-* 'conform (to)', 'comply (with)', *inan-* 'believe', *güven-* 'trust':

(76) [**Ayşe'nin geleceğin**]*-e* sevindik.
'We're glad *Ayşe's going to come.*'

(77) **Annemin isteğine** uymadım.
'I didn't comply *with my mother's wish.*'

(iii) The **complement** of:

(a) Certain bare postpositions, e.g. *doğru* 'towards', *göre* 'according to', *kadar* 'until' (see 17.2.2):

> (78) **Saat ikiye *kadar*** çalıştık.
> 'We worked *until two o'clock*.'

(b) Certain adjectives, e.g. *yakın* 'near', *uygun* 'suitable (for)' (see 15.5):

> (79) **Okula *yakın*** bir ev arıyorlar.
> 'They're looking for a house *near the school*.'

(iv) The 'causee' of a causative construction based on a transitive verb, i.e. the person who is made or allowed to perform the action (13.2.1):

> (80) Filiz bütün ev işlerini **kocasına** yaptırıyor.
> 'Filiz makes *her husband* do all the housework.'

14.3.3.4 The locative case marker

The locative suffix expresses physical or abstract location. A noun phrase in the locative case can function as one of the following:

(i) A time or place **adverbial**:

> (81) **O günler*de*** Selim çok sigara içiyordu.
> '*At that time* Selim was smoking a lot.'

> (82) İnsanlar artık komşularını bile tanımıyorlar **büyük kentler*de***.
> 'People don't even know their neighbours nowadays *in big cities*.'

(ii) The **oblique object** (13.1.2.2) of a small number of verbs, such as *karar kıl-* 'decide (on)', *ısrar et-* 'insist (on)':

> (83) [**Hepsini denemek**]-*te* ısrar etti.
> 'She insisted *on trying them all*.'

(iii) A **subject complement**:

(a) In linking sentences (12.1.1.2):

> (84) Anahtar **yerin*de*** değil.
> 'The key is not *in its place*.'

(b) In small clauses (24.5):

(85) [Onu **İstanbulda**] sanıyordum.
'I thought he was *in Istanbul.*'

(iv) The locational constituent of an existential sentence:

(86) **Köyde** elektrik var mıydı?
'Was there electricity *in the village?*'

(v) Within a larger noun phrase, a compound adjectival modifier expressing metaphorical 'location' in some kind of attribute (size, shape, colour, name, age, etc; see 15.3.2):

(87) **otuz metre derin-liğ-in-*de*** bir kuyu
thirty metre deep-N.DER-NC-LOC a well
'a well *thirty metres deep*'

14.3.3.5 The ablative case marker

The ablative case marker indicates that a noun phrase is functioning as one of the following:

(i) An **adverbial** associated with concepts such as departure, separation, source, or cause:

(88) Ali **oda*dan*** çıktı.
'Ali left *the room.*'

(89) Zavallı bunu **yorgunluk*tan*** yapmıştır.
'The poor thing must have done this *out of tiredness.*'

In association with the verb *geç-* 'pass' an ablative noun phrase indicates a place or space through which someone/something travels:

(90) Gelirken **şehir merkezin*den geç***tiniz mi?
'Did you *go through* the city centre on your way here?'

This usage is very frequent with the possessive-marked spatial postpositions (see 17.3.1.1 (iii)).

(ii) The **oblique object** (13.1.2.2) of certain verbs of emotion, especially those which reflect the concepts of aversion, e.g. *kork-* 'be afraid (of)', *iğren-* 'be disgusted (by)', *nefret et-* 'hate', *bık-* 'get fed up (with)', *hoşlan-* 'like':

> (91) **O adamdan** nefret ediyorum.
> 'I hate *that man.*'

> (92) Gürcan **yağmurlu havalardan** hoşlanır.
> 'Gürcan likes *wet weather.*'

Certain other verbs, notably *vazgeç-* 'give up', *faydalan-/yararlan-* 'benefit (from)' and *oluş-* 'consist (of)' also take ablative-marked objects:

> (93) Zerrin [**tenis oynamak**]-*tan* vazgeçti.
> 'Zerrin gave up [*playing tennis*].'

(iii) The **complement** of:

(a) Certain bare postpositions, e.g. *önce* 'before', *sonra* 'after', *başka* 'apart from', *dolayı* 'because of' (see 17.2.3):

> (94) **Okuldan sonra** genellikle futbol oynuyor.
> '*After school* he usually plays football.'

(b) Certain adjectives, e.g. *memnun* 'pleased (with)' (see 15.5):

> (95) **Hayatın-dan** *memnun* görünüyor.
> 'She seems *content with life.*'

(iv) Within a larger noun phrase, a **modifier** expressing

(a) The material from which something is made:

> (96) Padişahın {**som altından** bir taht}-ı vardı.
> 'The king had a throne *of solid gold.*'

(b) An entity, set or category of which the head constituent expresses a part or member (see **partitive constructions**, 14.5 below):

> (97) {**Çikolatalı pasta-dan** iki dilim} yedi.
> chocolate cake-ABL two slice
> 'He ate two slices *of the chocolate cake.*'

(v) A **subject complement** with partitive meaning:

(a) In nominal sentences (12.1.1.2):

(98) Osman {**yakın arkadaşlarımdan** (biri)} değildir.
'Osman is not *among*/(one of) *my close friends.*'

(b) In small clauses (24.5):

(99) {**Memleketin en iyi ressamlarından** (biri)} sayılır.
'S/he is regarded as *among*/(one of) *the best painters in the country.*'

(100) Ahmet Vefik Paşa'yı {**ilk Türk milliyetçilerinden** (biri)} addetmek mümkün.
'It is possible to regard Ahmet Vefik Paşa as *among*/(one of) *the first Turkish nationalists.*'

(vi) In adjectival or adverbial structures expressing comparison (see 15.4.2, 16.9), the **modifier** that expresses the object of comparison:

(101) Mustafa'nın evi **bundan** (daha) büyük.
'Mustafa's house is bigger *than this.*'

14.3.3.6 The genitive case marker

The basic function of the genitive case marker is to mark a noun phrase as denoting the possessor of some item expressed by another constituent. An important secondary function is to mark the subject of certain kinds of non-finite subordinate clause.

(i) As the expression of a possessor, a genitive-marked noun phrase can function as:

(a) The **modifier** in a genitive-possessive construction (a composite noun phrase whose head is marked by a possessive suffix, see 14.4 below):

(102) {**Bu çocuğun** annesi} nerede?
'Where is *this child's* mother?'

(103) {**Ayten'in** iki kız kardeşi} var.
'*Ayten* has two sisters.'

(**b**) A subject complement in nominal sentences (12.1.1.2):

> (104) Fotoğraf makinesi **benim** değil, **babamın**.
> 'The camera's not *mine*, it's *my father's*.'

(**c**) A subject complement in small clauses (24.5):

> (105) [Bu odayı artık **Fatma'nın**] sayıyorum.
> 'I now regard [this room as *Fatma's*].'

(**ii**) The types of non-finite subordinate clause in which an overt subject is genitive marked are:

(**a**) most non-finite noun clauses marked with *-mA*, *-DIK* or *-(y)AcAK* (see Chapter 24, especially 24.4.6):

> (106) [**Turgut-un** gel-me-sin]-i istiyorum.
> Turgut-GEN come-VN-3SG.POSS-ACC
> 'I want [*Turgut* to come].'

> (107) [**Bunun** bir roman olduğun]-u söylemişti.
> 'He said [*this* was a novel].'

(**b**) those types of relative clause whose verb is suffixed with *-DIK* or *-(y)AcAK* plus a possessive suffix (see 25.1.1.2):

> (108) [**Siz-in** söyle-dik-ler-iniz]-i beğendim.
> you-GEN say-PART-PL-2PL.POSS-ACC
> 'I liked [what *you* said].'

> (109) [**Anne-n-in** getir-eceğ-i] pasta yetecek mi?
> mother-2SG.POSS-GEN bring-PART-3SG.POSS cake
> 'Will the cake [*your mother*'s going to bring] be enough?'

14.4 THE GENITIVE-POSSESSIVE CONSTRUCTION

The genitive-possessive construction is a composite noun phrase constructed of two noun phrases marked as follows:

(noun phrase + genitive) + (noun phrase + possessive)

The first noun phrase, which carries genitive case marking, is the modifier and indicates the possessor. The second noun phrase, which carries possessive marking, is the head of the composite noun phrase and indicates the entity which is possessed:

Ali-**nin** oğl-**u**   'Ali's son'
Ali-GEN son-3SG.POSS
oda-**nın** kapı-**sı**   'the door of the room'
room-GEN door-3SG.POSS

The possessive suffix on the head has to agree in terms of grammatical person with the possessor-modifier, as illustrated below:

ben-im ev-**im**   'my house'
I-GEN house-1SG.POSS
Fatma-nın ev-**i**   'Fatma's house'
Fatma-GEN house-3SG.POSS

It is the possessive-marked head of the genitive-possessive construction that is the bearer of any case marking needed to indicate the relation of this composite noun phrase to other sentence constituents:

(110) Bu haber-i {Ali-nin oğl-un}-**dan** al-dı-m.
       this news-ACC Ali-GEN son-3SG.POSS-ABL get-PF-1SG
       'I heard this news *from* {Ali's son}.'

A genitive-possessive construction can itself function as the possessor constituent in a larger genitive-possessive construction:

(111) {{**Ayten-in anne-sin}-in ism-in**}-i biliyor musun?
       Ayten-GEN mother-3SG.POSS-GEN name-3SG.POSS-ACC
       'Do you know *Ayten's mother's name*?'

Where the possessed entity is singular and the possessor is plural, the 3rd person *singular* suffix is often used on the head, in order to avoid ambiguity with the parallel construction in which the entity possessed is plural:

(112) {Çocuk-lar-ın öğretmen-**i**} İngiliz.
       child-PL-GEN teacher-3SG.POSS
       'The children's teacher is English.'

(113) {Çocukların öğretmen-**ler-i**} İngiliz.
                        teacher-3PL.POSS/-3PL.POSS
       (**a**) 'The children's teachers are English.'
       (**b**) 'The children's teacher is English.'

Whereas sentences on the pattern of (112) clearly express the singularity of the possessed entity, the ambiguity of (113) shows that the plurality of an entity possessed by a plural possessor cannot be unambiguously articulated. However, (113a) represents the more typical sense in which this pattern is used.

One function of the genitive-possessive construction is to resolve ambiguities of the kind noted above in 14.3.2, where *Arkadaşlarına soralım* (46) was shown to be capable of four different readings. (114) demonstrates how the addition of a genitive-marked pronoun modifier, combined in (c) with the use of singular possessive marking, eliminates these ambiguities:

(114) (a) {**Sen-in** arkadaş-lar-ın}-a soralım.
     you-GEN friend-PL-2SG.POSS-DAT
     'Let's ask *your* friend*s*.'

(b) {**O-nun** arkadaş-lar-ın}-a soralım.
     s/he-GEN friend-PL-3SG.POSS-DAT
     'Let's ask *his/her* friend*s*.'

(c) {**Onlar-ın** arkadaş-ın}-a soralım.
     they-GEN friend-**3SG.POSS**-DAT
     'Let's ask *their* friend.'

(d) {**Onlar-ın** arkadaş-ların}-a soralım.
     they-GEN friend-PL.3PL.POSS-DAT
     'Let's ask *their* friend*s*.'

In informal styles, the head of a genitive-possessive construction is often left without possessive marking, particularly when the genitive-marked modifier is a 1st or 2nd person pronoun:

(115) Burası {**biz-im ev**}-den daha sıcak. (cf. (86) in Chapter 18)
     here we-GEN house-ABL more warm
     'It's warmer here than [in] *our house*.'

(116) Nerede {**senin çocuklar**}?
     'Where are *your children*?'

Such constructions occur only in contexts which fulfil the conditions governing the use of genitive-marked pronouns (see 18.1.5, 18.1.5.1). Note also that the omission of possessive marking on the head is not permissible in possessive existential sentences (12.1.1.2). Thus the possessive suffix on *araba* in (117) is obligatory:

(117) {**Siz-in araba-nız**} var mı?
     you-GEN car-2PL.POSS existent INT
     'Do you have a car?'

Apart from expressing possession, the genitive-possessive construction also articulates the relationship between different specimens of the same type. In this kind of genitive-possessive construction the genitive-marked noun phrase expresses either a particular specimen or specimens of the type, as in (118), or the type itself, as in (119). The nominal in the head position is usually a pronominalized determiner or adjectival (18.4):

(118) Bu araba {**benimkinin tam *aynısı***} değil.
      'This car is not *quite the same as mine.*'

(119) {**Bisikletin *motorlus*un**}-a motosiklet denir.
      '*The motorized version of a bicycle* is called a motorcycle.'

A further use of the genitive-possessive construction is to express a partitive relation (14.5.3).

14.5 PARTITIVE CONSTRUCTIONS

There are three composite noun-phrase constructions that are used to express part of a whole, or to select one or more items from a type or set.

	Modifier	+	Head
(i)	(noun phrase + ablative)	+	(bare noun phrase)
	şu elma-dan		*birkaç kilo*
	'a few kilos of these apples'		
(ii)	(noun phrase + ablative)	+	(noun phrase + 3rd person singular possessive)
	erkek öğrenciler-den		*bir tane-si*
	'one of the male students'		
(iii)	(noun phrase + genitive)	+	(noun phrase + 3rd person singular possessive)
	hesabımdaki para-nın		*büyük kısm-ı*
	'most of the money in my account'		

In each construction it is the genitive- or ablative-marked modifier constituent which expresses the whole or set, and the head constituent which expresses the part or the selected item(s). The head noun phrase is always indefinite (except in the case of one subtype of the bare-headed partitive; see 14.5.1 (i)), while the modifier noun phrase is definite, or sometimes generic.

14.5.1 THE BARE-HEADED PARTITIVE CONSTRUCTION WITH ABLATIVE-MARKED MODIFIER

Structurally, the distinguishing characteristic of this construction is that the bare noun phrase functioning as the head must itself be headed by one of the following: a proper name, a common noun, or the enumerator *tane* (15.8). There are three subtypes:

(i)   Partitives in which the head noun phrase is a proper name.
These differ from all other kinds of partitive constructions in that the head noun phrase is **definite**. The function of the ablative-marked modifier noun phrase here is to provide additional, descriptive information about the person or place identified by the proper name:

(120)   Bugünkü konuğumuz, {ülke-miz-in genç şair-ler-in-**den** *Küçük*
                                        country-1PL.POSS-GEN young poet-PL-
                                        3SG.POSS-ABL
        İskender}.
        'Our guest today is *Küçük İskender,* [*one*] *of our country's young poets.*'

(121)   {Batı Afrika ülkelerin**den** *Sierra Leone*}-de on yıldan beri iç savaş var.
        'In *Sierra Leone, a country in West Africa*, there has been civil war for ten years.'

This type of partitive construction occurs also in the question used to ask the day of the week:

(122)   Bugün {günler**den** *ne*}?
        '*What day* is it today?'

(ii)   Partitives in which the (bare) head noun phrase is itself headed by a common noun, and in which the meaning of the head noun phrase is relatively independent of the modifier noun phrase.
   The modifier noun phrase here may, as in type (i), have a descriptive rather than a truly partitive function:

(123)   Rehberimiz, {Abdülhamit dönemi mimari eserlerin**den** *bir mescid*}-e dikkat çekti.
        'Our guide drew attention to *a small mosque,* [*one*] *of the architectural works of Abdülhamit's reign.*'

However, it may also identify the individual(s) expressed by the head as belonging to a specific set:

(124) {Bu yılki misafirlerimiz**den** *yirmi otuz aile*} şimdiden gelecek yıl
için rezervasyon yaptılar.
'{*Twenty or thirty families from among our guests this year*} have
already made reservations for next year.'

Where the noun phrase defining the set has been mentioned in the immediately preceding context, the ablative-marked modifier is usually one of
the possessive-marked postpositions *iç-* or *ara-* 'among' (17.3.1.3):

(125) Bu yıl **bol misafirimiz** oldu. {*İçlerinden* yirmi otuz aile} de
şimdiden gelecek yıl için rezervasyon yaptılar.
'This year we had *a lot of guests*. {*From among them*, twenty or
thirty families} have already made reservations for next year.'

The forms with *iç-/ara-* are also preferred where the set is referred to in the
1st or 2nd person:

(126) {**İçimizden/Aramızdan** birkaç kişi} geziden memnun kalmadı.
'{Several *of our number*} were not satisfied with the tour.'

(**iii**) Partitive constructions in which the noun heading the head noun
phrase is either the enumerator *tane* (15.8) or a word expressing a concept
such as measure (e.g. *metre* 'metre', *dilim* 'slice', *şişe* 'bottle'), membership
of a category (e.g. *örnek* 'example'), or identity (e.g. *kopya* 'copy'):

(127) {Küçükler**den on** *tane*} yeter mi?
'Will {*ten of* the little ones} be enough?'

(128) {Şu kırmızı çiçekli kumaş**tan on** *metre*} alalım.
'Let's buy {*ten metres of* that material with red flowers on it}.'

In this third subtype of bare-headed partitives, the meaning of the head
noun phrase is highly dependent on that of the modifier, just as it is in the
-sI-marked constructions described in the next section. The item(s)
expressed by the head noun phrase in examples such as (127) and (128) are
not individuated; the emphasis is purely on quantification, and the referents are almost invariably non-human.
In this type of partitive construction it is even possible for the head noun
phrase to be omitted altogether. The ablative-marked noun phrase then
simply indicates some or any undefined quantity of the substance or set of
entities referred to:

(129) {Şu kırmızı çiçekli kumaş**tan**} alalım.
'Let's buy {[*some*] *of* that material with red flowers on it}.'

(130) {Bunlar**dan**} bizde de var.
      'We've got {[*some*] *of* these}, too.'

14.5.2 THE -*(s)I*-MARKED PARTITIVE CONSTRUCTION WITH ABLATIVE-MARKED MODIFIER

In this type of partitive construction there is a close semantic dependency of the head upon the modifier, indicated not only by the possessive suffix but also by the fact that the head noun phrase does not contain a semantically autonomous noun. The head noun phrase usually consists of one of the following items:

(i)   a numeral (suffixed with -*(s)I*)
(ii)   *kaç-ı* 'how many of' or *birkaç-ı* 'a few of', 'several of'
(iii) a numeral, *kaç* or *birkaç* followed by *tane-si*
(iv)   *bazı-sı/kimi-si/bir kısm-ı/bir bölüm-ü* 'some of'
(v)   *birçoğ-u* 'many of'
(vi)   *hangi-si* (or *hangiler-i* if a plural referent is intended) 'which of'
(vii) *hiçbir-i* 'none of'
(viii) a pronominalized adjectival (18.4 (i)), such as *en akıllılar-ı* 'the most intelligent (ones)'.

The function of this construction is to pick out one or more items from a distinct set:

(131) {Komşularımız**dan bazısı**} televizyonlarını çok açıyorlar.
      '*Some of* our neighbours turn their televisions on very loud.'

Under the same conditions as explained in 14.5.1 (ii), the modifier may be expressed by the ablative-marked form of a postposition based on *iç-* or *ara-*. For examples see (65), (69) in Chapter 19.

In the case of heads based upon *tane*, the choice between this construction and the bare-headed version described in (iii) of the previous section offers a distinction of meaning:

(132) (**a**) Bana {küçükler**den iki tane**} lazım.
          'I need {*two of* the small ones}.'

      (**b**) {Küçükler**den iki tane*si*}} bana lazım.
          'I need {*two of* the small ones}.'

In (132a) the ablative-marked modifier noun phrase is understood *generically*, i.e as referring to a type of thing rather than to a discrete set. The head noun phrase denotes simply a certain or approximate number of items of the type specified ('small ones'). In (132b), on the other hand, the presence of *-(s)I* on the head noun phrase imparts a *definite* meaning to the modifier noun phrase, making it refer to a particular set of 'small ones'.

When they are in the direct object role, *-(s)I*-marked partitives obligatorily take accusative case marking:

(133) {Bu ilaç-lar-**dan hangi-ler-in**}-*i* alıyorsun?
these medicine-PL-ABL which-PL-3SG.POSS-ACC
'{*Which (ones)* of these medicines} are you taking?'

14.5.3 THE *-(s)I*-MARKED PARTITIVE CONSTRUCTION WITH GENITIVE-MARKED MODIFIER

The third way of expressing a partitive relation is by means of the genitive-possessive construction (14.4). In many cases this is interchangeable with the *-(s)I*-marked partitive construction with ablative-marked modifier (14.5.2):

(134) {Komşularımız**ın bazısı**} televizyonlarını çok açıyorlar.
'*Some of* our neighbours turn their televisions up very loud.'

(135) {Bu ilaçlar**ın hangilerin**}-i alıyorsun?
'{*Which (ones)* of these medicines} are you taking?'

The partitive uses of the genitive-possessive construction include, however, another type of relation which cannot be expressed using an ablative-marked modifier. These are relations of *proportion* or *totality*, often involving one of the following items as the head:

(i)   *yarı-sı* 'half (of)'
(ii) *büyük kısm-ı/büyük bölüm-ü* 'the majority of', 'most of'
(iii) *çoğ-u* 'most of'
(iv) *hep-si* 'all of'
(v)   *tüm-ü/bütün-ü* 'the whole of', 'all of'
(vi) *her bir-i* 'every one of'
(vii) *her* followed by a numeral suffixed with *-(s)I*.

(136) {Dergiler**in hepsin**}-i Aysel'e geri verdim.
'I've given *all (of)* the magazines back to Aysel.'

(137) {Öğrenciler**in her birin**}-in ayrı bir mazereti vardı.
'{*Every one of* the students} had a different excuse.'

Fractions, being a precise kind of proportional relation, are expressed by an extended genitive-possessive construction (see 15.7.1).

14.5.4 OTHER FEATURES OF PARTITIVE CONSTRUCTIONS

It is possible for an adverbial to intervene between the two constituents of any type of partitive construction:

(138) {Güney Amerika ülkelerinden **en çok** Arjantin}'le ticaret yapıyoruz.
'Among the South American countries we do business *mostly* with Argentina.'

(139) {O kitaplardan **bugün** pek azı} kaldı.
'Very few of those books are left *today*.'

It is also possible for two separate heads to share a single partitive modifier (28.4.2.1 (iii)):

(140) Hafta sonlarında {çocuklarından **bazen *biri*, bazen *iki tanesi*}** geliyor.
'At the weekends *sometimes one*, *sometimes two* of his/her children come.'

14.6   STRESS IN NOUN PHRASES

In a noun phrase that contains an adjective, stress falls on the adjective unless it is itself modified (e.g. by *en* 'most' or *daha* 'more', see 15.4):

(141) {esKİ bir ev}
'an *old* house'

(142) {EN eski ev}
'the old*est* house'

If a noun phrase contains one of the quantifiers *birtakım* 'some', 'a number of', *biraz* 'a little' and *bir miktar* 'some', 'a certain amount of' (15.6.1 (ii)), but no adjectives, stress falls on the noun:

(143) bir miktar şeKER
'some *sugar*'

If a noun phrase contains any of the other indefinite determiners in 15.6.1 (other than *bir* 'a(n)'), a definite determiner (15.6.2) or a numeral (15.7), this constituent is stressed:

(144) {[sorusu olan] HER öğrenci}
'*every* student who has a question'

Note that these rules apply to noun phrases in isolation. When a noun phrase is uttered inside a sentence it may not be stressed at all, or it may be stressed on a different syllable. For the properties of sentence stress see Chapters 5 and 23.

15 ADJECTIVAL CONSTRUCTIONS, DETERMINERS AND NUMERALS

Adjectivals are words or constructions that modify noun phrases. Simple adjectivals consist of a single word, i.e. an **adjective** (see 7.1.1 (iii)):

(1) **küçük** evler
     '*small* houses'

(2) **beyaz** elbisem
     'my *white* dress'

Complex adjectivals vary in their degree of complexity. They range from structures consisting of a noun phrase marked with a suffix such as *-lI* or *-ki* to **relative clauses**, (as in (4)), which have a sentence-like structure:

(3) **bahçede*ki*** ağaç
     'the tree *in the garden*'

(4) [**manzarası olan**] bir ev
     'a house *which has a view*'

After a brief survey of the functions of adjectivals (15.1), and an overview of the ways in which adjectives can be formed in Turkish (15.2), section 15.3 examines the structure of complex adjectivals (except for relative clauses, for which see Chapter 25). The next two sections look at how adjectivals can be modified (e.g. *çok güzel* 'very nice', *daha küçük* 'smaller') or complemented (e.g. *buraya uygun* 'suitable for here').

In 15.6–15.8 we present other classes functionally related to adjectivals, namely **determiners** (e.g. *bir* 'a(n)', *bu* 'this'), numerals, the enumerator *tane* and measure terms. 15.9 explains how these items interact with adjectivals within the noun phrase.

15.1 FUNCTIONS OF ADJECTIVALS

Adjectivals express qualities that are ascribed to entities. In Turkish, as in other languages, they can be used **attributively**, that is as a modifier of a noun phrase, or **predicatively**, as the subject complement in a linking sentence (12.1.1.2) or small clause (24.5).

(i)   The attributive function:
In Turkish attributive adjectivals, whether simple or complex, always precede the noun they qualify:

yüksek *ağaç*	'*tall* tree'
şekerli *kahve*	'coffee *with sugar*'
beş yatak odalı *ev*	'*five-bedroomed* house'
yedi yaşında *bir çocuk*	'a *seven-year-old* child'
evin önündeki *arabalar*	'the cars *in front of the house*'

(ii)   The predicative function:
Predicative adjectivals, on the other hand, function as subject complements and therefore normally follow the noun phrase expressing the entity that they describe:

As subject complement in linking sentences (12.1.1.2):

(5)   Ağaç **yüksek**.
tree tall
'The tree is *tall*.'

(6)   Çocuk **yedi yaş-ın-da**.
child seven age-NC-LOC
'The child is *seven years old*.'

As subject complement in small clauses (24.5):

(7)   [Ev **beş yatak oda-lı**] say-ıl-ır.
house five bed room-ADJ consider-PASS-AOR
'The house can be considered *five-bedroomed*.'

(8)   [Selim-i **zengin**] say-mı-yor-um.
Selim-ACC rich regard-NEG-IMPF-1SG
'I don't regard Selim as *rich*.'

However, in accordance with the general principles affecting word order in the sentence, it is possible for a predicative adjective to precede the subject noun phrase; see 23.3.2, e.g. example (57).

15.2   ADJECTIVES

From the point of view of form we can divide adjectives into two main groups, according to whether or not they contain a **productive** derivational suffix (7.2). Adjectives such as *düşmanca* 'hostile', *başarılı* 'successful', or *bilimsel* 'scientific' are **derived** by means of a productive suffix (in this case *-CA*, *-lI* or *-sAl*), and therefore have a predictable semantic relationship with an item from another word class (in this case the nouns *düşman* 'enemy', *başarı* 'success' and *bilim* 'science').

15.2.1 FORMING ADJECTIVES BY MEANS OF DERIVATIONAL SUFFIXES

There are many suffixes which productively derive adjectives from nominal stems (principally from nouns) or from verb stems. The most commonly occurring suffixes that derive adjectives from nominal stems are *-CA*, *-CI*, *-lI*, *-lIk*, *-sAl* and *-sIz* (see 7.2.2.2):

(9) **yaz-lık** ev
summer-ADJ house
'holiday home'

-(y)IcI and *-(s)Al* are the most commonly occurring suffixes deriving adjectives from verb stems (see 7.2.1.1):

(10) **gör-sel** sanat-lar
see-ADJ art-PL
'*visual* arts'

15.2.2 INTENSIVE FORMS

Some adjectives have intensive forms produced by reduplication of the initial syllable:

yeni 'new'	→ **yepyeni**	'brand new'
başka 'different'	→ **bambaşka**	'completely different'

A full explanation of this process is given in 9.1, and a list of the adjectives (and adverbs) thus formed is provided in Appendix 1.

15.3 COMPLEX ADJECTIVALS

15.3.1 ADJECTIVE + NOUN

Adjectivals on this pattern are formed from a limited range of adjective-noun combinations. The nouns include *boy* 'size', *beden* 'size' (of clothing), *biçim* 'form', 'kind', *tarz* 'style':

(11) **küçük boy** kitaplar
'*small-format* books'

(12) **eski tarz** mobilya
'*old-style* furniture'

The noun *marka* 'make', 'brand' can be preceded in this type of structure
by a brand name instead of an adjective:

(13) **Opel marka** bir araba
'an Opel car'

15.3.2   LOCATIVE-MARKED NOUN PHRASE

This type of adjectival phrase expresses qualities such as age, size, shape,
colour, or style. The noun phrase to which locative case marking is attached
is either a *-(s)I* compound or has the form Adjective + Noun. Where used
attributively, this type of adjectival occurs only in indefinite noun phrases
(22.2):

(14) **dört yaş-ın-*da*** bir çocuk
four age-NC-LOC
'a *four-year-old* child'

(15) **geniş çap*ta*** bir arama
'a *wide-ranging* search'

15.3.3   ABLATIVE-MARKED NOUN PHRASE

Adjectivals on this pattern express the material from which something is
made:

(16) **som altın*dan*** bir taht
'a throne *of solid gold*'

(17) **gazete kağıdın*dan*** torbalar
'bags *made from newspaper*'

15.3.4   NOUN PHRASE MARKED WITH -*lI*

In addition to its function of forming derived adjectives from nouns, *-lI* is
highly productive in forming adjectivals from noun phrases. This suffix
means 'possessing', 'characterized by', or 'provided with' whatever is
expressed by the stem (see 7.2.2.2).

(18) **sarı saç-lı** kız
yellow hair-ADJ
'*blonde-haired* girl'

(19) **uzun boy-lu** adamlar
long stature-ADJ
'*tall* men'

If the head of the noun phrase to which *-lI* is suffixed is a *-(s)I* compound, the compound marker has to be deleted. Thus from *yatak oda-sı* 'bedroom' adjectival phrases such as *beş yatak oda-lı* 'five-bedroomed' are derived.

15.3.5   NOUN PHRASE MARKED WITH *-lIk*

Adjectivals of this type are formed from quantitative expressions of the form numeral + noun, and according to the meaning of this noun can express weight, length, capacity, duration, price, etc.:

(20) **beş metre*lik*** bir kablo
'a *five-metre* cable'

(21) **iki litre*lik*** bir kova
'a *two-litre* bucket'

When the noun to which *-lIk* is attached is *kişi* 'person', the adjectival usually has the meaning 'sufficient/suitable for ... people':

(22) Otobüste sadece **iki kişi*lik*** yer kalmış.
'It seems there are only two seats left on the bus.' (lit. 'space *for two people*')

Where *-lIk* is attached directly to a numerical expression, it denotes value or price (in Turkish lira, if not otherwise specified):

(23) Demet **beş yüz milyon*luk*** bir fotoğraf makinesi almış.
'Apparently Demet has bought a five-hundred-million (-lira) camera.'

15.3.6   LOCATIVE-MARKED NOUN PHRASE + *-ki*

This is an extremely productive construction (see 8.1.4), creating an attributive adjectival phrase from a locational expression (which without *-ki* could function only adverbially or predicatively). Adjectival phrases formed on this pattern are used predominantly in noun phrases that have definite status (22.1), sometimes also in those that are indefinite but specific (22.2.1):

(24) {**Bahçe-de-ki** (bazı) ağaç-lar} yapraklarını dökmeye başladı.
garden-LOC-ADJ (some) tree-PL
'{The/Some trees *in the garden*} have begun to shed their leaves.'

This construction occurs also with possessive-marked postpositions (17.3) that include the locative case marker:

(25) **Arka-mız-da-*ki*** (bir) araba bizi geçmek istiyor.
back-1PL.POSS-LOC-ADJ (a) car
'The/A car *behind us* wants to overtake us.'

(26) **Benim hakkımda*ki*** fikriniz yanlış.
'Your opinion *of me* is wrong.'

15.3.7   TEMPORAL ADVERBIAL + -*ki*

Any adverbial expressing location (as opposed to duration) in time (16.4.1.1) can similarly be converted into a defining adjectival phrase by the addition of -*ki* (8.1.4):

(27) **Bu sabah*ki*** gazetede okudum.
'I read (it) in *this morning's* paper.'

(28) Mehmet'in **o gün*kü*** halini çok iyi hatırlıyorum.
'I well remember the state Mehmet was in *that day*.'

15.3.8   NOUN PHRASE + *diye*

The word *diye* is the -*(y)A* converbial form (26.3.8) of the verb *de-* 'say'. Aside from its wide range of functions as a subordinator marking noun clauses (24.3.1) and adverbial clauses (26.1.1), *diye* has an adjectival function (not found in more formal registers) of indicating what something is called. Adjectivals constructed with *diye* are used exclusively in indefinite noun phrases (22.2):

(29) Bizim mahallede Güneş Gıda **diye** bir market var.
'In our neighbourhood there's a self-service shop *called* Güneş Gıda.'

(30) Mehmet **diye** bir oğlu daha var.
'S/he's got another son, *called* Mehmet.'

15.3.9 RELATIVE CLAUSE

Relative clauses are the most complex form of adjectival, having a sentence-like structure with a participle as their verb. These are fully discussed in Chapter 25.

(31) [Arka-mız-dan gel-**en**] araba bizi geçmek istiyor.
back-1PL.POSS-ABL come-PART car
'The car [*that's following* us] wants to overtake us.'

15.3.10 POSSESSIVE-MARKED NOUN PHRASE + ADJECTIVE (TRUNCATED RELATIVE CLAUSE)

This type of adjectival construction tends to occur with non-specific noun phrases (see 25.4.1.1 for details):

(32) [**sap-lar-ı kopuk**] birkaç çanta (cf. Chapter 25, (80)–(82))
handle-PL-3SG.POSS broken a.few bag
'a few bags *with broken handles*'

15.4 MODIFICATION OF ADJECTIVES

Adjectives can be modified by a preceding adverbial of degree (16.5) in order to indicate the intensity of the attribute denoted by the adjective. Most adverbials of degree, such as *çok* 'very' or *biraz* 'a little', relate to abstract notions of quantity, but two of them (*daha* 'more' and *en* 'most'), express respectively a comparative or superlative degree.

15.4.1 GENERAL MODIFICATION

15.4.1.1 By simple adverbials of degree

Simple adverbials of quantity and degree (listed in 16.5), such as *çok* 'very', 'too' and *biraz* 'a little', 'a bit', 'rather', occur as modifiers of adjectives:

(33) **çok** temiz
'*very* clean'

(34) **biraz** aptal
'*a bit* stupid'

15.4.1.2 By complex adverbials

The other means of general modification of adjectives is a phrase or clause headed by the postposition *kadar* 'as . . . as' (17.2.1 (iv)). This may be a postpositional phrase:

(35) **Filiz'in evi kadar** temiz
'*as clean as* Filiz's house'

Alternatively, it may be an adverbial clause (26.3.13):

(36) [**inan-ıl-a-ma-yacak kadar**] temiz
believe-PASS-PSB-NEG-CV
'*unbelievably* clean'

(37) [**bekle-diğ-imiz kadar**] temiz
expect-CV-1PL.POSS
'as clean [*as we expect(ed)*]'

15.4.2 COMPARATIVES

The comparative form of an adjective is formed by the adverb *daha* 'more'. *daha* precedes the adjectival constituent, and can itself be modified by the degree adverbs *çok* 'much' and *biraz* 'a little':

(38) (çok) **daha** rahat
'(much) *more* comfortable'

(39) (biraz) **daha** güzel
'(a little) pretti*er*'

daha usually takes an ablative-marked complement:

(40) bu araba-**dan daha** *geniş* bir araba
this car-ABL more spacious a car
'a *more spacious* car *than* this one'

(41) hepimiz**den daha** *hevesli* bir üye
'a member *more enthusiastic than* any of us'

Alternatively, it can be used with a phrase of comparison containing *kıyasla*, *oranla* or ∇*nazaran* 'compared with':

(42) Semra'**ya kıyasla daha** *becerikli*
'*more efficient than* Semra'

The complement of *daha* can be a non-finite noun clause (24.4):

(43) [**Beni son gördüğünüz**]-**den** daha iyiyim.
'I'm better *than* [*when you last saw me*].'

The complement of *daha* can be omitted when the person or object to which someone or something is compared is obvious from the context:

(44) Size (bu evden) **daha uygun bir ev** düşünemiyorum.
'I cannot think of *a more suitable house* for you (than this house).'

Alternatively, *daha* can be omitted if an ablative complement is present:

(45) Bu makine öbürün**den** ucuz.
'This machine is cheap*er than* the other one.'

The clitic *dA* (11.1.1.2, 28.3.1.1 (iiib)) inserted between the ablative complement and the adjective in the above type of construction has the sense of 'even':

(46) Bu makine öbürün**den** *de* ucuz.
'This machine is *even* cheap*er than* the other one.'

daha can modify an adjective which is the head of a genitive-possessive construction (14.4) or is otherwise being used pronominally (18.4):

(47) bu resm-*in* **daha** güzel-*i*
this picture-GEN more nice-3SG.POSS
'a nic*er* [version] of this picture'

(48) bu resimden **daha** güzel-i
'a picture nic*er* than this one'

To express the notion *less*, Turkish uses the phrase *daha az:*

(49) bizimkinden *daha az* **gürültülü** bir sokak
'a street *less noisy* than ours'

Note that *az* used without a preceding *daha* in a comparative construction is a colloquial and shortened form of *biraz* 'a little', and expresses 'a little more' (*not* 'less'). The same meaning is conveyed by *az daha*:

(50) bundan *az* (*daha*) **büyük** bir araba
'a car *slightly bigger* than this one'

15.4.3 SUPERLATIVES

The superlative form of an adjective defines the entity or set expressed by the following noun as the one which possesses (within a larger set of such entities) the highest degree of the attribute denoted by the adjective. The superlative form of an adjective is formed in Turkish by placing the adverbial *en* 'most' before it:

(51) **en** ilginç düşünce
'the *most* interesting idea'

(52) **en** küçük bardaklar
'the small*est* glasses'

Superlative adjectival constructions can be modified by one of the following:

(i) A locative expression with or without *-ki*:

(53) **listedeki** *en* başarılı çocuk
'the most successful child *on the list*'

(54) **[yarışmaya katılanlar] arasında/içinde** *en* başarılı çocuk
'the most successful child *among the ones* [*who entered the competition*]'

(ii) A genitive-marked noun phrase (forming a genitive-possessive construction (14.4) with the noun phrase that is qualified by the superlative adjective):

(55) **bu ilac-ın** *en* iyi taraf-ı
this medicine-GEN most good side-3SG.POSS
'the best thing *about this medicine*'

In the case of a few verbs of emotion such as *sev-* 'like', *beğen-* 'admire' and *kork-* 'fear', *en* can modify the verb in a relative clause directly (rather than modifying an adverb of degree such as *çok* 'much' which in turn modifies a verb; see 16.9):

(56) **[(benim)** *en* **sevdiğim]** tiyatro oyuncusu
'the actor [*I like the most*]'

En can modify an adjective which is the head of a genitive-possessive construction (14.4):

(57) bu resim-ler-**in** *en* güzel-**i**
these picture-PL-GEN most beautiful-3SG.POSS
'the *most* beautiful *of* these pictures'

15.5 COMPLEMENTATION OF ADJECTIVES

Certain adjectives, in at least some of their senses, require a noun phrase complement to complete their meaning. The case marking required on the complement is fixed for any given adjective. Some common examples of complement-taking adjectives are given below.

(i) Non-case-marked complement:

(58) Su **dolu** kova-lar
water full bucket-PL
'buckets *full of* water'

(ii) Dative-marked complement:

(59) ödü**le layık** bir öğrenci
'a student *worthy of* a prize'

(60) bu oda**ya uygun** bir tablo
'a picture *suitable for* this room'

(iii) Ablative-marked complement:

(61) öğrencilerin**den memnun** bir öğretmen
'a teacher *pleased with* his/her students'

(iv) Instrumental-marked complement:

(62) kar**la kaplı** sokaklar
'streets *covered in* snow'

(63) güvenlik**le ilgili** bir konu
'a matter *relating* to security'

15.6 DETERMINERS

The class of determiners in Turkish (see 14.1.2) consists of the items listed below. Many of these items also occur, either in the same form or with the addition of the 3rd person possessive suffix, as pronouns (18.4).

Determiners fall into two classes, indefinite and definite, according to the referential status they impart (see Chapter 22) to the noun phrase in which they occur.

15.6.1 INDEFINITE DETERMINERS

(i)   Indefinite article:

bir	'a(n)'

Note that in *bir*, and the items in the following list which contain *bir* (except *biraz*), the final 'r' is colloquially omitted before a consonant (e.g. *bi kadın* 'a woman').

(ii)   Quantifiers:

birkaç (tane)	'a few', 'several'
birtakım	'some', 'a number of'
birçok	'many', 'a lot of'
biraz	'a little'
bir miktar	'some', 'a certain amount of'
bazı/kimi/bir kısım	'some', 'certain'
bu kadar/şu kadar/o kadar	'this much', 'that much', 'so much'
çok	'a lot of', '(too) many', '(too) much'
çoğu	'most'
az	'not much', 'not enough'
fazla	'too much', 'too many'
hiçbir	'no', 'any' (see 20.5.2)
herhangi bir	'any' (see 20.5.2)

For the combinability of quantifying determiners with noun phrases denoting discrete or non-discrete entities, see 14.2. Several of the quantifiers cannot be used in a plural-marked noun phrase (see 14.3.1.1). *Bazı* and *kimi*, by contrast, are almost always used with plural marking on the head noun.

The quantifiers *bu kadar/şu kadar/o kadar* are derived from the demonstratives (15.6.2 (i)), and share the same differentiation in meaning (explained in 18.2).

(iii)   Interrogatives:

kaç (tane)	'how many'	(19.2.1.5)
ne kadar	'how much'	(19.2.1.6)

(iv) Markers of similarity and otherness:

böyle/şöyle/öyle (bir)	'such (a)'
başka (bir)	'(an)other'

The forms *böyle/şöyle/öyle* are derived from the demonstratives (15.6.2 (i)), and share the same differentiation in meaning (explained in 18.2).

15.6.2   DEFINITE DETERMINERS

(i)   Demonstratives:

bu	'this/these'
şu	'this/that/these/those'
o	'that/those'

For the pronominal use of the demonstratives see 18.2, where the semantic differences between the three forms are also explained.

(ii)   Universal quantifiers:

her	'every'
bütün/tüm	'all', 'the whole (of)'

(iii) Interrogatives:

hangi	'which'	(19.2.1.4)

(iv) Markers of identity or (exclusive) otherness:

aynı	'the same'
öteki/öbür/∇diğer	'the other'

(v)   Ordinal numerals (15.7.2) and the related items *ilk* 'first' and *son* 'last'

Noun phrases with definite determiners obligatorily have accusative case marking when functioning as direct objects (see 22.1 (iii)).

15.7 NUMERALS

15.7.1 CARDINAL NUMERALS

The cardinal numerals of Turkish are the following:

sıfır	'zero'	*yirmi*	'twenty'	*milyar*	'billion'
bir	'one'	*otuz*	'thirty'	*trilyon*	'trillion'
iki	'two'	*kırk*	'forty'	*katrilyon*	'quadrillion'
üç	'three'	*elli*	'fifty'		(= billion billion)
dört	'four'	*altmış*	'sixty'		
beş	'five'	*yetmiş*	'seventy'		
altı	'six'	*seksen*	'eighty'		
yedi	'seven'	*doksan*	'ninety'		
sekiz	'eight'	*yüz*	'(one) hundred'		
dokuz	'nine'	*bin*	'(one) thousand'		
on	'ten'	*milyon*	'million'		

The numerals from one to nine follow higher numerals to form the numerals from 11 to 99, and these follow any other higher numerals:

on iki	'twelve'
yetmiş üç	'seventy-three'
yüz kırk beş	'one hundred and forty-five'
bin yüz doksan dokuz	'one thousand one hundred and ninety-nine'

When the numerals from *yüz* '(one) hundred' to *katrilyon* 'quadrillion' are in their multiple forms, they are preceded by lower numerals:

üç yüz 'three hundred'
kırk iki bin 'forty-two thousand'
dokuz milyon altı yüz altmış bin 'nine million six hundred and sixty
   thousand'

yüz 'hundred' and *bin* 'thousand' are not preceded by *bir* when they indicate 'one hundred' and 'one thousand' (thus *yüz* 'one hundred', *bin* 'one thousand'), but *milyon, milyar, trilyon* and *katrilyon* are (i.e. *bir milyon* 'one million', etc.).

Turkish has three different words for *half. yarım* behaves just like a cardinal numeral, and is used only when referring to one half of an entity on its own: *yarım bardak* 'half a glass', *yarım portakal* 'half an orange'. The concept *and a half* is expressed by the word *buçuk*, e.g. *iki buçuk* 'two and a half'. The expression, *yarı* 'half' is (i) a noun used as the head of a partitive construction (see 14.5.3) and (ii) an adverb of degree (16.5). *çeyrek* 'a quarter' is the only numeral which needs a conjunction: *üç ve bir çeyrek* 'three and a quarter'. Note that a construction without the conjunction (and *bir*) indicates a totally different numeral: *üç çeyrek* 'three-quarters'.

'Quarter' can also be expressed as *dörtte bir* ('one out of four'). This structure, which contains the locative suffix *-DA*, is one of the means for expressing fractions: (3/4) *dörtte üç* 'three-quarters', (2/3) *'üçte iki* 'two-thirds'. The other way of expressing fractions is by using the expression *bölü* 'divided by': (2/5) *iki bölü beş* 'two-fifths/two over five'. Decimals are expressed by the whole number followed by *virgül* 'comma' or by a fraction: (3,32) *üç virgül otuz iki*, 'three point three two', (5,6) *beş onda altı* 'five [and] six-tenths'. *yüzde* expresses *per cent*: *yüzde beş* (%5) 'five per cent'. These structures are used as the heads of genitive-possessive constructions (14.4) when expressing either the full number or the entity or set of which the fraction is a part:

(64) yirmi-***nin*** sekiz-**de** yedi-***si***
     twenty-GEN eight-LOC seven-3SG.POSS
     'seven-eighths of twenty'

(65) para-mız-***ın*** yüz-**de** doksan beş-***i***'/%95'i
     money-1PL.POSS-GEN hundred-LOC ninety five-3SG.POSS
     '95% of our money'

When fractions follow whole numbers they are expressed without conjunctions: *üç onda dokuz* 'three [and] nine-tenths'. Conjunctions are also not used when two numerals are juxtaposed to give an approximation: *bir iki dükkan* 'one or two shops' (cf. 28.1).

It should be noted that, unlike determiners, numerals can occur in noun phrases that have either indefinite or definite status. They can be combined with some determiners (see 15.9.1). In general, a noun phrase containing a numeral cannot have plural marking (see 14.3.1.1).

15.7.2 ORDINAL NUMERALS

Ordinal numerals are formed by the suffix *-(I)ncI* (7.2.2.2), e.g. *altıncı* 'sixth', *yüzbeşinci* 'one hundred and fifth':

(66) **iki*nci*** öneri
     'the *second* proposal'

When ordinal numerals are used in titles they are written with a full stop following the numeral, e.g. 7. (= *yedinci* 'seventh'):

(67) 18. Uluslararası Tıp Kongresi
     'The 18th International Conference on Medicine'

Streets which are named numerically are expressed in ordinal numerals: *10. Sokak* (= *Onuncu Sokak*) '10th Street', *4. Cadde* (= *Dördüncü Cadde*) '4th Avenue'. *İlk* is another term for *birinci* 'first' (see 15.6.2):

(68) soldan **ilk** ev
      'the *first* house on the left'

15.7.3 DISTRIBUTIVE NUMERALS

Distributive numerals are formed by the suffix *-(ş)Ar* (7.2.2.2): *altışar* 'six each', *onar* 'ten each', *seksen ikişer* 'eighty-two each'. When added to numbers exceeding a thousand and denoting round numbers (such as two thousand, five million, seven billion, etc.) the suffix is attached to the first numeral: *sekizer bin* 'eight thousand each', *onar milyon* 'ten million each'. For multiples of a hundred, *-(ş)Ar* can be attached either to the first numeral, or to *yüz*:

(69) **üçer** yüz/üç **yüzer**
      'three hundred each'

The presence of a distributive numeral requires at least one plural noun phrase in the clause:

(70) Ahmet **çocuklara ikişer** hediye verdi.
      'Ahmet gave *the children two* gifts *each*.'

(71) ***Ahmet'le Mehmet*** Semra'ya **ikişer** hediye verdiler.
      '*Ahmet and Mehmet each* gave Semra *two* gifts.'

Distributive numerals are also used in pairs to form manner adverbials (16.4.3), e.g. *üçer üçer* 'in threes', *beşer onar* 'in fives and tens'.

15.8 THE ENUMERATOR *tane* AND MEASURE/TYPE TERMS

Cardinal numerals are often used with the enumerator *tane* (or (∇*adet*)), usually when modifying nouns denoting discrete, non-human entities:

(72) **on** *tane* tabak
      '*ten* plates'

Measure terms such as *şişe* 'bottle', *bardak* 'glass', *avuç* 'handful', *metre* 'metre', etc., and type terms such as *çeşit/tür* 'kind', *tip* 'type' are used in the same way:

(73) **sekiz *bardak*** su
      '*eight glasses* [*of*] water'

Tane and measure terms can also be used with distributive numerals:

(74) **ikişer *tane*** araba
      '*two* cars *each*'

Most of these terms can combine with the 3rd person singular possessive marker *-(s)I* (8.1.2) and function as heads of genitive-possessive constructions (14.4):

(75) **Limon-un *tane*-si** 20 peni.
      lemon-GEN ENUM-3SG.POSS
      '*The lemons* are 20p *each*.'

(76) **İpeğin *metre*si** ne kadar?
      'How much is *the silk per metre*?'

The possessive-suffixed forms also occur as pronominals (18.4 (iii)):

(77) Çok pahalı bir ilaç. **Şişesi** 100 sterlin.
      'It's a very expensive medicine. [It's] £100 *per bottle*.'

Dolusu '. . . ful' can also be used as a measure term when compounded with a preceding noun:

(78) **iki *oda dolusu*** eski gazete
      '*two roomfuls* of old newspapers'

The adverbials *yaklaşık olarak, aşağı yukarı* 'approximately', *hemen hemen* 'almost' can occur before any numerical expression:

(79) **Aşağı yukarı** 100 sayfa okudum.
      'I've read *about* 100 pages.'

15.9 THE POSITION OF DETERMINERS AND NUMERALS WITHIN THE NOUN PHRASE

The position of a determiner within the noun phrase depends both on the type of determiner involved and the type of adjectival construction(s) that are also present.

15.9.1 NUMERALS WITH DETERMINERS

The cardinal numerals follow most determiners:

> (80) **aynı üç** konuşmacı
> '*the same three* speakers'

> (81) **bu yedi (tane)** iskemle
> '*these seven* chairs'

The combination *her* + numeral, with or without the addition of the clitic *dA* (11.1.1.2) to the noun phrase head, is equivalent to 'all' + numeral in English:

> (82) **Her dört** daireyi (*de*) beğendik.
> 'We liked *all four flats*.'

Even if *her* is not present, placing *dA* after a noun phrase containing a numeral modifer has the effect of giving the phrase definite reference (cf. 18.4 (ii), 22.1):

> (83) (**Her**) **iki** çocuk *da* uyumuş.
> '*Both* children had gone to sleep.'

15.9.2 DETERMINERS OR NUMERALS WITH ADJECTIVES

Definite determiners and numerals normally precede adjectives:

> (84) **o** küçük dolap
> '*that* small cupboard'

> (85) **aynı** tatsız yemekler
> '*the same* tasteless food'

> (86) **üç** tarihi şehir
> '(the) *three* historic cities'

However, if the superlative marker *en* is present (15.4.3), the position of a numeral is after the adjective:

> (87) (**a**) **dört** başarılı öğrenci
> '*(the) four* successful students'

> (**b**) *en* başarılı **dört** öğrenci
> '*the four most* successful students'

The indefinite article *bir* usually follows the adjective, but can precede it:

(88) genç **bir** adam/**bir** genç adam
'*a* young man'

(89) açık **bir** pencere/**bir** açık pencere
'*an* open window'

There is a subtle difference in meaning between the two word orders with the indefinite article. Because modification within nominal phrases in Turkish operates from left to right, placing the adjectival to the left of *bir* has the effect of making the sequence {adjectival + head} be perceived as a semantic unit. Thus in (88) the form *bir genç adam* denotes a member of the class 'young man', whereas the form *genç bir adam* denotes a young member of the class 'man'. This latter order, which is much the more common, gives more prominence to the adjective.

Where *bir* means 'one' (usually in relation to an already mentioned set), it always precedes an adjective, is pronounced as [biɾ] or ↓ [bi] and receives stress:

(90) Burada ekonomik ve toplumsal sorunlarımızı konuşuyoruz. **BİR** önemli toplumsal sorunumuz da ailenin dağılmasıdır.
'We're talking about our economic and social problems here. *One* major social problem that we've got is the dispersal of the family.'

An adjective that is itself modified (15.4.1) has to precede *bir*, whether *bir* is being used in the article or the numeral function:

(91) *çok* önemli **bir/BİR** sorun
'*a/one very* important problem'

Indefinite determiners normally precede an adjective, but *birkaç, birçok, bazı* and *kimi* can sometimes follow it:

(92) **birkaç** kırık iskemle/kırık **birkaç** iskemle
'*a few* broken chairs'

15.9.3 DETERMINERS OR NUMERALS WITH COMPLEX ADJECTIVALS FORMED WITH *-DAn, -lI* OR *-lIk*

The situation with these adjectivals (15.3.3, 15.3.4, 15.3.5) is similar to that with simple adjectives, but here the post-adjectival position is more freely available, not only to all indefinite determiners but also to cardinal and ordinal numerals plus *ilk* and *son*.

(93) **birtakım** ceviz ağac-ın-***dan*** sehpa-lar/ceviz ağacın***dan*** **birtakım**
sehpalar
some walnut wood-NC-ABL small.table-PL
'*some* small tables *made of* walnut wood'

(94) **ilk** yüzme havuz***lu*** villa/yüzme havuz***lu*** **ilk** villa
'*the first* house *with* a swimming pool'

(95) **on tane** üçer dörder metre***lik*** heykel/üçer dörder metre***lik*** **on
tane** heykel
'*ten* statues, each three or four metres [high]'

As with adjectives (15.9.2), if a -*ll* adjectival is modified by the superlative
marker *en*, a numeral can only follow, not precede:

(96) *en* yüksek tirajlı **beş** Türk gazetesi
'*the five* Turkish newspapers with the high*est* circulation'

15.9.4 DETERMINERS OR NUMERALS WITH LOCATIVE-MARKED COMPLEX ADJECTIVALS

Locative-marked complex adjectivals (15.3.2) can occur with definite determiners only if -*ki* is added (15.9.5). Other determiners or numerals are
usually placed after the adjectival:

(97) Turhan Kural adın***da* bir** yazar
'*a* writer *by* the name of Turhan Kural'

(98) orta büyüklük***te* dört** patates
'*four* medium-size*d* potatoes'

15.9.5 DETERMINERS OR NUMERALS WITH ADJECTIVALS FORMED WITH -*ki*

In general, determiners and numerals have to follow -*ki* adjectivals (15.3.6,
15.3.7):

(99) gazetede***ki* öbür** resim
'*the other* picture in the paper'

(100) romanda**ki her** önemli kişi
'*every* important character in the novel'

If a determiner or numeral is placed before a locative + -*ki* construction, it
is usually understood as modifying the immediately following locative-

marked noun phrase rather than the larger one, of which the -*ki* adjectival is a part:

(101) **öbür** gazetede**ki** resim
       'the picture in *the other* paper'

(102) **her** romanda**ki** önemli kişi
       'the important character in *every* novel'

However, *bütün/tüm* 'all' and the demonstratives form exceptions to this general pattern. In the case of *bütün/tüm*, the determiner is understood as modifying the larger noun phrase, regardless of its position:

(103) **bütün** çekmecede**ki** para/çekmede**ki** **bütün** para
       '*all* the money in the drawer'

(104) **bütün** yedi yaşında**ki** çocuklar/yedi yaşında**ki** **bütün** çocuklar
       '*all* (the) seven-year-old children'

Placing a demonstrative before a locative + -*ki* adjectival creates a potential ambiguity as to whether the determiner forms part of the smaller or the larger noun phrase:

(105) **bu** masadaki kitaplar
       (**i**) 'the books on *this* table'
       (**ii**) (= masadaki **bu** kitaplar) '*these* books on the table'

In (i) *bu* is understood to modify *masa* 'table' and in (ii) to modify *kitaplar* 'books'.

In practice any potential ambiguity is usually eliminated by the way in which the words are uttered. If the demonstrative is intended as a modifier of the large noun phrase, it is unstressed and sometimes followed by a very slight pause. If, on the other hand, it is intended as a modifier of the noun closest to it, it is slightly stressed.

15.9.6   DETERMINERS OR NUMERALS WITH RELATIVE CLAUSES

Relative clauses (Chapter 25) behave rather similarly to -*ki* adjectivals in the way they interact with determiners and numerals. The position following the relative clause is the standard one for all these items:

(106) [Jale'nin sevdiği] **iki** yer
       '*two* places [Jale likes]'

(107) [Korkut'u o halde gör-müş olan] **bütün** arkadaşlarımız
'*all* our friends [who have/had seen Korkut in that state]'

However, under certain conditions the determiner or numeral can optionally precede the relative clause:

(**i**)   If the relative clause consists only of a verb (participle):

(108) **birkaç** (tane) [oynayan] çocuk/[oynayan] **birkaç** (tane) çocuk
'*a few* children [playing]'

(109) **şu** [gördüğünüz] kalabalık/[gördüğünüz] **şu** kalabalık
'*this* crowd [that you see]'

(**ii**)   If the relative clause is of the type marked by *-(y)An* (25.1.1.1), and
does not contain, apart from its verb, any constituent other than a one-
word, non-case-marked adverbial, as in (110), or a categorial direct object
(13.1.2.1, 22.3), as in (111):

(110) **her** [*hızlı* akan] nehir/[*hızlı* akan] **her** nehir
'*every* [*swiftly*-flowing] river'

(111) **kimi** [*ün* yap-an] oyuncular/[*ün* yap-an] **kimi** oyuncular
some fame make-PART actor-PL
'*some* actors [who become famous]'

(**iii**)   Demonstratives can be placed before any kind of relative clause, but
if this contains a noun phrase (other than a categorial direct object) there
is potential ambiguity of the kind noted for demonstratives preceding *-ki*
adjectivals (15.9.5):

(112) o çocuğun yaptığı resim
(**a**) [o çocuğ-un yap-tığ-ı] resim
that child make-PART-3SG.POSS picture
'the picture [(which) *that* child painted]'

(**b**) **o** [çocuğun yaptığı] resim (= [çocuğun yaptığı] **o** resim)
'*that* picture [(which) the child painted]'

As explained in the case of *-ki* constructions, the ambiguity is in practice
usually eliminated by the manner of utterance.

16 ADVERBIAL CONSTRUCTIONS

Adverbs (7.1.1 (iv)) are words that modify verbs, nominal predicates, adjectives, other adverbials, or whole sentences. '**Adverbial**' is a broader term used to cover all types of sentence constituent that perform the function of an adverb. Adverbials vary widely in structure (16.1), from single words (e.g. *herhalde* 'probably', *bugün* 'today') through noun phrases, with or without suffixes (e.g. *bu sabah* 'this morning', *iki gündür* 'for two days'), and postpositional phrases (e.g. . . . *rağmen* 'in spite of . . .') to adverbial clauses (e.g. *yanlışımı anlayınca* 'upon realizing my mistake'). The syntactic functions of adverbials are reviewed in 16.2. The following sections focus in turn on the various semantic roles that adverbial constructions play in the sentence, and are organized as follows: modal adverbials (16.3), adverbials of time (16.4.1), place (16.4.2), manner (16.4.3), quantity or degree (16.5) and respect (16.6), exclusive adverbials (16.7) and particularizing adverbials (16.8). Section 6.9 describes the modification of adverbs.

Postpositional phrases, which form a major type of relatively complex adverbials, are treated separately in Chapter 17. **Adverbial clauses** form the subject of Chapter 26, except for **conditional clauses**, which are discussed in Chapter 27.

16.1 TYPES OF ADVERBIAL CONSTRUCTION

16.1.1 SIMPLE ADVERBS

These are words whose sole or primary grammatical function is adverbial. Examples are *şimdi* 'now', *ancak* 'only', *çabuk* 'quickly', *maalesef* 'unfortunately'.

16.1.2 ADJECTIVES USED AS ADVERBS

Many lexical items whose primary function is adjectival (e.g. *güzel* 'beautiful', *kolay* 'easy', *yeni* 'new') can be made to function adverbially simply by placing them in the immediately preverbal position (for further examples see 23.2.1 (iii)).

(1) Özdemir o şarkıyı **güzel** söyledi.
     'Özdemir sang that song *well*.'

If there is a **categorial** direct object (22.3) the adverbial has to precede it:

(2) Özdemir **güzel *şarkı*** söyler.
     'Özdemir sings *(songs) well.*'

(3) Ben **zor *dikiş*** dikiyorum.
     'I sew [only] *with difficulty.*'

Not all adjectives can be used adverbially, even if their meaning is appropriate to the description of actions. With the exception of formations with *-lI* and *-sIz* (7.2.2.2), most derived adjectives (15.2.1) can modify verbs only indirectly, either by modifying a locative-marked noun phrase such as *bir biçimde/bir şekilde* 'in a ... manner', or by standing as complement to *olarak* (16.1.9):

(4) **Erkeksi *bir biçimde*** konuşur.
     'S/he talks *in a* masculine *way.*'

(5) Bu sorunu **bilimsel *olarak*** araştırmalıyız.
     'We must investigate this problem *scientifically.*'

The same restriction applies to adjectives of foreign origin:

(6) Başkan **demokratik *bir şekilde*** seçilmemişti.
     'The chairman had not been *democratically* elected.'

16.1.3 DOUBLED FORMS

Certain adverbials are formed by the reduplicated use of a noun, adjective or adverb (see 9.3). This is not a fully productive process, and the usage and/or meaning of such forms may be more restricted than the simple form. Thus *kolay kolay* 'easily' is used only in negative sentences, and *yavaş yavaş* always means 'slowly' or 'gradually', whereas the adjective *yavaş* can mean 'quiet' or 'gentle' in addition to 'slow'.

(7) Kimse buradan **kolay kolay** kaçamaz.
     'No one could *easily* escape from here.'

The temporal adverbials *sabah sabah* and *akşam akşam*, meaning approximately 'so early in the morning' and 'so late at night' respectively, are used with the implication that the performance of the action at the time in question is socially unacceptable.

(8) **Sabah sabah** ne diye bu kadar gürültü yapıyorsunuz?
     'Why are you making such a noise *at this unearthly hour*?'

16.1.4 NOUN PHRASES WITHOUT CASE MARKING

Non-case-marked noun phrases are used for certain types of time location (16.4.1.1), duration of time (16.4.1.2) and expressions of distance:

(9) **Beş kilometre** yürümüşüz.
'We seem to have walked *five kilometres*.'

16.1.5 NOUN PHRASES WITH OBLIQUE CASE MARKING

Noun phrases with dative, locative or ablative marking occur in a wide range of adverbial functions, discussed in 13.1.3, 14.3.3.3–5.

(10) Berna **koca-sın-*dan*** ayrıl-mış-tı.
Berna husband-3SG.POSS-ABL separate-PF-P.COP
'Berna had separated *from her husband*.'

16.1.6 NOUN OR ADJECTIVE SUFFIXED WITH -CA

For an overview of the functions of the unstressable suffix -*CA* (and its colloquial alternative -*CAK* (iii)) see 7.2.2.2. Here we illustrate the various adverbial meanings which -*CA* formations can express.

(i) Manner:

(11) **Yavaş-*ça*** Jale'nin koluna dokundu.
gentle-ADV
'S/he *gently* touched Jale's arm.'

(12) Osman **çocukça** davranıyor.
'Osman is behaving *childishly*.'

(13) Şarkıyı **Fransızca** söyledi.
'She sang the song *in French*.'

(ii) Long duration:

(14) Bu mektubu **haftalarca** beklemiştik.
'We had waited *weeks* for this letter.'

(iii) The collective or institutional agent of a passive verb (13.2.2.2):

(15) Yunus Emre [**Türk halkınca** sevilen] bir şairdir.
'Yunus Emre is a poet [loved *by the Turkish people*].'

(iv) Collective involvement in an action or state:

    (16) Onlar herşeyi **ailece** yaparlar.
        'They do everything *as a family*.'

(v) The respect in which a description is applicable:

    (17) Babası **dünyaca** meşhur bir ressamdı.
        'His/Her father was a *world*-famous painter.'

(vi) The viewpoint of a person:

    (18) **Bence** endişelenecek bir şey yok.
        '*In my view* there's nothing to worry about.'

16.1.7   NOUN PHRASE SUFFIXED WITH -*DIr*

This type of adverbial structure occurs only with noun phrases denoting a period of time (see 16.4.1.2 (iiib)).

16.1.8   POSTPOSITIONAL PHRASES

Postpositional phrases form the subject of Chapter 17. Their most characteristic function is adverbial (see 17.4.1):

    (19) **Evdeki durumdan *dolayı*** Filiz gelemeyebilir.
        '*Because of the situation at home* Filiz may not be able to come.'

16.1.9   CONSTRUCTIONS WITH *olarak*

Olarak, the converbial form of *ol-* 'be' formed with -*(y)ArAk* (26.3.8), has been lexicalized as a marker of certain types of adverbial phrase:

(i) It produces adverbials from adjectives, generally from derived adjectives (cf. 16.1.2).

    (20) Raporu **yazılı *olarak*** sunmuşlardı.
        'They had submitted the report *in writing*.'

(ii) Following a noun phrase, it forms an adverbial indicating:

(a) Status or classification:

    (21) Bunu sana **avukat *olarak*** değil, **arkadaş *olarak*** söylüyorum.
        'I'm saying this to you not *as a lawyer* but *as a friend*.'

(22) Şimdilik bu sandığı **masa *olarak*** kullanıyoruz.
'For the moment we're using this chest *as a table*.'

(23) **Meyva *olarak*** ne var?
'What is there *in the way of fruit*?'

(b) Collective involvement in an action or state (see -*CA*, 16.1.6 (iv)):

(24) **Aile *olarak*** müziğe meraklılar.
'*As a family*, they're interested in music.'

Where the group involved is expressed by a noun phrase containing a numeral modifier, *olarak* may be omitted (see 12.2.1, example (58)):

(25) Biz **üç arkadaş** (***olarak***) konuşuyoruz.
'We are chatting *as a group of three friends*.'

16.1.10 CONSTRUCTIONS WITH *olmak üzere*

olmak üzere, another converbial form of *ol-* 'be' (cf. 26.3.2, 26.3.12) is used to produce two kinds of adverbial:

(i) A construction indicating the internal composition of a set or group, in quantitative or proportional terms. The quantitative or proportional expression is marked with a 3rd person possessive suffix. This usage is rather formal.

(26) Biz-im koğuş-ta bazı-**sı** ağır ***ol-mak üzere*** on beş kadar hasta
we-GEN ward-LOC some-3SG.POSS serious be-CV 15 about patient
yat-ıyor-du.
lie-IMPF-P.COP
'In our ward there were about fifteen patients, some of them in a serious condition.'

(ii) A construction introduced by *başta* 'at the head', indicating the entity/entities to which a statement chiefly applies (see 16.8).

16.1.11 ADVERBIAL CLAUSES

Adverbial clauses are the most complex kinds of adverbial construction. Some types of adverbial meaning, such as reason, purpose, condition and concession, are expressed predominantly by means of adverbial clauses. For detailed discussion see Chapters 26 and 27.

16.2 SYNTACTIC FUNCTIONS OF ADVERBIALS

Adverbials play a modifying role within a sentence or clause. In broad terms what is modified is either (i) the sentence or clause as a whole, (ii) a verb, (iii) an adjective, or (iv) another adverb. Each of these patterns is illustrated below:

(i) Adverbial modifying the sentence or a clause as a whole:

(27) Telefon numaram sizde vardır **herhalde**.
'*I expect* you've got my telephone number.'

(ii) Adverbial modifying a verb (in the main clause or a subordinate clause, 13.1.3):

(28) [**Hızlı** yürüseydik] 19.10'daki trene yetişebilirdik.
'[If we had walked *fast*] we could have caught the 19.10 train.'

(iii) Adverbial modifying an adjective (15.4):

(29) Bu oda bana **oldukça** karanlık geldi.
'This room seems to me *quite* dark.'

(iv) Adverbial modifying another adverb (16.9):

(30) Çocuğa **fazla** sert davranıyor.
'S/he treats the child *too* harshly.'

16.3 MODAL ADVERBIALS

Modal adverbials express the speaker's stance towards the statement that is being made. Some of them, such as *yanılmıyorsam* 'if I'm not mistaken', *doğrusunu isterseniz* 'to tell you the truth', have the structure of a conditional clause (Chapter 27).

Modal adverbials fall into a number of functional groups:

(i) Adverbials indicating the speaker's degree of commitment to the truth of a statement:

gerçekten/hakikaten	'really'
sahiden	'really'
muhakkak/∇mutlaka	'definitely'

kesinlikle/kesin (olarak)	'definitely'
belli ki	'clearly', 'it's clear that . . .'
anlaşılan	'evidently'
dikkat edilirse	'it will be noted that . . .'
aslına bakılırsa	'the truth of the matter is that . . .'
herhalde	'probably', 'presumably', 'I expect'
bakarsın	'it might just happen that'
büyük bir ihtimalle/	'in all probability'
büyük bir olasılıkla	
yanılmıyorsam	'if I'm not mistaken'
galiba/sanırım	'I think'
∇*zannedersem*	'I think'
∇*zannediyorum*	'I think'
belki	'perhaps'
sözde/∇*güya*	'allegedly', 'supposedly'
bence (see 16.1.6)	'I think', 'in my opinion'
bana kalırsa	'my own view would be that . . .'

(31) [Herkesin para katkısında bulunması] isteniyor **anlaşılan**.
'*Evidently* everyone is expected [to make a financial contribution].'

(32) **Sanırım** Necla'nın sınavı bugün olacaktı.
'*I think* Necla's exam was going to be today.'

For the affinity of certain of this group of modal adverbials, such as *muhakkak*, *herhalde*, *belki*, with the aorist form of the verb and the generalizing modality marker -*DIr*, see the discussion of assumptions (modalized statements) in 21.4.1.4. For modal adverbs used in questions see 19.5.

(ii) Adverbials indicating the speaker's attitude towards the situation described by a statement:

inşallah	'God willing', 'hopefully', 'I hope'
umarım	'I hope'
Allahtan/bereket versin	'fortunately'
çok şükür	'thank goodness', 'fortunately'
iyi ki	'it's good (that . . .)', 'thank goodness'
maalesef/ne yazık ki	'unfortunately'
tabii (ki)/doğal olarak	'of course', 'naturally'

(33) Ambülans çabuk geldi **çok şükür**.
'*Fortunately* the ambulance came quickly.'

(iii) Politeness strategies:
This type of modal adverbial is used in order to mitigate the chance of a remark causing offence.

doğrusu/doğrusunu isterseniz,	'to be honest', 'to tell you the truth'
affedersiniz	'if you'll pardon the expression'
deyim yerindeyse	'if the expression is acceptable', 'if I can put it that way'

(34) **Doğrusunu isterseniz** ben hiçbir zaman Osman'ı o mevkiye layık görmemiştim.
'*To be honest*, I had never regarded Osman as worthy of that office.'

(iv) The modal adverb *meğer(se)*:
meğer (or *meğerse*) can be added to a sentence evidentially marked by *-mIş* or *-(y)mIş* in order to indicate that the statement expresses a revision of the speaker's earlier belief about a situation in the light of new information, new observation or new experience. The nearest English equivalent is usually 'it turns/turned out that . . .'.

(35) Anahtar palto-m-un ceb-in-de-**ymiş**
key coat-1SG.POSS-GEN pocket-3SG.POSS-LOC-EV.COP
meğerse.
it.turns.out
'It turned out that the key was in the pocket of my coat.'

16.4 CIRCUMSTANTIAL ADVERBIALS

In comparison with the class of modal adverbials, which consists of a limited range of expressions, the class of circumstantial adverbials is open. In addition to an inventory of fixed items, such as *şimdi* 'now', *ileri* 'forward', *çabuk* 'quickly', it includes a large range of grammatical strategies which can be freely used in the formation of more complex constructions.

In terms of their semantic functions, circumstantial adverbials express concepts such as time, place, manner, reason, purpose, condition and concession. Detailed discussion is here confined to the expression of time, place and manner. For the other categories the reader is generally referred to other chapters in which more complex adverbial structures are discussed.

16.4.1 TIME ADVERBIALS

In the following sections we look at the means by which various kinds of temporal relations are expressed: location in time (16.4.1.1), duration (16.4.1.2) and frequency (16.4.1.3). For the wide range of adverbial *clauses* which perform temporal functions see 26.1.2.1, 26.1.6 and 26.3.16.

16.4.1.1   Location in time

Temporal location is the time at which or within which an event happens or a state holds. In Turkish this is often, but by no means always, expressed by locative case marking. We first describe how clock time and dates are expressed in Turkish, and then proceed to consider more general aspects of the subject.

Clock time

The use of the word *saat* 'hour' is optional in all expressions of clock time, and if used must precede the numeral indicating the hour. Locations on the hour are expressed with the locative suffix on the numeral:

*(saat) altı-**da***   'at six (o'clock)'
(hour) six-LOC

For the half-hours, *buçuk* 'and a half' follows the numeral, and it is to this word that the locative suffix is attached:

*(saat) on buçuk**ta***   'at half-past ten'

An exception is that for 'half-past twelve' the word *yarım* 'half' is used:

*(saat) yarım**da***   'at half-past twelve'

For time locations less than thirty minutes after the hour, the word *geçe* (the -*(y)A* converb (26.3.8) of *geç-* 'pass') follows the number of minutes, which in turn follows the accusative-marked form of the hour numeral:

*(saat) iki**yi** beş **geçe***   'at five past two'

For time locations less than thirty minutes before the hour, the word *kala* (the -*(y)A* converb (26.3.8) of *kal-* 'be left') follows the number of minutes, which in this case follows the dative-marked form of the hour numeral:

*(saat) dörd-**e** yirmi **kala***   'at twenty to four'
(hour) four-DAT twenty to

The word *çeyrek* 'quarter' is used for 'quarter past' and 'quarter to':

*(saat) yedi**yi çeyrek** geçe*   'at quarter past seven'
*(saat) on iki**ye çeyrek** kala*   'at quarter to twelve'

As an alternative to all of the above, the conventions of the twenty-four hour clock may be used, with the locative suffix attached to the minute figure:

*(saat) yirmi otuz**da***   'at 20.30'

Days of the week

The name of the day may either be used on its own or made into a *-(s)I* compound (10.2) with *gün* 'day'. Case marking is generally not used when expressing time location with respect to a certain day of the week:

(36) **Çarşamba (gün-ü)** Konya'ya gidiyorum.
Wednesday (day-NC)
'I'm going to Konya *on Wednesday*.'

If reference is being made to future time, dative case marking is often added in colloquial usage. (Note that locative case marking is not used at all with days of the week.)

(37) Çarşamba-**ya** Konya'ya gidiyorum.
Wednesday-DAT
'I'm going to Konya on Wednesday.'

Dates

Time location involving dates always requires the locative suffix. In the expression of time location in a certain year, the number expressing the year may be compounded with *yıl* (or ∇*sene*) 'year'. Years are expressed just like simple numerals:

(38) (**a**) bin dokuz yüz doksan beş**te** (written *1995'te*)
(**b**) bin dokuz yüz doksan beş yılın**da** (written *1995 yılında*)
'in 1995'

Similarly, in the expression of location in a certain month, the name of the month may be compounded with *ay* 'month':

(39) şubat-**ta**/şubat ay-ın-**da**
February-LOC/February month-NC-LOC
'in February'

Time location on an exact date is expressed by placing the cardinal number before the name of the month, and adding the locative suffix to the latter. (Note that, in the case of an exact date, the name of the month is written with an initial capital.)

(40) on yedi haziran**da** (written *17 Haziran'da*)
'on the 17th of June'

If the year is expressed as well, this follows the name of the month, and the locative suffix appears on the year.

(41) sekiz kasım bin dokuz yüz seksen dört**te** (written *8 Kasım 1984'te*)
      'on the 8th of November 1984'

A more informal way of expressing the date of an event is to use a genitive-possessive construction (14.4):

(42) haziran-ın/haziran ay-ın-**ın** on yedi-**sin**-de
      June-GEN/June month-NC-GEN seventeen-3SG.POSS-LOC
      'on the 17th of June'

The year can be incorporated with the name of a month in one of two ways:

(**i**)   as a *-(s)I* compound:

(43) bin dokuz yüz seksen dört kasım**ın**da
      'in November 1984'

(**ii**) in a genitive-possessive construction:

(44) (**a**) bin dokuz yüz seksen dörd**ün** kasım**ın**da
      (**b**) bin dokuz yüz seksen dörd**ün** kasım ay**ın**da
      (**c**) bin dokuz yüz seksen dört yılı**nın** kasım ay**ın**da
               'in November 1984'

If the exact date is specified in an expression of the type exemplified in (44),
this is usually done by combining a genitive-possessive construction with
the pattern exemplified in (40) above:

(45) (**a**) bin dokuz yüz seksen dörd**ün** sekiz kasım**ın**da
      (**b**) bin dokuz yüz seksen dört yılı**nın** sekiz kasım**ın**da
               'on the 8th of November 1984'

Other less precise expressions of calendar time are illustrated below:

eylül/eylülün başında	'at the beginning of September'
nisanın ortasında	'in the middle of April'
ekim/ekimin sonunda	'at the end of October'
ay başında/sonunda	'at the beginning/end of the month'
ayın ortasında	'in the middle of the month'
ayın birinde	'on the first (day) of the month'
bin sekiz yüz otuzlarda	'in the 1830s'
(written *1830'larda*)	
bin sekiz yüz otuzlu yıllarda	'in the 1830s'
(written *1830'lu yıllarda*)	

Seasons of the year

Yaz 'summer' and *kış* 'winter' have special forms for expressing location: *yazın* 'in summer', *kışın* 'in winter' (7.2.2.2). *İlkbahar* (or *bahar*) 'spring' and *sonbahar* 'autumn', on the other hand, take the locative case marker:

(46) **Kışın** başlayan yağmurlar **ilkbaharda** da sürdü.
'The rain that began *in the winter* continued *in the spring*, too.'

Other phrases expressing location in time:

(i) The following adverbials express time locations in terms of their relation to the moment of speech (present, past, future):

(a) Present:

şimdi	'now'
şu anda	'at the moment', 'at this moment'
şu sıra(lar)da	'at the moment'
bu günlerde	'at the moment'
↓*şimdilerde*	'at the moment', 'these days'
bugün	'today'

(b) Past:

dün	'yesterday'
dün sabah	'yesterday morning'
dün akşam	'yesterday evening/night'
dün gece	'last night'
evvelsi gün	'the day before yesterday'
evvelki (hafta/ay/yıl)	'the (week/month/year) before last'
önceki (hafta/ay/yıl)	'last (week/month/year)', 'the (week/month/year) before last'
geçen gün	'the other day'
geçenlerde	'a few days ago'
geçen/geçtiğimiz (hafta/ay/yıl)	'last (week/month/year)'
... önce/∇evvel	'(amount of time) ago'
demin	'a few moments ago', 'just now'
son zamanlarda	'recently'
eskiden	'in the past', 'formerly'
bir zaman(lar)/∇bir vakitler	'in the past', 'formerly'
∇zamanında/∇vaktiyle	'in the past', 'formerly'

(c) Future:

akşama	'this evening', 'in the evening'
yarın	'tomorrow'
yarın sabah	'tomorrow morning'
yarın akşam	'tomorrow evening'
öbürsü gün	'the day after tomorrow'
haftaya	'next week'
gelecek/önümüzdeki (hafta/ay/yıl)	'next (week/month/year)'
seneye	'next year'
. . . sonra	'in (amount of time from now)'
yakında/biraz sonra	'soon'

(ii) The following adverbials express time locations without reference to how they relate to the moment of speech:

(a) Parts of the day:

sabah/↓sabahleyin	'in the morning', 'this morning'
öğleyin/öğle zamanı	'at midday'
öğleden sonra	'in the afternoon' 'this afternoon'
akşam üstü/üzeri	'in the early evening'
akşam/↓akşamleyin	'in the evening'
gece/↓geceleyin	'at night', 'in/during the night'

(b) More general expressions:

önce/∇evvela	'first', 'at first'
ilkönce	'first of all'
. . . önce/∇evvel	'(amount of time) before/ago'
(bir) önceki(gün/hafta/ay/yıl)	'the previous (day/week/month/year)'
sonra	'then', 'later'
daha sonra	'later (on)'
. . . sonra	'(amount of time) later'
sonraki/ertesi (gün/hafta/ay/yıl)	'the next (day/week/month/year)'
çok geçmeden	'before long'
o zaman	'then'
o zamanlar	'at that time'
o sırada	'at that point'
bu arada	'meanwhile'
bir ara	'at one point'

Expressions referring to present time

As shown in list (i) (a) above, there are several expressions that refer to a time location which includes the moment of speech, and can be translated by 'at the moment'. However, they differ in the range of time they express. *Şu anda* is the only one that can be focused on the actual moment of speech:

(47) **Şu anda** bir şey duyamıyorum, ama demin bir cızırtı vardı.
'At the moment I can't hear anything, but just now there was a crackling sound.'

The other three expressions refer to a much broader period of days or even weeks, extending both backwards and forwards from the moment of speech:

(48) Korkut **bu günlerde/şu sırada** tezini bitirmeye çalışıyor.
'Korkut is trying to finish his thesis *at the moment.*'

As for the adverb *şimdi* 'now', this does not always refer to present time. It can refer to the very near future:

(49) **Şimdi** gelirim.
'I'll be back *in a moment.*'

It can also refer to the immediate past, in which usage it receives stress (cf. 23.3.1):

(50) Ahmet Bey **ŞİMdi** çıktı.
'Ahmet Bey has *just* left.'

Synonymous with *şimdi* in this usage are ∇*henüz* and *yeni,* both of which can refer also to a *relative* immediate past, as in (51) below. All three of these adverbs are commonly reinforced by the modifier *daha* 'only' (16.4.1.4 (vc)):

(51) O sırada buraya **daha yeNİ** taşınmıştık.
'At that time we had *only just* moved here.'

önce 'before' and *sonra* 'after':
As shown in the above lists, *önce* and *sonra* as adverbials have a number of different usages. (For their functions as postpositions see 17.2.3 (vi)–(vii).)

(i) Used without modifiers, *önce* means 'first' or 'at first' and *sonra* 'then' or 'later':

(52) **Önce** bütün kitabı gözden geçir, **sonra** [önemli gördüğün] bölümlere geri dön.
   '*First* look over the whole book, *then* go back to the sections [you consider important].'

(ii) Both *önce* and *sonra* can be preceded by a noun phrase indicating an *amount of time*. The adverbial phrases thus formed can have as their reference points either the moment of speech or any other time location established in the preceding discourse:

(53) **(a)** *Yirmi yıl* **önce** burası tarlaydı.
     '*Twenty years ago* this was a field.'

   (b) Filiz Hanım yalnız yaşıyordu. Kocası *yirmi yıl* **önce** ölmüştü.
     'Filiz Hanım lived alone. Her husband had died *twenty years before*.'

(54) **(a)** *Beş gün* **sonra** sınavım var.
     'I've got an exam *in five days' time/five days from now*.'

   (b) *Beş gün* **sonra** sınava girdim.
     '*Five days later* I took the/an exam.'

(iii) When placed in the immediately pre-verbal position, *sonra* can mean '(only) later', 'not until afterwards'. In this usage it often takes ablative case marking:

(55) [Coşkun'un evli olduğun]-u **sonra(dan)** öğrendim.
   '*It was (only) later that* I found out [that Coşkun was married].'

Case marking (8.1.3) and its absence in expressing location in time

(i) No case marking:
The following nouns denoting parts of the day usually remain non-case-marked when they are used in the singular form to express location in time: *sabah* 'morning', *akşam* 'evening', *gece* 'night'. If used without a determiner (15.6), these words are understood as referring either to the day of the speech situation, or the previous night, or to another day on which attention is already focused.

(56) **Gece** yağmur yağmıştı, yerler ıslaktı.
   'It had rained *during the night*, [so] the ground was wet.'

This applies also to noun phrases in which the singular form of *sabah* 'morning', *akşam* 'evening', *gece* 'night', *gün* 'day', *hafta* 'week', *ay* 'month', *yıl/√sene* 'year' is preceded by one of the following determiners/adjectives or by an ordinal numeral: *bir* 'a(n)', *bu* 'this', *o* 'that', *geçen* 'last', *gelecek* 'next', *önceki* 'the previous', 'last', *sonraki* 'the next', *ertesi* 'the next', *ilk* 'the first', *son* 'the last':

> (57) **Bu sabah** bir öğrencim telefon etti.
>   'A student of mine rang *this morning*.'

> (58) **Gelecek hafta** boş vaktin var mı?
>   'Do you have any free time *next week*?'

(ii)   Dative case:
Where location in time is concerned, dative case marking (i.e. *-(y)A*) always produces (relative) future reference. This is a colloquial usage; the standard equivalents are also shown in (59); see also (36), (37).

> (59) [**Akşama/Akşam/O akşam** misafirlerimiz olacağı için] yemek
>   yapmakla meşguldük.
>   '[As we were expecting guests *that evening*] we were busy
>   cooking.'

(iii)   Locative case:
Apart from dates and clock time (hours and half-hours), locative case marking (i.e. *-DA*) occurs in noun phrases of which the head is the plural-marked form of one of any of the time nouns listed in (i) above, e.g. *son aylarda* 'in the last (few) months', *o yıllarda* 'in those years'. It also occurs in noun phrases of which the head is any other noun or noun compound denoting a period of time, e.g. *Osmanlı döneminde* 'in the Ottoman period', *çocukluğumda* 'in my childhood'.

   When locative case marking occurs in a quantified time expression, it indicates the time *within which* a task is (to be) performed, or within which a certain number of occurrences of an event are observed. The postposition *içinde* (17.3.1.2) is often used instead of simple locative case marking in such expressions:

> (60) **Üç haftada/Üç hafta içinde** bu kavşakta iki defa kaza oldu.
>   '*In the space of three weeks* there have twice been accidents at this
>   junction.'

(iv)   Ablative case:
Expressions of time location that include ablative case marking (i.e. *-DAn*) without any following postposition usually emphasize the earliness of the

time referred to. Fixed expressions of this kind include *erkenden* 'early', *önceden* 'beforehand', *şimdiden* 'already', *sabahtan* '(already) in the morning', *akşamdan* '(already) the evening before', *çoktan* 'long ago', 'long since':

(61) Ben **şimdi-*den*** üşüyorum.
      now-ABL
      'I'm *already* feeling cold.'

(62) Nermin'ler **sabah*tan*** gelmişler.
      'Apparently Nermin and her friends have been here *since this morning*.'

In the adverbial *sonradan* 'after the event', '(only) afterwards', the ablative case marking has the opposite effect of drawing attention to the *lateness* of the occurrence of an event (see (55) above).

Recurrent time locations

To express the regular occurrence of an event on a certain day of the week, or at a certain time of day, *-lAr-I* is added to the name of the day, or to any of the following expressions: *sabah* 'morning', *öğleden sonra* 'in the afternoon', *akşam* 'evening', *gece* 'night':

(63) **Pazartesi*leri*/Pazartesi gün*leri*** Taksim'deki ofisimizde çalışıyorum.
      '*On Mondays* I work at our office in Taksim.'

16.4.1.2   Duration

(i)   The duration of an activity may be expressed by a non-case-marked noun phrase:

(64) **Birkaç dakika** bekledik.
      'We waited *for a few minutes*.'

(ii)   Alternatively, an adverbial of quantity (16.5) may be used:

(65) Misafirler **az** oturdular.
      'The guests did*n't* stay *long*.'

(iii) To present a situation as having started some time ago/before, and still continuing (at the moment of speech or at some reference point in the past), one of the following is used:

(a)   the postposition *beri* (17.2.3 (ii))

(b) the suffix -*DIr* (8.3.3) attached to the noun phrase denoting the period:

> (66) **Üç yıldır/üç yıldan beri** burada çalışıyorum.
> 'I've been working here *for three years*.'

The rules governing the tense/aspect marking of a predicate modified by a -*DIr* adverbial are the same as those applying to predicates modified by *beri* phrases (see 17.2.3 (ii)).

(iv) Expressions of intended duration of stay, modifying a verb of motion, are constructed in one of two ways:

(a) with the postposition *için* 'for' (17.2.1 (ii))

(b) by attaching the suffix -*lIğInA* to the expression of duration:

> (67) Birkaç gün **için**/Birkaç gün**lüğüne** Fransa'ya gidiyorum.
> 'I'm going to France *for a few days*.'

16.4.1.3 Frequency

The principal adverbials expressing general notions of frequency are:

hep/her zaman	'always', 'all the time'
sık sık	'often', 'frequently'
çok defa	'many times', 'often'
genellikle	'usually', 'generally'
bazen	'sometimes'
kimi zaman	'sometimes'
kâh . . . kâh	'sometimes . . . sometimes'
arada bir/arasıra	'occasionally'
arada sırada	'occasionally'
zaman zaman	'from time to time'
seyrek	'seldom'
hiç	'never', 'ever'
hiçbir zaman	'never', 'ever'
asla/∇katiyen	'never'
pek	'very often' (only with negative verb)

Of these expressions, *hiç*, *hiçbir zaman*, *asla*, ∇*katiyen* and *pek* are discussed in 20.5.

Quantified frequency is expressed with locative marking of the noun expressing the relevant time unit (day, week, etc.), followed usually by *bir* 'once', otherwise by a numeral or quantifier followed by *kez*, *defa*, or *kere*, all meaning 'time' in the sense of 'instance of repetition':

(68) Şükran'la [**ay*da* bir** görüşmey]-e çalışıyoruz.
'Şükran and I try [to get together *once a month*].'

(69) Artık makine **yıl*da* dört beş kez/defa/kere** arızalanıyor.
'The machine is now breaking down *four or five times a year*.'

16.4.1.4 Other time adverbials

(i) *ancak*:
As a temporal adverb, *ancak* (see also 16.7) means 'only just [in time for something]', and is placed immediately before the predicate:

(70) Uçağa **ancak** yetiştik.
'We *only just* caught the plane.'

For *ancak* as an adversative connective see 28.3.4.2.

(ii) *artık*:
This indicates that a turning point has been reached.

(a) In affirmative sentences it is usually equivalent to 'now', but it is a 'now' that expresses the climax of some development in the past:

(71) **Artık** Türkçe'yi güzel konuşuyorsun.
'You *now* speak Turkish very well.'

(b) With a negative predicate it means 'no longer', 'any more':

(72) İstanbul'da evimiz yok **artık**.
'We *no longer* have a flat in İstanbul.'

(iii) *bir an önce*:
This is an informal expression meaning 'as soon as possible':

(73) Evi **bir an önce** satmak istiyoruz.
'We want to sell the house *as soon as possible*.'

A synonym not restricted to colloquial styles is *en kısa zamanda* 'in the shortest [possible] time'.

(iv) *bir daha*:
Literally 'once more', this expression is used in the sense of 'again'. It is used mostly in negative sentences, and is indeed the only means of expressing 'again' with a negative predicate:

(74) O adamı **bir daha** görmek istemem.
'I do*n't ever* want to see that man *again*.'

In affirmative sentences 'again' is usually expressed by *gene*, *yine*, ∇*tekrar* or *yeniden*, this last having sometimes the meaning of 'all over again':

(75) Binayı yıkıp **yeniden** yapacaklarmış.
'Apparently they're going to pull the building down and *re*build it.'

(**v**) *daha*:
This is an adverb with several meanings/functions. For its comparative function see 15.4.2, 16.9.

(**a**) With an affirmative predicate *daha* means 'still':

(76) Süleyman **daha** uyuyor.
'Süleyman is *still* asleep.'

(**b**) With a negative predicate it means 'yet', and in this function is synonymous with *henüz*, which is slightly more formal:

(77) **Daha/Henüz** hazır değilim.
'I'm not ready *yet*.'

(**c**) Placed before an adverbial expressing a time location prior to the moment of speech, *daha* emphasizes either the closeness or the distance of that time:

(78) Bu sorun **daha** *iki yıl önce* vardı.
'This problem *already* existed *two years ago*.'

(**vi**) *hâlâ*:
This conveys the notion 'still' more emphatically than *daha*:

(79) Yılmaz **hâlâ** aynı yerde çalışıyor.
'Yılmaz is *still* working in the same place.'

(**vii**) *hazır*:
As an adverb, *hazır* (primarily an adjective meaning 'ready', 'present') is used almost exclusively in converbial clauses marked by -*(y)ken* (26.2.3 (ii), 26.3.16 (iii)). It expresses the idea that the state of affairs described by the subordinate clause provides an opportunity for the performance of the action specified in the superordinate clause:

(80) [**Hazır** Ali buradayken] bilgisayar sorunumuzu ona soralım.
'[*Now that* Ali is here], let's ask him about our computer problem.'

(viii) *hemen,* ∇*derhal:*
These mean 'immediately', 'at once':

(81) Bardakları **hemen** yıka.
'Wash the glasses *immediately*.'

(ix) *neredeyse:*
This conveys that an event is expected imminently:

(82) Misafirler **neredeyse** gelir.
'The guests will be arriving *at any moment*.'

16.4.2 PLACE ADVERBIALS

In general terms, location in, on, or at a place is expressed by locative case marking of a noun phrase (14.3.3.4 (i), 13.1.3):

(83) Selim'in **Berlin-*de*** kızkardeşi varmış.
     Berlin-LOC
'Apparently Selim has a sister *in Berlin*.'

Movement to, into or on to a place is expressed by dative case marking of a noun phrase (14.3.3.3 (i), 13.1.3):

(84) Artık **ev-*e*** gidiyorum.
     house-DAT
'I'm going *home* now.'

Movement away from or out of a place is expressed by ablative case marking of a noun phrase (14.3.3.5 (i), 13.1.3):

(85) Arkadaşımı **havaalanın-*dan*** alacağım.
     airport-ABL
'I'm going to collect my friend *from the airport*.'

Other spatial relationships are expressed by the set of possessive-marked postpositions designated as group 1 in 17.3.1. *iç*-POSS-OBL and *üst*- POSS-OBL are often used in preference to simple case marking of the noun phrase where the difference between the concepts of *on* and *in* is felt to be important.

The attachment of the above case markers to the locative pronouns *bura-, şura-* and *ora-* (18.3.1) produces forms meaning 'here' and 'there':

(86) Bak, **şura*da*** yeni bir leke var.
'Look, there's a new mark *here*.'

(87) **Oray*a*** ne zaman gidiyorsunuz?
'When are you going *there*?'

Directional adverbials

The following adverbs, whether in their bare form or with dative case marking, express directional movement:

içeri	'inside'
dışarı	'outside'
yukarı	'up'
aşağı	'down'
ileri	'forward'
geri	'back'

(88) **İçeri(ye)** girelim mi?
'Shall we go *in*?'

(89) **Yukarı(ya)** çıktılar.
'They went *up(stairs)*.'

Locative and ablative case marking also occurs. The final vowel of *içeri*, *dışarı*, *yukarı* and *ileri* is usually dropped when the locative or ablative suffix is added:

(90) Annem **aşağı*da*** oturuyor.
'My mother lives *downstairs*.'

(91) **İçer(i)*den*** güzel yemek kokuları geliyordu.
'Nice smells of food were coming *from inside*.'

The word *öte* 'far side' is used adverbially only with locative, dative or ablative case marking:

(92) Makinalar çalışırken **öte*de*** durmak lazım.
'When the machines are working one has to stand *away*.'

The locative, dative and ablative forms of *her yer* 'everywhere' function as universal place adverbials:

(93) Artık **her yerde** McDonalds var.
'There are McDonald's *everywhere* now.'

16.4.3   MANNER ADVERBIALS

The following are some of the most common means of expressing the manner in which an action is performed:

(i)   A simple adverb, an adjective placed in the immediately preverbal position, or a doubled form (discussed in 16.1.1–3).

(ii)   A noun or adjective suffixed with -*CA* (see 16.1.6 (i)).

(iii)   One of the demonstrative adverbials *böyle* 'like this', *şöyle* 'like this', *öyle* 'like that'. (These are derived from the demonstrative pronouns *bu, şu* and *o* (18.2), and are differentiated from each other in similar ways. They also function as adverbials of degree (16.5) and as determiners (15.6.1 (iv)).)

(94) Kalemi **şöyle** tut.
      'Hold the pen *like this*.'

(95) [Mustafa'nın **öyle** konuşması] hoş olmadı.
      'It was unpleasant [that Mustafa talked *like that*].'

(iv)   A noun phrase marked with the comitative/instrumental marker -*(y)lA/ile* (8.1.4), the uses of which are explained in 17.2.1 (iii):

(96) Ömer okula **ablası***la* gidiyor.
      'Ömer goes to school *with his elder sister*.'

(v)   A postpositional phrase headed by *gibi*:

(97) **Öğretmen gibi** konuşuyorsun.
      'You're talking *like a teacher*.'

(vi)   Several types of adverbial clause (see 26.1.5, 26.3.8).

16.4.4   OTHER TYPES OF CIRCUMSTANTIAL ADVERBIAL

The range of adverbial relationships that can be expressed by postpositional phrases and adverbial clauses is extremely wide. Here we present an overview of the principal means available in Turkish for expressing four more circumstantial categories that are expressed mainly by postpositional phrases (Chapter 17) or adverbial clauses (Chapters 26 and 27).

Reason (or cause)

(i) Ablative case marking:
There are not many contexts in which this alone (without a post-position) is used to express cause. For examples see (43b) in Chapter 13 and (89) in Chapter 14.

(ii) A number of postpositions, all meaning approximately 'because of', 'as a result of': the bare postpositions *dolayı, ötürü*, taking ablative-marked complements (17.2.3) and the possessive-marked post-positions *sayesinde, nedeniyle, yüzünden* (17.3.2, 17.3.2.1 (viii)).

(iii) A finite adverbial clause marked with the subordinator *diye* (26.1.1.1), or a non-finite adverbial clause marked with *-DIğI için, -DIğIndAn*, etc., meaning 'because' (26.3.14).

Examples (i) and (iii) above are strategies for presenting two situations/events in a cause-result sequence.

(iv) A number of discourse connectives, all meaning 'because of this' or 'as a result', such as *onun için, dolayısıyla, bu nedenle, bu yüzden* (28.3.6).

(v) The discourse connective *çünkü* 'because' presents an explanation for a situation already stated (28.3.6), i.e. in a result-cause sequence.

Purpose

(i) The bare postposition *için* 'for' (17.2.1 (ii)).

(ii) The possessive-marked postposition *uğruna* 'for the sake of' (17.3.2, 17.3.2.1 (ix)).

(iii) A finite adverbial clause containing the subordinator *diye* (26.1.1.2) or *ki* (26.1.2.2) and having optative marking on the verb.

(iv) A non-finite adverbial clause marked with *-mAk için, -mAsI için, -mAyA* or *-mAk üzere* (26.3.12).

Condition

(i) A conditional clause marked with *-sA* or *-(y)sA* (Chapter 27).

(ii) A finite adverbial clause marked with *-DI mI* (27.6.2).

(iii) A non-finite adverbial clause marked with *-DIğI takdirde* or *-mAsI durumunda/halinde* (27.6.1).

(iv) The discourse connectives *o halde/öyleyse* 'in that case' (28.3.9 (ii)).

Concession

(i)   The bare postpositions *rağmen/karşın* 'in spite of', taking ablative-marked complements (17.2.3).

(ii) Non-finite adverbial clauses marked with *-DIğI halde, -mAsInA rağmen/karşın, -mAklA birlikte/beraber* (26.3.3).

(iii) The discourse connectives *bununla birlikte/beraber, buna rağmen/karşın*, all meaning 'in spite of this', 'nevertheless' (28.3.4.2).

16.5 ADVERBIALS OF QUANTITY OR DEGREE

The adverbials in this category differ from circumstantial adverbials in that they can modify adjectives and other adverbials as well as verbs. Some of them, (*en, ▽gayet, son derece, oldukça*) in fact, either cannot modify verbs at all, or are very restricted in the extent to which they can do this.

çok	'much', 'very', 'too (much)'
daha	'more'
en	'most'
pek	'very', 'much'
▽*(bir) hayli*	'very'
fazla(sıyla)	'too (much)', 'excessively'
aşırı (derecede)	'excessively'
▽*gayet*	'extremely'
son derece	'extremely'
yarı	'half'
▽*epey(i), epeyce*	'quite'
oldukça	'quite', 'fairly'
az	'not much'
biraz	'a little', 'a bit', 'rather'
böyle(sine)/şöyle(sine)/öyle(sine)	'such', 'so'
bu/şu/o kadar/derece/denli	'such', 'so', 'so much'
ne kadar	'how much', 'how'

The following examples illustrate the different kinds of modification performed by this type of adverbial:

(98) Bu dersi **biraz zor** buldum.   (*Biraz* modifies adjective)
      'I found this lesson *rather difficult.*'

(99) Bu dersi **biraz zor** yaptım.   (*Biraz* modifies adverbial)
      'I did this lesson *with some difficulty.*'

(100) [Bu dersi yaparken] **biraz zorlandım.**   (*Biraz* modifies verb)
      '*I struggled a bit* while [doing this lesson].'

Further examples may be found above in 16.2 (ii)–(iv).

As seen in 16.4.1.2, with verbs expressing a process that extends over time, adverbials of quantity express *temporal duration*:

(101) Meksika'da **az** kaldık.
'We did*n't* stay *long* in Mexico.'

Pek and *o kadar* have a particular affinity with negative sentences. Their uses are discussed in 20.5.4.2–3.

Other types of adverbials of quantity/degree are:

(i) Postpositional phrases with *kadar* following a non-case-marked (or genitive) complement (17.2.1 (iv)).
(ii) Non-finite clauses marked by *-(y)AcAk kadar/derecede* or *-DIğI/ -(y)AcAğI kadar* (26.3.13).

16.6 ADVERBIALS OF RESPECT

A number of strategies are available for indicating the respect in which, or point of view from which, a statement is regarded as applicable:

(i) The suffix *-CA* (16.1.6 (v)) is in restricted use for this purpose:

(102) Kağan **yaşça** küçük ama **vücutça** büyüktü.
'Kağan was small *in terms of age*, but big *in terms of physical size*.'

(ii) A variety of expressions and constructions incorporating the nouns *bakım* 'view', *açı* 'angle' or *yön* 'direction' are in much more common use:

(103) **Bir bakıma** [Ali'nin geç gelmesi] iyi oldu.
'*In a way* it was good [that Ali was late].'

(104) **O yönden/O açıdan** en büyük başarılarımızdan biriydi.
'*From that point of view* it was one of our greatest achievements.'

The forms *açısından* and *bakımından* are possessive-marked postpositions (see 17.3.2 and example (88) there).

(iii) The bare postposition *yana* (with ablative-marked complement, 17.2.3 (viii)) can be used in the same sense as *açısından* and *bakımından*, but is far less common.

16.7 EXCLUSIVE ADVERBIALS

The following are all used in the sense of 'only': *yalnız, ancak, sade(ce), sırf, salt, bir (tek)*. They restrict the applicability of what is being said to the **focused** constituent of a sentence (23.3.1). An exclusive adverbial is usually placed immediately before the focused constituent, which is typically either a noun phrase or a circumstantial adverbial.

(105) Mektubu **yalnız/bir tek** Mustafa'YA göstermiştim.
'I had shown the letter *only to Mustafa*.'

(106) **Ancak/yalnız/sadece** iKİ defa geldiler.
'They came *only twice*.'

(107) **Sırf** [üstünlüğünü kanıtlaMAK] amacıyla yapıyor bunları.
'He's doing all this [*merely in an effort to prove his superiority*].'

bir, tek and *bir tek* are used mainly with pronouns or proper nouns, where no possibility of ambiguity with the determiner or numeral senses of *bir* ('a(n)', 'one',) or the adjectival sense of *tek* 'single' arises. It is confined to informal styles:

(108) Bunun sırrını **bir (tek)** SEN biliyorsun.
'Only you know the secret of this.'

16.8 PARTICULARIZING ADVERBIALS

This small class of adverbials has a function somewhat similar to that of the exclusive adverbials, but are less absolute in their restrictive effect. The main items are *daha çok* 'mainly', *en çok* 'mostly', *asıl* 'really' and *özellikle/∇bilhassa* 'especially', 'particularly':

(109) Buraya **daha çok** üniVERsite öğrencileri geliyor.
'It's *mainly* university students who come here.'

(110) **En çok/Özellikle** AKdeniz ülkelerinde yetişir zeytin ağacı.
'The olive tree grows *mostly/particularly* in Mediterranean countries'.

For *özellikle/∇bilhassa* as conjunction/discourse connectives see 28.3.5 (iii).

asıl as a particularizing adverbial is quite colloquial:

(111) Bunu **asıl** senin AMcan iyi yapar.
'It's your uncle who would *really* make a good job of this.'

Another type of particularizing adverbial comprises those formed with the construction *başta ... olmak üzere* 'particularly', 'above all' (16.1.10). Here the identification of the particularized individual or group precedes the mention of the larger set of which it forms a part, and the particularized constituent is not focused:

(112) **Başta** kamu işçi-ler-i **olmak üzere** bütün işçi-ler sıkıntı-da.
head-LOC public.sector worker-PL-NC ADV all worker-PL
hardship-LOC
'All manual workers, especially the public sector workers, are suffering.'

16.9 MODIFICATION OF ADVERBS

The only kinds of adverbials that can be modified are adjectives functioning as adverbs (16.1.2), and the quantitative adverbs *çok* 'much', *fazla* '(too) much', *az* 'little' and *daha* 'more' (16.5). Note that while *fazla* on its own (at least in affirmative sentences) means 'too much', *daha çok* and *daha fazla* are synonymous, meaning 'more' (see (113)).

Modification of adverbs occurs in exactly the same way as modification of adjectives (see 15.4). Some examples are:

(113) Sen bu konu üzerinde (benden) *daha* **çok/fazla** çalıştın.
'You have worked *more* (than me) on this topic.'

(114) [Bu sorunu *en* **iyi** anlayan] kişi sizsiniz.
'You are the person [who understands this problem *best*].'

(115) Nazlı [*şaşılacak kadar*] **hızlı** yürür.
'Nazlı walks *amazingly fast*.'

See also (30) and (99) above.

17   POSTPOSITIONAL PHRASES

Turkish has no prepositions, but a large number of postpositions, which follow their complements. Turkish postpositions fall into two main categories: **bare postpositions** (17.2), which carry no suffixes, and **possessive-marked postpositions** (17.3), which are marked by a possessive suffix agreeing with the complement, and an **oblique** (dative, locative or ablative) **case marker**. After discussing all these types of postposition, and the principal members of each class, in 17.4 we consider the syntactic functions that postpositional phrases can perform.

17.1   STRUCTURE OF THE POSTPOSITIONAL PHRASE

A **postpositional phrase** consists of a noun phrase followed by a postposition. The postposition is the head of the phrase, and the noun phrase is its **complement**. In each of the examples below the postposition is shown in bold:

(1)   sen-in **için**
      you-GEN for
      '*for* you'

(2)   çıkış kapı-sın-a **doğru**
      exit gate-NC-DAT towards
      '*towards* the exit'

(3)   ev-imiz-in **arka-sın-da**
      house-1PL.POSS-GEN back-3SG.POSS-LOC
      '*behind* our house'

(4)   ben-im **yer-im-e**
      I-GEN place-1SG.POSS-DAT
      '*instead of* me'

Turkish postpositions may be classified according to the way in which they relate syntactically to their complements. There are two major subdivisions: bare postpositions, exemplified in (1) and (2) above and discussed in 17.2, and possessive-marked postpositions, exemplified in (3) and (4) above and discussed in 17.3.

17.2   BARE POSTPOSITIONS

Bare postpositions are invariable in form. They fall into distinct groups according to what case marking they require on their complements.

17.2.1   POSTPOSITIONS TAKING NON-CASE-MARKED OR GENITIVE COMPLEMENTS

There are four items in this group:

gibi	'like'
için	'for'
-(y)lA/ile	'with', 'by'
kadar	'as . . . as'

In general the complements of these postpositions are left in the non-case-marked form:

(5)   bizler **gibi**
      '*like* us'

(6)   başka bir kalem**le**
      '*with* another pen'

(7)   Atatürk **kadar** ünlü
      '*as* famous *as* Atatürk'

The only exception to this rule is that if the complement is one of the pronouns *ben* 'I', *sen* 'you', *biz* 'we', *siz* 'you', *bu* 'this', *şu* 'this'/'that', *o* 'that', *kim* 'who' it normally takes genitive case marking:

(8)   siz**in** için
      'for you'

This does not, however, apply to the plural-marked forms of these pronouns, *bizler, sizler, bunlar, şunlar, onlar, kimler*, which remain in the non-case-marked form, as seen in (5) above.

   The eight pronominal forms which require genitive case marking with *için, gibi, kadar* and *-(y)lA/ile* display the same property in respect of the possessive-marked postpositions discussed in 17.3. We shall refer to them as **genitive-attracting pronouns**, a term which should be understood as excluding their plural-marked forms.

   The usage of these four postpositions is discussed and/or illustrated individually below.

(i) *gibi* 'like':

(9) Fatma **senin gibi** çok çalışıyor.
'Fatma works very hard, *like* you.'

(10) [**Seninki gibi** bir çanta almay]-ı düşünüyordum.
'I was thinking of [buying a bag *like* yours].'

Note that the demonstrative pronouns *bu/şu/o* (18.2) can combine with *gibi* with or without genitive marking. These combinations are roughly synonymous with the determiners *böyle/şöyle/öyle* 'such' (15.6.1 (iv)):

(11) **O gibi/Onun gibi/Öyle** adamlar insanı kolaylıkla aldatabiliyorlar.
'Men *like that* can easily fool people.'

Combinations of *gibi* with the demonstratives can also be pronominalized by means of 3rd person possessive marking (cf. 18.4). In this case the demonstrative is genitive-marked:

(12) **Bu-nun gibi-ler-i** bence daha güzel.
this-GEN like-PL-3SG.POSS
'I think *the ones like this* are nicer.'

For *ne gibi* 'what kind of' see 19.2.1.9.

(ii) *için* 'for':

(13) Selim **benim için** bir şey bıraktı mı?
'Did Selim leave anything *for me*?'

The phrases *bunun için, onun için* often have the causal meaning 'because of this/that', 'so' (see 28.3.6 (ii)):

(14) Dün sürekli yağmur yağdı, **onun için** hiç sokağa çıkmadık.
'Yesterday it rained continually, *so* we didn't go out at all.'

With certain complements, such as *iş* 'work' and *para* 'money', a phrase headed by *için* can express purpose:

(15) Ferit **iş için** Arjantin'e gitmişti.
'Ferit had gone to Argentina *on business*.'

(iii) *-(y)lA/ile* 'with', 'by':
This postposition is also known as the comitative/instrumental marker (8.1.4). As a postposition *-(y)lA/ile* has four main meanings, the first two comitative and the other two instrumental:

(a)   in the company of a person or persons:

> (16) Ercan baloya **kimin*le*** gitmiş?
> '*Who* did Ercan go to the ball *with*?'

(b)   in a manner characterized by some quality:

> (17) Size **memnuniyet*le*** yardım ederim.
> 'I'll help you *with pleasure*.'

(c)   using an instrument:

> (18) Mehmet ekmeği **keskin bir bıçak*la*** kesti.
> 'Mehmet cut the bread *with a sharp knife*.'

(d)   using a means of transport or communication:

> (19) Jale işe **araba*yla*** gidiyor.
> 'Jale goes to work *by car*.'

> (20) Sonucu size **mektup*la*** bildiririz.
> 'We will inform you of the result *by letter*.'

For the use of *-(y)lA/ile* as a complement marker see 13.1.2.2, and for its use as a conjunction ('and') see 28.3.1.1 (ii); for subjects conjoined by *-(y)lA/ile* see 12.2.2.4, 13.2.3.2.

(iv)   *kadar* 'as . . . as':
This postposition has a comparative function, with two meanings:

(a)   the same degree of a certain quality
In this meaning the phrase that *kadar* forms with its complement modifies an adjective or adverb:

> (21) **Senin kadar** *akıllı* bir insan tanımıyorum.
> 'I don't know anyone *as clever as you*.'

> (22) Bugün Demet **kadar** *hızlı* koşabildim.
> 'Today I was able to run *as fast as* Demet.'

(b)   the same quantity of occurrence or performance
In this meaning the postpositional phrase modifies a verb:

> (23) Hülya Yücel **kadar** *öksür*müyordu.
> 'Hülya was not *coughing as much as* Yücel.'

Note that the demonstrative pronouns *bu/şu/o* (18.2) combine with *kadar* without genitive marking to form quantifier determiners (15.6.1) and adverbials of quantity or degree (16.5).

17.2.2 POSTPOSITIONS TAKING DATIVE COMPLEMENTS

(i) *doğru* 'towards':
This postposition can have either temporal or spatial meaning:

(24) **Akşam-a doğru** kar yağmaya başladı.
evening-DAT towards
'*Towards evening* it began to snow.'

(25) Kızlar **denize doğru** koşuyordu.
'The girls were running *towards the sea*.'

(ii) *göre* 'according to':
This postposition expresses the following types of relation:

(a) conformity

(26) **Hava raporuna göre** öğleden sonra yağmur yağacakmış.
'*According to the weather forecast* it's going to rain this afternoon.'

(b) comparison

(27) **Ötekine göre** bu otelin pek bir konforu yok.
'This hotel has few comforts *compared with the other*.'

(c) appropriateness

(28) Bu oda tam **sana göre**.
'This room is just *right for you*.'

(iii) *kadar* 'until', 'as far as':
When used with a dative-marked complement, *kadar* (and its much less used synonym *dek*) has either temporal or spatial meaning, in both cases involving a terminal point:

Temporal:

(29) **Saat bire kadar** beklerim.
'I'll wait *until one o'clock*.'

(30) **Cumaya kadar** biter.
'It will be finished *by Friday.*'

(31) **Beş dakikaya kadar** gelirim.
'I'll be back *within five minutes.*'

Spatial:

(32) **Van'a kadar** gidemedik.
'We weren't able to get *as far as Van.*'

For *kadar* with a non-case-marked or genitive complement see 17.2.1 (iv).

(**iv**) *karşı* 'against', 'towards':
This postposition expresses the following types of relation:

(**a**) opposition

(33) **Sana karşı** değiller.
'They're not *against you.*'

(**b**) attitude

(34) **Tarık Bey'e karşı** büyük saygım var.
'I have great respect *for Tarık Bey.*'

(**c**) proximity (in certain more or less fixed temporal expressions)

(35) **Sabaha karşı** fırtına dindi.
'*Towards morning* the storm died down.'

(**v**) *rağmen/karşın* 'in spite of':

(36) Şebnem **hastalığına rağmen** çalışmaya devam ediyor.
'Şebnem is carrying on working *in spite of her illness.*'

For *gelince* 'as for' see 23.3.3.1.

17.2.3 POSTPOSITIONS TAKING ABLATIVE COMPLEMENTS

(**i**) *başka/▽gayrı* 'apart from', 'other than':

(37) **Bundan başka** bir şey var mı?
'Is there anything *other than this*?'

(ii) *beri* 'since', 'for':
Postpositional phrases headed by *beri* always have temporal meaning. They express the duration, prior to a given reference point, of a state of affairs or a process which, at the point of time referred to, *is/was still continuing*. When *beri* has the sense of 'since', the complement noun phrase expresses the time at which the state or process began:

(38) **Pazartesiden beri** hasta-yım.
Monday-ABL since ill-1SG
'I've been ill *since Monday*.'

(39) Mehmet **ekim baş-ın-dan beri** yurtdışın-da-ydı.
Mehmet October beginning-NC-ABL since abroad-LOC-P.COP
'Mehmet had been abroad *since the beginning of October*.'

(40) Koray **1995'ten beri** Kanada'da yaşıyor.
'Koray has been living in Canada *since 1995*.'

When *beri* has the sense of 'for', the complement noun phrase expresses the amount of time that has/had elapsed since the start of the process or the onset of the state:

(41) **Üç günden beri** hastayım.
'I've been ill *for three days*.'

(42) Koray **birkaç yıldan beri** Kanada'da yaşamaktaydı.
'Koray had been living in Canada *for several years*.'

If (as in the above examples) the postpositional phrase headed by *beri* modifies the main predicate of the sentence, this predicate is usually presented in the form which expresses the state or process as ongoing at the reference point (see the discussion of imperfective aspect in 21.3.1–2). It can therefore be a nominal predicate, as in (38), (39), (41), or a verbal predicate with progressive aspect (*-(I)yor*, *-mAktA*), as in (40), (42). However, when *beri* has the sense of 'since', a quantified or negative predicate is often expressed with perfective aspect (*-DI*, *-mIş*):

(43) **O zamandan beri** arabamı *üç defa* değiştirdim.
'I've changed my car *three times since then*.'

(44) **Yıllardan beri** kendine yeni pabuç al*mamış*tı/almıyordu.
'S/he hadn't bought herself/himself any new shoes *for years*.'

In the case of a negative predicate there can be a clear difference in meaning between the perfective and imperfective versions of the same sentence:

(45) (a) Toplantı-dan beri konuş-**ma-mış**-lar.
meeting-ABL since speak-NEG-EV/PF-3PL
'Apparently they *haven't* spoken since the meeting.'

(b) Toplantı-dan beri konuş-**mu-yor**-lar-mış.
meeting-ABL since speak-NEG-IMPF-3PL-EV.COP
'Apparently they *haven't been* speak*ing* since the meeting.'

(iii) *bu yana* 'since':
This item is synonymous with *beri* in its 'since' meaning, except that the temporal reference point is usually the present moment, not a point of time in the past. Thus *bu yana* could be substituted for *beri* in (38) but not normally in (39). It is considerably less common than *beri* in informal speech.

(iv) *dolayı* 'because of':
This postposition has a synonym *ötürü*, which is less frequently used.

(46) **Üzüntüsünden dolayı** Ayşe o akşamki toplantımıza katılamadı.
'*Because of her distressed state* Ayşe wasn't able to join our gathering that evening.'

(v) *itibaren* 'from', 'with effect from':
This is a temporal postposition indicating the time at which some planned or anticipated state of affairs or process is or was due or expected to begin.

(47) Bu tarife, **1.10.2003 tarihinden itibaren** geçerlidir.
'This timetable is effective *from 1.10.2003*.'

(vi) *önce/∇evvel* 'before':

(48) Onlar **benden önce** gelmişler.
'They arrived *before me*.'

(vii) *sonra* 'after':

(49) **Her yemekten sonra** mutlaka bir fincan Türk kahvesi içer.
'S/he invariably drinks a cup of Turkish coffee *after every meal*.'

önce and *sonra* differ from other postpositions in that they can be modified by an immediately preceding adverbial, either an adverbial of quantity such as *çok* 'much' or *biraz* 'a little' (16.5), or an expression denoting a period of time, such as *beş dakika* 'five minutes' or *bir yıl* 'a year':

(50) **Yemekten *biraz* sonra** Ahmet işine döndü.
'*A little while after lunch* Ahmet returned to his work.'

(51) Onlar **benden *beş dakika* önce** gelmişler.
'Apparently they arrived *five minutes before me*.'

For the (non-postpositional) adverbial functions of *önce* and *sonra* see 16.4.1.1. For adverbial clauses formed with the subordinators *-mAdAn önce* and *-DIktAn sonra* see 26.3.16 (vi).

(**viii**) *yana* 'as regards', 'in favour of':

(52) Berna **akrabadan yana** şanslı sayılır.
'Berna can be considered fortunate *as regards relatives*.'

(53) **İdam cezasından yana** değilim.
'I'm not *in favour of capital punishment*.'

17.3 POSSESSIVE-MARKED POSTPOSITIONS

Possessive-marked postpositions are derived from nouns, and have the form noun + POSS + OBL. To the nominal stem (e.g. *arka* 'back', *yer* 'place') is added (a) a possessive suffix which shows person agreement with the complement noun phrase, and (b) an **oblique** case marker (dative, locative or ablative) or, in a few cases, the adverbial suffix *-CA* or the instrumental marker *-(y)lA*. In this chapter we use the abbreviation OBL to cover all of these suffixes.

A striking difference between postpositional phrases with bare and possessive-marked postpositions respectively is that the complement of a possessive-marked postposition is often not overtly expressed (see 18.1.5). This happens in cases where the possessive suffix is sufficient to identify the complement, in other words where its overt expression would take the form of a personal pronoun:

(54) (O-nun) **ön-*ün*-de** beş kişi vardı.
s/he-GEN front-3SG.POSS-LOC
'There were five people in front of *him/her*.'

Possessive-marked postpositions can be divided into two groups, which differ in respect of (i) whether, or under what circumstances, their complements take genitive case marking, and (ii) whether their own case marking is variable or fixed.

17.3.1 GROUP 1: SPATIAL RELATIONS

The postpositions in this group express spatial relations. Dative, locative or ablative case marking is selected according to the type of spatial meaning to be expressed. The nouns upon which this group is based are shown below, together with the postpositional meaning that they generate. Note that in their postpositional usages these nouns denote not only a particular part of a physical object but also a space situated in relation to that object. Thus *ön-* can mean 'the space in front', *üst-* 'the space above', *yan-* 'the space beside', etc.

ön	'front'	⇒ 'in front of'
arka	'back'	⇒ 'behind'
iç	'interior'	⇒ 'inside', 'in'
dış	'exterior'	⇒ 'outside'
üst	'top'	⇒ 'on top of', 'above', 'on'
alt	'bottom'	⇒ 'under', 'underneath', 'below'
yan	'side'	⇒ 'beside', 'next to'
karşı	'opposite side'	⇒ 'opposite'
ara	'space'	⇒ 'between', 'among'
etraf/çevre	'surroundings'	⇒ 'around'
öte	'far side'	⇒ 'beyond'

17.3.1.1 Group 1 possessive-marked postpositions with genitive complements

The postpositions in this group usually form a genitive-possessive construction (14.4) with their complement noun phrase.

(i)   As in the case of noun phrases in general (14.3.3.3 (i)), dative case marking is required where the postpositional phrase expresses the destination or target of an action:

(55) Küçük kız (ben-**im**) **yan-ım-***a* geldi.
　　　　　　　I-GEN side-1SG.POSS-DAT
　　　'The little girl came *over to* me.'

(56) Bu tabloyu kanepe**nin üstün***e* asalım.
　　　'Let's hang this picture *above* the sofa.'

(ii) Location requires locative case marking (14.3.3.4):

(57) Dolab-**ın arka-sın-***da* bir şey var mı?
cupboard-GEN back-3SG.POSS-LOC
'Is there anything *behind* the cupboard?'

(iii) Motion from, out of or through a space requires ablative case marking (14.3.3.5 (i)):

(58) Kanepe-**nin alt-ın-***dan* bir fare çıktı.
sofa-GEN bottom-3SG.POSS-ABL
'A mouse ran out *from under* the sofa.'

(59) Arabayla park**ın** **iç***inden geç*ilmez.
'One can't go *through* the park by car.'

17.3.1.2 Group 1 possessive-marked postpositions with non-case-marked complements

There are various contexts which require the complement of a group 1 possessive-marked postposition to be left in the non-case-marked form rather than being given genitive case marking. These are all contexts in which the complement is 3rd person, and even if it is plural (as in (67) and (68) below), the possessive marking on the postposition is always 3rd person singular.

(i) Contexts where the postposition is used in a non-physical sense, or with a metaphorical meaning. (60)–(62) show various such uses of *içinde* 'in':

(60) Bütün bunları **iki saat** *içinde* mi yaptınız? (cf. (60) in Chapter 16)
'Did you do all these *in two hours*?'

(61) **Ter** *içinde* kalmıştım.
'I was *covered in sweat*.'

(62) Seyhan **korku** *içinde* kapıya hafifçe vurdu.
'*In a state of fear*, Seyhan gently knocked on the door.'

Metaphorical uses of *altın(d)a* 'under' are also common:

(63) Bütün okullar **Bakanlık'ın denetimi** *altına* alındı.
'All schools were brought *under the control of the Ministry*.'

(64) Hep **babasının etkisi** *altında* yaşadı.
'He lived constantly *under the influence of his father.*'

(ii) Contexts where the complement is non-specific:

Non-specific indefinite complement (22.2.1):

(65) Bu hesapları **bir kağıt** *üstünde* yapmak daha kolay olacak.
'It will be easier to do these calculations *on a piece of paper.*'

Categorial complement (22.3):

(66) Sanık ne zaman **yargıç** *önüne* çıkar acaba?
'I wonder when the accused person will appear *before a judge?*'

Generic complement (22.4.2):

(67) Genellikle **kardeşler** *arasında* kuvvetli bir dayanışma olur.
'There is usually a strong solidarity *between siblings.*'

The two conditions described in (i) and (ii) above often occur together. For example, the complements of *içinde* in (61) and (62) are categorial, and the use of *arasında* in (67) is non-spatial.

17.3.1.3 Particular features of individual postpositions in Group 1

(i) *iç* + POSS + OBL can also be used in the non-physical sense of 'among', i.e. expressing inclusion in a set or group. In this particular sense it is interchangeable with *ara* + POSS + OBL:

(68) Ali'nin giysileri **içinde/arasında** işine yarayacak bir şey bulabilirsin.
'You may find something *among* Ali's clothes to fit your needs.'

For the partitive use of *iç* + POSS + ABL/*ara* + POSS + ABL see 14.5.1 (ii), 14.5.2, 18.4 (vi), 19.2.1.4–5.

(ii) Some speakers use the form *içeri* + POSS + OBL (e.g. *içerisinde*) in preference to *iç* + POSS + OBL (e.g. *içinde*). (For *içeri* in adverbial uses without possessive affixation see 16.4.2.)

(iii) *Üst* has a synonym V*üzer-*, which does not occur as a bare noun. It is interchangeable with *üst* in the postpositional function, but nowadays its usage is mainly confined to non-physical senses, as exemplified in (70) and (71).

(69) Masanın **üstünde/Vüzerinde** bir şey yok.
'There's nothing *on* the table.'

The dative forms *üstüne*/V*üzerine*, with a non-case-marked complement, can mean 'on' in the metaphorical sense of 'on the subject of':

(70) Gençlerde uyuşturucu kullanımı **üstüne/üzerine** araştırma yapıyor.
'S/he's doing research *on* the use of drugs among young people.'

Üzerine also means 'on', 'upon' in a temporal sense, expressing a sequential and causal relation between two events. In this usage also, the complement is left in the non-case-marked form (unless it is one of the genitive-attracting pronouns):

(71) Kocasının ölümü **üzerine** kendi memleketine döndü.
'*On* her husband's death she went back to her own country.'

For *bunun üzerine* as a temporal discourse connective see 28.3.8.

(iv) In addition to its literal meaning of 'beside', *yan* + POSS + OBL has a number of metaphorical senses. Most of these still belong to the realm of physical space, and require any definite or specific complements to be genitive-marked:

(72) Babalarının **yanında** sigara içmezler.
'They don't smoke *in* their father*'s presence*.'

(73) Çocuk daha çok anneannesi**nin yanında** kalıyor.
'The child lives mainly *with* his grandmother.'

(74) **Yanımda** beş kişi çalışıyor.
'I've got five people working *for me*.'

In the abstract sense of 'in comparison with', *yan* + POSS + LOC may or may not have a genitive-marked complement:

(75) [Ali'nin yaptıkları](-**nın**) **yanında** bunlar pek parlak değil.
'*Compared with* the ones Ali made/makes, these are not very wonderful.'

(v) In its sense of 'between', *ara* + POSS + OBL can take two or more conjoined complements. In the case of two complements, they are conjoined by *-(y)lA/ile* (28.3.1.1 (ii)):

(76) Benim odam*la* onunki **arasında** kalın bir duvar vardı.
'There was a thick wall *between* my room *and* his.'

In informal speech the second of the conjoined complements may be given genitive marking:

(77) Ahmet'*le* çocuklar(**ın**) **arasında** bir sorun mu var?
'Is there some problem *between* Ahmet *and* the children?'

If one of the complements conjoined by *ara* + POSS + OBL is a personal pronoun, it usually occurs as the second item, and if it is one of the genitive-attracting pronouns it must be genitive-marked:

(78) baba-sı-*yla* (biz-**im**) ara-**mız**-da
father-3SG.POSS-CONJ we-GEN between-1PL.POSS-LOC
'*between* his/her father *and* us/me'

In informal speech, some speakers may use a pronoun as the first of the two conjoined complements:

(79) **bizim*le*** babası arasında
'between *us* and his/her father'

As the examples above illustrate, *ara-* is marked with the same person as the *second* of the two complements (unlike the person marking of predicates with subjects conjoined by *-(y)lA/ile*, see 12.2.2.4 (ii)).

Where the pronoun is singular, the person marking on *ara-* is also singular:

(80) Ayşe-yle **sen-in** ara-**n**-da
Ayşe-CONJ you-GEN between-2SG.POSS-LOC
'between Ayşe and *you*'

Where the pronoun is 3rd person plural, the person marking on *ara-* may be (3rd person) singular or plural:

(81) Ayşe'yle **onlar(ın)** arasında/ara**larında**
'between Ayşe and *them*'

If there are more than two complements, the last two have to be conjoined by *ve* (not by *-(y)lA/ile*; see 28.3.1.1 (ii)):

(82) Babası, amcası **ve bizim** ara**mız**da eski bir dostluk vardı.
'There was a longstanding friendship *between* his father, his uncle *and* us.'

In the case of conjoined complements which are proper names of places, the use of an overt conjunction is optional, whether there are two or more complements:

(83) Diyarbakır **ile** Urfa arasında/Diyarbakır-Urfa arasında otobüs işletiyordu.
'He ran a bus service between Diyarbakır *and* Urfa.'

(84) Diyarbakır, Urfa, Gaziantep arasında otobüs işletiyordu.
'He ran a bus service between Diyarbakır, Urfa [*and*] Gaziantep.'

17.3.2   GROUP 2: ABSTRACT RELATIONS

Group 2 of the possessive-marked postpositions differ from those in group 1 in several ways:

(**i**)   Whereas the group 1 postpositions, at least in their literal senses, denote relations of physical space, the items in group 2 are mostly concerned with abstract relations.

(**ii**)   There is not always a clear connection between the meaning of the noun upon which the postposition is based and the meaning of the postposition, which may have evolved over time.

(**iii**)   The case marking of these postpositions is fixed, not variable as in group 1. In some instances the adverbial suffix *-CA* or the instrumental marker *-(y)lA/ile* replaces the case marker.

(**iv**)   With the exception of the genitive-attracting pronouns (17.2.1), the complements of these postpositions are almost always left in the non-case-marked form. (For further exceptions see 17.3.2.1.)

(**v**)   Where a 3rd person plural complement is overtly expressed, the possessive marker on the postposition is always 3rd person singular:

(85) **Çocuk-lar saye-*sin*-de** alışveriş işleri pek sorun olmuyor.
child-PL *saye*-3SG.POSS-LOC
'*Thanks to the children*, shopping is not really a problem.'

A list of the most common group 2 possessive-marked postpositions is given below. Because they are used mainly with 3rd person complements, they are shown here for convenience with the 3rd person singular possessive suffix. The examples with genitive-marked complements that appear immediately below the list include some with 1st and 2nd person possessive marking.

açı	'angle'	*açı-sın-dan*	'from the point of view of', 'in terms of'
ad	'name'	*ad-ın-a*	'in the name of', 'on behalf of'
aracılık	'mediation'	*aracılığ-ı-yla*	'through (the mediation of)'
bakım	'aspect'	*bakım-ın-dan*	'from the point of view of', 'in terms of'
boy	'length'	*boy-un-ca*	'all along', 'throughout'
gerek	'requirement'	*gereğ-in-ce*	'in accordance with'
hak	'right'	*hakk-ın-da*	'about'
∇*itibar*	'respect'	∇*itibar-ı-yla*	'in respect of', 'in terms of'
konu	'subject'	*konu-sun-da*	'on the subject of', 'about'
neden	'reason'	*neden-i-yle*	'because of'
saye (obs.)	'shadow'	*saye-sin-de*	'thanks to'
sıra	'time'	*sıra-sın-da*	'at the time of'
süre	'period'	*süre-sin-ce*	'during the period of'
taraf	'side'	*taraf-ın-dan*	'by' (an agent)
uğ(u)r	'good luck'	*uğr-un-a*	'for the sake of'
∇*vasıta*	'mediation'	∇*vasıta-sı-yla*	'through (the mediation of)'
yer	'place'	*yer-in-e*	'instead of'
yol	'way'	*yol-u-yla*	'by','by means of'
yüz	'reason'	*yüz-ün-den*	'because of'

Examples with genitive complements (genitive-attracting pronouns):

(86) Ömer ben-*im* **hakk-ım-da** neler söyledi?
      I-GEN *hakk*-1SG.POSS-LOC
    'What did Ömer say *about* me?'

(87) Bütün bunları siz-*in* **saye-niz-de** yapabildik.
          you- GEN *saye*-2PL.POSS-LOC
    'It is *thanks to* you that we have been able to do all this.'

Examples with non-case-marked complements:

(88) Sağlık **açısından/bakımından** bu kadar çikolata yemek doğru değil.
    '*From the* health *point of view* it's not good to eat so much chocolate.'

(89) Türkiye'deki depremler **konusunda** bir kitap yazmış.
    'S/he's written a book *about* earthquakes in Turkey.'

17.3.2.1 Particular features of individual postpositions in Group 2

(i) *aracılığıyla* and the synonymous ∇*vasıtasıyla* are unusual among the group 2 postpositions in that their complements are often genitive-marked. This is a matter of speakers' personal preference:

(90) Onlar Timur('un) **aracılığıyla**/Timur('un) **vasıtasıyla** tanışmışlar.
      'Apparently they first met *through* Timur.'

(ii) Unlike the other group 2 postpositions, *boyunca* can refer to a spatial dimension:

(91) Sahil **boyunca** küçük köyler vardı.
      '*All along* the coast there were small villages.'

Alternatively it can have temporal reference:

(92) Konferans **boyunca** fısıldaşmaya devam ettiler.
      'They continued to whisper to each other *throughout* the lecture.'

(iii) While in the sense of 'in respect of', 'in terms of', ∇*itibarıyla* has largely been replaced by *açısından* and *bakımından*, it also occurs in some formal registers as a synonym of *itibaren* (see 17.2.3).

(iv) *gereğince* is used only in legalistic language:

(93) Kanunun ilgili maddesi **gereğince** bir sözleşme hazırlanır.
      'A contract is drawn up *in accordance with* the relevant article of the law.'

(v) *konusunda* is not used with complements referring to human beings, except in the context of an organized exposition such as a book, an article or a lecture. Thus, for example, *yabancı öğrenciler* 'foreign students' could be substituted for *depremler* 'earthquakes' in (89) above.

(vi) *süresince* (and its obsolescent synonym (∇*müddetince*) differ from the temporal usage of *boyunca* (see (ii)) in that they do not emphasize the long duration of an activity or state:

(94) Yokluğum **süresince** komşum her gün uğrayıp kediye yiyecek verdi.
      '*During* my absence my neighbour came in every day and fed the cat.'

(vii) *tarafından* is used to express the agent of a passive verb (see 13.2.2).

(**viii**) In the expression of causality, *yüzünden* is used only when speaking of causes that have undesirable results:

> (95) Sıcak havalar **yüzünden** son zamanlarda işler yavaş gidiyor.
> '*Because of* the hot weather there has been slow progress recently.'

Causes that have desirable results can be expressed by *sayesinde*:

> (96) Sıcak havalar **sayesinde** denize bol bol girebildik.
> '*Because of* (*thanks to*) the hot weather we've been able to swim in the sea a lot.'

Nedeniyle is neutral in terms of the desirability of the outcome, but is restricted to relatively formal registers.

> (97) Yazların sıcaklığı **nedeniyle** bu bölgede muz ve hurma yetişmektedir.
> '*On account of* the hot summers, bananas and dates grow in this region.'

(**ix**) *uğruna* 'for the sake of' is used only with inanimate complements:

> (98) Güzellik **uğruna** bu kadar sıkıntıya katlanmaya değer mi?
> 'Is it worth suffering so much *for the sake of* beauty?'

17.4 SYNTACTIC FUNCTIONS OF THE POSTPOSITIONAL PHRASE

The range of syntactic functions that can be performed by a postpositional phrase depends upon the postposition that heads it. There are three possible functions: (i) adverbial, (ii) adjectival, (iii) predicative.

17.4.1 ADVERBIAL FUNCTION

The most characteristic function of a Turkish postpositional phrase is adverbial, either at the level of the sentence or within the verb phrase, and the great majority of examples already given in this chapter fall into this category. There are no postpositions that *cannot* head a postpositional phrase with adverbial function. Postpositional phrases headed by *kadar* (with non-case-marked or genitive complement), can also modify adjectives and adverbs (see (21) and (22) above, also 15.4.1.2).

17.4.2 ADJECTIVAL FUNCTION

Among the bare postpositions, the following can head postpositional phrases that function adjectivally within a noun phrase: *gibi*, *kadar* (with non-case-marked or genitive complement), *göre*, *başka*:

(99) **senin kadar** bir çocuk
'a child *of the same size/age as you*'

(100) tam **anneme göre** bir şapka
'a hat just *right for my mother*'

For other examples see (10), (11) and (37) above. Note that *başka* also occurs as an adjective meaning 'other', different'.

Postpositional phrases headed by *önce* and *sonra*, in common with other temporal adverbial phrases, can be converted from adverbial to adjectival function by the addition of *-ki* (see 15.3.7):

(101) bahçe-nin **yağmur-dan önce-*ki*** hal-i
garden-GEN rain-ABL before-ADJ state-3SG.POSS
'the state of the garden *before the rain*'

Postpositional phrases headed by possessive-marked postpositions can be used adjectivally only if the postposition has locative case marking, and again the addition of *-ki* is necessary to effect the conversion from adverbial to adjectival function (15.3.6):

(102) **Harun-la ara-mız-da-*ki*** gerginlik
Harun-CONJ between-1PL.POSS-LOC-ADJ tension
'the tension *between Harun and me/us*'

(103) **sendikacılık tarihi konusunda*ki*** araştırmalarınız
'your research *on* (*the subject of*) *the history of trade unionism*'

17.4.3 PREDICATIVE FUNCTION

Some types of postpositional phrase can be the subject complement in a linking sentence (12.1.1.2). All the bare postpositions whose phrases are used adjectivally can also occur in predicates. So also can *için*, *karşı*, *yana*, and the locative-marked forms of the possessive-marked postpositions:

(104) Bu çiçekler **sizin için**miş.
'Apparently these flowers are *for you*.'

For further examples see (28), (33) and (53) above.

In the case of the possessive-marked postpositions, it is only those that are locative-marked that can function predicatively:

(105) Can'ın arabası **evin önünde**.
'Can's car is *in front of the house*.'

The addition of -*ki* is not required unless pronominalization is intended (18.5):

(106) Can'ın arabası **evin önünde***ki*.
'Can's car is *the one in front of the house*.'

18 PRONOUNS

Pronouns are expressions that are used when referring to persons, things or states of affairs that have previously been mentioned, whose referents are obvious from the context or whose content is only partially specified, such as:

(1) **Onlar** eşyalarını daha toplamamış.
     '*They* haven't packed their luggage yet.'

(2) **Şuradakin**den de bir tane istiyorum.
     'I also want one of *the kind over there.*'

(3) Kapıda **birisi** var.
     'There's someone at the door.'

This chapter describes personal pronouns such as *ben* 'I', *kendim* 'myself', *birbir-* 'each other' (18.1), and the conditions under which they are used (18.1.5), demonstrative pronouns such as *bu* 'this (one)' (18.2), locative pronouns such as *şurada* 'here', 'over there' (18.3), pronouns formed by the suffix *-(s)I*, such as *iyisi* 'a nice(r) one', *bazısı* 'some (of them)' (18.4), pronouns formed by the suffix *-ki*, such as *benimki* 'mine', *öteki* 'the other (one)' (18.5), pronominal quantifiers such as *herkes* 'everyone', *bir şey* 'something', and other pronominal expressions (18.6).

Interrogative pronouns (e.g. *kim* 'who', *nerede* 'where') are discussed in 19.2, and pronominal quantifiers which interact with negation (e.g. *kimse* 'no one', 'anyone') are discussed in 20.5. Another type of pronominal construction, headless relative clauses, is discussed in 25.3.

18.1 PERSONAL PRONOUNS

18.1.1 SIMPLE PERSONAL PRONOUNS

The simple personal pronouns of Turkish are:

ben	'I'	*biz*	'we'
sen	'you' (familiar)	*siz*	'you' (plural), (formal singular)
o	'he', 'she', 'it'	*onlar*	'they'

biz:
biz 'we', which is the 1st person plural form, may also refer to the 1st person singular, either in very formal contexts where the speaker wishes to express his/her humble status as compared to the addressee(s), or ironically in imitation of such a stance:

(4) Efendim, **biz** sizin kadar bilemeyiz bu konuları tabii ki.
     'Naturally, **I** cannot know these subjects as well as you [do].'

siz and *sen*:
The 2nd person form *siz* is used in the following circumstances:

(i)   To indicate the plurality of the 2nd person (i.e. 'you both/all').
(ii) When addressing a person with whom one is on formal terms (in which case both parties normally address each other as *siz*).
(iii) When one is addressing a person who is taken to be of higher rank or status.

(5) **Siz** şu sıralarda sinemaya gittiniz mi?
     (a) 'Have *you (both/all)* been to the cinema lately?'
     (b) 'Have *you* (= formal, singular) been to the cinema lately?'

Children are almost always addressed as *sen*; older people are generally addressed as *siz*, and new acquaintances most commonly address each other as *siz*. Speakers who normally address each other as *sen* may, in a formal situation (such as a committee meeting), adopt the conventional formality of *siz*. However, the choice between *siz* and *sen* varies among speakers, since the notion of formality depends largely on the social background of the persons involved and, to some degree, on the speakers' attitude towards the norms of social hierarchy.

bizler and *sizler*:
biz 'we' and *siz* 'you' can combine with the plural suffix. Using *bizler* and *sizler* instead of *biz* and *siz* has only a marginally different effect, and is confined to the following circumstances:

(i)   Where the speaker wishes to individuate the members of a group, especially in cases where the speaker wants to indicate that the action was carried out, or the event experienced, individually, not as a group:

(6) **Bizler** kırık not alınca çok üzülürdük.
     '*We* (each of us) would be sad when *we* (each of us) got a bad mark.'

(ii) For referring to multiple groups of persons:

(7)   *Sizler,* **Ankara'lı ve İstanbul'lular**, Türkiye'nin geri kalanını
       tanımıyorsunuz.
       '*You, people from Ankara and Istanbul*, don't know the rest of
       Turkey.'

(iii) When talking to a person with whom one uses the formal *siz*, to indicate that one is referring to a group that that person belongs to (e.g. his/her
family or friends, etc.), and not to that person alone:

(8)   **Sizler** nasılsınız?
       'How are *you (both/all)*?'

o and *onlar*:
For the use of these forms as resumptive pronouns in relative clauses introduced by *ki*, see 25.6.

The inflection of simple personal pronouns
Pronouns, like other noun phrases, can be inflected for case, e.g. *beni* 'me',
onları 'them', *size* 'to you', *sende* 'on you'. The dative form of the 1st and
2nd persons singular is irregular, the stem vowel becoming 'a': *bana* 'to me',
sana 'to you'. Another irregularity concerns the 3rd person singular
pronoun *o*. The case markers and the plural suffix do not attach directly
to *o*, but do so only through the mediation of the consonant 'n': *ondan*
'from him/her/it', *onlar* 'they', etc. (6.2). The genitive case marker of the
1st person forms is *-Im*: *benim* 'my', *bizim* 'our'. For the combination of
simple personal pronouns with the comitative/instrumental marker *-(y)lA*
see 8.1.4.

18.1.2   *kendi*

The word *kendi* has five functions, one adjectival and the rest pronominal.
It usually refers to human beings but in its adjectival function (18.1.2.1) and
in its emphatic function (18.1.2.2 (ii)) it may refer to inanimate (usually
abstract) concepts.

(9)   **Plan-ın** *kendi-***sin-de** bir sorun var.
       plan-GEN self-3SG.POSS-LOC
       'There is a problem with *the plan itself*.'

Kendi (in its bare or inflected forms) can be *followed* by the noun phrase
which is its **antecedent** (i.e. the expression the pronoun refers to):

(10) **Kendi** fikriydi ***Ahmet'in*** mobilyaları değiştirmek.
'It was Ahmet's own idea to change the furniture.'

(11) **Kendinizi** anlatmadınız *siz* hiç.
'You haven't talked about yourself at all.'

18.1.2.1 Bare form *kendi*

In its bare form, *kendi* functions as an adjectival modifier of a possessive-marked noun phrase, and means 'own' (as in 'his own', 'our own'). In this usage *kendi* is not inflected for person or case. The possessive-marked noun phrase modified by *kendi* may form part of a genitive-possessive construction (14.4) in which the genitive-marked constituent is the antecedent:

(12) Hırsızlığı (**Erol'un**) *kendi* **şirket-in-**den biri yapmış.
                Erol-GEN own company-3SG.POSS-ABL
'It was apparently someone from *Erol's own company* who committed the burglary.'

(13) Erken emeklilik, (**ben-im**) *kendi* **isteğ-im-**di.
                I-GEN own wish-1SG.POSS-P.COP
'It was *my own wish* [to take early retirement].'

When the possessive-marked noun phrase is in the 3rd person (e.g. *anahtar-larını* 'his/her own keys' below), and does not have a genitive-marked modifier, *kendi* can refer to any 3rd person in the same clause, but it is most commonly understood as referring to the subject:

(14) Semra Elif'e *kendi* anahtar-lar-ın-ı vermiş.
                   own key-PL-3SG.POSS-ACC
'Semra gave Elif her own keys.'

The more likely intended meaning of (14) is that Semra gave Elif Semra's own keys; however, another possible meaning would be that she gave Elif Elif's own keys.
    The antecedent of adjectival *kendi* can denote an inanimate entity:

(15) Bu karışıklık, **sorun-un** *kendi* **özellik-ler-in-**den kaynaklanıyor.
                   problem-GEN own property-PL-3SG.POSS-ABL
'This confusion is a result of *the very properties of the problem*.'

(16) Bu, **evin** *kendi* rengi.
'This is *the original colour* of the house.'

18.1.2.2 Inflected *kendi-*: emphatic, reflexive, simple pronominal and resumptive usages

The pronoun *kendi-* can be inflected for person, in which case it combines with the possessive suffixes described in 8.1.2:

(17) *kendim* 1st person singular   *kendimiz* 1st person plural
     kendin 2nd person singular   *kendiniz* 2nd person plural,
           (familiar)   or formal singular
     kendi(si) 3rd person singular *kendileri* 3rd person plural

Note that in the case of the 3rd person, the person marker *-(s)I* is sometimes omitted.

The forms above can be further inflected for case, e.g. *kendi-m-den* 'from myself', *kendi-niz-i* '(you) yourself/yourselves' (formal/plural accusative), etc. Note that 'n' has to be attached to the 3rd person forms *kendi*, *kendisi* and *kendileri* when these are inflected for case, e.g. *kendine/kendisine* 'to him/her(self)', *kendilerinde* 'on them(selves)' (6.2, 8.1.3).

(i) Emphatic usage of inflected *kendi-*:
Kendi- inflected for person (i.e. the forms in (17)) can be used for purposes of emphasizing the subject pronoun of a main clause, as in *I myself*, *they themselves*, etc. In such emphatic constructions *kendi-* can be used with or without a pronoun matching it in person, but in all cases a matching person marker on the predicate is obligatory:

(18) Evde **(ben) kendim** oturacağım için bu renkleri seçtim.
         I self-1SG.POSS
      'I chose these colours because *I* will be living in the house *myself.*'

(19) **(O) kendi(si)** istemiş sınava girmeyi.
      '*S/he herself/himself* wanted to take an exam.'

The 3rd person forms *kendisi* and *kendileri* can have any type of noun phrase with a human referent (not only personal pronouns) as their antecedent', such as *müdürler* 'directors' and *Erol* below:

(20) **Müdür-ler kendi-leri** atıyorlar muavinlerini.
      director-PL self-3PL.POSS
      '*Directors* appoint their deputies *themselves.*'

(21) Arabayı **Erol kendisi** yıkayacak.
      '*Erol* is going to wash the car *himself.*'

In the 3rd person the antecedent may be given genitive marking:

(22) Arabayı **Erol'un kendi-si** yıkayacak.
     Erol-GEN/self-3SG.POSS
     'Erol is going to wash the car himself.'

On the other hand, the 1st and 2nd person pronouns as antecedents of emphatic *kendi-* can be genitive-marked only in noun clauses and relative clauses (see (27) and (28) below).

The form *kendisi* can be replaced by *kendi*. Where the antecedent is non-case-marked, this produces no difference of formality:

(23) Arabayı **Erol/o kendi** yıkayacak.
     Erol/he self

However, where the antecedent is genitive-marked, the use of *kendi* is informal:

(24) Arabayı **Erol-un kendi** yıkayacak.
     Erol-GEN self

Unlike the 1st and 2nd person emphatic forms, which, in main clauses, occur only as subjects, the 3rd person emphatic forms *kendisi* and *kendileri* can function as objects and adverbials. In these cases, the antecedent (*o, onlar* or any appropriate noun phrase) appears in the genitive form:

(25) Meclis'e belli bir saatte gidersen **Başbakan-ın kendi-sin-i** bile
     prime minister-GEN self-3SG.POSS-ACC
     görebilirsin.
     'If you go to parliament at a certain time you will be able to see the *Prime Minister himself/herself*.'

(26) Sonuçları **onlar-ın kendi-lerin-den** öğrenebilirsin.
     they-GEN self-3PL.POSS-ABL
     'You can find out the results from *them in person*.'

An emphatic construction with *kendi-* can be the subject of a noun clause (Chapter 24) or relative clause (Chapter 25). When it is the subject of a relative clause, the verb usually agrees with it (as in (27a)), but some speakers use 3rd person singular possessive marking on the verb (as in (27b)):

(27) (**a**) [(***ben-im***) **kendi-m-in** bile anla-ya-ma-dığ-*ım*] bir yazı
         I-GEN self-1SG.POSS-GEN even understand-PSB-NEG-
         PART-**1SG.POSS**

(b) [(**ben-im**) *kend-im-in* bile anla-ya-ma-dığ-*ı*] bir yazı
I-GEN self-1SG.POSS-GEN even understand-PSB-NEG-
PART-**3SG.POSS**
'an article that even *I* couldn't understand *myself*'

When an emphatic construction with *kendi-* functions as the subject of a
noun clause, the verb agrees with it. The antecedent (*siz* 'you' below)
usually has genitive marking, but it may also be non-case-marked (28a).
Kendiniz can also be used on its own in its non-case-marked form (28b):

(28) (a) [(*Siz-(in)*) **kendi-niz** oraya git-me-*niz*] gerekiyor.
you(-GEN) self-2PL.POSS there go-VN-**2PL.POSS**
'*You* should go there *yourself*.'

(b) [Oraya **kendi-niz** git-me-*niz*] gerekiyor.
'*You* should go there *yourself*.'

(ii) Reflexive usage of inflected *kendi-*:
kendi- is the standard means for expressing reflexivity (see also the reflexive
voice suffix, 8.2.1.3 and reflexive constructions, 13.2.3.1). Reflexive
sentences are sentences where the subject is also the recipient of the action,
as in *George likes himself*. In its usage as a reflexive pronoun, *kendi-* is
inflected for person and case.

(29) **Kendi-n-den** başkasına güvenemiyor musun?
self-2SG.POSS-ABL
'Can't you trust anyone but *yourself*?'

The antecedent of reflexive *kendi-* is usually the subject of its own clause:

(30) *Semra* aday olarak **kendi-sin-i/kendin-i** öne sürecekmiş.
'Apparently *Semra* is going put *herself* forward as a candidate.'

(31) [**Siz-in** *kendi-niz-i* eleştir-me-**niz**] ne kadar kolay-mış!
you-GEN self-2PL.POSS-ACC criticize-VN-2PL.POSS how easy-
EV.COP
'How easy *you* seem to find it to criticize *yourself*!'

This can be indicated simply by placing the appropriate person marker on
the predicate:

(32) **Kendi-m**-e bakamıyor-**um**.
self-1SG.POSS-DAT-1SG
'*I* can't take care of *myself*.'

A 3rd person antecedent whose identity is clear from previous mention similarly does not have to be expressed within the clause by an overt noun phrase:

(33) *Ninem* çok yaşlı. Artık **kendine** bakamıyor.
     'My granny's very old. She can't take care of *herself* any longer.'

The antecedent can also be a constituent other than the subject:

(34) Sanki *bana* **kendi-m-i** anlatıyorlardı.
     I(DAT) self-1SG.POSS-ACC
     '[It was] as if they were talking to *me* about *myself.*'

In the absence of an antecedent within the same clause, reflexive *kendi-* may refer to a person indicated in the superordinate clause:

(35) [**Kendimize** araba almak] istiyor**uz**.
     'We want to buy a car for *ourselves.*'

There are also cases where there is no antecedent in the sentence, yet a reflexive can still be used because the person to whom it refers is understood to be the subject of a non-person-marked verb, such as *almak* below:

(36) Bu durum-da [**kendi-niz-e** araba al-mak] çok zor olacak.
     this situation-LOC self-2PL.POSS-DAT car buy-VN very difficult
     be-FUT
     'Under these circumstances it is going to be very difficult [for you] to buy a car for *yourself.*'

There is a slight difference in the reflexive usage of the two 3rd person forms *kendi* and *kendisi*. The antecedent of *kendi* is more likely to be within the same clause, indicated either by a noun phrase or by person marking on the verb:

(37) (a) Erol [*Ziya'nın* **kendin-e** bir araba al-dığ-ın]-ı san-ıyor.
         Erol Ziya-GEN self-DAT a car buy-VN-3SG.POSS-ACC
         think-IMPF
         'Erol thinks *Ziya* bought a car for *himself.*'

     (b) Erol [**kendine** bir araba aldığın]-ı sanıyor.
         'Erol thinks *he* bought a car for *himself.*'

In (37a) Ziya is by far the most probable antecedent for *kendi*. In (37b), where the subject of the subordinate clause is not expressed by an overt noun phrase (hence the antecedent is the possessive marker), the most likely referent is Erol.

The 3rd person form *kendisi*, on the other hand, can refer either to an antecedent in its own clause, in which case it is used as a reflexive, or (much more freely than *kendi*) to an antecedent in the superordinate clause, in which case it is used as a simple personal pronoun (see (iii) below).

(38) **Erol [Ziya'nın kendi-sin-e** bir araba al-ma-sın]-ı söyle-di.
Erol Ziya-GEN self/s/he-3SG.POSS-DAT a car buy-VN-3SG.POSS-ACC tell-PF
(**i**) 'Erol told *Ziya* to buy a car for *himself.*'
(**ii**) 'Erol told Ziya to buy *him* a car.' (him = Erol or someone else)

(**iii**) Third person simple pronominal usage of inflected *kendi-*:
The 3rd person form *kendisi* can be used as a simple personal pronoun corresponding to *he* or *she*. In the contexts below, where the antecedent is a person mentioned in the preceding sentence, *kendisi* is interchangeable with, but slightly more formal than, *o*.

(39) Ahmet hala uyuyor. **Kendisi/o** bu günlerde çok yorgun.
'Ahmet is still asleep. *He*'s very tired at the moment.'

(40) A.– Kulüpteki arkadaşların nasıl?
'How are your friends at the club?'

B.– Bilmem, **kendi-lerin-i/onlar-ı** çoktandır görmedim.
s/he-3PL.POSS-ACC/they-ACC
'I don't know. I haven't seen *them* for a long time.'

kendisi and *o* are also interchangeable where the pronoun occurs in a subordinate clause and refers to a person mentioned in the main clause or in the preceding sentence:

(41) **Ahmet [kendisine/ona** hediye vermeyenler]-i sevmiyor.
'Ahmet doesn't like people who don't give him gifts.' (him = Ahmet/someone else)

Such sentences are therefore always potentially ambiguous where more than one possible antecedent is available.

kendileri can also be used with 3rd person singular reference as a deferential substitute for *kendisi*. In sentences with this usage of *kendileri*, all references to the person in question are made in the plural form. Note that in this usage *kendileri* cannot be replaced by *onlar*.

(42) Sayın Cumhurbaşkanı bugün yurda dönüyor**lar**. **Kendi-leri**
                                                       s/he-**3PL.POSS**
gezi-**lerin**-den çok verimli sonuçlarla dön-dük-**lerin**-i ifade et-ti-**ler**.
visit-**3PL.POSS**-ABL   return-VN-**3PL.POSS**-ACC say-PF-**3PL**
'The president is returning home today. S/he stated that s/he was
returning from his/her visit with very beneficial results.'

(iv) Usage of 3rd person *kendi-* as a resumptive pronoun:
The 3rd person form of *kendi-* (but not *o*) can optionally be used as a
resumptive pronoun in relative clauses with *-DIK* and *-(y)AcAK* where it
refers to the head of the relative clause (see 25.1.1.2 (ii)):

(43) [(***Kendi-lerin-i***) defalarca aradığımız] **yetkili-ler** telefonlarımıza
cevap vermediler.
s/he-3PL.POSS-ACC   person.in.charge-PL
'The persons in charge, whom we have rung many times, have not
responded to our calls.'

18.1.3 *kendi kendi-*

Kendi kendi-, which is obligatorily inflected for person and case, is an
emphatic version of *kendi-* in its reflexive usage, and occurs in the same
contexts:

(44) (**Kendi**) **kendimden** nefret ediyorum.
'I hate *myself*.'

The omission of *-(s)i* in the 3rd person occurs in less formal contexts.
    When *kendi kendi-* is in the dative case, it expresses the performance of
some action alone or unaided:

(45) Ahmet **kendi kendi-sin-e/kendin-e** yurt dışına çıkamaz.
             own self-3SG.POSS-DAT
'Ahmet cannot go abroad *on his own*.'

(46) Bu ütüler bir süre sonra **kendi kendi(leri)ne** kapanıyor.
'These irons switch *themselves* off after a while.'

As a result, there is a clear difference between a dative-marked *kendi-* and
a dative-marked *kendi kendi-*:

(47) (**a**) Biz **kendimize** yemek pişiriyoruz.
        'We are cooking a meal *for ourselves*.'

(b) Biz **kendi kendimize** yemek pişiriyoruz.
'We are cooking a meal *by ourselves*.'

18.1.4 THE RECIPROCAL PRONOUN *birbir-* 'EACH OTHER', 'ONE ANOTHER'

The pronoun *birbir-* is used in contexts where two parties act mutually (as is the case with the reciprocal suffix, 8.2.1.4, 13.2.3.2). *Birbir-* is obligatorily inflected for person by combining with the plural possessive suffixes (8.1.2) and with *-(s)i(n)* used as a 3rd person plural suffix:

birbirimiz	(1st person plural)
birbiriniz	(2nd person plural)
birbiri/birbirleri	(3rd person plural)

These forms can be further inflected for case, e.g. *birbirinizi* (2nd person plural accusative), *birbirimizden* (1st person plural ablative), etc. As in the case of *kendi-*, an 'n' appears before case suffixes in the 3rd person forms, as in *birbirinden*, *birbirlerine*, etc. (see 6.2).

birbiri and *birbirleri* are interchangeable when referring to two persons who are involved in a mutual activity:

(48) Ayşe'yle Semra **birbir-in-den/birbir-lerin-den** hiç hoşlanmıyor(**lar**).
each other-**3SG**.POSS-ABL/each other-**3PL**.POSS-ABL
'Ayşe and Semra don't like *each other* at all.'

When referring to interacting groups, again both forms can be used, but here *birbirleri* is the neutral form while *birbiri* is colloquial.

(49) Almanya ve Brezilya takımları **birbirlerinden** haklı olarak korkuyorlar.
'The German and Brazilian teams are justifiably scared *of each other*.'

When the antecedent of a reciprocal pronoun is the subject of that clause, it does not necessarily have to be expressed by an overt noun phrase. It may be omitted in accordance with the principles explained in 18.1.5:

(50) (*Siz*) **birbirinizle** çok iyi anlaşıyors**unuz**.
'*You* get along very well with *each other*.'

(51) **Birbir-lerin-i** iki yıldır gör-mü-yor-*lar*.
each.other-3PL.POSS-ACC two years see-NEG-IMPF-3PL
'*They* haven't seen *each other* for two years.'

The antecedent of a reciprocal pronoun can also be a constituent other than the subject:

(52) ***Biz-i* birbir-imiz-e** şikayet et-ti-n.
we-ACC each.other-1PL.POSS-DAT complain-PF-2SG
'You complained *to us* about *each other*.'

(53) ***Size* birbirinizden** hiç söz etmedim.
'I never talked to *you* about *one another*.'

The only context in which a reciprocal pronoun can function as the subject of a clause is a noun clause (Chapter 24) or a relative clause (Chapter 25). In these cases it is inflected for genitive case and its antecedent is in the superordinate clause:

(54) (**Siz**) [birbir**iniz**in yarışmayı kazanmasın]-ı mı istiyorsun**uz**?
'Do *you* want *each other* to win the competition?'

(55) (**Biz**) [birbir-**imiz-in** sev-diğ-i] renkleri sev-mi-yor-**uz**.
we each other-1PL.POSS-GEN like-PART-3SG.POSS colours like-
NEG-IMPF-1PL
'*We each* don't like the colours that *the other(s)* like(s).'

Note that the verb of a subordinate clause with *birbir-* as its subject is marked for 3rd person.

If there is no person in the superordinate clause either, *birbir-* may refer to persons who have been mentioned previously or who are salient in the context of the utterance:

(56) Amaç **birbirimizi** görmekti.
'The (= our) aim was to see *each other*.'

If there is an antecedent, it does not have to precede *birbir-*. It can come after it in the sentence as long as the general constraints on word order are not violated (see Chapter 23):

(57) **Birbirlerine** çok düşkün **Ayşe'yle Semra**.
'*Ayşe and Semra* are very attached to *each other*.'

18.1.5 THE OMISSION AND USAGE OF PERSONAL PRONOUNS

In this section we discuss the omission and usage of subject pronouns, and of genitive-marked modifiers of possessive constructions, both of which occur in association with person markers (on the predicate or possessed constituent). For the omission and usage of object pronouns see 28.4.2–3.

Note that the 3rd person pronouns *o(nun)* and *onlar(ın)* do not occur nearly as frequently as *ben(im)*, *sen(in)*, *biz(im)* and *siz(in)* to express a grammatical subject or a genitive-marked modifier. This is because a 1st or 2nd person pronoun is the only noun phrase that can be used to refer to the speaker (and his/her associates) and the hearer(s) (and any associated people) in any particular speech situation. For a 3rd person referent, on the other hand, a personal pronoun will often not provide sufficient identification, and a more explicit noun phrase (such as *Mehmet* or *şu büyük ağaç* 'that big tree') has to be used instead. *O* or *onlar* can be used only where an unambiguously identifiable referent is available. This will usually be as a result of immediately previous mention:

(58) Bugün Zeliha ve Hakan'la karşılaştım. **Onlar** taşınıyorlarmış.
'Today I ran into Zeliha and Hakan. It seems *they*'re moving.'

(i) Omission of subject pronouns in finite clauses:
In Turkish, main clause predicates are obligatorily marked for person, (12.2.1) and subject pronouns are not necessary. In the 3rd person singular person marking is effected by the *absence* of a person suffix (except for the optative/imperative *-sIn*, see 8.4, groups 3 and 4).

(59) O zaman öğrenci-ydi-**k**.
then student-P.COP-1PL
'We were students then.'

(60) Paris-e gid-ecek-miş.
Paris-DAT go-FUT-EV.COP
'Apparently s/he's going to go to Paris.'

(61) Öğleden sonra biz-e gel-**sin**.
afternoon we-DAT come-OPT.3SG
'Let him/her come round to us this afternoon.'

(ii) Omission of subject pronouns in non-finite clauses:
Subjects of noun clauses, relative clauses formed with *-DIK/-(y)AcAK* and some types of adverbial clause are indicated by the appropriate possessive marker (8.1.2) on the predicate. The use of personal pronouns referring to the subject is therefore not normally required in these clauses either:

(62) [Ev-e dön-me-**m**] zor olmadı.
home-DAT return-VN-1SG.POSS
'It wasn't difficult [for *me* to return home].'

(63) [Ev-e git-tiğ-**im**]-de kapılar açıktı.
home-DAT go-CV-1SG.POSS-LOC
'[When *I* arrived home] the doors were open.'

Subject pronouns can or must be omitted also in those types of adverbial clause whose predicates do not have person marking (see 26.2.2).

(**iii**) Omission of genitive-marked pronouns as modifiers of possessive noun phrases:
Like personal pronouns expressing subjects, genitive-marked personal pronouns expressing possessors, such as *benim* 'my', *sizin* 'your', are also normally omitted where matching possessive markers are present:

(64) Yeni palto-**m**-u gördün mü?
new coat-1SG.POSS-ACC
'Have you seen *my* new coat?'

A genitive-marked pronoun cannot be used as modifier of a possessive-marked noun phrase where the person to whom the pronoun refers is also the subject of the clause. Thus in (65) it would not be possible to use the pronoun *benim* to modify *anahtarlarım*:

(65) Anahtar-lar-**ım**-ı kaybet-ti-**m**.
key-PL-**1SG.POSS**-ACC lose-PF-**1SG**
'*I*'ve lost *my* keys.'

18.1.5.1   Conditions under which personal pronouns are used

(**i**)   Usage of subject pronouns in finite clauses:
A subject pronoun is used in the following circumstances:

(**a**)   Where a subject contrasts with that of the preceding sentence:

(66) Zeki bugün sokağa çıkmayacakmış. **Sen** bir yere gitmeyi düşünüyor muydun?
'It seems Zeki won't be going out today. Were *you* thinking of going anywhere?'

(**b**)   Where the subject is focused (see 23.3):

(67) Bu sabah çocukları **BEN** giydirdim.
'It was *I* who got the children dressed this morning.'

(68) **SEN** de çok güzel şarkı söylersin.
'*You* sing very nicely, too.'

(c) Where a 1st or 2nd person subject is one of a set of people actually or potentially involved in some action or situation:

(69) A.– Bu filmi seyretmek isteyen var mı?
'Does anyone want to watch this film?'

B.– **Ben** isterim.
'*I* do.'

(70) O gün **sen**, Ayten ve Yavuz sınava girmiştiniz.
'That day *you*, Ayten and Yavuz had had an exam.'

(See also 12.2.2.4.)

(d) Where a 3rd person subject is an entity that was introduced in a non-subject role in the previous sentence:

(71) Kitabı Zerrin'e verdim. **O** ne zamandır onu okumak istiyordu.
'I gave the book to Zerrin. *She* had been wanting to read it for ages.'

(For another example see (58) above.)

(e) Where, despite the continuance of the same subject, there is a shift from a statement about a specific event to a generalization (21.4.1.1) about the person involved:

(72) **Zeki** anahtarlarını kaybetmiş. **O** zaten oldum olası dağınıktır.
'*Zeki* has lost his keys. *He* has always been such a disorganized person.'

(73) Bilet almayı unuttu**m**. **Ben** böyle şeyleri unuturum hep ...
'*I*'ve forgotten to buy a ticket. *I* always seem to forget such things.'

(f) In the opening sentence of a conversation, or a sentence in which the speaker introduces a new topic of discussion:

(74) Ayşe, **ben** şimdi çıkıyorum.
'Ayşe, *I*'m going out now.'

(75) **Siz** herkesin konuştuğu şu İran filmini gördünüz mü?
'Have *you* seen this Iranian film that everyone's talking about?'

(ii) Usage of subject pronouns in non-finite clauses:
A subject pronoun is used in a noun clause or relative clause in the following circumstances:

(a) where it contrasts with the subject of the superordinate clause, the previous clause or a clause with an identical function:

(76) [*Zeki'nin* uçağa yetişmesi] [**benim** yetişmem]-den daha kolay.
'It is easier for *Zeki* to catch the flight than [for *me* (to catch it)].'

(77) [**Benim** yazdığım] mektubu almışlar. [**Senin** yazdığın] mektup daha ellerine geçmemiş.
'They've received the letter [that *I* wrote]. The letter [that *you* wrote] evidently hasn't reached them yet.'

(b) where the subject is focused:

(78) Yemeğin hazırlığına katılmış olmadığım için [bulaşıkları **beNİM** yıkamam] kararlaştırıldı.
'As I had taken no part in the preparation of the meal, it was decided [that *I* should do the washing-up].'

(c) where there is a shift of sentence topic (23.3.3) from the entity performing or undergoing an action (e.g. *Zeki* in (79) below) to the action itself (here *kaza geçirmesi* means 'his having an accident'):

(79) [Zeki'nin kaza geçirdiğin]i duydum. [**Onun** kaza geçirmesi] bütün planları altüst edecek.
'I've heard [that Zeki has had an accident]. [*His* having an accident] will upset all the plans.'

(d) in the opening sentence of a conversation, or a sentence in which the speaker introduces a new topic of discussion:

(80) Ayşe, [**benim** şimdi çıkmam] gerekiyor.
'Ayşe, *I*'ve got to go out now.'

(81) [**Sizlerin** yazın Amerika'ya gideceğiniz] doğru mu?
'Is it true [that *you* will be going to America in the summer]?

(**iii**) Usage of genitive-marked pronouns as modifiers of possessive noun phrases:

The referent of a 3rd person genitive-marked pronoun is always someone/ something *other* than the subject of the clause. For example, in both of the examples below *onun* 'his/her' indicates a person other than Semra:

(82) Semra **on-un** anahtar-lar-ın-ı kaybet-miş.
Semra s/he-GEN key-PL-3SG.POSS-ACC lose-PF/EV
'Apparently Semra lost *his/her* keys.'

(83) Semra **Elif**'e **onun** anahtarlarını vermiş. (cf. (15))
'Semra gave *Elif her/his* keys.'(her/his = Elif or any person other than Semra)

If it is intended that the possessive-marked noun phrase refer to the subject within the same clause (i.e. Semra in (84)), then *onun* is omitted. In such cases the possessive suffix can refer to any 3rd person in the clause or to some previously mentioned person:

(84) **Semra** anahtarlarını kaybetmiş.
'Apparently *Semra* lost *her* keys.' (most likely intended meaning: her = Semra)

(85) **Semra Elif**'e anahtarlarını vermiş. (cf. (15))
'Apparently *Semra* gave *Elif her/his* keys.' (most likely intended meanings: her = Semra or Elif)

A genitive-marked pronoun is used in the following circumstances:

(**a**) when the possessed entity is compared with something else:

(86) *Burası* **bizim evimiz**den daha sıcak.
'It's warmer *here* than [in] *our house*.'

(87) Zeki'nin arabası evin önündeymiş. **SeNİN** arabanı garaja soktum.
'Zeki's car is in front of the house. I put *your* car in the garage.'

(**b**) when the possessor is focused:

(88) Ahmet bugün çok sevinçli. Öğretmen en çok **oNUN** yazısını beğenmiş.
'Ahmet is very happy today. It seems the teacher liked *his* essay best.'

(c)   in the opening sentence of a conversation, or a sentence in which the speaker introduces a new topic of discussion:

> (89) Ayşe, **benim** anahtarım nerede?
> 'Ayşe, where's *my* key?'

> (90) **Bizim** başka bir haberimiz daha var.
> '*We*'ve got another piece of news, too.'

18.2   DEMONSTRATIVE PRONOUNS: *bu*, 'THIS (ONE)' *şu* 'THIS/THAT (ONE)', *o* 'THAT (ONE)'

The demonstrative pronouns are derived from the demonstrative determiners (15.6.2 (i)):

bu	'this (one)'	*bunlar*	'these'
şu	'this (one)', 'that (one)'	*şunlar*	'these', 'those'
o	'that (one)'	*onlar*	'those'

Note that the plural forms contain 'n' before the plural suffix. Similarly, when singular demonstrative pronouns are inflected for case, the case markers are preceded by 'n', as in *bunda* 'on/in this one', *şunu* 'that one (ACC)', *ona* 'to that one' (6.2, 8.1.3).

The difference between *bu*, *şu* and *o* is, from one point of view, a gradation in proximity. *Bu* refers to closer objects and *o* refers to ones that are furthest away. However, a major difference between *şu* and the others is that while *bu* and *o* usually refer to objects mentioned before, the referent of *şu* is almost always something to which the speaker is drawing attention for the first time. *şu* is therefore usually accompanied by an ostensive gesture, either a look in the direction of the item in question or pointing to it.

In the following examples the usage of *şu* implies that the referent, e.g. a particular bowl, has not been under discussion before this point, whereas in the case of *bu* there is no such implication.

> (91) Meyvaları **şuna** koyalım.
> 'Let's put the fruit in *this one*.'

> (92) Meyvaları **buna** koyalım.
> 'Let's put the fruit in *this one*.'

Similarly, the referent of *şu* can be a statement that the speaker is about to make. In the examples below, *bu* and *şu* are not interchangeable; *bu* stands for a statement that has just been made, whereas the referent of *şu* is to follow.

(93) On dakika sonra dükkanlar kapanıyor ve evde kahve yok.
En önemli sorun **bu**.
'The shops close in ten minutes and there's no coffee in the house. *This* is the most urgent problem.'

(94) En önemli sorun **şu**: on dakika sonra dükkanlar kapanıyor ve evde kahve yok.
'The most urgent problem is *this*: the shops close in ten minutes and there's no coffee in the house.'

O is used when a concrete item referred to is not within the visual field of the speaker or the addressee(s), but has been previously mentioned. Both *o* and *bu* can be used when an object, which is in the context, is topicalized (23.3.3).

(95) Adamın şapkasının rengini hatırlıyor musun? İşte **o/bu**, filmde çok önemli bir ayrıntıydı.
'Do you remember the colour of the man's hat? Now *that* was a very significant detail in the film.'

Şu ki and *o ki* can occur following a headless relative clause:

(96) Dediğim **şu ki**, bu tip boyalar ancak dış yüzeylerde kullanılabiliyor.
'What I'm saying is, these types of paint can only be used on exterior surfaces.' (lit. '. . . is *this*, *that* these types . . .')

(97) Görünen **o ki**, dünyanın iklimi değişiyor.
'It seems that the world's climate is changing.'

18.3 LOCATIVE AND DIRECTIONAL PRONOUNS

18.3.1 LOCATIVE PRONOUNS: *bura-* 'HERE', *şura-* 'HERE', 'OVER THERE' AND *ora-* 'THERE'

Locative pronouns are derived from *bu*, *şu* and *o*, and display similar differentiating characteristics in terms of their reference (18.2).

Like the question word *nere-* 'where' (19.2.1.3), *bura-* 'here', *şura-* 'here', 'over there' and *ora-* 'there' cannot be used in their bare form. They must have either a case suffix or a possessive suffix (or both), and either of these may be preceded by the plural suffix: *buraya* '(to) here', *oradan* 'from there', *şuran* 'this part of you', *şuramın* 'of this part of me', *buralarda* 'around here' (see 14.3.1.2 (viii)). The oblique-case-marked forms without possessive suffixes function adverbially (16.4.2).

The forms *burası* 'this place', *şurası* 'this place', 'that place over there' and *orası* 'that place (already mentioned)' are formed with the 3rd person possessive suffix *-(s)I* (8.1.2). Like their interrogative counterpart *neresi* 'what place' (19.2.1.3), they function as subjects:

(98) **Burası** çok kalabalık.
'[It] is very crowded *here*.'

(99) **Şurası** dinlenmek için ideal bir yer.
'*That (place over there)* is an ideal place to rest.'

The accusative and genitive forms *burasını(n)*, *şurasını(n)* and *orasını(n)* can be used instead of *burayı/buranın*, *şurayı/şuranın* and *orayı/oranın*:

(100) **Bura-sın-ı** çok sevdim; **bura-da** kalalım.
here-3SG.POSS-ACC   here-LOC
'I like [it] *here*; let's stay *here*.'

Bura-, *şura-* and *ora-* can also occur with the 1st and 2nd person possessive markers:

(101) **Şuranız**a bir düğme daha lazım.
'You need another button *here* (= on this part of you).'

Additionally, they can be modified by a genitive-marked noun phrase:

(102) ***Filmin* orası** çok önemliydi.
'*That part of the film* was very important.'

18.3.2   DIRECTIONAL PRONOUNS

Directional pronouns are formed by the attachment of the 3rd person possessive marker *-(s)I* to directional adverbials of place, such as *dışarı* 'outside' and *aşağı* 'down' (16.4.2):

(103) **Aşağısı** çok dağınık.
'*It*'s very untidy *downstairs*.'

When these forms are used as direct objects, accusative case marking is obligatory but the possessive marker may be omitted:

(104) Alıcılar **içeri-yi/içeri-sin-i** görmedi.
           inside-ACC/inside-3SG.POSS-ACC
'The buyers haven't seen *inside* yet.'

The form *ötesi* 'the far side' is usually used with a modifier:

(105) ***Köyün* ötesinde** bir dere var.
'There is a stream *beyond the village*.'

The usage of *beri* (and forms derived from it, e.g. *beriki* 'the other (one) (nearby)') is confined to provincial dialects. For *öteki* 'the other (one)', see 18.5.

18.4 PRONOMINALIZED ADJECTIVALS, NUMERALS AND DETERMINERS

The possessive markers (8.1.2) are the main device used for creating pronouns from a range of other grammatical forms. The pronouns are listed here in the 3rd person singular possessive form, which is by far the most common form they are used in, although forms containing 1st, 2nd and 3rd person plural possessive markers are also possible. Note that in all of the forms below an accusative case marker is obligatory when they are used as direct objects, see 14.3.3.2.

The possessive suffixes create pronominals from:

(i) Adjectives ((15.2); see also last section of 14.4): *eskisi* 'the old one', *çirkini* 'an uglier version':

    (106) Çamaşır makinası bozulmuş. **Yeni-sin-i** almamız lazım.
                                    new-3SG.POSS-ACC
          'The washing machine has broken down. We have to get *a new one.*'

Simple adjectives can be used with any of the possessive suffixes, including the 1st and 2nd person singular forms:

    (107) Kızkardeşin senin şişman**ın**.
          'Your sister is *a plumper version of you.*'

(ii) Numerals (15.7) (with or without the enumerator *tane* or measure terms (15.8); see also 14.5.2–3): *ikisi* 'two (of them)', *beş tanesi* 'five (of them)', *üç bardağı* 'three glasses (of it)'. (Numerals cannot be used with the 3rd person plural possessive suffix.)

    (108) Bütün kalemler kayboldu sanmıştım ama **ikisi/iki tanesi** burada.
          'I thought all the pencils were lost, but *two (of them)* are
          here.'

Note that the addition of *her* 'every' and/or the clitic *dA* (11.1.1.2) to pronominalized numerical expressions makes them definite. Thus, for example, *her ikisi* and *(her) ikisi de* mean 'both (of them)' (cf. 15.9.1).

(iii) The enumerator *tane* and measure terms (15.8): *tanesi* 'each one (of
...)', *şişesi* 'a bottle (of ...)'. (These cannot be used with any of the other
possessive suffixes.)

(109) **Kilosunu** on milyon liradan satacaklar.
'They're going to sell it for ten million liras *a kilogram*.'

Expressions consisting of a numeral followed by the enumerator *tane* or a
measure term can be used pronominally without the addition of a possessive suffix. This usage is generally confined to inanimate referents:

(110) Çamaşır makinası bozulmuş. **Yeni bir tane** almamız lazım.
'The washing machine has broken down. We must get *a new one*.'

(111) **İki kilo** versene.
'Give me *two kilograms*.'

(iv) Indefinite and definite determiners (15.6.1–2, 14.5.2–3): *aynısı* 'the
same (one)', *başkası* 'another (one)', *bazısı* 'some (of them)', *birçoğu* 'many
(of them)', *bir bölümü/bir kısmı* 'some (of it/them)', *biri(si)* 'someone', 'one
(of them)', *birkaçı* 'a few (of them)', *bütünü* 'all of it', *çoğu* 'most (of them)',
'most people', *diğeri* 'the other (one)', *hangisi* 'which (one)', *herhangi
biri(si)* 'any (one)', *hiçbiri(si)* 'none (of them)' (see also 20.5.2), *ilki* 'the first
(one)', *kaçı* 'how many (of them)', *kimisi* 'some (of them)', *ne kadarı* 'how
much (of it)', *öbürü/↓öbürkisi/ötekisi* 'the other (one)', *sonuncusu* 'the last
(one)', *böylesi* 'this kind', 'this way'. (Of these determiners, *birkaç*, *çok*,
hiçbir, *kaç* and *ne kadar* (except when this latter is used with adjectives
(19.2.1.6 (ii)) cannot be used with the 3rd person plural possessive suffix.
aynı can be used with any of the possessive suffixes, including the 1st and 2nd
person singular forms.)

(112) **Aynısını** istiyorum.
'I want [one of] *the same*.'

(113) **Bazılarımız** senin gibi düşünmüyor.
'*Some of us* wouldn't agree with you.'

(v) The adverbial *hep* 'always': *hepsi* 'all (of it/them)'. (*hep* cannot be
used with the 3rd person plural possessive suffix.)

(114) **Hepsini** katılımcılara mı vereceksiniz?
'Are you going to give *all of it/them* to the participants?'

(vi) Complex adjectivals formed by the attachment (to a verb stem) of the
participial suffix *-(y)An* (25.1.1.1) or one of its compound verb forms

(25.4.1) *-mAz olan, -mIş (olan)* or (less commonly) *-(y)AcAk (olan)*: *okunamayanı* 'the illegible one', *anlaşılmaz olanları* 'the ones which are incomprehensible', *kullanılmışı* 'a used one':

(115) **Boya-n-mış-ların**-da hatalar gözükmüyor.
     dye-PASS-PF-3PL.POSS-LOC
     'The mistakes are not visible on *the ones which have been dyed*.'

These are a specific kind of relative clause that looks deceptively similar to headless relative clauses (25.3):

Pronominalized complex adjectival:
(116) Opera **sev-me-yen-ler-i** Verona'da konaklamayacaklar.
        like-NEG-PART-PL-3SG.POSS
        '*Those [among them] who don't like* opera won't be staying (overnight) in Verona.'

Headless relative clause:
(117) Opera **sev-me-yen-ler** Verona'da konaklamayacaklar.
        like-NEG-PART-PL
        '*Those [people] who don't like* opera won't be staying (overnight) in Verona.'

Pronominalized complex adjectivals can be formed only from participles containing *-(y)An* (including compound forms such as *-mAz olan* and *-mIş (olan)*). Headless relative clauses, on the other hand, can be formed with the other participial suffixes (*-DIK* and *-(y)AcAK*) as well. Like other pronominalized adjectivals, pronominalized complex adjectivals draw attention to a subgroup or a specimen within another group (14.4–5). Headless relative clauses, by contrast, simply define a group or class without referring to a larger group of which it is a part.

Pronominalized complex adjectivals can be used in partitive constructions with ablative modifiers (14.5.2), particularly those formed from *iç-* and *ara-* (see 17.3.1.3):

(118) *İç-lerin-den* **en zor oku-n-an-ı** bana düşmüş.
        inside-3PL.POSS-ABL most difficult read-PASS-PART-3SG.POSS
        'I seem to have got *the least legible* [*one*] *of all*.'

(119) *Aralarında(n)* **opera sevmeyenleri** Verona'da
        konaklamayacaklar.
        '*Those among them who don't like opera* won't be staying (overnight) in Verona.'

They can also sometimes be used with genitive modifiers:

(120) *onlar-ın* **çalış-ma-yan-lar-ı**
they-GEN work-NEG-PART-PL-3SG.POSS
'the ones among them who/that don't work'

A rather unproductive type of pronominalized complex adjectival is one where the possessive marker does not refer to a subtype within another type but is used in its standard function of marking the *possessed* constituent. The unusual aspect of these constructions is that the genitive noun phrase in such a construction is the *direct object* of the verb inside the adjectival. These adjectival constructions are semi-lexicalized, since they usually contain the verb *sev-* 'like', 'love' (hence, *seven* 'lover', 'admirer') or other verbs of emotion such as *iste-* 'want', *beğen-* 'admire', *nefret et-* 'hate':

(121) **Opera-nın** *sev-en-i* çok.   (cf. Operayı seven çok.)
opera-GEN like-PART-3SG.POSS many
'[There] are many *lovers of opera*.' ('[There] are many [people] who love opera.')

18.5   PRONOMINAL EXPRESSIONS WITH *-ki*

The suffix *-ki* (8.1.4), which is used for forming attributive adjectives (15.3.6–7), has a pronominal function when used without a following noun phrase. This usage is possible only where the type of entity that is being talked about is obvious from the context:

(122) **Bahçe-de-ki-ler** yapraklarını dökmeye başladı. (cf. Chapter 15 (24))
garden-LOC-PRON-PL
'*The ones in the garden* have begun to shed their leaves.'

Note that any case suffixes attached to *-ki* have to be preceded by 'n' (6.2):

(123) **Bu sabahkinde** okudum. (cf. Chapter 15 (29))
'I read it *in this morning's (one)*.'

öteki/↓öbürki 'the other (one)' (15.6.2) can also be used pronominally:

(124) **Öteki** size daha çok uydu galiba.
'*The other one* seemed to suit you better.'

In addition, -*ki* can attach to any genitive-marked noun phrase to form a possessive pronominal expression. These forms cannot be used as modifiers of noun phrases:

(125) Yeni bir bilgisayar almam gerek. **Benimki** iyi çalışmıyor.
        'I have to buy a new computer. *Mine* isn't working properly.'

(126) Ayşe'nin arabası **Ahmet'inkiyle** karşılaştırılınca çok yeni duruyor.
        'Ayşe's car looks very new when compared *to Ahmet's*.'

18.6 OTHER PRONOMINAL EXPRESSIONS

18.6.1 PRONOMINAL QUANTIFIERS

The pronominal quantifiers of Turkish are *herkes* 'everyone', *her şey* 'everything', and *bir şey* 'something', 'anything'. All of these can be inflected for case and, with the exception of *herkes*, for person as well.

(127) Artık otobüslerde **herkesten** para alıyorlar, genç olsun, yaşlı
        olsun.
        'Nowadays they charge *everyone* on buses, whether they are
        young or old.'

(128) Yanına **her şeyini** aldın mı?
        'Have you taken *everything (that belongs to you)* with you?'

bir şey 'something', 'anything' can be used in the singular or in the plural form (14.3.1.1 (iii)), with both affirmative and negative predicates:

(129) Şu sıralar ilginç **bir şey/bir şeyler** okumuyor musun?
        'Aren't you reading *anything* interesting these days?'

(130) Söyleyecek **bir şeyim** yok
        'I have *nothing* to say.'

(131) Sabahtan beri **bir şey-ler-im-i** arıyorum ama bulamıyorum.
            something-PL-1SG.POSS-ACC
        'I've been looking for *some things of mine* all day.'

The expressions *kimse* 'no one', 'anyone', *hiç kimse* 'no one', *hiçbiri(si)* 'none (of them)', *hiçbir şey* 'nothing' are discussed in 20.5.

18.6.2 *insan* 'ONE'

İnsan 'person, human being' is used pronominally like the English generic pronoun 'one':

(132) **İnsan** bazen [hiçbir şey bilmediğin]-i sanıyor.
'Sometimes *one* thinks [one doesn't know anything].'

(133) Bazı günler her şey zor geliyor **insana**.
'Some days everything seems to be difficult (*for one*).'

18.6.3 *şey*

şey, literally 'thing', is probably one of the most commonly used expressions in colloquial Turkish, replacing anything from a word to a whole clause. It is used where the speaker cannot immediately call to mind the appropriate expression for what s/he intends to say. What it replaces may or may not follow in the conversation, depending on whether its referent is clear enough from the context.

(134) Ay arabanın **şeyini** kırmışlar!
'Oh God, they've broken the car's *thingumajig*!'

(135) **Şey** gibi olmasın ama, sana bir şey sormak istiyorum.
'I would like to ask you something, without sounding as if . . . you know . . .'

(136) Ziya'nın lafları biraz **şeysiz** kaçtı.
'Ziya's words lacked a bit of, how shall I put it . . .'

It can also be used as a 'filler' between sentences, or as a gradual start to a conversation, sometimes as a means of introducing a topic that the speaker finds difficult or embarrassing to broach.

(137) **Şey** . . . Biraz konuşmamız lazım.
'Uhmmm . . . we have to talk a bit.'

19 QUESTIONS

Questions in Turkish are formed either by the insertion of the question particle *mI*, which forms **yes/no questions** (19.1.1) and **alternative questions** (19.1.2), or by using a **wh-phrase** such as *ne zaman* 'when', *kim* 'who' or *hangi* 'which' (19.2).

- (1) Bahçeye ağaç dikecekler **mi**?
       'Will they plant trees in the garden?'

- (2) Otobüs durağı **nerede**?
       '*Where* is the bus stop?'

In 19.1.3 and 19.1.4 we describe the various positions that *mI* can occur in, and the effect this has on the content of the question. Sentences that contain a stressed phrase in addition to a *mI*-phrase (a phrase to which *mI* is attached) are the topic of 19.1.5. In 19.2.2 we describe the position of wh-phrases in a sentence. **Echo questions**, questions which simultaneously contain *mI* and a wh-phrase, are discussed in 19.3. 19.4 focuses on how phrases in subordinate clauses may be questioned, and 19.5 discusses **modal adverbs** that are used in questions. **Indirect questions** (questions in the form of noun clauses) are discussed in 24.4.3.2, and speculative conditional questions introduced by *ya* in 28.3.1.1 (vii).

19.1 QUESTIONS WITH *mI*

The particle *mI* is an unstressable clitic which forms yes/no questions and alternative questions. The phonological properties of *mI* and its location within a predicate are described in 11.1.1.5. Sentence stress usually occurs immediately before *mI* unless there are other factors affecting stress in the sentence (19.1.5). The exact position of stress within a word followed by *mI* is determined by the internal stress pattern of that word or phrase (Chapter 4).

19.1.1 YES/NO QUESTIONS

Yes/no questions are formed by inserting *mI* after a sentence or a phrase, or in some cases, within a phrase. There are two types of yes/no question: direct questions and tag questions.

19.1.1.1 Direct yes/no questions

In direct yes/no questions, the clitic *mI* attaches to the predicate when the entirety of a proposition is questioned:

(3) Kedi-ler iki konserve-yi de **bitir-miş-ler *mi*?**
     cat-PL two can-ACC both finish-EV/PF-3PL INT
     'Have the cats finished both tins?'

mI can also attach to a phrase within the sentence, with effects that are described in 19.1.4. A phrase to which *mI* is attached generally occurs just before the predicate. However, like other focused phrases (23.3.1), a *mI*-phrase can also occur in other positions, as long as it is not placed after the predicate:

(4) Zehra Londra-ya **eylül-de mi** gid-ecek?
     Zehra London-DAT September-LOC INT go-FUT
     'Is Zehra going to London in SEPTEMBER?'

(5) Zehra **eylülde mi** Londra'ya gidecek?
     'Is Zehra going to London in SEPTEMBER?'

The intonation of questions with *mI* usually comprises a high rise just before *mI*, followed by falling intonation (5.1), whether *mI* is placed at the end of the sentence or not:

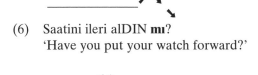

(6) Saatini ileri alDIN **mı**?
     'Have you put your watch forward?'

(7) BabasıNI **mı** özlemiş Hasan?
     'Is Hasan missing his father?'

There are, however, cases where questions with *mI* do not end with falling intonation. These are:

(i)   questions where *mI* is used for expressing surprise or disbelief (19.1.4 (iii))
(ii) questions where *mI* occurs with a wh-phrase (echo questions, 19.3)
(iii) questions where *mI* occurs with another stressed phrase (19.1.5).

19.1.1.2 Tag questions

A tag question is a question that is annexed to a statement and is used to seek confirmation of that statement. There are two forms of tag question:

(i) *değil mi*, which is a combination of the negative particle *değil* 'not' (20.2) and *mI*, and is most often pronounced [dí:lmɪ] ([dí:mɪ] or [dímɪ] in informal registers)

(ii) *öyle mi*, which is a combination of the demonstrative adverbial *öyle* 'like that' (16.4.3) and *mI*, and can also be pronounced [ö:lé mɪ]

Both forms can be tagged to affirmative or negative predicates which are verbal or nominal.

(8) Tiyatroya gitmeden önce yer **ayır-t-ma-mış-tı-n, *değil mi***?
  reserve-CAUS-NEG-EV/PF-P.COP-2SG not INT
  'You hadn't reserved seats before going to the theatre, had you?'

(9) Esra **Handan-ın abla-sı-ymış, *öyle mi***?
  Handan-GEN elder.sister-3SG.POSS-EV.COP thus INT
  'So Esra is Handan's elder sister, is that right?'

Questions with *değil mi* are unmarked tag questions, corresponding to 'isn't it', 'can you', etc. in English. This question type is used when the speaker seeks corroboration of a statement that s/he believes to be true.

(10) Cemal bugün okul-a git-me-di, **değil mi**?
  Cemal today school-DAT go-NEG-PF not INT
  'Cemal didn't go to school today, did he?'

Tag questions with *öyle mi* follow a much more tentative assertion, embodying information newly acquired by the speaker, or information that contradicts the speaker's previous assumption. *öyle mi* can also be used with the discourse connective *demek* 'so', which expresses an inference (28.3.7).

(11) (Demek) Cemal bugün okula gitmedi, **öyle mi**?
  'So Cemal didn't go to school today then?'

In (10) the speaker assumes that Cemal hasn't gone to school. In (11), on the other hand, the speaker voices surprise at the possibility of Cemal not having gone to school, implying an expectation that he would have done so.

öyle mi can be used on its own as a response to new information, especially where this has come as a surprise:

(12) A.– Bu yaz çok yağmur yağacakmış.
'Apparently there is going to be a lot of rain this summer.'

B.– Öyle mi?
'Really?'

Since the phrase *değil* is the standard form for negating the linking type of nominal sentence (20.2 and 12.1.1.2) the sequence *değil* + *mi* is potentially ambiguous between a direct yes/no question with a negative nominal predicate (13), and a tag question following an affirmative nominal predicate (14). In the spoken language these two sentences have different intonation patterns. A direct yes/no question has one intonational phrase: a high rise followed by a fall (5.1):

(13) Tiyatroya gitmeden önce yer ayırtmak lazım **deGİL mi**?
                                                    necessary not INT
'Isn't it necessary to reserve seats before going to the theatre?'

A sentence containing a tag question has two intonational phrases, sometimes separated by a pause before *değil*. The first intonational phrase has a slight rise followed by a fall (the pattern for statements), and the second one, consisting just of the tag question, has a high rise followed by a fall:

(14) Tiyatroya gitmeden önce yer ayırtMAK lazım, **deGİL mi**?
                                                    necessary not INT
'It's necessary to reserve seats before going to the theatre, isn't it?'

In the written language the ambiguity is resolved by using a comma before a tag question.

öyle and *değil mi* can be used together as a reinforced form of *değil mi* (i.e. *öyle değil mi*). These questions are only minimally different from tag questions with *değil mi*.

19.1.2 ALTERNATIVE QUESTIONS

These are questions which present two (or more) alternatives, equivalent to questions with 'or' in English. The particle *mI* is placed after each of the alternatives presented, which can optionally be connected by *yoksa* 'or' (28.3.3.1). The types of phrases *mI* can attach to are described in 19.1.3.

Where they are predicates, the second may simply be the negation of the first, as in (15)–(17):

(15) Cemal okula **git-ti** *mi*, (yoksa) **git-me-di** *mi*?
                   go-PF INT (or) go-NEG-PF INT
    'Did Cemal go to school or not?'

(16) Bu hastanede ameliyathane **var** *mı*, (yoksa) **yok** *mu*?
                          existent INT (or) non-existent INT
    'Is there an operating theatre in this hospital or not?'

(17) **Ankara-ya** *mı* **İstanbul-a** *mı* gitmek istiyorsun?
    Ankara-DAT INT Istanbul-DAT INT
    'Do you want to go to Ankara or to Istanbul?'

In alternative questions, each alternative has a high rise followed by a fall, sometimes with a rise in the juncture point between the two alternatives:

(18) *Tosca*-yı VERdi mi yazmıştı (yoksa) PucCİni mi?
    Tosca-ACC Verdi INT compose-EV/PF-P.COP (or) Puccini INT
    'Did Verdi or Puccini compose *Tosca*?'

19.1.3 POSITIONS FOR *mI* OTHER THAN THE END OF THE SENTENCE

In addition to attaching to predicates, *mI* can attach to subjects, objects and adverbials:

(19) Yalnız başına burada ***kitap*** **mı** okuyordun?
                     book INT
    'Were you reading a book here all alone?'

(20) ***Kedi-den*** **mi** korkuyorsun yoksa?
    cat-ABL INT
    'Are you afraid of cats, then?'

The position of the particle *mI* in a noun phrase is fixed: it attaches to the head of the phrase even when what is being questioned is one of the modifying constituents of that phrase. This is illustrated in (21):

(21) (a) {İki orta yaşlı adAM} *mı* çal-mış araba-yı?
two middle aged man INT steal-EV/PF car-ACC
'Did *two middle-aged MEN* steal the car?'

(b) {İKİ orta yaşlı adam} *mı* çalmış arabayı?
'Did *TWO middle-aged men* steal the car?'

It is the location of stress that indicates whether it is the entire noun phrase, as in (21a), or some particular part of it, as in (21b), that is questioned.

The unmarked position for *mI* in other types of phrases and constructions is at the end of that particular phrase or construction. This applies to postpositional phrases, genitive-possessive constructions and partitive constructions, as well as to compound verbs with free auxiliaries (13.3.1.2) and nominal-verb compounds (13.3.2):

(22) {*Murat-ın ev-i*} mi satılmış?
Murat-GEN house-3SG.POSS INT
'Has *Murat's house* been sold?'

However, it can also attach to the non-head constituents in these phrases:

(23) {*Murat' ın* mı evi} satılmış?
'Is it *Murat's* house that has been sold?'

(24) Sen şimdi o filmi **gör-müş** *mü* **ol-du-n**? (also 'görmüş oldun **mu**')
see-EV/PF INT be-PF-2SG
'Do you consider yourself as having seen that film now?'

(25) Sana **yardım** *mı* **et-ti** o adam? (also 'yardım etti **mi**')
help INT make-PF
'Did that man *help* you?'

It can also attach to the modifier in an adjectival or adverbial phrase:

(26) **Çok** *mu* **güzel** bir kız, bu sözünü ettiğin?
very INT beautiful a girl
'Is she a *really* pretty girl, this one you're talking about?'

(27) Umduğundan **daha da** *mı* **hızlı** yüzdün?
'Did you swim *even* fast*er* than you expected?'

In addition, *mI* can attach to subordinate clauses (12.3) or to the constituents inside them:

(28) (a) Aynur [**Zehra-yla buluş-tuk-tan sonra**] *mı* çocuk-lar-ı
Aynur Zehra-COM meet-cv.ABL before INT child-PL-ACC
okul-dan al-dı?
school-ABL pick.up-PF
'Was it [*after meeting Zehra*] that Aynur picked up the
children?'

(b) Aynur [**Zehra'yla** *mı* buluşmadan önce] çocukları okuldan
aldı?
'Was it [before meeting *Zehra*] that Aynur picked up the
children?'

19.1.4 THE EFFECT OF PLACING *mI* AFTER A PARTICULAR PHRASE

The placement of *mI* after a particular phrase serves three different
purposes. One of these is to narrow down the questioned part of a proposition and thus to question only a particular phrase within a sentence.
Alternatively, *mI* can be placed after a particular phrase to question the
whole proposition. Finally, it can be used as an expression of surprise at a
situation which has just come to the attention of the speaker.

(i) Using *mI* for questioning a specific part of a proposition:
One of the reasons why *mI* is inserted after a phrase is to focus on a particular part of a proposition, thereby making it the specific target of the
question. This generally implies that the information in the remainder of
the sentence is already assumed by the speaker.

(29) ***Ahmet* mi** para-lar-ı ev-de unut-muş?
Ahmet INT money-PL-ACC house-LOC forget-EV/PF
'Was it *Ahmet* who left the money at home?'

(30) Banka-ya ***sabah-leyin* mi** gid-ecek-sin?
bank-DAT morning-ADV INT go-FUT-2SG
'Will you be going to the bank *in the morning*?'

The intonation of these sentences is a high rise followed by a fall (5.1),
which is typical of direct yes/no questions (19.1.1.1):

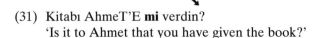

(31) Kitabı AhmeT'E **mi** verdin?
'Is it to Ahmet that you have given the book?'

(ii)   Using *mI* immediately before the predicate to question the whole proposition:

Placing *mI* after a particular phrase can also serve the purpose of questioning the whole proposition:

(32) Nermin okul-a **mı** git-miş?
      Nermin school-DAT INT go-EV/PF
      'Has Nermin gone to school?'

As noted in 19.1.1.1, questioning the whole proposition is also done by means of placing *mI* after the predicate:

(33) Nermin okula gitmiş **mi**?

However, although both of these questions involve the whole proposition, they cannot be used in the same context. The difference between them is that questions that have the structure of (32) are used when the speaker has an assumption about the situation s/he is asking about, usually because there are non-linguistic clues (visual, or perceptible by other senses) available to him/her. Those like (33), on the other hand, are out-of-the-blue questions, where the speaker has no assumptions about the situation. For example, a speaker can use (34a) upon seeing that the addressee is wearing a coat, a context which is totally unsuitable for (34b). (34b), on the other hand, is used in contexts where a speaker simply wants to know if the addressee will be going out that day or not, a context in which (34a) cannot be used.

(34) (**a**) Sokağa **mı** çıkıyorsun?
      (**b**) Sokağa çıkıyor **mu**sun?
              'Are you going out?'

The same phenomenon occurs in existential sentences as well:

(35) Bir sıkıntın **mı** var?
      'Are you worried about something?'

(36) Bir sıkıntın var **mı**?
      'Do you have any troubles?'

(iii) Using *mI* as an expression of surprise or disbelief:
mI can be placed after a particular constituent within a clause to highlight surprise or disbelief. In this case, the constituent just before *mI* is not the target of the question. Instead, the validity of the whole proposition is questioned. Such sentences have an intonation pattern similar to wh-questions (19.2), which is a slight rise followed by a fall-rise, but they usually start with a higher pitch than wh-questions. The phrase that *mI* is attached to usually occurs just before the predicate:

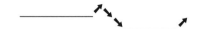

(37) Kitabı AhmeT'E **mi** verdin?
'You GAVE the BOOK to AHMET?'

19.1.5 YES/NO QUESTIONS CONTAINING A(NOTHER) STRESSED PHRASE

Although stress normally falls on the constituent immediately preceding the particle *mI*, there are cases where another constituent is stressed. In such questions *mI* attaches to the predicate, and the whole proposition is questioned:

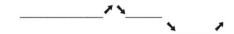

(38) Peki, sen hiç oPEra-ya git-ti-n **mi**?
well.then you ever opera-DAT go-PF-2SG INT
'Well then, have you ever been to the OPERA?'

Highlighting a particular constituent by stressing it in such sentences can serve to contrast it with another (previously mentioned) constituent. For example, (38) can be uttered after someone has mentioned that they have never been to the theatre.

The intonation pattern of these sentences, namely a fall after the stressed phrase, followed by another fall and then rising intonation at the end (see 5.1), is somewhat similar to that of wh-questions (19.2) and *mI* questions expressing disbelief (19.1.4 (iii)). A recent development is that this pattern is becoming quite commonly used in unmarked yes/no questions as well.

19.2 WH-QUESTIONS

Wh-questions are formed by using a question phrase (a wh-phrase) such as *kim* 'who', *nerede* 'where', etc. The wh-phrases in Turkish are the following:

kim	'who'
ne	'what'
hangi	'which'
nere-	'where'
hani	'where' (informal)
ne zaman	'when'
kaç	'how many', 'what time'
ne kadar	'how much'
nasıl	'how'
niye	'why'
neden	'why'
niçin	'why'

Wh-phrases are normally stressed, whether they are in the main clause or a subordinate clause. The only exception to this is when they occur with another stressed constituent (19.2.3). The intonation pattern of wh-questions is a slight rise followed by a fall-rise (5.1).

(39) **HANgi** tablo-yu müze-ye bağışla-mak ist-iyor-sun?
which painting-ACC museum-DAT donate-VN want-IMPF-2SG
'*Which* painting do you want to donate to the museum?'

(40) Ev-e **NE zaman** gid-ecek-sin?
home-DAT when go-FUT-2SG
'*When* will you be going home?'

19.2.1 WH-PHRASES

19.2.1.1 *kim* 'who'

kim is used in questions where the target of the question is a person. It can combine with all the inflectional suffixes that attach to nouns (8.1, 14.3) and usually occurs in the positions occupied by the corresponding noun phrases (Chapter 23):

(41) Resimleri **kim** değerlendirecek?
'*Who* will evaluate the paintings?'

(42) Şule'nin babası **kim**di?
'*Who* was Şule's father?'

kim obligatorily has accusative case marking when it functions as a direct object (see 22.1):

(43) Nuri **kim-i** görmüş?
    who-ACC
'*Who(m)* did Nuri see?'

kim can have plural marking when the speaker knows or assumes that more than one person or type of person is involved:

(44) En çok **kim-ler-in çocuk-lar-ı** okulda başarılı oluyormuş?
    who-PL-GEN child-PL-3SG.POSS
'*Whose children* (the children of what type of people) are the most successful at school?'

When *kim* combines with the comitative/instrumental marker *-(y)lA/ile*, the result is *kiminle* 'with whom' (8.1.4). However, *kimle* is also used in informal speech:

(45) En çok **kim-(in)-le** şakalaşmayı seviyorsun?
    who-(GEN)-COM
'*Who* do you most like to fool around *with*?'

19.2.1.2 *ne* 'what'

ne is used in questions where the target is an inanimate object, a substance, or an abstract concept. It can combine with all the inflectional suffixes that attach to nouns (8.1, 14.3), and it occurs in the positions occupied by noun phrases (Chapter 14):

(46) Bu kutunun içinde **ne-ler** var?
                what-PL
'*What's* in this box?'

(47) Serap Almanya'ya **ne-yle** gidiyor?
                what-INS
'*How* (= by what means) is Serap going to Germany?'

ne is also used when the modifier in a nominal compound is the target of a question:

(48) O adam *ne* **doktor-u**?
that man what doctor-NC
'What is the specialization of that doctor?' (lit. '*What sort of doctor* is that man?')

When used as a direct object, the non-case-marked *ne* indicates that the speaker has no preconceptions about the answer, whereas the accusative-case-marked *neyi* implies that the speaker expects the answer to fall within a specified set of items, usually concrete objects:

(49) **Ne** istiyorsun?
'*What* do you want?'

(50) **Neyi** istiyorsun?
'*What* do you want?'

The first question is a general inquiry about what the addressee wants, or expects to happen. The second question, on the other hand, would be asked in a situation where the speaker has a number of items in mind and expects the answer to refer to one of those items.

neli, nesiz
ne can combine with the suffixes *-lI* 'with' and *-sIz* 'without' (15.2.1) to form adjectives:

(51) **Ne-li** dondurma sev-er-sin?
what-ADJ ice.cream like-AOR-2SG
'*What kind* of ice cream do you like?'

It can also combine with the suffix *-CI* (7.2.2.2), most typically in its occupational sense, and much less commonly as denoting an ideology:

(52) Baba-sı **ne-ci**?
father-3SG.POSS what-DER
'*What* is the *occupation/ideology* of his/her father?'

nesi, neyi
nesi is the more commonly used 3rd person possessive form of *ne*, and *neyi* (6.2 (iii)) is slightly dated:

(53) Akdeniz-in **ne-si/√ney-i** insanları çekiyor?
Mediterranean-GEN what-3SG.POSS
'*What* is it *about* the Mediterranean that attracts people?'

ne and the idiom *ne biçim* 'what kind of . . .' can also be use in exclamations (12.4 (iv)).

19.2.1.3 *nere-* 'where'

The word *nere-* is used in its bare form only in non-standard dialects of Turkish. In standard Turkish it is always inflected. *Nere-* occurs in the positions occupied by noun phrases (Chapter 23), and it can combine with all the inflectional suffixes that attach to nouns (8.1, 14.3):

(54) Elbise-ler-in-i **nere-den** al-dı-n? (usually pronounced [nǽrdæn])
clothes-PL-2SG.POSS-ACC where-ABL buy-PF-2SG
'*Where* did you buy your clothes *from*?'

(55) En çok **nere-ler-i** görmek istiyorsun?
where-PL-ACC
'*What places* do you most want to see?'

(56) İğne-yi **nere-n-den** yap-acak-lar?
injection-ACC where-2SG.POSS-ABL make-FUT-3PL
'On what part of you? (lit. '*Where on you*?') are they going to do the injection?'

nerede, neresi
nerede (usually pronounced [nǽrdɛ]) is used when inquiring about the location of a person or object:

(57) Patagonya **nere-de**?
where-LOC
'*Where is* Patagonia?'

neresi is the form used when inquiring about a place itself, as opposed to the location of a particular object or person:

(58) Bura-sı **nere-si**?
here-3SG.POSS where-3SG.POSS
'*Where* are we?' (lit. '*What place* is this?')

neresi seeks as an answer a property or a characteristic that describes a location, rather than the whereabouts of a place. For example the response to a question like (59) would be a remark which contains a characteristic of Patagonia, such as *Arjantin'in güneyinde yarı kurak bir plato* '[It is] a semi-arid plateau in southern Argentina':

(59) Patagonya **nere-si**?
where-3SG.POSS
'*What and where* is Patagonia?'

The response to (57), on the other hand, is *Arjantin'de* 'In Argentina'.

19.2.1.4   *hangi* 'which'

hangi 'which' (15.6.2 (iii)) modifies a noun phrase:

(60) Ahmet *hangi* **doktora** güveniyor?
'*Which* doctor does Ahmet trust?'

A noun phrase containing *hangi* is always marked with the accusative case when it is the direct object:

(61) **Hangi** *kitab-ı* satın alacaksın?
which book-ACC
'*Which* book will you buy?'

Like most determiners, *hangi* can be pronominalized (18.4) by the addition of a possessive suffix:

(62) Kazanan **hangisi**ydi?
'*Which of them* (was the one who) won?'

(63) **Hangi-ler-iniz-den** para istediler?
which-PL-2PL.POSS-ABL
'*From which (ones) of you* did they ask for money?'

hangi can be used with an ablative- or genitive-marked modifier (14.5.2 and 14.5.3), including the ablative-marked forms of *iç-* or *ara-* 'among' (17.3.1.3):

(64) (*Asistanlardan*) **hangisi** bugün görevli?
'*Which one (of the assistants)* is on duty today?'

(65) *İçinizden/aranızdan* **hangisi** bu işte gönüllü olarak çalışmak
istiyor (sunuz)?
'*Which one among you* would like to work as a volunteer?'

For the agreement of a predicate with a subject containing a pronominalized determiner, see 12.2.2.3.

19.2.1.5   *kaç* 'how many'

kaç (15.6.1) is used for inquiring about the number of entities denoted by a noun phrase. It occupies the position of a numeral in a noun phrase (see 15.9.2) and can be used with the enumerator *tane* and measure terms such as *avuç* '(a) handful (of)' (15.8), and is followed by a noun without plural marking (14.3.1.1 (ii)).

(66) Günde *kaç* (**tane**) **çay** içiyorsun?
      '*How many* [*cups of*] *tea* do you drink a day?'

(67) Okula bu yıl *kaç* **kişi** alacaksınız?
      '*How many people* will you admit to the school this year?'

As a pronoun (suffixed with a possessive marker, see 18.4 (iv)) it can occur with modifiers, which are usually ablative-marked, but can also be genitive-marked (14.5.2–3):

(68) **Öğrencilerden** *kaçı* derse girmemiş?
      '*How many of the students* appear to have been absent?'

As in the case of *hangi* above, the modifier in the partitive construction can be an ablative-marked phrase based on *iç-* or *ara-* 'among' (17.3.1.3):

(69) *İçinizden* **kaçı** araba kullanmayı biliyor?
      '*How many of you* know how to drive?'

kaç is also used when asking about clock time:

(70) Saat **kaç**?
      'What time is it?'

(71) **Kaçla kaç** arasında arayayım seni?
      'Between what [times] should I call you?'

In questions about a person's age, *kaç* is the modifier in a *-sI* compound (10.2, 15.3.2):

(72) O çocuk **kaç** yaşında?
      'How old is that child?'

19.2.1.6 *ne kadar* 'how much'

ne kadar 'how much' is used for asking about the following:

(i)   The quantity of a particular (usually uncountable) inanimate entity:

   (73) Muhallebiye **ne kadar *şeker*** koyulur?
        '*How much sugar* is used in milk pudding?'

   (74) Bundan **ne kadar** istiyorsun?
        '*How much* of this do you want?'

(ii)   The degree to which a particular adjective or adverb is applicable:

   (75) Yeni bürosü acaba **ne kadar *büyük*?**
        '*How big*, I wonder, is his/her new office?'

   (76) Bu araba **ne kadar *hızlı*** gider?
        '*How fast* does this car go?'

(iii)   The price of an item:

   (77) Bu elbise **ne kadar**?
        '*How much* is this dress?'

(iv)   The quantity of time or space involved in a particular action, in which case it is used adverbially:

   (78) Bu sabah **ne kadar** koştun?
        '*How long/how much* did you run this morning?'

   (79) Ameliyat **ne kadar** sürecek?
        '*How long* will the operation last?'

ne kadar is usually used with *zaman* 'time' as the complement of temporal postpositions such as *içinde/∇zarfında* 'within', *önce* 'before' and *sonra* 'after' (16.4.1), when inquiring about the amount of time associated with a particular event:

   (80) Yemeğin altını, kaynadıktan **ne kadar (zaman) sonra**
        kapatıyorsunuz?
        '*How long after* the food comes to the boil do you turn off the heat?'

   (81) ***Ne kadar* (zaman)dır** Londra'da oturuyorsunuz?
        '*How long* have you been living in London?'

With the addition of a 3rd person possessive suffix, the pronominalized form *ne kadarı* (18.4 (iv)) can be used with a genitive-marked modifier (14.5.3):

(82) **İş-in *ne kadar-ın-ı*** Zeynep'e bırakacaksın?
job-GEN how.much-3SG.POSS-ACC
'*How much of the job* will you leave to Zeynep?'

Sentences with *ne kadar* can also be used as exclamations (12.4 (iv)).

19.2.1.7 *ne zaman* 'when'

ne zaman is used for questioning the time of an event.

(83) **Ne zaman** eve gidiyorsun?
'*When* are you going home?'

It also occurs in postpositional phrases where the complement is a time expression:

(84) *Ne zamandan* **beri** sigara içiyorsun?
'*Since when* have you been smoking?'

(85) *Ne zamana* **kadar** bekleyeyim?
'*When* shall I wait *till*?'

19.2.1.8 *neden, niye, niçin* 'why'

neden, *niye*, and *niçin* (pronounced [nitʃʰin] or [niːtʃʰin]) occur in questions which seek the reason or motive for an action or state of affairs:

(86) Kedilere **niye/niçin/neden** doğru dürüst yemek vermiyorsun?
'*Why* aren't you feeding the cats properly?'

19.2.1.9 *nasıl* 'how'

nasıl 'how' is used in questions which inquire about the manner in which an action is performed:

(87) Semra'nın evine **nasıl** gidiliyor?
'*How* does one go to Semra's house?'

(88) Bunu bana **nasıl** yapabildin?
'*How* could you do this to me?'

It can occur as a subject complement in linking sentences (12.1.1.2):

(89) **Nasılsın?**
'*How* are you?'

It can also occur as a determiner, often with a following *bir*. In this usage, it can be replaced by *ne gibi* 'what kind of':

(90) **Nasıl/ne gibi bir** *ev*e taşınmak istiyorsunuz?
'*What kind of house* do you want to move to?'

nasıl appears with *ol-* 'be' and *dA* in a number of phrases such as *nasıl oldu da/nasıl olmuş da* 'how come', 'how was it that', *nasıl oluyor da* 'how is it that':

(91) **Nasıl oldu da** bu kadar az çalışarak üniversiteyi bitirebildi?
'*How come* s/he worked so little and still managed to finish university?'

nasıl can also occur in exclamations (12.4 (iv)).

19.2.2 THE POSITION OF WH-PHRASES IN A SENTENCE

The most common position for a wh-phrase is immediately before the predicate:

(92) Semra'lar artık **nere-de** otur-uyor?
                where-LOC live-IMPF
'*Where* do Semra and her family live now?'

(93) Parti-de **kim-ler** var-dı?
party-LOC who-PL existent-P.COP
'*Who* was there at the party?'

Another frequently used position for wh-phrases is the position that their answers would occupy in the corresponding affirmative sentences:

(94) **Kim** onlar-ı okul-dan kaç-ar-ken gör-müş?
who they-ACC school-ABL run.away-AOR-CV see-EV/PF
'*Who* saw them running away from school?'

(95) Bu boya-lar-dan **hangi-sin-i** yan-da-ki dükkan-dan al-dı-n?
this paint-PL-ABL which-3SG.POSS-ACC next.door-LOC-ADJ
shop-ABL buy-PF-2SG
'*Which* of these paints did you buy from the shop next door?'

In informal speech a wh-phrase can be placed in other positions, as long as it is before the predicate:

(96) Erol'un **kim** doktor olduğunu söyledi?
'*Who* said Erol was a doctor?'

Unlike other wh-phrases, those corresponding to non-case-marked direct objects and oblique objects have a fixed position. These occur immediately before the predicate (see 23.2.1):

(97) Bugün hastalara öğle yemeğinde **ne** ver-di-ler?
what give-PF-3PL
'*What* did they give the patients today for lunch?'

(98) Necla **ne-den** korkuyor?
what-ABL fear-IMPF
'*What* is Necla scared *of*?'

Note that where *neden* means 'why' it can be in any position before the predicate.

The most common place for a wh-phrase that is a subject complement is at the end of the sentence, which is the unmarked position for predicates of linking sentences (23.1.2.1):

(99) Soru-lar-ı dağıt-acak ol-an kişi **kim**-di?
question-PL-ACC distribute-FUT be-PART person who-P.COP
'*Who* was the person that was supposed to distribute the questions?'

However, it can also occur at the beginning of a sentence:

(100) **Ne**-dir bana sormak istediğin soru?
what-GM
'*What* is the question you wanted to ask me?'

19.2.3 WH-PHRASES AND STRESSED PHRASES

In a wh-question it is possible for a phrase other than the wh-phrase to be stressed. This happens when the speaker wants the addressee to focus on a particular phrase in the question. In such cases the stressed phrase *precedes* the wh-phrase.

(101) Çocuk-lar ev-de değil-se *süt-Ü* **kim** iç-ti?
child-PL home-LOC not-COND.COP milk-ACC who drink-PF
'If the children aren't at home, then *who* drank the MILK?'

(102) **DuvarlaRI ne zaman** boyayacaklar?
'*When* will they paint the WALLS?'

19.2.4 MULTIPLE WH-PHRASES

In the event of two wh-phrases occurring in the same sentence, they appear in the order in which their corresponding responses would appear in an unmarked sentence (23.1). In such cases, the first question word has stress, and the sentence can have either the same intonation pattern as wh-questions (i.e. rising intonation at the end), or it may have falling intonation at the end:

(103) **KİM kime neyi** verdi?
'*WHO* gave *what to whom*?'

19.3 ECHO QUESTIONS

An echo question follows a question which has just been uttered, either because the initial question is unexpected and has come as a surprise, or because part of the initial question has not been heard or understood properly. Echo questions may also be used for inquiring about the validity of a question which has already been asked. Depending on the form of the initial question, they may contain a wh-phrase *and* the interrogative particle *mI*. The interrogative particle immediately follows a stressed wh-phrase, and the intonation is that of wh-questions, a slight rise followed by a fall-rise:

(104) **NEreye mi** gidiyorum?
(i) 'Are you asking me *where* I'm going?'
(ii) '*Where* am I GOING?'

If the wh-phrase is the subject complement, it occurs at the end and is not stressed. In these questions, stress falls on the phrase that *mI* is attached to.

(105) **HülYA mı kim**?
'Are you asking *who* Hülya is?/*Who* is HÜLYA?'

Echo questions following a statement have the same structure as ordinary wh-questions but are higher in pitch and do not contain a fall in intonation:

(106) **Nereye** gidiyorsun?
    (i) '*Where* did you say you were going?'
    (ii) 'You're going *WHERE*?'

19.4 QUESTIONING PARTS OF SUBORDINATE CLAUSES

The constituents of all types of subordinate clauses can be questioned, just like those of main clauses:

(107) Zehra [sen-in ***kim-i*** ara-dığ-ın]-ı sanıyormuş?
           you-GEN who-ACC look.for-VN-2SG.POSS-ACC
           '*Who* did Zehra think you were looking for?'

In (107) a constituent of a noun clause (Chapter 24) has been questioned. (108) shows the questioning of a constituent of a relative clause (Chapter 25):

(108) [***Nere-ye*** gid-en göçmen-ler] kolay kolay geri dönmüyorlar?
       where-DAT go-PART immigrant-PL
       '(The) (im)migrants going *where* don't easily return to their homeland?'

Finally, (109) exemplifies the questioning of a constituent of an adverbial clause (Chapter 26):

(109) [**Para-n-ı** *nere-de* **bul-a-ma-yınca**] telaşa kapıldın?
       money-2SG.POSS-ACC where-LOC find-PSB-NEG-CV
       '*Where* was it that when you couldn't find your money [there] you got worried?'

19.5 MODAL ADVERBS USED IN QUESTIONS

19.5.1 *hani*

hani is an interjection which means 'show me' or 'present me with':

(110) **Hani** çocukların kırdıkları vazo?
       '*So where is* the vase that the children broke?'

Questions with *hani* do not target the location of a particular object or person but seek confirmation of the presence of an entity of which both speech participants are aware. *hani* resembles the rhetorical usage of questions with 'where' in which the speaker does not actually ask for the whereabouts of a particular object but asks to be presented with it.

(111) **Hani** benim payım?
       'So where's my share, *then?'*

(112) Semra'ya aldığın hediye **hani**?
       'So where's the present you bought for Semra?'

Hani can be used in combination with the inflected forms of *nere-*. *Hani* and *nere-* are usually adjacent:

(113) Semra'ya aldığın hediye **hani nerede**?
       'So where's the present you bought for Semra?'

Constructions with *hani* at the beginning of a sentence and *nere-* at the end are also acceptable:

(114) **Hani** bana vereceğin para **nerede**?
       'So where is the money you were going to give me?'

Hani can also be used with other wh-phrases, in order to question the validity of a statement or to show disbelief:

(115) **Hani** *ne zaman* yaptın dersini?
       'When did you do your homework, *then?'*

(116) **Hani** *kim* görmüş çocukların camlara taş attığını?
       'So who saw the children throw stones at the windows, *then?'*

For the discourse-connective function of *hani* see 28.3.12.

19.5.2 *Acaba*

acaba indicates doubt or curiosity, and is roughly equivalent to 'I wonder (if)' in English. It can be used in wh-questions and yes/no questions, both verbal and nominal. It is generally placed either at the beginning or the end of a sentence, but can also occur in other positions (23.2.2).

(117) **Acaba** misafirler *saat kaçta* gelecek?
       'I wonder what time the guests will arrive.'

(118) Semra'ya hediye alsam **mı acaba**?
       'I wonder if I should buy a present for Semra.'

For the usage of *acaba* with deliberative *-sA* see 21.4.4.4.

19.5.3 *yoksa*

yoksa as an inferential connective (28.3.7) is typically used in yes/no questions. It indicates a sudden realization on the speaker's part that the situation might be different from what s/he expected:

> (119) **Yoksa** çocuklara daha yemek vermedin *mi*?
> 'Haven't you fed the children yet, *then*?'

> (120) Eski halılarını satıyor *mu*sun **yoksa**?
> 'Are you selling your old carpets, *then*?'

yoksa generally occurs at the beginning or at the end of a sentence, but it can occur in other positions as well (23.2.2), except when it is used for connecting alternative questions (19.1.2).

19.5.4 *bakalım*

bakalım 'let's see' is an expression of anticipation, usually indicating the speaker's curiosity about a prospective event. Except where it is used in commands, it occurs in sentences that contain either a wh-phrase or the question particle *mI*, but these sentences are not real questions, as they do not seek a response.

> (121) **Bakalım** doktorlardan *hangisi* o hastayı ameliyat edecek.
> '*Let's see which (one)* of the doctors will operate on that patient.'

> (122) Dersini zamanında bitirebilecek *mi*sin **bakalım**.
> '*Let's see if* you can finish your homework on time.'

19.6 RHETORICAL QUESTION FORMS IN NARRATIVE

In an informal narrative context, particularly in spoken narrative, yes/no questions containing an aorist or optative negative verb form (i.e. *-mAz*, *-mAyA-* or *-mAsIn*) are used to present an event or action as almost unbelievably perverse or outrageous:

> (123) Yepyeni şemsiyemi takside unut-**ma-ya-yım mı**?
> forget-NEG-OPT-1SG INT
> '*Would you believe it*, I left my brand new umbrella in the taxi!'

> (124) Bunun üzerine Turgut elindeki bardağı duvara doğru
> fırlat-**ma-sın mı**?
> hurl-NEG-OPT.3SG INT
> 'Then, *would you believe it*, Turgut hurled the glass in his hand against the wall.'

20 NEGATION

This chapter discusses the means of negating clauses in Turkish, and particular expressions which interact with negation. Sections 20.1–20.3 describe the conditions in which the markers of negation, *-mA*, *değil* and *yok*, are used. In 20.4 we discuss the negative connective *ne . . . ne . . .* 'neither . . . nor . . .', and in 20.5 expressions that occur mainly in negative sentences, such as *hiç* 'never', 'ever', 'at all', *kimse* 'no one', 'anyone', *hiçbir şey* 'nothing', 'anything', *asla* 'never', etc. Section 20.6 focuses on the usage of negative expressions in subordinate clauses.

20.1 *-mA*

The negative marker *-mA* (8.2.2) is an unstressable suffix. Its interaction with stress and intonation are discussed in 4.3.2 and 5.2.1. For the irregular combination of *-mA* with other suffixes see 8.2.3, and for converbial suffixes containing *-mA* see 8.5.2.2.

20.1.1 NEGATING CLAUSES WITH SIMPLE VERBS

-mA is the primary means used for negating verbal sentences and subordinate clauses.

(1) Ağaçları kes-**me**-yecek-ler.
          cut.down-NEG-FUT-3PL
    'They won't cut down the trees.'

(2) Ahmet [Zeki'yi gör-**me**-yeceğ-in]-i iddia ediyordu.
              see-NEG-VN-3SG.POSS-ACC
    'Ahmet was claiming that he wouldn't see Zeki.'

(3) [Ayşe-nin durumu bil-**me**-diğ-in]-i hiç bir zaman düşün-**me**-di-m.
                   know-NEG-VN-3SG.POSS-ACC think-NEG-PF-1SG
    'I never thought that Ayşe didn't know about the situation.'

In sentences with **small clauses** (24.5) the negation marker usually occurs once and can be either on the main clause verb or on the verb of the subordinate clause.

(4) [Zeki'yi Fransızca konuşuyor] addet-**mi**-yor-lar.
                           consider-NEG-IMPF-3PL
     'They don't consider Zeki a speaker of French.'

(5) [Zeki'yi Fransızca konuş-**mu**-yor] addediyorlar.
                     speak- NEG-IMPF
     'They consider Zeki unable to speak French.'

Where the main clause verb is *bil-* 'think' and the sentence contains a small clause, the negation marker is obligatorily on the verb of the subordinate (small) clause:

(6) [Nuran'ı daha ehliyetini al**ma**dı] biliyordum.
     'I was under the impression that Nuran hadn't got her driving licence yet.'

20.1.2 NEGATING CLAUSES WITH COMPOUND VERB FORMS

In compound verbs formed with free auxiliaries (13.3.1.2) the negative marker can be on either the **lexical verb** or the **auxiliary verb**. When it is on the lexical verb it negates the predicate, and this position of *-mA* indicates the non-performance of the action.

(7) İyi ki bakkal yiyecekleri eve yollayabiliyor. Bu yağmurda sokağa
     çık-*ma*-mış ol-du-k.
     go.out-NEG-PF be-PF-1PL
     'Fortunately, the grocer can do home deliveries of food. We avoided having to go out in this rain.' (lit. 'We ended up not having gone out . . .')

(8) Yakında bu kıyıdan denize **girile*mez* olacak.**
     'Soon it will be impossible to bathe in the sea along this shore.'
     (lit. '. . . going into the sea will be not be able to be done . . .')

The occurrence of the negative marker with a compound verb containing *bulun-* is rare but possible.

(9) O telaş içinde hastanın ateşine **bak*ma*mış bulundum.**
     'In the confusion I neglected to take the patient's temperature.'

The negative marker can also occur on the auxiliary verb *ol-* (but not *bulun-*). Placing the negative marker on the auxiliary verb expresses a denial that a particular action is/was fully performed:

(10) Bir yıl Çin'de kalmakla Çince **öğren-miş ol-*maz*-sın**.
learn-PF be-NEG.AOR-2SG
'You won't have learnt Chinese by staying in China for one year.'

The frequently used form *-mIş olmadı* indicates that the action has only been partially realized, usually because some component of the full meaning of the verb is considered by the speaker unfulfilled:

(11) Sokağa çıkalım diye tutturdun ama bir blok yürümekle sokağa
çık-mış ol-*ma*-dı-k.
go.out-PF be-NEG-PF-1PL
'You keep saying we should go out, but walking one block doesn't count as having gone out.' (lit. '. . . by walking one block we didn't end up having gone out')

Putting the negative marker on both verbs (as in the second of the two compound verbs below) is a means for denying the non-performance of an action:

(12) Böylesi daha iyi. Hem onları fazla **meşgul et-*me*-miş ol-ur-uz**
occupied make-NEG-PF be-AOR-1PL
hem de ziyaretlerine **git-*me*-miş ol-*ma*-yız**.
go-NEG-PF be-NEG-1PL
'It's better this way. We won't have taken up too much of their time, and on the other hand we won't have neglected to visit them.' (lit. '. . . we will not have not paid them a visit').

For the combination of *-mA* with compound verbs containing bound auxiliaries, see 8.2.3 (in particular *-(y)Iver* and *-(y)Abil*; see also *-yA*).

20.1.3 *-(y)Ip . . . -mA* 'WHETHER/IF . . . (OR NOT)'

-(y)Ip . . . -mA constructions correspond to 'whether/if . . . (or not)' in English. They are non-finite noun clauses (24.4) which contain two identical verbs, the first one affixed with the conjunctive suffix *-(y)Ip* (8.5.2.2, 28.2), and the second one affixed with the negative marker and one of the subordinating suffixes (*-DIK*, *-(y)AcAK*, *-mA*, *-mAK* or *-(y)Iş*, see 8.5). These constructions express affirmative and negative alternatives for the same situation. *-(y)Ip . . . -mA* constructions occur particularly commonly as objects of verbs of cognition such as *bil-* 'know', *anla-* 'understand' and *fark et-* 'notice' (24.4.3.2) or of the verbs *söyle-* 'say', *sor-* 'ask':

(13) [Çocukları tatile **götür-üp götür-me-mey**]-**e** henüz
take-CONJ take-NEG-VN-DAT
karar ver-**me**-di-ler.
decide-NEG-PF-3PL
'They haven't yet decided [*whether or not to take* the children on holiday].'

(14) Ahmet [Nuran'a Noel hediyesi **alıp almayacağın**]-ı bilmiyor.
'Ahmet doesn't know [*whether or not he will buy* Nuran a Christmas present].'

(15) Elif [**kalıp kalmayacağın**]-ı söyledi mi?
'Has Elif said [*whether or not she'll be staying*]?'

When used in sentences with nominal predicates, *-(y)Ip . . . -mA* constructions usually occur as the complement of the postposition *konusunda* 'about' (17.3.2):

(16) Osman [bu yaz tatile **çıkıp çıkmama**] *konusunda* tereddütlüymüş.
'Apparently Osman is hesitating about [whether to go on holiday this summer].'

20.2 *değil*

20.2.1 NEGATING NOMINAL SENTENCES

değil 'not' (pronounced [deil] or [di:l]) is primarily the means of negating the linking type of nominal sentence (12.1.1.2). It can combine with the suffixes that occur in nominal predicates, namely the copular markers (8.3.2), *-DIr* (8.3.3), the person markers belonging to group 2 (8.4) and the converbial marker *-(y)ken* (8.5.2.2):

(17) Nejat gençliğinde bu kadar *inatçı* **değil-di**.
stubborn not-P.COP
'Nejat wasn't so stubborn when he was young.'

(18) Bu yaptığın **çocukluk değil**(-**dir**) de nedir?
childishness not-GM
'This behaviour of yours is nothing but childish.' (lit. 'If this behaviour of yours is not childishness what is it?')

(19) [*Evde* **değil-sin**] sandık.
not-2SG
'We thought [you weren't at home].'

(20) [Anneleri **ev-de değil-ken**] çok daha derli toplu oluyorlar.
　　　　　　home-LOC not-CV
'They are much tidier [when their mother isn't at home].'

20.2.2　NEGATING VERBAL SENTENCES

değil can also be used for negating verbal sentences. In this case the verb is typically conjugated with the imperfective marker *-Iyor*, less commonly with the future marker *-(y)AcAK* or the perfective marker *-mIş* (see 8.2.3):

(21) Her yere taksiyle **gid-iyor** *değil*-**im**.
　　　　　　go-IMPF not-1SG
'It's not the case that I go everywhere by taxi.'

However, negating a verbal sentence with *değil* is different from negating it with *-mA* as in (22):

(22) Her yere taksiyle **git-*mi*-yor-um**.
　　　　　　go-NEG-IMPF-1SG
'I don't go everywhere by taxi.'

While negating a sentence with *-mA* simply asserts a state of affairs, negating a verbal sentence with *değil* repudiates an assumption which has either been overtly expressed or which the speaker attributes to the hearer. In the case of (21), the assumption is that the speaker regularly takes a taxi.

　değil can also occur with negated verb forms. Such sentences are affirmative as a result of being doubly negated:

(23) Bu sınavlarda neden bu kadar güçlük çekildiğini
　　　　anla-*mı*-yor *değil*-**im**.
　　　　understand-NEG-IMPF not-1SG
'I DO understand why [people] have so much difficulty with these exams.' (lit. 'It's *not* the case that I do*n't* understand . . .')

(24) Herhalde böyle önemli bir konuda ona akıl **danış*ma*yacak**
　　　　değiliz.
'We will naturally ask for his/her opinion on a matter as important as this.' (lit. 'It's *not* the case that we wo*n't* ask for his/her opinion on such an important matter.')

A verb inflected with the perfective marker *-DI* can be followed by *değil* only if it also has a negative marker. In this case any person marking has to attach to the verb instead of to *değil*:

(25) Olanları **gör-*me*-di-m değil**, ama tam hatırlayamıyorum.
　　　see-NEG-PF-1SG not
　　　'It's *not* that I did*n't* see what went on; it's just that I can't quite remember.'

20.2.3 *değil* IN ELLIPTICAL SENTENCES

değil can be used as a means of **ellipsis** (28.4.2), by replacing a particular part of a sentence. It replaces a (verbal) negative predicate in sentences which contain an identical (but affirmative) predicate. For example, a sentence such as (26) can be paraphrased as (27):

(26) Elma yemiyorum, armut yiyorum.
　　　'I'm not eating apples, I'm eating pears.'

(27) Elma **değil**, armut yi-yor-um.
　　　apple not pear eat-IMPF-1SG
　　　'I'm eating pears, *not* apples.'

The part that contains *değil* can also follow the main assertion:

(28) Armut yiyorum, elma **değil**.

In addition to replacing a predicate, *değil* can also replace a noun and its determiner (together with the predicate):

(29) Büyük **değil**, küçük bir elma iste-miş-ti-m.
　　　big not small a(n) apple want-PF-P.COP-1SG
　　　'I had asked for a small apple, *not* [a] big [one].'

Alternatively, *değil* can be used in a function semantically equivalent to *şöyle dursun* and *bir yana* (28.3.1.4), for contrasting or comparing two events or entities in terms of the scale of their improbability, in a similar way to 'let alone' in English. In these sentences *değil* precedes the constituent whose actualization is regarded as less probable, and this constituent usually precedes that to which it is contrasted. The intonation peak of such sentences is the contrasted constituent, which is almost always followed by *bile* 'even' (28.3.1.1 (iv)). The constituent to which something is contrasted is also stressed. Usually *değil* receives secondary stress:

(30) **Değil *sinema ya gitmek***, televizYON bile seyred-ecek
　　　not cinema-DAT GO-INF television even watch-PART
　　　zaman-ım yok.
　　　time-1SG.POSS non-existent
　　　'I don't even have time to watch TV, *let alone go to the cinema*.'

(31) Ahmet **değil** *saksafon*, ıslık bile çalamaz.
'Ahmet can't even whistle, *let alone* play *the saxophone*.'

20.3 *yok*

The negative existential expression *yok* 'non-existent' is the negated form of *var* 'existent' (12.1.1.2):

(32) Evde bir tane bile fazla ampul **yok**.
'There isn't even one spare light bulb in the house.'

(33) Çorbanın tuzu **yok**.
'The soup doesn't have any salt [in it].'

yok can also be used in a double negative construction with *değil*:

(34) Maaşımdan şikayetim **yok değil** ama idare ediyorum işte.
'I'm *not without* complaints about my salary, but I get by all the same.'

In colloquial speech, *yok* is commonly used as the negative response to a question, instead of *hayır* 'no':

(35) A.– Bugün sinemaya gidecek misin?
'Will you be going to the cinema today?'

B.– **Yok** (gitmeyeceğim).
'*No* (I won't).'

See 28.3.4.9 and 28.3.5 (ii) for the usages of *yok* as a connective.
Where a negative linking sentence includes a locative-marked expression, *yok* and *değil* are interchangeable (cf. 12.1.1.2, (19)–(20)):

(36) Semra **parti-de değil-di/yok-tu**.
party-LOC not-P.COP/absent-P.COP
'Semra wasn't at the party.'

Note that when *yok* is used, the position of the locative noun phrase (*partide* 'at the party') is not fixed in the sentence, whereas when *değil* is used the locative-marked noun phrase has to immediately precede it.

20.4 THE NEGATIVE CONNECTIVE *ne . . . ne* 'NEITHER . . . NOR'

ne . . . ne is a negative connective where each *ne* attaches to a phrase (either simple or complex). The last *ne* conjunct can be emphasized by using *de*:

(37) **Ne** yabancılar **ne** (**de**) mahalle halkı otobüs turlarından memnunlar.
'*Neither* the foreigners *nor* the locals are happy with the coach tours.'

(38) Görüşmeler hakkında **ne** hükümetten, **ne** iş adamlarından, **ne** (**de**) işçi sendikalarından bir bilgi alamadık.
'We weren't able to get any information about the negotiations from either the government, the businessmen *or* the trade unions.'

Sentences containing *ne . . . ne* can have either affirmative or negative predicates, but in each case they have a separate intonation contour and stress pattern. When the predicate is affirmative the first *ne* receives secondary stress, there is a rise in intonation after the first conjunct, and primary stress falls on the constituent before the predicate:

(39) Bu filmden **ne** kadınlar **ne** erkekLER hoşlandılar.
'*Neither* the women *nor* the men liked this film.'

If the predicate is negative, all of the *ne* conjuncts have an identical intonation contour, where both *ne* and the stressable syllable within the conjunct receive secondary stress, and primary stress falls on the predicate (on the syllable before the negative marker):

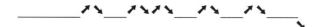

(40) Bu filmden **ne** kadınlar **ne** erkekler hoşLAN**madı**lar.
'*Neither* the women *nor* the men liked this film.'

The second conjunct can be placed after the predicate, but only when the predicate is affirmative:

(41) Bu sandviççide **ne** çay var, **ne de** kahve.
'There is *neither* tea *nor* coffee in this sandwich shop.'

(42) **Ne** yiyecek bulabildim **ne (de)** içecek.
'I couldn't find *either* food *or* drink.'

The *ne . . . ne* connective can conjoin pairs of any type of phrase, such as adverbial phrases, adjectival phrases, verb phrases, etc. It can also conjoin clauses:

(43) **Ne** tamir işleriyle uğraşır, **ne** yemek pişirmesini bilir, **ne (de)** çocuklarla ilgilenir.
'S/he *neither* does any repair jobs, *nor* knows how to cook, *nor* takes care of the children.'

(44) O kitaba sadece şöyle bir göz gezdirdim, yani **ne** okudum **ne** okumadım.
'I just glanced at that book, I mean I *neither* read [it] *nor* didn't read [it].'

20.5   EXPRESSIONS INTERACTING WITH NEGATION

There are a number of expressions which are very restricted in their ability to occur with affirmative predicates. They can occur in all types of negative sentence, and some can also occur in affirmative questions. These expressions are:

hiç	'never', 'ever', 'at all'
hiçbir (+ noun phrase)	'no/any . . .'
hiçbiri(si)	'none/any (of) . . .'
hiçbir şey	'nothing', 'anything'
hiçbir yer	'nowhere', 'anywhere'
hiçbir zaman	'never', 'ever'
hiçbir koşulda, hiçbir koşul/ şart altında, hiçbir durumda	'under no/any circumstances'
kimse/hiç kimse/hiçbir kimse	'no one', 'anyone'

Note that the negative meanings shown in the above list, such as 'never' and 'no one', are produced only by a combination of one of the expressions shown above with one of the markers of negation (*-mA*, *değil* or *yok*). This is illustrated in the following pair of examples:

(45) Evde **kimse** var mı?
no.one/anyone existent INT
'Is there *anyone* in the house?'

(46) Evde **kimse** *yok* mu?
    no.one/anyone not.existent INT
    'Is*n't* there *anyone*/Is there **no one** in the house?'

There are also certain other expressions which interact with negation. These are *artık* 'any more', *bir daha* 'once more', 'again', *daha/henüz* 'yet' (see 16.4.1.4).

20.5.1 *hiç* 'NEVER', 'EVER', 'AT ALL'

hiç is an adverb that is subject to different conditions depending on whether the sentence in which it occurs is a question or not. A sentence which is not a question and which contains *hiç* must also contain one of the markers of negation (*-mA*, *değil* or *yok*), and *hiç* intensifies this negative element:

(47) Bu adam **hiç** uyanık **değil**.
    at.all clever not
    'This man is*n't* clever *at all*.'

(48) Trende yer **yok**-muş **hiç**.
    place non-existent-EV.COP at.all
    'It seems there are*n't* any seats [left] *at all* on the train.'

hiç also occurs in yes/no questions with or without negative marking:

(49) **Hiç** sabah güneşin doğuşunu seyret-ti-n *mi*?
    ever   watch-PF-2SG
    'Have you *ever* watched the sun rise?'

(50) **Hiç** bin-**me**-di-n *mi* uçağa?
    ever board-NEG-PF-2SG
    'Have*n't* you *ever*/Have you *never* been on a plane?'

20.5.2 *hiçbir* 'NO', 'ANY', AND EXPRESSIONS CONTAINING *hiçbir* AND *herhangi bir* 'NO', 'ANY'

Hiçbir functions as a determiner in noun phrases (15.6.1):

(51) *Hiçbir* **çocuk** arkadaşından ayrılmak istemez.
    '*No child* would want to be separated from his/her friend(s).'

It also occurs in the following:

(i) the pronominalized form *hiçbiri(si)* 'none [of]', 'any [of]' (14.5.2–3, 18.4)

(ii) the composite expressions *hiçbir şey* 'nothing', 'anything', *hiçbir yer* 'nowhere', 'anywhere', *hiçbir zaman* 'never', 'ever', which incorporate the noun phrases *şey* 'thing', *yer* 'place' and *zaman* 'time'

(iii) the adverbials *hiçbir koşulda*, *hiçbir koşul/şart altında*, *hiçbir durumda* 'under no/any circumstances'.

All the forms that *hiçbir* appears in are found mainly in sentences containing one of the markers of negation (*-mA*, *değil* or *yok*):

(52) **Hiçbir yere** git*me*yin.
'Do*n't* go *anywhere*.'

(53) **Yolculardan hiçbiri(si)** yerini vermek iste*me*di.
'*None of the passengers* wanted to surrender their seats.'

(54) **Hiçbir zaman** mutlu *değil* miydi?
'Was*n't* s/he *ever* happy?'

(55) Dolapta **hiçbir şey** *yok*.
'There's *nothing* in the fridge.'

In informal speech some speakers use expressions containing *hiçbir* in affirmative questions as well. But the more common alternative, which is also the only way of expressing *any* in affirmative sentences that are not questions, such as (57), is *herhangi bir* 'any' (15.6.1, 18.4 (iv)):

(56) **Herhangi bir** yerde su *var* mı?/**Hiçbir** yerde su *var* mı?
'Is there [any] water anywhere?'

(57) Artık bunlardan **herhangi birini** alıp gidelim.
'Let's just take *any one* of these and go.'

20.5.3 *(hiç) kimse* 'NO ONE', 'ANYONE'

Like *hiç*, *kimse* and its reinforced form *hiç kimse* are subject to different conditions depending on whether the sentence in which they occur is a question or not. A sentence which is not a question and which contains *(hiç) kimse* must also contain one of the markers of negation (*-mA*, *değil* or *yok*):

(58) **(Hiç) kimseyi** içeri al*mı*yorlarmış.
'They are*n't* letting *anyone* in.'

(59) Bugün (**hiç**) **kimse** evinde **değil**.
'*No one* is at home today.'

In affirmative questions the simple form *kimse* is preferred:

(60) İçeride **kimse** var **mı**?
'Is there *anyone* inside?'

hiçbir kimse can be used as a further reinforcement of *hiç kimse*:

(61) Partiye **hiç(bir)** **kimse** gelmedi.
'*(Absolutely) No one* came to the party.'

Colloquially, the plural suffix is sometimes added to *(hiç) kimse*, producing a slightly intensified meaning (see 14.3.1.2 (v)):

(62) Beni artık (**hiç**) **kimseler** sevmiyor.
'*No one* loves me any more.'

An even more informal alternative is *(hiç) kimsecik(ler)* (for -CIK see 7.2.2.2).

When *(hiç) kimse* is the subject, the predicate has 3rd person singular marking. Similarly, when *kimseler* or *kimsecikler* expresses the subject, the non-specific reference of these pronouns precludes plural marking of the predicate (see 12.2.2.1 (iv)).

(63) Bu günlerde dükkanına **kimse(ler)** uğramıyor.
'*No one* has been going to his/her shop recently.'

Note that *kimse* and the forms containing it have accusative case marking when functioning as the direct object:

(64) Bu günlerde **kimseyi/kimseleri** görmüyorum.
'I have*n't* been seeing *anyone* recently.'

20.5.4   MODIFIERS OF NEGATION MARKERS

Apart from *hiç* (20.5.1), which intensifies the meaning of a negation marker, the following adverbials also modify the markers -*mA*, *değil* and *yok*: *artık* 'no longer', 'any more' (16.4.1.4 (iib)), *asla* 'never', ∇*katiyen* 'never', *pek* 'very' and *o kadar* 'so', 'such', 'all that'.

20.5.4.1 *asla* 'never', ∇*katiyen* 'never'

Both of these adverbs reinforce the meaning of a negative marker. However, unlike *hiç*, these express a determination on the part of the subject that the event described shall never occur. *asla* and ∇*katiyen* occur only in sentences that contain one of the markers of negation (-*mA*, *değil* or *yok*):

(65) Karısından **asla** özür dile**mez**.
'He *never* apologizes/will *never* apologize to his wife.'

(66) Onu bir daha ∇**katiyen** gör**me**yecek misin?
'Will you *never* see him/her again?'

20.5.4.2 *pek* 'much', 'very'

When *pek*, which is an adverb of degree (16.5), modifies one of the markers of negation (-*mA*, *değil* or *yok*), its function is not to intensify, but rather to reduce the absoluteness of the negative meaning:

(67) Odam **pek** büyük *değil*.
'My room's *not very* big.'

(68) O konuşmadan **pek** bir şey hatırla**m**ıyorum.
'I do*n't* remember *much* about that lecture.'

pek can also occur in affirmative sentences, but only where either (a) it modifies one of the determiners *çok* 'much' or *az* 'little', or (b) the sentence expresses an exclamation (12.4).

20.5.4.3 *o kadar* 'so', 'such', 'all that'

The degree adverb *o kadar* (16.5) has a particular function in negative sentences, where the quantity or degree it refers to may not have been explicitly specified in the preceding discourse, but is simply implied to be considerable:

(69) Aslında dondurmayı **o kadar** sev**m**iyorum.
'Actually I'm *not all that* keen on ice cream.'

(70) Onlar **o kadar** varlıklı *değil*lermiş.
'It seems they're *not so very* wealthy.'

20.6 EXPRESSIONS INTERACTING WITH NEGATION IN SUBORDINATE CLAUSES

20.6.1 EXPRESSIONS INTERACTING WITH NEGATION IN NOUN CLAUSES

When one of the expressions listed in 20.5 occurs in a noun clause (Chapter 24), the verb of the clause can be either affirmative or negative. The verb of a noun clause containing one of these expressions can be affirmative only if the main clause predicate has negative marking (i.e. -mA, değil or yok):

(71) [**Kimse**-nin bu kitab-ı oku-duğ-un]-u san-*m*-ıyor-um.
no.one-GEN this book-ACC read-VN-3SG.POSS-ACC
think-NEG-IMPF-1SG
'I do*n't* think *anyone* has read this book.'

(72) [**Hiçbir şey**in denize atılması] doğru *değil*.
'It is*n't* right for *anything at all* to be thrown into the sea.'

(73) [Hasan'ın sana yardım için **hiçbir şey** yaptığı] *yok*.
'Hasan does *absolutely nothing* to help you.'

The verb of a noun clause containing *hiç* 'never', 'ever', 'at all' (20.5.1) and *(hiç)kimse* 'no one', 'anyone' (20.5.3) can be affirmative also in questions:

(74) [**Kimse**nin kapıyı çaldığın]-ı duydun mu?
'Did you hear [anyone ring the door bell]?

20.6.2 EXPRESSIONS INTERACTING WITH NEGATION IN RELATIVE CLAUSES AND ADVERBIAL CLAUSES

When a relative clause (Chapter 25) or an adverbial clause (Chapter 26) contains one of the expressions listed in 20.5, the verb of that clause is obligatorily negative:

(75) [Ortalıkta **hiç** iz bırak*ma*yan] hırsız, yandaki evi de soymuş.
'It seems that the burglar, [who has*n't* left *any* traces], has also burgled the house next door.'

(76) Necla [kocasından **hiç** haber ala*ma*yınca] tutuklandığını sanmış.
'[When Necla did*n't* hear from her husband *at all*], she thought he had been arrested.'

One exception is clauses with -*(y)Ip*, which have to be left without negative marking if the verb in the superordinate clause is negative:

(77) Onunla **hiçbir zaman** görüşüp konuşa*ma*dık.
    'We never managed to see each other and talk.'

See 28.2 for details.

21 TENSE, ASPECT AND MODALITY

Tense, aspect and modality are grammatical categories mainly affecting the verbal constituent of a clause, although adverbials may also contribute to their expression. **Tense** (21.2) expresses the temporal location of the situation being talked about, indicating whether this is before, at, or after a particular reference point (usually, but not always, the moment of speech).

(1) (**a**) Okul-lar pazartesi açıl-**dı**.
      school-PL Monday open-PF
      'The schools *started* on Monday.'

     (**b**) Okul-lar pazartesi açıl-**acak**.
                                    -FUT
      'The schools *will start* on Monday.'

Aspect (21.3) indicates whether the situation is presented as completed, ongoing, or part of a recurring pattern.

(2) (**a**) Ahmet bir elma ye-**di**.
                        an apple eat-PF
      'Ahmet *ate* an apple.'

     (**b**) Ahmet bir elma yi-**yor**-du.
                        -IMPF-P.COP
      'Ahmet *was eating* an apple.'

     (**c**) Ahmet sabahları bir elma ye-**r**-di.
                              -AOR-P.COP
      'In the mornings *Ahmet used to eat* an apple.'

Modality (21.4) is a complex category, being concerned with possibility and necessity, with the speaker's degree of commitment to the factuality of a statement, and with the speaker's desire for something to happen or not happen.

(3) (**a**) Sevil bu konu-yu araştır-**abil-ir**.
                  this matter-ACC investigate-PSB-AOR
      'Sevil *can/could/may* look into this matter.'

(**b**) Sevil bu konuyu araştır-**mış-tır**.
　　　　　　　　　　-PF-GM
　　　'*Presumably* Sevil has looked into this matter.'

(**c**) Sevil bu konuyu araştır-**sın**.
　　　　　　　　　　-OPT.3SG
　　　'*I want* Sevil to look into this matter.'

In Appendix 2 we present an inventory of all the Turkish suffixes that
contribute to the expression of tense, aspect and modality. As in most
languages, there is considerable overlap between the articulation of the
three categories.

21.1 THE EXPRESSION OF TENSE, ASPECT AND MODALITY IN TURKISH

In Turkish tense, aspect and modality are marked by a combination of
suffixes from the following categories:

(**i**)　Verbal tense/aspect/modality suffixes (8.2.3)
(**ii**)　Copular markers and -*DIr* (8.3).

The copular markers are restricted in the range of tense/aspect/modality
meanings they cover. In order to make available in nominal sentences
(12.1.1.2) the full range of tense/aspect/modality specification, the copular/
auxiliary verb *ol-* is used as the carrier of suffixes of position 3 (see 12.1.1.3).

In verbal sentences the use of compound verb forms containing free
auxiliaries (13.3.1.2) makes possible combinations of tense/aspect/modality
marking that cannot be achieved on a single verb stem, and thus constitutes
an integral part of the overall system for the expression of these categories.
The role of compound verb forms is discussed in 21.5.

It is important to note that in Turkish tense, aspect and modality are only
fully articulated in finite verb forms. For discussion of the extent to which
tense, aspect and modality can be marked in the non-finite verb forms used
in subordinate clauses see 21.4.2.1–2, 24.4.7, 25.4.1, and 26.2.3.

21.2 TENSE

In this book we use the term 'tense' in the strict sense of the grammatical
marking of *location in time*.

In Turkish the primary tense differentiation is between past and non-
past. The suffixes involved in the expression of present and future tense
(-*(I)yor*, -*mAktA* and -*(y)AcAK*) are markers of **relative tense**. This means
that the expression of absolute present and future tense is dependent on

the *absence* of any other tense marker, such as the past copula -*(y)DI*, which would indicate a reference point other than the moment of speech.

21.2.1 PAST TENSE

The markers of past tense in Turkish are the verbal suffixes -*DI* and -*mIş* and the copular marker -*(y)DI* (with its relatively uncommon alternant *idi*).

(i) -*DI* and -*mIş*:
These suffixes express both past tense and perfective aspect (21.3), that is to say they express past events that are viewed as a completed whole.

(4) Ev-i sat-**tı**-nız mı?
house-ACC sell-PF-2PL INT
'*Did/Have you sold* the house?'

(5) Kerem'in babası ona biraz para ver-**miş**.
give-EV/PF
'Apparently Kerem's father *gave/has given* him some money.'

For the use of -*DI* and -*mIş* to express the completion of entry into a state, and thus the existence of that state of affairs at the moment of speech, see 21.3.3.

(ii) -*(y)DI*:
The past copula expresses past tense and imperfective aspect (21.3), that is to say it presents a situation as it was at some time in the past. This can be a state of affairs, as in the nominal sentences (6) and (7), or it can be an event which was ongoing (8) or anticipated (9) at the time referred to.

(6) Bodrum-da-**ydı**-k.
-LOC-P.COP-1PL
'We *were* in Bodrum.'

(7) Evde hiç para yok-**tu**.
non-existent-P.COP
'There *was* absolutely no money in the house.'

(8) Ayten bir bankada çalış-***ıyor*-du**.
work-IMPF-P.COP
'Ayten *was* work*ing* in a bank.'

(9) Yeni bir öğretmenimiz ol-***acak*-tı**.
be-FUT-P.COP
'We *were going to* have a new teacher.'

The suffixes *-DI* and *-mIş* and the copular marker *-(y)DI* differ not only in terms of aspect but also in terms of their precise tense values. Except for contexts in which it is not a tense marker at all but a marker of counter-factual modality (21.4.1.3, 27.2.3), the past copula *-(y)DI* expresses past tense in absolute terms; that is, it locates a situation in a time prior to the moment of speech. *-mIş*, by contrast, is a marker of relative past tense. When followed by *-(y)DI* or by the auxiliary verb *ol-*, it can refer to a time that is prior to *any* reference point established by the context:

(10) [Dön-düğ-üm-de] herkes yat-**mış-tı**.
     return-CV-1SG.POSS-LOC everyone go.to.bed-PF-P.COP
     '[When I came back] everyone *had* gone to bed.'

It is quite possible for this reference point to be after the moment of speech, i.e. in the future:

(11) İnşallah [ben dön-ünce-ye kadar] uyu-**muş** *ol-acak*-sın.
     I.hope I return-CV-DAT until sleep-PF AUX-FUT-2SG
     'I hope you *will have* gone to sleep [by the time I get back].'

As for *-DI*, its primary function in terms of tense is the same as that of *-(y)DI*, but in colloquial usage it can combine with *-(y)DI* in the sequence *-DIydI*, in which context (only) it acquires the relative tense value typical of *-mIş*. (For the position of a person marker in *-DIydI* forms see 8.4.)

(12) Ben sana bu sabah ↓söyle-**di-ydi**-m/↓söyle-**di**-m-**di**.
     I you-DAT this morning say-PF-P.COP-1SG/say-PF-1SG-P.COP
     'I *(had) told* you this morning.'

It should be noted that forms in *-mIştI* and *-DIydI* do not always locate an event prior to a specific reference point in the past. Sometimes, as in (12), the combination of two past tense markers simply serves to indicate that the situation being talked about is located in a past time that is quite separate from the speech context.

21.2.2 PRESENT TENSE

Turkish has no marker of present tense as such. In verbal sentences, present tense is indicated by a combination of

(i)   a marker of progressive aspect (21.3.2), usually *-(I)yor*, less commonly *-mAktA*, and
(ii) the absence of the past copular marker *-(y)DI*.

Progressive aspect, which presents a situation as ongoing at a particular point in time, is equivalent in tense terms to 'relative present'. (13) is the non-past version of (8) above:

(13) Ayten bir bankada çalış-**ıyor**.
     'Ayten *works/is working* in a bank.'

In nominal sentences without *ol-* (12.1.1.2), present tense is indicated simply by the absence of the past copula. (14) and (15) are the non-past versions of (6) and (7) above.

(14) Bodrum'da-yız.
             -1PL
     'We*'re* in Bodrum.'

(15) Evde hiç para yok.
     'There*'s* absolutely no money in the house.'

For the use of past tense perfective forms to express (entry into) a state ongoing at the moment of utterance see 21.3.3.

21.2.3 FUTURE TENSE

(i) Among the verbal suffixes, the only explicit marker of future tense is *-(y)AcAK*:

(16) Herkes bu roman-a bayıl-**acak**.
     everyone this novel-DAT love-FUT
     'Everyone will love this novel.'

In nominal sentences the auxiliary *ol-* (12.1.1.3) serves as the bearer of *-(y)AcAK*:

(17) [Geldiğiniz zaman] anahtar kapıcıda **olacak**.
     'The key *will be* with the caretaker when you arrive.'

Like *-mIş*, *-(y)AcAK* expresses tense in relative rather than absolute terms. When combined with the past copula, it locates an event or state at a time subsequent to some past reference point established by the discourse context. The future time to which the *-(y)AcAK* component of *-(y)AcAktI* refers may or may not be future in relation to the moment of speech:

(18) *Geçen/Önümüzdeki yıl* yeni bir öğretmen-imiz ol-**acak-tı**.
     last/next year new a teacher-1PL.POSS be-FUT-P.COP
     '*Last year/Next year* we *were going to* have a new teacher.'

(ii)   The imperfective aspect marker *-(I)yor* is regularly used with future reference when talking about events that are scheduled or fixed:

(19)   Yarın Londra'ya gid**iyor**uz.
       'We*'re* go*ing* to London tomorrow.'

(20)   Konser kaçta başlı-**yor**?
       'What time *does* the concert start?'

The use of *-(I)yor* for the expression of planned future events indicates a strong confidence on the speaker's part that events will indeed run according to the schedule. The use of *-(y)AcAK* in such contexts would suggest a more independent prediction, or would be used in the case of a schedule's breaking down. For example, (21) is more likely than (20) in the case of a concert that had not started at the scheduled time:

(21)   Konser kaçta başla**yacak**?
       'What time *is* the concert *going to* start?'

As in its other functions, *-(I)yor* in its future tense function is actually a marker of relative tense and, in the context of a narrative, the combination *-(I)yordu* expresses a scheduled event anticipated at some reference point in the past:

(22)   Füsun telaşlıydı. Birkaç gün sonra annesi gel**iyor***du*.
       'Füsun was agitated. Her mother *was coming* in a few days' time.'

(iii)   The aorist form of the verb often has future time reference, but any tense component of its meaning is conditioned by its primary function as a marker of various kinds of modality (see 21.4.1.4, 21.4.4.5–6).

(iv)   The construction *-mAk üzere* 'on the point of . . . ing' can be used to express action that is or was imminent:

(23)   [Sen telefon et-tiğ-in sıra-da] sokağ-a çık-**mak üzere**-ydi-m.
       you telephone-AUX-CV-2SG.POSS time-LOC street-DAT
       go.out-VN on-P.COP-1SG
       'I was *on the point of* going out [when you rang].'

For the converbial uses of *-mAk üzere* see 26.3.2, 26.3.12.

21.3   ASPECT

Aspect is that part of the grammar of a language which expresses the temporal viewpoint from which a situation is presented. It may be viewed 'from the outside', as a completed whole, with both its starting point and its endpoint visible. This is called **perfective** aspect. Alternatively it may be viewed 'from the inside', as being incomplete and ongoing at the time in question. This internal perspective, known as **imperfective** aspect, is also the typical viewpoint for the presentation of static situations (states).

At another level, imperfective forms are used for presenting any kind of situation (event or state) as occurring habitually, or as a general rule or pattern. In habitual statements it is the recurring pattern of events, rather than any individual event or state, that is presented as ongoing at the time in question.

21.3.1 PERFECTIVE AND IMPERFECTIVE

The distinction between perfective and imperfective applies mainly to sentences in the past tense. In Turkish, perfective aspect is expressed by the verbal suffixes -*DI* and -*mIş*, and imperfective aspect is expressed by the verbal suffixes -*(I)yor*, -*mAktA* and -*(A/I)r*, and by the past copular marker -*(y)DI*.

Perfective:

(24) (a) Geçen hafta her gün iki saat çalış-**tı**-m.
                                    work-PF-1SG
              'Last week I *worked* for two hours every day.'

        (b) İki saat çalış-**mış**-ım.
                  work-EV/PF-1SG
              'I *seem to have worked* for two hours.'

Imperfective:

(25) (a) Saat ikide çalış-**ıyor-du**-m.
                        work-IMPF-P.COP-1SG
              'At two o'clock I *was working.*'

        (b) Saat ikide ofis-te-**ydi**-m.
                      office-LOC-P.COP-1SG
              'At two o'clock I *was* at the office.'

        (c) Genellikle iki saat çalış-**ır-dı**-m.
                          work-AOR-P.COP-1SG
              'I *would* usually *work* for two hours.'

The forms -*mIştI* and -*DIydI* (21.2.1) combine elements of perfectivity and imperfectivity. They express the state ensuing upon the completion of an action or event.

21.3.2 SUBDIVISIONS OF IMPERFECTIVE: PROGRESSIVE AND HABITUAL

Within imperfective aspect there is a further distinction between **progressive** and **habitual**, which applies in both past and non-past contexts. Progressive aspect views a *specific situation* as incomplete. This situation may be dynamic (an event) or static (a state). In either case it is presented as being ongoing, or continuing, at the temporal reference point. Habitual aspect, on the other hand, indicates that a situation is incomplete in a different way: not at the level of any specific occurrence but in the sense that it is part of a *recurrent pattern*, which is shown as ongoing at the temporal reference point.

Of the three imperfective markers noted above, *-(I)yor* occurs with both progressive and habitual meaning, while *-mAktA* generally expresses progressive aspect but can occur with habitual meaning in relatively formal contexts. The difference between *-(I)yor* and *-mAktA* is largely stylistic, with *-(I)yor* being less formal and therefore much the more common in conversation. However, *-mAktA* may occur in relatively informal speech where a speaker wishes to emphasize the intensity of the ongoing event.

The range of aspectual meanings of *-(I)yor* and *-mAktA* in present-tense sentences is illustrated below:

Progressive: (event)

(26) A.– Şu an-da ne yap-**ıyor**-sunuz?
this moment-LOC what do-IMPF-2PL
'What *are* you *doing* at the moment?'

B.– Yemek yi-**yor**-uz.
meal eat-IMPF-1PL
'We*'re having* dinner.'

(27) Bugün aile yapı-sı hız-la değiş-**mekte**-dir.
today family structure-NC speed-INS change-IMPF-GM
'Today the structure of the family *is changing* rapidly.'

Progressive: (state)

(28) Sen Ömer-i ben-den daha iyi tanı-**yor**-sun.
you Ömer-ACC I-ABL more well know-IMPF-2SG
'You *know* Ömer better than me.'

(29) Çizgi-nin üst taraf-ın-da birkaç beyaz nokta gör-ül-**mekte**-dir.
line-GEN upper side-3SG.POSS-LOC several white spot
see-PASS-IMPF-GM
'Several white spots *can be seen* above the line.'

Habitual:

(30) Fatma genellikle Ankara-ya otobüs-le gid-**iyor**.
Fatma usually Ankara-DAT bus-INS go-IMPF
'Fatma usually *goes* to Ankara by bus.'

(31) Türkiye artık televizyon ihraç et-**mekte**-dir.
Turkey now television export AUX-IMPF-GM
'Now Turkey *exports/is exporting* televisions.'

A precisely similar range of meanings is seen in past-tense sentences with
-(I)yordu and *-mAktAydI*:

(32) Saat ikide çalış-**ıyor-du**-m.   (Progressive: event)
      -IMPF-P.COP-1SG
'At two o'clock I *was working*.'

(33) Sen Ömer'i benden daha iyi tanı-**yor-du**-n.   (Progressive: state)
                        -IMPF-P.COP-2SG
'You *knew* Ömer better than me.'

(34) Genellikle yazın bu rakam art-**makta-ydı**.   (Habitual)
                      -IMPF-P.COP
'This figure *would* usually *increase* in the summer.'

The aorist forms *-(A/I)r/-mAz* never express progressive aspect. In past
habituals *-(A/I)rdI/-mAzdI* are often interchangeable with *-(I)yordu* or
-mAktAydI (or their negative forms):

(35) **(a)** O zamanlarda Mehmet çok sigara iç-**iyor-du**.
                          -IMPF-P.COP
'At that time Mehmet was smoking a lot.'

   (b) O zamanlarda Mehmet çok sigara iç-**er-di**.
                          -AOR-P.COP
'At that time Mehmet smoked/used to smoke a lot/Mehmet
was a heavy smoker.'

The difference in meaning between the two past habitual forms *-(I)yordu*
and *-(A/I)rdI* reflects the 'general rule'/'observed facts' dichotomy between
the aorist and other finite forms, discussed in 21.4.1.1. *-(A/I)rdI* usually
refers to a long-term pattern of behaviour, which in the case of a human
subject is viewed as an inherent characteristic of that person. *-(A/I)rdI* is
potentially ambiguous between the past habitual meaning seen in (35b) and

the counterfactual meaning 'would have . . .' (21.4.1.3), which occurs most typically in the main clause of certain types of conditional sentence.

21.3.3 EVENTS AND STATES

There is a close interaction between aspect marking and the event/state distinction. Although both events and states can be presented from an imperfective viewpoint, perfective aspect occurs only in the expression of events. A number of Turkish verbs, particularly those expressing a bodily posture or a psychological state (perception, cognition or emotion) have a dynamic (event) meaning when used in a perfective form, and a stative (state) meaning when used in a progressive form. Some examples are given below.

	Event	*State*
dur-	'stop'	'stand'
otur-	'sit down'	'be sitting'
yat-	'lie down', 'go to bed'	'lie', 'be in bed'
uyu-	'fall asleep'	'be asleep'
tanı-	'recognize'	'know'

The effect of aspect marking on the meaning of these verbs is illustrated below:

(36) (a) Tülay yan-ım-a ***otur*-du**.   (Event)
Tülay side-1SG.POSS-DAT sit-PF
'Tülay *sat down* beside me.'

(b) Yemek-te Tülay yan-ım-da ***otur*-uyor-du**.   (State)
dinner-LOC Tülay side-1SG.POSS-LOC sit-IMPF-P.COP
'Tülay *was sitting* beside me at dinner.'

In the case of psychological verbs, such as *sevin-* 'be glad' (and some others, such as *üşü-* '(begin to) feel cold'), there is often a high degree of interchangeability between a perfective *-DI* or *-mIş* (expressing entry into a state) and a progressive *-(I)yor* (expressing the state itself):

(37) (a) [Mehmet-in gel-eceğ-in]-e ***sevin*-di**-m.   (Entry into state)
Mehmet-GEN come-VN-3SG.POSS-DAT be.glad-PF-1SG
'I *was/I'm glad* [to hear] that Mehmet's coming.'

(b) [Mehmet'in geleceğin]-e ***sevin*-iyor**-um.   (State)
-IMPF-1SG
'I'*m glad* Mehmet's coming.'

(38) (a) ***Anla-dı*-**n mı?   (Entry into state)
             -PF-2SG INT
             '*Have* you understood?'/'*Do* you understand?'

       (b) ***Anlı-*yor** mu-sun?   (State)
             -IMPF INT-2SG
             '*Do* you understand?'

In the case of some of the verbs that have this dual event/state quality, in particular those involving physical states, it is possible for perfective forms to indicate not just entry into the state (of sleep, sitting, etc.) but the maintenance of that state over a period of time:

(39) Sekiz saat ***uyumuş***um.
       'I *seem to have slept* for eight hours.'

(40) Bütün gün evde ***otur***duk.
       'We *sat* at home all day.'

Turkish also has a small class of verbs which can directly express *only* the entry into a state. The existence of the state at some particular time is expressed by a perfective form. The most important verbs in this class are *acık-* 'get hungry', *susa-* 'get thirsty', *yorul-* 'get tired', *bık-* 'get tired (of)/bored (with)', *kız-* 'get angry', *kal-* 'be left':

(41) Susa-**dı**-m.
       get.thirsty-PF-1SG
       '*I'm* thirsty.'

21.3.4   ASPECT IN NOMINAL SENTENCES

Aspectual marking in nominal sentences requires the presence of the copular verb *ol-* (12.1.1.3) to act as the bearer of one of the aspectual suffixes discussed in 21.3.1. Two particular forms are aspectually significant: *oldu* (contrasting with *-(y)DI/idi* and *vardı*) and *oluyor*.

21.3.4.1   The distinction between *oldu* and *-(y)DI/idi* or *vardı*

In its copular functions the verb *ol-* can have either dynamic or stative meaning, a distinction that generally corresponds to the distinction between 'become' and 'be' in English. The past copular marker *-(y)DI/idi*, on the other hand, being a marker of imperfectivity, can only express states ('be'). This means that the distinction between *oldu* and *-(y)DI/idi* often corresponds to that between 'became' and 'was':

(42) 1994'te Ahmet derneğin başkanı **oldu**.
'In 1994 Ahmet *became* president of the society.'

(43) 1994'te Ahmet derneğin başkanı**ydı**.
'In 1994 Ahmet *was* president of the society.'

However, there are certain kinds of nominal sentence in which *oldu* does not express a change of state (as 'become' does), but rather the outcome of some kind of process of evaluation or ranking.

(44) Geçen hafta-ki toplantı çok sıkıcı **ol-du**.
last week-ADJ meeting very boring be-PF
'Last week's meeting *was* very boring.'

This usage of *oldu* often involves a sequential ordering item such as *ilk* 'first', *son(uncu)* 'last', *ondan sonraki* 'the next', or an ordinal numeral (15.7.2):

(45) Gürkan [bana bu olay-dan bahsed-en] *üçüncü* kişi **ol-du**.
Gürkan I(DAT) this incident-ABL mention-PART third person be-PF
'Gürkan *was* the *third* person [to mention this incident to me].'

The superlative marker *en* 'most' (15.4.3) is another typical element of these evaluative sentences:

(46) [*En* beğenilen] tablo bu **oldu**.
'The picture [that was *most* admired] *was* this one.'

In existential sentences *oldu* expresses the event of coming into existence rather than the (past) state of existing.

(47) Partide [seni soran]lar **oldu**.
'There were people [asking after you] at the party.' (See 25.3.)

(48) Fatma'nın bir kızı **oldu**.
'Fatma (has) had a daughter.'

The same aspectual distinction applies to *olmuş* and *-(y)mIş/imiş*.

21.3.4.2 Habitual aspect in nominal sentences

Habitual aspect in nominal sentences is marked by *oluyor* in non-past contexts and by *oluyordu* or *olurdu* in past contexts. The pairs of sentences below illustrate the difference between a single state that obtains/obtained at some particular moment, and a habitually recurring state:

(49) (a) Şu anda ev-de-yim.
             home-LOC-1SG
             'At the moment I'm at home.'

      (b) Bu saatte ev-de **ol-uyor**-um.
             home-LOC be-IMPF-1SG
             'I'm [usually] at home at this time [of day].'

(50) (a) Ögrenciler o gün neşeli-**ydi**-ler.
             cheerful-P.COP-3PL
             'The students were cheerful that day.'

      (b) Öğrenciler neşeli **ol-uyor**-lar-**dı/ol-ur**-lar-**dı**.
             cheerful be-IMPF-3PL-P.COP/be-AOR-3PL-P.COP
             'The students were (usually/always) cheerful.'

(51) (a) Bu akşam film var.
             'There's a film this evening.'

      (b) Bazı akşamlar film **oluyor**.
             'Some evenings there's a film.'

21.3.4.3 Other meanings of *oluyor*

The copular form *oluyor* is sometimes used in sentences expressing an identification or classification, and has the effect of making a statement sound less abrupt or less categorical. This is a stylistic refinement which is in decreasing use:

(52) Halil benim dayızadem (**oluyor**).
       'Halil is my cousin.' (son of my maternal uncle)

(53) En ucuzu bu (**oluyor**) galiba.
       'This one seems to be the cheapest.'

In some instances of this optional usage of *oluyor* an element of habituality can be detected.

(54) Ortak dilimiz Fransızcaydı/Fransızca **oluyordu**.
       'Our common language was French.'

Another optional usage of *oluyor* occurs where a speaker wants to emphasize the ongoing, subjective experience of a situation, process or activity.

(55) Anne babaları arasındaki bu gerginlik, çocuklar için zor (**oluyor**) tabii.
'This tension between their parents is, of course, hard for the children.'

21.4 MODALITY

Unlike tense and aspect, modality is not related to the concept of time. It is concerned with whether a situation is presented as a directly known fact, or in some other way. A main clause that is marked by one of the following tense/aspect/modality suffixes is *modally neutral*, that is to say it is presented as reflecting a fact directly known to the speaker:

(**i**)   in verbal sentences: *-DI*, *-(I)yor*, *-mAktA*
(**ii**)   in nominal sentences: no marker or *-(y)DI*.

Modalized utterances are of various kinds. They may present:

(**i**)   a generalization, general rule, or statement of principle: *-(A/I)r/ -mAz*, *-DIr* (21.4.1.1)
(**ii**)   an assumption or hypothesis: *-(A/I)r/-mAz*, *-DIr*, *olacak*, *olmalı* (21.4.1.3–4)
(**iii**)   a statement concerning the possibility or necessity of the occurrence of an event or state: *-(y)Abil/-(y)AmA*, *-mAlI* (21.4.2)
(**iv**)   a statement based upon knowledge acquired indirectly: *-mIş*, *-(y)mIş* (21.4.3)
(**v**)   an expression of desire or willingness for an event or state to occur: imperative, optative, conditional and aorist forms (21.4.4).

The suffixes *-mIş* and *-(y)AcAK* have modal force in some contexts but not in others. In the case of *-mIş* this is grammatically determined: *-mIş* becomes purely a tense/aspect marker when followed by *-(y)DI*, *-DIr* or *ol-*. By contrast, whether *-(y)AcAK* is to be understood as marking (unmodally) future tense or (modally) an assumption or an instruction depends on the speech context in a more general way.

21.4.1   GENERALIZATIONS AND HYPOTHESES

The Turkish system of modality marking allows for a distinction to be made between (neutral) statements that reflect the direct experience, knowledge or observation of the speaker, and (modal) statements that make assertions of a more general, theoretical nature, or express assumptions or hypotheses. The grammatical markers that express these types of modality are predominantly the aorist forms *-(A/I)r/-mAz* in verbal sentences and the generalizing modality marker *-DIr* in nominal sentences.

21.4.1.1 Statements of permanent or generalized validity

Verbal sentences with aorist

In reviewing the types of generalization that are expressed by the aorist, we shall compare statements expressed in this form with the corresponding statements marked with the imperfective marker *-(I)yor*. In its habitual aspect sense (21.3.2), *-(I)yor* expresses a different kind of generalization from the aorist, one that refers to a state of affairs which has been directly observed or experienced by the speaker, without implying that it has the status of a rule or principle.

There are four main types of generalization expressed by the aorist:

(**i**) Scientific and moral axioms:

    (56) İki, iki daha dört ed-**er**.
           two two more four make-AOR
           'Two and two make four.'

    (57) Para mutluluk getir-**mez**.
           money happiness bring-NEG.AOR
           'Money doesn't bring happiness.'

In contrast with (57), which claims to be a universal truth, (58) reflects the speaker's own experience or observation from life.

    (58) Para mutluluk getir-mi-**yor**.
                     -NEG-IMPF
           'Money doesn't bring happiness.'

(**ii**) Normative or prescriptive statements:

The use of the aorist is standard in text types ranging from constitutions to recipes, that lay down a procedure that is to be followed. However, such statements are usually capable of either a descriptive or a prescriptive reading:

    (59) Başbakan, Cumhurbaşkanı tarafından görevlendiril**ir**.
           'The Prime Minister is appointed by the President.'

    (60) Burada musluk suyu içil**mez**.
           'One doesn't drink the tap water here.' (lit. 'the tap water is not drunk')

The corresponding form with *-(I)yor*, on the other hand, is more descriptive:

    (61) Burada musluk suyu içil**miyor**.
          'Here people do not drink the tap water.' (lit. 'the tap water is not drunk')

The passive of the negative aorist form is regularly used in public notices expressing prohibitions:

    (62) *Girilmez*   'No entry'
           Park yapılmaz   'No parking'

(**iii**)   Generic statements about the characteristic qualities or behaviour of a class:

    (63) Kaplumbağa yavaş yürür.
          'A tortoise walks slowly.'

    (64) Amerika'lılar çok süt içer.
          '(The) Americans drink a lot of milk.'

The substitution of *-(I)yor* for the aorist in sentences like (63), where the subject is bare, changes the reference of this noun phrase from generic to specific (see 22.7). Thus in (65) *kaplumbağa* refers to a specific tortoise:

    (65) Kaplumbağa yavaş yürü**yor**.
          'The tortoise *walks/is walking* slowly.'

In (66) the plural-marked *Amerika'lılar* could retain its generic reading (see 22.7), but could also refer to a specific group of Americans:

    (66) Amerika'lılar çok süt iç**iyor**.
          'The Americans *are drinking/drink* a lot of milk.'

(**iv**) Statements about the characteristic qualities or behaviour of an individual:

    (67) Ali sigara iç-**mez**.
                    -NEG.AOR
          'Ali doesn't smoke.'

    (68) Ali sigara iç-**mi-yor**.
                    -NEG.IMPF
          'Ali doesn't smoke.'

(67) could be paraphrased as 'Ali is a non-smoker'. Its counterpart (68) merely describes Ali's observed habitual behaviour. This difference in meaning is underlined by the fact that an adverbial restricting the time span to which the statement applies, such as *bu günlerde* 'at the moment' (16.4.1.1), would be possible only with *içmiyor*:

(69) Ali *bu günlerde* sigara iç-**mi-yor**.
'Ali's not smoking *at the moment*.'

Nominal sentences with -*DIr*

One of the functions of the generalizing modality marker -*DIr* in a nominal sentence is to define or classify a subject, or to ascribe certain permanent qualities or inherent characteristics to it. However, this usage of -*DIr* is nowadays largely confined to formal language.

(70) Antropoloji, [insan topluluklarını inceleyen] bir bilim(**dir**).
'Anthropology is a science which studies human communities.'

Where a generalization ascribes a certain quality to an entire class, and the subject complement is adjectival, the informal counterpart of -*DIr* is not the absence of a marker, as above, but *olur* or *oluyor* (cf. 21.3.4.2 for *oluyor* as a marker of habitual aspect). These forms give the statement a less absolute, more modest tone than -*DIr*. Like other -*(I)yor* forms, *oluyor* conveys the idea that the utterance reflects the speaker's own experience:

(71) Çocuklar bencil **ol-ur/ol-uyor**.
be-AOR/be-IMPF
'Children are selfish.'

21.4.1.2   The use of -*DIr* in formal writing

In academic and other formal writing, and in official announcements made orally (for example on radio and television), the use of -*DIr* is by no means confined to nominal sentences. -*DIr* is also regularly affixed to the following finite verbal forms: -*mIş*, -*(y)AcAK*, -*mAlI*, -*mAktA*.

(72) Osmanlı Türkleri de bu kültüre katkıda bulun*muş*lar**dır**.
'And the Ottoman Turks contributed to this culture.'

(73) Bu teknik, [[yüzeysel yapıları farklı olan] eserlerin karşılaştırılmasın]-ı kolaylaştır**acaktır**.
'This technique will facilitate the comparison of works [which have different surface structures].'

In terms of their tense/aspect values, the following correspondences hold:

-mIştIr	*-DI*	past tense, perfective aspect
-(y)AcAktIr	*-(y)AcAK*	future tense
-mAktAdIr	*-(I)yor, -mAktA*	present tense, progressive or habitual aspect

It should be noted that the *-mIş* component of *-mIştIr* has no (evidential) modality value of its own; it is purely past/perfective. The modal function of *-DIr* in these verbal sentences is to indicate that a claim of some signif-icance is being made, and that this is based on some well-founded authority which gives it a kind of permanence that transcends the explicit tense marking of its content.

21.4.1.3 Hypothetical and counterfactual situations

Hypothetical and counterfactual situations imply the fulfilment of some condition (27.2.3–6):

(74) Koşma, düşersin.
'Don't run; you'll fall over.' (i.e. Don't run; if you do . . .)

(75) Senden iyi mühendis ol**ur**.
'You would make a good engineer.' (lit. 'From you [a] good engineer would come into existence.')

Counterfactual situations differ from hypotheticals in that the condition upon which they depend is known to be unrealizable. They are expressed by *-(A/I)rdI/-mAzdI* or *-(y)AcAktI*:

(76) Ben bu reng-i seç-**mez-di**-m.
I this colour-ACC choose-NEG.AOR-P.COP-1SG
'I wouldn't have chosen this colour.'

-(y)AcAktI is an option only where reference is to a pre-planned or sched-uled event:

(77) [O konser-e git-mek] hoş ol-**ur-du**/ol-**acak-tı**.
that concert-DAT go-VN nice be-AOR-P.COP/be-FUT-P.COP
'It *would have* been nice [to go to that concert].'

In counterfactual utterances the past copula *-(y)DI* is as much a marker of modality as of tense, and the reference is not always to past time (27.2.3.2).

21.4.1.4 Assumptions

In Turkish the principal markers of non-factual probability judgements are the aorist and *-DIr*. Assumptions expressed with these forms are usually also marked by a modal adverbial (16.3) such as *kesinlikle* 'definitely', *herhalde* 'probably', 'presumably', 'I expect', or *belki* 'perhaps', which expresses the strength of the speaker's confidence in the soundness of the assumption. Where no modal adverbial is used the utterance will usually be understood as having the medium strength of an assumption marked by *herhalde*. It is important to note that assumptions do not have to be grammatically marked in Turkish. The non-factual modality of such utterances is often indicated simply by the presence of a modal adverbial. We include within the category of assumptions expressions of hope marked by the modal adverbial *umarım* 'I hope' or *inşallah* 'God willing', 'hopefully'.

(i) Verbal sentences with *-(A/I)r/-mAz*:
Assumptions expressed with the aorist always have future time reference, and denote events that are not envisaged as planned or predetermined:

(78) Mehmet geç gel-**ir**.
     late come-AOR
   'Mehmet will (probably) be late.'

(79) ***Umarım*** Semra vazonun yokluğunu farket-**mez**.
              notice-NEG.AOR
   'I hope Semra won't notice the absence of the vase.'

(ii) Nominal and verbal sentences with *-DIr*:
A striking feature of assumptions expressed with *-DIr* is that in this type of utterance *-DIr* is attached not only to 3rd person but also to 1st and 2nd person predicates (see 8.3.3).

(80) ***İnşallah*** hasta değil-im-**dir**.
   hopefully ill not-1SG-GM
   '*I hope* I'm not ill.'

(81) ***Herhalde*** bir yerlerde karşılaş-**mış**-ız-**dır**.
             -PF-1PL-GM
   'We *have probably* met somewhere or other.'

(82) ***Mutlaka*** bugün telefon ed-**ecek**-ler-**dir**.
           -FUT-3PL-GM
   'They *will definitely* ring today.'

-(y)AcAKtIr expresses the assumption that the predicted action is planned or otherwise predetermined. (82) therefore expresses greater confidence in the realization of the prediction than if the aorist had been used.

(iii) Probability statements with *olsa gerek*:
This construction (the conditional form of the copular/auxiliary verb *ol-* followed by *gerek* 'necessary') is used mostly in the 3rd person:

(83) En iyisi bu **olsa gerek**.
'This one is *probably* the best.'

olsa gerek occurs also in compound verb forms (21.5).

(iv) Non-future predictions with *olacak*:
The future form of *ol-* can be used with present tense reference to make a confident statement about an entity that is not within sight at the moment of speech, but is near enough for the prediction to be immediately verified:

(84) A.– Zarflar nerede?
'Where are the envelopes?'

B.– İkinci çekmecede **olacak**lar.
'They'*ll be* in the second drawer.'

For the occurrence of this usage of *olacak* in compound verb forms, see 21.5.1.

(v) Assumptive use of *olması gerek/lazım*:
The construction *-mA*-POSS *gerek/lazım* is one of the means of expressing objective necessity, as explained in 21.4.2.2. The 3rd person form with the copular/auxiliary *ol-* as the verb can have the secondary function of expressing a strong assumption based upon knowledge of other relevant facts. The time reference is either present or, where there is a preceding verb form with *-mIş*, past:

(85) Bu saatte [Ali'nin işte **olması**] **lazım**.
'Ali *must be* at work at this hour.' (I know his hours of work.)

(86) [Herkesin afişi gör***müş* olması**] **gerek**.
'Everyone *must have* seen the notice.' (It was in an obvious place.)

(vi) Deductions with *olmalı*:
The obligative form (see below, 21.4.2.2) of the copular/auxiliary verb *ol-* expresses an inference drawn about a past or present event or state from

strong circumstantial evidence. In nominal sentences the time reference is present tense:

(87) Kapı açık, evde **olmalı**lar.
'The door's open; they *must be* at home.'

For the use of *olmalı* following the *-mIş* or *-(I)yor* form of another verb, see 21.5.1–2.

21.4.2 POSSIBILITY AND NECESSITY

The concepts of possibility and necessity differ from other types of modality in having objective components that are independent of the speaker's perception or attitude. *Ahmet can swim two kilometres* and *The card has to be inserted slowly* are examples respectively of **objective possibility** and **objective necessity**.

21.4.2.1 The expression of possibility

The suffixes which mark possibility and impossibility are the verbal suffixes *-(y)Abil* and *-(y)AmA* (the latter incorporating the negative marker *-mA*). The markers of possibility and impossibility enter into a wide range of combinations with the markers of tense, aspect, and other types of modality. Non-finite verb forms can also be marked for (im)possibility:

(88) konuş-**abil**-mek
talk-PSB-VN
'to *be able to* talk'

(89) gör-**e-me**-yen-ler
see-PSB-NEG-PART-PL
'those *unable to* see'

Where *-(y)Abil* is added to the negative stem of a verb, it denotes the possibility of the action *not* occurring, or the freedom of the subject not to perform it:

(90) söyle-***me*-yebil**-mek
say-NEG-PSB-VN
'to *be able not to* say'

Objective possibility and the question of actualization

Objective possibility denotes either the ability of a person to perform a certain action, or the absence of any impediment to the occurrence of an event. In statements of objective possibility the choice of tense/aspect/ modality marking (following *-(y)Abil/-(y)AmA*) determines whether the possibility or impossibility is understood as **actualized** (taking effect) or not.

Statements with aorist marking simply assert that the possibility of some-thing happening exists or does not exist, leaving the question of actualization open. Aorist-marked (im)possibility statements fall into one or other of the categories of modalized statement typically expressed by the aorist:

(i)   Statements of generalized validity (21.4.1.1):

    (91) Kaplumbağa hızlı yürü-**ye-mez**. (cf. (63))
                    walk-PSB-NEG.AOR
        'A tortoise *can't* walk fast.'

(ii)   Hypothetical statements (21.4.1.3):

    (92) Masayı şuraya koy**abilir**iz.
        'We *can/could* put the table here.' (If we so decide(d).)

The combination of aorist *-(y)Abilir* or *-(y)AmA(z)* with the past copular marker *-(y)DI* produces counterfactual meaning, i.e. implies that an action envisaged as having been possible at some time in the past was not actualized:

    (93) Daha uygun bir saat seç**ebilirdi**niz.
        'You *could have* chosen a more convenient time.' (Implies that you didn't.)

(iii) Assumptions and conjectures with future time reference (21.4.1.4 (i)):

    (94) Belki bunca zamandan sonra birbirimizi tanı-**ya-ma**-yız.
                              recognize-PSB-NEG-1PL
        'Maybe we *won't be able to* recognize each other after all this time.'

In contrast to possibility statements with aorist marking, those marked with *-DI*, *-mIş*, *-(I)yor* or *-mAktA* (with or without a following *-(y)DI*) always imply the actualization of the possibility or impossibility:

    (95) Geçen yıl Bodrum'a dört defa gid-**ebil-*di***-k.
                             go-PSB-PF-1PL
        'Last year we *were able to* go to Bodrum four times.'
        (Implies that we did this.)

(96) Filiz o gün oğluyla konuş-**a-ma-*mış*-*tı***.
                      talk-PSB-NEG-PF-P.COP
     'Filiz *hadn't been able to* talk to her son that day.'
     (Implies that she had not talked to him.)

In future contexts the question of actualization does not arise. The combination of (im)possibility marking with the future marker *-(y)AcAK* simply indicates that a possibility (or the lack of it) is or was regarded as certain to occur at some time in the future:

(97) Yeni evimizden işime bisikletle gid**emey*eceğ*im**.
     'From our new house I *shan't be able to* go to work by bicycle.'

The form *-(y)Abiliyor* can additionally be used to express the fact that a situation tends to occur from time to time:

(98) Plastik parçalar zamanla aşın**abil*iyor***.
     'The parts made of plastic *can/tend to* erode with time.'

Speaker-generated possibility
Speaker-generated possibility (as distinct from objective possibility) is of two types: **permissive** and **speculative**.

(i) Permissive possibility:
The granting of permission by the speaker to the hearer(s) or to a third party is expressed by *-(y)Abilir*:

(99) Bilgisayarımı [ne zaman istersen] kullan-**abil-ir**-sin.
                                  use-PSB-AOR-2SG
     'You *can* use my computer [whenever you like].'
     (I give you permission to do so.)

Prohibition is expressed by *-(y)AmAz*:

(100) Burada otur-**a-maz**-sınız.
            sit-PSB-NEG.AOR-2PL
      'You *can't* sit here.' (I/We don't allow it.)

Requests for permission are expressed with the 1st person interrogative of the above forms:

(101) Bir şey sor**abilir** miyim?
      '*Can/May* I ask something?'

(ii) Speculative possibility:
A statement of speculative possibility expresses a judgement about the possibility of some event occurring. It is usually expressed with -(y)Abilir:

(102) Bugün yağmur yağ**abilir**.
'It *may/could* rain today.'

Occasionally, speculative possibility is expressed with -(y)AbileceK. The use of this form effectively neutralizes the distinction between objective and speculative possibility, and gives a greater sense of authority to a statement about the possible occurrence of a future event:

(103) Bu evler birkaç yıl sonra yıkıl**abilecek**.
'These houses *may* be demolished in a few years' time.'

Speculations with -(y)Abilir can be expressed about negative or (objectively) impossible situations as well as positive ones:

(104) Yağmur yağ-***ma*-yabil-ir**.
NEG-PSB-AOR
'It *may not* rain.'/'It'*s possible (that)* it wo*n't* rain.'

(105) Coşkun'u ikna ed-***e-me*-yebil-ir**-im.
AUX-PSB-NEG-PSB-AOR-1SG
'I *may not* be able to persuade Coşkun.'

With verbs in general the negative possibility aorist form -(y)AmAz does not occur with speculative meaning. However, in the case of the copular/auxiliary *ol-* 'be', this form can be used to negate a speculative possibility on the basis of other known facts:

(106) Osman Ankara'da ol**amaz**.
'Osman *can't* be in Ankara.' (e.g. because I saw him in London an hour ago)

(107) Sen bu ceketimi daha önce gör-***müş*** ol-**a-maz**-sın.
see-PF AUX-PSB-NEG.AOR-2SG
'You *can't have* seen this jacket of mine before.'
(e.g. because I have only just bought it)

Ambiguity of -*(y)Abilir*
In sentences expressing events in which human agency is involved, the sequence -(y)Abilir is potentially ambiguous between objective, speculative and permissive readings:

(108) Ahmet tez-in-i bu oda-da yaz-**abil-ir**.
          thesis-3SG.POSS-ACC this room-LOC write-PSB-AOR
(**a**) 'Ahmet *can/could* write his thesis in this room.' (There is nothing to prevent him from doing this.) (*objective*)
(**b**) 'Ahmet *can* write his thesis in this room.' (I permit him to use the room for this purpose.) (*permissive*)
(**c**) 'Ahmet *may* write his thesis in this room.' (I consider it possible that he will decide to do so/Perhaps he will do so.) (*speculative*)

The expression of possibility in subordinate clauses formed with -*DIK*/-*(y)AcAK*

As explained elsewhere in this book, certain types of subordinate clause in Turkish involve a choice between -*DIK* and -*(y)AcAK* as the verbal marker:

(**i**)   noun clauses expressing indirect statements and questions (24.4.3)
(**ii**)   certain types of relative clause (25.1.1.2)
(**iii**) certain types of adverbial clause (26.2, 26.3).

The distinction in meaning between these two forms is generally one of tense, with -*DIK* expressing relative present or relative past, and -*(y)AcAK* relative future. However, where one of these suffixes is combined with a possibility marker, the -*DIK*/-*(y)AcAK* distinction often involves modality as much as tense. The combinations -*(y)AbildiK* and -*(y)AmAdIK* always express actualized possibility/impossibility:

(109) [Selim-in neden bun-u anla-**ya-ma-dığ**-ın]-ı bilmiyordum.
      Selim-GEN why this-ACC understand-PSB-NEG-VN-3SG.POSS-ACC
      'I didn't know [why Selim *couldn't* understand this].'
      (Implies that he did not understand it.)

By contrast, the combinations -*(y)AbileceK* and -*(y)AmAyAcAK* have a number of different modal values in subordinate clauses:

(**i**)   An objective possibility (or impossibility) that is expected to be actualized at some (relative) future time. This usage is equivalent to -*(y)AbileceK* in finite clauses:

(110) [Toplantıya katıl-**a-ma-yacağ**-ım]-ı söyledim.
                attend-PSB-NEG-VN-1SG.POSS-ACC
      'I said [I *wouldn't be able to* attend the meeting].'

(111) Kartı [herkesin gör-**ebil-eceğ**-i] bir yere koymuştu.
      see-PSB-PART-3SG.POSS
  'S/he had put the card in a place where everyone *would be able
to* see it.'

(**ii**) Two of the kinds of objective possibility that are articulated by the
aorist combinations *-(y)Abilir* and *-(y)AmA(z)* in finite clauses, in which
the question of actualization is unresolved:

Generalizations:

(112) [Yaşlıların gençleri kıskan**abilecek**lerin]-i herkes bilir.
  'Everyone knows [that the old *can* be jealous of the young].'

Hypothetical situations:

(113) [O çocuğun yap**amayacağ**ı] hiçbir şey yok.
  'There is nothing [that boy *couldn't* do].' (If he set his mind to it)

(**iii**) Counterfactual situations (expressed in finite clauses by *-(y)Abilirdi*
and *-(y)AmAzdI*):

(114) Osman [Ali'ye yardım ed**ebileceğ**i halde] hiçbir şey yapmadı.
  ['Although Osman *could have* helped Ali], he did nothing.'

(**iv**) Permissive possibility and its denial:

(115) Özdemir'e [bilgisayarımı kullan**abileceğ**in]-i söyledim. (cf. 99))
  'I told Özdemir [that he *could* use my computer].'

(**v**) The affirmative form *-(y)AbileceK* (attached to a positive or negative
stem) can express speculative possibility:

(116) [Başkanlık konusunda Coşkun'u ikna ed***emeyebileceğ***im için]
  başka kişiler üzerinde de durmamız gerekiyor. (cf. (105))
  '[As I *may not be able to* persuade Coşkun about the
  chairmanship,] we have to consider other people too.'

As in the case of aorist impossibility forms in finite clauses, the subordinate impossibility combination *-(y)AmAyAcAK* can be used in a
speculative context only when attached to the copula/auxiliary *ol-*:

(117) [Osman'ın Ankara'da ol**amayacağ**ın]-ı biliyordum. (cf. (106))
  'I knew [that Osman *couldn't* be in Ankara].'

21.4.2.2   The expression of necessity/obligation

The grammatical marker of necessity (or obligation) in Turkish is the suffix
-mAlI.

> (118) (a)   Ankara-ya git-**meli**-yim.
> Ankara-DAT go-OBLG-1SG
> 'I *must* go to Ankara.'

Necessity is also regularly expressed by lexical means. This involves articulating the action that is considered necessary as a non-finite noun clause
(24.4.1–2), which is then treated in one of the following ways:

(i)   As the subject of a nominal sentence with *gerek/lazım* 'necessary' or
şart 'essential' as the complement:

> (118) (b)   [Ankara-ya git-me-m] **lazım/gerek/şart**.
> Ankara-DAT goVN-1SG.POSS necessary/essential
> 'I have to go to Ankara.'/'It's essential for me to go to
> Ankara.' (lit. '[My going to Ankara] is *necessary/essential*.')

(ii)   As the subject of a verbal sentence with *gerek-* 'be necessary' as the
predicate:

> (118) (c)   [Ankara'ya git-me-m] **gerek**-iyor.
> go-VN-1SG.POSS be.necessary-IMPF
> 'I have to go to Ankara.' (lit. '[My going to Ankara] is
> *necessary*.')

(iii)   As the modifier in a *-(s)I* compound of which the head is *zor/
∇mecburiyet* 'compulsion' or *durum* 'situation':

> (118) (d)   [Ankara'ya git-mek] **zor**-un-da-yım/**durum**-un-da-yım.
> go-VN compulsion-NC-LOC-1SG/
> situation-NC-LOC-1SG
> 'I have to/am obliged to go to Ankara.' (lit. 'I am in the
> *compulsion/situation* of [going to Ankara].')

Note that *zorunda* also has an obsolescent synonym *∇mecburiyetinde* (from
mecburiyet 'obligation'). The use of *durumunda* in this construction is
slightly more formal than *zorunda*, and is not favoured by all speakers.

   All four versions of the statement in (118) refer to an obligation that is
presented as existing at the moment of speech but not (yet) fulfilled. In
many contexts they could be used interchangeably. However, apart from
the fact that the constructions with *şart* and *zorunda* express a stronger,

more unavoidable obligation than those with *gerek*, *lazım* or *gerek-*, there is a more fundamental difference between *-mAlI* (118a), on the one hand, and all the lexicalized constructions (118b–d) on the other. *-mAlI* expresses an obligation perceived or imposed by the speaker (**speaker-generated**), while the lexicalized constructions present an **objective** obligation, that is, one arising from external factors operating independently of the speaker. The difference corresponds roughly to that between 'must' and 'have to' in English.

In addition to the personalized forms illustrated in (118), objective necessity can also be expressed impersonally, with a *-mAk* clause (24.4.1.1) as the subject of *lazım* or *gerek-*:

(119) [Burasını da doldurmak] **gerek**iyor mu?
       '*Is it necessary to/Does one have to* fill in this part as well?'

Speaker-generated obligation: *-mAlI*
A sentence marked with *-mAlI* that has a 1st person subject expresses an action which the speaker feels obliged (often morally obliged) to perform (but has not yet done so):

(120) Mustafa'ya yardım et**meli**yiz.
       'We *must* help Mustafa.'

Where the subject is 2nd or 3rd person the utterance is tantamount to the speaker's imposing an obligation on that other person or persons:

(121) Önce annene sor**malı**sın.
       'You *must* first ask your mother.'

Sometimes the 3rd person singular form is used with impersonal meaning:

(122) Bence bu sorunu bir an önce hallet**meli**.
       'If you ask me, this problem *ought to* be solved as soon as possible.' (lit. 'one ought to solve . . .')

The affixation of *-mAlI* to a negative stem expresses an obligation *not* to behave in a certain way:

(123) [Beni gördüğün]-ü hiç kimseye söyle-*me*-**meli**-sin.
                                    tell-NEG-OBLG-2SG
       'You *mustn't* tell anyone [that you saw me].'

The addition of the past copular marker *-(y)DI* to *-mAlI* produces one of two possible meanings:

(i)   In the great majority of cases it gives a counterfactual reading (cf. 21.4.1.3). In other words, it indicates that an obligation perceived by the speaker was not fulfilled at the time that it obtained.

(124)   O para-yı geri ver-**meli-ydi**-n.
that money-ACC back give-OBLG-P.COP-2SG
'You *ought to have* given that money back.' (But you didn't.)

(ii)   In the context of a narrative, *-mAllydI* sometimes projects an obligation on to an actor at a particular juncture in the narrative. The outcome of this obligation is unknown at this point in the story, i.e. the question of actualization remains open:

(125)   Hüseyin artık karar ver**meliydi**. Herkesi bu kadar oyalaması ayıptı.
'Hüseyin *must* now take a decision. It was disgraceful for him to keep everyone waiting so long.'

Deductions expressed with *olmalı* (discussed above in 21.4.1.4 (vi)) constitute a quite different kind of speaker-generated necessity.

Objective necessity and its actualization
As in the case of objective possibility, the choice of grammatical marking for the predicate not only indicates tense and aspect, but also distinguishes between statements or questions which imply the actualization (fulfilment) of the obligation and those which do not carry such an implication.

Non-actualized obligation
The means of expressing a non-actualized obligation existing at the moment of speech were discussed above in connection with (118). In a narrative context, an obligation that arose in the past can similarly be presented without indicating whether the obligation was fulfilled or not. This is done by adding the past copular marker to any of the structures exemplified in (118), as in (126), where the listener/reader is not informed at this stage whether or not the narrator actually went on to say something:

(126)   Herkes bana bakıyordu. Artık bir şey söylemem
gerekiyor*du*/söylemek **zorunday***dım*.
'Everyone was looking at me. Now I *had to* say something.'

The forms *lazımdı* and *gerekiyordu* can also be used counterfactually, like *-mAllydI*, discussed above:

(127)   Dünkü toplantıda bu konuyu konuşmamız **gerekiyordu**.
'We *were supposed to* discuss this at yesterday's meeting.'
(But we didn't.)

Actualized obligation
The suffixes *-DI*, *-mIş* and *-(y)AcAK* imply the actualization of an obligation (because of its unavoidable nature). The suffix *-(I)yor*, on the other
hand, is ambiguous with regard to actuality. The constructions that occur
with actualizing meaning are:

(**i**)   *-mA*-POSS *gerek-*
(**ii**) V-*mA*-POSS *lazım gel-*
(**iii**) *-mAk zorunda kal-*

Examples of actualized obligation using the above forms are given below:

(**i**)   A specific event in the past:

>   (128) (**a**) [Zeki-ye yüz dolar ver-***me-m***] ***gerek***-ti.
>   Zeki-DAT hundred dollar give-VN-1SG.POSS be.necessary-PF

>   (**b**) [Zeki-ye yüz dolar ver-***mek***] ***zor-un-da kal***-dı-m.
>   give-VN compulsion-NC-LOC be.left-PF-1SG
>   'I *had to* give Zeki a hundred dollars.' (And therefore I did.)

(**ii**)   Recurrent obligation:
The only forms which unambiguously imply the actualization of a recurring
obligation are *-mAk zorunda kalıyor(du)*:

>   (129) **Her ay** Zeki'ye yüz dolar ver-***mek zor***-un-da kal-ıyor-um/
>   -IMPF-1SG/
>   kal-ıyor-du-m.
>   -IMPF-P.COP-1SG
>   'I *have/had to* give Zeki a hundred dollars *a month*.'
>   (And therefore I do/did.)

The use of *vermem gerekiyor(du)* would be equally grammatical in (129),
but would make the sentence ambiguous as to whether the obligation was
fulfilled or avoided. (See (118c), (126) and (127) above for sentences where
gerekiyor(du) has been given a non-actualized or even (in the case of (127))
a counterfactual interpretation.)

(**iii**)   Firmly expected future (or relative future) obligation:
Actualization is not an issue in future contexts, because of their inherent
unknowability. The marking of an obligational expression with *-(y)AcAK*
simply indicates that the obligation itself is or was regarded as certain to
occur at some time in the future:

(130) Yakında yeni bir televizyon al-***ma-mız gerek*-ecek**(-ti).
                                   buy-VN-1PL.POSS be.necessary-FUT-
                                   P.COP
        'Soon we shall (would) have to buy a new television.'

The expression of necessity in subordinate clauses
In subordinate clauses necessity and obligation can be expressed only by using one of the constructions with *gerek-* (or ∇*lazım gel-*), *zorunda kal-* or (for obligations that are in existence at the time on which attention is focused) *zorunda ol-*. The distinctions between objective and speaker-generated, and between actualized and non-actualized, necessity are neutralized in these non-finite constructions.

(131) (**a**) Adam [gitmesi **gerek**-tiğ-in]-i söyledi.
                           be.necessary-VN-3SG.POSS-ACC
       (**b**) Adam [gitmek **zor-un-da ol**-duğ-un]-u söyledi.
                           compulsion-NC-LOC be-VN-3SG.POSS-ACC
        'The man said [he *had to* go].'

For the omission of genitive marking on the subject of a noun clause such as that in (131) see 24.4.6 (iii).

21.4.3 EVIDENTIALLY MARKED STATEMENTS WITH
      -mIş OR *-(y)mIş*

Another major category of speaker-generated modality consists of statements based upon knowledge acquired indirectly. This is called **evidential** modality, and is marked in Turkish by the verbal suffix *-mIş*, which (as explained in 21.2.1 and 21.3.1) also marks relative past tense and perfective aspect, and the copular suffix *-(y)mIş*, which is purely a marker of evidential modality. The source of the indirect knowledge upon which these statements are based is usually either a statement made by someone else (in speech or in writing) or a resultant state (e.g. a flat tyre as an indicator of the tyre having burst). In the case of *-(y)mIş* the modality marker sometimes simply indicates that the statement expresses a new discovery on the part of the speaker, which has not yet been fully assimilated to his/her existing stock of knowledge.

For the use of the modal adverbial *meğer(se)* in evidentially marked statements see 16.3 (iv).

21.4.3.1 Information-based evidential statements

When speakers are transmitting information that they have received verbally from any other source (oral or written), they give their statement evidential marking. Use of evidential marking is not a matter of choice in Turkish. Failure to use it when making a statement about a situation of which one has no direct knowledge is a breach of conversational conventions, because it suggests that a different kind of knowledge (personal experience or observation) is involved. The English equivalents of *-mIş/ -(y)mIş* in this usage are expressions like 'apparently', 'it seems', 'I gather'.

The way in which the verbal suffix *-mIş* replaces *-DI* in the verbal transmission of information is illustrated in (132), which represents three separate, consecutive encounters between the individuals involved:

(132) **(a)** (Ali, to Gül): Bahçe-ye bir meşe ağac-ı dik-**ti**-m.
garden-DAT an oak tree-NC plant-PF-1SG
'I've planted an oak tree in the garden.'

(b) (Gül, to Orhan): Ali bahçe-sin-e bir meşe ağacı dik-**miş**.
garden-3SG.POSS-DAT   -EV/PF
'Ali has *apparently* planted an oak tree in his garden.'

(c) (Orhan, to Ali): Sen bir meşe ağacı dik-**miş**-sin, bana
              -EV/PF-2SG
göstersene.
'*I've heard* you've planted an oak tree; why don't you show it to me?'

(133a) could be from a newspaper report:

(133) **(a)** İki tarafın temsilcileri Hilton Oteli'nde bir araya gel**di**ler.
'Representatives of the two sides met at the Hilton Hotel.'

(b) (Ahmet, having read this news, relaying it to Gürkan:)
İki tarafın temsilcileri Hilton Oteli'nde bir araya gel**miş**ler.

If the information received and transmitted by a speaker is anything other than a completed, past-tense event, the evidential copular marker *-(y)mIş* is used. Unlike the verbal suffix *-mIş*, the copular *-(y)mIş* has no tense or aspect content. The aspectual meaning of a sentence with *-(y)mIş* is identical with that of the same sentence without evidential marking. However, the fact that not more than one copular marker may appear together on one verb gives rise to an ambiguity of tense reference (non-past/past) in *-(y)mIş* sentences, which can be resolved only by a time adverbial or by the discourse context:

(134) **(a)** (Ayşe, to Çiğdem): Annem biraz rahatsız.
              'My mother is not very well.'

(b) (Çiğdem, to Nesrin): Ayşe'nin annesi biraz rahatsız-**mış**.
　　　　　　　　　　　　　　　　　　　　unwell-EV.COP
　　　　　'*It seems* Ayşe's mother is not very well.'

(135)　**(a)**　(Ayşe, to Çiğdem): *O gün* annem biraz rahatsız**dı**.
　　　　　　　'My mother was not very well *that day*.'

　　　　(b)　(Çiğdem, to Nesrin): *O gün* Ayşe'nin annesi biraz rahatsız**mış**.
　　　　　　　　'*Apparently* Ayşe's mother was not very
　　　　　　　　well *that day*.'

The information-based evidential is relatively uncommon in the 1st and
2nd persons. In 1st person utterances it may express information that the
speaker has acquired from others about what s/he did when too young to
remember, or while asleep or unconscious:

(136)　[Bir yaş-ın-da-yken] kalp ameliyat-ı ol-**muş**-um.
　　　　one age-NC-LOC-CV heart operation-NC AUX-EV.COP-1SG
　　　　'I had a heart operation [when I was a year old].'

Alternatively, it may express what the speaker presents as a view of him/her
held by other people:

(137)　Sözde inatçı-**ymış**-ım.
　　　　supposedly obstinate-EV.COP-1SG
　　　　'I am supposedly obstinate.'

An information-based 2nd person evidential utterance presents to the
hearer some information about himself/herself that the speaker has
acquired from another source.

(138)　Siz babamla tanışıyor**muş**sunuz galiba.
　　　　'*I believe* you know/knew my father.'

21.4.3.2　Result-based evidential statements

Another use of the verbal suffix *-mIş* is to express the occurrence of an
event that the speaker did not witness but is able to infer from its result,
to which s/he has direct access. For example, any comment on a manufac-
tured item which refers to something that was evidently done or not done
during the course of its production requires to be expressed in this form.
The same applies to the reporting of an accidental event such as a burst or
breakage, which the speaker did not witness but whose result s/he has
encountered.

(139) (Commenting on a painting)
Ressam iki figürün arasını boş bırak**mış**.
'The painter has left the space between the two figures empty.'

(140) (On finding one's glasses are not in one's bag/pocket)
Gözlüğümü yanıma alma**mışım**.
'I *seem* not to have brought my glasses with me.'

21.4.3.3 Use of the evidential copula to express a newly discovered state of affairs

Another use of the evidential copula *-(y)mIş* is to indicate that the state of affairs described is a new discovery as far as the speaker is concerned. There is often an element of surprise.

(141) (On opening the fridge)
Aaa, yiyecek hiçbir şey yok**muş**.
'Oh, there's absolutely nothing to eat.'

(142) (First comment to a friend after meeting his sister)
Kardeşin pek tatlı**ymış**.
'Your sister is lovely.'

21.4.3.4 Evidentiality in questions

The function of an evidential marker in a question differs from its function in a statement in one fundamental respect. Here it is not the speaker's own knowledge but the hearer's that is being marked as indirect. If the speaker anticipates that, in answering his/her question, the hearer will be passing on information gained indirectly, or presenting a new discovery, s/he will recognize this by marking the question evidentially:

(143) (Addressed to someone reading the financial page of the newspaper)
Bugün dolar ne kadar**mış**?
'How much *does it say* the dollar is today?'

(144) (Addressed to someone who has gone into the kitchen)
Fasulye ol**muş** mu?
'Do the beans *seem* to be done?'

21.4.4 VOLITIONAL UTTERANCES

Volitional utterances are not statements, but expressions of the speaker's (or in interrogative forms the hearer's) will or desire in relation to the situation expressed.

21.4.4.1 Wishes: -sA(ydI)

Apart from being used adverbially to express conditions (Chapter 27), the verb forms -sA/-sAydI express wishes.

(i) 1st person forms of -sA can express a fully realizable wish to perform some action:

(145) Bu akşam güzel bir film seyret-**se**-k.
                      watch-COND-1PL
      '*It would be nice* to watch a good film this evening.'

(ii) -sA can also express wishes whose fulfilment is beyond the speaker's control, and may be actually impossible. These correspond to constructions with 'if only' in English, and are optionally marked by the particle *keşke* 'if only', or by the adverbial *bir* 'once' (which, if present, usually occupies the immediately pre-verbal position).

(146) *Keşke* daha çok param ol**sa**.
      '*If only* I had more money.'

(147) Bu soğuklar (*bir*) bit**se** artık . . .
      '*If only* this cold weather would come to an end . . .'

(iii) -sAydI (or its informal alternative (-(y)AydI, see 8.2.3.3), again often combined with *keşke*, expresses a counterfactual wish or regret, usually but not always relating to past time:

(148) *Keşke* Hülya'ya söyleme**seydi**n.
      '*If only* you hadn't told Hülya.'

Wishes expressed by -sAydI/(-(y)AydI can have a reproachful, quasi-obligative tone:

(149) [Madem uykun vardı], misafir çağırma**saydı**n/çağırmaya**ydı**n.
      '[Since you were sleepy], you *would have done better* not *to* invite guests.'

21.4.4.2 Commands

(i) Basic commands: no marker or *-(y)In(Iz)* (See 8.4, group 4.)
These standard imperative forms express straightforward commands.

(150) Bu para-yı baba-n(ız)-a ver(**-in**).
this money-ACC father-2SG/PL.POSS-DAT give(IMP)(-2PL)
'Give this money to your father.'

The longer 2nd person plural form *-(y)InIz* is used mainly for formal public commands:

(151) Lütfen kemerlerinizi bağla**yınız**.
'Please fasten your seatbelts.'

In ordinary social situations *-(y)In* is the standard plural/polite imperative.

(ii) 3rd person instructions: *-sIn(lAr)*:
The 3rd person imperative forms (8.4, group 4) express instructions for something to be done by someone other than the hearer.

(152) Çocuklar burada kal**sın**(**lar**).
'*Let* the children stay here.'/'*I want* the children to stay here.'/'*See to it that* the children stay here.'

If the speaker is only interested in getting an action done (or preventing its being done) a passive form may be used:

(153) Artık bura-ya afiş as-ıl-ma-**sın**.
from.now.on here-DAT notice hang-PASS-NEG[-IMP]-3SG
'*Let* no notices be put up here from now on.'/'*I* don't *want* any notices put up from now on.'/'*See to it that* no notices are put up here from now on.'

When a 3rd person imperative form is used in a question, the speaker is consulting the hearer as to whether s/he wishes a certain action to be performed or a situation to occur:

(154) Çocuklar burada *mı* kal**sın**(**lar**)?
'*Should* the children stay here?'/'*Do you want* the children to stay here?'/'*Do you think it would be best* for the children to stay here?'

(iii) Persuasive commands: ↓*-sAnA*, ↓*-sAnIzA* (8.4, group 4):
Utterances with ↓*-sAn(Iz)A* are not so much commands but pointers to, or reminders of, something that needs to be done. They often express a certain

impatience on the part of the speaker that the action indicated, the desirability of which is obvious to him/her, has not been performed by the hearer(s) of their own accord.

Forms with ↓–*sAn(Iz)A* are rarely used in sequence, i.e. a single utterance would normally not contain more than one of them.

(155) Artık yat**san(ız)a**, uyukluyorsunuz.
       '*Why don't you go to bed* now, you're nodding off.'

(iv) Imperative use of the future marker *-(y)AcAK*:
Aside from its main function of expressing an expectation about future events on the factual plane, *-(y)AcAK* can also express the other kind of expectation, i.e. an action that someone in a position of authority or power expects others to perform:

(156) Oraya bir daha gitme**yecek**sin, anladın mı?
       'You're not *going to* go there again, do you understand?'

This type of volitional modality can be projected into the past:

(157) Bütün bunlar at-ıl-**acak-tı**.
       all these throw.away-PASS-FUT-P.COP
       'All these *were supposed to* be thrown away.'

21.4.4.3 Suggestions: first person optative forms *-(y)AyIm*, *-(y)AlIm*

The 1st person singular optative *-(y)AyIm* expresses an action that the speaker proposes to perform. It often accompanies the actual performance of the action.

(158) Sana yardım ed**eyim**.
       '*Let me* help you.'

The 1st person plural form *-(y)AlIm* expresses action that the speaker proposes for performance jointly with the hearer(s) and/or other people.

(159) Biraz konuş**alım**.
       '*Let's* have a bit of a chat.'

(160) Hediyeleri Mehmet'e göster-me-**ye-lim**.
                        show-NEG-OPT-1PL
       '*Let's* not show Mehmet the presents.'

In questions, both of the above forms become consultative, asking the hearer(s) whether or how they would like the proposed action to be performed:

(161) Sana yardım ed**eyim** *mi*?
'*Shall I* help you?'

(162) Şu tabakları *nereye* koy**alım**?
'*Where shall/should we* put these plates?'

(163) Hediyeleri Mehmet'e gösterme**yelim** *mi*?
'*Should we* not show the presents to Mehmet?'/'*Don't you want us* to show the presents to Mehmet?'

21.4.4.4 Deliberation about possible action: questions with -sAm, -sAk

When a finite verb with the conditional suffix *-sA*, marked for 1st person, is used in a question, it has consultative force. The difference between questions with the conditional suffix and questions with the optative forms discussed in 21.4.4.3 is that in the case of the conditional forms the speaker regards the decision to be taken as more problematical. S/he is not clear in his/her own mind about the desirability of the proposed action, or the form that it should take, and s/he does not expect the hearer to be able to provide a simple answer. Because of this uncertainty, questions with *-sAm/-sAk* are usually marked with the modal adverbial *acaba* 'I wonder' (19.5.2):

(164) Bu konuda **kim**e danışsam *acaba*?
'*I wonder who* I *should* consult about this?'

(165) *Acaba* başka bir yere **mi** gitsek?
'*I wonder if* we *should* go somewhere else?'

21.4.4.5 Requests and offers: second person aorist interrogative

Requests and offers are identical in form.

Requests:

(166) Ben-im-le hastane-ye gel-**ir mi-sin**?
I-GEN-COM hospital-DAT come-AOR INT-2SG
'*Would you* [*please*] come with me to the hospital?'

The addition of the possibility suffix *-(y)Abil* makes the request more tentative:

(167) Bana biraz yardım ed**ebil**ir misiniz?
'*Could* you [please] give me a bit of help?'

Offers:

(168) Çay iç**er misiniz**?
'*Will you* have/*Would you* like some tea?'

Offers cast as a negative question are more persuasive in tone:

(169) Otur-**maz mı-sınız**?
sit.down-NEG.AOR INT-2PL
'*Won't you* sit down?'

21.4.4.6   Expression of commitment: first person aorist

The 1st person (usually singular) of the aorist is used to express a commitment or promise entered into at the moment of, and by the act of, the
utterance itself. This may well be a response to a request (also expressed
in the aorist, as explained in 21.4.4.5):

(170) A.– Benimle evlen**ir** misin?
        '*Will* you marry me?'

        B.– Evlen**ir**im
        'Yes, I *will*.'

In some contexts, ambiguity between the modality of commitment and the
modality of probability (21.4.1.4) may undermine the degree of confidence
inspired by a 1st person aorist utterance. The modally neutral *-(y)AcAK*
form in (171b), presenting the promised action as a matter of future fact,
may carry more conviction, because it indicates a pre-existing plan on
the part of the speaker, and also suggests that s/he has checked its practi-
cability.

(171) (**a**) Akşama kadar dön**er**im.   (Promise)
        'I'*ll* be back by this evening.'

        (**b**) Akşama kadar dön**eceğ**im.   (Statement of plan/
        'I'm *going to* be back by this evening.' firm prediction)

(172) Hiç kimseye söyle-**me**-m.   (Promise)
                tell[-AOR].NEG-1SG
        'I *won't* tell anyone at all.'

21.5 TENSE, ASPECT AND MODALITY IN COMPOUND VERB FORMS

Compound verb forms consisting of a lexical verb followed by the auxiliary *ol-* (or *bulun-*, see 13.3.1.2) provide within a single verbal complex two verb stems which are separately (and nearly always differently) marked for tense, aspect and/or modality. The lexical verb is marked for relative tense or for aspect, as follows:

PERFECTIVE/RELATIVE PAST	*-mIş*
RELATIVE FUTURE	*-(y)AcAK*
PROGRESSIVE	*-(I)yor*
HABITUAL	*-(A/I)r* or *-mAz*

The auxiliary form that follows adds a further dimension of tense or aspect, or some kind of modality:

oldu	past tense, perfective aspect
olmuş	(relative) past tense, perfective aspect, evidential modality
oluyor	habitual aspect
olacak	(i) (relative) future tense
	(ii) non-fact modality (assumption)
	(iii) volitional modality (command)
olur	non-fact modality (assumption or hypothesis)
olsa gerek	non-fact modality (probability)
olmalı	non-fact modality (deduction)
olabilir	non-fact modality (speculative possibility)
olsa	volitional modality (wish)
olayım/olalım	volitional modality (1st person)
olsun	volitional modality (3rd person)

The number of possible combinations that can occur in compound verb forms is extremely large, and we do not attempt to offer an exhaustive list. The table below shows, for each finite form of *ol-*, which suffixes commonly occur on the lexical verb preceding it.

-mIş, -(y)AcAk, -(A/I)r, -mAz	*oldu*
-(A/I)r, -mAz	*olmuş*
-mIş, -(y)AcAk	*oluyor*
-mIş, -(I)yor	*olacak*
-mIş	*olur*
-mIş, -(I)yor	*olsa gerek*
-mIş, -(I)yor	*olmalı*

-mIş, -(I)yor	*olabilir*
-(I)yor	*olsa*
-mIş	*olayım/olalım*
-mIş	*olsun*

21.5.1 COMPOUND FORMS IN WHICH THE LEXICAL VERB IS MARKED WITH *-mIş*

-mIş is the most frequently occurring marker of the lexical verb in compound verb forms. In general terms it presents an event as being completed prior to some reference point.

The auxiliary form *oluyor* signals a habitually recurring reference point:

(173) Genellikle *saat yediye kadar* dükkanı kapat**mış oluyor**uz.
'We *have usually* shut the shop *by seven o'clock*.'

olacak indicates that the reference point is in the future:

(174) *O zamana kadar* herkes git**miş olacak**.
'Everyone *will have* gone *by then*.'

In the case of modal forms expressing assumptions, such as *olsa gerek* (21.4.1.4 (iii)), *olmalı* (21.4.1.4 (vi)) and *olabilir* (21.4.2.1), the reference point is usually the moment of speech:

-mIş olsa gerek

(175) [Bahçeyi bu hale getirmek için] aylarca uğraş**mış olsa**n gerek.
'You *must have* worked for months [to get the garden looking like this].'

-mIş olmalı

(176) Kayseri'yi gör**müş olmalı**yım ama hiç hatırlamıyorum.
'I *must have* seen Kayseri, but I don't remember [it] at all.'

-mIş olabilir

(177) Ayşe bu fotoğrafı Hatice'ye göster**miş olabilir**.
'Ayşe *may have* shown this photograph to Hatice.'

In some occurrences of the *-mIş olacak* combination, *olacak* can have one of the modal values noted elsewhere in this chapter:

(i)   Non-future prediction (21.4.1.4 (iv)):
This usage is rather rare.

> (178)   A.– Turgut bana selam vermedi.
> 'Turgut didn't say hello to me.'
>
> B. – Seni o kıyafette tanımamış **olacak**.
> 'He *won't have* recognized you in that outfit.'

(ii)   Volitional modality (expectation) (21.4.4.2 (iv)):

> (179)   Akşama kadar bütün bu gazeteler paketlen**miş olacak**.
> 'All these newspapers *are to* be (lit. *are to have been*) parcelled up by this evening.'

Compounds formed with *-mIş olur* present a hypothetical situation, such as one dependent upon the fulfilment of a condition:

> (180)   [Daha geç bir saatte gitsek] sokaklar boşal**mış olur**.
> '[If we went later in the day] the streets *would* be less crowded.'
> (lit. '*would have* emptied')

With *olmalı* an obligative reading is possible in addition to the assumptive one noted above:

> (181)   6.30'a kadar yola çık**mış olmalı**yız.
> 'We *must be* on the road (lit. *must have* set out) by 6.30.'

The optative forms *olayım/olalım* and the 3rd person imperative forms *olsun(lar)* can combine with *-mIş* to express the suggestion or (in a noun clause, 24.2, 24.3) the wish that an action be completed by a certain time:

> (182)   [Bu akşama kadar bu odayı bitir**miş olalım**] istiyoruz.
> 'We want [*to have* finished this room by this evening].'

21.5.1.1   The resultative usage of compound verb forms with *-mIş*

A further element of meaning that is present in some instances of compound forms with *-mIş* is that the event is presented as happening as the *result* (intentional or not) of the performance of some other act. This meaning is always present in the combination *-mIş oldu*, which expresses, as a completed event, *entry into* the state of having done something (a concept difficult to express in English, cf. 21.3.3):

(183) Dördüncü bölümün bitmesiyle kitabın yarısı yazıl**mış oldu**.
'With the completion of the fourth chapter, half of the book
has been written.'

The resultative function of -*mIş* can occur also with *oluyor*, *olacak* and *olur*:

(184) Bu tür davranışlarla onu küçük düşür**müş oluyor**sun.
'You humiliate him/her by this kind of behaviour.'
(You *are habitually* in the state of *having* humiliated him/her.)

(185) [Beni bu yükten kurtarmakla] bana büyük bir iyilik yap**mış**
olacaksınız.
'You *will have* done me a great favour [by ridding me of this
burden].'

With resultative -*mIş*, *oluyor* does not always express habitual aspect. It can
simply mark (relative) present tense, imparting a sense that the impact of
the completion of the event is/was very much current at the reference point.
Thus -*mIş oluyor* is virtually synonymous with -*mIş oldu* in all instances
where the reference point is the moment of speech, as in (183) above:

(186) Bu bölümün bitmesiyle kitabın yarısı yazıl**mış oluyor**.
'With the completion of this chapter, half of the book *has*
been written.'

Finally, resultative -*mIş* can occur with the optative/imperative forms of
ol-. (187) could be an explanation given retrospectively for the purchase of
a large number of different perfumes:

(187) [Bu kokuların her birini birer defa dene**miş olayım**] demiştim.
'I thought [*I would like to have* tried each of these perfumes
once].'

21.5.2 COMPOUND FORMS IN WHICH THE LEXICAL VERB IS MARKED WITH -*(I)yor*

These forms indicate that an event is/was/will be ongoing at some reference
point.

-*(I)yor olacak* marks the reference point as being in the future:

(188) Saat altıda çalış**ıyor olacağım**.
'I *shall be* work*ing* at six o'clock.'

Combinations of *-(I)yor* with *olsa gerek*, *olmalı*, and *olabilir* express assumptions or conjectures about a situation current at the moment of speech:

(189) Çok gürültü var, yukarıda birisi matkap kullan**ıyor olmalı/olsa gerek**.
'There's such a noise; someone upstairs *must be* us*ing* a drill.'

(190) Ali'nin patronu onu sev**miyor olabilir**.
'*It's possible* Ali's boss doesn't like him.'

-(I)yor olsa articulates a counterfactual wish about the present state of affairs:

(191) Keşke sıcak bir ülkede yaşı**yor olsam**.
'If only I *were* liv*ing* in a hot country.'

21.5.3 COMPOUND FORMS IN WHICH THE LEXICAL VERB IS MARKED WITH *-(y)AcAk*

This pattern is in very restricted use in main clauses, although it is highly productive in conditional clauses (27.2.1.3, 27.2.6) and in relative clauses (25.4.1). The combination *-(y)AcAk oldu* expresses an action that a person decided (somewhat hesitantly) to perform. It is nearly always followed by a statement expressing or implying the reversal of that decision:

(192) Bir şey söyle**yecek oldu**m, ama tam o anda kapı çaldı.
'I *was about to* say something, but just at that moment the door (bell) rang.'

Compounds with *-(y)AcAk oluyor* give the same kind of situation a habitual context:

(193) Bazen bir şey söyle**yecek oluyor**um ama bir türlü çıkmıyor.
'Sometimes I *get almost to the point of* saying something, but it just doesn't come out.'

21.5.4 COMPOUND FORMS IN WHICH THE LEXICAL VERB IS MARKED WITH *-(A/I)r* OR *-mAz*

Aorist marking of the lexical verb is restricted to compounds in which the auxiliary has perfective marking (the modally neutral *-DI* or evidential *-mIş*).

(i) *-(A/I)r oldu/olmuş*:

The affirmative aorist form followed by *oldu/olmuş* expresses the fact that an event began or has begun to happen recurrently, or as a matter of habit:

(194) Son zamanlarda sık sık tiyatroya gid**er olduk**.
     'Recently we *have started* go*ing* to the theatre a lot.'

(ii) *-mAz oldu/olmuş*:

The negative aorist form with *oldu/olmuş* expresses the fact that a formerly recurrent event (has) ceased to happen:

(195) O olaydan sonra Hakan bir süre bize uğra**maz oldu**.
     'After that incident Hakan *stopped* call*ing* on us for a while.'

21.5.5 THE ADDITION OF THE PAST COPULA *-(y)DI* TO COMPOUND VERB FORMS

The past copula *-(y)DI* (21.2.1 (ii)) can be added to the auxiliary component of any compound verb form. It has one of two functions:

(i) In most cases it provides a reference point in absolute past time (time prior to the moment of speech) for the relative tense or aspect marked on the lexical verb:

(196) Genellikle saat yediye kadar dükkanı kapat**mış oluyordu**k.
     'We *had* usually shut the shop by seven o'clock.'

(ii) The other function of *-(y)DI* is to indicate counterfactuality. This occurs only with the modal forms *olur* (21.4.1.3), *olabilir* (21.4.2.1), *olmalı* (21.4.2.2) and *olsa* (21.4.4.1).

olmalıydı expresses an unfulfilled obligation (21.4.2.2). The reference is not necessarily to a past time:

(197) Bu saatte çalışıyor **olmalıydı**m.
     'I *should/ought to be* work*ing* at this time of day.'

In the case of the aorist there can be ambiguity between past and counterfactual meaning. For example, (198) could be understood as expressing either a habitual state of affairs in the past, or a state of affairs that did not occur but would have if some condition had been fulfilled:

(198) Saat dörde kadar mektuplar postalan**mış olurdu**.
     'By four o'clock the letters *would have* been posted.'

22 DEFINITENESS, SPECIFICITY AND GENERIC REFERENCE

This chapter deals with the referential function of noun phrases. Speakers can use noun phrases with specific or non-specific reference, and if they are referring to specific entities they can use various means to indicate whether or not they expect their hearers to be able to identify the person(s) or thing(s) they are talking about. In Turkish the **referential status** of a noun phrase depends on one or more of the following factors:

(i)   what kind of determiners, if any, are present (15.6)
(ii)   the use or non-use of accusative marking on direct objects (14.3.3.2)
(iii) word order (22.5)
(iv) sentence stress (22.6)
(v)   the tense, aspect and modality of the predicate (22.7)

Four referential statuses can be identified in Turkish, and these are explained in detail in the successive sections of this chapter. Both **definite** (22.1) and **indefinite** (22.2) noun phrases are always marked for number:

(1)   {**Çocuk-lar**} {**araba**}-yı yıkadılar.
      child-PL   car-ACC
      DEF.PL   DEF.SG
      '{*The children*} washed {*the car*}.'

(2)   {**Bir oda**}-da {**birtakım kutu-lar**} vardı.
      a room-LOC some box-PL
      INDEF.SG   INDEF.PL
      'There were {*some boxes*} in *a room*.'

This is in contrast to the second non-definite status that exists in Turkish, namely **categorial** (22.3), in which the distinction between singular and plural is neutralized and the noun phrase indicates merely the 'kind' to which reference is being made:

(3)   Sen daha {**çocuk**}sun.
      'You're still {*a child*}.'

The fourth referential status, **generic** reference (22.4), involves the use of a noun phrase in a generalizing function, to refer to an entire class of entities, or to a(ny) typical member of that class:

(4) Eskiden {çocuk}, büyüklerine saygı gösterirdi.
     'In the past, {a child} showed respect to his/her elders.'

Specificity is a category that overlaps the boundary between definite and indefinite. All definites are specific, but, as explained in 22.2, indefinites may be either specific or non-specific. All categorial noun phrases are non-specific, as (in a somewhat different sense) are all noun phrases used generically.

22.1 DEFINITE STATUS

A noun phrase marked as definite refers to a specific entity or entities that the speaker assumes to be unambiguously identifiable by the hearer. In Turkish the minimal requirements for a noun phrase to be interpreted as definite are:

(i) the absence of an indefinite determiner (15.6.1)

(ii) accusative case marking where the noun phrase is functioning as direct object.

In (5) all three of the noun phrases are definite:

(5) {**Garson**} {**temiz tabak-lar**}-ı {**masa**}-ya koydu.
     waiter clean plate-PL-ACC table-DAT
     '*The waiter* put *the clean plates* down on *the table*.'

The following classes of noun phrase are inherently definite:

(i) The proper names of people, places and institutions:

(6) **Osman'ı** dün gördük.
     'We saw *Osman* yesterday.'

(7) **Ankara'yı** severim.
     'I like *Ankara*.'

(8) **Anıtlar Yüksek Kurulu'nu** bundan sorumlu tutuyorum.
     'I hold *the High Commission on Monuments* responsible for this.'

(ii) Most pronouns, specifically:

(a) The simple personal pronouns (18.1.1):

(9) Murat **sen*i*** seviyor.
     'Murat loves *you*.'

(b)   The demonstrative pronouns (18.2):

> (10) **Şunları** da yıkamamız lâzım.
> 'We've got to wash *these*, too.'

(c)   The pronominal quantifiers *herkes* 'everyone' and *her şey* 'everything'
(18.6.1):

> (11) Ömer **herkesi** sinirlendirdi.
> 'Ömer got on *everyone*'s nerves.'

(d)   The interrogative *kim(ler)* 'who' (19.2.1.1), and the expression *kimse
(ler)* 'no one', 'anyone' (20.5.3):

> (12) **Kim-ler-i** görüyorsunuz?
> who-PL-ACC
> '*Who* do you see (nowadays)?'

> (13) Pek **kimseyi** görmüyorum.
> 'I don't see *anyone* much.'

(e)   *öbürü/öteki* 'the other (one)', and their plural forms *öbürleri/ötekiler*
(18.4–5):

> (14) Bir anahtar burada, **öbürünü** gördün mü?
> 'One key is here; have you seen *the other(one)*?'

(iii) A noun phrase that includes one of the definite determiners
(15.6.2):

> (15) Bana {**bu** oda}-**yı** ver-di-ler.
> I(DAT) this room-ACC give-PF-3PL
> 'They have given me {*this* room}.'

> (16) Siz {**hangi** kitab}-**ı** daha yararlı buldunuz?
> '{*Which* book} did you find more useful?'

22.2   INDEFINITE STATUS

If a noun phrase includes *bir* ('a(n)') or any of the other indefinite determiners (15.6.1) it is unambiguously indefinite. A noun phrase that includes
a cardinal or distributive numeral is also interpreted as indefinite unless (i)
a definite determiner (15.6.2) is also present, or (ii) the noun phrase is

followed by the clitic *dA* (see 15.9.1). Finally, noun phrases that include neither a determiner nor a numeral but are marked with the plural suffix *-lAr* have indefinite status in some contexts but not in others. They are unambiguously indefinite where they occur as non-case-marked direct objects, as in (17c). Otherwise, their referential status (definite, indefinite or generic) is determined by the word order (22.5), stress pattern (22.6) or modality (22.7) of the sentence.

(17) (a) Çekmece-de **bir** defter bul-du-k.
  drawer-LOC a notebook find-PF-1PL
  'We found *a* notebook in the drawer.'

   (b) Çekmecede **dört (tane)** defter bulduk.
    four ENUM notebook
    'We found *four* notebooks in the drawer.'

   (c) Çekmecede defter-**ler** bulduk.
    notebook-PL
    'We found notebook*s* in the drawer.'

   (d) Çekmecede **birtakım** defter-**ler** bulduk.
    some notebook-PL
    'We found *some* notebook*s* in the drawer.'

Note that *şey* 'thing' and *yer* 'place' do not occur in the plural-marked form as indefinites unless preceded by either an adjective or a determiner. See also 14.3.1.1.

As indefinite noun phrases always express new information, they very often occupy the immediately preverbal position (see 23.3.1). If they are non-case-marked direct objects, as in (17), they are obligatorily placed in this position (see 23.2.3, and exceptions noted in 23.2.1).

22.2.1 SPECIFIC AND NON-SPECIFIC INDEFINITES

A noun phrase marked as indefinite can perform one of two referential functions:

(i) It can refer to a **specific** entity (or set of entities) known to the speaker, which is being introduced into the discourse as a new item, and which is assumed not to be familiar to, or not to be identifiable by, the hearer:

(18) Dün sokakta {çok eski **bir** arkadaşım}-la karşılaştım.
  'Yesterday I bumped into {*a* very old friend of mine} in the street.'

(19) Yarınki toplantıya {**birkaç** kişi} gelemeyecekmiş.
'It seems {*several* people} are not going to be able to get to the
meeting tomorrow.'

(**ii**)   It can denote a **non-specific** entity (or set of entities), whose identity
is unknown or unknowable to the speaker. Non-specific indefinites occur
mainly in clauses expressing a future or hypothetical event, or in negative
statements or questions.

(20) [{Daha büyük **bir** araba} almay]-ı düşünüyoruz.
'We're thinking of [buying {*a* larger car}].'

(21) {Yeni **bir** şey} söyle-me-di.
new a thing say-NEG-PF
'He didn't say {*any*thing new}.'

The distinction between specific and non-specific indefinites is reflected in
certain features of Turkish grammar.

(**a**)   In direct objects the use of plural marking without a determiner is
largely confined to specific indefinites. Thus the plural-marked indefinite form in (22) refers to specific shirts that have been purchased:

(22) Dün Korkut-a **yeni gömlek-*ler*** al-dı-k.
yesterday Korkut-DAT new shirt-PL buy-PF-1PL
'Yesterday we bought *(some) new shirts* for Korkut.'

If the predicate were changed in such a way that the shirts lost their
specificity, the categorial form (without plural marking, see 22.3)
would be preferred to the indefinite form:

(23) (**a**) Korkut'a **yeni gömlek** almamız lazım.
'We need to get *a new shirt/(some) new shirts* for Korkut.'

(**b**) Korkut'a **yeni gömlek** almadık.
'We didn't buy Korkut [*any*] *new shirts*.'

(**c**) Korkut'a **yeni gömlek** aldın mı?
'Did you buy Korkut [*a*] *new shirt/*[*any*] *new shirts*?'

(**b**)   The omission of *olan* in relative clauses whose verb is of the form
-*mIş olan* or -*(y)AcAk olan* is preferred where the relativized
constituent is a non-specific noun phrase (see 25.4.1.1 for details):

(24) (a) {[Masaya **bırakılmış**] bir not} yeterli olurdu.
'{A note [*left* on the table]} would have been enough.'

(b) {[Masaya **bırakılmış** *olan*] bir not}-ta kaloriferler,
çöplerin toplanması, pencerelerin kilitlenmesi gibi
konularda bilgiler vardı.
'In {a note [*that had been left* on the table]} there was
information about the central heating, rubbish
collection, locking of windows, etc.'

In (24a) no note has been left; the subject noun phrase therefore
represents a purely hypothetical entity. This noun phrase is thus non-
specific, and *olan* is omitted from the relative clause modifying it.
In (24b), on the other hand, the factual and affirmative past tense
predicate *vardı* indicates that a specific note is being described.

(c)   In a limited range of contexts, where there is ambiguity between a
specific and a non-specific interpretation of a direct object, the use of
accusative marking favours the specific reading:

With verbs such as *iste-* 'want' and *ara-* 'look for':

(25) (a) {Gürcistan folkloruyla ilgili bir kitap} arıyorum.
'I'm looking for {a book about Georgian folklore}.'

(b) {Gürcistan folkloruyla ilgili bir kitab}-ı arıyorum.
'I'm looking for {a book about Georgian folklore}.'

(25a) implies that the speaker would be interested in *any* book about
Georgian folklore that might be available. (25b), on the other hand,
where the object is given accusative marking, implies that the speaker
has a specific title in mind.

A recurrent pattern of events:

(26) (a) Bazen masaya {bir örtü} yayardık.
'Sometimes we would spread {a cloth} on the table.'

(b) Bazen masaya {[sarı çiçeklerle işlenmiş] bir örtü}-(yü)
yayardık.
'Sometimes we would spread on the table {a cloth
[embroidered with yellow flowers]}.'

(c) Bazen masaya {[Ayşe-nin biz-e Meksika-dan getir-diğ-i]
        Ayşe-GEN we-DAT Mexico-ABL bring-PART-3SG.POSS
bir örtü}-(yü) yayardık
a cloth-ACC.
'Sometimes we would spread on the table {a cloth [that Ayşe
had brought us from Mexico]}.'

The three sentences in (26) show a gradation from total ambiguity with
regard to specificity in (a) to unambiguous specificity in (c). In (a) the
speaker has not provided the cloth with any descriptors at all. The likelihood of accusative marking being used here is extremely small. In (b) the
cloth is given quite a detailed description, and it seems likely that one
specific tablecloth is intended. In (c) the specificity of the cloth is virtually
assured through its linkage to the action of a specific individual. However,
although accusative marking is much more acceptable in (b) and (c) than
in (a), it is important to note that the non-case-marked version of these
sentences is also perfectly acceptable, and if used it would not force a non-
specific reading. In other words, accusative marking is not a requirement
for giving the direct object in such sentences a specific reading, but if used
it does lend weight to that interpretation.

A conjecture about the future:

(27) (a) Program-da {bazı değişiklik-ler} yap-ma-mız
programme-LOC some change-PL make-VN-1PL.POSS
gerek-ebil-ir.
be.necessary-PSB-AOR
'It may be necessary for us to make {some changes} to the
programme.'

(b) Programda {[şu anda akılda olmayan] bazı değişiklik-ler}(-i)
                                some change-PL(-ACC)
yapmamız gerekebilir.
'It may be necessary for us to make {some changes} to the
programme [that are currently unpredictable].'

(c) Programda {[yetkililerin istediği] bazı değişiklikler}(-i)
yapmamız gerekebilir.
'It may be necessary for us to make {some changes} to the
programme [that are required by the authorities].'

(27a–c) are modalized statements about a hypothetical possibility
(21.4.2.1), and in such a context it would be very difficult to understand the
indefinite direct object in anything but a non-specific sense. (27) shows,

then, that accusative marking is not necessarily linked to specificity, but can simply be a function of the complexity of the noun phrase itself. The kind of complex modification provided by a relative clause, in particular, considerably increases the tendency towards the use of accusative marking.

As explained in 14.3.3.2, certain types of indefinite direct object (notably those occurring to the left of the verb but not in the immediately preverbal position, and those marked for possession) obligatorily take accusative marking. It should be noted that this grammatically conditioned accusative marking is quite independent of the specific/non-specific distinction. The direct objects in (28) and (29) both have a non-specific interpretation.

(28) {Birçok şey}-**i** şu raflara koyabiliriz.
'{A lot of things} we can put on these shelves.'

(29) İsterse Ahmet {bir arkadaşın}-ı getirebilir.
'Ahmet can bring {a friend (of his)} if he wants.'

22.3 CATEGORIAL STATUS

A categorial noun phrase is not marked for number. It denotes an unspecified quantity, or number of items of a certain kind, or an unspecified quantity of a certain substance. Note that, unlike generic noun phrases (22.4), categorial noun phrases do not refer to a class of entities *as a whole*, or to a *typical* member of a class. Categorial noun phrases are used in contexts where distinctions of number or quantity are simply irrelevant:

(30) Şu anda konuşamayacağım, **müşteri** var.
'I can't talk now; I've got *customers/a customer*.'

(31) O gün **kar** yağmıştı.
'*Snow* had fallen on that day.'

The formal characteristics of noun phrases used with categorial status are that:

(i) They cannot be modified by any determiners.
(ii) They cannot be plural-marked.
(iii) When functioning as subject they have to occupy the immediately preverbal position (see 23.2.1).
(iv) When functioning as direct object, they do not receive accusative case marking unless topicalized (see 23.3.3).

There are certain contexts in which the use of the categorial form is regularly preferred to a number-marked form:

(i) A subject complement expressing the gender, nationality, occupation or social status of a person or persons:

(32) Oğlumun bütün öğretmenleri **kadın**.
'All of my son's teachers are *women*.'

(33) Biz [onları **Türk**] sanıyorduk. (See 24.5.)
'We thought [they were *Turks*].'

Note that if the subject complement is a plural-marked noun phrase, as in (34b), it acquires definite status:

(34) (a) Onlar **dokTOR-muş**(-lar).
doctor-EV.COP(-3PL)
'Apparently they're *doctors*.'

(b) Onlar **doktor-LAR-mış**.
doctor-PL-EV.COP
'Apparently they're *the doctors*.'

In (34a) the suffix *-lar* is the group 2 person marker (3rd person plural) (8.4), affixed to the evidential copular suffix *-(y)mIş* (8.3.2). It refers to the plurality of the subject *onlar*. In (34b), on the other hand, *-lar* is the nominal plural marker (8.1.1) affixed to the noun phrase *doktor*.

(ii) The subject of an interrogative or negative existential sentence (12.1.1.2):

(35) **Kardeş**iniz var mı?
'Have you any *brothers or sisters*?'

(36) Bizim apartmanımızda hiç **çocuk** yok.
'There are no *children* at all in our block of flats.'

(iii) The non-specific subject or direct object of an interrogative or negative verbal sentence:

(37) **Misafir** mi gelecek?
'Are you expecting *guests*?' (lit. 'Are *guest(s)* going to come?')

(38) Amerika'lılar oraya **asker** göndermemişti.
'The Americans had not sent *(any) troops* there.'

(iv) The direct object of sentences in which attention is focused on an action or activity rather than on the entity/entities affected or produced by it:

(39) Ne güzel **şarkı söylü**-yor-sun!
how beautiful song sing-IMPF-2SG
'How beautifully you *sing*!'

(40) Ayşe bütün gün **kitap oku**yor.
'Ayşe *reads books* all day.'

Many verbal expressions of the form bare noun + verb, where the bare noun is the direct object, have been lexicalized as expressions that will be found in dictionaries. Some other examples are: *ders çalış-* 'study', 'do one's homework', *yemek ye-* 'eat', 'have a meal', and *sigara iç-* 'smoke'. The fact that these lexicalized expressions exist does not in any way prevent the same noun being used with the same verb but with a different referential status. For example, the direct object noun phrase *o şarkıyı* below is definite, referring to a specific song that the speaker assumes the hearer can identify.

(41) **O şarkı-yı** ne güzel söyledin!
that song-ACC
'How beautifully you sang *that song*!'

In (42), on the other hand, *iki sigara* is indefinite; the identity of the cigarettes in question is not of interest:

(42) Bugün yalnız **iki sigara** içtim.
'I have smoked only *two cigarettes* today.'

(v) The subject of a sentence in which attention is focused on an action, or the impact of that action, rather than on the identity of the person or thing doing it:

(43) Geçen kış evimize **hırsız** girdi.
'Last winter our house was burgled.' (lit. '[a] *burglar/burglar[s]* got into our house')

(44) Tatildeyken beni **arı** soktu.
'While on holiday I was stung by a bee.' (lit. '[a] *bee/bee[s]* stung me')

Outside the types of context identified in (i)–(v) above, the choice between categorial and indefinite reference depends on how much importance the speaker attaches to the number aspect of the entity s/he is talking about.

(45) (a) Dayım bize **hediye** getirmişti.
       'My uncle had brought us *a present/presents.*'

   (b) Dayım bize **bir hediye** getirmişti.
       'My uncle had brought us *a present.*'

   (c) Dayım bize **hediyeler** getirmişti.
       'My uncle had brought us *presents.*'

In (a) attention is focused on the uncle's action rather than on the present(s) brought. (b) and (c), on the other hand, suggest that the speaker is going to go on to say something more about the actual present(s).

22.4 GENERIC REFERENCE

A noun phrase is said to have generic reference when it refers not to any specific entity or entities but to *an entire class*, or to *a typical member* of that class. In Turkish, generic reference can be effected by both singular and plural noun phrases.

22.4.1 GENERIC REFERENCE BY SINGULAR NOUN PHRASES

22.4.1.1 The bare generic

The bare generic is a noun phrase without either *bir* or plural marking, which is used with generic reference. Among the different forms of generic reference, the bare generic evokes most strongly the idea of the 'class' as a single whole, as opposed to the class viewed as a collection of separate individuals. It is the form used for the expression of laws of nature (46), definitions and classifications (47), and proverbs (48). In general it produces a more absolute, unqualified axiom than the other forms.

(46) **Kuş** uçar.
    '*Birds* fly/*A bird* flies.'

(47) **Balina** memeli bir hayvan-dır.
    whale mammal an animal-GM
    '*The whale* is a mammal.'

(48) **Dert** gitmez, değişir.
'*Problems* don't go away, they change.'

(49) **Hırsız** pencereden girer.
'*Burglars/a burglar* come(s) in through windows/a window'.

The use of *insan* 'human being' in the sense of the English generic
pronoun 'one' (see 18.6.2) is a special instance of the bare generic:

(50) **Para sıkıntısı *insan-a*** üzüntü ver-ir.
money problem person-DAT distress give-AOR
'*Money problems* cause *one* distress.'

22.4.1.2   The indefinite generic

The indefinite generic is a noun phrase marked with *bir* that has generic
reference. It expresses a typical member of a class. It occurs mainly in the
following contexts:

(i)   A noun phrase that includes adjectival modifiers (Chapter 15):

(51) {*Akıllı* **bir insan**} borçlanmaktan kaçınır.
'{*A wise person*} avoids getting into debt.'

(52) {[*Yurtdışında okumak isteyen*] **bir öğrenci**}, iyi İngilizce
öğrenmeli.
'{*A student* [*who wants to study abroad*]} must learn English well.'

Because generics are inherently non-specific, the adjectival can be a relative clause with *olan* omitted (see 22.2.1, 25.4.1.1):

(53) {[*Elli yaşını geçmiş*] **bir insan**}-ın bu memlekette iş bulması kolay
değil.
'It's not easy for {*a person over fifty*} to find work in this country.'

(ii)   A noun phrase that includes one of the indefinite determiners
herhangi bir 'any' or *böyle bir/şöyle bir/öyle bir* 'such a' (15.6.1):

(54) {*Herhangi bir* **anne**} bu sorunu tanır.
'{*Any mother*} would recognize this problem.'

(55) {*Öyle bir* **okul**}-da okumak zor.
'It's hard to study in {*such a school*}.'

(iii) A noun phrase followed by *bile* 'even' (see 28.3.1.1):

> (56) Bunu {**bir çocuk**} *bile* anlayabilir.
> '*Even {a child}* could understand this.'

22.4.2 GENERIC REFERENCE BY PLURAL NOUN PHRASES

The plural generic, consisting of a plural-marked noun phrase, is closer in meaning to the indefinite generic than to the bare generic, in that it also generalizes from individual to class rather than vice versa. It makes reference to the collectivity of individuals that are seen as constituting a class. In comparison with the bare generic, the plural generic makes a less absolute kind of generalization, hinting at the possibility that it will not apply equally to all members of the class.

The plural generic could be substituted for the indefinite generic in all the examples given in 22.4.1, with the exception of (54) (because *herhangi* has to be followed by *bir* and a singular noun phrase). The plural equivalents of (51) and (55) are given below:

> (57) {**Akıllı insan*lar***} borçlanmaktan kaçınır.
> '{*Wise people*} avoid getting into debt.'

> (58) {**Öyle okul*lar***}-da okumak zor.
> 'It's hard to study in {*such schools*}.'

The plural generic is the form preferred for making generalizations about classes of human beings:

> (59) **İtalyanlar** konuşkandır.
> '*(The) Italians* are talkative.'

> (60) Kimse **politikacılar**a güvenmez.
> 'No one trusts *politicians*.'

The 'individuation' conveyed by the plural generic makes it appropriate for the expression of quite modest or homely generalizations based upon the speaker's personal observation or experience:

> (61) **Kalorifersiz evler** nispeten ucuz oluyor.
> '*Flats without central heating* are relatively cheap.'

> (62) Bugün **gençler** [yemek yapmasın]-ı bilmiyorlar.
> '*Young people* today don't know [how to cook].'

22.4.3   GENERIC NOUN PHRASES AS DIRECT OBJECTS

Bare generics are usually non-case-marked in the direct object function:

(63)   Sen **çocuk** sevmezsin.
       'You don't like *children*.'

(64)   Ayten **şapka** seviyor.
       'Ayten loves *hats*.'

In sentences where a direct object with no determiner has accusative marking, the referential status of the noun phrase is usually definite:

(65)   Ayten **şapkayı** seviyor.
       'Ayten loves *the hat*.'

However, such noun phrases can also be open to a generic interpretation:

(66)   Ayten **şapkayı** başkalarında seviyor, ama [saçları güzel olduğu için] kendisi pek giymiyor.
       'Ayten likes *hats* on other people, but [because she has beautiful hair] she herself doesn't wear [them] much.'

A bare generic direct object is particularly likely to be accusative-marked where (a) it denotes animate beings, and (b) the subject of the sentence is itself a bare generic:

(67)   **Kedi köpeği** kovar.
       '*A cat* drives away/can drive away *a dog*.'

(68)   **Mühendis mimarı** kıskanır.
       '*The/An engineer* is usually jealous of *the/an architect*.'

Two other types of bare generic also have to be accusative-marked when they are direct objects:

(**i**)   *-sI* compounds (10.2) whose modifier constituent is a noun of nationality:

(69)   Arkadaşım **Türk kahvesini** sevmiyor.
       'My friend doesn't like *Turkish coffee*.'

(**ii**)   Noun phrases expressing entities regarded as social 'institutions':

(70)   Kızın ailesi [**okulu** önemsemiyor] görünüyor.
       'The girl's family appears [not to regard *school* as important].'

Indefinite and plural generics occurring as direct objects are obligatorily accusative-marked:

(71) Ahmet o anda [**koşuya hazırlanan**] **bir atlet***i* andırıyordu.
'At that moment Ahmet looked like {*an athlete* [*preparing for a race*]}.'

(72) Ali **doktorları** sevmez.
'Ali doesn't like *doctors*.'

22.5 THE EFFECT OF WORD ORDER ON REFERENTIAL STATUS

In the case of a subject noun phrase, its position in the sentence can have a determining effect on its referential status. In (73), where the noun phrase is not plural-marked, the difference in word order gives a categorial reading in (a) and a definite reading in (b). This is because a categorial subject has to occupy the immediately preverbal position (23.2.1 (v)), whereas the usual position for a definite subject is at the beginning of the sentence (23.1). While it is possible for a definite subject to be placed in the immediately preverbal position for purposes of emphasis or contrast (23.3), the likelihood of (a) being uttered with the meaning of 'It was *the burglar* (not anyone else) who got in through here' is small.

(73) (**a**) Buradan **hırsız** girmiş. (cf. (43))
'*A burglar/Burglars* got in through here.'

(**b**) **Hırsız** buradan girmiş.
'*The burglar* got in through here.'

In (74) the subject noun phrase has plural marking, which gives the possibility of an indefinite or (contrastive) definite reading in (a), but exclusively a definite reading in (b). As explained in 23.2.1, a plural-marked indefinite subject without determiner has to occupy the immediately preverbal position.

(74) (**a**) Arka sıra-lar-da **öğrenci-ler** otur-acak.
back row-PL-LOC student-PL sit-FUT
(**i**) '*Students* will sit in the back rows.'
(**ii**) 'It's *the students* who will sit in the back rows.'

(**b**) **Öğrenciler** arka sıralarda oturacak.
'*The students* will sit in the back rows.'

22.6 THE EFFECT OF STRESS ON REFERENTIAL STATUS

In a sentence that consists only of a plural-marked subject noun phrase and a verb, differential stress patterns determine the referential status of the noun phrase. It is understood as indefinite if it bears sentence stress itself, as in (a) below, and as definite if the stress is on the verb, as in (b).

(75) (a) Rapor**LAR** yazıldı.
'*Reports* were written.'

(b) Raporlar yazıl**DI**.
'*The reports* were written.'

22.7 THE EFFECT OF TENSE, ASPECT AND MODALITY ON REFERENTIAL STATUS

The tense/aspect/modality of the predicate is the most important indicator of whether a subject noun phrase has definite or generic reference. A bare generic subject noun phrase almost always occurs with one of the predicate types identified in 21.4.1.1 as expressing permanent or generalized validity, namely verbal predicates containing the aorist suffix -(A/I)r/-mAz, and nominal predicates, optionally marked by -DIr. A generic interpretation is often not possible with finite verb forms that express perfective aspect (21.3.1) or (definite) future tense, i.e. -DI, -mIş and -(y)AcAK. The contrast between (76a) and (76b) below shows that only in the case of predicates that can be applied holistically to an entire class of entities is the use of one of these forms compatible with a generic interpretation:

(76) (a) **Bilgisayar** hepimizin işini kolaylaştır**dı**.
'*The computer* has made things easier for all of us.'

(b) **Bilgisayar** Kenan'ın odasına kon**du**.
'*The computer* was put in Kenan's room.'

(76a) is capable of either a generic or a definite reading (computers in general, or a particular computer), while (76b) must refer to a specific computer, because 'putting' is an action that can only be performed on individual entities, not on an entire class.

(77) below has the aorist marking characteristic of sentences which make generalized statements about behaviour or qualities regarded as typical of a class of entities, and translation (i) expresses this generic interpretation. However, since the aorist is used equally to express the characteristic behaviour or qualities of an individual (21.4.1.1), (77) can also be understood as a statement about a particular cat (translation (ii)):

(77) **Kedi** süt iç*er.*
    (**i**) '*Cats* drink milk.'/'*A cat* drinks milk.'
    (**ii**) '*The cat* drinks milk.'

The substitution of -*(I)yor* for the aorist in (78) eliminates altogether the possibility of a generic reading. *Kedi* here has to have definite reference to a specific cat.

(78) **Kedi** süt iç*iyor.*
    (**i**) '*The cat* is drinking (some) milk.'
    (**ii**) '*The cat* drinks milk.'

However, there are contexts in which -*(I)yor* is readily compatible with a generic subject. As shown above in (61)–(62), this usage is particularly common in statements with plural generic subjects, for which only a limited degree of generality is claimed, and which reflect the speaker's own experience rather than a universal law.

(79) (**a**) {**Bu makineler**} iyi kesmiyor.
       '{*These machines*} don't cut well.'

    (**b**) {**Bu tür makineler**} iyi kesmiyor.
       '{*This kind of machine*} doesn't cut well.'

(79a) is ambiguous between a generic interpretation ('machines of this kind') and a definite one (referring to a specific set of machines known to both speaker and hearer). The replacement of the simple demonstrative by the explicitly generic modifier *bu tür* 'this kind (of)' eliminates the ambiguity. Other explicitly generic modifiers derived from the demonstratives are *bu/o gibi* 'this/that kind of' and *böyle/şöyle/öyle (bir)* (see 22.4.1.2 (ii) and examples (55) and (58)). These modifiers occur only with plural and indefinite generics.

(80) illustrates the effect of the generalizing modality marker -*DIr* on the referential status of a noun phrase in a nominal sentence. The noun phrase *hanımelinin* is in a possessor/modifier role in this sentence, but the same effect would be observable in a subject.

(80) (**a**) **Hanımeli**-nin koku-su çok güzel.
       honeysuckle-GEN smell-3SG.POSS very beautiful
       'The smell of *(the)* honeysuckle is lovely.'

    (**b**) **Hanımeli**nin kokusu çok güzel-*dir.*
                           -GM
       'The smell of *honeysuckle* is lovely.'

(c) **Hanımeli**nin kokusu çok güzel-*di*.

-P.COP

'The smell of *the honeysuckle* was lovely.'

(a) is ambiguous between a generic reading (honeysuckle plants in general) and a definite one (referring to a particular honeysuckle plant). The addition of -*DIr* in (b) forces the generalized reading. (c), on the other hand, shows that, just as in verbal sentences perfective aspect is usually incompatible with generic reference, so in nominal sentences past tense marking usually excludes the generic interpretation. The latter would be possible only in the case of a change in the situation of an entire class of entities over time, as in (81):

(81) 1920'lerde **otomobil** yaygın değil*di*.
       '*Cars* were not common in the 1920s.'

23 WORD ORDER

In Turkish word order is variable. Changing the order of the constituents in a sentence is used as a means of distinguishing new information from background information and of making a certain constituent prominent in the discourse. Shifting the position of sentence stress also serves a similar purpose. Hence variations in word order, together with the position of sentence stress, affect the meaning of a sentence. Although there are many possible arrangements for the stressed and unstressed constituents in a sentence, here we discuss only the most common patterns of word order variation.

Which particular syllable receives stress within a constituent that requires to be stressed is determined by the rules of word stress explained in Chapter 4.

23.1 gives an overview of the unmarked order of sentence constituents, and 23.2 explores this topic in more detail. Variations in word order are discussed in 23.3. Section 23.4 looks at constituents that are dislocated from phrases and from subordinate clauses.

23.1 UNMARKED SENTENCES: WORD ORDER AND STRESS

Major constituents can occur in any order in Turkish, but the unmarked order is *subject (– object) – predicate* (SOV) in verbal sentences and *subject – predicate* in nominal sentences. The term **unmarked order** refers to the ordering of constituents in the opening sentence of a dialogue or discourse, where no information is presupposed.

(1) Terzi elbise-m-i bitir-miş.
    SUBJECT OBJECT PREDICATE
    dressmaker dress-1SG.POSS-ACC finish-EV/PF
    'Apparently the dressmaker has finished my dress.'

(2) Hava çok soğuk.
    SUBJECT PREDICATE
    weather very cold
    'The weather is very cold.'

Utterances in the unmarked order have no particular part which is more prominent than the others. The main properties of an unmarked sentence are given below:

(i)   The predicate is at the end.
(ii)   The subject is at the beginning.
(iii) A non-case-marked direct object, or any indefinite constituent with the occasional exception of an animate subject, occurs immediately before the verb.
(iv)   An oblique object is placed immediately before the verb.
(v)   Modal adverbials occur either at the very beginning of the sentence, or after the subject.
(vi)   Sentence stress falls on the constituent before the predicate in verbal and affirmative existential sentences, on the subject complement in affirmative linking sentences, on *değil* in negative linking sentences and on *yok* in negative existential sentences.

In this chapter (and occasionally elsewhere in this book) stress is indicated by capital letters. Bold type and/or italics do *not* indicate stress.

23.1.1   VERBAL SENTENCES

The unmarked order in verbal sentences is:

SUBJECT/MODAL ADVERBIAL – ACCUSATIVE-MARKED DIRECT OBJECT – OTHER ADVERBIALS – OBLIQUE OBJECT/NON-CASE-MARKED DIRECT OBJECT – VERB

(3)   Çocuk-lar belki akşam televizyon-da film seyred-er-ler.
       child-PL perhaps evening television-LOC film watch-AOR-3PL
       'The children will perhaps watch a film on television tonight.'

In unmarked verbal sentences, sentence stress falls on the constituent immediately before the predicate:

(4)   Erol bu sabah otobüste **Sema-YA** rastla-dı.
                             Sema-DAT come.across-PF
       'Erol came across Sema on the bus this morning.'

There are two instances where a sentence is unmarked, yet stress falls on a constituent other than the one immediately before the predicate:

(i)   When there are clitics and other unstressable items (4.3.2):

(5)   Ev-e GİT-me-di-m.
       house-DAT go-NEG-PF-1SG
       'I didn't go home.'

(ii)   When there are certain adverbs of degree (16.5), such as *en* 'most', *daha* 'more' and *çok* 'very':

(6) ÇOK yavaş kitap okurum.
very slowly book read-AOR-1SG
'I read books *very* slowly.'

23.1.2 NOMINAL SENTENCES

23.1.2.1 Linking sentences

In linking sentences (12.1.1.2), the predicate is placed at the end and the subject at the beginning. Sentence stress falls on the part of the predicate which is before the copular marker (*müdür* 'director' in (7), and the possessive suffix -*ü* in (8)).

(7) Rezan bu banka-da **müDÜR**-dü.
        this bank-LOC director-P.COP
'Rezan was a director at this bank.'

(8) Rezan bu banka-nın **müdür-Ü**-ydü.
        this bank-GEN director-3SG.POSS-P.COP
'Rezan was the director of this bank.'

Stress falls on the nominal predicate irrespective of whether there is an overt copular marker or not:

(9) Rezan on yıldır **piLOT**.
'Rezan has been a pilot for 10 years.'

When there is an adjective modifying the nominal predicate, stress falls on the adjective:

(10) Rezan **iYİ** bir pilot.
'Rezan is a good pilot.'

23.1.2.2 Existential sentences

In existential sentences (12.1.1.2) the initial position is occupied by a locative or genitive noun phrase. The subject occupies the position immediately before the predicate. Stress falls on the subject if the sentence is affirmative, and on the predicate if it is negative.

(11) Bu köy-de çoktandır genetik **bir hastaLIK** var-mış.
     this village-LOC for.a.long.time genetic a disease existent-EV.COP
'There has been a genetic disease in this village for a long time.'

(12) Hasan-ın imza yetki-si **YOK**.
Hasan-GEN signature authorization-3SG.POSS non-existent
'Hasan does not have authorization to sign.'

23.2 THE UNMARKED ORDER OF MAJOR CONSTITUENTS

23.2.1 THE IMMEDIATELY PREVERBAL POSITION

There are certain types of constituent that obligatorily occupy the position immediately before the verb. The only items that can come between such phrases and the predicate are the question particle *mI*, adverbial clitics such as *bile* 'even', *dA* 'also', etc. (Chapter 11), and (in the case of (iv)–(vi) below) adverbial expressions such as *çok* 'very much' and wh-phrases. The types of phrase in question are:

(i) Subject complements (12.1.1.2):

(13) Meral çabucak **hasta** oldu.
'Meral quickly became *ill*.'

(ii) Small clauses (24.5):

(14) Ben [**Meral-i hasta**] sanıyordum.
'I thought *Meral [was] ill*.'

(iii) Adjectives used adverbially (16.1.2):

(15) Bu yemek odası takımı mutfakta **iğreti** duruyor.
'This dining room set looks *out of place* in the kitchen.'

(16) Nilgün problemleri **yavaş** çözer.
'Nilgün solves (the) problems *slowly*.'

(iv) Non-case-marked direct objects (which may be indefinite (22.2) or categorial (22.3) noun phrases):

(17) Dün bana **başka bir telefon numarası** vermiştin.
'Yesterday you gave me *a different telephone number*.'

(v) Categorial subjects:

(18) Elimi **cam** kesti.
'*Some glass* cut my hand.'

(**vi**) Plural-marked indefinite subjects without a determiner:

> (19) Yukarıya **yeni kiracılar** taşınmış.
> '*New tenants* have apparently moved in upstairs.'

There are certain other types of phrase that also tend to occur in the immediately preverbal position:

(**i**) Oblique objects, unless there is also an adverb:

> (20) İnsanların çoğu **ölümden** korkar.
> 'Most people fear *death*.'

> (21) Sen **babama** *hep* kızardın.
> 'You *always* got angry with *my father*.'

(**ii**) Adverbial clauses of manner (26.3.8):

> (22) Neslihan elbiselerini [**üstüne denemeden**] alır.
> 'Neslihan buys her clothes [*without trying them on*].'

(**iii**) Case-marked indefinite noun phrases:

> (23) Dün sokakta **bir hırsız-ı** kovala-mış-lar.
>   a thief-ACC chase-EV/PF-3PL
> 'Apparently they chased *a thief* in the street yesterday.'

> (24) Müdür resmi evrakları **bir sekreter-e** verdi.
>   a secretary-DAT give-PF
> 'The director gave the official documents *to a secretary*.'

(**iv**) Indefinite animate and inanimate subjects:

> (25) Sabah eve **bir adam** geldi.
> '*A man* came to the house this morning.'

> (26) Dolabın arkasına **bir şey** düşmüş.
> '*Something* seems to have fallen down behind the cupboard.'

23.2.2 SUBJECTS AND MODAL ADVERBS

In most cases, the position of modal adverbs and subjects is interchangeable:

(27) *Meğer* **Hasan** çoktan tıbbı bitirmişmiş.
as.it.turns.out Hasan
'It turns out that Hasan completed his medical studies a long
time ago.'

(28) **Necla** *galiba* artık bankada değil.
Necla I.think
'I don't think Necla is with the bank any more.'

In existential sentences the modal adverb usually precedes the subject or
the possessive-marked noun phrase within the subject:

(29) Biz-de *sahiden* **video** yok.
we-LOC really
'We really don't have a video player.'

(30) Biz-im *gerçekten* **video-muz** yok.
we-GEN really video.player-1PL.POSS
'We really don't have a video player.'

23.2.3 OBJECTS

Non-case-marked direct objects and oblique objects occur in the immediately preverbal position when they precede the predicate. The only
exception to this is when they are followed by certain clitics or adverbials
(see 23.2.1):

(31) **Bir çay** *da* bana ver.
'Give me *a (glass of) tea, too.*'

(32) Ahmet'ten **mektup** *mu* aldın?
'Have you had *a letter* from Ahmet?'

Definite and other accusative-marked direct objects usually occur near
the beginning of the sentence, following the subject noun phrase and/or
modal adverbial, if present:

(33) (Ahmet herhalde) **bütün para-yı** bir haftada bitirir.
'(Ahmet)/[He] would (probably) get through *all the money* in a
week.'

(34) (Öğretmen) {[**dersi baltalayan**] **öğrencilerden birkaç tanesin**}-i
idareye bildirdi.
'(The teacher)/[S/he] reported *several of the students* [*who had
disrupted the class*] to the authorities.'

In sentences which contain both an accusative-marked direct object and an oblique object, the former has to precede the latter:

(35) Hasta anne-sin-**i** ye-mey-**e** zorla-dı.
sick mother-3SG.POSS-ACC eat-VN-DAT force-PF
'S/he forced his/her sick mother to eat.'

Otherwise there are generally no clear-cut rules determining the ordering of two or more case-marked noun phrases (objects or adverbials) in relation to one another, *where all or both are definite*. The general principle is that the more predictable a constituent is (e.g. from previous mention or from presence in the speech context) the earlier in the sentence it is likely to appear.

(36) Ahmet öğrenci-ler-**e** sınav kağıt-ların-**ı** verdi.
student-PL-DAT exam paper-3PL.POSS-ACC
'Ahmet gave the students their exam papers.'

(37) Şu masa-**yı** yandaki oda-**ya** götür.
table-ACC   room-DAT
'Take this table into the room next door.'

If a sentence has two accusative-marked or two dative-marked noun phrases (because there are two clauses in the sentence), then each noun phrase occupies its unmarked position within its own clause (see also 13.2.1.1 (38)):

(38) Ahmet **sen-i** [**ben-i** tanı-mı-yor] san-dı.
you-ACC I-ACC know-NEG-IMPF think-PF
'Ahmet thought you didn't know me.'

(39) **Doktor-a** [**hasta-ya** bak-ma-sın]-ı söyle-di.
doctor-DAT patient-DAT check-VN-3SG.POSS-ACC tell-PF
'S/he told the doctor [to check the patient].'

23.2.4 ADVERBIAL PHRASES

Adverbial phrases of time generally precede those expressing location, which in turn precede those expressing manner:

(40) Ben **şimdi** derslerimi **aşağıda bilgisayar-la** veriyorum.
now   downstairs computer-INS
'*Now* I'm giving my lectures *downstairs with a computer.*'

Adverbials expressing reason or purpose often occur at the beginning of the sentence, and can precede the subject:

(41) [**Mehmet borcunu ödemediği için**] Ali **bu yıl** kendi borçlarını **zor**
     ödeyecek.
     '[*Because Mehmet hasn't paid his debt*] Ali will pay his own debts
     with great difficulty this year.'

(42) [**Bozulmasın diye**] annem köfteyi buzdolabına koymuştu.
     'My mother had put the meatballs in the fridge [*so that they
     wouldn't go off*].'

Most adverbials of time may also precede the subject:

(43) **Dün** annem doktora gitti.
     '*Yesterday* my mother went to the doctor.'

(44) **Hafta sonları** çocuklar burada olmuyor.
     'The children are not here *at the weekends.*'

Where two adverbials of time or place occur together, the one with the
broader meaning precedes the other:

(45) **Her gün 14.30-da** uçak kalkıyormuş.
     every day 14.30-LOC
     'It seems a plane goes *at 14.30 every day.*'

23.3   WORD ORDER VARIATIONS

The major constituents of a sentence can appear in any order, provided that
none is indefinite. For example, a sentence containing a subject, a direct
object (with an accusative case marker) and a verb has six possible orders
(with the further possibility of inserting adverbials at the beginning, the end
or between constituents):

(46) **(a)** Ali ev-i sat-tı.
         Ali house-ACC sell-PF
         'Ali sold the house.'

     (b) Evi Ali sattı.
     (c) Ali sattı evi.
     (d) Evi sattı Ali.
     (e) Sattı Ali evi.
     (f) Sattı evi Ali.

Although these sentences are equally grammatical, they are used in
different contexts. For example, (b) and (c) are interchangeable if *Ali* is

stressed, a strategy which guides the hearer to focus his/her attention on Ali, and indicates that it was Ali who sold the house. (e) and (f) emphasize the selling of the house, as a verb which is at the beginning of a sentence obligatorily carries stress. On the other hand, (b) and (d) are more or less interchangeable if *evi* 'the house (ACC)' bears stress. These sentences are used in circumstances when the emphasis is placed on this constituent, e.g. to draw attention to the fact that it is the house and not some other building that Ali sold. This interpretation applies to (a) as well if *evi* 'the house' bears stress. These are a few of the possible interpretations of (a)–(f).

Changing the order in which constituents appear in unmarked sentences, i.e. **scrambling** them, has three general purposes:

(i) Emphasizing a particular constituent:
This strategy, which is called **focusing**, is used to highlight the information provided by the constituent in question. This may be because it is new information, i.e. refers to something that has not previously been mentioned, or because the speaker wishes to contrast this item of information with another (perhaps previously mentioned).

(ii) De-emphasizing a particular constituent or constituents:
Some of the constituents in a sentence may have relatively less informative value than others, generally as a result of having been mentioned earlier, or simply because they are uttered as an afterthought. Such pieces of information are described as **backgrounded**.

(iii) Making a particular constituent the pivot of the information in a sentence:
A particular constituent may act as the information centre in terms of signalling what the sentence is about. This is called a **topic**.

Placing (or not placing) sentence stress on a constituent plays as important a role in determining its information value as scrambling does. For example, focused constituents are almost always stressed, while backgrounded constituents never are. Those signalling topics usually take secondary stress (see 5.2.2).

In many cases the acoustic quality of stress in sentences with scrambled order is different from the stress of unmarked sentences. In particular, a focused constituent usually gets heavy stress, with an accent higher in pitch than the stressed constituent of an unmarked sentence. However, we do not attempt to indicate such differences in this book.

The following conditions apply to scrambled constituents:

    (i) Focused phrases bear heavy stress.

(ii) Focused phrases appear in the area preceding the predicate, either immediately to the left of the predicate or in their unmarked position.

(iii) Backgrounded information follows the predicate and is never stressed.

(iv) Topics (sometimes followed by topic shifters) usually occur at the beginning of a sentence.

(v) The predicate is obligatorily stressed (and focused) if it is at the beginning of a sentence.

(vi) Certain semantic properties of noun phrases, such as definiteness, specificity and animacy, also affect word order, as discussed in 22.5, 23.2.1 and 23.3.3.

23.3.1 THE POSITION OF FOCUSED CONSTITUENTS: THE PREVERBAL AREA

All types of constituents can be focused. Focused constituents can occur in any position before the predicate, but their most typical position in verbal sentences is immediately in front of the verb. They bear heavy stress wherever they may occur:

(47) Fatma çiçek-ler-i **BUgün** sula-yacak.
Fatma flower-PL-ACC today water-FUT
'Fatma will water the plants TODAY.'

(48) Bazı günler ön bahçe-de **çocuk-LAR** oynu-yor.
some day-PL front garden-LOC child-PL play-IMPF
'Some days CHILDREN play in the front garden.'

A less common strategy for focusing a constituent is to place stress on it in its unmarked position:

(49) **BUgün** çiçekleri sulayacaksın.
'You will water the plants TODAY.'

The most typical strategy for focusing a constituent in an existential sentence is to place stress on it in its unmarked position:

(50) **Ahmet'İN** iki arabası var.
'AHMET has two cars.'

In linking sentences the preferred strategy is to place the focused constituent just before the predicate:

(51) Ahmet'in babası **HER gün** hasta.
'Ahmet's father is ill EVERY DAY.'

Focused constituents can be used with focus-sensitive adverbials and connectives such as *ancak* 'only', *dA* 'also' and *bile* 'even' (see 16.7, 28.3.1.1).

(52) ***Ancak öZEL izin-le*** gir-il-ebil-iyor-muş kulis-e.
only special permit-INS enter-PASS-PSB-IMPF-EV.COP
back.stage-DAT
'One can only go back stage *by special permit*.'

(53) **KomşuLAR** *da* bazı günler ön bahçede oturuyor.
'Some days *the neighbours* too sit in the front garden.'

Like any other constituent, predicates can be focused by placing stress on them. When stressed, they can occupy any position, including their unmarked sentence-final position:

(54) Onlar-ın hep-si **öğretMEN**. (Cevapları tabii ki bilecekler.)
they-GEN all-3SG.POSS teacher
'They are all TEACHERS. (Of course they'll know the answers.)'

(55) Ama ben bütün mektupları dün **yırtTIM**.
'But I TORE UP all the letters yesterday.'

23.3.2 THE POSITION OF BACKGROUND INFORMATION: THE POSTVERBAL AREA

The area following the predicate, generally referred to as the postverbal area, is the site for information which is backgrounded, information which is assumed to be shared by the speaker and the hearer, or which has only just been mentioned in the discourse. Placing constituents here also has the effect of rendering another constituent more prominent, sometimes leaving this latter as the only phrase before the predicate. Note that the strategy of backgrounding is restricted to spoken and informal written Turkish. In formal written styles constituents are not normally placed after the predicate.

(56) Hiç seyahat-e GİT-me-miş **yalnız başına daha önce**.
never trip-DAT go-NEG-EV/PF alone before
'Apparently s/he's never been on holiday *alone before*.'

(57) GüZEL-miş **bu ev**.
nice-EV.COP this house
'It's nice, *this house*.'

The relative positioning of the constituents in the postverbal area is insignificant. More than one constituent can follow the predicate, and these can occur in any order. If all the constituents in a sentence follow the predicate then the predicate is obligatorily stressed. The sentences below are informationally identical:

(58) (a) Bitir-Dİ **Fatma üniversite-yi bu yıl**.
finish-PF Fatma university-ACC this year
'Fatma FINISHED university this year.'

(b) BitirDİ **üniversite-yi bu yıl Fatma**.

(c) BitirDİ **bu yıl Fatma üniversite-yi**.

No constituent occurring in the postverbal area can bear stress; as a result, the postverbal area cannot host stress-requiring elements such as wh-phrases (19.2.1) or *mI*-phrases (19.1). (Note that *mI*-phrases can appear after the predicate in alternative questions, in cases where the second mention of a shared verb is omitted; see example (18) in 19.1.2.)

The types of constituents that are most commonly backgrounded are definite noun phrases and adverbials. However, it is possible for a non-definite noun phrase to be placed in the postverbal position if it refers to an entity or category that has been mentioned (or implied) in the immediately preceding discourse:

(59) Ayşe senin arkadaşlarınla ne kadar rahat konuşuyordu.
Üniversiteye girdiği yıl bil-mi-yor-du hiç **İngilizce**.
                                  know-NEG-IMPF-P.COP any English
'How fluently Ayşe was talking to your friends. She didn't know any *English* the year she entered university.'

(60) Bana da getir **bir kahve**.
I(DAT) too bring a coffee
'Bring me *a coffee*, too.'

(61) Var-mış **siz-in bakkal-da kopya kağıd-ı**!
existent-EV.COP you-GEN grocer-LOC carbon paper-NC
'Your grocer DOES sell carbon paper!'

Backgrounding can also take place within a noun clause:

(62) [(. . .) Piyano çal-dığ-ın-ı **Ayşe-nin**] bil-mi-yor-du-m.
piano play-VN-3SG.POSS-ACC Ayşe-GEN know-NEG-IMPF-P.COP-1SG
'I didn't know [*Ayşe* played the piano].'

23.3.3 THE TOPIC POSITION

The initial position in a sentence is often used to indicate what the sentence is 'about', in other words its topic. As explained in 23.1, in unmarked sentences it is usually the subject (if overtly expressed) that occupies the topic position. However, through scrambling it is possible to topicalize any constituent except those that obligatorily occur in the immediately preverbal position (see 23.2.1). In some of the translations in this section passivization has been used in order to reflect the informational effect of topicalizing a non-subject constituent.

> (63) **Erol-a** sonunda Spor Birliği bir maDALya ver-di.
>   Erol-DAT finally sports association a medal give-PF
>   '*Erol* was finally awarded a medal by the Sports Association.'

Where a non-definite direct object is topicalized, it has to be given accusative marking if it is no longer in the immediately preverbal position (see 14.3.3.2 (ii)).

> (64) **Suluboya-yı** ancak usTA bir ressam böyle kullan-abil-ir.
>   watercolour-ACC only highly.skilled a painter like.this
>   use-PSB-AOR
>   '*Watercolours* can only be used like this by a highly skilled painter.'

An indefinite noun phrase can be topicalized only if it refers to a member or members of a group or category that has been mentioned or implied in the preceding discourse:

> (65) Misafirlerin çoğu bahçeye çıkmıştı. **Birkaç çocuk** orada babamla konuşuyordu.
>   'Most of the guests had gone out into the garden. *Several children* were talking to my father out there.'

> (66) **Bir tane** de bana ver.
>   'Give me *one*, too.'

Noun phrases with categorial status (22.3) cannot be topicalized as *subjects*. This means that subject noun phrases that occur in the topic position without plural marking and without a determiner are always interpreted as definite (see 22.5) or generic (see 22.7).

It should be noted that not all sentences in Turkish have overtly expressed topics. The continuation of a subject-topic from one sentence to another is signalled by the *absence* of a noun phrase referring to the subject in the second and subsequent sentences in the sequence (see 18.1.5).

Topicalization can also take place within a noun clause:

(67) Ayşe [**yaprağ-ı** annesi (...) sar-ıyor] san-dı.
Ayşe vine.leaf-ACC mother-3SG.POSS stuff-IMPF think-PF
'Ayşe thought *the vine leaves* were being stuffed by her mother.'

23.3.3.1 Topic shifters

There are a number of markers in Turkish which signal a change of topic: the clitics *dA* and *-(y)sA/ise* and the postposition *gelince* 'as for ...' (the *-(y)IncA* converbial form of *gel-* 'come', i.e. 'when one comes to ...'). *-(y)sA/ise* and *gelince* are placed immediately after the new topic at the beginning of a sentence. The position of a *dA* marked topic is somewhat less rigid, and although as a topic shifter *dA* most commonly appears after the first constituent in a sentence, it can also occur in other positions.

(i) The clitic *dA* is the least emphatic marker of topic shift. It signals a continuity or connection between two events or situations, and is usually equivalent to 'and' or 'so' in English (see also 28.3.1.1 (iiia)).

(68) Kimse Semra'ya gel dememiş, o **da** evDE oturacakmış.
'No one asked Semra to come, *so* she'll be staying at home.'

A non-focused *subject* combined with *dA* may occur in the post-verbal position:

(69) Derslerini yapmamışlar. Onları UYARDIM ben **de**.
'It seems they haven't done their homework. *So* I've warned them'.

For other functions of *dA*, see 28.3.1.1 (iiib), 28.3.2 and 28.3.4.3.

(ii) The clitic *-(y)sA/ise* sends a stronger signal, indicating that a significantly different point is going to be made about the new topic. This may be a direct contrast with what has been said about the previous topic:

(70) Sen hep kolayına kaçıyorsun, ben**se** her işi en iyi şekilde yapmaya çalışıyorum.
'You always take the easy way out, *whereas* I try to do everything in the best way possible.'

Alternatively, it may be a rather striking, perhaps even surprising, further development of the same theme:

(71) Kağıtları ancak toparlayabildim. Kitaplar**sa** hala kutularda duruyor.
'I have only managed to tidy up the papers. *As for* the books, they are still in their boxes.'

(72) Ahmet Semra'yı hiç aramıyormuş. Semra'nınsa buna hiç aldırdığı
yok (see 24.4.3.3 (i).
'Apparently Ahmet doesn't call Semra any more. Semra, *for her
part*, couldn't care less.'

(iii) *gelince* phrases correspond to 'as for . . .' constructions in English.
They have dative-marked complements which act as antecedent to an obligatory pronoun later in the sentence. This construction occurs less frequently
than topics marked with *dA* or *-(y)sA*, and signals that the speaker wishes
to draw particular attention to the statement that is about to be made.

(73) Hayri ve Faruk bugün babalarına hediye alacaklarını söylediler.
Ahmet'e *gelince*, o nasıl olsa çok düşünceli-dir. Al-mış-tır bile.
Ahmet-DAT as.for he anyway very thoughtful-GM
Buy-PF-GM already
'Hayri and Faruk said they would be buying their father a
present/presents today. *As for Ahmet*, well, *he*'s very considerate
in any case. He will have bought [one] already.'

All topic-shift markers, with the topics that they mark, form intonational
phrases ending in a slight rise (5.1 (iii)). There is usually a short pause after
gelince; this may also occur after *-(y)sA*, but is not normally heard after *dA*.

23.4 DISLOCATED CONSTITUENTS

In addition to the possibility of placing any major constituent after the predicate, some constituents can cross the boundaries of the phrase or the clause
of which they are part.

23.4.1 DISLOCATED ADJECTIVAL PHRASES

Adjectival phrases which are parts of indefinite noun phrases can be placed
in the position following the predicate. This usually occurs where the modifying phrase is added as an afterthought. In the examples below the
unmarked position for the dislocated phrase is indicated by (. . .).

(74) Burada (. . .) bir elbise-m var-dı **eteğ-i sökük**.
here a dress-1SG.POSS existent-P.COP hemline-3SG.POSS unstitched
'I had a dress here, *with its hemline unstitched*.'

(75) Bütün zeytinyağlı-lar-da (. . .) şeker var-dır **bir iki kaşık**.
all cold.vegetable.dish-PL-LOC sugar existent-GM one two spoonful
'All cold vegetable dishes have sugar in them, [just] *one or two
spoonfuls*.'

23.4.2 DISLOCATED CONSTITUENTS OF NOUN CLAUSES

Mostly subjects, but also other constituents of a noun clause can be dislocated and placed at the end of the sentence:

(76) [(. . .) Piyano çal-dığ-ın]-ı bil-mi-yor-du-m **Ayşe'nin.**
      piano play-VN-3SG.POSS-ACC know-NEG-IMPF-P.COP-1SG
      Ayşe-GEN
      'I didn't know [*Ayşe* played the piano].'

(77) [Zerrin'in (. . .) (. . .) gör-me-sin]-i iste-mi-yor-du-m
      Zerrin-GEN see-VN-3SG.POSS-ACC want-NEG-IMPF-P.COP-1SG
      hediye-sin-i şimdiden.
      present 3SG.POSS-ACC yet
      'I didn't want [Zerrin to see *her present yet*].'

Alternatively, constituents of a noun clause can be placed at the beginning of a sentence for topicalization:

(78) **Yaprağ-ı** Ayşe [herhangi biri-nin (. . .) sar-abil-eceğ-in-e]
      vine.leaf-ACC Ayşe anyone-GEN stuff-PSB-VN-3SG.POSS-DAT
      inan-mı-yor-du.
      believe-NEG-IMPF-P.COP
      'Ayşe didn't believe [that (just) anyone could stuff *vine leaves*].'

24 NOUN CLAUSES

Noun clauses are clausal noun phrases. They are subordinate clauses that perform within the larger sentence (within the main clause or another subordinate clause) the same functions as noun phrases, i.e. those of subject, object, etc. (see Chapter 14). Structurally they may be one of two types:

(i)   **finite** (i.e. identical in structure to a full sentence, see 12.3):

   (1)   [Üniversite-ye gid-e-yim] isti-yor.
         university-DAT go-OPT-1SG want-IMPF
         'S/he wants [me to go to university].'

(ii)   **non-finite** (i.e. with their verbal constituent marked by one of the subordinating suffixes *-mAK, -mA, -DIK, -(y)AcAK* or *-(y)Iş*, see 12.3):

   (2)   [Konu-yu iyice anla-**mak**] gerek.
         topic-ACC thoroughly understand-VN necessary
         'One has to understand the topic thoroughly.'

Within the finite category a further division exists: **bare finite noun clauses** (24.2) are simply juxtaposed to, or inserted within, the **superordinate** clause, as in (1) above, while **finite noun clauses** with a **subordinator** (24.3; see also 12.3) are linked to their superordinate clause by a preceding *ki* or a following *diye* or *gibi*:

   (3)   [Sen Londra-da-sın **diye**] *bil*-iyor-du-m.
         You London-LOC-2SG SUB think-IMPF-P.COP-1SG
         'I thought [you were in London].'

In 24.4 we present a detailed account of the wide range of non-finite noun clause patterns and functions in Turkish. 24.5 is devoted to the special kind of noun clause known as a **small clause**, the subject of which is also a constituent of the superordinate clause. The chapter concludes with a brief discussion of noun clauses as modifiers in noun compounds (24.6).

In the interests of clarity we have confined both the discussion and the examples in this chapter to sentences in which the noun clause is embedded directly in the main clause. However, it should be borne in mind that all types of noun clause, with the exception of those formed with *ki* (24.3.2), regularly occur embedded in other clauses which are themselves subordinate to the main clause (see 12.3).

24.1 FINITE AND NON-FINITE NOUN CLAUSES

The subordinating suffix that is attached to the predicate of non-finite noun clauses gives them a much more recognizably *nominal* structure than a finite noun clause can have. In all noun clauses marked with *-DIK* or *-(y)AcAK*, and in most that are marked with *-mA* or *-(y)Iş*, the subject is indicated by a possessive suffix attached to the verbal noun. The subject may also be referred to more explicitly by a genitive-marked noun phrase, which gives the noun clause the overall structure of a genitive-possessive construction. (For omission of genitive marking on the subject see 24.4.6.)

(4) [(Sen-**in**) piyano çal-**dığ-ın**]-ı bilmiyordum.
you-GEN piano play-VN-2SG.POSS-ACC
'I didn't know [you played the piano].'

(5) [(Sen-**in**) piyano çal-**ma-n**]-ı beklediler.
you-GEN piano play-VN-2SG.POSS-ACC
'They expected [you to play the piano].'

Non-finite noun clauses have the same kind of mobility within the sentence as noun phrases (see 23.3). Some types of finite noun clause, on the other hand (especially the bare type and those formed with *ki*), are considerably more restricted in the positions that they can occupy in relation to the main predicate.

In general terms the non-finite types of noun clause are more universally acceptable than their finite equivalents (where these indeed exist). Except for the presentation of direct speech (24.2.1 (i)), and the use of *ki* clauses with cognitive verbs (24.3.2.2), the use of finite noun clauses is largely confined to informal styles of speech and writing.

24.2 BARE FINITE NOUN CLAUSES (FINITE NOUN CLAUSES WITHOUT A SUBORDINATOR)

These occur as subjects or objects of the verbs *de-* 'say', *iste-* 'want', and verbs of cognition.

24.2.1 SUBJECT OR OBJECT OF THE VERB *de-*

de- 'say' occurs only with finite noun clauses. It can be used not only to express a spoken utterance but also for the expression of unspoken thoughts. Here we shall discuss three different uses of *de-*.

(i) The most straightforward use of *de-* is in representations of direct speech, where the speaker claims to present the exact words spoken in another context by himself/herself or someone else. It should be noted that *de-*, whether in a finite form or a non-finite one such as *diye* (24.3.1), is the *only* verb that can be used for this purpose. The quotation itself occupies the immediately preverbal position.

(6) O gün Suzan "Artık dayan-a-m-ıyor-um" **de**-miş-ti bana.
that day Suzan now bear-PSB-NEG-IMPF-1SG say-PF-P.COP
I(DAT)
'That day Suzan had *said* to me "I can't bear [it] any longer".'

(7) Bana genellikle "Sen küçüksün, gelemezsin" **de**-n-iyor-du.
say-PASS-IMPF-P.COP
'I was usually *told* "You're too young; you can't come".'

(ii) The second use of *de-* differs only slightly from the first. Here the subordinate clause is not claimed to present the exact words uttered by a specific person on a specific occasion, but rather to encapsulate the gist of a more generalized utterance, attributed to unspecified people. Quotation marks are not found with this usage of *de-*.

(8) [New York ağustosta çekilmez] **di**-yor-lar.
say-IMPF-3PL
'People *say* [New York is unbearable in August].'

(iii) The use of *de-* to express thoughts rather than utterances is very common in informal registers. Although the context may imply that the thought is articulated in speech, quotation marks are not used, because the emphasis is on the substance of the thought rather than on a particular utterance of it.

(9) [Tören bir saat sürer] **di**yelim.
'Let's *suppose* [the ceremony will last an hour].'

Where the verb in the subordinate clause is marked with one of the optative forms *-sIn*, *-(y)AyIm*, *-(y)AlIm* or the conditional *-sA*, the thought is also a desire for something to happen (see 21.4.4).

(10) [Herkes kendi yiyeceklerini kendi getir**sin**] **di**yorum ben.
'I *think* [everyone *should* bring their own food].'

(11) [Bu belirsizlik bit-*se* artık] **di**-yor-du-k.
this uncertainty end-OPT now say-IMPF-P.COP-1PL
'[*If only* this uncertainty *would* end], we *thought*.'

Note that the verb *söyle-*, the other verb in Turkish which means 'say', contrasts with *de-* in terms of the type of noun clause that can be used with it. *Söyle-* can only be used with non-finite clauses (see 24.4.2.2 and 24.4.3.1); moreover, it always denotes a *spoken* utterance.

24.2.2 INTERROGATIVE SENTENCE AS SUBJECT OR OBJECT OF A VERB OF COGNITION

A finite question clause can be the subject or object of a verb of cognition such as *bil-* 'know', *anla-* 'understand'. The main verb is usually negative or interrogative:

(12) [Çocuğ-un baba-sı kim] **bil**-in-iyor mu?
child-GEN father-3SG.POSS who know-PASS-IMPF INT
'Is it *known* [who the child's father is]?'

(13) [Ertan'ı neden bu kadar beğeniyorsun] **anla**yamıyorum.
'I can't *understand* [why you admire Ertan so much].'

For the use of finite *statements* as the objects of certain cognition verbs see 24.5. A number of fixed forms such as *sanırım* 'I think', *umarım* 'I hope', *bakarsın* 'you'll see' are modal adverbials (16.3).

24.2.3 SUBJECT OR OBJECT OF THE VERB *iste-*

A sentence whose main verb is *iste-* 'want' can also have a finite noun clause as its subject or object, although here the verb in the subordinate clause is always suffixed with one of the optative forms *-sIn*, *-(y)AyIm* or *-(y)AlIm* (21.4.4.2–3).

(14) [Birer birer gir-*e-lim*] **iste**-n-iyor-muş.
one.by.one go.in-OPT-1PL want-PASS-IMPF-EV.COP
'Apparently they *want* [us to go in one by one].'

(15) [Her taraf mermerle kaplan*sın*] **isti**yor.
'He *wants* [everywhere to be covered in marble].'

24.3 FINITE NOUN CLAUSES WITH A SUBORDINATOR

The subordinators that mark certain types of finite noun clauses are *diye*, *gibi* and *ki*.

24.3.1 CLAUSES FORMED WITH *diye*

The subordinator *diye* is the *-(y)A* converbial form of the verb *de-* 'say'
(26.3.8), and its functions are quite clearly derived from the various meanings of *de-* discussed in 24.2.1. *diye* is of very common occurrence in the
formation of both noun and adverbial clauses (26.1.1). It always stands at
the end of its clause. Noun clauses with *diye* function as subject or object
of the following classes of verbs:

(i)   Verbs of communication other than *de-*
(ii)   Verbs of cognition and perception
(iii) Verbs of emotion.

(i)   Verbs of communication other than *de-*:
Where a piece of direct speech is presented as the subject or object of a
main verb other than *de-*, such as *sor-* 'ask', *bağır-* 'shout' or *yaz-* 'write',
diye has to intervene between the quotation and this main verb:

(16) "Akşam-a gel-ecek mi-sin?" **diye** *sor-*du anne-m bana.
      evening-DAT come-FUT INT-2SG SUB ask-PF mother-1SG.POSS
      I(DAT)
      ' "Will you be coming back tonight?" my mother *asked* me.'

As the object of *konuş-* 'talk', a *diye* clause expresses action that has been
agreed upon by two or more people; this need not be treated as a quotation:

(17) [Herkes bir yemek yapıp getirsin **diye**] *konuş*muştuk.
      'We had *agreed* [*that* everyone should make and bring one dish].'

(ii)   Verbs of cognition and perception:
The principal verbs of cognition and perception that occur with *diye-*
marked objects are: *bil-* (in this context meaning not 'know' but 'think'
(= suppose)), *düşün-* 'think' (= speculate, be of the opinion that), *bekle-*
'expect', *duy-* 'hear', *işit-* 'hear', *oku-* 'read'.

(18) [Bir torununuz olmuş **diye**] *duy*dum.
      'I *heard* [*that* you have had a grandchild].'

See also example (3).

(iii) Verbs of emotion:
All verbs of emotion that take an oblique object (13.1.2.2) can alternatively
have a clausal object which is marked by *diye*:

(19) Teoman [memur onu azarladı **diye**] çok **sinirlen**mişti.
'Teoman *was very annoyed* [*that* the official had reprimanded him].'

In the case of *kork-* 'be afraid', the verb in the subordinate clause receives the conditional suffix *-(y)sA*:

(20) Meral, [Turgut onu Selim'le gör-ür-*se* **diye**] **kork**-uyor-du.
　　　　　　　　　　see-AOR-COND.COP SUB be.afraid-IMPF-P.COP
'Meral *was afraid* [*that* Turgut would see her with Selim].'

24.3.2 CLAUSES FORMED WITH *ki*

Unlike other noun clauses in Turkish, which can be placed either before or after the main predicate, *ki* clauses obligatorily follow the main predicate:

(21) Sanıyorum [**ki** iş-in-i bırak-mak isti-yor].
I.think that job-3SG.POSS-ACC leave-VN want-IMPF
'I think [(*that*) s/he wants to leave his/her job].'

The use of a *ki* clause rather than either of the other types of finite noun clause has the effect of highlighting the main predicate, thus drawing attention to the status of what is about to be uttered: an obvious fact, a surmise on the part of the speaker, a desire, etc. (For the stress-related properties of *ki* see 4.3.2.1.) Note that the main predicate preceding a *ki* clause is rarely cast in an interrogative or negative form.

Speakers also use *ki* structures as an organizational device to gain time for articulating the substantive content of their communication. Although of common occurrence, *ki* clauses are perceived as marked structures, and therefore do not normally occur repeatedly within a single utterance or paragraph.

24.3.2.1 Subject or object of the verb *de-*

The use of *de-* 'say' followed by a *ki* clause is an alternative to the type of structure discussed in 24.2.1, where *de-* immediately follows the clause expressing the utterance or thought. *ki* clauses occur in all the three functions of *de-* identified in 24.2.1:

(i) Representations of direct speech (cf. (6) and (7)):

(22) O gün Suzan bana **de**-miş-ti **ki**: "Artık dayan-a-m-ıyor-um".
that day Suzan I(DAT) say-PF-P.COP SUB now bear-PSB-NEG-IMPF-1SG
'That day Suzan had *said* to me "I can't bear [it] any longer".'

(23) Bana genellikle **deni**yordu **ki**: "Sen küçüksün, gelemezsin".
'I was usually *told* "You're too young; you can't come".'

(**ii**) Generalized sayings (cf. (8)):

(24) **Di**yorlar [**ki** New York ağustosta çekilmez].
'People *say* [*(that)* New York is unbearable in August].'

(**iii**) Thoughts and wishes (cf. (10)):

(25) Ben **di**yorum [**ki** herkes kendi yiyeceklerini kendi getir*sin*].
'I *think* [(that) everyone *should* bring their own food].'

There is no difference in formality between the two alternative structures with *de-*. Sentences in which *de-* is used to express thoughts rather than utterances are less likely to be structured with a *ki* clause unless, as in (25), they can be construed as containing both speech and thought elements simultaneously.

24.3.2.2 Subject or object of a verb of perception or cognition

ki clauses can occur with all verbs of perception, and also with verbs such as *inan-* 'believe', *san-* 'think', *iddia et-* 'claim', *kabul et-* 'accept', *tahmin et-* 'guess', 'imagine', which express an attitude towards the truth of a proposition.

(26) *Anlaşılı*yor [**ki** Fransızca'ya olan talep iyice azalmış].
'*It's clear* [*that* the demand for French has considerably declined].'

(27) Bir gün *duy*duk [**ki** adam taşınıp gitmiş].
'One day we *heard* [*that* the man had moved away].'

In constructions of this kind the demonstrative adverbial *öyle* 'like that' (16.4.3 (iii)) is sometimes inserted before the main verb:

(28) (*Öyle*) **san**ıyorum [**ki** arkadaşlarımızın çoğu ağustosta gelemeyecekler].
'I *imagine* [*that* most of our friends won't be able to come in August].'

This *öyle* is seen in the lexicalized expression *öyle gel-* 'seem (to someone)', which is always used in combination with the dative-marked form of a personal pronoun:

(29) **Bana öyle gel**-iyor [**ki** Ömer'le ablasının araları pek iyi değil].
   I(DAT) seem-IMPF SUB
   'It *seems to me* [*that* Ömer and his sister don't get on very well].'

This construction is identical in meaning to ... *gibi gel-* constructions (24.3.3).

Where a *ki* clause expresses a discovery made on performing a certain action, the verb of perception itself may be omitted:

(30) Kapıyı açtım [**ki** içerisi insan dolu].
   'I opened the door [*and saw*] [*that* the place was full of people].'

24.3.2.3   Subject or object of the verb *iste-*

As in the case of bare finite noun clauses with *iste-* (24.2.3), the verb in a *ki* clause which is dependent on the verb *iste-* 'want' is always suffixed with one of the optative forms *-sIn*, *-(y)AyIm* or *-(y)AlIm* (21.4.4.2–3).

(31) İsteniyormuş [**ki** birer birer gir**elim**]. (cf. (14))
   'Apparently what they want is [for us to go in one by one].'

(32) Aslında istiyor [**ki** her taraf mermerle kaplan**sın**]. (cf. (15))
   'Actually what he wants is [for everywhere to be covered in marble].'

24.3.2.4   Subject of adjectival predicates

In sentences like (33) and (34) the *ki* clause is technically the subject of a linking sentence (12.1.1.2), of which the predicate is the adjective at the beginning of the sentence (*tabii* 'natural', *belli* 'clear, 'obvious').

(33) Tabii [**ki** ben hiç öyle bir şey kastetmemiştim].
   'Of course I had meant nothing of the sort.'

(34) Belli [**ki** birbirini çekemiyorlar].
   'It's obvious [*that* they can't stand each other].'

However, the combinations of adjectives such as *tabii* and *belli* with *ki* have become frozen forms which really function more as modal adverbials (16.3).

24.3.3   CLAUSES FORMED WITH *gibi*

The role of *gibi* as a subordinator is derived from its primary function as a postposition meaning 'like' (17.2.1). As a subordinator it occurs mainly in adverbial clauses (26.1.5), but when it stands between a finite subordinate clause and a main verb which is *gel-* it marks a noun clause.

The informal idiom *gibi gel-*, combined with the dative-marked form of a personal pronoun or of any noun phrase referring to (a) human being(s), means 'seem (to someone)' (just like *öyle gel-* with a *ki* clause, 24.3.2.2). The finite noun clause immediately preceding *gibi* is the subject of the sentence.

(35) [Meryem yeni işine pek ısınamadı] **gibi gel**-iyor **bana**.
　　　　　　　　　　　　　　　　seem-IMPF I(DAT)
'*It seems to me* [*that* Meryem is not very happy in her new job].'

(36) **Sana** [bu işi büyütüyorum] **gibi gel**ebilir.
'*It* may *seem to you* [*that* I'm making too much fuss about this].'

An even more informal variant of this construction, occurring only in the first person and giving a rather more tentative meaning, is *gibime gel-* (used in lieu of *bana . . . gibi gel-*):

(37) [O çocukta bir tuhaflık var] **gibi-m-e gel**-iyor.
　　　　　　　　　　　　　　　　gibi-1SG.POSS-DAT *gel*-IMPF
'*I have a feeling* [there's something odd about that child].'

Note that other verbs meaning 'seem', such as *gibi dur-/gibi görün-/gibi gözük-*, behave differently from *gibi gel-* (see 24.5).

24.4　NON-FINITE NOUN CLAUSES

In the following sections we describe in turn the functions of noun clauses formed with each of the following subordinating suffixes: *-mAK, -mA, -DIK, -(y)AcAK, -(y)Iş.*

24.4.1　CLAUSES FORMED WITH *-mAK*

The verb form suffixed with the subordinator *-mAK* (8.5.2), often called the **infinitive**, is the 'citation' form of the verb, used when talking about a verb as a lexical item:

(38) Öyle bir hareket için 'sıyrıl**mak**' fiilini kullanırız.
'We use the verb *sıyrılmak* for such an action.'

Noun clauses formed with *-mAK* are used primarily (i) for talking about an activity, action or state in general terms, or (ii) with main verbs that express a subject's behaviour or attitude towards an action or activity that s/he her/himself performs or may perform.

The crucial difference beween -*mAK* clauses and those with -*mA* is that -*mA* clauses in the majority of cases contain their own subject (see 24.4.2), whereas -*mAK* clauses do not. A -*mAK* clause usually has an *understood subject*, which is indicated by a noun phrase or person marker occurring in the superordinate clause (see 24.4.1.1 for details). For example, in (39) the subject of the -*mAK* clause is indicated by the 1st person marking on the main verb:

(39) [Sokağa çık-**mak**] isti-yor-**um**.
             go.out-*mAK* want-IMPF-1SG
       'I want [to go out].'

The subject of a -*mA* clause, on the other hand, cannot be the same as the subject of the superordinate clause:

(40) [Sokağa çık-**ma-n**]-ı isti-yor-**um**
             go.out-*mA*-2SG.POSS-ACC want-IMPF-1SG
       'I want [*you* to go out].'

In the following sections we review the functions of -*mAK* constructions with and without case marking.

24.4.1.1   The non-case-marked form -*mAk*

Like all non-case-marked noun phrases (14.3.3.1), a noun clause containing -*mAk* without the addition of any case suffixes can function as subject (41), subject complement (42), or direct object (43) within the clause in which it is embedded. The only verb which regularly takes a -*mAk* clause as its direct object is *iste-* 'want' (43). Other transitive verbs require the accusative-marked form -*mAyI* (24.4.1.2).

(41) [Türkçe öğren**mek**] zor.
       '[Learn*ing* Turkish] is difficult.'/'It's difficult [*to* learn Turkish].'

(42) Hayattaki en büyük nimetlerden biri [sevil**mek**]-tir.
       'One of the greatest blessings in life is [*to* be loved].'

The question of what is understood to be the subject of the -*mAk* clause depends on whether the main clause (or another clause in which the -*mAk* clause is embedded) is verbal or nominal.

(i)   Where the superordinate clause is **verbal**, the subject of the -*mAk* clause can be one of the following constituents of this superordinate clause:

(a)   the subject:

(43) ***Sen*** [nereye git**mek**] istiyor***sun***?
'Where do *you* want [*to* go]?'

For another example see (39) above, and for passive -*mAk* clauses which are the subject of their superordinate clause see 24.4.1.4.

(b)   the direct object:

(44) [Bütün gün müze gez**mek**] ***biz***i çok yormuştu.
'[Go*ing* round museums all day] had worn *us* out.'

(c)   the oblique object:

(45) [Ev taşı**mak**] ***Nevin***'e çok kolay geldi.
'[Mov*ing* house] came very easily to *Nevin*.

(ii)   Where a -*mAk* clause forms part of a nominal sentence, the subject of the -*mAk* clause may or may not be identifiable:

(a)   If the -*mAk* clause is the subject of the sentence, the subject of the noun clause may be made explicit by the use of a postpositional phrase with *için* 'for' in the main clause:

(46) [Kimseye bir şey söyleme**mek**] kolay olmayacak **ben**im için.
'[Not tell*ing* anyone anything] is not going to be easy for *me*.'

In the absence of an *için* phrase, the subject of the noun clause may be inferable from the context. In (47) it is the speaker:

(47) [Sizinle konuş**mak**] hoş oldu.
'It's been nice [talk*ing* to you].'

In (48), on the other hand, it is either the addressee or some third party:

(48) [Bütün gece otur**mak**] çok zor olmuştur.
'It must have been very hard [sitt*ing* up all night].'

A -*mak* clause that is the subject of a sentence can also denote an activity, action or state in the abstract, without relation to any particular subject:

(49) [Bir çocuğa öyle bir şey söyleme**mek**] lazım.
'One shouldn't say such a thing to a child.'

For the use of *-mAk* clauses in impersonal obligative expressions such as that in (49) see 21.4.2.2, and example (119) in that chapter.

(**b**)   If the *-mAk* clause is the subject complement, and the subject of the sentence is marked with a possessive suffix, the subject of the noun clause will be understood to be the person referred to by that suffix:

(50) Amac-*ım*, [beş yıl içinde zengin ol-**mak**]-tı.
aim-1SG.POSS five years within rich be-VN-P.COP
'*My* aim was [*to* get rich in five years].'

Where, in a sentence of this type, the main clause subject has no possessive marking, the subject of the noun clause may be inferable from the context:

(51) Amaç, [beş yıl içinde zengin ol**mak**]-tı.
'The aim was [*to* get rich in five years].'

In some cases, as in (42) above, the noun clause has no identifiable subject, and is understood to be applicable to human beings in general.

24.4.1.2   The accusative-marked form *-mAyI*

This form (sometimes spelt *-mAğI*, see 8.5.1.2) occurs where the noun clause is the direct object of any transitive verb (although with *iste-* 'want' it is formal and much less common than *-mAk*).

(52) Şükrü [yemek yap-**may**]-*ı* bil-iyor mu?
Şükrü food make-VN-ACC know-IMPF INT
'Does Şükrü know [how to cook]?'

(53) [Bu yaz İtalya'ya git**mey**]-*i* düşünüyoruz.
'We're thinking of [going to Italy this summer].'

In informal usage with a small number of main verbs, notably *bil-* 'know (how)', *öğren-* 'learn' and *sev-* 'like', the noun clause is sometimes marked with *-mAsInI* rather than *-mAyI*, with no change in meaning. The 3rd person possessive suffix has no obvious referent in such sentences.

(54) Şükrü [yemek yap-**ma-sın**]-*ı* bil-iyor mu?
Şükrü food make-VN-3SG.POSS-ACC know-IMPF INT
'Does Şükrü know [how to cook]?'

(55) Ahmet [araba kullan**masın**]*ı* sever.
'Ahmet likes [driving].'

24.4.1.3 The oblique case-marked forms: *-mAyA, -mAktA* (*-mAdA*) and *-mAktAn*

(**i**) These forms occur where the verb in the main clause is one that requires an oblique object (13.1.2.2). The dative-marked form *-mAyA* is sometimes spelt *-mAğA* (8.5.1.2). Verbs such as *başla-* 'begin', *karar ver-* 'decide', *devam et-* 'continue', *çalış-* 'try' require the dative case:

(56) [Her gün beş sayfa yaz-**may**]-*a çalış*-ıyor-um.
every day five page write-VN-DAT try-IMPF-1SG
'I *try* [to write five pages every day].'

Some verbs such as *zorla-* 'force', *ikna et-* 'persuade' require a human direct object in addition to the oblique object:

(57) **Beni** [konuş**may**]-*a zorla*ma!
'Don't *force me* [to talk]!'

Verbs such as *diren-/diret-/ısrar et-* 'insist (on)' and *yarar gör-* 'see benefit/ point (in)' require the locative case:

(58) Demet [otobüs-le git-**mek**]-*te diren*-**iyor**.
Demet bus-INS go-VN-LOC insist.on-IMPF
'Demet is *insist*ing *on* [going by bus].'

Some speakers use the form *-mAdA* in the same function as *-mAktA*.

Verbs such as *vazgeç-* 'stop', 'decide not (to)', *kork-* 'be afraid (of/to)', *çekin-* 'be reluctant (to)', *kaçın-* 'avoid', *nefret et-* 'hate' take an ablative-marked object:

(59) [Sigara iç-**mek**]-*ten vazgeç*-meli-siniz.
cigarette smoke-ABL give.up-OBLG-2SG/PL
'You must *give up* [smoking].'

A few verbs take as their oblique object a *-mAk* clause marked with the comitative/instrumental marker *-(y)lA*, such as *övün-* 'boast (of)', *suçla-* 'accuse [s.o.] (of)':

(60) Ayten'i [eski bilgisayarını bana ver**mek**]-*le* suçluyorlar.
'They are *accus*ing Ayten *of* [giving her old computer to me].'

(ii) Locative marking occurs also in existential sentences with ∇*fayda/ yarar* 'benefit', 'point', 'use' as the subject. As with non-case-marked *-mAk* (24.4.1.1), the subject of the noun clause in these constructions may be entirely unspecified, as in (61), or may be implied in the context, as in (62).

(61) [Yaşlıları dinle**mek**]-*te fayda var.*
'*There is benefit in* [listening to old people].'

(62) [Babana bir kere daha sor**mak**]-*ta yarar var.*
'*It's worth* [asking your father once more].'

However, the negative versions of such sentences are more often cast as a possessive existential with the genitive-marked form of *-mA* (see 24.4.2.1 (ii)).

(iii) Ablative case marking also occurs where the noun clause expresses an object of comparison (14.3.3.5 (iv)):

(63) [Evi kendim temizle**mek**], [başkasına temizlet**mek**]-*ten* daha kolay geliyor.
'I find it easier [to clean the house myself] *than* [to get someone else to clean [*it*]].'

24.4.1.4 Passive *-mAk* clauses as subjects

When a passive *-mAk* clause is the subject of the superordinate clause, the verb of the superordinate clause, usually *iste-* 'want', 'try' or *çalış-* 'try', is obligatorily passive. In these sentences the subject of the *-mAk* clause (e.g. *toplantı* in (64), *biz* in (65)) behaves as if it is also the subject of the main clause.

(64) [***Toplantı*** [müdür gel-meden] başla-t-*ıl*-**mak**] iste-*n*-di. (cf. Toplantıyı . . . başlatmak istediler.)
meeting director come-CV start-CAUS-PASS-VN want-PASS-PF
'An attempt was made [to start the meeting [before the director arrived]].'

The majority of these clauses have 3rd person subjects, but other persons may also be used. Note that agent phrases (containing *tarafından* or *-CA* 'by', 13.2.2.2) can occur in these constructions:

(65) ***Biz*** [yürüyüş sırasında önce polis, sonra düzenleyici-ler ***tarafından*** we demonstration during first police then organizer-PL by
dur-dur-*ul*-**mak**] iste-**n**-di-**k**.
stop-CAUS-PASS-VN want-PASS-PF-1PL
'During the demonstration attempts were made to stop us, first *by* the police, then *by* the organizers.'

When the verb of the -*mAk* clause is intransitive (as in the case of *git*- 'go' below), the whole sentence becomes an impersonal passive construction (13.2.2.3):

(66) [Deprem bölgesine gid-**il**-mey]-e çalış-**ıl**-ıyor.
go-PASS-VN-DAT try-PASS-IMPF
'People are trying [to reach the earthquake area].'

24.4.2 CLAUSES FORMED WITH -*mA*

In general terms noun clauses formed with -*mA* are less abstract in meaning than those formed with -*mAK*. One result of this is that many -*mA* verbal nouns have become lexicalized as ordinary nouns with concrete meanings (see 7.2.1.1). When -*mA* is used as a productive inflectional suffix, by far the most common pattern is for it to be followed by a possessive suffix referring to the subject of the noun clause (24.4.2.2). However, there are two types of -*mA* clause in which possessive suffixes do not occur, and we deal with these first.

24.4.2.1 -*mA* without possessive suffixes

(i)   The plural form -*mAlAr*
This is a not very common pattern, used to form the subject of a sentence describing repeated instances of an action or activity performed or undergone by unspecified subjects:

(67) O sıralarda [sabahın köründe polis tarafından
uyan-dır-ıl-**ma-lar**], [karakola götür-ül-**me-ler**], [gözaltına al-ın-
ma-lar]
wake.up-CAUS-PASS-VN-PL   take-PASS-VN-PL detain-PASS-VN-PL
günlük olaylardandı.
'At that time [being woken up by the police in the early hours of
the morning, being taken to the police station, and being detained
in custody] were daily occurrences.'

(ii)   The genitive-marked form -*mAnIn*
This form behaves exactly as if it were the genitive-marked form of -*mAK*. Like -*mAK* it is either used to denote an activity, action or state in general terms, or it can have an implied subject inferable from the speech context. These genitive-marked noun clauses occur as modifiers in genitive-possessive constructions where the possessive-marked noun phrase is an abstract noun such as *anlam* 'meaning', 'sense', ∇*fayda/yarar* 'benefit', *zarar* 'harm', *neden*/∇*sebep* 'reason', *amaç* 'purpose':

(68) Ben-ce {[Ali-yi çağır-**ma**]-*nın anlam*}-*ı* yok.
I-ADV Ali-ACC summon-VN-GEN sense-3SG.POSS non-existent
'I don't think *there's any point in* [asking Ali to come].'

(69) {[Sigarayı bırak-**ma**]-*nın fayda-sın*}-ı ilk günlerde görmeyebilirsin.
'You may not experience *the benefit of* [*giving up smoking*] in the first few days.'

For similar constructions with possessive-marked -*mA* clauses see 24.4.2.2.

24.4.2.2 -*mA* with possessive suffixes

A noun clause with possessive-marked -*mA* as its verbal constituent denotes an action, activity or state that is predicated of a certain subject. This subject may be more explicitly referred to by a genitive-marked noun phrase, which if present usually stands at the beginning of the clause:

(sizin) bu evi beğenmeniz	'your liking this house'
Can'ın erken gelmesi	'Can's coming early'
kapının güzel kapatılmaması	'the door not being shut properly'

In contrast to sentences containing noun clauses marked with -*DIK* or -*(y)AcAK* (24.4.3), which are to do with factual perception, knowledge or communication, sentences constructed with -*mA* clauses deal with states and events in terms of description or evaluation, of causation processes in which they are involved, or of people's attitudes towards them or attempts to bring them about.

Below we describe the typical functions that -*mA* clauses can have in different grammatical roles within the sentence.

(**i**)   As subject:

(**a**)   Description/evaluation:

(70) [Fatma Hanım-**ın** üç kat merdiven çık-**ma-sı**] *çok zor.*
    -GEN three storey stairs go.up-VN-3SG.POSS very difficult
    'It's *very difficult* [for Fatma Hanım to go up three flights of stairs].'

Subject -*mA* clauses are one of the major means in Turkish of expressing necessity or obligation (see 21.4.2.2):

(71) [8.30'ta havalimanında ol**mamız**] *gerek*iyor.
    'We have to be at the airport at 8.30.'

The sequence *olması gerek/lazım* can also express an assumption (see 21.4.1.4).

(b)   Causation:

> (72)   [Ayla'**nın** işten hep geç ve yorgun gel**mesi**] evde gerginlik
> yaratıyordu.
> '[The fact that Ayla always got back from work late and
> tired] was creating tension in the house.'

(c)   Desired action or state:
A fuller treatment of this type is given in (iiia) below, dealing with
-*mA* clauses as direct objects. Where the -*mA* clause is the subject,
the main predicate is usually the passivized form of *iste-* 'want':

> (73)   [Herkes-**in** birer hikaye anlat-**ma-sı**] iste-***n***-iyor-muş.
> everyone-GEN one.each story tell-VN-3SG.POSS want-PASS-
> IMPF-EV.COP
> 'It seems they want [everyone to tell a story].'

(d)   Indirect commands, requests and recommendations:
These are the passivized versions of the type of sentence discussed in
(iii)(b) below:

> (74)   [Bu ürünün elde yıkan**ması**] tavsiye ed*i/i*r.
> 'It is recommended [that this product be washed by hand].'

(ii)   As subject complement:
All of the functions performed by -*mA* clauses as subjects can also be
performed when they are in the subject complement role (12.1.1.2):

> (75)   Önemli olan [siz**in** bu evi beğen**meniz**].
> 'The important thing is [that you (should) like this house].'

> (76)   Bizim ricamız [toplantı**nın** haftaya ertelen**mesi**] olacak.
> 'Our request is (lit. will be) [that the meeting be postponed to
> next week].'

(iii)   With accusative case marking as direct object:
Like all noun phrases marked for possession, possessive-marked -*mA*
clauses always take accusative case marking when they are in the direct
object role (see 14.3.3.2).

(a)   Desired action or state:
In sentences expressing a desire for something to happen, the -*mA*
clause is usually the object of the verb *iste-* 'want':

(77) [Bu tablo-**nun** şura-ya as-ıl-ma-**sın**]-*ı* isti-yor-uz.
this picture-GEN here-DAT hang-PASS-VN-3SG.POSS-ACC
want-IMPF-1PL
'We want [this picture to be hung here].'

Other volitional verbs that can take a -*mA* clause as their direct object
are *bekle-* 'expect' and *dile-* '(express the) wish (that)'. For the distinction between this construction and -*mAk iste-*, see 24.4.1, examples
(39) and (40).

(b) Indirect commands, requests and recommendations:
These are sentences in which the -*mA* clause is the direct object of a
verb that expresses an attempt to secure the performance of an action
by others. The principal main verbs involved are *söyle-* 'tell', *emret-*
'order', *iste-* 'ask', *rica et-* 'request', and *tavsiye et-* 'recommend',
'advise'.

(78) Otel müdürü [oda-yı hemen boşalt-**ma-ların**]-*ı* söyle-di.
hotel manager room-ACC immediately
vacate-VN-3PL.POSS-ACC say-PF
'The hotel manager told [*them* to vacate the room
immediately].'

Often, as in (78), the addressee of this type of utterance is not explicitly mentioned, and is assumed to be identical with the subject of the
noun clause. It is, however, possible for a different addressee to be
named:

(79) Ceyda **anne-m-e** [herkes-**in** kalın giysiler-le gel-**me-sin**]-*i*
söyle-miş.
Ceyda mother-1SG.POSS-DAT everyone-GEN thick
clothes-COM come-VN-3SG.POSS-ACC say-EV/PF
'Ceyda told *my mother* [that *everyone* was to come with
warm clothes].'

In the case of *iste-* and *rica et-*, the addressee is expressed (if at all)
by an ablative-marked noun phrase:

(80) [Turgut **biz-den** [taşınacağı gün kendisine yardım
we-ABL   help
et-**me-miz**]-*i* istedi.
AUX-VN-1PL.POSS-ACC
'Turgut has asked *us* [to help him on the day he moves].'

(c) Causation:
A process that facilitates or obstructs the occurrence of the situation expressed by the noun clause has as its main predicate a verb such as *sağla-* 'ensure', *kolaylaştır-* 'make (it) easy (for)', *zorlaştır-* 'make (it) difficult (for)', *engelle-* 'hinder', *önle-* 'prevent'.

(81) İlkbahardaki yağmurlar [mahsul**ün** bol ol**masın**]-*ı* sağladı.
'The spring rains have ensured [that the harvest is plentiful].'

(d) Object of verbs expressing attitude:
Some of the most commonly occurring verbs in this category are *beğen-* 'like', 'approve of', *kına-* 'deplore', *affet-/bağışla-* 'forgive', *hoş gör-* 'condone':

(82) [Kocas**ının** kendisine yalan söyle**mesin**]-*i* affedemiyordu.
'She couldn't forgive [her husband's lying to her].'

(e) For *-mA* clauses as objects of verbs of cognition and perception see 24.4.5.1.

(iv) As oblique object:

(a) Emotional attitude:
A *-mA* clause marked for dative or ablative case or with the instrumental marker can function as the oblique object of a verb of emotion (see 13.1.2.2, also 24.4.5.2).

(83) Mehmet, [Ali-**nin** kendisini çağır-ma-**ma-sın**]-*a* gücendi.
      Ali-GEN   invite-NEG-VN-3SG.POSS-DAT
'Mehmet was offended *by* [Ali's not inviting him].'

(84) [Tülay'**ın** sürekli kendisinden söz et**mesin**]-*den* sıkılıyorum.
'I get bored *by* [Tülay talking about herself all the time].'

(b) Causation:
Dative-marked *-mA* clauses occur as oblique objects of verbs such as *neden*/∇*sebep ol-* 'cause', *yol aç-* 'cause', *yardım et-* 'help', ∇*müsaade et-/izin ver-* 'allow':

(85) Sıcak havalar, [meyvalar-**ın** erken olgunlaş**masın**]-*a* yol açtı bu yıl.
'The hot weather has caused [the fruit to ripen early] this year.'

(86) Çocuklar [burayı topla**manız**]-*a* yardım etsinler.
'The children should help [you to clear up in here].'

(87) Ev sahibimiz [kedi ya da köpek besle**memiz**]-*e* izin
vermiyordu.
'Our landlady didn't allow [us to have a cat or dog].'

(v) With genitive marking:

Possessive-marked -*mA* clauses with genitive case marking on the verbal
noun occur in the same kinds of structures as clauses with -*mAnIn*
(24.4.2.1). If a possessive suffix is added to the verbal noun in a sentence
such as (68) above the noun clause acquires a specific subject:

(88) Ben-ce {[Ali-yi çağır-ma-**mız**]-*ın anlam*}-*ı* yok
I-ADV Ali-ACC summon-VN-**1PL.POSS** -GEN sense-3SG.POSS
non-existent
'I don't think there's any point in [*us* asking Ali to come].'

24.4.3 CLAUSES FORMED WITH -*DIK* OR -*(y)AcAK*

The subordinating suffixes -*DIK* and -*(y)AcAK* are obligatorily followed
by a possessive suffix referring to the subject of the noun clause. -*DIK* and
-*(y)AcAK* alternate with each other on the basis of the *tense* component of
their meanings: -*DIK* refers to a time simultaneous with, or earlier than,
that referred to by the superordinate predicate, while -*(y)AcAK* refers to
a time later than that referred to by the superordinate predicate. In other
words, -*DIK* expresses relative present or relative past tense and -*(y)AcAK*
relative future tense (21.2):

(89) (a) [Orhan-**ın** bir şey yap-ma-**dığ**-ı] belliydi.
Orhan-GEN anything do-NEG-VN-3SG.POSS
'It was obvious [that Orhan *wasn't doing/hadn't done*
anything].'

(b) [Orhan-**ın** bir şey yap-ma-**yacağ**-ı] belliydi.
Orhan-GEN anything do-NEG-VN-3SG.POSS
'It was obvious [that Orhan *wouldn't do/wasn't going to do*
anything].'

The fact that noun clauses with -*DIK* and -*(y)AcAK* are marked for tense
points to the crucial difference between them and (possessive-marked)
-*mA* clauses. -*DIK*/-*(y)AcAK* clauses are used almost exclusively in
sentences that have to do with the *factual status* of an event or state (the
truth or otherwise of its occurrence or of some aspect of its occurrence

(who, what, where, etc)). The main or superordinate predicate in such sentences, if nominal, as in (89), expresses concepts such as truth or false-hood, certainty or uncertainty. If verbal, it is typically a verb expressing some cognitive process (knowledge, understanding, belief, opinion, etc.) or communication (saying, asking, etc.). The types of sentence in which -*DIK/-(y)AcAK* clauses occur are thus principally those known as **indirect statements** and **indirect questions**. In both types the noun clause can occur either as subject, as direct object (with obligatory accusative case marking) or as oblique object.

24.4.3.1 Indirect statements

In an indirect statement, the content of the noun clause would, if formu-lated as an independent sentence, constitute a statement. The sentence as a whole may, however, take the form of either a statement or a question:

(**i**)   With the noun clause as subject:
The superordinate predicate may be either nominal, as in (90a), or verbal, as in (90b):

>   (90) (**a**) [Ayşe-**nin** ameliyat ol-**duğ-u**] doğru mu?
>   Ayşe-GEN operation AUX-VN-3SG.POSS true INT
>   'Is it true [*that* Ayşe has had an operation]?'
>
>   (**b**) [Ayşe-**nin** ameliyat ol-**duğ-u**] söyle-n-iyor. (cf. Ayşe ameliyat
>   say-PASS-IMPF
>   olmuş.)
>   'It is (being) said [*that* Ayşe has had an operation].'

The verbal predicate of a sentence with a -*DIK/-(y)AcAK* clause as its subject is the passivized form of a verb such as those listed in (ii) below.

(**ii**)   With the noun clause as direct object:
This occurs with main verbs such as *bil-* 'know', 'think', *anla-* 'understand', 'realize', *san-* 'think', *düşün-* 'think', *söyle-* 'say', *yaz-* 'write', *duy-/işit-* 'hear', *öğren-* 'learn':

>   (91) O gün Suzan bana [artık dayan-a-ma-**yacağ-ın**]-*ı* söylemişti.
>   bear-PSB-NEG-VN-3SG.POSS-ACC
>   (cf. (6) and (22) above)
>   'That day Suzan had told me [that she couldn't bear [it] any longer].'

Where the noun clause is the object of *bil-* 'know', 'think', the factual status of its content depends on the position of stress within the sentence.

When stress is placed on the main verb *bil-*, it means 'know', and the content of the noun clause expresses an established fact:

(92) [Sen-in abla-n-ın yanında ol-duğ-un]-u bi**L-İ**yor-du-m.
　　 you-GEN sister-2SG.POSS-GEN with be-VN-2SG.POSS-ACC know-
　　 IMPF-P.COP-1SG
　　 'I knew [you were with your sister].'

When, on the other hand, stress is placed within the noun clause, *bil-* is interchangeable with *san-* 'think', and the noun clause expresses a supposition that may turn out (or have turned out) to be false:

(93) [Senin **AB**lanın yanında olduğun]-u biliyordum/sanıyordum.
　　 'I thought [you were with your sister].'

(iii) With the noun clause as oblique object:
This occurs with *inan-* 'believe' (dative marking) and *emin ol-* 'be sure' (ablative marking):

(94) [Bize o kadar büyük bir para ver-**ecek-lerin**]-*e* inanmamıştım.
　　　　　　　　　　　　　　　　 give-VN-3PL.POSS-DAT
　　 'I never believed [*that* they would give us such a large amount of money].'

A *-DIK/-(y)AcAK* clause also occurs with ablative marking as the oblique object of existential possessive expressions (12.1.1.2) with *haber* 'knowledge (of)', 'awareness (of)' as subject:

(95) [Ahmet-in evlen-**diğ-in**]-*den* haber-**im** yok-tu.
　　 Ahmet-GEN marry-VN-3SG.POSS-ABL knowledge-1SG.POSS
　　 non-existent-P.COP
　　 'I had no idea [*that* Ahmet had got married].'

(iv) With genitive marking on the noun clause:
This occurs with the expressions *farkında/ayırdında/bilincinde ol-* 'be aware that', where the noun clause becomes the possessor constituent in a genitive-possessive construction (14.4):

(96) [Bu iş-in iki günde bit-me-yebil-eceğ-i]-**nin** fark-**ın**-da-yım.
　　　　 finish-NEG-PSB-VN-3SG.POSS-GEN aware-3SG.POSS-LOC-1SG
　　 'I am aware [*that* this job may not be finished in two days].'

24.4.3.2   Indirect questions

Indirect questions are distinguished from indirect statements by the fact that the content of the noun clause would, if converted into an independent sentence, express a question.

The structures by which the various types of questions in simple sentences (or main clauses) are expressed in Turkish are explained in Chapter 19. The corresponding structures for questions expressed indirectly in *-DIK/-(y)AcAK* clauses are as follows:

(i)   'Whether (or not)' questions are expressed using the *-(y)Ip . . . -mA* construction (20.1.3):

(97)   Annem bana [akşama **gel*ip* gel*me*yeceğim**]-*i* sordu.
'My mother asked me [*if* I would be coming back that night (or not)].'

In terms of simple-sentence equivalents, these correspond both to yes/no questions (compare (97) with the direct-speech version in (16) above) and to the kind of alternative questions in which the alternative presented is simply the negation of the predicate (= 'or not') (19.1.2).

(ii)   Alternative questions involving an alternative which is not simply the negation of the predicate are expressed in a manner exactly parallel to that in simple sentences (19.1.2), with the interrogative particle *mI* placed after each of the alternative items. (98) contains the non-finite equivalent of example (18) in Chapter 19:

(98)   [*Tosca*'yı Verdi'**nin** mi, (yoksa) Puccini'**nin** mi yaz**dığın**]-*ı* bilmiyorum.
'I don't know [*whether* it was Verdi or Puccini who composed *Tosca*].'

(iii)   Wh-questions are expressed simply by including the appropriate wh-phrase (19.2) in the noun clause:

(99)   [Çocuğ-un baba-sı-**nın** *kim* ol-**duğ-u**] bil-in-iyor mu? (cf. (12) above)
child-GEN father-3SG.POSS-GEN who be-VN-3SG.POSS know-PASS-IMPF INT
'Is it known [*who* the child's father is]?'

(100)   [Ertan'ı *neden* bu kadar beğen**diğin**]-**i** anlayamıyorum. (cf. (13) above)
'I can't understand [*why* you admire Ertan so much].'

24.4.3.3   Other functions of -DIK/-(y)AcAK clauses

(i)   Clauses with -DIK (not -(y)AcAK) also occur as the subject of sentences which comment on the frequency of a certain event or situation. The main verb here is usually ol- 'occur', görül- 'be seen', or duyul- 'be heard'.

(101)   O günlerde [akşamları birlikte çay içtiğimiz] çok olurdu.
'In those days it was common [for us to have tea together in the evenings].'

(102)   [Gökhan'ın içkiyi fazla kaçırdığı] hiç görülmemişti.
'Gökhan had never been known [to have had too much to drink].'

Colloquially, this type of utterance can also be cast in the form of an interrogative or negative existential sentence:

(103)   [Ahmet-i gör-düğ-ün] var mı bu günlerde?
Ahmet-ACC see-VN-2SG.POSS existent INT recently
'Have you seen anything of Ahmet recently?'

(ii)   Although -DIK/-(y)AcAK clauses cannot, in general, be used to express evaluations or descriptions of events (cf. 24.4.2.2), the specific combination of -DIK with iyi ol- 'be good' does occur:

(104)   [Bunu konuşmamız/konuştuğumuz] iyi oldu.
'It's good [that we have talked about this].'

(iii)   Another use of genitive-marked -DIK clauses is in genitive-possessive constructions of which the head is a unit of time:

(105)   [Adana-ya gel-diğ-im]-in ikinci gün-ü Turhan'la görüştük.
Adana-DAT arrive-VN-1SG.POSS-GEN second day-3SG.POSS
'Turhan and I met on the second day after [my arrival in Adana].'

24.4.4   CLAUSES FORMED WITH -(y)Iş

While productive as a derivational suffix forming abstract or semi-abstract nouns (7.2.1.1), as a subordinator -(y)Iş is more restricted in its functions than any of the other suffixes discussed in this chapter. It is almost always used to refer to an action or state predicated of a particular subject (indicated, as usual, by the affixation of a possessive suffix). It therefore cannot be used in any of the functions of -mAK. It also cannot be used in sentences that bear upon the factual status of a proposition, nor in those that express a volitional stance (desire, command, request, permission, etc.) towards a situation. It is therefore excluded from most of the contexts in which *-DIK/-(y)AcAK* or *-mA* are used.

The verbal noun formed with *-(y)Iş* has two functions that are not shared by any of the other forms discussed in this chapter. It can express (i) the *manner* in which an action is performed, or (ii) a *single instance* of an event or action. In both of these functions *-(y)Iş* forms can have a status that is more noun-like than the other verbal nouns. This is illustrated in (106), where *sokuluş* 'manner of snuggling up', while remaining sufficiently verb-like to retain its oblique object *insana* 'to one', is preceded by the sequence *hoş bir* (ADJ *bir*) 'a nice', which occurs only in noun phrases.

(106) [O kedinin insana **hoş bir sokuluşu**] vardı.
'That cat had *a nice way of snuggling up* to one.'

Similarly, in the *single instance* reading, *-(y)Iş* clauses, unlike those formed with *-mA* or *-DIK/-(y)AcAK*, are countable:

(107) [Zehra'yı **her** gör-**üş**-ün]-ü ayrı bir zevkle hatırlıyordu.
　　　　　　 every see-VN-3SG.POSS-ACC
'S/he remembered with a separate pleasure *each occasion on which* s/he had seen Zehra.'

(108) [Türkiye'ye ikinci ve üçüncü gid**işler**imiz] 1982'de oldu.
'Our second and third *visits* to Turkey took place in 1982.'

24.4.5 OVERLAPPING USES OF *-mA*, *-DIK/-(y)AcAK* AND *-(y)Iş*

24.4.5.1 As direct object of verbs of perception or cognition

All noun clause types capable of taking possessive suffixes can occur as objects of verbs of perception such as *gör-* 'see', *duy-* 'hear', *anla-* 'understand', *hatırla-* 'remember', and *unut-* 'forget'. However, the choice of subordinator in these cases has a clear effect on the meaning. While the use of *-DIK/-(y)AcAK* expresses the perception of a situation merely as a *fact*, the use of *-mA* or *-(y)Iş* expresses rather the perception of an inherent quality of the event or state. We illustrate this with two contrasting examples:

(109) (a) [Çocuğ-un ağaç-tan düş-**tüğ**-ün]-ü gör-dü-m.
　　　 (b) [Çocuğ-un ağaç-tan düş-**me**-sin]-i gör-dü-m.
　　　 (c) [Çocuğ-un ağaç-tan düş-**üş**-ün]-ü gör-dü-m.
　　　　　 child-GEN tree-ABL fall-VN-3SG.POSS-ACC see-PF-1SG

All of the sentences in (109) could be translated 'I saw the child fall from the tree'. However, (a) is also open to the interpretation 'I saw that the child had fallen from the tree', where the fact is perceived only after the event has taken place; (b) and (c), on the other hand, tell us that the speaker witnessed the process of the child's fall. In a sense, therefore, both -*mA* and -*(y)Iş* in such contexts evoke more the idea of *how* something happens than the fact *that* it happens. Indeed, neither (109b) nor (109c) could be used in a context in which the fact of the child's fall had not already been established.

(110) (a) Hakan [anne-sin-i sev-me-**dig**-imiz]-i anlı-yor-du.
Hakan mother-3SG.POSS-ACC love-NEG-VN-1PL.POSS-ACC
understand-IMPF-P.COP
'Hakan was aware [*that* we didn't like his mother].'
(b) Hakan [annesini sev-me-**me**-miz]-i anlıyordu.
(c) Hakan [annesini sev-me-**yiş**-imiz]-i anlıyordu.
'Hakan understood [our not liking his mother].'

In (110) the (a) sentence states Hakan's understanding of a situation at the factual level, whereas the (b) and (c) versions relate his understanding to the situation itself, implying that he understood *why* the speaker and others felt this way.

24.4.5.2   As oblique object of verbs of emotion

The semantic contrasts noted in 24.4.5.1 are neutralized where the noun clause is the object of a verb of emotion, such as *sevin-* 'be glad' or *üzül-* 'be sorry'. The -*DIK/-(y)AcAK* forms are fully interchangeable with -*mA* in such contexts, as shown below:

(111) Hepimiz [çocuğ-un öyle bir suç işle-**me**-sin]-e üzüldük.
Hepimiz [çocuğ-un öyle bir suç işle-**dig**-in]-e üzüldük.
boy-GEN such a crime commit-VN-3SG.POSS-DAT
'We were all distressed [*that* the boy had committed such a crime].'

(112) [Hediyelerini beğen-me-**me**-miz]-den korkuyorlardı galiba.
[Hediyelerini beğen-me-**yeceğ**-imiz]-den korkuyorlardı galiba.
like-NEG-VN-1PL.POSS-ABL
'I think they were afraid [we wouldn't like their present].'

-*(y)Iş* clauses also can express the object of a verb of emotion, provided (as always in the case of this suffix) that the situation is one that is *actualized*, i.e. has happened or is ongoing at the moment of speech. The use of -*(y)Iş* also tends to be avoided with affirmative transitive verbs (such as *işle-* in (111)), unless the sense of manner is intended. (113) is an example with a negativized transitive verb, where all three forms would be acceptable (cf. (83) for the *-mA* version):

(113) Mehmet, [Ali-**nin** kendisini çağır-ma-**yış-ın**]-**a** gücendi.
        Ali-GEN   invite-NEG-VN-3SG.POSS-DAT
'Mehmet was offended by [Ali's not inviting him].'

24.4.6 OMISSION OF GENITIVE MARKING ON THE SUBJECT OF CLAUSES FORMED WITH POSSESSIVE-MARKED *-mA* OR *-DIK/-(y)AcAK*

There are certain exceptions to the rule (24.1) that a noun phrase expressing the subject of a non-finite noun clause receives genitive case marking. In this section we discuss four types of subject that do *not* normally receive case marking.

(**i**)   A noun phrase with **categorial** status (22.3):
This is the only type of noun clause subject where the addition of the genitive suffix affects the meaning of the sentence, by changing the referential status of the subject from categorial to definite:

(114) (**a**) [Buraya **araba** çarptığın]-ı tahmin ediyorum.
             'I guess [*a car* bumped here].'

        (**b**) [Buraya **araba-*nın*** çarptığın]-ı tahmin ediyorum.
                    car-GEN
             'I guess [*the car* bumped here].'

(115) (**a**) [Çocuğa **para** verilmesi] yanlış olur.
             'It would be wrong [for the child to be given *money*].'

        (**b**) [**Para*nın*** çocuğa verilmesi] yanlış olur.
             'It would be wrong [for the child to be given *the money*].'

In types (ii)–(iv) below, on the other hand, genitive case marking, while unusual in (ii) and (iii), could be added without any effect on the meaning.

(**ii**)   The subject of an existential clause:

(116) [Filiz'in odasında **yeşil perdeler** ol-duğ-un]-u hatırlıyorum.
            'I remember [that there were *green curtains* in Filiz's room].'

(**iii**) A possessive-marked *-mA* clause which is the subject of a *-DIK/ -(y)AcAK* clause expressing necessity:

(117) {Ahmet'in gel**mesi** [gerek**tiğin**]}-i düşünüyorum.
            'I think Ahmet *ought to* come.'

(iv) The indefinite subject of a passive verb in a noun clause which is itself the subject of an expression of necessity or desire:

(118) [**Bir şey(-in)** yap-ıl-ma-sı] lazım.
something(-GEN) do-PASS-VN-3SG.POSS necessary
'*Something* has got to be done.'

(119) [Bu konuda **bir iki sayfa(nın)** yaz-ıl-ma-sı] iste-n-iyor-muş.
                   write-PASS-VN-3SG.POSS want- PASS-IMPF-EV.COP
'Apparently they want [*a few pages* to be written on this subject].'

24.4.7 THE USE OF AUXILIARY *ol-* IN NON-FINITE NOUN CLAUSES

As in the case of other types of non-finite subordinate clause (relative clauses 25.4.1, adverbial clauses 26.2.3) the auxiliary verb *ol-* is widely used in all types of non-finite noun clauses to add components of tense and aspect to the meaning of the clause. Where the auxiliary *ol-* is used, the lexical verb in the noun clause receives one of the tense/ aspect suffixes shown below, and the subordinating suffix is shifted on to the auxiliary.

PERFECTIVE/PAST	*-mIş*
FUTURE	*-(y)AcAK*
PROGRESSIVE/HABITUAL	*-mAktA* and *-(I)yor*
HABITUAL	*-(A/I)r/-mAz*

(For a full discussion of tense and aspect in Turkish see 21.2–3. For compound verb forms with *ol-* in finite clauses see 21.5.)

By far the most common tense/aspect suffix to be used in non-finite noun clauses is *-mIş*. The inclusion of *-mIş* in a noun clause conveys that the event in question is envisaged as having been completed prior to a reference point specified or implied elsewhere in the sentence:

(120) [Çocukluğunda Atatürk'ü gör-**müş ol-mak**] kendisi için bir gurur
                        see-PF AUX-VN
kaynağı idi.
'[*To have* seen Atatürk in his/her childhood] was a source of pride for him/her.'

(121) [Yarın akşama kadar kitapların yarısını gözden geçir**miş**
olacağımız]-ı tahmin ediyoruz.
'We estimate [that we *shall have* gone through half of the books by tomorrow evening].'

The use of -*(I)yor* or -*mAktA* in the noun clause can have one of two meanings:

(i)   The situation in question is presented or envisaged as ongoing at the given reference point:

(122)   [Filiz'in bu saatte çalış-**ıyor ol-ma**-sı] lazım.
                                           work-IMPF AUX-VN-3SG.POSS
  (a) 'Filiz should/ought to *be* work*ing* at this hour.' (Obligation, 21.4.2.2)
  (b) 'Filiz must *be* work*ing* at this hour.' (Assumption, 21.4.1.4)

(123)   [Toplantının devam et**mekte olduğu**n]-u söylediler.
  'They said [the meeting *was* [still] go*ing* on].'

(124)   [Tam o sırada Dekan'la görüş**üyor olacağı**mız]-ı tahmin ediyordum.
  'I reckoned [that we *would be* talk*ing* to the Dean at exactly that time].'

(ii)   The situation is presented as occurring recurrently in a timespan that includes the reference point:

(125)   [Tülay'ın hafta sonları Ankara'ya gid**iyor olduğu**n]-u sanıyorum.
  'I think [Tülay goes to Ankara at the weekends].'

It should be noted that the combination -*(I)yor olduK*- is in declining use. Many speakers would use the simple form *gittiğini* in (125).
  The use of -*mAktA olduK*- in a context of habituality is formal (cf. 21.3.2):

(126)   [Bazı denetim işlerinin düzenli yapılma**makta olduğu**] belliydi.
  'It was clear [that some checks *were* not be*ing* carried out regularly].'

Compound forms with *ol*- can be used to resolve the temporal ambiguity inherent in the subordinator -*DIK* (24.4.3):

(127)   **(a)** [Ali'nin bu kitabı oku**duğu**n]-u sanıyorum.
    'I think [Ali *has read/is reading* this book].'

    (b) [Ali'nin bu kitabı oku**yor**/oku**makta olduğu**n]-u sanıyorum.
    'I think [Ali *is reading* this book].'

    (c) [Ali'nin bu kitabı oku**muş olduğu**n]-u sanıyorum.
    'I think Ali [*has read* this book].'

-(y)AcAk ol- is rare in noun clauses, but *-(A/I)r/-mAz olduK-* is the equivalent of *-(A/I)r/-mAz oldu* in finite clauses (21.5.4):

(128) [Koray'la Hakan'ın görüş**mez olduk**ların]-ı işittim.
'I've heard that Koray and Hakan *have stopped* seeing each other.'

24.5 SMALL CLAUSES

Small clauses are a variant kind of finite noun clause. They are unusual in that one of their constituents, the subject, is also a constituent (subject or object) of the main clause. The contexts in which small clauses occur are sentences where the main predicate is one of the types of transitive verb described below, or an intransitive verb meaning 'seem', 'appear'.

24.5.1 SMALL CLAUSES OCCURRING WITH MAIN CLAUSE TRANSITIVE VERBS

The types of transitive verb which take small clauses are the following:

(i)   verbs of perception/cognition:
    (a)   *san-/∇zannet-* 'think', *bil-* 'think'
    (b)   *say-/addet-/∇farzet-* 'consider'
    (c)   *bul-* 'find', *gör-*, 'find', *iste-* 'want'

(129) Biz [***sen-i* okul-u bitir-di-(*n*)**] added-iyor-uz.
we you-ACC school-acc finish-PF(-2SG) consider-IMPF-1PL
'We thought [*you had left*].'

(130) [***Delikanlı-yı* yakışıklı**] buldum.
'I found [*the young man handsome*].'

(ii)   verbs expressing an act performed on an object which is or may be subject to a process of change; in this case the predicate of the small clause is an adjective expressing the state of the object at the time when the action is performed, e.g. *ye-* 'eat', *iç-* 'drink', *kaldır-* 'put [s.t.] away', *as-* 'hang', *bırak-* 'leave [s.t.]'

(131) Tülin [***çayını* soğuk**] içiyor.
'Tülin drinks [her tea cold].'

(iii)   verbs expressing an action which gives someone or something status or quality, expressed by a noun, e.g. *yap-*, 'make', *seç-* 'elect', *boya-* 'paint'

(132) [***Mehmet'i* başkan**] seçtik.
'We elected [*Mehmet (as) chairman*].'

When the main clause verb is transitive, the *subject* of a small clause (italicized in (129)–(132)) functions as the direct object of the main clause, marked with the accusative case. The verbs in (ia) and (ib) can occur with small clauses with nominal or verbal predicates. The verbs in (ic), (ii) and (iii) occur only with small clauses with nominal predicates.

The subordinator *diye* (24.3) can be used after a small clause when the main clause verb is *bil-* 'think'. Note that the verbs in (ia) (in the case of *bil-* 'think', only for some speakers) can also have finite complements (see 24.2):

(133) Biz [*sen* **git-ti-*n***] san-dı-k.
       we you go-PF-2SG think-PF-1PL
       'We thought [*you had left*].'

24.5.2 SMALL CLAUSES OCCURRING WITH MAIN CLAUSE INTRANSITIVE VERBS

When the main clause verb is intransitive (either in its root form or through passivization), the subject of the small clause (in bold italics immediately below) also functions as the subject of the main predicate.

(134) [***Mehmet*** **iyi**] görün-üyor-du.
       Mehmet fine seem-IMPF-P.COP
       '*Mehmet* was looking *fine.*'

(135) [***Biz*** kurs-u tamamla-dı-**(k)**] addediliyor**uz**.
       we course-ACC complete-PF(-1PL) consider-PASS-IMPF-1PL
       '*We* are considered [to have completed the course].'

Small clauses occurring with *benze-* 'look as if' as the main clause verb are idiosyncratic in that their own verb cannot be inflected for person. A further peculiarity of *benze-* is that it requires dative marking of the small clause predicate:

(136) [(**Sen**) güneş-te fazla kal-mış]-*a benzi*-yor-**sun**
       (you) sun-LOC too.much stay-PF-DAT look-IMPF-2SG
       'You look [as if *you stayed too long in the sun*].'

24.5.3 TENSE/ASPECT AND PERSON MARKING

Tense/aspect marking

The verbal predicate of a small clause is marked with one of the suffixes *-mIş, -(I)yor, -(y)AcAK, -(A/I)r* and *-DI* (see (135) and (136) above). Small clauses do not contain copular markers or *-DIr*, except when the main clause predicate is *san-/∇zannet-* 'think', in which case it may be marked with a past copula.

Person marking

The occurrence of person marking on the predicate of a small clause depends on (a) the predicate of the main clause, and, (b) whether the small clause has a verbal or nominal predicate. The main clause predicates which allow person marking in the small clause when this latter has a verbal predicate are the ones in (ia) and (ib):

(137) Biz [sen-i git-ti-(**n**)] sandık.
       we you-ACC go-PF(-2SG)
       'We thought [*you had left*].'

The optionality of person marking applies to the passive forms of these verbs as well; see (135).

When the small clause has a nominal predicate, it can have person marking only if the main clause predicate is *san-/∇zannet-* 'think' and, for some speakers, *bil-* 'think':

(138) Onlar [bizi farkında değil(**iz**)] sanıyorlar.
       'They think we aren't aware [of the situation].'

In sentences with small clauses, the *main clause* predicate is obligatorily inflected for person, except where the main verb is one of the following: the passive forms of *san-/∇zannet-* 'think' (i.e. *sanıl-/∇zannedil-* 'thought [to be]', *gibi dur-/gibi görün-/gibi gözük-* 'seem', 'appear'. With these verbs, person marking may be attached either to the main verb or to the small clause predicate:

(139) (**a**) [*Siz* hayat-ınız-dan memnun] **gibi dur**-uyor-*sunuz*.
             you life-2PL.POSS-ABL happy like seem-IMPF-2PL
             '*You* seem [to be *happy with your life*].'

       (**b**) [*Siz* hayatınızdan memnun-*sunuz*] **gibi dur**-uyor.
                          happy-2PL like seem-IMPF
             'It seems that *you are happy with your life*.'

Note that *gibi gel-* 'seem' (24.3.3) cannot be used with person marking on the main verb, i.e. could not be used in a sentence like (139a).

24.6   NOUN CLAUSES AS MODIFIERS IN -*(s)I* COMPOUNDS

Finite and non-finite noun clauses can function as modifiers in -*(s)I* compounds (10.2). In these compounds not only does the modifier, in this case the noun clause, make more particular the meaning of the head noun, it also provides the content of the head noun. The nouns that occur most commonly as the heads of these complex -*(s)I* compounds generally denote one of the following:

(i)   an utterance, e.g. *soru* 'question', *komut* 'order', *iddia* 'claim'

(ii)   a belief or perception, e.g. *düşünce* 'thought', *inanç* 'belief', *beklenti* 'expectation', *duygu* 'feeling', *kaygı* 'anxiety', *umut/∇ümit* 'hope'

(iii)   a state of affairs, e.g. *sorun/∇mesele* 'problem', *konu* 'issue'

(iv)   a desire, e.g. *istek/∇arzu* 'wish', 'desire', *özlem/hasret* 'longing'

(v)   possibility or necessity, e.g. *olasılık/∇ihtimal* 'possibility', *gereksinim/∇ihtiyaç* 'need', *zorunluk/∇mecburiyet*

(vi)   a pattern of behaviour, e.g. *alışkanlık* 'habit', *eğilim* 'tendency', *gelenek* 'tradition'

(vii)   time, e.g. *zaman/vakit* 'time (general)', *saat* 'time (by the clock)'.

Head nouns in categories (i)–(iii) above can be modified by either a finite or a non-finite noun clause. (140)–(142) contain -*(s)I* compounds with finite-clause modifiers. These are generally more informal than their non-finite counterparts.

(140) Nuri Bey, emekli olduktan sonra [**ben artık hiçbir işe yaramıyorum**] *kaygı-sın*-a kapıldı.
                            anxiety-NC-DAT
    'After he retired, Nuri Bey began to feel that he lacked purpose.' (lit. 'started feeling [*an*] *"I'm no use any more"* *anxiety.'*)

(141) Herkesin kafasında [**seçim-ler ne zaman yap-ıl-acak**] *soru-su* var.
                       election-PL when make-PASS-FUT question-NC existent
    'The question on everybody's mind is: when are the elections going to be held?' (lit. 'On everybody's mind is *the question* *"When will the elections be held?"*')

(142) ["**Saat altıda hazır ol-un**"] *komut-un*-u aldık.
               ready be-IMP.2PL order-NC-ACC
    'We received *the order "Be ready at six o'clock".'*

The finite noun clauses in the above three examples are a statement (140), a question (141) and a command (142). Their non-finite counterparts will therefore be respectively an indirect statement (24.4.3.1), an indirect question (24.4.3.2) and an indirect command (24.4.2.2 (iiib)):

(143) Nuri Bey, emekli olduktan sonra [**artık hiç bir işe yarama*dığı***] **kaygısı**na kapıldı.
    'After he retired, Nuri Bey began to feel that he lacked purpose.' (lit. 'started feeling [*an*] anxiety [*that he was no use any more*]')

(144) Herkesin kafasında [**seçimler*in* ne zaman yapıl*acağı*] **sorusu** var.
'The question on everybody's mind is when the elections are
going to be held.' (lit. 'On everybody's mind is *the question of*
[*when the elections will be held*].')

(145) [**Saat altıda hazır ol*ma***] **komutun**-u aldık.
'We received *the order* [*to be ready at six o'clock*].'

Where the head noun of the *-(s)I* compound falls into one of the categories listed (iv)–(vii) above, a finite noun clause modifer is usually not
possible, although with category (iv) a finite clause with optative or conditional marking may occur colloquially:

(146) İçimde [**Ahmet-i gör-ebil-se-m**] *özlem-i* depreşti.
        Ahmet-ACC see-PSB-COND-1SG longing-NC
'*The longing* [*that I might be able to see Ahmet*] overwhelmed
me again.'

Otherwise, the form that a clausal modifier takes with one of these heads
is a non-finite clause with *-mA* or *-mAk*. It should be noted that *-mA* is
generally preferred to *-mAk* in noun clauses that function as modifiers of
compounds.

(147) Aysel [**oğlunu Amerika'da okut*ma*(*k*)**] **isteğ**ini yenemiyordu.
'Aysel couldn't overcome *the/her desire* [*to get her son educated
in America*].'

(148) Öğleden sonra [**kardeşimin gel*me*(*k*)/gel*mesi***] **ihtimali** var.
'In the afternoon there's *a possibility* [*that my brother/sister
will come*].'

(149) [**Başkalarından saygı bekle*me*(*k*)**] **alışkanlığı** insanı düş
kırıklığına uğratır.
'*The habit of* [*expecting respect from others*] leads to
disappointment.'

(150) [**Bu yanlış uygulamayı düzelt*memiz***] **zamanı** geldi.
'*The time* has come for [*us to correct this wrong practice*].'

In this type of compound, person marking of the *-mA* verbal noun is
possible only with highly impersonal heads such as *olasılık/ihtimal* 'possibility' or *zaman/vakit* 'time' (see (148), (150). In other cases, person
marking can attach only to the head:

(151) [Başkalarından saygı bekleme(k)] alışkanlı**ğımız** bizi düş
kırıklığına uğratıyor.
'*Our* habit of [expecting respect from others] causes us
disappointment.'

25 RELATIVE CLAUSES

Relative clauses are complex adjectival constructions that modify noun phrases. The most typical type of relative clause is non-finite (12.3), and contains one of the participle suffixes *-(y)An*, *-DIK*, or *-(y)AcAK*, corresponding to the relative pronouns 'who', 'which', 'that', 'whom', 'whose', 'where', etc. in English. Finite relative clauses, incorporating the subordinator *ki* (11.1.1.4), also occur, but the range of this type is quite limited. For this reason, the whole of this chapter, with the exception of the last section (25.6), is devoted to non-finite relative clauses. With the exception of *ki* clauses, all relative clauses *precede* the noun phrase they modify, in the same way that adjectives precede the noun they modify:

(1)   küçük kız
      'the little girl'

(2)   **oyuncak-lar-ın-ı kır-*an*** (küçük) kız
      toy-PL-3SG.POSS-ACC break-PART little girl
      'the (little) girl *who* breaks/has broken her toys'

(3)   **her gün okul-da gör-*düğ*-üm** kız
      every day school-LOC see-PART-1SG.POSS girl
      'the girl *whom* I see at school every day'

(4)   **anne-si-yle tanış-*acağ*-ım** kız
      mother-3SG.POSS-COM meet-PART-1SG.POSS girl
      'the girl *whose* mother I'm going to meet'

(5)   **baş-ın-da şapka ol-*an*** kız
      head-3SG.POSS-LOC hat be-PART- girl
      'the girl *who* has a hat on her head'

Section 25.1 describes the principles of relativization and the function of the participle suffixes. Section 25.2 discusses the distinction between restrictive and non-restrictive relative clauses, and 25.3 deals with headless relative clauses. 25.4 examines the expression of tense and aspect in relative clauses, and the conditions under which *olan* (where this is the relevant participial form) may be omitted. For the ordering of a non-finite relative clause with respect to other adjectivals and determiners in the noun phrase see 15.3.9.

25.1 PRINCIPLES OF RELATIVIZATION

The noun of the noun phrase that a relative clause modifies, i.e. the head noun, can have one of several different relationships with the relative clause. For example, in (2) the relationship of the target of relativization, the head noun *kız* 'girl', to the relative clause is that of subject of the verb *kır-* 'break' (cf. **kız** *oyuncaklarını kırdı 'the girl* broke her toys'), whereas in (3) it is the direct object of the verb *gör-* 'see' (cf. *her gün **kızı** okulda görüyorum* 'I see *the girl* at school every day'). In (4), on the other hand, *kız* is the possessor of *anne-si* 'her mother' (cf. the genitive-possessive construction **kız-ın** *anne-si 'the girl*'s mother'). These processes are referred to as 'relativizing the subject', 'relativizing the direct object', 'relativizing the possessor', etc. The participle suffix used in non-finite relative clauses is selected on the basis of the nature of the relationship of the head noun to the relative clause in any particular instance.

When relativizing a constituent of a nominal sentence (12.1.1.2) the suppletive form *ol-* of the copula (12.1.1.3) is used as the bearer of the participle suffixes:

(6) [ağır yaralı *ol*-**an**] hastalar
 seriously injured be-PART patients
 'the patients [*who are* seriously injured]'

(7) [çocukların evde *ol*acağı] bir gün
 'a day [*when* the children *will be* at home]'

The construction in (6) corresponds to the nominal sentence *Hastalar ağır yaralı* 'The patients are seriously injured'.

The verb *bulun-* 'be (found)' can also be used when relativizing one of the constituents of a nominal sentence, especially where location is involved:

(8) iç-in-de üç top *bulun*-**an**/*ol*-**an** kutu (cf. Kutunun içinde üç top var.)
 inside-3SG.POSS-LOC three ball be-PART box
 'the box [*which has/had* three balls inside it]'

25.1.1 MARKERS OF NON-FINITE RELATIVE CLAUSES: THE PARTICIPLE SUFFIXES

25.1.1.1 *-(y)An*

A non-finite verb form which contains *-(y)An* does not get inflected for case or person, except in headless relative clauses (see 25.3). This participle occurs in the following circumstances:

(i)   In clauses where the relativized constituent is the *subject* of the verb in the relative clause:

(9)   [burada sat-ıl-**an**] *kitap-lar* (cf. *Kitaplar* burada satılıyor.)
      here sell-PASS-PART book-PL
      '*the books* [(*which* are) sold here]'

(10) [öğretmen ol-**an**] *Haydar* (cf. *Haydar* öğretmen.)
      teacher be-PART Haydar
      '*Haydar*, [*who* is a teacher]'

(ii) In clauses where the relativized constituent is the possessor (14.4) of some constituent of the relative clause:

(a)   Where this possessor is part of the subject of the verb in the relative clause, the relative clause begins with a non-case-marked noun phrase marked with a 3rd person possessive suffix. For example, in (11) below *komşumuz* 'our neighbour', which is the relativized constituent, is the possessor of *araba-sı* 'his/her car', and would thus be the modifier in the corresponding genitive-possessive construction *komşumuz-un araba-sı* 'our neighbour's car', which is understood to be the subject of *çalın-* 'be stolen' (cf. *Komşumuzun arabası çalındı* 'Our neighbour's car has been stolen').

      (11) [araba-*sı* çal-ın-**an**] *komşu-muz*
            car-3SG.POSS steal-PASS-PART neighbour-1PL.POSS
            '*our neighbour* [*whose* car was stolen]'

      (12) [rol*ü* büyük olma**yan**] *oyuncu* (cf. *Oyuncunun* rolü büyük değil.)
            '*the actor* [*whose* part isn't big]'/'the actor [who does not have a big part]'

      Note that in the pattern represented in (12), where the verb in the relative clause is *ol-* (corresponding to an expression with 'have' in English), it is unusual for the possessive-marked constituent to be preceded by any modifiers. Any adjectival descriptors associated with this noun, such as *büyük* 'big', are preferably given a predicative role within the relative clause, which thus corresponds in form to a linking sentence rather than to an existential one (see 12.1.1.2).

(b)   Where this possessor is part of some constituent of the relative clause other than its subject, the relative clause must have a non-definite (i.e. categorial or indefinite) subject. (Otherwise, if the subject is definite, a -*DIK/-(y)AcAK* construction is used; see 25.1.1.2 (iii). The possessor can be part of any non-subject constituent, such as:

A direct object:

> (13) [koyun-ların-ı *kurt* kap-**an**] köylü-ler (cf. Köylülerin koyunlarını kurt kaptı.)
> sheep-PL.3PL.POSS-ACC wolf catch-PART villager-PL
> 'the villagers [*whose* sheep were caught by wolves]'
> (lit. 'whose sheep wolves caught')

An adverbial:

> (14) [çatı-sın-dan birkaç küçük *kiremit* düş-**en**] ev
> roof-3SG.POSS-ABL a.few small tile fall-PART house
> 'the house [from the roof of *which* a few small tiles fell]'

A possessive-marked postposition:

> (15) [arka-sın-da *adam* ol-**an**] çocuk (cf. Çocuğun arkasında adam var.)
> back-3POSS.SG-LOC man be-PART child
> 'the child [behind *whom* there is a man]'

In (13) the relativized constituent *köylüler* 'villagers' is the possessor of *koyun* 'sheep', and would thus be the modifier in the corresponding genitive-possessive construction *köylülerin koyunları*, which itself functions as the direct object of *kap-* 'seize and devour' (cf. *Köylülerin koyunlarını kurt kaptı* 'Wolves devoured the villagers' sheep'. The non-definite subject may be modified (e.g. by a determiner and/or adjective, such as *birkaç* 'a few' and *küçük* 'small' in (14)).

In these constructions the subject of the relative clause (i.e. *kiremit* 'tiles', *kurt* 'wolves', *adam* 'man' in the examples above) is non-definite, and is placed immediately before the verb (see 23.2.1). The constituent towards which the relativized constituent stands in a possessor relation (*koyunlarını* 'their sheep' (ACC), *çatısından* 'from the roof of which', *arkasında* 'behind whom') is positioned at the beginning of the relative clause and is marked by a 3rd person possessive suffix.

(iii) In clauses where the relativized constituent is a possessed item (a noun phrase with possessive marking):

-*(y)An* is used only in cases where the possessed item is part of the subject of the verb in the relative clause. Otherwise -*DIK/-(y)AcAK* are used (see

25.1.1.2 (iv)). For example, in (16) below, the relativized constituent *arabası* 'car-3SG.POSS' is the possessed item in the genitive-possessive construction *komşumuz-un araba-sı* 'our neighbour's car', which is itself the subject of *çalın-* 'be stolen' (cf. *Komşumuzun arabası çalındı* 'Our neighbour's car was stolen').

(16) [komşu-muz-un çal-ın-**an**] araba-sı
neighbour-1PL.POSS-GEN steal-PASS-PART car-3SG.POSS
'our neighbour's car, [*which* was stolen]'/'our neighbour's stolen car'

(17) [oyuncunun büyük olma**yan**] rolü (cf. Oyuncunun rolü büyük değil.)
'the actor's part, [*which* isn't/wasn't big]'

(**iv**) In clauses where the relativized constituent is a noun phrase expressing the location of the activity expressed by the relative clause:

In these constructions the relative clause itself contains a subject with categorial status (22.3), and the verb has passive marking:

(18) [*kitap* imzala-**n**-**an**] yer (cf. O yerde kitap imzalanıyor.)
book sign-PASS-PART place
'the place [*where* books are signed]'

(19) [*içki* iç-*il*-ebil-ecek (ol-**an**)] lokantalar (cf. O lokantalarda içki içilebiliyor.)
alcoholic.beverage drink-PASS-PSB-FUT AUX-PART restaurants
'restaurants [*where* alcohol can be drunk]'

25.1.1.2   -DIK and -(y)AcAK

These participles have identical structural properties in terms of their role in relative clauses, but they differ in terms of tense. In very general terms, *-(y)AcAK* refers to future situations:

(20) [Fatma'nın yarın gör-**eceğ**-i] film
Fatma-GEN tomorrow see-PART-3SG.POSS film
'the film [*that* Fatma is *going to* see/*will* be seeing tomorrow]'

-DIK, on the other hand, mainly refers to past or ongoing situations:

(21) [Fatma-**nın** doku-duğ-**u**] halı
Fatma-GEN weave-PART-3SG.POSS rug
'the rug [*that* Fatma is/was weaving/wove/has woven]'

Temporal adverbs (such as *dün* 'yesterday', *şu anda* 'at the moment') are used in contexts where an explicit differentiation between past and present is necessary. See 25.4 for a more detailed description of the tense and aspectual properties of relative clauses.

Clauses with *-DIK* and *-(y)AcAK* have the structure of genitive-possessive constructions (14.4), i.e. the participle has possessive marking agreeing with the subject, and the subject, if separately expressed by a noun phrase, as in (20) and (21) above, is in the genitive case. For the conditions under which the subject of a clause may be omitted see 18.1.5.

-DIK and *-(y)AcAK* are used in the following circumstances:

(i) In clauses where the relativized constituent is the direct object of the verb in the relative clause:

(22) [bil-**diğ**-im] bir turizm şirketi (cf. Bir turizm şirketi biliyorum.)
    know-PART-1SG.POSS a tourism agency
    'a tourist agency [(*that*) I know]'

(23) [gönder**ecek**leri] temsilci (cf. Bir temsilci gönderecekler.)
    'the representative [(*whom*) they *will* send]'

(ii) In clauses where the relativized constituent is the oblique object or the adverbial modifier of the verb in the relative clause (see 13.1.2.2 and 13.1.3):

(24) [benim kork**tuğ**um] bazı hayvanlar (cf. Bazı hayvanlardan korkuyorum.)
    'some animals [*of which* I am/was afraid]'

(25) [Turhan-ın et-i kes-**eceğ**-i] bıçak (cf. Turhan eti bıçakla kesecek.)
    Turhan-GEN meat-ACC cut-PART-3SG.POSS knife
    'the knife [*with which* Turhan *will/would* cut the meat]'

In this construction type, where the relativized constituent refers to a human being and is in the 3rd person (as in the case of *birisi* 'someone' and *kişiler* 'people' in the examples below), a resumptive pronoun (*kendisi* in the case of 3rd person singular and *kendileri* in the case of 3rd person plural, see 18.1.2.2 (iv)) can appear in the relative clause. *Kendisi* and *kendileri* carry the case marker or the postposition that the relativized constituent would be associated with in a corresponding finite clause:

(26) [Erol-un] (kendi-si-**yle**) konuş-abil-**eceğ**-i birisi (cf. Erol öyle birisi**yle** konuşabilir.)
    Erol-GEN *kendi*-3SG.POSS-COM talk-PSB-PART-3SG.POSS someone
    'someone [*with whom* Erol can/could/would be able to talk]'

(27) [(bizim) (kendilerin*den*) nefret et**tiğ**imiz] kişiler (cf. Biz öyle
kişiler*den* nefret ediyoruz.)
'the people [*whom* we hate/hated]'

(iii) In clauses where the relativized constituent is the possessor (14.4) of
some constituent of the relative clause other than its subject, as exemplified below:

The direct object:

(28) [usta-nın ***kapı-sın-ı*** değiştir-**eceğ**-i] çamaşır makinası
(cf. Usta *çamaşır makinasının kapısını* değiştirecek.)
engineer-GEN door-3SG.POSS-ACC change-PART-3SG.POSS
washing machine
'the washing machine [*of which* the engineer is/was going to
change the door]'

An adverbial:

(29) *[kız-ın-a* piyano ders-i ver-**diğ**-im] hanım (cf. *Bir hanımın kızına*
piyano dersi veriyorum.)
daughter-3SG.POSS piano lesson-NC give-PART-1SG.POSS lady
'the lady [*to whose daughter* I give/gave piano lessons]'

A possessive-marked postposition:

(30) [***ön-ün-den*** köprü-nün geç-**tiğ**-i] ev-ler (cf. Köprü *evlerin önünden*
geçiyor.)
front-3SG.POSS-ABL bridge-GEN be.situated-PART-3SG.POSS
house-PL
'the houses [*in front of which* the bridge is situated]'

The crucial difference between this strategy for relativizing a non-subject
possessor and the one with *-(y)An* described above in 25.1.1.1 (ii)b is
that while the latter permits only non-definite subjects, the use of *-DIK/
-(y)AcAK* allows definite subjects, such as *usta* 'the engineer' in (28), 'I' in
(29) (expressed by the possessive marking on the verb), and *köprü* 'the
bridge' in (30).

In (31), the *-(y)An* construction parallel to (30), the subject *köprü* has
the non-definite meaning 'a bridge/bridges':

(31) [***ön-ün-den*** köprü geç-**en**] ev-ler
front-3SG.POSS-ABL bridge be.situated-PART house-PL
'the houses [*in front of which* a bridge is situated]'

As a result of this difference, a relative clause of this type which has a proper noun as its subject (e.g. *Semra* below) is only grammatical with the *-DIK-/(y)AcAK* strategy:

(32) [*arkasında* Semra-nın otur**duğu**] çocuk
'the child [*behind whom* Semra is/was sitting]'

While a relative clause with a categorial subject has to be expressed with *-(y)An* (as in (31), also (13) and (15)), in the case of an indefinite subject (i.e. one in which a numeral or indefinite determiner is present), either kind of participle is possible:

(33) (a) [*içine* birkaç çiçek konmuş ol**an**] bir vazo
 (b) [*içine* birkaç çiçeğin konmuş ol**duğu**] bir vazo
 'a vase [*into which* a few flowers have/had been put]'

The tendency for the *-DIK-/(y)AcAK* strategy to be preferred with an indefinite subject increases with the degree of particularization given to the subject. Below, for example, it would be almost obligatory:

(34) [*içine* [Handan'ın bahçesinden toplanmış] birkaç çiçeğin konmuş ol**duğu**] bir vazo
 'a vase [*into which* a few flowers [*picked from Handan's garden*] had been put]'

(iv) In clauses where the relativized constituent is a possessed item (a noun phrase with possessive marking):

-DIK/-(y)AcAK are used only in cases where the possessed item is *not* part of the subject of the verb in the relative clause. Otherwise *-(y)An* is used (see 25.1.1.1 (iii)). (35) and (36) are examples of this type of *-DIK/-(y)AcAK* clause, in which the possessed constituent is respectively part of a direct object (*arabanın sol aynası* 'the left mirror of the car') and an oblique object (*ev sahibinin köpeği* 'the landlord's dog'):

(35) [araba-nın kır-**dığ**-ın] sol ayna-sı (cf. *Arabanın sol aynasını kırdın.*)
 car-GEN break-PART-2SG.POSS left mirror-3SG.POSS
 'the left mirror of the car, [*which* you broke]'

(36) [ev sahib-in-in kork-**tuğ**-um] köpeğ-i (cf. *Ev sahibinin köpeğinden korkuyorum.*)
 landlord-NC-GEN fear-PART-1SG.POSS dog-3SG.POSS
 'the landlord's dog, [*which* I'm afraid of]'

(v) Special usages of *-DIK/-(y)AcAK*:
Where the relativized constituent is the non-definite (i.e. categorial or indefinite) object of the verb in the relative clause, *-(y)AcAK* can also appear without any person marking:

(37) [çayla yi**yecek**] bir şeyler (cf. Çayla insan bir şeyler yer/yiyebilir.)
'things [*to* eat with tea]'

The relativized constituent in this type of construction can also, as in the case of *yaş* 'age' in (38), have an adverbial relation to the relative clause. For an example with *zaman* 'time' see (30) in Chapter 20.

(38) [seni anla**yacak**] **yaş**(ta değil) (cf. Bu yaşta seni anlayamaz.)
'(s/he is not) old enough (lit. 'at an age') [to understand you]'

Although it is not overtly marked, the verbs in these constructions express possibility, a value normally associated with the modality suffix *-(y)Abil*. The lack of person marking on the verb indicates that the clause lacks an agent. As a result, those where the relativized constituent is a direct object can generally be interchanged with clauses where the verb is in the passive voice:

(39) **(a)** [Hasan'a yönelt-**ecek**] soru (cf. Hasan'a birisi soru yönelt(ebil)ir.)
direct-PART
'a question/questions [to direct to Hasan]'

(b) [Hasan'a yönelt-**il-ecek**] soru
direct-PASS-PART
'a question/questions [to be directed to Hasan]'

Some *-(y)AcAK* participles have been lexicalized as nouns or adjectives (e.g. from *yak-* 'burn' *yakacak* 'fuel', see 7.2.1.1).
    -DIK has a similar lexical usage. When it is used with no other suffix, it is highly unproductive, and forms nouns or adjectives (e.g. *tanıdık bir yüz* 'a familiar face'). Its negativized form *-mAdIk* is more productive (e.g. *bakmadık* 'unsearched'); see 7.2.1.1.

25.1.1.3 Summary of strategies of relativization

(i)	Relativizing subjects	*-(y)An*	25.1.1.1 (i)
(ii)	Relativizing direct objects	*-DIK/-(y)AcAK*	25.1.1.2 (i), (v)
(iii)	Relativizing oblique objects	*-DIK/-(y)AcAK*	25.1.1.2 (ii)
(iv)	Relativizing adverbials	*-(y)An*	25.1.1.1 (iv)
		-DIK/-(y)AcAK	25.1.1.2 (ii)

(v) Relativizing possessors

(a) which are part of subjects	*-(y)An*	(25.1.1.1 (ii–a))
(b) which are not part of subjects	*-(y)An*	(25.1.1.1 (ii–b)
or	*-DIK/-(y)AcAK*	(25.1.1.2 (iii))

(vi) Relativizing possessed constituents

(a) which are part of subjects	*-(y)An*	(25.1.1.1 (iii))
(b) which are not part of subjects	*-DIK/-(y)AcAK*	(25.1.1.2 (iv))

25.1.2 RELATIVE CLAUSES WITH EMBEDDED NOUN CLAUSES

These are constructions where the relativized constituent (e.g. *kız* 'girl' in (40)) is a constituent of a noun clause (Chapter 24). The choice between *-(y)An* and *-DIK/-(y)AcAK* on the verb of this complex type of relative clause depends on whether the particular embedded noun clause is the subject of the relative clause or not. If it is, *-(y)An* is used; otherwise *-DIK/ -(y)AcAK* are used. The pattern here thus follows the general pattern described above (25.1.1):

(40) [[İstanbul-da otur-duğ-u] san-ıl-**an**] kız
Istanbul-LOC live-VN-3.SG.POSS think-PASS-PART girl
'the girl [*who* is/was thought [to be living in Istanbul]]'

In this example, the relativized constituent *kız* belongs to the noun clause *(kızın) İstanbul'da oturduğu* 'that (the girl) lives/lived in İstanbul'. The noun clause itself is the subject of the passive verb *sanıl-* 'be thought'. Therefore *-(y)An* is selected.

Similarly, in the examples below the noun clauses *herkesin (bir konu) bilmesi* 'everyone's knowing a subject' and *(misafirlerin) gelmeleri* 'the guests' arrival' are each the subject of the relative clause within which they are embedded:

(41) [[herkesin bilmesi] gerek**en**] bir konu
'a subject [*which* everyone should know about]'

(42) [[gelmeleri] beklen**en**] misafirler
'the guests [*who* are expected [to arrive]]'

In the following example, on the other hand, the noun clause *(kızın) İstanbul'da oturduğun-u* 'that she lives/lived in Istanbul-ACC' is not the subject of the verb *san-* 'think', but its direct object. Therefore *-DIK/-(y)AcAK* are selected:

(43) [(ben-im) [İstanbul-da otur-duğ-un]-**u** san-**dığ**-ım] kız
I-GEN Istanbul-LOC live-VN-3SG.POSS-ACC think-PART-1SG.POSS
girl
'the girl [*who* [I think/thought lives/lived in Istanbul]]'

The embedded verb in the noun clause takes whatever subordinator
(*-mA, -mAK, -(y)Iş, -DIK/-(y)AcAK*) may be required by the verb of which
it is a complement. Thus *-DIK* in *otur-duğ-un-u* (43) and *-(y)AcAK* in
evlen-eceğ-in-i below, are *not* participle suffixes but verbal noun markers:

(44) [Erol-un [evlen-**eceğ**-in]-i san-**dığ**-ı] kız
Erol-GEN marry-VN-3SG.POSS-ACC think-PART-3SG.POSS girl
(**i**) 'the girl [Erol thinks/thought [he (= Erol) will/would marry]]'
(**ii**) 'the girl [Erol thinks/thought [will/would get married]]'

In the first interpretation of (44) the subject of the noun clause [(*Erol'un*)
evleneceği] 'that he (= Erol) will marry' is the same as the subject of
the relative clause [*Erol'un . . . sandığı*] '(that) Erol thought . . .'. The two
can also be distinct, as in the second interpretation of (44), where the
relativized constituent (*kız* 'girl') is understood to be the subject of the
noun clause, or in (45), where the relative clause has a 1st person singular
subject:

(45) [[Erol'un evleneceğin]-i düşündüğ**üm**] kız
'the girl [(*that*) I thought [Erol would marry]]'

In constructions where the noun clause subordinator is *-mA*, the two clauses
always have separate subjects (see 24.4.2.2):

(46) [[al-***ma***-nız]-ı tavsiye et-tiğ-**im**] ilaç
take-VN-2PL.POSS-ACC suggest-PART-1SG.POSS medication
'the medication [that *I* suggested [*you* take]]'

25.2 RESTRICTIVE AND NON-RESTRICTIVE RELATIVE CLAUSES

Restrictive relative clauses express a limitation on the reference of the
noun they modify, and thus have an identifying function. For example, the
relative clause in *yaprakları dökülen ağaçlar* 'trees that lose their leaves'
limits the reference of 'trees' to those that lose their leaves. Non-restrictive
relative clauses, on the other hand, add new information about referents
that are in no need of identification, and thus have a merely descriptive
function. For example, the relative clause in *damadıyla hiçbir zaman iyi
geçinmemiş olan Hayriye Hanım* 'Hayriye Hanım, who had never got on
well with her son-in-law', provides additional information about Hayriye
Hanım, a person whom the hearer is assumed to be able to identify.

In Turkish the typical usage of a relative clause with a participle suffix is
restrictive. Thus (47) is more likely to be interpreted as 'the trees (that) I
like' rather than 'the trees, which I like so much'.

(47) sev-**diğ**-im ağaç-lar
      like-PART-1SG.POSS tree-PL

As a result, in the spoken language proper nouns do not often occur as the relativized constituent of a relative clause, since their referents are not usually in need of identification. If a proper noun does occur in conversation as the head of a relative clause, this is again usually with a restrictive meaning. In (48) the usage of *bu* 'this' in the subsequent mention of the name makes the identifying function explicit:

(48) [Kenan'ın evleneceği] **Ayşe**, işte **bu Ayşe**.
      'This is the Ayşe [that Kenan is going to marry].'

However, the non-restrictive usage of relative clauses is quite common in the written language, where it can be used as a stylistic device to avoid a monotonous succession of finite clauses:

(49) [Bugün yurda dön**en**] *Cumhurbaşkanı*, saat 16'da bir basın
      toplantısı düzenleyecek.
      'The *president*, [who is returning to the country today], will hold a
      press conference at 4 p.m.'

The omission of *olan* from a relative clause containing a compound verb form makes a non-restrictive interpretation unlikely (see 25.4.1.1). On the other hand, finite relative clauses with *ki* occur mainly in the non-restrictive function (see 25.6).

25.3 HEADLESS RELATIVE CLAUSES

These are constructions where the head noun that a relative clause modifies is omitted from the sentence, because the referent of the relative clause is either clear from previous mention, or is essentially self-identifying. Such clauses correspond to expressions such as 'the one(s) that', 'the person who', 'those who', 'what', 'anything that', etc. In these clauses the number and case markers that would otherwise be attached to the noun appear on the participle itself, as illustrated in the (b) examples below:

(50) (**a**) [opera-yı sev-me-yen]-**ler-e** (şaşıyorum).
            opera-ACC like-NEG-PART-PL-DAT
            '(I am surprised) at *those* [*who* don't like opera].'

      (**b**) [operayı sevmeyen] kişi-**ler-e** . . .
                              person-PL-DAT
            '. . . at people [who don't like opera]'

(51) (**a**) [Biz-im dik-ecek]-**ler**-imiz-de (hata var).
we-GEN sew-PART-PL-1PL.POSS-LOC
'(There is a fault) with *the ones* [*that* we shall be making].'

(**b**) [biz-im dik-eceğ-imiz] elbise-**ler-de** . . .
'. . . with the dresses [*that* we shall be making]'

Note that, in the case of *-DIK/-(y)AcAK*, the marker for plural associated with the omitted head noun (e.g. *elbise*-**ler** 'dresses' in (51b)) occurs *before* the person marker in the headless relative clause, following the order of nominal inflectional suffixes (8.1).

There is also a highly productive use of headless relative clauses as the subject of an existential sentence.

(52) Öğleden sonra ara-yan ol-ma-dı. (cf. . . . arayan birisi olmadı.)
call-PART be-NEG-PF
'No one called in the afternoon.' (lit. 'There was no one who . . .'.)

(53) Bu konuda bil-diğ-im yok. (cf. . . . bildiğim bir şey yok.)
know-PART-1SG.POSS non-existent
'I don't know anything about this matter.' (lit. 'There is nothing I know.')

See 18.4 (vi), examples (116)–(117) for a comparison of headless relative clauses and pronominalized complex adjectivals.

25.4 THE EXPRESSION OF TENSE AND ASPECT IN RELATIVE CLAUSES

None of the participle suffixes *-(y)An*, *-DIK* and *-(y)AcAK* have a unique time reference. They attach directly to a verb stem which is uninflected for tense and aspect (8.2.3), and therefore using any of them on their own may result in ambiguity. For example, *yüz-en kadın* (swim-PART woman) can mean 'the woman who is/was swimming', or 'the woman who swims/ swam/has swum', and *çiz-**diğ**-im resim* (draw-PART-1SG.POSS picture) can mean 'the sketch I am/was making/make/made/have made'.

In order to indicate the time location of the situation in a relative clause either time adverbials are used, or a compound verb form is constructed by means of the auxiliary *ol-* (13.3.1.2), in order to enable the addition of certain tense and aspect markers (25.4.1).

-(y)An typically refers to non-future situations:

(54) [*dün* başla-**yan**] fırtına
yesterday start-PART storm
'the storm [that started *yesterday*]'

(55) [*iki yıldır* süren] kuraklık
'the drought [that has been going on *for two years*]'

(56) [*şu anda* çalan] parça
'the piece [that is playing *at the moment*]'

In informal registers it can also refer to the future:

(57) [*Yarın* çık-**an**] gazete-de önemli bir yazı bulun-acak.
tomorrow appear-PART paper-LOC important an article be-FUT
'There will be an important article in the paper [that comes out *tomorrow*].'

-*DIK* also typically refers to non-future situations:

(58) [*geçen hafta* bitir-**diğ**-im] roman
last week finish-PART-1SG.POSS novel
'the novel [I finished *last week*]'

(59) [*şu sırada* oku**duğum**] roman
'the novel [I am reading *at the moment*]'

It can also refer to situations which precede or are simultaneous with a future situation referred to in the superordinate clause:

(60) Sonunda [git-**tiğ**-in] okul nasıl olsa bir spor akademi-si ol-acak.
in.the.end go-PART-2SG.POSS school in any case a sports academy-NC be-FUT
'In the end, whatever school [you go to], it will be a sports academy.'

-*(y)AcAK* refers to future situations. The futurity may be in relation to the time of utterance:

(61) [yarın oku-**yacağ**-ım] makale
tomorrow read-PART-1SG.POSS article
'the article [that I'm *going to* read tomorrow]'

Or it may be futurity with respect to any other point in time, which may itself be in the past:

(62) [Dün oku-**yacağ**-ım] makale-yi ancak bugün oku-yabil-di-m.
yesterday read-PART-1SG.POSS article-ACC only today read-PSB-PF-1SG
'The article [that I *was to* read yesterday], I managed to read only today.'

(63) [Geçen hafta göre**ceğ**im] film *Mavi Kadife*'ydi.
'The film [that I *was going to* see last week] was *Blue Velvet*.'

25.4.1 THE USE OF AUXILIARY *ol-* IN RELATIVE CLAUSES

The strategy used for indicating finer specifications of tense and aspect in relative clauses is to attach the participle suffixes to the auxiliary verb *ol-*, producing the forms *olan, olduK-* and *olacaK-* (see 13.3.1.2). This strategy allows the verb of the relative clause to combine freely with some of the tense and aspect markers, producing compound forms such as *bak-mış olan* 'who has looked', *bak-maz ol-duğ-um* 'that I have stopped looking at', etc. However, it should be noted that even this strategy is, at times, insufficient, and verbs in relative clauses may not express tense and aspect as fully as their finite counterparts do.

The attachment of the participle suffixes to the auxiliary *ol-* makes it possible to express the following tenses and aspects in a relative clause:

PERFECTIVE/PAST:	*-mIş*
FUTURE:	*-(y)AcAK*
PROGRESSIVE/HABITUAL:	*-mAktA* and *-(I)yor*
HABITUAL:	*-(A/I)r/-mAz*

(i) *-mIş olan, -mIş olduK-, -mIş olacaK-*:
-mIş, which in some finite clauses marks perfective aspect, relative past tense and evidential modality (21.4.3), loses its modality value when followed by *ol-* (8.2.3.3, 21.5). In relative clauses, as in other subordinate clauses (cf. 24.4.7, 26.2.3 (i)), it locates a situation unambiguously in a time period prior to that of another time referred to in the sentence. For example, one of the readings associated with (64a) below, namely the imperfective 's/he lost the book (that) s/he was reading', is not a possible interpretation of (64b), which contains *-mIş olduK-*.

(64) (**a**) [Oku-**duğ**-u] kitabı kaybetti.
read-PART-3SG.POSS
'S/he lost the book [(that) s/he was reading/read/had read].'

(**b**) [Oku-*muş* **ol**-**duğ**-u] kitabı kaybetti.
read-PF AUX-PART-3SG.POSS
'S/he lost the book [(that) s/he *had* read].'

The form *-mIş olacaK-* is equivalent to the finite compound form *-mIş olacak* (21.5.1). Thus a relative clause which contains *-mIş olacaK-* is aspectually different from one that just contains a *-(y)AcAK* participle. For example, while (65a) identifies a certain book in terms of the occurrence of a future event, (65b) identifies it in terms of a future situation in which that event will already have been completed:

(65) (a) [yarın bitir**eceğ**im] kitap
'the book [that I'm *going to* finish tomorrow]'

(b) [yarın bitir***miş** ola***cağ*ım] kitap
the book [that I *will have* finish*ed* tomorrow]'

However, a relative clause with *-mIş olan* or *-mIş olduK-* is sometimes just a slightly more formal variant of a relative clause marked simply by *-(y)An* or *-DIK*:

(66) [kızı dün gel**en**] kadın/[kızı dün gel***miş** ol***an**] kadın
'the woman [whose daughter came yesterday]'

(67) [Sizin dün gör**düğ**ünüz/gör***müş** ol***du*ğunuz] filmi ben yarın göreceğim.
'The film [(that) you saw yesterday] I'm going to see tomorrow.'

(ii) *-(y)AcAk olan*, *-(y)AcAk olduK-*:
The suffix *-(y)AcAK* indicates relative future tense (see 21.5.3).

The combination of the tense suffix *-(y)AcAK* with *olan* is the standard means of expressing relative future tense in relative clauses that require *-(y)An* marking. (Compare the informal alternative strategy exemplified in (57) above.)

(68) [Yarın çık-***acak ol*-an**] gazete-de önemli bir yazı bulun-acak.
tomorrow come.out-FUT AUX-PART paper-LOC important an article be-FUT
'There will be an important article in the paper [that's *going to* come out tomorrow].'

(69) [Dün gösteril***ecek ol*an**] filmde sakıncalı sahneler bulunmuş.
'It seems that improper scenes were found in the film [that *was going to* be shown yesterday].'

Relative clauses with *-(y)AcAk olduK-* occur rather infrequently. They are identical in meaning to their counterparts with the participle suffix *-(y)AcAK*:

(70) (**a**) [arkadaş-lar-ın al-**acak**-ları] televizyon
      friend-PL-GEN buy-PART-3PL.POSS television

      (**b**) [arkadaş-lar-ın al-*acak ol*-**duk**-ları] televizyon
      friend-PL-GEN buy-FUT AUX-PART-3PL.POSS television
      'the television [that [our] friends *are/were going to* buy]'

(**iii**) *-mAktA olan, -mAktA olduK-,* and *-(I)yor olacaK-*:
Both *-mAktA* and *-(I)yor* mark imperfective (progressive or habitual)
aspect (21.3.2). In relative clauses *-mAkta* is more typically used with *olan*
and *olduK-*, while *-(I)yor* is used with *olacaK*. Although verb forms with
-mAktA ol- resolve ambiguities as described below, they are not favoured
in everyday speech.

In the absence of an adverbial expressing frequency (such as *her gün*
'every day') these forms are understood to have progressive meaning:

(71) [Oku-*makta ol*-**duğ**-u] kitabı kaybetti. (cf. (64a) above)
      read-IMPF AUX-PART-3SG.POSS
      'S/he lost the book [(that) s/he *was* read*ing*].'

The use of a *-mAktA ol-* form of participle resolves the ambiguity of *-(y)An*
and *-DIK* with regard to perfectivity in favour of the imperfective (progressive) meaning.

Where the relative clause contains a time adverbial that denotes an
ongoing situation, such as *şu anda* 'at the/this moment' or *o sırada* 'at that
time', the verb will be understood as progressive, whether *-mAktA
olan/olduK-* are used or the simple *-(y)An* or *-DIK* participles. The use of
-mAktA ol- in such cases is more formal:

(72) (**a**) [*şu anda* Erol-a mektup yaz-*makta ol*-**an**] kız
      at this moment Erol-DAT letter write-IMPF AUX-PART girl

      (**b**) [şu anda Erol-a mektup yaz-**an**] kız
                              write-PART
      'the girl [who *at this moment* is writing a letter to Erol]'

(73) (**a**) [*o sırada* seyret-*mekte ol*-**duğ**-um] videolar
      at that time watch-IMPF AUX-PART-1SG.POSS videos

      (**b**) [o sırada seyret-**tiğ**-im] videolar
                              watch-PART-1SG.POSS
      'the videos [I was watching *at the time*]'

-(I)yor olacaK- marks progressive or habitual aspect in the (relative) future. The interpretation depends on contextual clues, in particular the type of time adverbial used:

(74) [[***Erol geldiği sırada***] seyred*iyor ol*acağım] film eskilerden biri olacak(tı).
      The film [that I *will (would) be* watch*ing at the time of Erol's arrival*] will (would) be one of the old ones.' (Progressive)

(75) [Yakında ***her gün*** gör*üyor ol*acağım] terapist acaba bana dayanabilecek mi?
      'I wonder if the therapist [that I *will* soon *be* see*ing every day*] will be able to put up with me.' (Habitual)

(iv) *-(A/I)r olduK-, -mAz olan, -mAz olduK, -mAz olacaK:*
The aorist marker *-(A/I)r*, which in finite clauses can have aspectual or modal meaning (21.3.2, 21.4.1), in relative clauses is an aspectual marker with habitual meaning. It occurs only with *olduK-*:

(76) [Artık sık sık görüş*ür ol*duğumuz] komşularımızı başta hiç sevmemiştik.
      'At first we didn't like our neighbours, [whom we see quite often now].'

-mAz, the negative counterpart of *-(A/I)r*, is used with all three forms of the participle, to express a habitually non-occurring action or state:

(77) Semra [yakında giy-e-mez ***ol-acağ***-ı] giysilerini bu günlerde
               soon wear-PSB-NEG.AOR AUX-PART-3SG.POSS
      özellikle giymek istiyor.
      'Semra particularly wants to wear now the clothes [that she *will* soon *not* be able to *wear*].'

25.4.1.1 The omission of *olan*: truncated relative clauses

olan can be omitted from the forms *-mIş olan* (25.4.1 (i)) and *-(y)AcAk olan* (25.4.1 (ii)), in a way somewhat similar to the omission of 'who is', 'which was', etc. in some kinds of relative clause in English:

(78) [kömür-de piş-**miş**] patlıcan (cf. kömürde piş**miş olan** patlıcan)
      coal-LOC cook-PF aubergine
      'aubergine [cooked on coal]'

(79) [iki kilometre yüz-**ecek**] birisi (cf. iki kilometre yüz(**ebil**)ecek **olan** birisi)
two kilometre swim-FUT someone
'someone [attempting/able to swim two kilometres]'

Note that *olan* cannot be omitted from relative clauses in which the verb is suffixed with *-mAktA*, *-(I)yor* or *-mAz*. However, it can be omitted from clauses which have nominal predicates and relativized possessors:

(80) [kapağ-ı boyalı] bir kutu (cf. kapağı boyalı **olan** bir kutu)
lid-3SG.POSS painted a box
'a box with a painted lid' (lit. 'whose lid is painted')

(81) [önü bahçeli] ev (cf. önü bahçeli **olan** ev)
'a house/houses with (a) garden(s) in front'

There are semantic differences between a relative clause which contains *olan* and a 'truncated' one where it is omitted. Truncated relative clauses are nearly always of the restrictive type (see 25.2). Moreover, there is a tendency for the head of a truncated relative clause to have non-specific reference. It may be a non-specific indefinite noun phrase (22.2.1), such as *bir öğrenci* in (82), denoting any member of the class *öğrenci* that fits the description provided by the relative clause:

(82) [Notu düşük] **bir öğrenci** bu sınavı alamaz.
'*A student* [who has a low grade] cannot take this exam.'

Alternatively, it can be a generic noun phrase (22.4), such as *bebek* below, in which the truncated relative clause narrows down the class 'baby' in such a way as to designate only those that have eaten their food.

(83) [Yemeğ-in-i ye-miş] **bebek** ağlamaz.
food-3SG.POSS-ACC eat-PF
'*A baby* [that has eaten its food] doesn't cry.'

However, truncated relative clauses are sometimes used with *specific* noun phrases (definite or indefinite) as their head. This occurs mainly where the relative clause contains *-(y)AcAk*:

(84) [Sınava girecek] **öğrenciler** burada.
'*The students* [who will be taking the exam] are here.'

Relative clauses which contain *olan*, on the other hand, may be either restrictive, as in (85), or non-restrictive, as in (86):

(85) [Yemeğini ye**miş olan**] bebek ağlamaz.
      '*A* baby [*that has* eaten its food] doesn't cry.'

(86) [Yemeğini ye**miş olan**] bebek hemen uykuya daldı.
      '*The* baby, [*which had* eaten its food,] immediately fell asleep.'

25.5 OTHER COMPLEX ADJECTIVAL CONSTRUCTIONS

The suffixes -*(y)IcI* and -*(A/I)r* can also be used in complex adjectival constructions. Clausal formations with these suffixes are very rare in comparison with participial relative clauses, see 7.2.1.1 for examples.

25.6 FINITE RELATIVE CLAUSES WITH *ki*

Relativization with *ki* is a quite different strategy for forming relative clauses. In a reversal of the order in non-finite relative clauses, the relativized constituent precedes *ki* and the finite clause (12.3) it introduces. The subordinator *ki*, here functioning somewhat like a relative pronoun, is used mostly to form non-restrictive relative clauses, i.e. simply to add new information about the referent of the head noun (see 25.2). It may also be used in restrictive relative clauses and parenthetical expressions.

25.6.1 *ki* IN NON-RESTRICTIVE RELATIVE CLAUSES

The head noun in these constructions almost always functions as the subject of the main clause. It is also usually 3rd person singular or plural:

(87) *Ayşe*, [**ki** şu anda mutfakta yemek pişiriyor,] birazdan ortaya çıkacak.
      '*Ayşe*, [*who* is cooking in the kitchen at the moment,] will appear soon.'

(88) *Komşu-muz*, [**ki** oldukça tanınmış bir piyanist-miş,]
      neighbour-1PL.POSS RP quite well.known a pianist-EV.COP
      evinde sık sık oda müziği konserleri düzenliyor.
      '*Our neighbour*, [*who* is apparently quite a well-known pianist,] often organizes chamber music concerts at his home.'

Finite relative clauses with *ki* are also used for emphatic purposes. In these constructions the main clause can contain a reiterated subject, identical to the head and followed by *bile* 'even'. These constructions may also have 1st or 2nd person pronouns as their head:

(89) **Sen** [**ki** herkesin doğum gününü hatırlarsın], **sen bile**
Semra'nınkini unuttun.
'*Even you*, [*who* remember everyone's birthday], forgot about
Semra's.'

In certain circumstances a 3rd person head either may or must be reiterated within the *ki* clause by a resumptive pronoun:

(**i**)   If the head is the subject of the relative clause, and refers to someone
whom the speaker holds in respect, one of the pronouns *kendisi* or *kendileri* (18.1.2.2 (iii), (iv)) may be added:

(90) **Komşumuz**, [ki **kendisi** oldukça tanınmış bir piyanist-miş] . . .
(cf. (88))
'*Our neighbour*, [*who* is apparently quite a well-known pianist] . . .'

The personal pronoun *o* can also be used instead of *kendisi* in such cases,
but this usage is less common and it lacks the respectful tone. Where the
head refers to more than one person *onlar* or *kendileri* can be used:

(91) **Bodrum'da tanıştığımız bir çift**, [ki **onlar** öğretmenmiş] . . .
'*A couple that we met in Bodrum*, [*who* apparently are teachers]
. . .'

(**ii**)   If the head is not the subject of the relative clause, but instead functions within it as an object or adverbial, this function is made explicit by
an appropriately case-marked 3rd person pronoun, *o/onlar* or *kendisi/
kendileri*, within the *ki* clause:

(92) Sınıflarında Gülten diye çok şımarık bir kız vardı, [**ki** Hülya
ondan/kendisinden nefret ederdi].
'There was a very self-indulgent girl in their class called Gülten,
[*whom* Hülya hated].'

(93) Dayımın çocukları, [**ki** biz **onlarla/kendileriyle** her yaz
buluşurduk], çok güzel tenis oynuyorlardı.
'My cousins, [*whom* we used to meet every summer], were very
good at playing tennis.'

25.6.2 *ki* IN RESTRICTIVE RELATIVE CLAUSES

ki also has a certain limited usage in forming restrictive relative clauses. In
such constructions (which have a rather literary flavour), the head is usually
the subject of the relative clause, and the verb of this clause is negative and
has optative marking. The main clause is also usually negative:

(94) Bizim okulda hiçbir öğrenci **yok** [**ki** Bilge Hanım'dan azar
işitmemiş ol**sun**].
'There is no student in our school [*who* has not been
reprimanded by Bilge Hanım].'

If the head is not the subject of the main clause a resumptive pronoun has
to be used, such as *ona* in (95):

(95) Bir ahçı [**ki** baklava yap-may-ı bil-me-**sin**,] ben **on-a** ahçı de-me-m.
a cook RP baklava make-VN-ACC know-NEG-3SG.OPT I s/he-DAT
cook call-[AOR.]NEG-1SG
'A cook [*who* can't make baklava]! I don't call *that* a cook.'

25.6.3 COMMENT USAGE OF *ki*

ki clauses can also be used, in a way somewhat similar to a certain use of
'which' in English, to introduce a comment on, or expansion of, something
that has just been said. The clause introduced by *ki* usually contains some
kind of demonstrative, such as the pronoun *bu* 'this' (18.2), or the adverbial *öyle* 'like that' (16.4.3), which refers to the entire situation expressed
in the previous clause:

(96) Ziya beni görmek istemiyormuş, [**ki** bunu daha önce söylemişti].
'Apparently Ziya doesn't want to see me, which he said before.'

This kind of *ki* clause often occurs parenthetically within a sentence,
following an adverbial clause, on the content of which it provides a
comment. For example, in (97) *ki* follows a conditional clause and in (98)
it follows a temporal clause.

(97) [Parası yoksa,] [*ki* **öyle** olduğunu tahmin ediyorum,] şirketi
kurtaramaz.
'[If s/he doesn't have any money,] [*which* I think is the case,]
s/he won't be able to save the company.'

These *ki* clauses often do not correspond to relative clauses in English, and
they do not always contain a demonstrative:

(98) [Ahmet'ler gelinceye kadar,] [*ki* geç gelebilirlermiş,] çıkmayız.
'We won't go out [until Ahmet and his friends come] (*and*
apparently they may be late).'

Following an adverbial clause of time, the demonstrative in the *ki* clause
may either be a pronoun or a time adverbial such as *o zaman* 'then', reit-
erating the time expressed by the adverbial clause:

(99) [Uçağa bindiğimiz zaman,] [*ki* **ona** daha iki saat var,]
      rahatlayacağım.
      '[When we get on the plane] (*and that* is still two hours away) I
      shall relax.'

(100) [Buraya taşındığımızda,] [*ki* ben **o zaman** sekiz yaşındaydım,]
       etrafta başka hiç ev yoktu.
       '[When we moved here] (*and* I was *then* eight years old) there
       were no other houses in the vicinity.'

See 11.1.1.4 for other functions of *ki*.

26 ADVERBIAL CLAUSES

Adverbial clauses are subordinate clauses that perform an adverbial function (see Chapter 16) within another clause. In Turkish, adverbial clauses can be finite or non-finite (see 12.3), but the non-finite forms are much more numerous and, in general, more widely used.

Finite adverbial clauses (26.1) are all marked by subordinating conjunctions. Those which are introduced by the Persian-derived *ki* or a compound of it are structurally similar to Indo-European-type adverbial clauses:

(1) Koca-sın-a düşkün ol-malı [**ki** masa-sın-da o-nun üç tane
     resm-i var].
     husband-3SG.POSS-DAT very.fond be-OBLG SUB desk-3SG.POSS-
     LOC he-GEN three ENUM picture-3SG.POSS existent
     'She must be very fond of her husband, [*because* there are three
     pictures of him on her desk.]'

Non-finite adverbial clauses have subordinating suffixes on the verb, and in some cases the verb is also followed by a postposition or noun phrase (usually with oblique case marking):

(2) [Masa-sın-da koca-sı-nın üç tane resm-i ol-**duğ-un-a göre**] on-a
     düşkün ol-malı.
     desk-3SG.POSS-LOC husband-3SG.POSS-GEN three ENUM
     picture-3SG.POSS be-CV-3SG.POSS-DAT according.to he-DAT
     very.fond be-OBLG
     '[*Seeing that* there are three pictures of her husband on her desk,]
     she must be very fond of him.'

The subordinate verb forms that occur in non-finite adverbial clauses are called **converbs** (8.5). More information about the structural features of these clauses is given in 26.2. Section 26.3 is devoted to a discussion of the functions of specific converbs, classified according to meaning.

Conditional clauses, which are also adverbial in function, have a different structure from other adverbial clauses and are discussed separately in Chapter 27.

26.1   FINITE ADVERBIAL CLAUSES

These clauses are formed with *diye*, *ki*, *madem(ki)*, *nasıl ki*, *(sanki)* ...
-mIş/-(y)mIş gibi and *-DI mI*. It should be noted that those formed with *ki*,
madem(ki), *nasıl ki* and *-DI mI* can only modify the main clause of a
sentence.

26.1.1   CLAUSES FORMED WITH *diye*

Diye is itself the *-(y)A* converbial form (26.3.8) of the verb *de-* 'say'. In its
function as a subordinator it marks both noun clauses (24.3.1) and adverbial clauses. It always stands at the end of its clause:

(3)   [Çocukları getir-*ir-ler* **diye**] porselen eşyayı ortadan kaldırmıştı.
          bring-AOR-3PL SUB
      '[*Thinking* they would bring the children], she had put the china
      pieces away.'

Adverbial clauses with *diye* are used in relatively informal registers to
express reason, purpose, precaution, or understanding, as explained in the
following sections. The sense of 'saying' (or, more usually, 'thinking', cf.
24.2.1 (iii)) is detectable in all of them, which gives them a subjective tone
not found in their non-finite counterparts.

26.1.1.1   Reason

The kind of reason expressed by a *diye* clause is one which exists in the
perception of the subject of the main verb.

(4)   [Kalabalık olacağız **diye**] bir ekmek daha almıştım.
      (**i**)   '[*As* there were going to be a lot of us], I had bought another
            loaf.'
      (**ii**) '[*Thinking* there were going to be a lot of us], I had bought
            another loaf.'

As indicated by the second translation above, the speaker may be aware
that this perception is or was incorrect. This element of meaning differentiates reason clauses expressed with *diye* from those expressed by non-finite
means (26.3.14). A form such as *olacağımız için* could not be substituted
for *olacağız diye* in (4) if interpretation (ii) was intended.

26.1.1.2   Purpose

In this meaning the verb in the subordinate clause is always in the optative
form (8.2.3.3):

(5) [Kışın üşü-me-*ye-lim* **diye**] kalorifer yaptırdık.
    'We've had central heating installed [*so that* we shan't be cold in winter].'

26.1.1.3 Precaution

In this meaning (equivalent to English 'in case . . .') the verb in the subordinate clause takes the form of an open conditional (27.2.1.1), i.e. aorist + *-(y)sA*:

(6) [Bir daha görüş-e-*mez-se-k* **diye**] anahtarları sana şimdiden
                    see.each.other-PSB-NEG.AOR-COND.COP-1PL SUB
    veriyorum.
    '[*In case* we don't have the chance to see each other again],
    I'm giving you the keys now.'

26.1.1.4 Understanding

This type of *diye* clause expresses how the subject of the main clause understands a situation that is relevant to the performance of the action in the main clause:

(7) Ali o işe [geceleri çalışılmıyor **diye**] girmişti.
    'Ali had gone into that job [*on the understanding that* there was no night working].'

Where the subject is plural, this understanding may represent an agreement made between the people referred to (cf. *diye* clauses as object of *konuş-*, 24.3.1 (i), and non-finite adverbial clauses with *-mAk üzere*, 26.3.2).

(8) [[Tülin İstanbul'a gelince] yeniden buluşuruz **diye**] ayrılmışlar o gün.
    'Apparently they had parted that day [*on the understanding that* they would meet again [when Tülin came to Istanbul]].'

26.1.2 CLAUSES FORMED WITH *ki*

Adverbial clauses formed with *ki* share two basic structural features with noun clauses (24.3.2) and relative clauses (25.6) formed with this subordinator: (i) they always *follow* the main clause, and (ii) *ki* itself always stands at the beginning of its clause. (Note that these characteristics are not shared by clauses formed with *madem(ki)*, *nasıl ki* and *sanki*.)

(9) Kalorifer yaptırdık [**ki** kışın üşü-me-ye-lim]. (cf.(5))
                    SUB in.winter be.cold-NEG-OPT-1PL
    'We've had central heating installed [*so that* we shan't be cold in winter].'

There are three main types of adverbial *ki* clause, expressing respectively location in time, purpose, and the basis for a deduction.

26.1.2.1 Location in time

In this type of clause *ki* is equivalent to 'when'. The verb in the main clause is marked by *-(I)yordu* (21.3.2), *-mAktAydI* (21.3.2) or *-mIştI* (21.2.1), and the verb in the *ki* clause is marked perfectively by *-DI*. The reversal of the more usual order of time clause followed by main clause, and the special phonological properties of *ki* (4.3.2.1; cf. 24.3.2) give these sentences a much more dramatic quality than equivalent constructions involving non-finite adverbial clauses of time. This is often reinforced by the use of the adverb *tam* 'just' or (with *-mIştI*) *yeni* 'only just':

(10) **Tam** yemeğ-e otur-**uyor-du**-k [**ki** bangır bangır kapı vur-ul-du].
just meal-DAT sit-IMPF-P.COP-1PL SUB violently door knock-PASS-PF
'We were *just* sitting down to [our] meal [*when* there was a violent banging on the door].'

26.1.2.2 Purpose

As in the corresponding construction with *diye* (26.1.1.2), the verb in purpose clauses with *ki* is always in the optative form. Some speakers add *diye* itself to the end of this type of *ki* clause:

(11) Çantamı dolaba koydum [**ki** kimse al-ma-sın (*diye*)].
SUB no.one take-NEG-3SG.OPT
'I've put my bag in the cupboard, [*so that* no one will take it].'

26.1.2.3 Result

Result clauses introduced by *ki* follow a main clause in which one of the following adverbials of quantity/degree is present: *öyle* 'so', 'such', *öylesine* 'so', 'such', *o kadar*, 'so (much)' (16.5):

(12) Ali'nin odası *o kadar* dağınıktı [**ki** oturacak yer bulamadık].
'Ali's room was *so* untidy [*that* we couldn't find anywhere to sit down].'

(13) **Öylesine** şaşırdım [**ki** ne söyleyeceğimi bilemedim].
'I was *so* astonished [*that* I didn't know what to say].'

In this type of construction the content of the *ki* clause can be deleted, leaving an exclamatory sentence of the pattern *o kadar/öyle(sine)* . . . *ki* (12.4 (iv)).

26.1.2.4 Basis for deduction

This type of *ki* clause follows a deduction expressed by the obligative form of the auxiliary/copular *ol-*, *olmalı* (21.4.1.4 (vi), 21.5.1–2). It expresses the evidence upon which the deduction is based:

(14) Korkut gitmiş *olmalı* [**ki** odasında hiçbir şey kalmamış].
      'Korkut *must* have gone, [*because* there's nothing left in his room].'

For another example see (1) above.

26.1.3 CLAUSES FORMED WITH *madem(ki)*

madem, or its alternative form *mademki*, expresses the piece of information upon which the speaker bases the question or modalized utterance (21.4) contained in the main clause:

(15) [**Madem** biliyordun] neden söylemedin?
      '[*Since* you knew], why didn't you say?'

(16) [**Mademki** seksen yaşındaki komşum bilgisayar kullanmayı öğrenmiş,] ben de öğrenebilirim.
      '[*Seeing that* my eighty-year-old neighbour has learned to use a computer], I can learn too.'

26.1.4 CLAUSES FORMED WITH *nasıl ki*

Clauses introduced by *nasıl ki* express a similarity between the situation described in the subordinate clause and that described by the superordinate clause. They are synonymous with one of the types of universal conditional described in 27.5. (17) is a modified version of (93) in 27.5, with the addition of *ki* and the deletion of the conditional copular marker:

(17) [**Nasıl ki** Hakan akşamları garsonluk yapıyor], sen de derslerine engel olmayacak bir iş bulabilirsin.
      '[*Just as* Hakan works in the evenings as a waiter], you too could find a job that wouldn't interfere with your academic commitments.'

26.1.5 CLAUSES FORMED WITH (sanki) . . . -mIş/-(y)mIş gibi

Finite adverbial clauses ending in the postposition *gibi* (17.3.1) express the manner in which an event occurs, an action is performed, or a person behaves, either by comparison with another (imagined) event or action or by suggesting an underlying motivation or emotion. The verb in the subordinate clause is marked with the evidential perfective suffix *-mIş* or the evidential copular marker *-(y)mIş*. The optional addition of the subordinating conjunction *sanki* 'as if' at the beginning of the clause provides early warning to the hearer of the non-factual status of the content of the clause.

(18) Adam [hayalet gör-**müş gibi**] sapsarı kesil-di.
man ghost see-EV/PF like very.pale become-PF
'The man turned very pale, [*as if* he had seen a ghost].'

(19) Ertan küskün duruyor, [(**sanki**) biz ona kötü davran-ıyor-**muş**-uz
gibi].   we he-DAT bad behave-
IMPF-EV.COP-1PL
like 'Ertan is looking resentful, [*as if* we were treating him badly].'

Where the marker on the verb in the *gibi* clause is evidential perfective *-mIş*, person marking on this verb is optional:

(20) **Sen** o anda [hayalet gör-**müş(-sün) gibi**] sapsarı kesil-di-**n**.
you that moment ghost see-EV/PF(-2SG) like pale become-PF-2SG
'You went very pale at that moment, [*as if* you'd seen a ghost].'

This structural variability of *-mIş gibi* places it in a borderline category between finite and non-finite (cf. *-(A/I)r gibi*, 26.3.8 (ii)).

For *gibi dur-/gibi görün-/gibi gözük-* 'seem', 'appear' see 24.5.

26.1.6 CLAUSES FORMED WITH -DI mI

Adverbial clauses formed with the perfective *-DI* form of a verb (8.2.3.3) followed by the clitic *mI* (11.1.1.5) have either temporal or conditional function (for the latter see 27.6.2). In its temporal meaning it is equivalent to 'as soon as', and can be used in sentences that have either future or habitual time reference:

(21) [Köşeyi dön-**dü-nüz mü**] sinemayı göreceksiniz.
turn-PF-2SG/PL INT
'[*As soon as* you turn the corner] you'll see the cinema.'

(22) [Kapılar açıl**dı mı**] kalabalık içeri dalar.
'[*As soon as* the doors open] the crowd surges in.'

26.1.7 CLAUSES FORMED WITH *dA*

An adverbial clause in which a finite verb is followed by the clitic *dA* (11.1.1.2) is used to draw attention to the fact that the action it expresses *precedes/preceded* that expressed by the main clause:

(23) [Yemek yeDİM **de**] geldim.
'I came [having [*already*] eaten].'

A subordinate clause marked by *dA* always precedes the main verb of the sentence, and is the stressed constituent. For *-(y)Ip dA* see 28.2 (13).

26.2 NON-FINITE ADVERBIAL CLAUSES: STRUCTURAL CHARACTERISTICS

The verbal marking of non-finite adverbial clauses takes widely differing forms. In some cases, e.g. *-(y)ArAk*, *-(y)IncA*, a distinctively converbial suffix is added directly to the verb (8.5.2.2). In other cases (e.g *-mAk için*, *-DIğI zaman*) the converbial marker is composite, consisting of one of the multi-functional subordinators, such as *-mAK* or *-DIK*, followed by a case marker and/or postposition or a nominal form (8.5.1).

The most important structural distinction among converbs is between those that are marked for person and those that are not. Only those formed with the suffixes *-DIK*, *-(y)AcAK* and *-mA* can be marked for person. Except in the cases of *-DIkçA* and *-DIktAn sonra*, where person marking does not occur, this marking is obligatory, and is effected by the possessive suffixes (8.1.2):

(24) çalış-***ma*-mız *için***
work-CV-1PL.POSS for
'in order for us to work'

(25) telefon et-***tiğ*-in sıra-*da***
telephone AUX-CV-2SG.POSS time-LOC
'at the time you ring/rang'

(26) otel-den ayrıl-***acağ*-ınız *zaman***
hotel-ABL leave-CV-2PL.POSS time
'when you are/were about to leave the hotel'

The form *-mAdAn önce* can optionally occur with person marking where the converb has a separate subject. This affects the position of stress; see 26.3.16 (vi).

Converbial forms that obligatorily include a possessive suffix are conventionally cited in the 3rd person singular form, e.g. *-mAsI için, -DIğI halde.*

26.2.1 GENITIVE CASE MARKING OR ITS ABSENCE IN THE SUBJECT OF A NON-FINITE ADVERBIAL CLAUSE

The overt subject of most kinds of non-finite adverbial clause is non-case-marked:

(27) [*Zehra* torununu görmek iste-**diğ-i için**] Bursa'ya uğradık.
Zehra   want-CV-3SG.POSS for
'[*Because Zehra* wanted to see her grandchild] we stopped off in Bursa.'

In the following types, however, the subject receives genitive case marking:

(i)   clauses that have the subordinator *-mA*:

(28) [*Zehra-nın* torununu gör-ebil-**me-si için**] ne yapabiliriz?
Zehra-GEN   want-PSB-CV-3SG.POSS for
'What can we do [*in order for Zehra* to be able to see her grandchild]?'

(ii)   clauses formed with *-DIğI/-(y)AcAğI gibi* expressing manner (26.3.8 (iii)), but not those expressing addition (26.3.1) or time (26.3.16 (iv)):

It should be noted that the absence of subject case marking differentiates (most) adverbial clauses with *-DIK* and *-(y)AcAK* from relative clauses (25.1.1.2) and most noun clauses (24.4.3, 24.4.6) formed with the same subordinators.

26.2.2 POSSIBILITY OF THE ADVERBIAL CLAUSE HAVING A SEPARATE SUBJECT FROM THAT OF THE SUPERORDINATE CLAUSE

In most converbial constructions there is complete freedom for the subjects of the subordinate and superordinate clauses to be either the same or different:

(29) Makine [tamir ed-il-**dikten sonra**] yeniden bozul-du.
machine repair AUX-PASS-CV after again break.down-PF
'[*After* being repaired], the machine broke down again.'

(30) [Makine tamir ed-il-**dikten sonra**] iş-e yeniden başla-dı-**k**.
machine repair AUX-PASS-CV after job-DAT again begin-PF-**1PL**.
'[*After* the machine was repaired] *we* began the job again.'

(31) [Haberi duy**duğunuz sırada**] burada mıydınız?
'Were you here [*at the time you* heard the news]?'

(32) [Haberi duy**duğunuz sırada**] *Filiz* burada mıydı?
'Was *Filiz* here [*at the time you* heard the news]?'

There are, however, certain exceptions to this general rule:

(**i**)   Adverbial clauses whose converb includes the subordinator *-mAK* cannot contain within them an overtly expressed subject. Their *understood* subject is, in the majority of cases, identical with the subject of the superordinate clause:

(33) *Çocuk*, [dondurma al-**mak için**] biz-den para iste-di.
child ice.cream buy-CV for we-ABL money ask.for-PF
'*The child* asked us for money [to buy an ice cream].'

However, in the case of purpose clauses expressed with *-mAk için/üzere* (26.3.12), some speakers use a noun phrase occurring in a non-subject role in the superordinate clause as the understood subject:

(34) *Çocuğ-a* [dondurma al-**mak için**] para ver-di-k.
child-DAT ice.cream buy-CV for money give-PF-1PL
'We gave *the child* money [to buy an ice cream].'

(**ii**)   Converbs formed with *-mAsI için*, also expressing purpose, are used with a subject *different from* that of the superordinate verb. The person-marked converb as in (35) would therefore be an acceptable alternative in (34) but not in (33):

(35) *Çocuğ-a* [dondurma al-**ma-sı için**] para ver-di-k.
'We gave *the child* money [for *him/her* to buy an ice cream].'

(**iii**)   The use of the conjunctive converb *-(y)Ip* (26.3.5, 28.2) with a subject different from that of the superordinate clause is possible but relatively unusual.

(**iv**)   The manner converbs *-(y)A . . . -(y)A* and *-(y)ArAk* (26.3.8) similarly do not often occur with a subject different from that of the superordinate verb. Where they do, it is usually in contexts where the subject of the adverbial clause is marked by a possessive suffix referring to the subject of the superordinate clause:

(36) [Palto-*su*-nun etek-ler-i yer-ler-e sürün-**erek**] yürüyordu.
coat-3SG.POSS-GEN skirt-PL-3SG.POSS ground-PL-DAT trail-CV
'*S/he* was walking [with the tail of *his/her* coat trailing along the ground].'

Where the subject of a non-finite adverbial clause is the same as that of the superordinate clause, it does not receive separate overt expression (18.1.5):

(37) **Ahmet** [yeni eve geçtik**ten sonra**] daha rahat olacak.
'*Ahmet* will be more comfortable [*after* moving/*after he* moves to the new house].'

Note that where an adverbial clause contains no overt subject there is potential for ambiguity. Thus in (37) the adverbial clause could also mean '... [after we/you/they move ...].'

26.2.3 TENSE AND ASPECT MARKING IN NON-FINITE ADVERBIAL CLAUSES

The extent to which tense and aspect are marked in non-finite adverbial clauses varies from one type to another. For example, such marking is far less usual in clauses of manner and time than in clauses expressing concession or reason.

Any tense marking in non-finite adverbial clauses is interpreted in the light of the semantic relationship between the subordinate and superordinate clauses. It may be relative either to the time of utterance or to some other point in time.

Four different kinds of tense/aspect marking occur:

(i) Adverbial clauses can be marked for relative tense or for aspect by the use of compound verb forms incorporating the auxiliary *ol-* (13.3.1.2). (For a full discussion of tense and aspect in Turkish see 21.2–3. For compound verb forms with *ol-* in finite clauses see 21.5.)

(38) Musa [gece geç vakte kadar çalış*mış ol*duğu için] bitkindi.
(Perfective aspect/relative past tense)
'[*Because* Musa *had* work*ed* late into the night] he was exhausted.'

(39) Musa [dün bütün gün çalış*ıyor **olduğu için*] bizimle plaja
gelemedi. (Progressive aspect/relative present tense)
'[*Because* Musa *was* working all day yesterday] he couldn't come
to the beach with us.'

(ii) In the case of *-(y)ken* (8.5.2.2, 26.3.16 (iii)), the converbial suffix incor-
porates the copula *-(y)-* and can therefore be suffixed to a range of tense/
aspect/modality markers in position 3 on the verb (8.2.3.3), as well as to
non-verbal subject complements. *-(y)ken* is itself tense/aspect-neutral, and
produces converbs whose meaning in terms of relative tense and aspect is
determined by what precedes the suffix.
When suffixed to an aorist-marked stem (less commonly *-(I)yor*) or to a
nominal, a converb with *-(y)ken* expresses a situation that is either cotermi-
nous with, or temporally includes, the time of the situation expressed by the
superordinate clause. This is by far the most common function of *-(y)ken*:

(40) [Çalış-*ır*-**ken**] radyoyu hep açık tutarım.
work-AOR-CV
'I always keep the radio on [*while/when (I am)* work*ing*]'.

(41) [Ahmet Türkiye'de**yken**] Londra'daki evine hırsız girmiş.
'Apparently [*while* Ahmet *was* in Turkey] his house in London
was burgled.'

A converb in which *-(y)ken* is suffixed to the perfective marker *-mIş*
expresses a situation that is/was completed prior to the time referred to by
the superordinate clause:

(42) [Bunca çaba göster*miş*ken] projeden kolay kolay vazgeçemiyorlar
tabii.
'[*Having* put in so much effort], they naturally can't give up the
project easily.'

The combination of *-(y)ken* with *-(y)AcAk*, on the other hand, marks
the verb in the subordinate clause as referring to a situation that has/had
not yet occurred (but is/was expected or planned to occur) at some time
understood from the context. The superordinate clause often expresses the
non-realization of the expectation or plan:

(43) [Deniz otobüsüyle gel-*ecek*-ler-**ken**] fırtınadan dolayı arabayla
come-FUT-3PL-CV
gelmek zorunda kaldılar.
['*Although they were going to (have)* come by hydrofoil], because
of the storm they had to come by car.'

(iii) In some converbial forms there is a choice between -DIK and -(y)AcAK, the former expressing relative past or present, the latter relative future tense:

(44) Sen [cumartesi burada ol-ma-**dığ-ın için**] Mehmet'le
you Saturday here be-NEG-CV-2SG.POSS for Mehmet-COM
tanış-a-ma-dı-n.
meet-NEG-PSB-PF-2SG
'[*As* you *were* not here on Saturday] you were not able to meet Mehmet.'

(45) Sen [cumartesi-ler-i burada ol-ma-**dığ-ın için**] Mehmet'le henüz
Saturday-PL-NC here be-NEG-CV-2SG.POSS for
tanışamadın.
'[*As* you *are*n't here on Saturdays] you haven't been able to meet Mehmet yet.'

(46) [Sen cumartesi burada ol-ma-**yacağ-ın** için] Mehmet pazar günü
be-NEG-CV-2SG.POSS for
gelmeyi kabul etti.
(i) '[*As* you *won't* be here on Saturday] Mehmet has agreed to come on Sunday.'
(ii) '[*As* you *were* not *going to* be here on Saturday] Mehmet agreed to come on Sunday.'

For the modal differences between -DIK and -(y)AcAK in subordinate clauses expressing possibility, see 21.4.2.1.

(iv) In temporal clauses (26.3.16) -(y)AcAK has a much more restricted function than in other types of non-finite adverbial clause. It is used only in cases where the situation expressed by the adverbial clause is in the future with respect to the time of the situation expressed by the superordinate clause:

(47) [Misafir gel**eceği zaman**(lar)] Fatma Hanım çok telaşlanıyor.
'Fatma Hanım gets very agitated [*when* guests *are going to* come].'

In the much more usual case where, of two situations in the future, the one expressed by the temporal clause either precedes or is contemporaneous with the other, -DIK is used:

(48) [Misafirler gel**diği zaman**] onlara önce kahve ikram edeceğiz.
'[*When* the guests come] we shall first offer them coffee.'

(49) [Misafirler gel**diği zaman**] çocuklar evde olmayacak.
'The children will not be at home [*when* the guests come].'

26.3 NON-FINITE ADVERBIAL CLAUSES: SEMANTIC CLASSIFICATION

In this section we present specific converbs in fourteen categories determined by meaning. The categories are arranged alphabetically.

26.3.1 ADDITION

Converbs formed with *-mAktAn başka* (much less commonly *-DIktAn başka*) or *-mAktAn* ∇*gayrı* mean 'apart from', 'in addition to'. These constructions are based on the postpositions *başka/*∇*gayrı* 'apart from' (17.2.3). A near synonym is *-mAktAn öte* 'beyond'.

(50) Hakan [beni sinirlendir**mekten başka**] bir de çalışmamı engelliyordu.
'[*Apart from* irritating me], Hakan was also hindering my work.'

Where the subject of the adverbial clause is different from that of the superordinate clause, the form *-mAsındAn başka* has to be used:

(51) [Hakan'*ın* çene çal**masından başka**] [çocukların koşuşması] da beni deli ediyordu.
'[*Apart from* Hakan's chattering], [the children's dashing around] was also driving me mad.'

The construction *-DIğI/-(y)AcAğI gibi* can be used additively in the sense of 'not only ... (but also)'. The superordinate clause always includes an additive connective (28.3.1), such as *dA* in the example below:

(52) Kayhan [arabasını sat-**tığ-ı gibi**] evini *de* ipotek ettirmiş.
               sell-CV-3SG.POSS just.as
'*Not only* has Kayhan sold his car, he has *also* mortgaged his house.'

26.3.2 AGREEMENT

-mAk üzere (see also 26.3.12) is used to express the substance of a planned action agreed upon by two or more parties:

(53) [Tülin İstanbul'a gelince yeniden buluş**mak üzere**] ayrılmışlar o gün. (cf. (8))
'Apparently they had parted that day [*on the understanding that* they would meet again when Tülin came to Istanbul].'

26.3.3 CONCESSION

The two concessive converbial forms in most frequent use are those marked with *-DIğI/-(y)AcAğI halde* 'although' and *-mAsIna rağmen/karşın* 'in spite of the fact that', the latter being based on the postpositions *rağmen/karşın* 'in spite of' (17.2.2):

(54) Osman, [[Ali'ye yardım et-me-si] gerek-**tiğ-i halde**]
help AUX-VN-3SG.POSS be.necessary-CV-3SG.POSS although
hiçbir şey yapmadı.
'[*Although* Osman should have helped Ali], he did nothing.'

(55) [Hayatında bazı çok kötü şeyler yap-mış ol-**ma-sın-a rağmen**]
do-PF AUX-CV-3SG.POSS-DAT despite
Şule'yi severim.
'[*Despite the fact that* she has done some very bad things in her life], I like Şule.'

Where the subject is the same as that of the superordinate clause, *-mAklA birlikte/beraber* is occasionally used, mainly with verbs denoting states rather than events:

(56) [Ahmet bu konuda çok şey bil**mekle birlikte**] bütün ayrıntıları
anlamış değil.
'[*Although* Ahmet knows a lot of things on this subject],
he doesn't understand all the details.'

The converb marker *-(y)ken* 'while', which has a primarily temporal function (26.3.16 (iii)), is sometimes used to draw a contrast between two situations:

(57) [Herkes Nazlı'nın son resimlerine bayıl-**ır-ken**] ben onları ruhsuz
adore-AOR-CV
buldum.
'[*While* everyone [else] was in raptures about Nazlı's latest paintings], I found them lifeless.'

26.3.4 CONDITION

Converbs marked with *-DIğI takdirde* 'in the event that' and *-mAsI halinde/durumunda* 'in the case of' form clauses with conditional meaning equivalent to those formed with the suffixes *-sA/-(y)sA*. See 27.6.1 for discussion.

The converb marker *-mAk/-mAsI şartıyla* 'on condition that' expresses the kind of condition that one party to a transaction may impose on the other:

(58) Biz size [iki ay içinde geri ö**demek şartıyla**] on milyarlık borç
verebiliriz.
'We can give you a loan of ten billion [lira], [*on condition that*
[you] pay it back within two months].'

26.3.5 CONJUNCTION

The converbial suffix -*(y)Ip* has a conjunctive rather than a modifying function, that is to say it conjoins two clauses that are semantically of equal
status in the sentence. Its use is therefore discussed in 28.2, along with the
conjunctive use of -*(y)ArAk*, a suffix that also marks adverbial clauses of
manner (26.3.8).

26.3.6 DISMISSAL

The suffix -*mAsInA* is used only in association with a finite form of the same
verb. It indicates that the action expressed by the main verb is regarded as
abortive or likely to be so. The use of -*mAsInA* is generally triggered by a
prompt or enquiry from another speaker, and the whole construction is
usually linked to the following sentence by an adversative conjunction such
as *ama*, *dA* or *ya* (28.3.4):

(59) A.– Bugün Hüseyin doktora gidecekti galiba.
'I think Hüseyin was going to go to the doctor today.'

B.– Gitmiş [git**mesine**], **ama** doktor gelmemiş.
'I gather he did go, but the doctor didn't come.'

(60) A.– Fatma'yla konuşacak mısın?
'Are you going to talk to Fatma?'

B.– [Konuş**masına**] konuşacağım **da**, bakalım o dinleyecek mi?
'Yes, I'm going to talk to her, but let's see if she'll listen.'

26.3.7 INFORMATION BASE FOR AN UTTERANCE

The forms -*DIğInA*/-*(y)AcAğInA göre* 'since', 'in view of the fact that' have
a function somewhat similar to that of *madem(ki)* (26.1.3), in that
they express the information upon which the utterance contained in the
main clause is based. The main clause can express the following types of
utterance:

A deduction:

(61) [Ali Antalya'ya gitmek isteme**diğine göre**] başka bir planı var
demek.
'[*Since* Ali doesn't want to go to Antalya], *that means* he's got
some other plan.'

A modalized utterance (21.4):

(62) [Ali Antalya'ya gitmek isteme**diğine göre**] başka bir yer
düşün**meli**yiz.
'[*In view of the fact that* Ali doesn't want to go to Antalya],
we'll *have to* think of somewhere else.'

A question:

(63) [Bayramda ofis kapalı ol**acağına göre**] sen bu işi *nasıl*
bitireceksin?
'[*As* the office will be closed during the public holiday], *how* are
you going to finish this job?'

26.3.8 MANNER

Converbs expressing the manner of an action may be divided into four
groups:

(**i**) *-(y)ArAk* and *-(y)A . . . -(y)A* express manner directly, in terms of an
accompanying action or state:

(64) Çocuklar [koş**arak**] içeri girdiler.
'The children came in [runn*ing*].'

The construction *-(y)A . . . -(y)A* occurs either with identical verb stems or
different ones (8.5.2.2). Its use is less widespread than that of *-(y)ArAk*,
and its meaning is more emphatic, stressing the continuous or repeated
nature of the action it expresses. The forms involving two different verb
stems are for the most part lexicalized pairs.

(65) Genç kadın [ağla**ya** ağla**ya**] hikayesini anlattı.
'The young woman wept continually as she told her story.' (lit.
'told her story, [weep*ing continually*]')

(66) Adam [it**e** kak**a**] öne geçmeye çalışıyordu.
'[Push*ing* and shov*ing*], the man was trying to get to the front.'

(ii) The forms *-(A/I)r gibi*, *-(A/I)rcAsInA*, *-mIş gibi* and *-mIşçAsInA* 'as if' express manner by evoking similarity with another, purely imagined action by the same subject, or by suggesting an underlying motivation or emotion. These forms produce clauses that have the same function as the finite *gibi* clauses discussed in 26.1.5, and like them can be reinforced by *sanki* 'as if':

> (67) [(Sanki) uyku-da gez**er gibi**] dolaştım birkaç gün.
>   sleep-LOC go.around-CV as.if
>   'For several days I wandered around [*as if* sleepwalking].'

> (68) [Hiçbir şey anla-ma-**mış gibi**] konuşuyorsun.
>   understand-NEG-CV as.if
>   'You're talking [*as if* you hadn't understood a single thing].'

> (69) Demet [dediklerimi duyma**mışçasına**] konuşup duruyordu.
>   'Demet kept on talking [*as if* she hadn't heard a word I said].'

(iii) *-DIğI/-(y)AcAğI/-mAsI gibi*

(a) The construction *-DIğI/-(y)AcAğI gibi* expresses manner in terms of conformity to another known action or psychological state. The subject of this type of clause takes genitive case marking:

> (70) Pastayı [anne-m-**in** anlat-**tığ-ı gibi**] yapmaya çalıştım.
>   mother-1SG.POSS-GEN describe-CV-3SG.POSS as
>   'I tried to make the cake [*the way* my mother had described].'

(b) The construction *-mAsI gibi* simply draws attention to a similarity between two situations:

> (71) [Turhan'**ın** kızıp ofisi birbirine kat**ması gibi**] Ahmet de düşünmeden istifa etti.
>   '[*Just as* Turhan became irate and caused havoc in the office], Ahmet resigned without thinking.'

This structure produces the same meaning as finite clauses introduced by *nasıl ki* (26.1.4). For the use of universal conditional clauses with *nasıl* 'how' in the same function, see 27.5.

(iv) Converbs formed with *-mAdAn*, *-mAksIzIn*, both meaning 'without', express manner negatively, in terms of what is not done. Note that the *-mA* in *-mAdAn* is the negative suffix, and generates stress on the preceding syllable (see 8.5.2.2 (i)):

(72) Çocuklar, [baĞIR**madan**] oynayın!
'Children, play [*without* shouting]!'

(73) Kemal Bey bütün bir günü [televizyon seyRET**meden**] geçirebilmiş.
'It seems that Kemal Bey has managed to spend a whole day [*without* watching television].'

The form -*mAksIzIn* is rare except in relatively formal registers.

26.3.9 MEANS

The means by which some goal is sought or result achieved can be expressed by -*(y)ArAk* (26.3.8 (i)) or more formally by -*mAk* ∇*suretiyle/yoluyla* 'by (means of)':

(74) Ayten [her gün yürüyüş yap**arak**/yap**mak** ∇suretiyle] kilo verdi.
'Ayten lost weight [*by* going for a walk every day].'

The form -*mAklA* can express a similar meaning at a more generalized level:

(75) Sadece [yürüyüş yap-**makla**] kilo ver-il-mez.
simply walk do-CV weight lose-PASS-NEG.AOR
'One can't lose weight simply [*by* walking].'

-*mAklA* also expresses an action by the performance of which a certain result was produced, whether intentionally or not:

(76) [Öyle söyle-**mekle**] bana hakaret et-miş ol-uyor-sun.
thus say-CV I.DAT insult AUX-PF AUX-IMPF-2SG
'You insult me [*by* saying that].'

For the use of compound verb forms with -*mIş* in the main clause of such sentences see 21.5.1.1.

26.3.10 PREFERENCE

Adverbial clauses marked with -*mAktAnsA* 'rather than' are used in sentences expressing preference:

(77) [Kimsenin beğenmediği bir filmi seyret**mektense**] evde kalmayı tercih ederim.
'I'd prefer to stay at home [*rather than* watch a film that no one likes].'

26.3.11 PROPORTIONALITY

One of the functions of the converbial suffix *-DIkçA* is to indicate that one
event happens in proportion to the occurrence of another:

(78) [Çikolata ye**dikçe**] kilo alırsın.
       '[*The more* chocolate you eat], *the more* you'll put on weight.'

For *-DIkçA* in the sense of 'whenever' see 26.3.6 (ix). More formal means
of expressing proportionality are *-DIğI ∇nispette*, *-DIğI oranda* and *-DIğI
ölçüde*:

(79) İnsanlar [sağlıklarına dikkat et-**tik-leri oran-da**] uzun yaşarlar.
                                            care-AUX-CV-3PL.POSS proportion-LOC
       '[*The more* people take care of their health], *the longer* they live.'

26.3.12 PURPOSE

Where the subject of a non-finite clause expressing purpose is the same as
that of the superordinate clause, the converbial marker *-mAk için* 'in order
to' (or its more formal counterpart *-mAk üzere*) is used:

(80) [Kışın üşü-me-**mek için**] kalorifer yaptırdık. (cf. (5), (9))
       in.winter be.cold-NEG-CV for
       'We've had central heating installed [*so as* not to be cold
       in winter].'

As explained in 26.2.2 (i), this converb can also be used where the *understood* subject of the purpose clause is a noun phrase occurring in a
non-subject role in the superordinate clause. However, where the purpose
clause has an overt separate subject, *-mAsI için* 'in order that/for', 'so that'
is used:

(81) [***Anne-m-in*** kışın üşü-me-**me-si için**] acaba ne yapabiliriz?
       mother-1SG.POSS-GEN in.winter be.cold-NEG-CV-3SG.POSS for
       'I wonder what we can do [*so that* my mother won't be cold in
       winter]?'

In same-subject contexts where the superordinate verb is *git-* 'go' or *gel-*
'come' *-mAk için* is usually replaced by the dative-marked form of *-mAk*,
namely *-mAyA* (see 8.5.1.2):

(82) Ayşe [kızını gör**mey**]-**e** gitti.
       'Ayşe has gone [*to* see her daughter].'

26.3.13 QUANTITY OR DEGREE

Like simple adverbials of quantity or degree (16.5), this type of adverbial clause expresses either (a) the quantity in which an event happens, or (b) the degree to which the quality expressed by an adjective, or the manner expressed by an adverb, applies.

(i) *-(y)AcAk kadar/derecede*:
This construction can express the fact that the degree of the event or state in the superordinate clause is sufficient to produce a certain result (intended or not). The version with *derecede* is relatively uncommon and rather formal:

(83) [Komşuları uyutma**yacak kadar**] gürültü yapıyorlardı.
'They were making *enough* noise [*to* keep the neighbours awake].'

(84) Sevim [hepimizi şaşırt **acak derecede**] güzel konuştu.
'Sevim spoke *so* well [*that* she surprised us all].'

Some constructions of this type (notably *şaşılacak kadar* 'amazingly' and *inanıl(a)mayacak kadar* 'incredibly') are semi-lexicalized as modifiers of adjectives and adverbs (for examples see 15.4.1.2, 16.9).

(ii) *-DIğI/-(y)AcAğI kadar*:
This construction specifies the quantity or degree of the event or state in the superordinate clause in terms of commensurability with another event or state:

(85) Burada [iste**diğin kadar**] kalabilirsin.
'You can stay here [*as long as* you like].'

(86) Su [herkesin güvenle kullanabil**eceği kadar**] temiz olmalı.
'The water must be clean [*enough for* everyone to be able to use it with confidence].'

26.3.14 REASON

By far the most commonly occurring converbial marker expressing reason or cause is *-DIğI/-(y)AcAğI için* 'because', 'as':

(87) [Bana kız**dığın için**] öyle söylüyorsun.
'You're saying that [*because* you're angry with me].'

(88) [Bu para yetme**yeceği için**] Gürkan'dan borç isteyeceğim.
'[*As* this money won't be enough] I'm going to ask Gürkan for a loan.'

Other forms with more or less identical meaning are: *-DIğIndAn/ -(y)AcAğIndAn (dolayı/ötürü), -mAsIndAn dolayı, -mAsI yüzünden.*

26.3.15 SUBSTITUTION

-(y)AcAğInA and *-mAk yerine* both mean 'instead of' (as does the post-position *yerine*, 17.3 2):

(89) Seni [azarla**yacağına**] rahatlatmaya çalışmalıydı.
'[*Instead of* scolding you] s/he should have tried to reassure you.'

(90) [[Düzenli ye**mek yerine**] durmadan atıştırmak] hiç akıl işi değil.
'[Eating snacks all the time [*instead of* having regular meals]] is not at all sensible.'

26.3.16 TIME

Temporal clauses specify the time of the situation expressed by the super-ordinate clause by reference to how it relates to the time of some other situation (event or state). The number of converbial forms in this class far exceeds that in any other, permitting a wide range of temporal relations to be expressed.

(i) *-(y)IncA* 'when' expresses a sequential relation between two events:

(91) [Yağmur yağmaya başla**yınca**] içeri girdik.
'[*When* it began to rain] we went inside.'

Similar in meaning, but confined to rather formal usage, is *-mAsI üzerine*, which requires its subject to be different from that of the superordinate clause:

(92) [Meclis**in** tatile gir**mesi üzerine**] başkentteki faaliyet azaldı.
'[*When* parliament went into recess], activity in the capital decreased.'

(ii) Although *-DIğIndA* and *-DIğI zaman* 'when' are sometimes used interchangeably with *-(y)IncA*, their more characteristic function is to indicate that the situation described by the superordinate clause is/was ongoing at the time of the event expressed by the adverbial clause:

(93) [Uçaktan indiğimiz**de**/indiğimiz **zaman**] kar yağ-**ıyor-du**.
fall-IMPF-P.COP
'[*When* we came out of the plane] it *was* snow*ing*.'

Virtually synonymous with the above two forms is *-DIğI sırada* 'at the time (that ...)'. For the restricted use of future-tense marking in temporal converbs see 26.2.3 (iv).

(iii) *-(y)ken* 'while', 'as', 'when' is usually attached to the aorist suffix or to a subject complement, although other tense/aspect markings are possible, as explained in 26.2.3 (ii) above. The combination *-(A/I)rken*, as also the combination of *-(y)ken* with a non-verbal predicate, expresses a situation that is ongoing. The temporal relationship between the two clauses may be of two kinds, according to whether the predicate of the superordinate clause is perfective or imperfective:

(a) If the superordinate clause has a perfective predicate, it expresses an event which takes place (and is completed) during the period of continuance of the situation in the clause marked by *-(y)ken*:

> (94) [Orman-da dolaş-**ır-ken**] bir tilki gör-***dü***-m.
> forest-LOC walk.about-AOR-CV a fox see-PF-1SG
> '[*While* walking in the forest] I *saw* a fox.'

> (95) Ahmet o kitabı [öğrenci-**yken**] oku-***muş***.
> student- CV read-EV/PF
> 'It seems Ahmet *read* that book [*when* he was a student].'

(b) If the superordinate clause has an imperfective predicate, it expresses a situation which is ongoing during the period of continuance of the situation in the clause marked by *-(y)ken*:

> (96) [Sen ormanda onu ara**rken**] Bahri burada-***ydı***.
> here-P.COP
> '[*While* you were looking for him in the forest], Bahri *was* here.'

> (97) [Adana'da**yken**] Şule ile sık sık görüş-***ür-dü***-k.
> see.each.other-AOR-P.COP-1PL
> '[*When* (I was/we were) in Adana] I/we used to see Şule often.'

(iv) The juxtaposition of the positive and negative aorist stems of the same verb in the converb *-(A/I)r ... -mAz* gives the meaning 'as soon as':

> (98) [Su kayna-**r** kayna-**maz**] altını kıs.
> boil-AOR boil-NEG.AOR
> '[*As soon as* the water boils] turn down the heat (under it).'

-DIğI gibi (see 26.3.1, 26.3.8) also sometimes occurs in the temporal sense of 'as soon as'. Another near synonym is *-DIğI anda* 'at the moment that'.

(v) The forms ↓*-(y)AlI (beri)* and *-DIğIndAn beri* 'since' are the clausal equivalents of postpositional phrases with *beri* 'since', discussed in 17.2.3, and the tense/aspect marking of the superordinate clause (if finite) has the same pattern as described there.

(99) [Kocası ↓öl-**eli (beri)**/öl-**düğ-ün-den beri**] ablasının yanında
        die-CV since/die-CV-3SG.POSS-ABL since
      kal-*ıyor*.
      stay-**IMPF**
      'She*'s been* stay*ing* with her sister [*since* her husband died].'

(100) [Çiğdem Almanya'ya taşın-**dığ-ın-dan beri**] ondan bir haber
                          move-CV-3SG.POSS-ABL since
      al-a-***ma-dı***-m.
      get-PSB-**NEG-PF**-1SG
      '[*Since* Çiğdem moved to Germany] I *haven't* heard anything
      from her.'

Colloquially, greater emphasis can be given to the temporal relationship between the two situations by doubling the verb in the subordinate clause, and marking the first verb with *-DI* and the appropriate person marker. The sequence ↓*-DI . . . -(y)AlI* is roughly equivalent to 'ever since':

(101) [O köpeği al-**dı-*k*** al-**alı**] hiç rahat yüzü görmedik.
                  buy-PF-1PL buy-CV
      '[*Ever since* we bought that dog] we've had no peace.'

(vi) *-mAdAn (önce/∇evvel)* and *-DIktAn sonra* are the converbial counterparts of the postpositions *önce* 'before' and *sonra* 'after' (17.2.3). As in the case of *-mAdAn* 'without' (26.3.8), the stress in *-mAdAn (önce)* falls on the syllable before *-mA*:

(102) Sorunlar [ben GEL**meden (önce)**] başlamış.
      'The problems seem to have started [*before* I came].'

(103) Sorunlar [sen git**tikTEN sonra**] başladı.
      'The problems began [*after* you left].'

Just as in their postpositional function, *önce* and *sonra* in these converbial constructions can be modified by an adverbial of quantity (16.5) or an expression denoting a period of time:

(104) Ali, [babası öl**dükten** *iki ay* **sonra**] doğdu.
'Ali was born [*two months after* his father died].'

Where the adverbial clause has a separate subject, the person-marked forms *-mAsındAn önce/sonra* are sometimes used instead of the forms shown above. In this case the subject takes genitive marking (see 26.2.1), and the *-mA* has no stress-producing effect:

(105) (**a**) Bu haber [mektup-lar postaLA-N-**madan (önce)**] gelmişti.
           letter-PL post-PASS-CV (before)

(**b**) Bu haber [mektup-lar-*ın* postala-n-**ma-sın-DAN önce**]
           letter-PL-GEN post-PASS-CV-3SG.POSS-ABL before
gelmişti.
'This news had arrived [*before* the letters were posted].'

A formal alternative to *-mAsındAn sonra*, in contexts where the superordinate clause expresses a durative situation rather than a single event, is *-mAsındAn itibaren* 'from the time that', based on the postposition *itibaren* (17.2.3):

(106) [Yeni sistemin yürürlüğe gir **mesinden sonra/itibaren**] bu sorunlar yaşanmayacaktır.
'[*After/From the time that* the new system goes into operation], these problems will not be encountered.'

(**vii**) The forms *-(y)IncAyA kadar/değin/dek* and ↓*-(y)AnA kadar* have two meanings, both involving a terminal point:

(**a**) 'until'

(107) Fatma artık [[öl**ünceye dek**] burada kalmak] istiyordu.
'Fatma now wanted to stay here [*until* she died].'

(**b**) 'by the time (that ...)'

(108) [Bu iş bit**inceye kadar**] hepimiz yaşlanmış olacağız.
'We shall all have grown old [*by the time* this work is finished].'

kadar is in much more frequent use in these constructions than *değin* or *dek*.

(**viii**) The converb *-DIkçA*, in addition to its proportionality meaning (26.3.11), can mean 'whenever':

(109) [Osman'a kaza hakkında bir şeyler sorul**dukça**] kafası daha da
karışıyordu.
'[*Whenever* Osman was asked (things) about the accident], he
would become even more confused.'

'Whenever' can also be expressed by a universal conditional construction
(27.5).

(**ix**) The converbial forms -*DIğI sürece/(müddetçe* mean 'throughout the
time (that)':

(110) [O evde kal**dığım sürece**] kimse benimle tek kelime konuşmadı.
'[*Throughout the time* I stayed in that house] no one said a word
to me.'

27 CONDITIONAL SENTENCES

From the functional point of view, conditional clauses are a sub-type of adverbial clauses (Chapter 26). However, their expression in Turkish differs from that of other adverbial clauses in that the subordinating verb forms they contain are more closely related to finite verb forms than to converbs. Person marking of the predicate of a conditional clause is effected not by the use of possessive suffixes but by one of the sets of person markers used on finite verbs (8.4):

(1) [Şura-da otur-**sa-nız**]daha rahat ed-er-siniz.
     here-LOC sit-COND-2PL more comfortable be-AOR-2PL
     'You'd be more comfortable [if you sat here].'

(2) [Öykü-yü daha bitir-me-di-**niz-se**] daha sonra da
     story-ACC yet finish-NEG-PF-2SG/PL-COND.COP later also
     oku-yabil-ir-im.
     read-PSB-AOR-1SG
     '[If you haven't finished [writing] the story yet] I can read it
     later.'

This chapter begins with a brief review of the grammatical marking of conditional clauses, devoting most attention to the suffixes -*sA* and -*(y)sA* and their distribution (27.1). Since the choice of conditional marker depends upon the function of the conditional clause in relation to the sentence as a whole, we proceed to discuss three main functional types of conditional sentence. **Predictive conditionals**, which express a predictable relation between two situations, are explained in 27.2. Then in 27.3 we look at **knowable conditions**, which usually serve as background for an inference, a question, or some kind of volitional utterance (e.g. a command or request). Section 27.4 deals with further uses of -*sA* and -*(y)sA* as subordinators, including concessive forms with *dA* and *bile*, and 27.5 discusses **universal conditional clauses**, which contain a question phrase in addition to a conditional marker. Finally in 27.6 we review alternative types of conditional construction which do not involve conditional suffixes.

27.1 THE GRAMMATICAL MARKING OF CONDITIONAL CLAUSES

27.1.1 THE VERBAL SUFFIX -sA AND THE COPULAR MARKER -(y)sA (OR ise)

We use the term 'conditional clause' to denote the subordinate clause in a conditional sentence, that is the one corresponding to the 'if' clause in an English conditional sentence. With the exception of the constructions described in 27.6, all conditional clauses in Turkish are marked in one of two ways:

(i)   The attachment of the suffix -sA (one of the tense/aspect/modality markers described in 8.2.3.3) to a verb:

(3)   [Biraz erken gel-**se**-n] iyi ol-ur.
a.bit early come-COND-2SG good be-AOR
'It would be good [if you came a bit early].'

(4)   [Telefon et-**se**-ydi-k] belki bekle-r-ler-di.
telephone AUX-COND-P.COP-1PL perhaps wait-AOR-3PL-P.COP
'[If we had telephoned], perhaps they would have waited.'

(ii)   The use of the copular marker -(y)sA, or its free-standing alternate *ise*, following (a) one of the position 3 tense/aspect/modality markers (8.2.3.3), (b) a subject complement (12.1.1.2), (c) the negative particle *değil*, (d) one of the existential expressions *var/yok* or (e) one of the copular markers -(y)DI or -(y)mIş. (For a fuller explanation of the attachment properties of -(y)sA see 8.3.2, 8.4.)

(5)   [Yabancı bir dil öğren-ir-**se**-niz] dünya-nız genişle-r.
foreign a language learn-AOR-COND.COP-2PL world-2PL.POSS expand-AOR
'[If you learn a foreign language] your world will expand.'

(6)   [Yorgun-lar-**sa**] yarın-a bırak-abil-ir-iz.
tired-3PL-COND.COP tomorrow-DAT leave-PSB-AOR-1PL
'[If they're tired] we can leave [it] till tomorrow.'

Note that the attachment of -(y)sA to the past copula -(y)DI in nominal predicates is a usage accepted by some but not all speakers:

(7)   [Para-sı var-dı-**ysa**] ev-e neden hiç bak-ma-mış?
money-3SG.POSS existent-P.COP-COND.COP house-DAT why at.all look-NEG-EV/PF
'[If he had money], why did he not look after the house at all?'

The use of the non-suffixed copular form *ise* is nowadays rare in ordinary conditional sentences, particularly in those where the conditional clause contains a verb. However, it is quite often used for purposes of emphasis in the type of concessive clause discussed in 27.4.2.2, where the conditional copula is followed by *dA*. For the use of *ise* as a topic shifter see 23.3.3.1 (ii).

The two conditional suffixes differ not only in the kind of stem to which they can be attached, but also in their stressability. *-sA* is a regular stressable suffix (4.3.1), whereas *-(y)sA*, like all the copular markers, is unstressable (4.3.2).

(8) [Arabayı sat-**SA**] hepimiz rahat**LA**rız.
        sell-COND
        '[If he sold the car] it would be a relief to all of us.'

(9) [Arabayı sat-**AR-sa**] hepimiz rahat**LA**rız.
        sell-AOR-COND.COP
        '[If he sells the car] it will be a relief to all of us.'

-sA occurs only in the predictive type of conditional. *-(y)sA*, on the other hand, occurs in both predictive and knowable conditional sentences.

27.1.2 THE CONDITIONAL CONJUNCTIONS *eğer* AND ∨*şayet*

These two conjunctions, both of Persian origin, are grammatically redundant in Turkish conditional clauses, but are sometimes added for emphasis, or (particularly at the beginning of a long and complex sentence containing other subordinate clauses) to signal at an early point the conditionality of what is being said. Of the two, *eğer* is much the more common, and is neutral in terms of the type of conditionality it expresses (like 'if' in English). It therefore appears in all kinds of conditional clauses, but is extremely rare with *-sA*, except where this is affixed with *-ydI*:

(10) [***Eğer*** çocuk yaşa-**sa-ydı**] çok iyi bir mimar olacaktı.
          live-COND-P.COP
          '[If the boy had lived] he would have been a very good architect.'

In informal styles *eğer* can occur at the end of its clause:

(11) [Hasan bu mektubu okuduy**sa** ***eğer***], çok kötü olmuştur.
          '[If Hasan has read this letter] he must be feeling terrible.'

The obsolescent ∇*şayet* is more tentative, meaning something like 'if by any chance'. It occurs only with -*(y)sA*:

(12) [*Şayet* karşı tarafı düşünebiliyor**sanız**], Bostancı'da güzel bir ev gördüm geçen gün.
'[If *by any chance* you can contemplate [living on] the other side], I saw a nice place in Bostancı the other day.'

27.2 PREDICTIVE CONDITIONALS

The predictive type of conditional sentence asserts that if one event takes (or took) place another will (or would) follow it. The first event is presented as causing or making possible the second. There are four possible markings for the subordinate clause of a predictive conditional:

(i)   -*(y)sA* (usually attached to aorist -*(A/I)r* or -*mAz*)
(ii)   -*sA*
(iii) -*sAydI* (-*sA* + past copula)
(iv)   -*sAymIş* (-*sA* + evidential copula).

Although there are clear differences in meaning between some of these forms, there are also areas of overlap. (i) expresses a condition deemed capable of fulfilment, (iii) expresses a condition known to be incapable of fulfilment, while (ii) and (iv) are ambiguous in this regard. We shall discuss each form in turn, and the kinds of contexts in which they occur.

27.2.1 AORIST + -*(y)sA*

Conditional clauses with the aorist are of two types. The first, which is more obviously 'predictive', is called an **open** conditional. In this type both the condition expressed and its consequence are in the future. The second type itself embraces two closely related kinds of statement, **generic** and **habitual**. In this type the predictability relates not to the relationship between a pair of future events but to that in a recurrent *pattern* of events. Where the verb in the main clause is also in the aorist form there is potential ambiguity between the two types:

(13) [Mehmet geç yat-**ar-sa**] zor kalk-*ar*.
Mehmet late go.to.bed-AOR-COND.COP difficult get.up-AOR
(i)   '[If Mehmet goes to bed late] he'll have difficulty getting up.' (Open)
(ii) '[If Mehmet goes to bed late] he has difficulty getting up.' (Habitual)

27.2.1.1 Open conditionals

In open conditionals the speaker does not know whether or not the condition will be fulfilled, but treats it as a real possibility rather than a merely hypothetical one. When the main clause expresses a statement, its verb is marked by either *-(y)AcAK* or the aorist. *-(y)AcAK* is used if the event is regarded as certain to follow the fulfilment of the condition, perhaps because of some prior decision (see 21.2.3):

(14) [Kayıt-lar onbeş-i bul-**maz-sa**] ders aç-ıl-ma-**yacak**.
registration-PL fifteen-ACC reach-NEG.AOR-COND.COP course open-PASS-NEG-FUT
'[If registrations do not reach fifteen], the course will not be run.'

The use of the aorist in the main clause, on the other hand, presents the consequence of the fulfilment of the condition more as an assumption or probability (21.4.1.4):

(15) [8-de-ki otobüs-e bin-**er-se**] uçağ-a rahat rahat yetiş-*ir*.
8-LOC-ADJ bus-DAT take-AOR-COND.COP plane-DAT comfortably catch-AOR
'[If s/he takes the 8 o'clock bus] s/he'll catch the plane comfortably.'

Whereas in other predictive conditionals the main clause has to be either a statement or a question, in open conditionals the main clause can also be a volitional utterance (12.4 (iii), 21.4.4):

(16) [Engin'i gör**ürse**n] benden selam söyle.
                                        say [IMP.2SG]
'[If you see Engin], say hello to him from me.'

(17) [Kezban gel**mezse**] onu bir daha çağır-ma-*ya-lım*.
                                        invite-NEG-OPT-1PL
'[If Kezban doesn't come], let's not invite her again.'

When an open conditional construction occurs in the course of a narrative, reflecting a situation that was in the future at that particular point in the story, the past copula *-(y)DI* is added to the main clause (but not to the conditional clause):

(18) Hüseyin zor durumdaydı. [Amerika'ya gid**erse**] Jale onunla gitmeyebilir*di*.
'Hüseyin found himself in a difficult situation. [If he *went* to America], Jale *might* not go with him.'

27.2.1.2 Generic and habitual conditionals

(i) Generic conditionals:
Generic statements concern the characteristic qualities or behaviour of a class of entities, and are regularly expressed with the aorist (21.4.1.1). In conditional sentences there can be ambiguity between a generic and an open predictive reading. In the example below, *kedi* 'cat' and *köpek* 'dog' are understood generically (see 22.4.1.1) in (i), whereas in (ii) they are understood as referring to a specific cat and dog.

(19) [Kedi-yle köpek bir arada büyüt-ül-**ür**-ler-**se**] dövüş-mez-ler.
cat-CONJ dog together bring.up-PASS-AOR-3PL-COND.COP fight-
NEG.AOR-3PL
  (i) '[If a cat and a dog are brought up together] they don't fight.'
    (Generic)
  (ii) '[If the cat and the dog are brought up together] they won't
    fight.' (Open)

(ii) Habitual conditionals:
While generics generalize about the behaviour or qualities of a whole class, habituals generalize about the behaviour or qualities of specific entities or groups. Non-past habituals usually have *-(I)yor* in the main clause (21.3.2), which entirely disambiguates them from open predictive conditionals:

(20) [Ahmet evliliklerinin yıldönümünü unut**ursa**] Şebnem çok kız**ıyor**.
    'Şebnem goes into a temper [if Ahmet forgets their wedding
    anniversary].'

(21) [Vaktim ol**ursa**] okula kadar yürü**yor**um.
    '[If I have time] I walk to school.'

Where a habitual conditional sentence has past time reference, the main clause receives past tense marking, whereas the conditional clause does not:

(22) Padişah [bir vezirinden memnun kal**mazsa**] onu idam et-tir-ir-***di***.
                                  execution AUX-CAUS-AOR-P.COP
    '[If the sultan *was* not pleased with one of his viziers], he would
    have him executed.'

(23) [Sınavdaki puan ortalaması düşük çık**arsa**] bir ayarlama
    yap-ıl-abil-iyor-***du***.
    make-PASS-PSB-IMPF-P.COP
    '[If the average mark in the exam turn*ed* out low], an adjustment
    could be made.'

27.2.1.3 Compound forms with *olursa*

Compound verb forms in conditional clauses are generally analogous in terms of their relative tense and aspect values to their counterparts in finite clauses (see 21.5).

(i) In open conditionals:
The combination *-mIş olursa* indicates that the event in the conditional clause is envisaged as being completed *before* a specified reference point:

(24) [O zaman-a kadar anne-leri gel-me-**miş ol-ur-sa**]
that time-DAT by mother-3PL.POSS come-NEG-PF AUX-AOR-COND.COP
siz çocuk-lar-la kal-abil-ir mi-siniz?
you child-PL-COM stay-PSB-AOR INT-2SG/PL
'[If their mother *has*n't come back by then], would you be able to stay with the children?'

-(I)yor olursa presents the event as being *ongoing* at a certain reference point:

(25) [Saat 5'te toplantı hala sür**üyor olursa**] sessizce kalkıp giderim.
'[If the meeting *is* still go*ing* on at 5 o'clock], I'll quietly get up and go.'

The combination of *-(y)AcAk* with *olursa* has two different functions in open conditions. Its less common function is analogous to that of the two preceding combinations, postulating a situation in which an event is *about to happen*. In such cases the event expressed by the main clause is envisaged as taking place *before* the conditional event:

(26) [Ev-in-i sat-**acak ol-ur-sa**-n] ban-a haber ver.
house-2SG.POSS-ACC sell-FUT AUX-AOR-COND.COP-2SG I-DAT
news give [IMP.2SG]
'[If you *are [ever] about to* sell your house], let me know.'

More commonly, however, *-(y)AcAk olursa* is used in a sense close to that of the simple aorist + *-(y)sA*, but more tentative. In this type of sentence the chronological sequence of *main clause event following conditional event* is the same as in sentences with aorist + *-(y)sA*:

(27) [Mustafa fikrini sonra değiştir**ecek olursa**] hoş karşılamalıyız.
'[If Mustafa *should* subsequently change his mind], we must accept (this).'

(ii) In habitual conditionals:

In this type of conditional the functions of *-mIş*, *-(I)yor* and *-(y)AcAk olursa* are fully transparent. The 'tentative-making' function of *-(y)AcAk olursa* does not occur:

(28) [Yemeği Turgut yap**mış olursa**] bulaşığı Lale yıkıyor**du**.
   '[If Turgut *had* cooked the meal], Lale would do the washing up.'

(29) [Geç vakit çalış**ıyor olursa**k] bir yerlerden sıcak yemek getirtiyoruz.
   '[If we'*re* work*ing* late], we get hot food brought in from somewhere.'

(30) [Remziye işten sonra arkadaşlarıyla buluş**acak olursa**] yanına başka giysiler alıyor.
   '[If Remziye *is going to* meet up with friends after work], she takes different clothes with her.'

27.2.2 OPEN AND HABITUAL CONDITIONALS EXPRESSED WITHOUT AORIST MARKING

Certain kinds of open or habitual conditional clause can be expressed without the use of the aorist:

(i) Where the conditional clause has a nominal predicate, the conditional copula may be attached directly to this predicate, without recourse to the copular verb *ol-*. Thus the following forms are interchangeable:

olursa	*-(y)sA/varsa*
olmazsa	*değilse/yoksa*

Open conditionals:

(31) Yarın [ev fazla soğuk **ol-maz-sa/değil-se**] burada çalış-abil-ir-iz.
   tomorrow house too cold be-NEG.AOR-COND.COP/
   not-COND.COP work-PSB-AOR-1PL
   'Tomorrow [if the house *is* not too cold] we can work here.'

(32) [Başka işim **olmazsa/yoksa**] gelirim.
   'I'll come [if I have no other commitments].'

Habitual conditionals:

(33) [**Yorgun ol-ur-sa**-m/**yorgun-sa**-m] yemek yap-mı-yor-um.
   tired be-AOR-COND.COP-1SG/tired-COND.COP-1SG food cook-
   NEG-IMPF-1SG
   '[If *I'm* tired] I don't cook.'

(ii) Where the conditional clause has a verbal predicate marked with *-mIş* or *-(I)yor*, the conditional copula may be attached directly to this predicate, without creating a compound verb form as described in 27.2.1.3.

Open conditionals:

(34) [Kırmızı satıl **mış olursa**/satıl**mışsa**] maviyi alırım.
       '[If the red one *has* been sold], I'll buy the blue one.'

(35) [Oraya gittiğim zaman çalış **ıyor olursa**/çalış **ıyorsa**] bir merhaba deyip dönerim.
       '[If *he's* work*ing* when I get there], I'll just say hello and come back.'

Habitual conditionals:

(36) Her yazdığımızı Mustafa Bey'e sunuyorduk. [Eğer herhangi bir şeyi yanlış **yazmış olursak**/**yazmışsak**] o düzeltiyordu.
       'We would submit everything we wrote to Mustafa Bey.
       [If we *had* got anything wrong] he would correct it.'

27.2.3   -sA

27.2.3.1   -sA used without past copular marking of the main clause

The distribution and the range of meanings of the verbal suffix *-sA* in conditional clauses is somewhat complex. (For its main-clause functions see 21.4.4.1 and 21.4.4.4.) The key to its interpretation in any particular conditional sentence lies in whether or not the main clause is marked by the past copula *-(y)DI*. If the main clause does not contain *-(y)DI*, the condition expressed in the subordinate clause is understood to be capable of fulfilment, but is presented more as a hypothetical possibility than as one which the speaker locates in the 'real' future. For this reason the verb in the main clause is almost always in the aorist form (see also 21.4.1.3).

-sA is often used when talking about action that is being considered in a detached or abstract way (compare the 'deliberative' sense of the conditional interrogative in main clauses, 21.4.4.4). (37) could represent an early contribution to a discussion about how to get to the airport in time for a particular flight:

(37) [9-da-ki otobüs-e bin-**se**-k] uçağ-a yetiş-ir mi-yiz acaba?
       9-LOC-ADJ bus-DAT take-COND-1PL plane-DAT catch-AOR INT-1PL I.wonder
       'Would we, I wonder, catch the plane [if we took the 9 o'clock bus]?'

-*sA* is also used where the utterance challenges the validity of something that has been said or assumed, or the appropriateness of an action intended or in progress:

(38) [9'daki otobüse bin**sek**] yetişmez miyiz?
'Wouldn't we catch [it] [if we took the 9 o'clock bus]?'

(39) [İğneyi şöyle tut **san**] dikişler bu kadar göze batmaz.
'[If you held the needle this way] the stitches wouldn't be so obvious.'

Another very widespread use of the -*sA* conditional is to express an evaluation (usually positive) of a certain possible action, often with the strong implication that the speaker wants or expects this action to be performed:

(40) [Bugün burada temizlik yap-ıl-**sa**] iyi ol-ur.
today here cleaning do-PASS-COND good be-AOR
'It would be good [if some cleaning were done here today].'

This usage is semantically close to the main clause use of -*sA* to express wishes (21.4.4.1).

27.2.3.2 -*sA* used with past copular marking of the main clause

In sentences where the conditional clause is marked by -*sA* and the verb in the main clause contains the past copula -*(y)DI*, the sentence has counterfactual meaning, that is to say it expresses a situation that is contrary to the actual state of affairs. Note that in this modal function as a marker of counterfactuality -*(y)DI* does not necessarily refer to past time, as shown in the first example below:

(41) [Vakt-im ol-**sa**] ben de yarın siz-ler-e katıl-ır-**dı**-m.
time-1SG.POSS be-COND I also tomorrow you-PL-DAT join-AOR-P.COP-1SG
'[If I had time] I would join you tomorrow.' (But I don't, and therefore I won't.)

(42) Ali [[çocuğun kötü bir şey yaptığın]-ı bil**se**] bana söyler**di**.
'[If Ali knew [the child had done something bad]], he would have told me.' (Therefore I assume that he didn't know.)

The counterfactual use of -*sA* occurs mainly with verbs expressing states, such as *ol-* 'be', 'exist' or *bil-* 'know'. With event verbs, counterfactuality is usually expressed either by -*sAydI* (27.2.4) or by compound forms with *olsa* (27.2.6). However, where the main clause is of the evaluative kind, noted in 27.2.3.1, event verbs can also occur in this pattern. In such utterances the counterfactuality is less absolute than in identical sentences with *-sAydI*. The possibility that the desired event might still happen in the future is not completely excluded.

(43) [Ahmet de gel-**se**] ne iyi ol-ur-***du***.
Ahmet too come-COND how nice be-AOR-P.COP
'How nice it would be/have been [if Ahmet came/had come too].'

(44) [Buraya birkaç ağaç dikil**se**] çok fark eder***di***.
'It would make/have made a lot of difference [if a few trees were/had been planted here].'

27.2.4 *-sAydI*

Conditional clauses marked with *-sAydI* always have counterfactual meaning, and therefore always have the past copula in their main clauses.

(45) [9-da-ki otobüs-e bin-***se-ydi***-n] uçağ-a yetiş-mez-**di**-n. (cf.(37)-(38))
9-LOC-ADJ bus-DAT take-COND-P.COP-2SG plane-DAT catch-NEG.AOR-P.COP-2SG
'[If you had taken the 9 o'clock bus] you wouldn't have caught the plane.'

As in the case of *-(y)DI* in counterfactual main clauses, a conditional clause marked with *-sAydI* does not necessarily refer to past time:

(46) [Vaktim ol***saydı***] ben de yarın sizlere katılır**dım**. (cf. (41))
'[If I had had time] I would have joined you tomorrow.'

Although the main clause of a counterfactual conditional is most commonly marked by *-(A/I)rdI* (or its negative counterpart *-mAzdI*), the form *-(y)AcAktI* is also possible where reference is being made to a firmly planned action, a scheduled event, or a situation regarded for some other reason as certain to have resulted if the condition had been fulfilled:

(47) [Temmuz-da gel-ebil-**se**-ler-**di**] biz onlar-ı bir hafta
July-LOC come-PSB-COND-3PL-P.COP we they-ACC one week
gezdir-***ecek-ti***-k.
take.sightseeing-FUT- P.COP-1PL
'[If they had been able to come in July], we *were going to* take them sightseeing for a week.'

27.2.5 -sAymIş

The form -sAymIş is a combination of -sA and the evidential copula -(y)mIş, the use of which in main clauses is explained in 21.4.3. A conditional clause marked with -sAymIş is always followed by a main clause also marked with -(y)mIş:

(48) [Dişçi-ye birkaç ay önce git-**se-ymiş**-im]
      dentist-DAT few month earlier go-COND-EV.COP-1SG
      diş-im-i kurtar-abil-ecek-**miş**.
      tooth-1SG.POSS-ACC save-PSB-FUT-EV.COP
      '*Apparently* [if I had gone to the dentist a few months earlier]
      s/he would have been able to save my tooth.'

The ambiguity of tense reference which is a feature of all sentences marked with -(y)mIş is seen in these conditionals also:

(49) [Filiz Türkiye'de ol**saymış**] nikahınıza gelir**miş**.
      (i) 'Filiz *says that* [if she *were* in Turkey] she would come to your wedding.'
      (ii) 'Filiz *says that* [if she *had been* in Turkey] she would *have* come to your wedding.'

It should be noted that because of the impossibility of combining the conditional copula and the evidential copula on one stem, the only kinds of conditional clauses that can be evidentially marked are the hypothetical and counterfactual predictives. In other types of conditional sentences, such as the open conditional in (50), only the main clause can be evidentially marked:

(50) [Hava kötü ol**ursa**] Cemil gelmeyecek**miş**.
      '*Apparently* Cemil's not going to come [if the weather's bad].'

27.2.6 COMPOUND FORMS WITH *olsa/olsaydı/olsaymış*

Compound forms with *olsa-* are analogous in terms of their relative tense and aspect values to their counterparts with *olursa* (27.2.1.3). They can occur in either hypothetical or counterfactual contexts. The counterfactual versions are differentiated by past copular marking of the main clause, as in (51b) and (c), and by the interchangeability of *olsa* and *olsaydı* in the conditional clause.

The three sentences below illustrate the combinations with *-mIş*. (51a) might be uttered in the course of planning a conference. (51c) could only be uttered after the conference had ended. (51b) could be used in either situation, but if uttered in the planning stage this would be as an argument against a decision that had already been taken.

(51) (a) [Kongre öğle zamanı bit-**miş ol-sa**]
conference noon end-PF AUX-COND
katılan-lar-ın çoğ-u aynı gün ev-e dön-ebil-*ir*.
participant-PL-GEN most-3SG.POSS same day home-DAT
return-PSB-AOR
'[If the conference *had* ended at noon], most of the participants *would* be able to get home the same day.'

(b) [Kongre öğle zamanı bit**miş olsa**] katılanların çoğu aynı gün eve dönebil-*ir-di*.
          AOR-P.COP
'[If the conference *had* ended at noon], most of the participants *would have* been able to get home the same day.'

(c) [Kongre öğle zamanı bit-**miş ol-sa-ydı**]
          AUX-COND- P.COP
katılanların çoğu aynı gün eve dön-ebil-*ir-di*.
'[If the conference *had* ended at noon], most of the participants *would have* been able to get home the same day.'

A similar gradation of meaning occurs in the case of sentences with -*(I)yor ol*-:

(52) (a) [İstanbul'da otur**uyor olsa**m] her akşam tiyatro ya da konsere gidebil*ir*im.
'[If I *were* liv*ing*/liv*ed* in Istanbul] I *would* be able to go to a theatre or concert every evening.'

(b) [İstanbul'da otur**uyor olsa**m] her akşam tiyatro ya da konsere gidebil*irdi*m.
'[If I *were/had been* liv*ing* in Istanbul], I *would* be/*have* been able to go to a theatre or concert every evening.'

(c) [İstanbul'da otur**uyor olsaydı**m] her akşam tiyatro ya da konsere gidebil*irdi*m.
'[If I *had been* liv*ing* in Istanbul], I *would have* been able to go to a theatre or concert every evening.'

The relative-future meaning of -*(y)AcAk ol*- is seen in the next trio of sentences:

(53) (a) [Herhangi bir gün geleme**yecek olsa**m] size önceden
bildir*ir*im.
'[If on any day I *were* not *going to* be able to come] I *would*
let you know in advance.'

  (b) [Herhangi bir gün geleme**yecek olsa**m] size önceden
bildir*irdi*m.
'[If on any day I *were* not *going to* be able to come] I *would*
have let you know in advance.'

  (c) [Herhangi bir gün geleme**yecek olsaydı**m] size önceden
bildir*irdi*m.
'[If on any day I *had* not *been going to* be able to come] I
would have let you know in advance.'

For some speakers, the form -*(y)AcAk olsa* has another function, parallel
to the 'tentative' use of -*(y)AcAk olursa* (27.2.1.3), in which the event
expressed by the conditional clause is not subsequent to that of the main
clause. In this case the tentativeness is compounded by the hypotheticality
of the conditional element *olsa*:

(54) [[Sözleşme imzalandıktan sonra] arkadaşın çekil**ecek olsa**] sen
yanarsın.
'[If your friend *were to* pull out [after the contract is signed]],
you'd be ruined.'

The form -*mIş olsaydı* is often used synonymously with -*sAydI*, to express
a counterfactual condition without any 'relative tense' component in its
meaning:

(55) [Mehmet üniversiteyi kazan**saydı**/kazan**mış olsaydı**] babası ona
Ankara'da ev tutacak**tı**.
'[If Mehmet had got into university], his father was going to rent
a flat for him in Ankara.'

The evidentially marked *olsaymış* can occur in all compound forms where
the context requires it (see 27.2.5):

(56) [Ben şapka giy-**ecek ol-sa-ymış**-ım] o da giy-ecek-miş.
I hat wear-FUT AUX-COND-EV.COP-1SG s/he also wear-FUT-
EV.COP
'*Apparently* s/he would have worn a hat [if I was going to].'

27.3 KNOWABLE CONDITIONS

The potential for fulfilment of the condition expressed by a predictive conditional clause is 'unknowable', in that the condition refers to the unforeseeable future, or to a hypothetical world, or to an event that is known *not* to have happened. The knowable type of condition, on the other hand, is one about whose fulfilment or non-fulfilment information is in principle available, because it refers either to present or past time, or to planned or scheduled future events.

The conditional marker in a knowable condition is always the conditional copula, attached to one of the following:

(**a**) a position 3 tense/aspect/modality suffix (8.2.3.3) (not the aorist)
(**b**) any constituent functioning as a subject complement (12.1.1.2)
(**c**) the particle *değil*
(**d**) one of the existential expressions *var/yok*
(**e**) the past or evidential copula.

Present tense:

(57) [Tanju futbol oyn-**uyor-sa**] iyileş-miş ol-malı.
Tanju football play-IMPF-COND.COP get.better-PF AUX-OBLG
'[If Tanju is playing football], he must have got better.'

(58) [Meşgul-**se**-niz] rahatsız etmeyeyim.
busy-COND.COP-2SG/PL
'[If you're busy] let me not disturb [you].'

(59) [Para-sı yok-**muş-sa**] neden ev almaya kalkmış?
money-POSS.3SG non-existent-EV.COP-COND.COP
'[If (as is claimed) he has no money], why has he taken it into his head to buy a flat?'

Past tense:

(60) Fasulye [yarım saat piş-**ti-yse**] ol-muş-tur artık.
beans half hour cook-PF-COND.COP be.done-PF-GM by.now
'[If the beans have cooked for half an hour], they'll be done by now.'

(61) [Ali o sırada burada **idi-yse**] neden ondan yardım istemedin?
here P.COP-COND.COP
'[If Ali was here then], why didn't you ask him for help?'

(62) Meryem [[bunu Sevgi'nin yaptığın]-ı bil-**iyor-du-ysa**] bize
　　　　　　　　　　　　　　 know-IMPF-P.COP-COND.COP
söylemeliydi.
'[If Meryem knew [it was Sevgi who did this]], she should have
told us.'

Future tense (planned or scheduled events):

(63) [Şükrü gel-me-**yecek-se**] bir yedek bilet-imiz var demek.
Şükrü come-NEG-FUT-COND.COP one spare ticket-1PL.POSS
existent it.means
'[If Şükrü's not going to come], that means we've got a spare
ticket.'

(64) [Uçak 17.00'de kalk**ıyorsa**] 15.00'te havaalanında olmamız lazım.
'[If the plane is taking off at 17.00], we have to be the airport at
15.00.'

Some knowable conditions do not imply any knowledge on the part of
the speaker as to whether the reality of the situation fulfils the condition.
This is particularly the case where the condition relates to a present-tense
situation:

(65) [Vaktiniz var**sa**] biraz deniz kenarında yürüyelim.
'[If you have time], let's go for a little walk along the seashore.'

(66) [Ahmet çalışıyor**sa**] rahatsız edilmek istemez.
'[If Ahmet's working], he won't want to be disturbed.'

This type of knowable condition has the same kind of relation to the situation in the main clause (causing or enabling it) as that which is found in
predictive conditionals.

In most knowable conditions, however, the relation between the two
clauses is different, and much freer. The conditional clause expresses some
information that the speaker has newly acquired, either from another
participant in the conversation or from some other source within the shared
situation of the speech participants. Such a condition is more or less known
to be fulfilled. It is presented as a working assumption, and as the background to what the speaker says in the main clause. Certain kinds of
utterance occur frequently in the main clause of a knowable condition: an
inference, as in (57), (60), (63); a suggestion, request, or other volitional
utterance, as in (58), (65); an expression of obligation, as in (62), (64); or a
question, as in (59), (61). Questions following conditions that are presented
as working assumptions are usually, as in these examples, reproachful in

tone, pointing to an incongruity between the situation assumed in the conditional clause and some observed behaviour or action.

27.4 FURTHER USES OF -sA AND -(y)sA AS SUBORDINATORS

Subordinate clauses marked with -sA or -(y)sA do not always express conditional meaning. In this section we look at some other ways in which these suffixes are used.

27.4.1 -sA . . . -sA

The doubled use of the -sA form of the same verb, with the same person marker, produces a special kind of **concessive conditional** clause which restricts the potential applicability of the main predicate to the constituent immediately preceding it, at the same time expressing the likelihood of non-occurrence of even this event. The main predicate is always from the same root as the conditional verbs, and marked for the same person. It is usually in the aorist form, expressing a generalization (21.4.1.1) or assumption (21.4.1.4).

(67) Sabah-lar-ı [**ye-se-m ye-se-m**] bir dilim ekmek ye-r-im.
morning-PL-3SG.POSS eat-COND-1SG eat-COND-1SG a slice bread
eat-AOR-1SG
'[If I eat anything in the mornings], it's just a slice of bread.'

(68) Bun-u [**yap-sa yap-sa**] Gürkan yap-ar.
this-ACC do-COND do-COND Gürkan do-AOR
'[If anyone can do this], it'll be Gürkan.'

The form *olsa olsa* has been lexicalized as an adverbial, meaning 'if anyone', 'if anything' or 'if at all'. It can be substituted for the verbal -sA forms in sentences like (67) and (68), and also has more general application, as in:

(69) Nazan **olsa olsa** cumartesi sabahı gelebilirmiş.
'Apparently the only time that Nazan could possibly come would be Saturday morning.'

27.4.2 -sA AND -(y)sA/ise WITH dA

27.4.2.1 -sA with dA

The combination of -sA with the clitic dA (11.1.1.2) in a subordinate clause can have one of three different functions:

(i)   A single occurrence of *-sA* or *-sAydI* with *dA* has the concessive conditional meaning 'even if' (cf. 28.3.1.1 (iiib)):

(70) Ahmet artık [çalışsa **da**] sınavı geçemez.
'By now, [*even if* Ahmet works] he won't be able to pass the exam.'

(71) [Beni çağırmasalar**dı da**] gidecektim.
'I was going to go [*even if* they hadn't invited me].'

The clitic *bile* 'even' (11.1.1.1, 28.3.1.1 (iv)) is interchangeable with *dA* in this function:

(72) Ahmet artık [çalışsa **bile**] sınavı geçemez.
'By now, [*even if* Ahmet works] he won't be able to pass the exam.'

The position of the clitic is not always after the word containing the *-sA* suffix. Where there is a compound verb form the clitic can be placed between the two components of this:

(73) [Ömer o zamana kadar üniversiteyi bitirmiş **de** olsa/bitirmiş olsa **da**] Ankara'da bir eve ihtiyacı olabilir.
'[*Even if* Ömer has finished university by that time], he may need a flat in Ankara.'

(74) [Borca girecek **bile** olsam/girecek ols**am** bile] o arsayı almaya kararlıyım.
'[*Even if* it means going into debt] I am determined to buy that piece of land.'

It can also be placed after a non-verbal focused constituent (23.3.1):

(75) [*Bahçemizi* **de/bile** alsalar] biz buradan çıkmayacağız.
'[*Even if* they take away *our garden*], we're not going to move from here.'

The distinction of meaning between aorist + *-(y)sA* and *-sA* noted in the context of predictive conditionals is neutralized in concessive conditionals, and the combination of *-(A/I)rsA/-mAzsA* with *dA* or *bile* is quite rare. Thus *-sA dA* can even occur in sentences with habitual meaning:

(76) Banu [toplantılarımıza gel**se de**] pek bir şey söylemiyor.
'[*Even if* Banu comes to our meetings] she doesn't say much.'

(ii) With *olur* 'it will be all right' as the main clause, the combination of
-sA and *dA* expresses the possibility or acceptability of an alternative
course of action:

(77) [Sen gelme**sen de**] olur.
'It's not essential for you to come.' (lit. 'It will be all right [if you
don't come].')

(78) [Raporu pazartesi **de** versek] olurmuş.
'Apparently it will be all right [if we hand the report in on
Monday].' (e.g. as opposed to today)

(iii) *dA* can mark each of two alternative conditions in a predictive conditional sentence ('whether ... or'), indicating that the outcome will be the
same whichever of them is fulfilled (cf. 28.3.2):

(79) Ahmet artık [çalış**sa da** çalışma**sa da**] sınavı geçemez. (cf. (72))
'By now, [*whether* Ahmet works *or* not] he won't be able to pass
the exam.'

(80) [Evde **de** otursam sokağa **da** çıksam] hep içimde o acı var.
'[*Whether* I sit at home *or* I go out], there is always that pain
inside me.'

27.4.2.2 *-(y)sA/ise* with *dA*

A subordinate predicate marked by the conditional copula *-(y)sA* can be
followed by the clitic *dA* to produce a **concessive** clause, equivalent to an
English clause introduced by 'although'. (For the kinds of constituent to
which *-(y)sA* can attach see 27.1.1 (ii).) The meaning produced by this
construction is *factual* (not conditional). Note, however, that combinations
of the aorist-conditional forms *-(A/I)rsA/-mAzsA* with *dA* (which are rare),
mean 'even if', not 'although' (see 27.4.2.1 (i)).

(81) Banu [toplantılarımıza gel-**iyor-sa da**] pek bir şey söylemiyor.
come-IMPF-COND.COP
(cf. (76))
'[*Although* Banu comes to our meetings] she doesn't say much.'

(82) [Mehmet'i birkaç defa sokakta gör-**dü**-m-**se de**/gör-**dü-yse**-m **de**]
see-PF-1SG-COND.COP *dA*/see- PF-COND.COP-1SG *dA*
konuşmadık.
'[*Although* I've seen Mehmet in the street a few times], we
haven't talked.'

(83) [Parası var**sa da**/var **Vise de**] harcamak istemiyor.
'Although s/he's got money, s/he doesn't want to spend [it].'

It is possible for clauses marked with -*(y)sA dA* to be introduced by *(her) ne kadar* (see 27.5). Although this adds nothing to the meaning, it enables the speaker to signal at the beginning of the sentence that the message of the first clause is subsequently going to be overridden by a conflicting or contrasting statement to come in the main clause:

(84) [***Her ne kadar*** Banu toplantılarımıza gel**iyorsa da**] pek bir şey söylemiyor.
'*Although* Banu sometimes comes to our meetings, she doesn't say much.'

For alternative ways of expressing concessive clauses see 26.3.3.

27.5 UNIVERSAL CONDITIONAL CLAUSES (CONTAINING A QUESTION PHRASE)

Where a conditional clause contains a question phrase (wh-phrase, see 19.2), its meaning is equivalent to a clause with 'whoever', 'wherever', etc. in English. We refer to this type of conditional clause as universal, because (except where the question phrase is *hangi* 'which') there is no limit to the range of conditions that it encompasses. A striking feature of these clauses is that -*sA* occurs interchangeably with various verbal -*(y)sA* combinations:

(85) [***Kim***e sor-du-k-**sa**/sor-**sa**-k] aynı cevab-ı al-dı-k.
who-DAT ask-PF-1PL-COND.COP/ask-COND-1PL same answer-ACC get-PF-1PL
'[Whoever we asked] we got the same answer.'

(86) Hayriye Hanım [***nereye*** giderse/gitse] köpeğini de yanında götürüyordu.
'[*Wherever* Hayriye Hanım went] she took her dog with her too.'

(87) [Bu resimlerden ***hangi***sini seçerseniz] hemen çerçeveletiriz.
'[*Whichever* of these pictures you choose], we'll get [it] framed straight away.'

As in the case of -*sA* with *dA* (27.4.2.1), in universal conditionals also -*sA* can occur with habitual meaning:

(88) Necla [***ne zaman*** sınava girse] heyecan çekiyor.
'[*Whenever* Necla takes an exam] she gets nervous.'

Occasionally the wh-phrase in the subordinate clause is echoed by a **resumptive pronoun** in the main clause:

(89) [***Kim**e sorduksa*] ***hepsin**-den* aynı cevabı aldık. (cf. (85))
                  all.of.them-ABL

(90) Hayriye Hanım [***nereye** giderse*] köpeğini de ***oraya*** yanında
     götürüyordu. (cf. (86))

(91) [Bu resimlerden ***hangi**sini seçerseniz*] hemen çerçeveletiriz
     onu. (cf. (87))

If the question phrase is *kim* 'who', *ne* 'what' or *nere-* 'where', the idea of universality can be reinforced by placing *her* 'every' before this item:

(92) Hayriye Hanım [***her nereye** giderse*] köpeğini de yanında
     götürüyordu.

Universal conditionals with *nasıl* 'how' are often used in a sense removed from any kind of conditionality, to express simply a similarity between two situations:

(93) [***Nasıl** Hakan akşamları garsonluk yapıyorsa*] sen de derslerine
     engel olmayacak bir iş bulabilirsin. (cf. (17) in Chapter 26)
     '[*Just as* Hakan works in the evenings as a waiter], you too could
     find a job that wouldn't interfere with your academic
     commitments.'

If, on the other hand, *nasıl* actually modifies the verb in the subordinate clause, it is echoed by *öyle* 'so', 'in that way' in the main clause:

(94) [Bir baba çocuklarını ***nasıl** severse*] Mustafa da köpeklerini *öyle*
     seviyor.
     'Mustafa loves his dogs [*in the same way that* a father loves his
     children].'

27.5.1 UNIVERSAL CONDITIONAL CONCESSIVES

Many universal conditional constructions express a concessive relation, particularly the failure (predicted or actual) to achieve an objective in spite of the efforts expressed in the conditional clause. Two alternative strategies may optionally be used to reinforce this concessive meaning:

(i)   *dA* may be placed after the conditional verb:

(95) [Bu konuda **ne kadar** iyi bir kitap yaz**san** (*da*)] meşhur
olamayacaksın.
'[*However* good a book you write on this subject], you won't
become famous.'

(96) Adam [**ne** söyledi**yse** (*de*)] karısını suçsuz olduğuna inandıramadı.
'[*Whatever* the man said], he couldn't convince his wife that he
was innocent.'

(97) [Kemal bana **kaç** defa anlat**sa** (*da*)] gene anlamayacaktım.
'[*However* many times Kemal explained [it] to me] I still wouldn't
have understood.'

Note that *dA* is generally not used where the verb in the conditional clause
has aorist marking.

(**ii**)   If the conditional clause is in the form aorist + -(*y*)*sA*, the imperative
or optative form of the same verb (in the same grammatical person) may
be inserted immediately after the conditional form. This additional verb
form is, strictly speaking, the main clause that the universal conditional
modifies, but in practice it serves to reinforce the meaning of the universal
conditional clause itself.

(98) [**Ne kadar** konuş-**ur**-lar-**sa**] konuş-*sun*-lar hiçbir zaman
what amount talk-AOR-3PL-COND.COP talk-IMP.3PL
anlaşamayacaklar.
'*However long* they go on talking, (let them talk;) they're never
going to be able to agree.'

(99) [**Nere-ye** gid-er-se-niz] gid-*in* bu fiyata bu kadar güzel bir kanepe.
where-DAT go-AOR-COND.COP-2SG/PL go-IMP.2SG/PL
bulamazsınız.
'(Go) *no matter where* you go; you won't find such a fine sofa at
this price.'

As noted in 27.4.2.2, (**her**) **ne kadar** in a conditional-marked clause does
not always mean 'however much/long', as it has become lexicalized as a
general marker of concessive clauses with -(*y*)*sA dA*.

27.6   CONDITIONAL CONSTRUCTIONS WITHOUT CONDITIONAL SUFFIXES

There are a number of constructions that express the same meaning as aorist
+ -(*y*)*sA*, i.e. predictive open and habitual conditional clauses (27.2.1.1–2),
without the use of either of the conditional suffixes.

27.6.1 -DIğI takdirde, -mAsI durumunda/halinde

Conditional clauses whose verbs are marked with these forms structurally resemble the other non-finite adverbial constructions discussed in 26.3. They are characteristic of relatively formal styles, and approximate to 'in the event of/that'. Note that in -DIğI *takdirde* the subordinator is always -DIK, not -(y)AcAK.

(100) [Aday-lar-dan hiçbir-i çoğunluk
      candidate-PL-ABL none-3SG.POSS majority
      sağla-ya-ma-**dığ-ı takdirde**] ikinci tur-a geç-il-ecek-tir.
      secure-PSB-NEG-CV-3SG.POSS *takdirde* second round-DAT
      move-PASS-FUT-GM
      '[*In the event of* none of the candidates being able to secure a majority], [the process] will continue into a second round.'

(101) [Yapılaşma denetim altına alınma**ması durumunda/halinde**] kıyı bölgeleri kısa zamanda bozulmaktadır.
      '[If building development is not brought under control], coastal regions are rapidly spoilt.'

27.6.2 -DI mI

By contrast, -DI mI (the perfective finite verb form followed by the interrogative clitic) is a very informal alternative to the aorist conditional. It is used only where the speaker wishes to impart a rather dramatic tone to a conditional utterance:

(102) [O kağıdı imzala**dık mı**] artık yakamızı hiç kurtaramayız.
      '[If we once sign that piece of paper] we'll never be able to escape.'

Subordinate clauses with -dI mI also occur with temporal meaning (26.1.6).

28 CONJUNCTIONS, CO-ORDINATION AND DISCOURSE CONNECTION

In Turkish a number of devices are used for co-ordinating phrases and/or sentences:

(i)   The juxtaposition of two or more constituents (28.1)
(ii) The subordinating suffixes -(y)Ip and -(y)ArAk (28.2)
(iii) Conjunctions and connectives (28.3).

Certain items may be omitted when two or more phrases or clauses are conjoined. These are discussed in 28.4.

28.1 THE JUXTAPOSITION OF TWO OR MORE CONSTITUENTS

One of the most common methods of co-ordinating two or more phrases or sentences is simply to list them without using an overt co-ordinator. Note that Turkish uses simple juxtaposition in many cases where English uses 'and' or 'or':

(1)   **siyah beyaz** bir film
      'a black [*and*] white film'

(2)   Öğleyin **ekmek peynir** yedim.
      'I had bread [*and*] cheese at lunch time.'

(3)   **Gece gündüz** çalışıyoruz.
      'We're working night [*and*] day.'

Apart from semi-lexicalized pairs such as those shown in (1)–(3), and juxtaposed numeral pairs such as *iki üç* 'two [or] three' (15.7.1), constituents co-ordinated in this way are often separated by a pause in speech, and at the end of all but the last of the conjoined items there is rising intonation. In writing, listing in this manner requires a comma:

(4)   güzel, büyük, deniz manzaralı bir oda
      'a beautiful, large room with a view of the sea'

(5) Ziya pabuçlarını, paltosunu giydi, eline şemsiyesini aldı, işe gitti.
     'Ziya put on his shoes [*and*] coat, picked up his umbrella [*and*]
     left for work.'

28.2 THE SUBORDINATING SUFFIXES -(y)Ip AND -(y)ArAk

-(y)Ip (8.5.2.2) is a regular means of conjoining clauses which are semantically of equal status with respect to tense/aspect/modality. *-(y)ArAk* (8.5.2.2
and 26.3) can also be used for the same purpose. These suffixes are attached
to all verbs but the last in a series of conjuncts, in place of all
tense/aspect/modality suffixes and all other suffixes following them:

(6) Sinemaya gid**ip** güzel bir film seyret**sek**. (cf. Sinemaya
     git**sek ve** . . .)
     'We should go to the cinema *and* watch a good film.'

(7) Başbakan İzmir'e gid-**erek** bazı işadamlarıyla görüş**tü**.
                        go-CONJmeet-PF
     (cf. İzmir'e git**ti ve** . . .)
     'The Prime Minister went to Izmir *and* met some businessmen.'

In subordinate clauses *-(y)Ip* and *-(y)ArAk* replace other subordinating
suffixes (8.5) and any other suffixes that follow them:

(8) [Kendin gel-**ip** gör-**ünce**] anlayacaksın. (cf. gel**ince ve** . . .)
                come-CONJ see-CV
     '[When you come *and* see for yourself], you will understand.'

(9) [Konuyu bil-**ip** fark ettir-me-**diğ-in**]-**i** tahmin ediyorum.
                  know-CONJ give.away-NEG-VN-2SG.POSS-ACC
     (cf. bil**diğini fakat** . . .)
     'I have a feeling [that you know about the matter *but* you're not
     giving it away].'

For the *-(y)(I)p* . . . *-mA* construction that occurs on identical verb stems in
noun clauses, see 20.1.3.

Where the verb in the superordinate clause contains a negative suffix,
the verb containing *-(y)Ip* is also typically understood to have negative
meaning:

(10) Bu havada herhalde evde otur-**up** televizyon seyret-**me-yeceğ-iz**!
                              stay-CONJ   watch-NEG-FUT-1PL
(= ... evde otur-**ma-yacağ-ız** ve ...)
                 stay-NEG-FUT-1PL and ...
'We'll hardly be staying indoors *and* watching the telly in this weather!'

It is also possible, however, for the verb containing *-(y)Ip* to have affirmative meaning despite negative marking of the superordinate verb, as seen in (9) above. If the clitic *dA* follows *-(y)Ip* in such contexts it serves to emphasize an adversative relation between the two verbs (28.3.45):

(11) Ahmet mesajı bul-up **da** anla-***ma***-mış mı acaba?
                       find-CONJ *dA* understand-NEG-EV/PF
'I wonder if Ahmet found the message *but* didn't understand [it]?'

The verb containing *-(y)Ip* can itself be negative-marked only where the superordinate verb is not:

(12) Bu havada evde otur-**ma-yıp** yürüyüşe çık-malı-yız.
                       stay-NEG-CONJ   go.out-OBLG-1PL
'In this weather we must not stay indoors *but* go out for a walk.'

Where a verb containing *-(y)Ip* is followed by *dA* and is *stressed*, the clause in which it occurs is exactly equivalent to a finite subordinate clause marked by *dA* (26.1.7), i.e. it emphasizes the fact that the action it expresses *precedes/preceded* that articulated by the main clause:

(13) [Yemek yi**YIP** de] geldim. (cf. (23) in Chapter 26)
'I came [having [already] eaten].'

Although it is rather unusual, some speakers use *-(y)Ip* when conjoining clauses with different subjects, especially when they both have 3rd person subjects:

(14) Tam o saat-te Semra iş-i bırak-**ıp** Ahmet işbaşı yap-**ıyor**.
exactly that time-LOC Semra work-ACC leave-CONJ Ahmet clocking.on do-IMPF
'At exactly that time Semra leaves work and Ahmet goes on duty.'

28.3 CONJUNCTIONS AND DISCOURSE CONNECTIVES

Conjunctions are expressions such as *ve* 'and', *fakat* 'but', and *ya da* 'or', which join two or more items that have the same syntactic function. These can be phrases, subordinate clauses or sentences. The conjoining function of **discourse connectives**, on the other hand, is minimally to join two sentences. Discourse connectives such as *aksine* 'on the contrary', *üstelik* 'moreover' and *sonuç olarak* 'as a result' can be used for purposes of forming a cohesive link between concepts expressed by entire groups of sentences. Another difference between the two classes is that while a conjunction always joins two (or more) linguistic items, this is not always the case with discourse connectives, which can sometimes be used on their own if the context presents a situation (e.g. a recent experience shared by speaker and hearer) to which a cohesive link can be made.

The various semantic functions of Turkish conjunctions and discourse connectives are explained below. Some expressions (e.g. *yoksa* 'or', 'otherwise') can function both as conjunctions and as discourse connectives, and some fulfil more than one role even as discourse connectives. For example, *dA* has additive, enumerative and adversative functions, all of which are discussed under different subsections below. Quite a number of discourse connectives are adverbial in form, for example those such as *bununla birlikte* 'in spite of this', *onun için* 'for that reason', which consist of a postpositional phrase with a demonstrative pronoun as its complement.

28.3.1 ADDITIVE

The common characteristic of the items in this group is that they signal the addition of a new item without changing the direction of the discourse.

28.3.1.1 *ve, -(y)lA/ile, dA* 'and', *dA* 'too', *bile* 'even', *ve de* 'and what's more', *bir de* 'and also', *ya* 'and what . . .'

(i) *ve*, a particle borrowed from Arabic, conjoins all types of phrases and clauses, and can function both as a conjunction and as a discourse connective.

> (15) Arapça ve Farsça
> 'Arabic and Persian'

> (16) [Paris'e gittiğin]-e **ve** [müzeleri gezdiğin]-e çok seviniyor.
> 'S/he is very happy [that s/he went to Paris *and* visited the museums].'

In its function of conjoining two clauses, *ve* is often replaced by *-(y)Ip* or (less commonly) by *-(y)ArAK* (28.2).

(ii)   The clitic *ile* and its suffixal counterpart *-(y)lA* (8.1.4), unlike *ve*, attach only to non-case-marked noun phrases and to noun clauses formed with *-mAK* (24.4.1) and *-mA* (24.4.2). They can join only conjuncts, and they cannot occur as discourse connectives.

(17)   Arapça'**yla** Farsça
'Arabic and Persian'

(18)   [Ahmet'in bu kitabı okuması]-**yla** [okumaması] arasında bir fark olacağını sanmıyorum.
'I don't believe there will be a difference between [Ahmet's reading this book] and [his not reading [it]].'

Another difference between *ve* and *-(y)lA/ile* is that *ve* is exclusive, whereas *-(y)lA/ile* can be either exclusive or inclusive. Where the conjunction is *ve*, a plural pronoun (such as *biz* 'we' below) does not include within its reference the noun phrase conjoined to it:

(19)   **Zehra ve biz** kolay anlaşıyoruz.
'*We and Zehra* get along well.' (*We* get along well *with Zehra*.)

-(y)lA/ile, on the other hand, can be either inclusive or exclusive, i.e. the conjoined noun phrase may or may not denote a member of the group that the plural pronoun refers to:

(20)   **Zehra'yla biz** eve gidiyoruz.
(**a**)   '*Zehra and I* are going home.'
(**b**)   '*We and Zehra* are going home.' (*We* are going home *with Zehra*.)

(See also 12.2.2.4 and 13.2.3.2 for subjects conjoined by *ve* or *-(y)lA/ile* and 17.2.1 for *-(y)lA* as a postposition.)

(iii)   In its additive usages, the clitic *dA* (11.1.1.2) is a discourse connective occurring in the second conjunct (cf. the usages described in 26.1.7, 28.3.4.5 (i)). It has different functions according to the type of constituent it is attached to. It can be attached either to a non-focused constituent or to a focused one.

(**a**)   *dA* attached to a non-focused (i.e. unstressed) constituent
A non-focused constituent to which *dA* is attached is usually the first constituent in a sentence. In this case *dA* has a primarily continuative function, indicating that the events described in successive sentences are connected, but it may also signal a change in topic (23.3.3.1 (i), as in the case of *Semra'ya* in (21)). In this usage *dA* corresponds to 'and':

(21) Sana bugün iki mektup geldi. *Semra'ya* **da** bir paKET.
'Two letters arrived for you today. *And* a package for Semra.'

(22) Balığı kızarttım. Biraz sonra **da** yiyeCEğim.
'I have fried the fish *and* will eat it in a few minutes.'

(b) *dA* attached to a focused (i.e.stressed) constituent
This can be any constituent in the sentence, including the predicate.
In this function *dA* corresponds to 'too', 'also':

(23) Kışın ortasında Bodrum'a gitti, deniZE **de** girdi.
'S/he went to Bodrum in the middle of winter, *and* swam in the sea, too.'

(24) Hep İzlanda'ya gitmek isterdi, sonunda gitTİ **de**.
'S/he always wanted to go to Iceland, *and* in the end s/he went, too.'

dA can sometimes attach to the stressed constituent within a phrase:

(25) Bebek ne tatlı. ÇOK **da** uslu maşallah.
'The baby is so sweet. And *very* well-behaved, *too!*'

See 28.3.2 for enumerating *dA* . . . *dA*, 28.3.4.5 (i) for the adversative function of *dA*, 27.4.2 for combinations of *dA* with the conditional markers -*sA* and -*(y)sA*, and 26.1.7 for *dA* as a subordinator.

(iv) *bile* 'even', 'already' attaches to any constituent that can receive stress:

(26) Nuri, **sokaĞA** *bile* **çıkmak** istemiyor.
'Nuri doesn't *even* want to go out [of the house].'

When *bile* attaches to a predicate in a finite clause, it can mean 'even', but more often corresponds to 'already':

(27) Bazen o pis köpeği okŞUyor **bile**.
'Sometimes s/he *even* strokes that filthy dog.'

(28) O filmi görDÜM **bile**.
'I have *already* seen that film.'

(v) *ve de* is an emphatic form of *ve*, mostly in its function as a sentence co-ordinator, and is used mainly to highlight the significance of the comment that follows:

(29) 80 yaşında Almanca öğrenmeye başladı **ve de** bundan çok
      memnun.
      'S/he has started learning German at 80, *and what's more* s/he's
      very happy about it.'

(vi) *bir de* can follow or precede the second conjunct. It sometimes signals
that the item it introduces is an afterthought:

(30) Evde tuz kalmamış, **bir de** süt.
      'We are out of salt . . . *and* milk.'

(31) İtalya'ya gitmek istiyorum, İspanya'ya **bir de**.
      'I want to go to Italy . . . *also* to Spain.'

(vii) *ya* as an additive is a discourse connective which has the sole function
of introducing a speculative question involving a conditional clause. The
verb is always marked with one of the conditional suffixes *-sA* or *-(y)sA*
(Chapter 27). The sentence may be left without a main clause, in which case
it corresponds to questions expressed with '(And) what if . . .' in English:

(32) **Ya** bir kazaya uğradı**ysa**?
      '*(And) what if* s/he's had an accident?'

If there is a main clause, it is always in the form of a wh-question (19.2):

(33) **Ya** [ben evde olma**saydım**] seni *kim* kurtaracaktı?
      '*And who* would have rescued you [*if* I hadn't been at home]?'

28.3.1.2 *üstelik, üstüne üstlük, hem, hem (de), buna ek olarak, ayrıca, kaldı ki* 'and (what's more)', 'also', *sonra* 'and then'

These connectives do not merely conjoin two sentences; they also draw
attention to the speaker's conscious decision to add something to what has
already been said. As seen in the examples below, they are often combined
with *dA*. They can be situated at the beginning or at the end of the second
sentence:

(34) Nota okumayı sevmiyormuş. **Üstelik** piyanist!
      'S/he doesn't like reading scores. *And* she's a pianist!'

(35) Erken buluşalım. **Hem** birşeyler **de** yeriz.
      'Let's meet early. *Then* we could have something to eat as well.'

28.3.1.3 *hatta, dahası* 'even', 'indeed'

These discourse connectives introduce a statement that reinforces the previous statement, usually by making an even more convincing point. They occur at the beginning of the second conjunct, and are often combined with *bile* (28.3.1.1 (iv)):

(36) [Erol'un Korkut'u sevmediği] belli. **Hatta** bunu açıkça söylüyor.
      'It's obvious [that Erol doesn't like Korkut]. *Indeed*, he says so quite openly.'

(37) Akşam kurslarına gitti. **Dahası** tatillerde *bile* ders çalıştı.
      'S/he went to evening classes. S/he *even* studied in the holidays.'

hatta also occurs as a conjunction:

(38) [Sıcaktan bayılanlar], **hatta** [ölenler] olmuş.
      'Apparently there were [people who fainted], *and even* [some who died of the heat].'

28.3.1.4 *şöyle dursun/bir yana/bırak(ın)* 'let alone'

These expressions, which function as conjunctions, occur only in negative sentences, and are placed at the end of the first conjunct. Their effect is to reinforce the negativity of the assertion involving the first conjunct by drawing a comparison with the negativity of another situation regarded as inherently more realizable. The second conjunct almost always includes *bile* 'even' (28.3.1.1 (iv)). Note that if, as in (39), the comparison is between two clauses (rather than two noun phrases), the first is expressed as a *-mAk* clause (24.4.1.1):

(39) Diplomasını almak **şöyle dursun/bir yana**, tezini **bile** daha yazmamış.
      'S/he hasn't *even* written her thesis yet, *let alone* received his/her degree.'

For the use of the negative particle *değil* in a similar function see 20.2.3.

28.3.2 ENUMERATING

dA . . . dA, hem . . . hem, gerek . . . (ve) gerek(se de) 'both . . . and'

The items in this group of reduplicated conjunctions emphasize the equal status and function in an utterance of two or more persons, objects or events. *dA* is attached to the end of each of the phrases involved, whereas *hem* and *gerek* precede the phrases or clauses they connect:

(40) Dünya Kupasında **Güney Kore** *de* **Türkiye** *de* yarı finale kaldı.
'*Both* South Korea *and* Turkey have reached the semi-finals of the World Cup.'

(41) Necla *hem* **Boğaziçi Üniversitesi** *hem de* **Bilkent**'e girebiliyormuş.
'Necla has been admitted to *both* Boğaziçi University *and* Bilkent.'

In the last occurrence of *hem*, *dA* can be used for emphasis, as in (41) above. The last occurrence of *gerek* can be replaced by *gerekse*, *gerekse de* or *ve gerekse de*:

(42) *Gerek* **İngiliz takımı**, *gerekse* (*de*) **Fransızlar**, bu Dünya Kupası yarışmasına iddialı giriyorlar.
'*Both* the English team *and* the French are entering this World Cup competition with high hopes.'

Where *dA* ... *dA*, *hem* ... *hem* or *gerek* ... *(ve) gerek (se de)* are used in sentences with a negative predicate, they are equivalent to *ne* ... *ne* 'neither ... nor' (20.4).

28.3.3 ALTERNATIVE

This group of items conjoins phrases, clauses or sentences that express objects, persons, events or situations presented as alternatives.

28.3.3.1 *ya da, veya, ∇(ve) yahut (da), yoksa* 'or', *ya* ... *ya (da)* 'either ... or'

Of the various terms expressing 'or' in Turkish, *ya da*, *veya* and *∇(ve) yahut (da)* are interchangeable in most contexts, both as conjunctions and as discourse connectives:

(43) Evde meyva **veya/ya da** tatlı var mı?
'Is there any fruit *or* any [sort of] sweet in the house?'

When *ya da* is used as a discourse connective it can be placed after the second conjunct:

(44) Necla sinemaya gitmek istemiyor. **Ya da** öyle söylüyor./
Öyle söylüyor **ya da**.
'Necla doesn't want to go to the cinema. *Or* that's what she says.'

When used as a conjunction, *ya da* can occur either on its own or with another *ya* preceding the first conjunct:

(45) O konuyu (**ya**) Ahmet'(le) **ya da** karısıyla konuşabilirsin.
      'You can discuss that matter (*either*) with Ahmet *or* with his wife.'

Alternatively, *ya . . . ya* can be used to express 'either . . . or'.

Note that *ya* used on its own can function as an additive connective introducing conditional questions (28.3.1.1 (vii), an adversative connective (28.3.4.5 (ii) and 28.3.4.7), or a reminding connective (28.3.12).
   yoksa as an alternative conjunction occurs only in alternative questions (19.1.2). As a discourse connective it can introduce a question expressing surprise at an inference drawn (19.5.3), or it can have the conditional sense of 'otherwise' (28.3.9).

28.3.3.2 *ister . . . ister, olsun . . . olsun, ha . . . ha, ama . . . ama* 'whether . . . or'

These reduplicated conjunctions indicate the speaker's indifference towards the alternatives mentioned.

(**i**) *ister . . . ister* conjoins imperative or optative verb forms (21.4.4.2–3), or nominal predicates. Each conjunction is placed before the constituent it conjoins:

(46) **İster** kal, **ister** git, yeter ki bugün şu işi bitir. (For *yeter ki* see 28.3.9.)
      '*Whether* you stay *or* leave, make sure you finish off the job today.'

(47) Nazlı **ister** kursa yazılsın **ister** yazılmasın, bir şekilde Fransızca öğrenmesi gerekiyor.
      '*Whether* she joins a class *or not*, Nazlı has to learn French somehow.'

(**ii**) *olsun . . . olsun*, which is a combination of the copular verb *ol-* 'be' (12.1.1.3) and the 3rd person optative form (8.4), is used with nominal predicates. Each conjunction is placed after the constituent it conjoins:

(48) Büyük **olsun** küçük **olsun**, evlerin sorunları bitmiyor.
      'Big *or* small, houses always have problems.'

ister . . . ister can occur with *olsun . . . olsun*:

(49) **İster** büyük **olsun, ister** küçük **(olsun)**, evlerin sorunları bitmiyor.
'Whether big *or* small, houses always have problems.'

(iii) *ha ... ha* and *ama ... ama* are both colloquial conjunctions which
precede the constituents they conjoin:

(50) **Ha** Boğaziçi'ne gitmişsin **ha** Bilkent'e. İkisi de iyi üniversite.
'*It doesn't matter whether* you go to Boğaziçi *or* to Bilkent. They
are both good universities.'

(51) Bu tip fırınlarda genellikle ızgara olmuyor, **ama** yerli **ama**
yabancı.
'*Whether* they are made in Turkey (lit. locally) *or* imported, these
ovens don't usually have grills.'

28.3.4 ADVERSATIVE

Adversative conjunctions signal a turning of the discourse in a direction
contrary to what has been previously established.

28.3.4.1 *ama, fakat, ancak, yalnız* 'but'

Fakat and *ama* are interchangeable. They conjoin clauses whose combined
content expresses some kind of conflict or contradiction:

(52) Semra hep gezmek istiyor **ama/fakat** zamanı yok. (Conflict)
'Semra always wants to travel, *but* she doesn't have the time.'

(53) Sonbahar geldi **ama/fakat** ağaçlar hâlâ yeşil.   (Contradiction)
'Autumn is here, *but* the trees are still green.'

When *ama* is used as a discourse connective, in other words when the
second conjunct is uttered as a separate statement from the first, *ama* can
also be placed at the end of the second conjunct:

(54) Kitabı hevesle satın aldım. Okuyamadım **ama**.
'I bought the book with great enthusiasm. I haven't managed to
read it, *though*.'

Ama and *fakat* can also conjoin adjectival constructions:

(55) Sıcak **ama** [bunaltıcı olmayan] bir havası var Ankara'nın.
'The weather in Ankara is hot *but* not suffocating.'
(lit. 'Ankara has a hot but not suffocating climate.')

ancak and *yalnız* (which as adverbials mean 'only' (16.7)) are slightly more restricted in their occurrence as adversative connectives than *ama* or *fakat*. They are used mainly to introduce a sentence expressing inability, failure, obligation, or some other disadvantageous situation:

(56) Ahmet aslında çok iyi bir mimar. **Ancak/Yalnız** aksiliği yüzünden müşterileri kaçırıyor. (For *aslında* see 28.3.4.6.)
'Ahmet is actually a very good architect. *But* he loses customers because of his bad temper.'

28.3.4.2 Gene (de)/yine (de) '(and) yet', '(and) still', bununla birlikte/beraber, buna karşın/rağmen 'despite this', 'nevertheless'

These discourse connectives are more emphatic adversatives than those in 28.3.4.1. *gene de/yine de* are often used together with *ama* or *fakat* (for an example see (68) below). *gene/yine* also occur as adverbials meaning 'again'; the addition of *de* eliminates potential ambiguity.

(57) Rusça çok zor bir dilmiş, **gene de** onu öğrenmeye kararlıyım.
'Russian is said to be a very difficult language, *yet* I am determined to learn it.'

(58) Ahmet nezle olmuş. **Buna rağmen** yüzmek istiyor.
'Ahmet's got a cold. *Despite this*, he wants to go swimming.'

28.3.4.3 ne (var) ki/∇mamafih, 'however'

These items are confined to rather formal registers, and highlight the speaker's conscious intention to articulate a conflictual or contradictory state of affairs:

(59) İlköğretimi tamamlayanların sayısında önemli bir artış olmuş. **Ne var ki** rakamlara ayrıntılı bakıldığında bölgesel farklılaşma da dikkat çekmektedir.
'There has evidently been a significant increase in the number of those completing primary education. *However*, when one looks at the figures in detail, one is also struck by regional differentiation.'

28.3.4.4 halbuki/oysa (ki), 'whereas', 'however'

The discourse connectives *halbuki/oysa (ki)* sometimes merely point to a contrast between two states of affairs:

(60) Sen [bütün duvarların düz beyaz kalmasın]-ı istersin, **oysa** ben
      [bazı odalarda değişik renkler olsun] isterim.
      'You want [all the walls to stay plain white], *whereas* I want [there
      to be different colours in some rooms].'

In this function a sentence with *halbuki/oysa (ki)* could be paraphrased with
-(y)sA (23.3.3.1 (ii)). The more distinctive function of *halbuki* and *oysa (ki)*
is to signal a contradiction between a *factual* state of affairs and a *belief* or
claim concerning it. The connective always appears at the beginning (or
end) of the second conjunct, but this may be the one expressing either the
factual or the supposed state of affairs:

(61) (**a**) Necla [evini sattığında] bunalıma girdi. **Halbuki/Oysa**
              [bu fikre çoktandır alıştı] sanıyordum.
              'Necla became very depressed [when she sold her house].
              Whereas I thought [she had got used to the idea].'

      (**b**) Necla [evini satma fikrine alıştı] sanıyordum. **Halbuki/Oysa**
              [bir alıcı çıktığında] bunalıma girdi.
              'I thought [Necla had got used to the idea of selling her
              house]. *However*, [when a buyer appeared] she became
              very depressed.'

28.3.4.5 *dA, ya* 'but', *-(y)sA/ise* 'as for', 'whereas'

These are conjunctions which contrast a situation presented in the second
conjunct to the situation presented in the first one.

(**i**) *dA* is placed after the predicate of the first conjunct, and produces
stress on the last syllable of the predicate, even if this position is not the
normally stressable position of that word (4.3.2.1):

(62) Öğrencilerin hepsinin adlarını bilmiyoRUM **da** yüzlerini
      tanıyorum.
      'I don't know the names of all the students, *but* I know their faces.'

(63) Sen GİT **de** ben gelmeyeceğim.
      'You go, *but* I'm not coming.'

Note that adversative *dA* does not produce primary stress on *-(y)Ip* (28.2):

(64) Ahmet mesajı bul**up da** yanLIŞ anlamış meğerse.
      'It turns out that Ahmet had found the message *but*
      misunderstood [it].'

(ii)   *ya* is used in colloquial speech as a contrastive adversative conjunction:

(65) Toplantıya katılırım **ya** [ne diyeceğim]-i bilemem.
      'Join the meeting I will, *but* I won't know [what to say].'

(iii)   The contrastive function of *-(y)sA/ise* (11.1.1.3) is to switch the attention of the speaker to a new topic; this is explained in 23.3.3.1 (ii)).

28.3.4.6   *gerçi/∇hoş* 'it's true that', 'admittedly', 'actually', *aslında* 'actually'

The function of this group of adversative discourse connectives is concessive. While marking the statement they introduce as contradictory to what has previously been said, they also signal that the speaker regards this contradiction as illusory, reparable or otherwise tolerable. *gerçi* arouses an expectation that the statement it introduces will be followed by another introduced by a conflictive adversative (such as *ama* 'but'), which will counterbalance the concession made, and cancel out its effect:

(66) Uludağ'a gidiyorlarmış. **Gerçi** Ziya kayak yapmayı sevmez **ama
      yine de** gidecekmiş.
      'They are going to Uludağ. *Actually* Ziya doesn't like skiing, *but*
      he is still going.'

hoş is used in the same way as *gerçi*, but is a slightly dated expression, used only in colloquial speech. As for the very common expression *aslında* 'actually', this can be used either in the same way as *gerçi* or on its own, as in (67), leaving the concession unrepaired:

(67) [Bakkala gittiğinde] gazete de alır mısın? **Aslında** birazdan ben
      de çıkacağım.
      'Can you buy a paper [when you go to the corner shop]?
      Actually I shall be going out soon, too.'

28.3.4.7   *ki* and *ya*

As adversative connectives, *ki* and *ya* complement each other, and have a repudiative function. Both challenge the previous statement or question, or the presupposition of the previous speaker, but whereas *ki* occurs in negative statements and in questions, *ya* as a repudiator occurs only in affirmative statements. They both occur after the predicate and usually at the end of a sentence, placing stress on the preceding syllable, even in those cases where this position is not the normally stressable syllable of a word (4.3.2.1):

(68) Ahmet gezide fotoğraf çekecekti **ama** makinasını yanına
almaMIŞ **ki**!
'Ahmet was supposed to take photographs on the trip,
but apparently he hadn't taken his camera with him!'

(69) A.– Sana [bu sabunu kullan] demedim mi?
'Didn't I tell you [to use this soap]?'

B.– KullanDIM **ya**!
'*But* I did!'

The discourse connective function of *ki* described here is related to one of
its subordinating functions, in which it introduces clauses expressing
purpose (26.1.2.2). For this reason, repudiative *ki* can be followed by an
optative-marked verb (which would usually have no counterpart in the
English version of the sentence):

(70) A.– Hani alışverişe gidecektin?
'I thought you were going to go shopping?'

B.– Dükkanlar daha açılmamıŞTIR ki (gideyim).
'*But* the shops won't be open yet.'

For the various other (non-conjunctive) functions of *ki* and *ya* see 11.1.1.4
and 11.1.1.6.

28.3.4.8 *peki* 'but'

The most common function of *peki* is to express the speaker's agreement
with a proposal or instruction articulated by the addressee. In this usage it
means 'all right', and can stand on its own as a complete utterance. As a
discourse connective *peki* is used only in questions, and indicates that the
speaker is not satisfied with the information conveyed in a previous statement, and requires more information:

(71) A.– Bütün yazı çalışarak geçirmem gerekiyor.
'I have to spend the whole summer working'.

B.– **Peki**, sen bu yaz evini satmayacak mıydın?
'*But* weren't you planning to sell your house this summer?'

28.3.4.9 *yok* 'but'

Yok can be used as an adversative discourse connective in the second of
two consecutive conditional sentences. In each sentence the conditional

verb is marked with *-(y)sA* (27.1–3), and the two conditions expressed are mutually exclusive. *Yok* is placed at the beginning of the second sentence, and may optionally be followed by the conditional conjunction *eğer* 'if' (27.1.2):

(72) [Mehmet ikiye kadar gelir**se**] iyi. [**Yok** (**eğer**) o saate kadar
   gelmemiş**se**] daha fazla bekleyemeyiz.
   '[If Mehmet arrives by two o'clock], that's fine. [*But* if he hasn't
   come by that time], we won't be able to wait any longer.'

28.3.5 EXPANSIVE

This group of conjunctions and connectives are used to signal an expansion of the speaker's statement. Expansion may take the form of exemplification, particularization, analogy, explanation, justification, correction or (in the case of a negative statement) amplification. *Şöyle ki* always precedes the comment it introduces; the others, with the exception of the expansive suffixes in (ii), are likewise often placed at the beginning of the second conjunct, but in colloquial speech they can also follow the second conjunct or can occur in some position within it.

(**i**)   *örneğin/mesela/sözgelişi/sözgelimi* 'for example'
örneğin and its Arabic synonym *mesela* are the most frequently used expressions in the exemplifying group:

(73) Nane bazı şeylerle çok iyi gidiyor, **örneğin** kuzu etiyle.
   'Mint goes very well with some things. With lamb, *for example*.'

(**ii**)   *-(y)DI . . . -(y)DI, -(y)mIş . . . -(y)mIş, yok . . . yok* '. . . and the like', 'etc.'
In colloquial usage these reduplicative forms perform another kind of exemplifying function, listing some of the possible items in a set. Two of the connectives in this group are the copular markers *-(y)DI* and *-(y)mIş* (8.3.2). The listed items marked in this manner usually precede the general term (indicated by italics below) referring to them:

(74) Yanına **kağıttı**, **kalemdi**, *sınav için ne gerekliyse* al.
   'Take with you *all that you need for the exam, paper, pencils and what have you*.'

(75) **Koşmakmış**, **yüzmekmiş**, hiç öyle *spor*la filan uğraştığı yok.
   'S/he is not interested in *sports* at all, like running, swimming, etc.'

Reduplicated *yok*, also an informal way of listing items, is used in a different way. It allows the speaker to express his/her frustration with a particular situation. Each statement that follows *yok* is presented by the speaker as an untenable excuse or an unrealistic wish. These statements often contain the evidential copula *-(y)mIş*.

(76) Hep bir bahanesi var. **Yok** hava kötü**ymüş**, **yok** parası yetmez**miş**, **yok** vakti yok**muş** ... Yani anlayacağın, bizimle tatile gitmemek için elinden geleni yapıyor.
'S/he always has an excuse ... *Either* the weather is bad, *or* s/he doesn't have enough money, *or* s/he doesn't have time ... In short, s/he does whatever s/he can to avoid going on holiday with us.'

(iii) *hele* 'in particular', 'above all' and *özellikle/∇bilhassa* 'particularly', 'especially' single out one of the alternatives within a set:

(77) Nimet Hanım torunlarını çok seviyor. En küçüğe **hele** bayılıyor.
'Nimet loves her grandchildren. She *particularly* adores the youngest one.'

(78) Annem Afrika'yı, **özellikle** güney Afrika'yı çok seviyor.
'My mother loves Africa, *especially* southern Africa.'

(iv) *nitekim/nasıl ki* 'just as', 'similarly' expand by way of analogy:

(79) Her yıl okullarımızda büyük bir öğretmen sıkıntısı yaşanıyor, **nitekim** hastanelerimizdeki sağlık personelinin sayısı da yetersiz.
'Every year there is a great shortage of teachers in our schools, *just as* the number of health professionals in our hospitals is insufficient.'

(v) *başka bir deyişle* 'in other words', *yani* 'I mean', 'in other words', 'i.e.' These explanatory conjunctions/connectives introduce a phrase, clause or sentence in which the speaker reformulates his/her message in a different way. *başka bir deyişle* is used in formal contexts, and is limited to introducing a straightforward paraphrase:

(80) Babıali, **başka bir deyişle** Osmanlı hükümeti ...
'The Sublime Porte, *in other words* the Ottoman government ...'

yani, on the other hand, which is in much more general use, may introduce any kind of paraphrase or explanation, including the provision of further information:

(81) Seninle salı günü, **yani *bu iş bittikten sonra*** görüsebiliriz.
 'You and I can get together on Tuesday, *i.e. after this job is finished.*'

yani is a very common expression in conversation. It is often used by a speaker who is trying to express himself/herself more articulately, but has not yet found the appropriate words to use:

(82) Evden hiç çıkmak istemiyor. **Yani** . . . ne bileyim . . .
 'S/he doesn't want to leave the house. *Well* . . . I don't know . . .'

(vi) *şöyle ki* '[the situation is] as follows'
Şöyle ki is used in formal contexts, and generally introduces a sequence of sentences which as a whole expand on the previous remark of the same speaker.

(vii) *bir kere* 'for one thing', *sonra* 'for another thing', 'and then (again)'
These discourse connectives introduce statements which expand on the speaker's previous statement in terms of providing justification for the attitude or opinion expressed. If just one justificatory point is made, *bir kere* is used:

(83) Necla'ya güvenemem. **Bir kere** doktor değil.
 'I can't trust Necla. *For one thing*, she's not a doctor.'

If a further point is added this is introduced by *sonra*:

(84) Bence başkanlığı en iyi Osman yapar. **Bir kere** herkes ona güveniyor, **sonra** bilgi ve deneyimi var.
 'In my view Osman would be the best chairman. *For one thing* everyone trusts him, *for another* he has the knowledge and experience.'

(viii) *daha doğrusu* 'or rather'
The conjunction/discourse connective *daha doğrusu* has a corrective function. It is used when the speaker wants to reformulate a phrase, clause or sentence that s/he has uttered, and wants the hearer to disregard all or part of the first conjunct:

(85) Yusuf pilavı çok sever. **Daha doğrusu** annesinin yaptığı pilavı çok sever.
 'Yusuf loves rice, *or rather* the rice that his mother cooks.'

(ix) *aksine, tersine,* ∇*bilakis* 'on the contrary'
These connectives introduce a statement that amplifies the statement in the first conjunct, which is always negative:

(86) Erol Semra'yı görmek iste**mi**yor. **Aksine**, görecek diye ödü kopuyor.
'Erol doesn't want to see Semra. *On the contrary*, he dreads seeing [her].'

28.3.6 CAUSAL

These connectives link two statements that are connected to each other by a causal link.

(i) *çünkü/*∇*zira* 'because'
Situated either at the beginning or (*çünkü* only) at the end of the second conjunct, these connectives present the cause of an event or state expressed by the first conjunct.

(87) Partiye gelmek istemiyor, **çünkü** kimseyi tanımıyormuş.
'S/he doesn't want to come to the party, *because* s/he says s/he doesn't know anyone.'

(88) Antalya'ya gidemedim. Param yoktu **çünkü**.
'I wasn't able to go to Antalya. *Because* I didn't have any money.'

As a strategy for expressing the cause of a situation, the use of *çünkü/*∇*zira* is mainly confined to informal registers. In more formal styles the use of a non-finite causal clause (26.3.14), which places the cause before the result, is generally preferred. Informally also, adverbial clauses, whether finite (with *diye*, 26.1.1.1) or non-finite, are regularly used for the expression of reason. The use of a separate sentence introduced by *çünkü* is preferred where (a) the reason is added as an afterthought, or (b) the reason is a fact not known to the hearer, to which the speaker wishes to give as much informational value as to the resultant event or state.

(ii) *bunun için/onun için/bundan dolayı/dolayısıyla/bu nedenle/bu yüzden/sonuç olarak* 'because of this/that', 'as a result'
This group of discourse connectives presents the result of a state of affairs described in the preceding sentence(s):

(89) Ahmet'in ehliyeti yok. **Dolayısıyla** araba kullanamaz.
'Ahmet doesn't have a driving licence. *As a result* he is not allowed to drive.'

For *dolayı* as a postposition see 17.2.3.

28.3.7 INFERENTIAL

demek (ki) 'that means', 'so' stands at either the beginning or the end of the sentence in which it is located, and indicates that this sentence expresses an inference drawn from what has been said previously:

(90) Görgü şahidi olarak mahkemeye çağırılmışsın. **Demek** sen de kaza yerindeydin!
'I hear you've been summoned as an eye witness. *So* you were at the scene of the accident as well!'

(91) Orhan artık Amerika'ya iyice alışmış **demek ki**.
'*So* Orhan is well and truly settled in America, it seems.'

For the inferential connective *yoksa* see 19.5.3.

28.3.8 TEMPORAL

This group of discourse connectives includes *önce* 'first', *sonra* 'then', *daha sonra* 'later', *ondan/bundan sonra* 'then', *onun/bunun üzerine* 'upon this/that', *derken* 'just then':

(92) Ücretlerinde bir artış olmadı. Onlar da **bunun üzerine** grev yapmaya karar verdiler.
'They got no pay increase, *upon which* they decided to go on strike.'

The informal connective *derken* introduces an event that comes as the climax of a process or series, or a situation that creeps up on someone without their realizing it:

(93) Bütün gün ev baktık. Osmanbey, Şişli, Mecidiyeköy, Beşiktaş'ta dolaşıp durduk. **Derken** saat beş olmuş.
'We spent all day looking at flats. We went round and round Osmanbey, Şişli, Mecidiyeköy [and] Beşiktaş. *And suddenly* it was five o'clock.'

For a fuller discussion of temporal adverbials see 16.4.1, and for *önce* and *sonra* as postpositions see 17.2.3.

28.3.9 CONDITIONAL

The discourse connectives in this group express what conditionality, if any, attaches to one or other of the conjuncts.

(i) *yeter ki* 'all that is needed is . . .', introducing the second conjunct, expresses a condition that needs to be fulfilled in order for the state of affairs described in the *first* conjunct to be fully realized:

(94) Sana iş bulacağım. **Yeter ki** sen bulduğum işi beğen.
'I will find you a job. *All that is needed is* for you to like the job I find.'

(ii) Other connectives perform the opposite function, of specifying the conditionality (or lack of it) of the *second* conjunct. They fall into three groups:

(a) *o halde/öyleyse* 'in that case' and *o zaman* 'then' treat the content of the first conjunct as a **knowable condition** (27.3), which is assumed to be fulfilled:

(95) A.– Dükkanlar saat 5'te kapanıyormuş. (cf. Dükkanlar . . . kapanıyorsa)
'Apparently the shops close at 5 o'clock.'

B.– **O halde** bugün alışveriş yapamayacağız.
'*In that case* we won't be able to do any shopping today.'

(b) *yoksa, aksi halde/takdirde* and *sonra* 'otherwise', by contrast, treat the relation between the two sentences as a **predictive conditional** (27.2) in which the second conjunct predicts what the consequence would be if the state of affairs were *other than* what is described in the first conjunct:

(96) Herhalde evde oturmaktan çok sıkıldı. **Yoksa** bu soğukta sokağa çıkmazdı.
'S/he must have got very bored staying indoors. *Otherwise* s/he would never have gone outside in this cold weather.'

aksi takdirde is formal. On the other hand, *sonra* in this usage is very informal, and the sentence that it marks usually follows a command:

(97) Haydi ceketini giy. Üşürsün **sonra**.
'Come on now, put your jacket on. *Otherwise* you'll get cold.'

(c) *nasılsa/nasıl olsa/zaten* 'in any case', 'anyway'
These items indicate that the statement to which they are attached is independent of *any* conditionality:

(98) A.– Benim yüzümden boş yere para harcadın diye
      üzülüyorum.
      'I feel bad about you spending money unnecessarily on my
      account.'

      B.– Yok canım, ben **ZAten/NAsılsa** yeni bir bavul
      alacaktım.
      'That's nonsense; I was going to buy a new suitcase
      anyway.'

These items are always stressed. For unstressed *zaten* see 28.3.11.

(**d**) The expression *ne de olsa* 'after all' has universal conditional concessive meaning (27.5.1):

(99) Sevil'in bunu bilmesi gerekir. **Ne de olsa** fizikçi.
      'Sevil ought to know this. *After all*, she is a physicist.'

28.3.10 ORGANIZATIONAL

This class of connectives provides organizational clues as to how an utterance is to be understood.

(**i**) *işte* has a resumptive or summarizing function. It very often co-occurs
with one of the demonstratives (e.g. *bu* 'this') or their derivatives (e.g. *böyle*
'like this'), and is used to link some previously mentioned item to
the speaker's present statement, which may be a summary of a longer
utterance:

(100) Ortalık karmakarışıktı. Yerlerde gazete kağıtları, kitaplar. Bir
       gün önce de evde kızkardeşimin doğum gününü kutlamıştık.
       Bulaşık bile daha yıkanmamıştı. **İşte** karışıklık derken **bundan**
       söz ediyorum.
       'The house was in a real mess. Newpapers and books strewn
       around. The previous day we had celebrated my sister's birthday
       in the flat. Even the dishes hadn't yet been washed. *Now this* is
       what I mean by a mess.'

In the spoken language the cohesive link provided by *işte* is often to the
visual environment of the speech situation:

(101) **İşte** cuma akşamları toplandığımız yer **burası**.
       '*This* is the place [*that I mentioned earlier*] where we gather on
       Friday evenings.'

Another function of *işte* can be to indicate that the speaker does not wish to continue discussion of the topic in question:

(102) Gitmek istemiyorum **işte**.
'*Well*, I don't want to go.' (As I have already told you)

(**ii**) The expressions ∇*velhasıl/kısacası/özetle/özet olarak* 'in short' introduce a summary of what the speaker has been saying, without the resumptive dimension given by *işte*:

(103) Karısı yemeklerini yapıyor, çamaşırını yıkayıp ütülüyor, telefonlarına bakıyor, **kısacası** hayatını kolaylaştırmak için her şeyi yapıyor.
'His wife cooks his meals, does his washing and ironing, answers the phone for him, *in short* does everything to make his life easy.'

özetlersek/özetleyecek olursak 'to sum up' are much more formal alternatives, used in lectures, etc.

(**iii**) *konumuza dönersek/dönecek olursak* 'to return to our topic' is used to indicate the end of a digression, or the intention of bringing the discussion back to what the speaker wants to talk about.

(**iv**) As an organizational connective the informal expression *neyse* 'well anyway', 'oh well' expresses the speaker's feeling that discussion (of a certain topic, or in total) has gone on long enough, and should be concluded:

(104) Sabah erkenden trene yetişmem gerekiyordu. Kalktım, ortalığı topladım. Bu arada kediler de yemek istiyorlardı. Bir ara kapıya birisi geldi. Meğer postacıymış. İmza gerektiren bir paket varmış. **Neyse**, 8.50 trenine yetişebildim.
'I had to catch an early train. I got up and tidied the house. Meanwhile the cats were wanting to be fed. Then someone came to the door. It turned out to be the postman. There was a packet that had to be signed for. *To cut a long story short*, I did manage to catch the 8.50.'

(105) **Neyse**, ben gitmeliyim artık.
'*Well anyway*, I must be going now.'

For another function of *neyse* see 28.3.13.

28.3.11 CORROBORATIVE

zaten 'in any case', 'well' occurs at the beginning or end of the second conjunct, and presents a statement which makes the first conjunct predictable, thus corroborating or overriding it:

(106) Oraya trenle gidemezsin. **Zaten** bugün trenler çalışmıyor.
'You can't go there by train. *In any case*, the trains aren't running today.'

(107) A.– Ben o kadar aç değilim.
'I'm not all that hungry.'

B.– Sen yemek yemiştin **zaten**.
'*Well*, you had [already] eaten.'

Note that in this usage *zaten* is unstressed. For stressed *zaten* see 28.3.9.

28.3.12 REMINDING

The discourse connectives in this group occur in the first of the two conjuncts. They are used by the speaker to remind the hearer of a person, thing or situation within their shared knowledge, in order that the speaker may go on to say something on that topic. The expressions in question are as follows:

(i) for recalling an event or state: *(hani) . . . ya* (used with *ya* placed immediately after the predicate)
(ii) for recalling people or things: *(hani) . . . var ya/yok mu*.

All of these correspond to phrases such as 'you know' and 'remember' in English:

(108) (**Hani**) geçen gün okula gitmemiştim **ya**, meğer okul zaten tatilmiş.
'*Remember* I didn't go to school the other day? Well, it turns out it was a holiday anyway.' (For *meğer* see 16.3 (iv).)

(109) (**Hani**) şu marangoz İbrahim **var ya/yok mu**? İşte onun dükkanından söz ediyorum. (For *işte* see 28.3.10 (i).)
'*You know* İbrahim the joiner? I'm talking about his shop.'

28.3.13   CONSTRUCTIVE

The function of this group of discourse connectives is to present constructive interpretations of, or responses to, undesirable situations that have been described, or which are part of the shared knowledge of speaker and hearer(s):

(i)   *neyse* 'oh well' has two constructive functions:

(a)   It points to a redeeming feature of a seemingly undesirable state of affairs:

> (110)   Hafta sonunda hep yağmur yağdı. **Neyse**, okuduğum
> romanı bitirebildim.
> 'It rained all weekend. *Oh well,* I was able to finish the
> novel I was reading.'

(b)   It expresses acceptance or resignation:

> (111)   **Neyse**, bizim yapabileceğimiz bir şey yok.
> '*Oh well,* there's nothing we can do.'

(ii)   *hiç olmazsa, hiç değilse, en azından* and *bari* all mean 'at least'. *hiç olmazsa, hiç değilse* and *en azından* are used interchangeably, and can introduce statements of all modalities. *Bari,* on the other hand, can be used only in volitional utterances (21.4.4):

> (112)   **Hiç olmazsa** birimiz bileti kullanabildik.
> 'One of us was *at least* able to use the ticket.'

> (113)   **Bari/Hiç olmazsa** birimiz bileti kullanabilseydik.
> '*I wish* one of us could *at least* have used the ticket.'

28.4   THE EFFECTS OF CO-ORDINATION AND DISCOURSE CONNECTION

When identical items occur in co-ordinated constructions all but one of them may be omitted to avoid repetition. This kind of omission is called **ellipsis**. In Turkish, suffixes and clitics can be elided (28.4.1) as well as phrases (28.4.2). Ellipsis of noun phrases can also occur across sentence boundaries when a referent can be identified by the hearer from previous mention (28.4.3).

28.4.1 THE ELISION OF SUFFIXES AND CLITICS IN CO-ORDINATED CONSTRUCTIONS

If a series of conjoined phrases or clauses contain certain identical suffixes and/or clitics, these may be omitted in all of the conjuncts except the last one. For example, in (114) the copular marker *-(y)DI*, which appears on *gider**di***, can be omitted in the first two predicates, leaving *giyer* and *alır* as 'incomplete' forms in terms of the meaning expressed:

> (114)   Ziya her sabah paltosunu **giyer**(. . .), şemsiyesini **alır**(. . .) ve işe **gider***di*.
> 'Every morning Ziya *would put on* his coat, *pick up* his umbrella and *leave* for work.'

This is known as 'suspended affixation'. Below we explain the most common types of suspended affixation.

28.4.1.1   Omission of copular markers and person markers

A person marker (8.4) from group 2 can be omitted if it is directly attached to one of the markers from position 3 on the verb:

> (115)   Eskiden Kayseri'ye gitmiş(. . .), hatta orada yaşamış**lar**.
> '*Apparently* at one time *they* went to Kayseri and even lived there.'

If the predicate contains a copular marker (8.3.2) and/or the generalizing modality marker *-DIr* (8.3.3) these can only be omitted together with any person marker that is present (8.4). The conjunct which is 'incomplete' can be either a subject complement, as in (116), or a verb inflected with one of the position 3 suffixes, as in (117):

> (116)   Öğretmen(. . .) ve bilim insanı-**ymış**.
> teacher and scientist-EV.COP
> '*Apparently* s/he is/was a teacher and a scientist.'

> (117)   Hem sinema-ya git-miş(. . .) hem de biraz gez-miş-**ti-m**.
> both cinema-DAT go-PF both also a.little go.around-PF-P.COP-1SG
> '*I* had both gone to the cinema and walked around a bit.'

In alternative questions (19.1.2) which contain the combination copular marker + person marker, usually the suffixes in the *last* conjunct are omitted.

(118) Öğretmen mi**siniz** (yoksa) öğrenci mi(. . .)?
'*Are you* a teacher, or a student?'

Of the position 3 suffixes, those which can occur in suspended affixation constructions are *-(I)yor, -mIş, -(A/I)r, -(y)AcAk, -mAlI* and *-mAktA*. Note that in 1st person negative aorist verb forms (which do not contain an aorist suffix, eg. *oyna-ma-m* (play-NEG-1SG) 'I don't/won't play') suspended affixation is not possible, and these have to occur in their full form in conjoined constructions.

28.4.1.2 Omission of nominal inflectional markers

In noun phrases, the following suffixes can be suspended:

(i)   The plural suffix (8.1.1) can be suspended, but only if any other suffixes following it are also suspended.

(119) bütün kitap(. . .) ve defter**lerimiz**
'all *our* book*s* and notebook*s*'

(ii)   Case markers (8.1.3), the comitative/instrumental marker *-(y)lA/ile* (8.1.4) and the suffix *-sIz* 'without' (7.2.2.2) can be suspended on their own:

(120) Vapur hem Napoli(. . .) hem Venedik'**e** uğruyormuş.
'Apparently the boat stops *at* both Naples and Venice.'

(121) kitap(. . .) ya da defter**siz**
'*without* books or notebooks'

(122) öğretmen-ler(. . .) ve öğrenci-ler-**le**
teacher-PL and student-PL-COM
'*with* (the) students and (the) teachers'

If one of these suffixes occurs with the plural marker and a possessive suffix, all three can be suspended:

(123) köy(. . .), kasaba(. . .) ve kent**lerimizden**
'*from our* village*s*, small town*s* and citie*s*'

(iii)   *-ki* can be suspended either on its own or with a preceding locative or genitive marker:

(124) bilgisayar(. . .) ve yazıcı**nınki**
'*the one belonging to* the computer and printer'

28.4.1.3   Omission of other items: *-(y)ken, bile, mI, ki*

The following are also often omitted from all but the final item in a series of conjuncts:

(i)   The adverbial marker *-(y)ken* (26.3.16 (iii)):

(125)   insanlar **küçük**(. . .) ve **daha konuşmaz-*ken***
'*when* people are small and can't yet talk'

(ii)   The connective *bile* 'even' (28.3.1.1 (iv)):

(126)   Dersini **çalış-mış**(. . .) ve odanı **topla-mış-*sa-n bile*** sokağa çıkamazsın.
'You can't go out *even if you* have done your homework and tidied your room.'

(iii)   The interrogative marker *mI* (11.1.1.5):

(127)   **Gittin** (. . .) ve **gördün *mü*?**
'Have you gone and seen (it)?'

(iv)   The subordinator *ki* (11.1.1.4):

(128)   **Gördüm** (. . .) ve **biliyorum *ki*** . . .
'I have seen and know *that* . . .'

28.4.2   THE ELISION OF PHRASES IN CO-ORDINATED CONSTRUCTIONS

The following constituents can be elided when they are in co-ordinated constructions within the sentence:

(i)   Determiners and adjectives:

(129)   **yeşil bir** atkı ya da (. . .) şapka
'*a green* hat or (*a green*) scarf'

(ii)   Adverbs and modifiers of adjectives and adverbs:

(130)   **yavaşça** oturup (. . .) kalk-
'sit down (*slowly*) and get up *slowly*'

(131)   **çok** şeker ve (. . .) cana yakın bir çocuk
'a *very* sweet and (*very*) lovable child'

(**iii**) Postpositions:

(132) karısı (. . .) ve kendisi **için**
'*for* his wife and (*for*) himself'

(**iv**) Verbs and verb phrases (see also 20.2.3).

(133) (a) Ali odayı (. . .), Mehmet balkonu **temizledi.**/ Ali odayı
temizledi, Mehmet balkonu (. . .).
Ali *cleaned* the room and Mehmet (*cleaned*) the balcony

(b) Ali **odayı temizledi**, Mehmet de (. . .) (. . .).
Ali *cleaned* the room, and so [*did*] Mehmet

28.4.2.1 The elision of noun phrases in co-ordinated constructions

Noun phrases in subject, complement and possessor-modifier functions can
be elided in co-ordinated constructions within the sentence:

(**i**) Subjects (see 18.1.5):

(134) **Nuri** geldi ve (. . .) karşıma oturdu.
'*Nuri* came and sat opposite me.'

(**ii**) Complements:
Elision of complement noun phrases occurs regularly where they have identical referents and case markers:

(135) **Semra'yı** gördüm ve (. . .) çok sevdim. (Direct object)
'I have seen *Semra* and liked [*her*] very much.'

(136) Zeki **köpekten** hem nefret ediyor, hem (. . .) korkuyor.
(Oblique object)
'Zeki both hates and fears *dogs*.'

If the second or subsequent occurrence of a complement requires a
different case marker from that used on its first occurrence, then a pronoun
with the appropriate case marker is usually used. For example, *Semra* below
is in the accusative case when it first occurs, but since the verb *hayran kal-*
'admire' requires a dative-marked noun phrase, the form *ona* 'for her' is
likely to be used in the second conjunct:

(137) **Semra'yı** tanıdım ve (**ona**) hayran kaldım.
'I got to know *Semra* and became full of admiration for *her*.'

(iii)   Genetive and ablative modifiers (see also 14.5.4, example (140)):

(138) **Esra'nın** anne(si) ve (. . .) babası
       'Esra's mother and father'

28.4.3   The elision of noun phrases in other contexts

Unlike other types of phrase, noun phrases are regularly omitted in contexts other than co-ordinated constructions, wherever (a) the identity of the referent is unambiguous, and (b) (in the case of subjects or possessors) no contrast is involved or emphasis required:

(139) Bugün **Ayşe**'yi gördüm. (. . .) Sana selam söyledi.
       'I saw *Ayşe* today. *She* sent you her love.'

For the conditions governing the omission of subject pronouns, and of genitive-marked pronouns expressing possessor-modifiers, see 18.1.5.

Direct object noun phrases are are also regularly omitted after their first mention, for as long as the identity of the referent can still be assumed to be unambiguously identifiable by the hearer:

(140) ***Beyaz Kale'yi*** ilk defa 1990'da okudum ve (. . .) çok sevdim.
       Geçen hafta [Handan (. . .) bana verince] (. . .) yeniden okudum.
       'I first read *The White Castle* in 1990 and liked [*it*] very much. Last week [when Handan gave [*it*] to me] I read [*it*] again.'

Noun phrase ellipsis also crosses the boundary beween the utterances of different speakers, and occurs regularly in answers to questions:

(141) A.– **Kitabını** buldun mu?
       'Have you found *your book*?'

       B.– (. . .) Aramadım ki.
       'I haven't looked for [*it*].'

Another context in which noun phrase ellipsis occurs is where the referent is identified by non-linguistic means:

(142) A. (pointing at something) – (. . .) Gördün mü?
       'See?' (lit. 'Have you seen [*it*]?')

       B.– Tabii. Ben (. . .) yaptım.
       'Sure. I did [*it*].'

APPENDIX 1:
REDUPLICATED STEMS

List of emphatically reduplicated stems (9.1) starting with a consonant (all stems starting with a vowel are reduplicated with 'p'):

başka	bambaşka
bayağı	basbayağı
bedava	besbedava
belli	besbelli
beter	besbeter
beyaz	bembeyaz
boş	bomboş
bok	bombok
buruşuk	bumburuşuk
bütün	büsbütün
canlı	capcanlı, capacanlı
cavlak	cascavlak
cıbıldak	cıscıbıldak
cıvık	cıscıvık
çabuk	çarçabuk
çevre	çepçevre, çepeçevre
çıplak	çırçıplak, çırılçıplak
dar	dapdar
daracık	dapdaracık
derin	depderin
dik	dimdik
diri	dipdiri
doğru	dosdoğru
dolu	dopdolu
duru	dupduru
düz	dümdüz (adj., adv.) düpedüz (adv.)
düzgün	düpdüzgün
genç	gepgenç
geniş	gepgeniş
gündüz	güpegündüz
güzel	güpgüzel
kalın	kapkalın
kara	kapkara
karanlık	kapkaranlık

katı	kaskatı
kırmızı	kıpkırmızı
kısa	kıpkısa
kıvrak	kıskıvrak
kızıl	kıpkızıl
kirli	kipkirli
koca	koskoca
kocaman	koskocaman
kötürüm	кösкötürüm
koyu	kopkoyu
kuru	kupkuru
mavi	masmavi
mor	mosmor
parça	paramparça
pembe	pespembe
perişan	perperişan
sağlam	sapasağlam
sarı	sapsarı
sebil	sersebil
sefil	sersefil
serin	sepserin
sıcacık	sımsıcacık
sıcak	sımsıcak
sıkı	sımsıkı
silik	sipsilik
sivri	sipsivri
siyah	simsiyah
soğuk	sopsoğuk
şirin	şipşirin
tamam	tastamam
taze	taptaze
temiz	tertemiz
toparlak	tostoparlak
yanlış	yapyanlış, yapayanlış
yalnız	yapayalnız
yassı	yamyassı
yaş	yamyaş
yeni	yepyeni
yeşil	yemyeşil
yumru	yusyumru
yuvarlak	yusyuvarlak
zayıf	zapzayıf

APPENDIX 2: TENSE/ASPECT/ MODALITY SUFFIXES

The following list shows all the suffixes used in Turkish to express tense, aspect and/or modality (Chapter 21), together with a brief indication of their meanings. Except where otherwise shown (by 'or' or the use of roman numerals), the various elements of meaning shown for each suffix are present simultaneously in every usage of that form. For example, every usage of *-DI* involves past tense, perfective aspect and factual modality. Individual occurrences of *-(A/I)r/-mAz*, on the other hand, while they may be open to more than one interpretation, may also fall into just one of the three patterns of meaning shown.

VERBAL TENSE/ASPECT/MODALITY SUFFIXES (8.2.3)

-(y)Abil
Possibility (21.4.2.1):

  (1)   Hasan Fransızca oku-**yabil**-iyor.
        'Hasan can read French.'

  (2)   Yağmur yağ-**abil**-ir.
        'It may rain.'

-(y)A-mAz
Negative possibility (21.4.2.1):

  (3)   Oraya gid-**e-mez**-sin.
        'You can't go there.'

-DI
Past tense (21.2.1)
Perfective aspect (21.3, 21.3.1)
Neutral modality (direct knowledge) (21.4):

  (4)   Arabamı sat-**tı**-m.
        'I sold/have sold my car.'

-mIş
Relative past tense (21.2.1)
Perfective aspect (21.3, 21.3.1)
Evidential modality (indirect knowledge) (21.4.3)

> (5) Burada yağmur yağ-**mış**.
>   'Apparently it rained/It seems to have rained here.'

The modality component of the meaning of *-mIş* is neutralized when the past copula *-(y)DI* is added, or the auxiliary verb *ol-* follows:

> (6) O hafta çok yağmur yağ-**mış-*tı***.
>   'It had rained a lot that week.'

-(I)yor

(**i**) Imperfective aspect (progressive or habitual) (21.3.1–2)

Progressive:

> (7) Şu anda Ahmet futbol oyn-**uyor**.
>   'Ahmet is playing football at the moment.'

> (8) Sen telefon ettiğinde Ahmet futbol oyn-**uyor-*du***.
>   'Ahmet was playing football when you rang.'

Habitual:

> (9) Cumartesileri Ahmet futbol oyn-**uyor**(-*du*).
>   'On Saturdays Ahmet plays (used to play) football.'

(**ii**) Scheduled future tense:

> (10) Yarın Paris'e gid-**iyor**-uz.
>   'We're going to Paris tomorrow.'

-mAktA
Imperfective aspect (progressive or habitual) (21.3.1–2)

Progressive:

> (11) Şu sıralarda konferansımı hazırla-**makta**-yım.
>   'At the moment I'm preparing my lecture.'

Habitual:

(12) Cep telefonlarının kullanımı uçağın iletişim sistemini kötü yönde
etkile-**mekte**-dir.
'The use of mobile phones adversely affects the plane's
communication system.'

-(y)AcAK

(**i**)   Relative future tense (21.2.3):

(13) Burada dört ev yap-ıl-**acak**(*-tı*).
'Four houses are/were going to be built here.'

(**ii**)   Non-fact modality (assumption) (*ol-* only) (21.4.1.4):

(14) Kapı çaldı, Hasan ol-**acak**.
'The door bell rang; that'll be Hasan.'

(**iii**)   Volitional modality (command) (21.4.4.2 (iv)):

(15) Herkes saat ikide burada ol-**acak**, anlaşıldı mı?
'Everyone is to be here at two o'clock; is that clear?'

-(A/I)r/-mAz (Aorist)

(**i**)   Imperfective (habitual) aspect (21.3.2) + generalizing modality
(21.4.1.1):

(16) Burada çok yağmur yağ-**ar**.
'It rains a lot here.'

(17) Para mutluluk getir-**mez**.
'Money doesn't bring happiness.'

(18) Öğrenciler çok kahve iç-**er**.
'(The) students drink a lot of coffee.'

(**ii**)   Hypothetical modality (21.4.1.3):

(19) Sen oradaki havayı beğen-**mez**-sin.
'You wouldn't like the atmosphere there.'

(iii)   Future tense + non-fact modality (assumption) (21.4.1.4):

   (20)   Oradan iki saatte gel-**ir**-siniz.
       'From there you'll get here in two hours.'

(**iv**)   Volitional modality (21.4.4.5–6):

   (21)   Bana yardım ed-**er** misiniz?   (Request)
       'Would you [please] help me?'

   (22)   Bunu kimseye söyle-**me**-m.   (Promise)
       'I won't tell anyone about this.'

-mAlI

(**i**)   Speaker-generated obligation (21.4.2.2):

   (23)   Artık git-**meli**-yim.
       'I must go now.'

(**ii**)   Non-fact modality (deduction) (*ol-* only) (21.4.1.4):

   (24)   Bu ceket senin ol-**malı**.
       'This jacket must be yours.'

-sA

(**i**)   Volitional modality (wish) (21.4.4.1):

   (25)   Daha büyük bir arabamız ol-**sa**.
       'If only we had a bigger car.'

-sAm/-sAk

(**ii**)   (1st person forms only, in questions) volitional modality (deliberation) (21.4.4.4):

   (26)   Bu akşam ne yap-**sa**-k acaba?
       'What should we do this evening, I wonder?'

(zero), *-(y)In(Iz)*, *-sIn(lAr)* (Imperative)
Volitional modality (command) (21.4.4.2 (i), (ii)):

   (27)   Bu parayı Kaya'ya ver.
       'Give this money to Kaya.'

   (28)   Düğmeye bas-**ın**-(**ız**).
       'Press the button.'

(29) Ayşe bu akşam bana telefon et-**sin**.
'I want/Tell Ayşe to ring me this evening.'

-(y)AyIm, -(y)AlIm (Optative, 1st person forms)
Volitional modality (suggestion) (21.4.4.3):

(30) Sana yardım ed-**eyim**.
'Let me help you.'

(31) Biraz otur-**alım** mı?
'Shall we sit down for a while?'

COPULAR MARKERS (USED IN NOMINAL AND VERBAL SENTENCES) (8.3.2)

-(y)DI

(i) Past tense (21.2.1):

(32) Herkes bahçe-de-**ydi**.
'Everyone was in the garden.'

(33) Eğlen-iyor-**du**-k.
'We were having a good time.'

(ii) Counterfactual modality:

(34) Sen bu işi daha güzel yapar-**dı**-n.
'You would have done this job better.'

(35) Baştan söyle-**se-ydi**-n.
'If only you had said [so] at the start.'

-(y)mIş
Evidential modality (indirectly or newly acquired knowledge) (21.4.3):

(36) Aysel'in babası mühendis-**miş**.
'Apparently Aysel's father is/was an engineer.'

(37) Her yaz Amerika'ya gid-iyor-lar-**mış**.
'It seems they go/went to America every summer.'

(38) Burası gerçekten güzel-**miş**.
'This really is a beautiful place.'

THE GENERALIZING MODALITY MARKER -*DIr* (*8.3.3*)

(**i**)   Generalizing modality (21.4.1.1–2):

>   (39) Demir ağır-**dır**.
>   'Iron is heavy.'

>   (40) İnsanlar tembel-**dir**.
>   'People are lazy.'

(**ii**)   Non-fact modality (assumption) (21.4.1.4):

>   (41) Yorgun-sun-**dur**.
>   'You must be tired.'

>   (42) Toplantı artık bit-miş-**tir**.
>   'The meeting will have finished by now.'

GLOSSARY OF GRAMMATICAL TERMS

ablative	one of the five **case markers** (*-DAn*), often expressing concepts such as *from, out of, through*
accusative	one of the five **case markers** (*-(y)I*), indicating a **direct object** which is **definite** or **specific**
active	(of a verb form or sentence) which expresses the concept of someone or something performing an action: *Peter Smith wrote a book*; opposed to **passive**
addressee	the person to whom a speaker is speaking, also called the hearer
adjectival (phrase)	any linguistic structure that performs the function of an adjective
adjective	a word that ascribes some property, quality or status to the entity denoted by a noun (e.g. *blue, good, democratic, imaginary*)
adverb	a word that modifies (i.e. further specifies the meaning of) a verb, an adjective, another adverb, or a whole sentence (e.g. *easily, very, now, probably*)
adverbial (phrase)	any linguistic structure that performs the function of an adverb
adverbial clause	a finite or non-finite subordinate clause that performs an adverbial function in relation to its superordinate clause
affirmative	not negative
affricate	(consonant) produced by the gradual opening of the vocal tract after complete closure
agent	the item expressing the person(s) or thing(s) that perform the action of the verb; identical with the **subject** in an **active** sentence, but either suppressed or expressed as an optional constituent in a **passive** sentence
agreement	the requirement for the **predicate** to be marked for **person** and **number** in accordance with the person and number of the **subject**
allophone	a variant form of pronunciation of a **phonological unit**

alveolar	articulated with the tip or blade of the tongue against the alveolar ridge (the bony ridged area just behind the upper front teeth)
antecedent	a linguistic item (usually a noun phrase) which identifies the person(s) or thing(s) referred to by a pronoun
aorist	a **finite verb form** marked by the suffix *-(A/I)r* (or its negative counterpart *-z*); the aorist expresses either habitual aspect or various kinds of modality: generalizing, hypothetical, presumptive (with future time reference) or volitional
aspect	the temporal viewpoint from which an event is presented; see **perfective** and **imperfective**
aspirated	(of a **voiceless consonant**) whose articulation is followed by an escape of breath
attributive	(of an adjectival) occurring as part of a **noun phrase** (e.g. *pahalı bir araba* 'an *expensive* car'); cf. **predicative**
auxiliary verb	a verb that cannot stand on its own, but occurs either suffixed to another verb (bound auxiliary) or compounded with another verb or a nominal (free auxiliary)
back	(of a vowel) articulated with the tongue positioned at the back of the oral cavity
bilabial	(consonant) articulated by bringing both lips together
case marker/suffix	a nominal inflectional suffix attached to the **head** of a **noun phrase** to indicate the relationship of that noun phrase to other constituents of the sentence *ay-**a** bak* 'look *at* the moon'
categorial	the status of a noun phrase that is not marked for number (i.e. is **transnumeral**), and denotes an unspecified quantity/number from a designated class of persons or things
causative suffix	a suffix that turns an **intransitive** verb into a **transitive** one (e.g. *öl-* 'die', *öl-**dür-*** 'kill') or that expresses the concept of causing, securing or allowing the performance of the action of the root verb; a clause in which the verb is marked with a **causative suffix**
causee	in a causative construction, the noun phrase expressing the person (or machine, etc.) that is made to perform the action expressed by the root verb

clause	a syntactic structure that is either grammatically a *complete* sentence, or resembles a sentence in having a subject (overt or implied) and a predicate
clitic	a linguistic item which (although in most cases written as a separate word) cannot stand on its own, is dependent on the phrase that it follows (in Turkish), and is unstressed (e.g. the interrogative particle *mI*)
comitative	expressing the concept *(together) with/in the company of*
comitative/ instrumental marker	the suffix -*(y)lA* or its free-standing counterpart *ile*
complement	a noun phrase that 'completes' the meaning of another constituent, e.g. a verb (as in ***Filmden** hoşlandım* 'I enjoyed *the film*'), an adjective (as in ***spora** meraklı* 'interested *in sport*') or a postposition (*o **günden** beri* 'since *that day*'); see also **subject complement**
complex sentence	a sentence which, in addition to its **main clause**, contains at least one **subordinate clause**
compound verb form	a composite verb form in which a **lexical verb** marked for relative tense or aspect is followed by one of the free **auxiliary verbs** *ol-* or *bulun-*, the auxiliary verb carrying either supplementary tense/aspect/modality marking or a **subordinating suffix**
concessive	(of an adverbial clause) expressing a situation that is in apparent contradiction to the superordinate clause (expressing the concept *although*); (of a discourse connective) marking the speaker's recognition that s/he is making an observation that appears to contradict what has been said before, but not irreparably (e.g. *actually, admittedly*)
conditional clause	an adverbial clause expressing the concept *if*
conjunct	one of the items joined by a conjunction
conjunction	a word that joins two or more items that have the same syntactic function (e.g. *and, or, but*)
connective	see **discourse connective**
constituent	any linguistic unit viewed as part of a larger construction
converb	the non-finite verb of an **adverbial clause**
co-ordination	the linking of two or more phrases or clauses that are equivalent to each other in terms of syntactic function (e.g. ***Londra** ve **Paris** 'London* and *Paris*', ***ucuz** ama **iyi** bir otel* 'a *cheap* but *good hotel*')

copula	forms which express the concept *be* (see 8.3.1)
copular markers	markers that contain the *-y-* form of the copula: the unstressable suffixes *-(y)DI*, *-(y)mIş* and *-(y)sA*
counterfactual	(of a conditional clause or a main clause that implies the fulfilment of a condition) expressing what is known not to have happened, or not to be the case (e.g. *(If you had told me) I would have come*)
dative	one of the five **case markers** *(-(y)A)*, often expressing concepts such as *to, into, on to*
definite	the status of a noun phrase that refers to a specific entity or entities which the speaker assumes to be unambiguously identifiable by the addressee(s) (e.g. *France, the first house, these plates*)
demonstrative	a **determiner** or **pronoun** that has (literally or figuratively) a 'pointing' function (e.g. *this, those*)
dental	articulated with the tip of the tongue against the upper front teeth
denti-alveolar	articulated with the tip or blade of the tongue at the junction between the top teeth and the alveolar ridge
derivation	the creation of a new **lexical item**, by suffixation (e.g. *iyileş-* 'get better', *tuzlu* 'salty'), compounding (e.g. *karabiber* 'black pepper, *futbol takımı* 'football team') or reduplication (*simsiyah* 'jet black')
derivational suffix	a suffix which, when added to a stem, produces a new **lexical item** whose meaning is connected to that of the stem (e.g. *-lAş-* 'become', *-lI* 'having', 'characterized by')
derived	(of a word) that contains one or more (usually derivational) suffixes in addition to the root
determiner	a word whose function is to specify the limitation (or lack of limitation) of the potential referent of a noun phrase (e.g. ***this*** *city,* ***some*** *daily newspapers,* ***every*** *university student*)
direct object	the **complement** of a **transitive** verb, as in *John is building* ***a boat***, *I've finished* ***my work***
discourse connective	a word or phrase which provides a cohesive link between two sentences or larger pieces of discourse, indicating how the content of what is newly uttered relates to what has gone before (e.g. *what's more, however, or rather, in short*); sometimes just called a **connective**

distributive numeral a form of numeral expressing *one each*, *two each*, etc.

echo question a question which partly (or in full) repeats a statement just made by another speaker, e.g. A: *John's bought a crocodile.* B: *He's bought what?/John's bought a crocodile?*

ellipsis (or **elision**) the omission of a linguistic item that is readily identifiable from the context, e.g. *our* in *our friends and (. . .) neighbours*) or *I'm* in *Where are you? (. . .) Here.*

epenthetic vowel a **high** vowel that appears in the second syllable of certain nouns, only in the **root** form or when a suffix beginning with a consonant is added (e.g. *resmi* 'his/her picture', but *resim* 'picture', *resimler* 'pictures')

evidential a type of **modal** marking (with *-mIş* or *-(y)mIş*) which indicates that a statement is based upon knowledge acquired by the speaker indirectly

existential sentence a **nominal sentence** which asserts (or, in the negative, denies) the existence or presence of some entity or entities; there are two types: **locative**, expressing the basic notion *there is an x (in y)*, and **possessive**, expressing the basic notion *x has y* (where *is* and *has* stand for any form of the verbs *be* and *have* respectively)

finite clause a clause whose predicate is either a **finite verb** or identical in form to a **nominal sentence**

finite verb form a verb form that can occur in a **simple sentence** or **main clause**

focused (of a sentence constituent) emphasized by being pronounced with heavy stress

fricative (consonant) produced through friction in the vocal tract resulting from two organs (e.g. tongue and teeth) coming very close together

front (of a vowel) articulated with the tongue positioned at the front of the oral cavity

generic the status of a noun phrase that (in any given utterance) is used with a generalizing function, to refer to an entire class of entities, or to a(ny) typical member of that class (e.g. *drugs* in *Drugs can kill* or *the tiger* in *The tiger is a carnivore*)

genitive one of the five **case markers** (*-(n)In*), marking a noun phrase either as the possessor of another entity expressed in the sentence, or as the **subject** of certain types of **subordinate clause**

genitive-attracting pronouns a set of pronouns which, when not plural-marked, require genitive case marking with certain postpositions

genitive-possessive construction a composite **noun phrase** consisting of a **genitive-marked** noun phrase followed by a noun phrase marked with a **possessive suffix**: *ben-im ad-ım* 'my name', *kitab-ın fiyat-ı* 'the price of the book'

glide a consonant whose articulation does not involve any closure or friction, also called a semi-vowel

glottal stop consonantal sound produced by the audible release of a complete closure at the glottis (the aperture in the larynx between the vocal cords)

habitual (of an **imperfective** verb form) presenting a situation as part of a recurring pattern

hard palate the hard bony area in the roof of the mouth between the **alveolar** ridge and the **velum**

head (i) the obligatory constituent (cf. **modifier**) of certain types of phrase: in particular, the verb in a **verb phrase** and the constituent furthest to the right in a **noun phrase**;
(ii) the last constituent of a **noun compound**

high vowel a vowel produced by raising the tongue above its neutral position

imperative a **finite verb form** expressing a command

imperfective (of a verb form) expressing a situation from an internal temporal **aspect**, as being in some sense incomplete and ongoing (e.g. *gidiyordum* 'I was going', 'I used to go'); see **progressive** and **habitual**

impersonal passive a form that occurs in Turkish but not in English, namely the **passive** form of an **intransitive** verb (e.g. *sevinilir* 'one is pleased', 'people are pleased')

indefinite the status of a noun phrase that either
(i) refers to a **specific** entity (or set of entities) known to the speaker, but assumed not to be familiar to, or identifiable by, the addressee(s) (e.g. *a tiger* in *we saw a tiger today*)
or (ii) denotes a **non-specific** entity (or set of entities), whose identity is unknown or unknowable to the speaker (e.g. *a tiger* in *I've never seen a tiger*)

indirect command a noun clause whose content would, if converted into an independent sentence, express a command (e.g. *to wait there* in *They told me to wait there*)

indirect question a noun clause whose content would, if converted into an independent sentence, express a question

(e.g. *where Louise is* in *I don't know where Louise is*)

indirect statement   a noun clause whose content would, if converted into an independent sentence, express a statement (e.g. *you're right* in *I know you're right*)

inflected   (of a word) that contains at least one inflectional suffix

inflection   alteration of the grammatical form of a word by the addition (to the lexical form) of one or more **inflectional suffixes**

inflectional suffix   a suffix which changes the grammatical form of a word; in verbs, inflectional suffixes express categories such as voice, negation, tense, aspect, modality and person/number; in nominals they express categories such as number, possession and case

instrumental   the concept *with* denoting use of an instrument, or *by* denoting use of a means of transport or communication

intonational phrase   a unit of speech (one, or more usually, several words) containing one **primary stress** and a single **intonation contour**

intonation contour   one of a number of distinctive patterns of rise and fall in the pitch of the voice

intransitive verb   a verb that either takes no complement (e.g. *laugh, walk, sleep*), or takes an **oblique object** (expressed in English using a preposition, e.g. *look (at/after/for)*

labio-dental   (consonant) articulated with the lower lip against the upper front teeth

lateral   (consonant) produced by air flowing around a complete closure formed in the mouth

lexical item   a linguistic form that one would expect to find as an item in a dictionary of the language; normally the uninflected form of a word

lexicalized   a term applied to an **inflected** word or phrase which, through usage, has acquired the status of a **lexical item** (e.g. *diye, olarak, gelince*)

lexical verb   in a **compound verb form** the first of the two verbs, and the one that provides the lexical (dictionary) meaning

linking sentence   a **nominal sentence** expressing the basic notion *x is y* (or, in the negative, *x is not y* (where *is* stands for any form of the verb *be*)

locative	one of the five **case markers** (*-DA*), expressing spatial, temporal or abstract location (*in, on, at*)
locative existential	see **existential sentence**
low vowel	a vowel produced by lowering the tongue below its neutral position
main clause	in a **complex sentence**, the clause which includes, and is **superordinate** to, all the others
mid vowel	a vowel produced with the tongue at a level intermediate between **high** and **low**
modal adverbial	an adverbial expressing the speaker's stance towards the utterance that is being made (e.g. *belki* 'perhaps', *maalesef* 'unfortunately')
modality	a grammatical category whose expression is linked with that of **tense** and **aspect**, and which concerns the speaker's degree of commitment to the truth of a statement, the speaker's attitude towards the potential occurrence of an event, or general notions of possibility or necessity
modifier	a non-obligatory constituent of certain types of phrase, which 'modifies' (i.e. makes more specific) the meaning of the **head**; nouns and noun compounds can be modified by determiners, numerals and adjectivals (*o dört büyük ağaç* 'those four big trees'), while verbs, adjectives and adverbs can be modified by adverbials (*erken gel-* 'come early', *fazla büyük* 'too big', *fazla erken* 'too early')
nasal	(sound) produced while the **velum** is lowered to allow the audible escape of air through the nose; in the case of nasal consonants, such as /m/ and /n/, there is complete closure of the oral cavity
nominal	a word belonging to one of the following (related) classes: noun, pronoun, adjective and adverb
nominal sentence	a sentence whose main or only clause either contains no verb or whose verb is one of the forms of the **copula**; the two types of nominal sentence are **linking sentences** and **existential sentences**
nominalized forms	forms derived from verbs by means of a **subordinating suffix** (such as *-DIK* or *-mA*), and functioning as nominals
nominal-verb compound	a **lexical item** functioning as a **verb**, which is formed by the combination of a nominal with a free **auxiliary** such as *et-* or *ol-* (e.g. *mücadele et-* 'fight', *memnun ol-* 'be pleased')

non-definite	**indefinite** or **categorial**
non-finite clause	a **subordinate clause** in which the verb is non-finite, i.e. marked with a **subordinating suffix**
non-specific	see under **indefinite**; also used as a cover term for **categorial** and **generic**
noun	a word that denotes a class of things or persons, a member of such a class, a substance, an abstract concept, or the proper name of a person or place (e.g. *table, girl, water, knowledge, Ahmet, Turkey*)
noun clause	a finite or non-finite subordinate clause that performs the function of a **noun phrase** within its superordinate clause
noun compound	a word-like unit which is made up of two nouns (e.g. *kız kardeş* 'sister', *balık lokantası* 'fish restaurant)' or an adjective and a noun (e.g. *ilkbahar* 'spring'); the majority of noun compounds in Turkish are *-(s)I* **compounds**
noun phrase	any word or sequence of words that can function as the subject or object in a sentence (e.g. *it, the others, a very loud noise, Mary's uncle, the car you usually drive*); the **head** of a noun phrase may be a **noun**, a **noun compound**, or a **pronoun**
number	the distinction between singular and plural
object	see **direct object**, **oblique object**
oblique case markers	this term is applied to the dative, locative and ablative case markers, and sometimes also to the comitative/instrumental marker
oblique object	the **complement** of an **intransitive** verb, marked in Turkish by one of the **oblique case** markers, or by the **comitative/instrumental marker**: *Bun-a çok sevindim* 'I'm very pleased *about this*', *Mehmet'le alay ettiler* 'They made fun *of Mehmet*'
optative	a **finite** verb form expressing the speaker's (or, in questions, the hearer's) will or desire
ordinal numeral	a numeral which indicates an ordered position in a series (*first, second*, etc.)
palatal	(consonant) articulated with the blade of the tongue against the **hard palate**
palatalization	the pronunciation of a consonant as palatal in a front-vowel environment, or the pronunciation of a back vowel in a relatively fronted position in the environment of certain palatal consonants
participle	the non-finite verb of a **relative clause**

partitive construction	a composite **noun phrase** (made up of a modifier noun phrase followed by a head noun phrase) used to express part of a whole, or to select one or more items from a type or set; the modifier has either **ablative** or **genitive** case marking, and the head may or may not have a 3rd person **possessive suffix**
passive	(a verb form) which expresses that an action *is (or was) done* rather than that someone or something *does (or did)* it (although an **agent** may optionally be expressed within the clause): *A book was written (by Peter Smith)*
perfective	(of a verb form) expressing an event from an external temporal **aspect**, as a completed whole (e.g. *gittim* 'I went')
person	in a grammatical context this term refers to the distinction between 1st person (referring to the speaker or a group including the speaker), 2nd person (referring to the addressee(s)), and 3rd person (referring to other entities)
person marker	a suffix attached to the predicate to indicate the **person** of the **subject**
phonological unit	any one of the consonants and vowels that can be distinguished functionally (i.e. in terms of creating differences of meaning) in a particular language
phrase	a syntactic unit (word group) that is less than a **clause**; the name of a particular type of phrase indicates either the class of word that constitutes its **head** (as in **verb phrase**, **postpositional phrase**), or the function of the phrase as a whole within the sentence (as in **adjectival phrase**, **adverbial phrase**), or it may include both of these meanings (as in **noun phrase**)
plosive	(consonant) produced by the sudden opening of the vocal tract after complete closure
possessive existential	see **existential sentence**
possessive suffix	one of a set of nominal infectional suffixes attached to the **head** of a **noun phrase**; while the 3rd person singular possessive suffix has other additional functions, the function shared by all possessive suffixes is to indicate the grammatical person (1st, 2nd, 3rd, singular/plural) of the possessor of the entity denoted by the noun phrase: *evimiz* 'our house', *kapısı* 'his/her/its door'

post-alveolar	(consonant) articulated towards the back of the alveolar ridge (see **alveolar**)
postposition	a word which, together with the noun phrase complement that it follows, forms a phrase with an adverbial or adjectival function: *bütün bunlardan sonra* 'after all this', *dolabın üstünde* 'on top of the cupboard'; Turkish postpositions usually correspond to prepositions in English
predicate	in a verbal sentence or subordinate clause, the **verb**; in a nominal sentence or non-verbal small clause, the **subject complement** plus (if present) the **copula**
predicative	occurring as (part of) a nominal **predicate**, i.e. as a **subject complement**
primary stress	the acoustically most prominent syllable in an **intonational phrase**
productive	(of a suffix) that regularly has a particular meaning and can be used freely with a particular type of stem
progressive	(of an **imperfective** verb form) expressing an event or state as ongoing at a specific reference point
pronoun	an expression used when referring to persons or things that have previously been mentioned, whose referents are obvious from the context or whose content is only partially specified (e.g. *he, those, I, herself, someone, anything*)
quantifier	**determiner** or **pronoun** that expresses quantity in non-numerical terms (e.g. *many, much, some, all; someone, everything*)
reduplication	the repetition of a word or part of a word, as a lexical or grammatical process (e.g. *bambaşka* 'quite different', *birer birer* 'one by one', *rahat rahat* 'comfortably')
referent	the person(s) or thing(s) referred to by a speaker in a particular instance of the use of a noun phrase
referential status	the status of a **noun phrase**, on any particular occasion of its use, in terms of the type of reference it makes to entities in the world; see **definite, indefinite, categorial, specific, generic**
register	a variety of language defined by its use in particular social situations or text types (e.g. colloquial, formal, legal)
relative clause	a finite or non-finite subordinate clause that performs an **adjectival** or, in the case of headless

	relative clauses, a pronominal function within its superordinate clause
relative tense	**tense** marking that locates an event as prior to, simultaneous with, or subsequent to, any reference point established by the context
resumptive pronoun	a pronoun referring (i) in sentences with certain types of relative clause, to the head of the noun phrase qualified by the relative clause, and (ii) in the superordinate clause of a universal conditional clause, to the entity or class defined by the conditional clause
root	the minimal form of a word, not including any suffixes, whether derivational or inflectional
rounded	(of a vowel) produced with the lips in a rounded position
-(s)I compound	a **noun compound** consisting minimally of two juxtaposed nouns, the second of which (the **head**) is marked with the 3rd person possessive suffix *-(s)I* (e.g. *otobüs durağı* 'bus stop')
simple sentence	a sentence consisting of just one clause (a **main clause**)
small clause	a type of **finite noun clause** whose subject is also the subject or object of the **main clause**
specific	a term encompassing both **definite** and one of the two types of **indefinite**; see also **non-specific**
stem	any linguistic item to which suffixes can be added, whether a simple root or a combination of a root plus suffix(es)
stress	the high pitch and loudness with which a syllable is uttered relative to others in the same word or sequence of words
subject	in an **active** sentence or clause, the item expressing the person(s) or thing(s) that perform the action of the verb: *Susan plays tennis*, or are described by the **predicate**: *The children are happy*; in a **passive** sentence or clause, the item expressing the person(s) or thing(s) that undergo the action of the verb: *Susan was beaten in today's match*
subject complement	a noun phrase or adjectival phrase that forms (part of) the **predicate** of a **linking sentence** (e.g. *Siz komşumsunuz* 'You are *my neighbour*') or of a **small clause** (*Sizi komşu sayıyorum* 'I consider you *a neighbour*')

subordinate clause	a clause which forms a constituent within a **complex sentence**; there are three functional types: **noun clauses**, **relative clauses**, and **adverbial clauses**
subordinating suffix	one of a range of suffixes (e.g. *-mAK*, *-(y)An*, *-(y)ken*) that mark a predicate as **non-finite**, and thus the clause in which it occurs as a **subordinate clause**; apart from *-(y)ken* and the conditional copula marker *-(y)sA*, subordinating suffixes can be attached only to verbal predicates
subordinator	any linguistic item that marks a **subordinate clause**, whether a separate word such as *diye* or *ki*, or a **subordinating suffix**
suffix	a linguistic item that cannot stand on its own, but is added to the right of a **root** or **stem** to form part of the same word; see **derivational suffix** and **inflectional suffix**
superordinate clause	the clause within which a **subordinate clause** occurs; this may be either the main clause of the sentence or another subordinate clause
tap	consonant produced by a single rapid contact between the tongue and the roof of the mouth
tense	the grammatical marking of location in time: past, present or future (see also **relative tense**)
topic	a constituent taken as indicating what the sentence is 'about'; this usually occurs at the beginning of the sentence, but if marked by the topic-shifter *dA* it can occur in other positions also
topic shifter	a linguistic item which marks a change of **topic**
transitive verb	a verb (such as *al-* 'take', *iste-* 'want') that requires to be complemented by a **direct object** expressing an entity or entities directly affected by its action; the direct object can be omitted in Turkish if it is obvious from the context
transnumeral	(of a noun phrase) neutral with regard to **number**
universal conditional clause	a Turkish conditional clause that includes a **wh-phrase**; such clauses express the concepts *whoever*, *wherever*, etc.
universal quantifier	**quantifier** denoting an entire class (e.g. *all*, *each*, *everyone*)
unmarked order	the most neutral order of sentence constituents, found in contexts in which no information is presupposed, and no constituent is given special emphasis

velar	(consonant) articulated with the back of the tongue against the **velum**
velum	the mobile fleshy area at the back of the mouth, behind the hard palate; also known as the soft palate
verb	a word that expresses an action, event, process or state, and which, in Turkish, takes verbal suffixes, such as the infinitive suffix *-mAk* or the imperfective suffix *-(I)yor*: *yaz-* 'write', *düş-* 'fall', *eri-* 'melt', *görün-* 'seem'
verbal noun	the non-finite verb of a **noun clause**
verbal sentence	a sentence whose main or only clause has a finite verb (other than *ol-* in its copular function) as its predicate
verb phrase	that part of a clause which consists of the verb together with its complement(s) and any modifying adverbials
voiced consonant	a consonant pronounced while the vocal cords are vibrating (e.g. /b/, /d/, /g/, /z/)
voiceless consonant	a consonant pronounced while the vocal cords are not vibrating (e.g. /p/, /t/, /k/, /s/)
voice suffix	collective term for the **causative**, **passive**, reflexive and reciprocal suffixes, which precede all other inflectional suffixes on the verb stem
volitional utterance	a type of sentence (distinguished from statements and questions) which expresses the speaker's (or in interrogative forms the hearer's) will or desire (e.g. *Buraya gel!* 'Come here!' *Gidelim mi?* 'Shall we go?')
wh-phrase	a questioning expression used in questions other than yes/no questions or alternative questions; so named because most of the Engish expressions in this class (*who, where, which*, etc.) begin with *wh-*

BIBLIOGRAPHY

Ahmet Cevat [Emre] (1931) *Yeni bir Gramer Metodu Hakkında Layıha*, vol. 1. İstanbul: Devlet Matbaası.

Akar, D. (1988) 'Some syntactic properties of Turkish interjections', in S. Koç (ed.) *Studies on Turkish linguistics: Proceedings of the Fourth International Conference on Turkish Linguistics*, 265–74. Ankara: METU.

Atalay, B. (1942) *Türk Dilinde Ekler ve Kökler üzerine bir Deneme*. İstanbul: Matbaai Ebüzziya.

Aygen, G. (2002) 'Finiteness, case and clausal architecture'. Doctoral dissertation. Harvard University.

Bainbridge, M. (1980–1987) A Comprehensive Turkish Course (in four stages, each consisting of five books plus cassettes). SOAS, University of London ms.

Banguoğlu, T. (1974) *Türkçenin Grameri*. İstanbul: Baha Matbaası.

Bozşahin, C. (2003) 'Gapping and word order in Turkish', in A.S Özsoy, D. Akar, M. Nakipoğlu-Demiralp, E.E. Erguvanlı-Taylan and A. Aksu-Koç, (eds) *Studies in Turkish Linguistics: Proceedings of the Tenth International Conference on Turkish Linguistics*, 95–104. İstanbul: Boğaziçi University Press.

Bussmann, H. (1996) *Routledge Dictionary of Language and Linguistics* (translated and edited by G. P. Trauth and K. Kazzazi). London: Routledge.

Charette, M. (2004) 'Defining the structure of Turkish words', in A. Bellem and K. Rowan (eds) *SOAS Working Papers in Linguistics* 13. London: SOAS.

Charette, M. and Göksel, A. (1998) 'Licensing constraints and vowel harmony in Turkic languages,' in E. Cyran (ed) *Structure and Interpretation: Studies in Phonology*, 65–88. Lublin: Folium.

Crystal, D. (1991) *A Dictionary of Linguistics and Phonetics* (3rd edition). Oxford: Blackwell.

Demiray, K. (1994) *Temel Türkçe Sözlük* (3rd edition). İstanbul: İnkılâp Kitabevi.

Demircan, Ö. (1978) *Türkiye Türkçesinin Ses Düzeni, Türkiye Türkçesinde Sesler*. Ankara: Türk Dil Kurumu Yayınları.

Demircan, Ö. (2000) *Türkçenin Ezgisi*. İstanbul: Yıldız Teknik Üniversitesi Vakfı Yayınları.

Denwood, A. (2002) 'K~Ø: Morpho-phonology in Turkish' in C. Colella, and S. Hellmuth (eds) *SOAS Working Papers in Linguistics* 12. London: SOAS.

Deny, J. (1921) *Grammaire de langue turque (dialecte osmanli)*. Paris: Leroux.

Dizdaroğlu, H. (1976) *Tümcebilgisi*. Ankara: Türk Dil Kurumu Yayınları.

Ediskun, H. (1963) *Yeni Türk Dilbilgisi*. İstanbul: Remzi Kitabevi.

Ediskun. H. (1985) *Türk Dilbilgisi*. İstanbul: Remzi Kitabevi.

Elöve, A. U. (1941) *Türk Dili Grameri (Osmanlı Lehçesi)*. İstanbul: Maarif Matbaası. [Turkish translation of Deny 1921, with additional notes.]

Emre, A. C. (1945) *Türk Dilbilgisi*. Ankara: Türk Dil Kurumu Yayınları.

Erkman-Akerson, F. and Ozil, Ş. (1998) *Türkçe'de Niteleme: Sıfat İşlevli Yan Tümceler*. İstanbul: Simurg Yayınları.

Enç, M. (1986) 'Topic switching and pronominal subjects in Turkish', in D. I. Slobin and K. Zimmer (eds) *Studies in Turkish Linguistics*, 195–208. Amsterdam: John Benjamins.

Enç, M. (1991) 'The semantics of specificity'. *Linguistic Inquiry* 22.1: 1–25.

Erdal, M. (1998) 'On the verbal noun in *-(y)Iş*', in *Doğan Aksan Armağanı*, 53–68. Ankara: Ankara Üniversitesi Basımevi.

Erdal, M. (2000) 'Clitics in Turkish', in A. Göksel and C. Kerslake (eds) *Studies on Turkish and Turkic Languages; Proceedings of the Ninth International Conference on Turkish Linguistics*, 41–55. Wiesbaden: Harrassowitz Verlag.

Ergin, M. (1989) *Türk Dil Bilgisi*. İstanbul: Bayrak Basım-Yayın-Tanıtım.

Erguvanlı, E. E. (1984) *The Function of Word Order in Turkish Grammar*. Berkeley: University of California Press.

Erguvanlı-Taylan, E. (1986) 'An odd case in the causative construction in Turkish'. Papers from the 15th Annual Regional Meeting of the Chicago Linguistics Society. Chicago: University of Chicago Press.

Erguvanlı-Taylan, E. (2000) Structure of Modern Turkish (class notes). Boğaziçi University ms.

von Gabain, A. (1988) *Eski Türkçe'nin Grameri* (translated by M. Akalın). Ankara: Türk Tarih Kurumu Basımevi.

Gencan, T. N. (1971) *Dilbilgisi* (2nd edition). Ankara: Türk Dil Kurumu Yayınları.

Golstein, Bernard (1999) *Grammaire du Turc: Ouvrage pratique à l'usage des francophones* (2nd edition). Paris and Montreal: L'Harmattan.

Göknel, Y. (n.d. [1974?]) *Modern Türkçe Dilbilgisi*. İzmir: Hür Efe Matbaası.

Göksel, A. (1993) 'Levels of representation and argument structure in Turkish'. Doctoral dissertation, SOAS, University of London.

Göksel, A. (1998) 'Linearity, focus and the postverbal position in Turkish', in L. Johanson with É. Á. Csató, V. Locke, A. Menz and D. Winterling (eds) *The Mainz Meeting*, 85–106. Wiesbaden: Harrossowitz Verlag.

Göksel, A. and Özsoy, A. S. (2000) 'Is there a focus position in Turkish?', in A. Göksel and C. Kerslake (eds) *Studies on Turkish and Turkic*

Languages; Proceedings of the Ninth International Conference on Turkish Linguistics, 219–28. Wiesbaden: Harrassowitz Verlag.

Göksel, A. and Özsoy, A. S. (2003) '*dA*: a focus/topic associated clitic in Turkish'. *Lingua* 113, no.11: 1143–67. (Special Issue on *Focus in Turkish*, edited by A. S. Özsoy and A. Göksel)

Haig, G. (1997) *Relative Constructions in Turkish*. Wiesbaden: Harrassowitz Verlag.

Hankamer, J. (1986) 'Finite state morphology and left to right phonology'. *Proceedings of the West Coast Conference on Formal Linguistics* 5: 41–52.

Hankamer, J. and Knecht, L. (1976) 'The role of the subject/non-subject distinction in determining the choice of relative clause participle in Turkish'. *Harvard Studies in Syntax and Semantics*, 2: 197–219.

Hazai, G. (1978) *Kurze Einführung in das Studium der türkischen Sprache*. Budapest: Akadémiai Kiadó.

Hengirmen, M. (1995) *Türkçe Dilbilgisi*. Ankara: Engin Yayınevi.

Inkelas, S. (1996) 'The interaction of phrase and word rules in Turkish'. *Linguistic Review* 13: 193–217.

Inkelas, S. (1999) 'The exceptional stress-attracting suffixes in Turkish: Representations versus the grammar', in R. Kager, H. van der Hulst and V. Zonneveld (eds) *The Prosody-Morphology Interface*, 134–87. Cambridge: Cambridge University Press.

Inkelas, S. and Orgun, O. (1995) 'Level ordering and economy in the lexical phonology of Turkish'. *Language* 71: 763–93.

Johanson, L. (1990) 'Studien zur türkeitürkischen Grammatik' in G. Hazai (ed.) *Handbuch der Türkischen Sprachwissenschaft*, Teil I: 146–301. Wiesbaden: Otto Harrassowitz.

Kabak, B. (2001) 'Suspended affixation in verbal coordinate constructions in Turkish'. University of Delaware ms.

Kabak, B. and Vogel, I. (forthcoming) 'The phonological word and stress assignment in Turkish'. To appear in *Phonology*.

Kelepir, M. (2000) 'To be or not to be faithful', in A. Göksel and C. Kerslake (eds) *Studies on Turkish and Turkic Languages: Proceedings of the Ninth International Conference on Turkish Linguistics*, 11–18. Wiesbaden: Harrassowitz.

Kelepir, M. (2001) 'Topics in Turkish syntax: clausal structure and scope'. Doctoral dissertation, MIT.

Kerslake, C. (1998) 'Ottoman Turkish', in L. Johanson and É. Á. Csató (eds) *TheTurkic Languages*, 179–202. London: Routledge.

Kerslake, C. (2001) 'Does Turkish prefer events to states?' *Turkic Languages* 5: 198–215.

Kerslake, C. (2003) 'A new look at conditional constructions in Turkish', in A. S. Özsoy, D. Akar, M. Nakipoğlu-Demiralp, E. E. Erguvanlı-Taylan, A. Aksu-Koç (eds) *Studies in Turkish Linguistics*, 215–26. İstanbul: Boğaziçi University Press.

Kılıçaslan, Y. (2003) 'Syntax of information structure in Turkish'. *Linguistics* 42/4: 717–65.

Kissling, H. J. (1960) *Osmanisch-türkische Grammatik.* Wiesbaden: Otto Harrassowitz.

Kononov, A. N. (1956) *Grammatika Sovremennogo Tureckogo Literaturnogo Jazika.* Moskva: Izdatel'stvo Akademii Nauk SSSR.

Kornfilt, J. (1996) 'On copular clitic forms in Turkish', in A. Alexiadou, N. Fuhrkop, P. Law and S. Löhken (eds) *ZAS Papers in Linguistics* 6: 96–114. Berlin: Zentrum für Allgemeine Sprachwissenschaft.

Kornfilt, J. (1997) *Turkish.* London: Routledge.

Kural, M. (1994) 'Scrambling in Turkish'. UCLA ms.

Kural, M. (1997) 'Postverbal constituents in Turkish and the linear correspondence axiom'. *Linguistic Inquiry* 28: 498–521.

Lees, R. B. (1961) *The phonology of Modern Standard Turkish.* Uralic and Altaic Series 6, Bloomington: Indiana University.

Lewis, G. (1999) *The Turkish Language Reform: A Catastrophic Success.* Oxford: Oxford University Press.

Lewis, G. (2000) *Turkish Grammar* (2nd edition). Oxford: Oxford University Press.

Matthews, P. H. (1997) *The Concise Oxford Dictionary of Linguistics.* Oxford: Oxford University Press.

Moser-Weithmann, B. (2001) *Türkische Grammatik.* Hamburg: Helmut Buske Verlag.

Nakipoğlu, M. (2002) 'Case and delimitedness: Meeting the interpretive requirements of the interfaces'. Paper presented at the 11th International Conference on Turkish Linguistics, August 7–9, 2002, Eastern Mediterranean University, Famagusta/Gazimagusa.

Nash, R. (1973) *Turkish Intonation; An Instrumental Study.* The Hague: Mouton.

Özbek, N. (2000) '*Yani, işte, şey, ya*: interactional markers of Turkish', in A. Göksel and C. Kerslake (eds) *Studies on Turkish and Turkic Languages; Proceedings of the Ninth International Conference on Turkish Linguistics*, 393–401. Wiesbaden: Harrassowitz Verlag.

Özel, S. (1977) *Türkiye Türkçesinde Sözcük Türetme ve Bileştirme.* Ankara: Türk Dil Kurumu Yayınları.

Özge, U. (2003) 'A tune-based account of Turkish information structure'. M.Sc. dissertation, METU, Ankara.

Özsoy, A. S. (1999) *Türkçe.* İstanbul: Boğaziçi Üniversitesi Yayınları.

Özsoy, A. S. (2002) 'On "small clauses", other "bare" verbal complements and feature checking', in E. E. Erguvanlı-Taylan (ed.) *The Verb in Turkish*, 213–38. Amsterdam: John Benjamins.

Özsoy, A. S. (2004) *Türkçe'nin Yapısı – I; Sesbilim.* İstanbul: Boğaziçi Üniversitesi Yayınları.

Öztürk, B. (1999) 'Turkish as a non-pro-drop language', in E. E. Erguvanlı-Taylan (ed.) *The Verb in Turkish*, 239–59. Amsterdam: John Benjamins.

The Redhouse Turkish-English Dictionary (1999). İstanbul: SEV Matbaacılık ve Yayıncılık A. Ş.

Rona, B. (1972) Lectures given on the structure of Modern Turkish at Boğaziçi University, İstanbul.

van Schaaik, G. (1999) 'The order of nominalizations in Turkish'. *Turkic Languages* 3: 87–120.

van Schaaik, G. (2000) 'Higher order compounds in Turkish: some observations', in A. Göksel and C. Kerslake (eds) *Studies on Turkish and Turkic Languages, Proceedings of the Ninth International Conference on Turkish Linguistics*, 113–120. Wiesbaden: Harrassowitz Verlag.

Schroeder, C. (1997) '"Relative" *ki*-clauses and the structure of spoken Turkish', in K. İmer and N.E. Uzun (eds) *Proceedings of the VIIIth International Conference on Turkish Linguistics*, 347–362. Ankara: Ankara Üniversitesi Basımevi.

Schroeder, C. (1999) *The Turkish Nominal Phrase in Spoken Discourse*. Wiesbaden: Harrassowitz Verlag.

Sebüktekin, H. (1971) *Turkish-English Contrastive Analysis*. The Hague: Mouton.

Sebüktekin, H. (1975) *An Outline of English-Turkish Contrastive Phonology: Segmental Phonemes*. İstanbul: Boğaziçi Üniversitesi.

Sebüktekin, H. (1997) *Turkish for Foreigners/Yabancılar için Türkçe*, vols. 1–2 (2nd edition). İstanbul: Boğaziçi Üniversitesi Yayınları.

Sezer, E. (1986) 'An autosegmental analysis of compensatory lengthening in Turkish', in L. Wetzels and E. Sezer (eds) *Studies in Compensatory Lengthening*, 227–50. Dordrecht: Foris.

Sezer, E. (1978) 'Eylemlerin çoğul öznelere uyumu'. *Genel Dilbilim Dergisi*, 25–32. Ankara: Ankara Dilbilim Çevresi Derneği.

Sezer, E. (2002) 'Finite inflection in Turkish', in E. E. Erguvanlı-Taylan (ed.) *The Verb in Turkish*, 1–46. Amsterdam: John Benjamins.

Slobin, D.I. and Aksu, A.A. (1982) 'Tense, aspect and modality in the use of the Turkish evidential', in P.J. Hopper (ed.) *Tense-Aspect: Between Semantics and Pragmatics*, 185–200. Amsterdam: John Benjamins.

Swift, L. B. (1963) *A Reference Grammar of Modern Turkish*. The Hague: Mouton.

Şener, S. and İşsever, S. (2003) 'The interaction of negation with focus: *ne ... ne ...* phrases in Turkish'. *Lingua* 113/11: 1089–117. (Special Issue on *Focus in Turkish*, edited by A. S. Özsoy and A. Göksel.)

Tansu, M. (1963) *Durgun Genel Ses Bilgisi ve Türkçe*. Ankara: Türk Tarih Kurumu Basımevi.

Tekin, T. (2000) *Orhun Türkçesi Grameri*. (Türk Dilleri Araştırmaları Dizisi 9.) Ankara: Yayınları.

Underhill, R. (1976) *Turkish Grammar.* Cambridge, Mass.: MIT Press.

Underhill, R. (1986) 'Bibliography of modern linguistic work on Turkish', in D. I. Slobin and K. Zimmer (eds), *Studies in Turkish Linguistics*, 23–51. Amsterdam: John Benjamins.

Underhill, R. (1988) 'A lexical account of Turkish accent', in A. Sezer (ed.) *Studies on Turkish Linguistics.* Ankara: METU Press.

Uygun, D. B. (2000) 'The question particle and movement in Turkish'. MA dissertation, Boğazici University, İstanbul.

Zimmer, K. and Orgun, O. (2000) 'Turkish' in *Handbook of the International Phonetic Association*, 154–5. Cambridge: Cambridge University Press.

INDEX

This index is arranged according to the Turkish alphabet (for which see pp. xxxviii–xxxix). The following abbreviations have been used:

adj.   adjectival marker
adv.   adverbial marker
der.   derivational suffix
d.n.   de-nominal derivational suffix (i.e. derivational suffix attached to a nominal root)
d.v.   de-verbal derivational suffix (i.e. derivational suffix attached to a verbal root)
NP   noun phrase
pl.   plural
poss.   possessive
sg.   singular
sub.   subordinator

A

-*A* (d.n.) 57; (d.v.) 53
Ablative case marker, *see -DAn*
Ablative-marked NP **179–81**, 186–9
   as adjectival 194, 209–10
   as adverbial 144, 215, 228–9, 233–4, 251
   as complement 143, 198–9, 201, 246–9, 416, 422, 425
   as object of comparison 181, 240, 417
acaba 308, 362
-*(A)C* (d.n.) 59; (d.v.) 53
-*(A)cAn* (d.v.) 53
Accusative case marker, *see -(y)I*
Accusative-marked NP 141–2, **175–6**, 371–2, **375–7**, 383–4
   position of 393–4, 400
   see also Direct object
Adjectival (construction) **Ch. 15** *passim*
   attributive/modifier 163, 191–2
   dislocated 402
   position within NP 162, 208–12
   predicative 121, 191–2
   pronominalized 281–4
Adjective **50, Ch. 15** *passim*
   complement of 201
   used adverbially 213–14, 391

intensive forms 98–9, 100–1, 193, 539–40
   modification of 98–9, **197–201**
   with noun compound 107–8
   pronominalized 185, 199, 281
   and reduplication 98–9, 100–1
   position within NP 208–9
Adjective-noun compound 103
Adverb 27, 50, 100–1, **213–14**
   modification of 98, **240**
   and reduplication 98, 100–1, 214
   and word order 389–93
Adverbial 144–5, **Ch. 16** *passim*, 258, **Ch. 26** *passim*
   as modifier 144–5, 197–201, 218, 240
   and word order 389–93, **394–5**
   see also Adverb, Adverbial clause, Directional, Distance, Manner, Modal, Place, Purpose, Reason, Time
Adverbial clause 235–7, **Ch. 26** *passim*
   questioning part of 307
Agent (of passive verb) 149–50
Agreement (subject-predicate) **127–35**, 266–7, 272
-*AğAn/-AgAn* (d.v.) 53
-*(A/I)cIK,* 31, 60; *see also -CAK*
-*(A/I)klA* (d.v.) 56